Lecture Notes in Computer Science 8001

Commenced Publication in 1973
Founding and Former Series Editors:
Gerhard Goos, Juris Hartmanis, and Jan van Leeuwen

Nachum Dershowitz   Ephraim Nissan (Eds.)

Language, Culture, Computation

Computing - Theory and Technology

Essays Dedicated to Yaacov Choueka
on the Occasion of His 75th Birthday, Part I

Springer

Volume Editors

Nachum Dershowitz
Tel Aviv University, School of Computer Science
Ramat Aviv, Tel Aviv 69978, Israel
E-mail: nachumd@tau.ac.il

Ephraim Nissan
University of London, Goldsmiths College
Department of Computing
25–27 St. James, New Cross, London SE14 6NW, UK
E-mail: ephraim.nissan@hotmail.co.uk

Cover illustration: Jacob et Rachel près d'une fontaine (drawing of painting),
1830 Etienne Achille Réveil.
Source: Museum of Painting and Sculpture: or, Collection of the Principal Pictures,
Statues and Bas-reliefs in the Public and Private Galleries of Europe.
Authors: Etienne Achille Réveil, Jean Duchesne; Publisher: Bossange, 1830

Photograph on p. VII: The photograph of the honoree was taken by Yoni Shveka.
Used with permission.

ISSN 0302-9743   e-ISSN 1611-3349
ISBN 978-3-642-45320-5   e-ISBN 978-3-642-45321-2
DOI 10.1007/978-3-642-45321-2
Springer Heidelberg New York Dordrecht London

Library of Congress Control Number: 2013955036

LNCS Sublibrary: SL 3 – Information Systems and Application, incl. Internet/Web
and HCI

© Springer-Verlag Berlin Heidelberg 2014

Typesetting: Camera-ready by author, data conversion by Scientific Publishing Services, Chennai, India

Printed on acid-free paper

Springer is part of Springer Science+Business Media (www.springer.com)

Yaacov Choueka

tabula gratulatoria

Tres libros amicorum istos,

illi Magistro excelso plaudentes dedicaverunt

Aldo Franco Dragoni, Amihood Amir, Amir Kantor, Andrey Rosenberg, Antonio A. Martino, Antonio Toral, Ariel Gorfinkel, Aviezri Fraenkel, Carmelo Asaro, Claudia Soria, Dany Y. Farook, David Harel, David Peleg, David Rydeheard, Dina Goren-Bar, Dov Gabbay, Dov Winer, Edward Reingold, Efrat Manisterski, Ephraim Nissan, Erick Fredj, Ghil῾ad Zuckermann, Gian Piero Zarri, Howard Barringer, Ian Lancashire, Idan Spektor, Ido Dagan, Jacob Goldenberg, Jihad El-Sana, John Zeleznikow, Judit Bar-Ilan, Julia Sheidin, Kendall Lister, Kfir Bar, Klaus Schmidt, Leon Sterling, Liad Tal, Lyle Ungar, Mark Cohen, Massimo Zancanaro, Meir Bar-Ilan, Mona Diab, Monica Monachini, Moshe Fresko, Moshe Goldstein, Moshe Koppel, Moshe Lewenstein, Moshe Vardi, Nachum Dershowitz, Nadav Kashtan, Nicoletta Calzolari, Noa Lewenstein, Oded Netzer, Ofir Tzvi Erlich, Olivier Finkel, Oliviero Stock, Raz Lin, Rebecca J. W. Jefferson, Ronen Feldman, Roy Bar-Haim, Ruth Kannai, Sadek Jbara, Sarit Kraus, Shahar Kats, Shmuel T. Klein, Solomon Eyal Shimony, Subha Chandra, Tsvi Kuflik, Uri J. Schild, Valeria Quochi, Willard McCarty, et Yaakov HaCohen-Kerner.

From the editors   to the authors:

Popóscimus,   accucurrístis.
Cunctáti erámus,   pepercístis.

We asked,   you came running.
We were delayed, you forgave.

To our Maker:

וִיהִי נֹעַם הי אֱ-לֹהֵינוּ עָלֵינוּ
וּמַעֲשֵׂה יָדֵינוּ כּוֹנְנָה עָלֵינוּ
וּמַעֲשֵׂה יָדֵינוּ כּוֹנְנֵהוּ

Psalms 90:17

Yaacov Choueka
(Photo taken by Yoni Shveka, son of the honoree)

Preface

Yaacov Choueka celebrated his 75th birthday in 2011. The present three-volume *liber amicorum*, several years in gestation, honors this outstanding Israeli computer scientist and is dedicated to him and to his scientific endeavors. Yaacov's research has had a major impact not only within the walls of academia, but also (as we are going to show in the three separate prefaces of this volume-set) in the daily life of lay users of such technology that originated from his research. An especially amazing aspect of the temporal span of his scholarly work is that half a century after his influential research from the early 1960s (when you use a search engine to search the Web, think of him with gratitude for his early efforts), a project in which he is currently involved is proving to be a sensation, as will become apparent from what follows.

Yaacov began his research career in the theory of computer science, dealing with basic questions regarding the relation between mathematical logic and automata theory. From formal languages, Yaacov moved to natural languages. He was a founder of natural-language processing in Israel, developing numerous tools for Hebrew. He is best known for his primary role, together with Aviezri Fraenkel, in the development of the Responsa Project, one of the earliest full-text retrieval systems in the world. More recently, he has headed the Friedberg Genizah Project, which is bringing the treasures of the Cairo Genizah into the Digital Age.

The three volumes are organized thematically and differ from one another. Volume I is entitled "Computing – Theory and Technology," as it covers a range of topics in computer science. The title of Volume II is "Computing for Humanities, Law, and Narratives," and is devoted to those application areas. Volume III is entitled "Computational Linguistics and Linguistics," and the thematic progression therein fits between the two poles indicated in its title. Within each individual volume, the reader will find headings in the table of contents that state the narrower theme shared by the articles appearing under that rubric. Admittedly, sometimes a paper could have also been placed in another cluster, but we trust that the thematic clusters as defined will be found helpful for orientation.

Volume I is loosely organized according to the many areas of interest of Yaacov. It begins with a tribute by Aviezri Fraenkel, based on the banquet talk delivered at the Bar-Ilan Symposium on Foundations of Artificial Intelligence in honor of Choueka's 65th birthday (Jerusalem, June 2001) and with Yaacov's biography (written with his cooperation) and a résumé of his academic career and publications. That section, "The Jubilarian," is followed, under the rubric "Theory of Computation," by papers on theory and algorithms, several of which deal with automata on infinite strings, an area in which Choueka's early papers are required reading.

The cluster of articles about theory is followed by a section on "Science Computing and Tools for Engineering." It comprises a paper on an information agent interacting with the Cyc knowledge base, then an article in evolutionary computing applied to bio-molecular chemistry, and a long study in artificial intelligence for refuelling design in nuclear reactor cores. A few more words about the cluster of papers on e-science and engineering. The title of the Yaacov Choueka Jubilee set is "Language, Culture, Computation." Engineering is culture when it is done by humans, rather than bees or termites. (One of us was once told by a rather wooden linguist, who had watched with a face like that of Ramses II's mummy a lecture in knowledge engineering: "This is poetry!" The one who was challenged retorted: "Engineering *is* poetry." The interlocutor was baffled by this, but the description is accurate, because of how engineering makes choices when handling degrees of freedom.) Also doing mathematics is a signal example of a cultural practice (historians of mathematics, and their colleagues from ethnography, the ethnomathematicians, know that all too well). It is the one manner that the exact sciences have to peer into the logical structure that, some feel, may have existed before the physical universe, and now expresses the constraints on its shape. Yaacov's biography makes this quite clear. And science stands to culture as culture stands to nature. It is the most self-conscious form of human culture.

The following section, "Information Retrieval," is longer; it comprises both overviews and original research papers, and one of its themes is ontologies, a subject also covered in two of the sections of Volume III (the other papers are included there because they combine ontologies with the lexicon). Moreover, in Volume II there is a "Review of Ontology-Based Storytelling Devices." Whereas in the first volume, under "Information Retrieval," there is an article about character recognition applied to the Arabic script, Arabic natural-language processing is the subject of two papers in the third volume. That same section "Information Retrieval" (in which one finds such papers that also deal with any of the following: ontologies, Web technology, data mining, and e-commerce) concludes with the fullest treatment to date of the CuProS metadata language, a precursor of XML independent of SGML (the ancestor of XML). The most developed applications of CuProS were in computational linguistics (another one was to law), but when CuProS and, earlier on, the deeply nested database relations whose structure CuProS described were originally proposed, this was out of character with the nested relations school within database-design research, because at that time two or three levels of nesting inside relations were favored by the mainstream of that school of research. The success of XML has certainly vindicated CuProS, and in Volume III a few of the papers discuss its applications. The syntax of CuProS was first described in an appendix of a doctoral dissertation supervised by Yaacov.

Apart from that culture-bound significance, the importance of full-text online search worldwide is for all to see, and yet, Yaacov had to argue for it, when it had not yet become popular, as he explains in his article about natural-language processing in Volume III. After one of us expressed to Aviezri Fraenkel astonishment ("These are not scholars with a shred of gratitude to their precursors") that an up-and-coming scholar in information retrieval, enjoying his moment of fame, reacted with ignorant arrogance when approached (upon the advice of a colleague of his), Aviezri pointed out informally in reply, in an email of 16 March 2008: "It doesn't surprise me at all that most people don't know about our 'google' engine that was working decades before the present Google engine. I know that." The top scientists at Google, on the other hand, are well aware of the pioneering work of Yaacov and Aviezri. And the fine authors who contributed their articles to the present initiative know that, too. The older ones – in their respective fields – have been prominent players in a gloriously pioneering age in the history of computing. Just stop to consider how privileged we are in having been participants in the advancement of this stage in the development of technology and its allied sciences.

The contents of the other two volumes of the Yaacov Choueka Jubilee volume-set will be presented separately.

September 2013   Nachum Dershowitz
                                                            Ephraim Nissan

Table of Contents – Part I

The Jubilarian: Yaacov and His Oeuvre

From the Alleys of Cairo to the Internet Highways. An Intellectual
Journey: Languages, Information and Intelligence 1
    Yaacov Choueka

Yaacov Choueka: A Profile (and List of Publications) 19
    Nachum Dershowitz and Ephraim Nissan

Integrating and Rejuvenating Old and New Gems 37
    Aviezri S. Fraenkel

Theory of Computation

Topological Complexity of Context-Free ω-Languages: A Survey 50
    Olivier Finkel

From Löwenheim to PSL and SVA 78
    Moshe Y. Vardi

Reactivity and Grammars: An Exploration 103
    Howard Barringer, David Rydeheard, and Dov Gabbay

Modal Scenarios as Automata 156
    David Harel and Amir Kantor

Immunity against Local Influence 168
    David Peleg

The Development of the Strategic Behavior of Peer Designed Agents ... 180
    Efrat Manistersky, Raz Lin, and Sarit Kraus

A New Approach to Alphabet Extension for Improving Static
Compression Schemes 197
    Shmuel T. Klein

Four Apt Elementary Examples of Recursion 213
    Edward M. Reingold

Science Computing and Tools for Engineering

Integrating a Lightweight Information Agent with the Cyc Knowledge
Base 225
    Kendall Lister and Leon Sterling

A Knowledge-Based Approach to Initial Population Generation
in Evolutionary Algorithms: Application to the Protein Structure
Prediction Problem 252
    Erick Fredj and Moshe Goldstein

Nuclear In-core Fuel Reload Design: The Trajectory of a Sequence
of Projects 263
    Ephraim Nissan

Information Retrieval

Hypertext Searching - A Survey 364
    Amihood Amir, Moshe Lewenstein, and Noa Lewenstein

Search Engines and Hebrew - Revisited 382
    Judit Bar-Ilan

Matching with a Hierarchical Ontology 395
    Yaacov Choueka, Nachum Dershowitz, and Liad Tal

Analyzing Product Comparisons on Discussion Boards 399
    Ronen Feldman, Moshe Fresko, Jacob Goldenberg, Oded Netzer,
    and Lyle Ungar

Benchmarking Applied Semantic Inference:
The PASCAL Recognising Textual Entailment Challenges 409
    Roy Bar-Haim, Ido Dagan, and Idan Szpektor

A Retrospective of a Pioneering Project. Earlier Than XML, Other
Than SGML, Still Going: CuProS Metadata for Deeply Nested
Relations and Navigating for Retrieval in RAFFAELLO 425
    Ephraim Nissan and Jihad El-Sana

Arabic Character Recognition 584
    Nachum Dershowitz and Andrey Rosenberg

Author Index 603

From the Alleys of Cairo to the Internet Highways
An Intellectual Journey:
Languages, Information and Intelligence[*]

Yaacov Choueka

Department of Computer Science, Bar-Ilan University, Ramat Gan, Israel
The Computerization Unit of the Friedberg Genizah Project, Jerusalem
www.genizah.org

To Sarah, my wife and life companion since my graduating days,

Who shared with me many days of happiness and a few moments of painful sorrow,

Whose unbound love, infinite dynamism and energy, and constant smile and optimism, brightened my days, my nights, and my heart

"Start from the beginning, and when you get to the end... stop!".

A wise advice indeed, given by the rabbit to Alice in "Alice in the Wonderland". Here, however, I would rather begin from the very end of the journey, i.e. from the publication of this book.

It is a great privilege and a no less great pleasure to start this exposition by thanking my long time friends Nachum Dershowitz and Ephraim Nissan, for their generous initiative and for the hard work they put in compiling, editing and publishing this book.

These thanks are no less due to many more colleagues, many of them former students, and all of them now my masters (each in his respective area of research)[1]. At the painful risk of omitting important and dear names, I would like to mention and thank Marty Golumbic. Ariel Frank, Ido Dagan, David Harel, Aviezri Fraenkel, Amir Amihood, Uri Schild and Moshe Vardi that have been showering on me so kind gestures of friendship and appreciation since the early 2000s, with the approach of my formal retirement from Bar-Ilan University, where I taught and did research in mathematics and computer science for almost forty years. They were kind enough to associate my name with the BISFAI (Bar-Ilan International Symposium on the Mathematical Foundations of Artificial Intelligence) Conference in 2001, celebrating

---

[*] The Responsa Project was awarded the prestigious Israel Prize (*Prass Israel*) in 2007.

[1] At the painful risk of omitting important and dear names, I would like to mention and thank Marty Golumbic. Ariel Frank, Ido Dagan, David Harel, Aviezri Fraenkel, Amir Amihood, Uri Schild and Moshe Vardi.

N. Dershowitz and E. Nissan (Eds.): Choueka Festschrift, Part I, LNCS 8001, pp. 1–18, 2014.
© Springer-Verlag Berlin Heidelberg 2014

my then 35 years of teaching and research, which was then followed by a series of invited plenary talks in various scientific meetings, among them ISCOL (Israel Society for Computational Linguistics) 2004 and BISFAI 2007, and finally by contributing such interesting papers to this book.

Whether I deserve that or not, this is a typical situation in which I gladly follow the wise saying of Rabbi Yossi, son of Halafta, one of the elders of the Galilee in the second century, as quoted in the Talmud (Tractate Shabbath, folio 118 b): "Rabbi Yosi said: "I never acted against my colleagues dicta. I know that I am not a Cohen; still if my friends would tell me "you are, indeed, so go to the pulpit and bless us with the Cohen blessing", I would do so".

Back in 2001, when I was asked by the BISFAI 2001 organizers to give the keynote lecture at that conference, I finally had a reasonably good excuse to spend some time reflecting peacefully - in a kind of introspective mood – on the way my academic life started and the way in which it unfolded for almost fifty years.

What I discovered really startled and baffled me. My surprise was in finding out, first, how much of what I did and of what I became was deeply rooted in my boyhood years in the alleys of Cairo, to which my family emigrated at the turn of the twentieth century from Aleppo in Syria, and where I was born and spent my childhood and my teen years. Then also, by how much of my academic life has been shaped by chance, by random encounters, or by immediate and lightly taken decisions. The feeling I got can be best described by that verse in Ezekiel, talking about the angels (I, 16): " ... and their looks and actions were as would be the wheel within the wheel...", and even more so by the following one (paraphrased) from Proverbs (V, 6), describing life "...its wheels are spinning, and you wouldn't know...". I even felt then how, in the words of Shakespeare in King Lear, "... the wheel has come full circle...".

It has appeared to me, therefore, that, rather than boring my readers with yet another tagger or parser or text categorizer with 94.37 precision and 95.62 recall, I would better share with them some personal feelings and reflections about these three successive Ws "Wheels Within Wheels", interweaving them with a few remarks on the way various branches of computer science with which I was mainly involved, namely Automata Theory (AT), Information Retrieval (IR), and Natural Language Processing (NLP), inspired and shaped these forty years. So please bear with me if I will be somewhat personal and intimate in the following lines; this exposition shouldn't thus be read as a "paper" but rather as a "by-the-fire chat" between friends.

Looking at the sub-title of my talk, one would hardly notice any mathematical content in it; at the most, this title conceals only a sixth mathematical part, since "languages" - which is one third of it – denotes, beside natural languages, also "formal languages", an area which is certainly mathematical in its methodology, content and spirit.

And yet, I am basically a mathematician, by inclination, by state of mind, by whatever talents I have, and certainly by formation, since both my M.Sc. and my Ph.D. theses were in mathematics. Not that I had then, however, any better alternative, since, in the early sixties, computer science was not yet firmly established or recognized as an independent and legitimate scientific domain of teaching and research, at least not yet in Israel.

The first spark in my love for mathematics – and more especially for logic and foundations of mathematics - was kindled in me when I was probably less than twelve years old by my uncle Avraham Choueka, then a young bachelor in his mid-twenties.

Avraham finished his high school studies in Cairo in the late thirties with brilliant results, and was immediately marked by the Jewish Community there as a talent to cultivate, encourage and nurture, seeing in him a potential candidate for the next Chief Rabbi of Egypt position; the more so since his grandfather (i.e. my great grandfather) was Chief Rabbi of Aleppo in the eighties of the nineteenth century.

Endowing him with a generous grant, the Jewish Community Council sent him to what was then Palestine, to complete his studies in the Rabbinical Academies ("Yeshivoth") of Jerusalem and Tel Aviv and to get there also an academic degree from the Hebrew University, in whatever field he chose. His choice was mathematics and philosophy.

Whenever he visited us, Avraham used to tease me with riddles and puzzles in mathematics, mostly with natural numbers. One day (it was in the late forties) he asked me to try and define precisely what is the number 2 or, for that matter, the number 1, and when I failed, naturally, he introduced me step by step to the idea that the best way to deal with the natural numbers is to look upon them as a set of abstract entities governed by a very small set of self evident rules, in fact what is known as Peano systems. I even remember vividly the name "Peano" being then mentioned. I was probably one of the youngest boys ever introduced to Peano systems (at least in Egypt...).

He explained to me the proof of the proposition "2 + 2 = 4", after which he asked me how can we be sure that nobody will ever prove also that "2 + 2 = 5". "Of course nobody can prove that", I replied confidently, "since this is false". He tried then to introduce me to the difference between truth and provability, falsehood and un-provability, which, needless to say, I couldn't fully understand at that age. It took me many years of studying, and what is more, many years of teaching and discussing these concepts with my most challenging students, that I finally came to really understand them, in the deep sense of the word. Indeed I always felt that the elucidation of the concept of mathematical truth, of consistency and completeness, of provability vs. un-provability, and of computability vs. un-computability, achieved by the mathematical geniuses of Hilbert, Godel, Turing, Church, Tarski, and others, to be one of the greatest intellectual achievements of the twentieth century, on a par with Einstein theory of relativity, Bohr, Heisenberg and others' atomic and quantum theory, or Chomsky insights in linguistics.

No wonder then that about twenty years later I designed and taught for many years a first-year course on Set Theory and Number Systems, including of course Peano systems (one of the first ever in universities in Israel), at Bar-Ilan University Mathematics and, later, Computer Science Departments.

This story however has a surprising epilogue.

In 1957, the year we came to settle in Israel, more than ten years after this episode, I was in my first year of studies at the Hebrew University Mathematics Department, attending a course on Set Theory given by Prof. Avraham Fraenkel, the mathematician of international fame from the Zermelo-Fraenkel model of Set Theory. We were told that it was the last course this great, wise and nice man was going to teach at the university before retiring, so nobody wanted to miss it.

As every true "professor", Fraenkel (of German origin) was notoriously absent-minded. He used to wear a large hat, and whenever he entered the classroom he would put it on the table, give his lecture, and then leave the room, with us running after him to give him the hat he forgot. His wife apparently heard about that, so she stitched a hook on his shirt, and whenever he entered the classroom he would put his hat on the hook, give the lecture, and leave the room with the hat on the hook, with us running (again) after him to remind him to take it from the hook and wear it... .

Anyway, at the end of the year, we were standing in line in front of his desk, about a hundred of us, with our students' cards, waiting for him to sign the card attesting that we indeed attended his class, as was required then by the university regulations. Needless to say this was a completely formal procedure, since no professor could ever recognize the faces of some one-hundred first year students. Prof. Fraenkel was therefore mechanically signing all the cards presented to him, not even raising his eyes to look at us. My turn finally came and I handed him the card; he began signing it, when he suddenly froze, looked at me silently for a few seconds, then asked me with his German accent: "Your name is Yaacov Choueka?" I was already shaking, not knowing what did I do wrong, and how on earth does he know anything about me, replying with a hesitant "Yes", when he asked me: "Do you have a relative named Avraham Choueka who studied mathematics here about fifteen years ago?" I said, somewhat more confidently, "Yes, that was my uncle". He was then all smiles, saying: "Please give him my best regards; he is a mathematical genius!" This is how I, coming from Egypt, heard the praise of the man who was the trigger to my early attachment to mathematics, from the lips of this famous mathematician, coming from Germany, who remembered him so many years after he was his student, even though he (Avraham) had to return to Egypt after only three years of studies and before graduating.

One more detail, and the whole story will get its true effect.

As it happens, Prof. Avraham Fraenkel was none but the uncle of Prof. Aviezri Fraenkel, from the Computer Science Department of the Weizman Insitute of Science, a colleague and personal friend for many years, and the one asked, by pure chance, by the BISFAI 2001 Program Committee to speak at the BISFAI banquet convened in my honor. Neither the Program Committee nor Aviezri himself knew a word of this story. And this is how it came to be that, forty-three years after his uncle (from Germany) praised my uncle (from Egypt), we were both standing at this banquet (in Jerusalem) with him toasting me...

And this is how the first wheel "has come full circle"

My real fascination with mathematics, however, begun in the last couple of years of my high school studies at the *Lycée Français* in Cairo (1948 - 1952), and the additional year I spent there studying almost only mathematics, in preparation for the entrance examinations to the *"Grandes Écoles"* of Paris. Before going further on this, however, I would like first to spin yet another wheel within this wheel. I was then fifteen years old, my Hebrew was then, and I hope still is, excellent, and my French was, but alas is no more, very good. Many of the students in the *Lycée* were Jewish, but none of them knew really Hebrew. I therefore thought of doing something useful in this situation, and began translating poems from the romantic nineteenth century French poets such as Victor Hugo, Lamartine and Alfred de Musset, to Hebrew, going as far as translating also *L'Avare* of Molière, while compiling, at the same time, a Hebrew-French dictionary. Needless to say everything was done then manually, FAHQT (Fully Automatic High-Quality Translation) not being available then, as it is not yet available now, fifty years later, and as (read my lips) it will not be available probably in the next fifty years. This, despite the claim in a leaflet I picked up at an NAACL conference in Pittsburgh in 2001 publicizing an Automatic Translation Product whose design "follows Fully Automatic High Quality Translation design concepts". Little did they know, probably, that the acronym FAHQT was invented by the late Yehoshua Bar Hillel from the Hebrew University in the mid-sixties in his famous ALPAC report, just to emphasize that such a design is *not* possible, and you have either to drop the FA (Fully Automatic) or the HQ (High Quality) part to make it feasible.

Anyway, going back to my Hebrew-French dictionary project, I began writing down in strict alphabetical order all the Hebrew words I knew, being careful to begin every new letter with a new page, and to leave a few empty lines between each two consecutive words, just in case I will have to add later in between some forgotten word. As you can imagine, after a few days my notebook became so crammed, with a lot of arrows pointing everywhere and with no empty places to add new words, that I became desperate about ever finishing the project, and had to admit that I miserably failed in it. Little did I know then that you could write the words on 3×5 cards and then simply sort the cards alphabetically, which shows either that this is indeed a genial idea, or that I was too dumb then for such a project.

This said, I took my revenge on this failure, with flying colors, some forty five years later, when, as the culmination of an eight-year project *("Rav-Milim")* for the intelligent processing of modern Hebrew, I published in 1997 a new and comprehensive 6-volume dictionary of modern Hebrew built upon modern lexicographical principles, which was quite revolutionary in terms of Hebrew dictionary making, and in which the computer played an absolutely primordial role.

Let me note *en passant* that part of the *Rav-Milim* project was the development of an automatic vocalizer for modern Hebrew, a complex and tough task even for knowledgeable native speakers of the language, usually taught to first-year university students of Hebrew linguistics, which, despite the very high proportion of ambiguous forms in an ordinary Hebrew text, performed remarkably well, and won me and my team (headed by Yoni Neeman) the Israel Information Processing Association Annual Prize for Best Scientific and Technological Application of Computers, in 1992, and, a year later, the Israel Prime Minister Prize for Computing.

Though very dear to me, I have to refrain from giving more details about the *Rav-Milim* project and *Rav-Milim* dictionary here.

How could I have imagined back then, in 1952, in Cairo, while playing soccer with my friends using a small ball made of old socks stitched together, that some forty years later I would be living in Jerusalem, in an independent Jewish state, compiling such a dictionary, with the help of magical tool called a computer?

And this is how the second wheel has come full circle.

Coming back to my years at the *Lycée Français*, I should first mention that all the teachers there were French, *agrégés* of the *Grandes Écoles*, and all of them were just excellent and first-rate educators. What I learned there in terms of mathematics, logic, philosophy of science, methodical thinking, and the scientific way of approaching and solving problems, as taught by Descartes in his famous *"Discours de la Methode"*, shaped my whole intellectual life, and helped me manage successfully some of the large projects in IR and NLP, as well as other daring computerization projects that I was fool enough to initiate, but was somehow always lucky to bring to a successful end.

It is there that I came to appreciate the beauty of a mathematical proof. I was taught then by my teacher *"Monsieur Thenos"* that such a proof has to be not only correct, but also clear, elegant, short and natural. It is not enough to be able to follow a proof or to be able to check it mathematically; you have to "understand" it, you have to feel that it is flowing naturally and gracefully, like a gentle stream of clear water in a small country garden. Which reminds me of the following wonderful quotation from an 18th century essay on the French language by *de Rivarol*: *"Ce qui n'est pas clair, n'est pas Français"*, "Whatever is not clear, is not French" (Antoine de Rivarol, *Discours sur l'Universalité de la Langue Française, 1784*).

In the same vein, I can add: any proof that is not crystal-clear is probably not yet the ultimate proof.

In my teaching career, I probably taught more than thirty different courses in mathematics and computer science, some of them in really thorny subjects with complex theorems, such as real analysis, classical analysis, differential equations, beside courses in advanced set theory, mathematical logic, computability, and the like. I always made it a point in all of these courses never to give the lecture with the help of written notes, as my students can indeed testify. My belief has always been that if you cannot reconstruct the proof on the spot and present it smoothly to your students, then you probably don't really understand it, or maybe something is not quite right or natural in the proof itself. Contrary to what my students apparently thought, it is not a question of memorizing, but of understanding.

This obsession, because it is indeed an obsession, of always trying to shorten and simplify a proof, to make it more natural, clear and elegant, which I learned at the Cairo *Lycée*, is at the core of much of what I did or published in mathematics, including parts of my Ph.D. thesis. I could give scores of examples on that, but I will give just a very peculiar, illuminating and interesting one. While I was working on my doctoral thesis under the supervision of Michael Rabin, Rabin was then in the process of polishing the first draft of his paper on the theory of automata on infinite trees, a theory as powerful as it is complex. He gave me the paper's draft, asking me to look into it. I spent a couple of months trying to understand and analyze that very long and unusually complex proof, dissecting it, so to speak, lemma by lemma and argument by argument. Finally I met him and gave him a two-hour presentation of his paper, at the end of which he remained silent for a couple of minutes, then said: "You know, Yaacov, this is the first time I really understand my proof...". And that was the sweetest compliment I could ever aspire to from one of the brightest minds in computer science, and one of the best teachers and lecturers I ever heard.

Without going into any technical details, I would like to mention two (among many others) of these simplification ideas. Because he apparently didn't need it explicitly in his theory, Rabin didn't bother to mention or to prove that the intersection of two regular sets of infinite trees (whatever this is) is a regular set of the same type. Still, in three different places of the proof, he was building some very complex automata that had to simultaneously satisfy several different conditions. By just proving the intersection property first, and this is a very easy and quite trivial lemma to prove, and using it later in the various needed automata constructions, the proof would have been much simpler, shorter, clearer and more elegant. In another crucial and hair-splitting part of the proof, I noticed that Rabin was in fact working hard to prove simultaneously a general Koenig-like combinatorial lemma on infinite trees, which has absolutely nothing to do with finite automata, while applying it at the same time to his automata model. By extracting this lemma from the proof, proving it independently and then applying it just where needed, both the lemma's proof and its application to the needed construction were, again, considerably simplified and shortened (this lemma was later published by me independently of the automata theory context, mentioning of course that the idea and proof were extracted from Rabin's paper).

And this is how the third wheel has come its full circle.

Finally, to go back for the last time to Cairo and to the *Lycée*, I was not able then, at the end of these years, to go to Paris and present my candidature to the *Grandes Écoles*, and I had, instead, to work for three years as accountant in a wholesale company, to support the family. Mind you, these were not wasted years; I used the sound accounting principles I learned there to manage some of the largest projects that I directed, and in which considerable amounts of money were flowing in and out.

Having paid tribute to the streets of Cairo, I would like now to move on to an episode from my years as a graduate student at the Hebrew University.

Let me first mention a quotation, which, since ever I saw it for the first time, has been on my mind and gave me support and moral strength in many of the research projects in which I was to be involved later. This quotation has, however, a story, and I have to begin with that story first.

I already mentioned that our teacher for Set Theory at the first year was the famous Avraham Fraenkel. Our other teachers were no less famous. We were taught Linear Algebra by Avraham Robinson, probably the most important logician of the fifties and sixties of the twentieth century, Analytic Geometry by S. Amitsur, author of the famous Amitsur combinatorial lemma, Infinitesimal Calculus by B. Amira, the general editor of the famous *Journal d'Analyse Mathématique*, one of the most aristocratic, selective and elegant of mathematical journals. Rarely can one boast of having such a dream team of teachers for his first year at the university. The same goes for Differential Equations (S. Agmon), Probability and Linear Spaces (A. Dvoretzki), Mathematical Logic, Computability and Automata (M. Rabin) and Theory of Games (Nobel-Prize Winner I. Aumann). I shall forever be indebted to the Hebrew University for allowing me to study at the feet of such masters.

In my final year there I was working on my master thesis, also supervised by Michael Rabin, studying a complicated set-theoretic construction, the ultraproduct, and its special case, the ultrapower, which can be useful in model theory, a branch of mathematical logic. Somewhere along the line I got the feeling that this subject is strongly connected to the Non-Standard Analysis theory created a few years earlier by Avraham Robinson, and still under further development by him at that time. I read then everything Robinson wrote about the subject, and got caught by the daring concept, the beauty and elegance of the new treatment of infinitesimals, in which clean algebraic and logical notions and notations replaced the very cumbersome and annoying *"epsilon-delta"* apparatus. So much so, in fact, that in my final test on Differential Equations in 1962, when I was asked to prove the existence and uniqueness of a solution to a certain differential equation, I did it by using Non-standard Analysis techniques, and I was probably the first ever student to do such a thing in a test.

Anyway I was able to prove in this thesis a simple meta-theorem in non-standard analysis, which had as corollaries many theorems previously proved by Robinson. He got interested in my thesis and as a consequence we developed then a close relationship and met several times and for many years. I was many times deeply impressed by a rather sad and depressed look in his eyes. His daring, breathtaking and beautiful theory was not well received or recognized, at that time, neither by mathematicians nor by logicians. The mathematicians couldn't follow his logical arguments, since few of them ever learned mathematical logic, and the logicians were not interested in the new mathematical applications.

A few years later, in 1974, he published a new book on Non-Standard Analysis, with the following French quotation (taken from the essay of the French philosopher Montaigne "On the Solitude") appearing on the book front:

"Souvienne vous de celuy a qui, comme on demanda a quoi faire il se peignoit si fort en un art qui ne pouvoit venir a la cognaissance de guerres de gents, "j'en ai assez de peu", repondit-il, "j'en ai assez d'un, j'en ai assez de pas un".

"Remember the one who, when asked why is he toiling so hard on an art that cannot reach the knowledge of other people, replied, "Few of them are enough for me, one of them is enough for me, none of them is enough for me".

So many times I had this loneliness feeling; the feeling that you are alone in your endeavors, that very few indeed are aware of what you are doing or achieving, to say nothing about appreciating it. This quotation would then give me the needed support: very few of them should be enough for you, one of them should be enough for you, none of them should be also enough for you.

This may shed some light on why I emphasize sometimes, in what follows, that "this was the first time" that so-and-so was achieved. Indeed, some of my results went largely unnoticed at the time by the academic community, to be put again into focus only much later, sometimes twenty years or more later, when the subject finally became fashionable.

Although this feeling was more persistent in my work in IR and NLP, still a got a first taste of it when I developed and then published my results in the theory of finite automata on infinite tapes. The subject was mainly looked upon then as an interesting abstract mathematical "game", which can be useful for solving some decision problems in mathematical logic. Very few researchers were indeed interested in such a topic at that time. Slowly it became apparent however that these constructions have an interesting and rich structure of their own. And so, a growing body of literature began to emerge on these structures and their properties. Suddenly, however, about the mid-eighties, I began receiving a torrential rain of requests for reprints of my basic paper in this topic, and I couldn't understand what was really happening here. I soon learned, however, that it was discovered that automata on infinite tapes are exactly the right context to develop some special theories of program verification (with "really" practical applications), and so this subject became fashionable (one of the leaders of this trend was Moshe Vardi, who attended as a graduate student a course on Automata Theory which I gave at the Weizmann Institute, and was so caught by the beauty and elegance of the subject that he decided to make it one of his main areas of research). So much so in fact that a textbook on Program Verification written by a Bell Labs researcher and published in 1994 included several chapters devoted solely to that paper and to what the author called "Choueka flag construction". I was very happy to see that, since I do believe – unlike maybe some of my colleagues – that the ultimate recognition for a piece of research is whether it is eventually integrated in a textbook. This is in the same spirit of what S. Agnon, the Nobel Prize laureate in literature and the most famous Hebrew writer of modern times, said once, that of all the possible prizes, the one he is most aspiring to is that a few lines of what he ever wrote would eventually find their way into the Jewish prayer book.

If I have some regret about how my research career developed, it is that, because of other occupations and responsibilities, I had to neglect the automata topic shortly before it became so important and fashionable, and when so many mathematically beautiful results were achieved in it. I would have immensely enjoyed working in it and maybe contributing something to it, since I feel that I understood and mastered those topics, at that time, quite deeply.

In any case, the lesson is that science trends and fashions have their own surprising turns and detours; just be patient!

Coming back now to the sub-title of my talk "Languages, Information and Intelligence", you have probably already noticed that every word in it has at least a double connotation: "Languages" denote both natural and formal languages, "Information" encompasses both the content of communication and the material to be stored, processed and retrieved, and "intelligence" denotes both natural and artificial intelligence. It should be obvious how communicated information is connected to natural languages. After all, communication between human beings is achieved mainly through natural language, despite the fact that some communication can be indeed achieved through gestures, body language and the like. But what about language and intelligence? For that, let me refer you to my other paper in this book, about natural language processing. There I quote the quite widespread claim that language may be the main property that differentiates between man and all other living or non-living entities, and that it is therefore the essence of his "intelligence". It seems, though, that only now, in the computer age, do we begin to really appreciate the extraordinary complexity of the natural language (any natural language) world, and our inherent inability to find the necessary algorithms that would lead the computer to process it in a truly intelligent way.

Let me now then spin in this context a fourth wheel, that of morphology. My involvement with morphology goes back to 1962. After graduating in the summer of 1962 from the Hebrew University, I began my regular military service in the IDF,

Israel Defense Forces, and was immediately sent to a computer-programming course, the first ever organized in Israel. By and large, there were in Israel at that time only two computers: one at the Weizmann Institute of Science, the other at IDF. Returning to my unit, I was given my first assignment and this is how my commander, Lieutenant Colonel Meir Shapira, put it. "Look", he said, "computers are being more and more powerful and are being applied to a host of applications, including text manipulation (this was 1962!). We have to prepare ourselves to a time when computers will play a crucial role in text analysis, performing tasks that will require probably deep linguistic knowledge, and we have to begin mastering the needed methodologies and technologies. So let us first begin with a language we know well, Hebrew, and with the most elementary step needed, which is morphological analysis and lemmatization. Your assignment therefore is to build a computerized morphological analyzer and lemmatizer for Hebrew, and to integrate it in a package for the automatic production of concordances, where the entries are sorted by lemmas, or even by roots, rather than by forms".

This assignment was met with very fierce opposition by all the other officers in that unit, who thought that it was a lunatic and useless task, and that Meir was just "wasting the talents" of a "rare bird" (me…), who just got his M.Sc. with High Distinction in Mathematics, who is fluent – besides Hebrew – also in Arabic, French and English, and so could be of use in so many other more important tasks. Meir, who had as background a solid British military training, stood his ground firmly, and so was it decided. I pay here tribute to the memory of that intelligent man, who always saw ten steps ahead of everyone else around him, and thus was often left alone in many of his daring decisions.

It took me about a year and a half to complete my assignment, check it, and declare it ready. I did the linguistic analysis, the system analysis, the programming, the debugging, the checking, in fact everything except the actual input of the fully tagged dictionary into the computer, which was done by a typist. The program was written in Assembler language, for the simple reason that no high level language, not even Fortran, was available and ready at that time for such a task. This was 1962, when computers didn't even have upper and lower case characters, and this was Hebrew, a Semitic language with a very rich and complex morphology. I would like to emphasize that the system was not built as a toy system, or as a prototype or a "proof of concept" module. It was a fully operational, comprehensive and accurate system that performed as well as any linguist would do, and was tested by the automatic construction of a concordance of the first 80 pages of "Tsiklag Days", an important and quite difficult book by the modern Israeli writer S. Izhar. Except, of course, that I didn't handle the word-sense disambiguation problem. So every ambiguous form that could be attributed, when out of context, to several different lemmas, indeed appeared in the concordance under each of these different lemmas (this was my first encounter with the word-sense disambiguation problem).

This was probably the first fully operational, complete and accurate morphological analyzer and lemmatizer ever developed for any language.

It should be mentioned here that – for reasons to be detailed later - morphology was not fashionable in the sixties, seventies, and up to the mid-eighties of the last century. In fact, as late as the early nineties (so almost thirty years after my first work for Hebrew), there was no portable, fully operational, comprehensive and accurate lemmatizer for English, certainly the most common language researched.

Many years ago I had a heated argument on this point with Ken Church at one of the ACL conferences. When I asked how is it that till then no comprehensive, accurate and operational lemmatizer existed for English, he replied that everybody knows that it can be done, and there is no real challenge in doing it. Indeed. That is why people were developing partial and incomplete solutions such as formal stemmers, comparing the performance of various stemmers, computing precision and recall of such stemmers, and so on and so forth. With a very small fraction of the talent, time, energy and resources spent on that, a fully operational and exact lemmatizer could have been already built and put at the service of all.

Why then didn't I do it myself, you may ask? Well, because it is none of my business. I was willing to put a lot of time and energy in building the infrastructure needed for the intelligent processing of Hebrew, so that when new successful technologies would be available for high-level text processing and understanding, the ground will be ready for applying them to Hebrew. I care about Hebrew, and it was obvious that if we don't do the job ourselves, nobody is going to do it for us. Otherwise, my research in NLP was never specific to any language, but was rather developed to be applicable to any "reasonable" language, as can be noticed by looking at my work on collocations, word-sense disambiguation or the embedding of linguistic components in text -retrieval systems.

In any case, things changed dramatically in the nineties, when a lot of projects (and accordingly a lot of papers), were produced on morphology, a clear case, in my opinion, of over-killing. The morphology pendulum was swinging too fast, from almost no activity, to hyper-activity.

To sum up my view on that point: morphology is a problem that has to be completely, accurately and comprehensively solved, without sparing any efforts required for that. Once solved, however, it should be looked upon as a black box, and there shouldn't be much to say about it after that, unless you are interested in comparative linguistics or in high-level abstract linguistic models, which is rarely the case in NLP.

Spinning now the morphology wheel, it was because of what I did in my military unit in 1962/63 that Aviezri Fraenkel, who was initiating a large full-text retrieval system in the mid-sixties, known since then as the Responsa Project, asked me to join his team and contribute the linguistic component to that full-text system. This is how I got introduced, through this project, to the world of information retrieval, and the rest, as far as I was concerned is, as they say, history.

In fact I contributed two different morphological systems to the Responsa Project: the first one, in the late sixties, adapted to the batch (off-line) retrieval system then operational, and the second one, in the mid-seventies, adapted to the online system then under preparation, and which became operational in 1980. My ultimate version of a morphological analyzer and lemmatizer for modern Hebrew, however, was completed in 1989 as a component of the large *Rav-Milim* project mentioned above. This program, *Milim*, is now by and large the standard morphological component available and embedded in most advanced Hebrew full-text systems currently operational in Israel.

With this, almost thirty years after my first step in computational morphology, I finally put my interest in this topic to rest, bringing the fourth wheel full circle.

What happened with morphology is symptomatic to what happened to many other topics that are now considered as essential elements of NLP, and were totally neglected in the sixties, seventies and up to the mid eighties. Many reasons can be cited for that, but the main one seems to me to be Noam Chomsky's attitude. In the sixties and seventies Chomsky was king. His theories, his approach, his word, were the law in linguistics, including in computational linguistics. I don't have to reiterate here the unique and unparalleled contributions of Chomsky to our understanding of the language structure, and the way he opened for us new intellectual horizons in this context. We are all his disciples and his admirers. Being myself extremely enthusiastic then about this new world, I contributed in 1969 a paper in Hebrew presenting some of Chomsky ideas and formalism and applying them to formalize some parts of Hebrew morphology. I know personally a few heads of departments of Hebrew Linguistics who got their introduction to Chomsky theories through that paper.

Unfortunately, there was no place in Chomsky theories for morphology, dictionaries, collocations or word-sense disambiguation. More importantly, corpora and probability, the two most important tools of current NLP, were considered by him and his school to be absolute Taboo.

In the late seventies, there was already an uneasy feeling about the situation in Computational Linguistics. Beautiful and deep as much as the theoretical models were, they were sterile as practical solutions to computerized language understanding. Most of what was produced then consisted of formidable and practically unusable parsers. In the mid-eighties, a decisive change happened, which can be best described by this subtle shift in terminology from Computational Linguistics to Natural Language Processing. Again there were many reasons why this happened about that time, some of them related to technological innovations in hardware, software and networks, but to single just one major different reason, the reins of research and development in languages and computers changed hands, from linguists trying to build models of language and being assisted by programmers, to computer scientists interested in solving practical problems being assisted (when needed) by linguists.

Where and how did the Responsa Project team, and I, as part of it, fit in this picture in those years?

As I mentioned before, I spent quite some time working on Hebrew, and I paid a price for that. There is a limit to the number of papers that deal with Hebrew that you can present to international conferences in the pre-1995 period, when "globalization" was not even a recognized word. You could stretch this limit a little bit by claiming from time to time that the technologies presented could be applied to Arabic too; you would get then a listening ear, since Arabic is where the potentially big markets are and where the big money is.

From the price I paid, however, I got every penny back. Because we were lucky enough to work in two quite complex environments - Hebrew on one hand, Rabbinical historical documents on the other - we became aware much earlier than others about crucial problems in IR and NLP, for which we had to devise adequate solutions. Hebrew is an unvocalized Semitic language based on roots and patterns, with a rich morphology, a very flexible word order in its syntax, a very large collocational component, an exceptionally high degree of ambiguity, with no upper/lower case differentiation, and more. On the other hand, we were busy researching the Responsa system, one of the very first full-text retrieval systems to be developed for Humanities' scholars, with a huge corpus of (at that time) about seventy million words of Rabbinical documents spanning one thousand years and originating from more than fifty different countries, with a sophisticated linguistic component embedded in it, with a small but sophisticated group of users with whom we were interacting on a daily basis, and who pushed us to always do better and satisfy their advanced needs.

As I mentioned before, the project was initiated in the mid-sixties by Prof. Aviezri Fraenkel and was led by him (as a join project of the Weizmann Institute and Bar-Ilan University) till 1975, when, upon transferring the project completely to Bar-Ilan, I replaced him as the Project Head till 1986.

Working in these environments exposed us already in the seventies and early eighties to a host of interesting IR and NLP problems, which have become hot topics of research only much later. I detail in what follows a partial list of such topics that we researched at that time. Many of the results achieved were published (mostly in conference proceedings), but many also (may be even many more) were not, for reasons partially mentioned above.

The topics researched (and for every such item, it can be easily explained why and how it was raised by the described environments) included, in NLP: morphological analysis and lemmatization, word-sense disambiguation, collocations extraction and processing, names' recognition, and in IR: embedding linguistic components in full-text systems, feedback techniques, text compression, full-text inverted files architecture and compression, hypertext systems, OCR automatic error checking and correction, and more.

Even the concept of a full-text system itself was hardly recognized at that time by the IR community as a legitimate academic concept, worthy of research and implementation, and I am sure that Aviezri shared with me the feeling of isolation and frustration caused by the IR community being totally geared at that time towards the Salton SMART vector systems.

I vividly recall an anecdote related to this situation. In the summer of 1975 I visited Prof. Salton - then the Guru and the father figure of IR - in his office at Cornell University, to discuss with him our ideas about full-text systems and the results we achieved with it so far. His reaction was quite fierce. He was so furious that anyone would dare develop IR systems which were not according to the SMART design, that he began shouting at me that we don't know what we are doing, that we are mixing apples with oranges, and that this approach can never, and will never, work. Finally we made some shaky peace when he invited me to spend the evening with him at his lovely home near the lake.

Was our idea of full-text for IR such a wrong one? Just ask yourself what is the main method with which you — and millions of others — extract information from the Internet. On a more practical plan, if you wish, Bar-Ilan has been commercializing the full-text Responsa system, corpus and retrieval engine, very successfully, for the last twenty years, selling the expensive CD-ROM and its never-ending new versions to tens of thousands of users all over the world.

The vast Talmudic literature, from which the Responsa literature cites abundantly, is replete with collocations and sequences of words that are both common and with unique, many times idiomatic. meanings. It was therefore natural for our team to try and find adequate approaches for the automatic extraction of such collocations from the very vast corpus of tens of millions of words then available in the Responsa system. Our approach, developed in the late seventies and published in 1983, based on some mathematical modeling, was quite unique and we did not see it replicated, even in spirit, in the prolific literature on collocations that began to appear about ten years later. The paper also reported the results of an experiment in which native language speakers helped in deciding whether an extracted "collocation" was indeed a collocation, by trying to guess the entire sequence of words given its beginning, again an approach that was apparently quite unique.

This intriguing question of automatic retrieval of collocations obsessed me ever since. In 1986/87 I spent a sabbatical year at Bellcore (Bell Communications Research, an advanced private research company in NJ). There I had the very good fortune of being part of a group of gifted NLP researchers such as Mike Lesk, Don Walker, Bob Amsler and others, and of being able to process the there available computerized corpus of the daily New York Times text covering about nine years and containing almost ten million words, a notably large corpus at these times. Keeping the basic idea of our original approach but eliminating the mathematical apparatus, I developed a new algorithm for collocations' extraction in which I restricted myself to processing the available text only, ignoring any potentially helpful tools such as dictionaries, stemmers, lemmatizers, morphological analyzers, parsers and the like.

While preparing the paper that was supposed to describe the approach and its results, and which I was planning to submit to the RIAO 88 Conference in Cambridge Mass., I got a polite call from Bellcore's lawyers asking me to please omit any specific details about the algorithm from that paper (assuming probably that it may have some meaningful market value...). Reluctantly, I had to comply with this request.

Intrigued by the omission of such details while inspecting at the same time the quite stunning results achieved both in terms of "recall" (thousands of genuine collocations) and "precision" (relatively very few "false drops"), my listeners/readers had to assume that a quite formidable algorithm is behind these results. The algorithm, on the contrary, was deceptively simple, one of its main tricks being the ability to recognize both "New York Times" and its subsequence "New York" as collocations, while rejecting "York Times" as one, although it has the same frequency as "New York Times" (the hint is simple: it is rejected *just* because it has the same frequency!). I was asked then by the editor of the IR&M Journal to publish the full paper with the detailed algorithm in that journal, and I promised to do so once out of Bellcore. Unfortunately, as my colleagues can guess, new ideas, new projects and new challenges, postponed this promise's fulfillment year after year, until it became quite irrelevant. Anyway, the paper, published in the Proceedings of that conference, turned out apparently to be some landmark in this area, and I know about many M.Sc. and Ph.D. theses that used this paper as a starting point for further refinements and developments in automatic collocations' extraction approaches.

I can add an interesting final touch to this episode.

Bellcore's lawyers were not really so much off the mark. A short time after my talk a representative of some agency of the US Air Force Intelligence visited me at my Bellcore office, asking for the details of the algorithm which they were thinking of applying to solve one of their vexing problems. They have to scan in short times hundreds of thousands of scientific papers and abstracts from various sources, in order to pinpoint new emerging technologies, scientific issues or problems (such as, say, "global warming", "gene replication", etc) that were in the focus of research of these sources and of which they are, maybe, unaware, through the detection of recurring collocations in this corpus. This visit was followed by many others in which the algorithm was further refined and adapted to these needs.

That wonderful year at Bellcore provided me with the opportunity of using this *New York Times* corpus to check yet another idea that I developed in the early seventies in the framework of the Responsa Project, and to check whether it works for English corpora too.

In the early seventies, one of the users of the system asked us to retrieve documents that deal with "witness", "testify" etc., including all their grammatical variants (in Hebrew all these words have the same root). That was apparently an easy query, because of the morphological module that was embedded in the system. We run it on the then batch system, and the output, being quite voluminous, was sent to the user with a messenger. He came back to us very angry, claiming that almost all of the output was totally irrelevant, as indeed we found out immediately, the reason being that the two-letter word denoting "witness" in Hebrew can also function as the very common preposition denoting "until"…

The question then presented itself, how can we help the system to discern automatically, at least for most of the occurrences of this form, which is which. Especially so since in Hebrew most written words are ambiguous in a similar way, "mother" (*em,* written with the letters *aleph* and *mem*) is also "if" i*m,* written with the same letters *aleph* and *mem*), "brother" is also "hearth" (same spelling and pronunciation), "father" is also the name of a Hebrew month (same spelling and pronunciation), "uncle" (*dod*) is also "vat" (*dud,* the spelling being DWD), and so forth.

I spent long nights looking at that output and the occurrences of this and similar words in the corpus, and I came to two conclusions:

(a) in most cases the word preceding or following the ambiguous one can easily disambiguate its meaning correctly,

(b) by compiling a list of all frequent different common neighbors, manually specifying the meaning according to this neighbor in these different cases and then spreading this disambiguation decision to all occurrences of the ambiguous word with that specific neighbor, the system can in fact disambiguate most occurrences of that ambiguous word.

I didn't have then the opportunity to quantify these findings, until a few years later, when I spent a sabbatical at the University of Montreal. There, together with Serge Lusignan, we checked these findings very thoroughly on a French book that was then (1980) available electronically. The findings, published only in 1985 (the editor writing to us three years after the paper's submission that he lost it...), confirmed that indeed these findings – which we were able then to quantify - are valid also for French, and this is how "Short-context Disambiguation" ("Short is Beautiful") was born, when word-sense disambiguation was not a really hot issue yet. The idea then presented itself of building a special Disambiguation Dictionary, in which the entries are all ambiguous words (with different semantic fields) in the language, each entry containing its most common neighbors as extracted automatically from large corpora, the neighbors being tagged (manually) with the correct meaning. This dictionary can then grow automatically by applying it to large corpora, harvesting new words close to the ambiguous one and tagging them with the neighbor's tag, again and again, in a kind of "boot-strapping" technique. The idea unfortunately was never implemented or published. The short context approach was not even implemented in the Responsa system ("if it is working and selling well, why bother improve it?...").

That year at Montreal was successful in yet another aspect. The problem of an efficient implementation for the processing of prefix or infix truncation such as in *mycin or in M*h*m*d (where * stands for any sequence of characters) was considered in the late seventies as very complex and an obstacle to the further development of advanced IR systems, and in fact was listed by Salton in his Chairman's Message in the ACM SIGIR Forum in 1980 as one of the outstanding problems in IR.

Working with Paul Bratley there, we devised a very elegant, efficient, fast and easily programmable (no more than a few lines) algorithm for its solution, although its correctness proof is not very direct. The paper, published in 1982, won us the Israel Information Processing Association Annual Prize for Best Research Paper in Computer Science.

Shortly after this paper's publication I was asked by Lexis, then the most important and largest full-text retrieval system in the US, to come and explain the algorithm to their programmers. Though quite superfluous, since everything was very clearly explained in the paper, I met with their programmers and then pocketed the fattest check I ever received for a couple of hours of consulting...

Back to Bellcore and short-context disambiguation, I used the New York Times corpus there to check how well this can work for English texts, analyzing the occurrences of "party" (= political party, celebration, group of people such as in "the president party", etc). And indeed it was found that about thirty neighbors – clearly disambiguating this word – account for a huge proportion of the occurrences of "party" in the corpus (the results were never published).

What does all this have to do with Artificial Intelligence?

Well, it is quite fashionable now to include NLP activities under this rather impressive banner, and maybe rightly so. If natural language is associated with natural intelligence as was claimed above, then it is fit that computerized – that is artificial – understanding of language should be associated with artificial intelligence.

So where are we heading now with NLP research? This is the topic of my other paper in this book, so I won't expand more on that here.

Let me now spin the Hebrew wheel its full circle, bringing it to its stopping point. Towards the end of the twentieth century's nineties, noticing that many of my best friends in the computer science department are joining emerging start-ups of various kinds, or even building their own, I decided to jump on the galloping wagon, and after some shopping around I joined a young start-up that had a very challenging target, which would include anything someone like me would dream of: web crawling, text categorization, information extraction, natural language processing, dialogue systems, information retrieval, and machine learning. Except that, as the company's president warned me in our first meeting, with a menacing raised finger, "No Hebrew here, Yaacov!"

Soon after retiring formally from the university, I had the unbelievable chance of finally spinning the "Grand Wheel": back to Cairo!

The Cairo Genizah is a staggering collection of Hebrew manuscripts, discovered mostly about 1900 in a loft of an old synagogue in the medieval part of Cairo. Spanning almost a thousand years, and comprising some 350,000 fragmentary texts, the Cairo Genizah is an incredibly rich and important collection of documents that outlines the history of the Jewish communities in the Middle East, containing very important religious sources (Bible, Talmud, rabbinical writings, etc) as well as personal letters, reports, court decisions, and what not. Residing now in more than sixty different public and university libraries all over the world, about 60% of its contents are currently at Cambridge University Library, the major other collections being in Oxford, in London, in New York, in Paris, and in various other European cities. Though extensively researched in the last hundred years, it goes without saying that the task is far from being finished. Through a generous grant by Mr. Dov Friedberg from Canada, the Friedberg Genizah Project was initiated about ten years ago, to give a real boost to Genizah research. Many attempts were made to harness computers and computer technology to this effort, but they stumbled on the difficult question of what is there really to computerize and how to do it. Asked towards the end of 2005 to try and meet this challenge, and arming myself with all the experience

I managed to get by many years of researching the interaction between computers, texts, languages, Hebrew, IR and NLP, I designed a strategy and a well-detailed plan, which I started to implement with a team of programmers and researchers early 2006. This is by far one of the most complex, challenging and satisfying projects I ever directed. The results achieved so far, available through the website (www.genizah.org) - in terms of producing new tools and new and efficient ways for studying the Genizah – seem indeed to be quite remarkable, and in the words of many of the most prominent Genizah scholars, will revolutionize the Genizah research world in the coming years.

Like the Sphinx near Cairo, which has been silent for so many thousands of years, so it seems the Cairo Genizah was silently waiting for one of its own children to come and help her speak out its so far buried legacy.

Looking back now at what I did in these forty-plus years in the domains of AT, IR and NLP, and asking myself what were my best achievements, I feel inclined to say: first my students, then my projects (three of which – out of ten – were mentioned here), and finally my papers (no more than about ten of them).

I was triply lucky in my academic life: I had the best masters, the best colleagues, and the best students. How easily and naturally I endorse the 2,000-year Talmudic saying (Tractate Makkot, folio 10a) by Rabbi Yehuda Hanassí (Rabbi Judah the Ethnarch, also known as "Rabbi" for short), the spiritual and communal leader in the Land of Israel at the beginning of the third century: "Said Rabbi: I learned much from my masters, even more from my colleagues, and the most from my students".

May you, my patient reader, who had the courage to reach these lines, always get deep satisfaction from every day of your research, and may your colleagues and students be as smart, talented, challenging and loyal as mine were.

Yaacov Choueka: A Profile

The Editors[1]

Yaacov Choueka was born in 1936 in Cairo, Egypt to a family of renowned rabbis who had emigrated from Aleppo to Cairo in the early years of the twentieth century. Yaacov's great grandfather, Hakham Aharon, had been Chief Rabbi of Aleppo, Syria, in the 1870).

In Egypt, Choueka absorbed – and learned to cherish – the Arabic language, on the literary as well as the colloquial level, and developed an appreciation of Egyptian cultural heritage, especially musical heritage. He is quite a *maven* in classical Arabic music, with its unique modalities of *maqamat*, and in the Egyptian musical scene of the 1920s through the 1970s, in particular the musical world of the genial composer Mohammed Abdel Wahab and the inimitable diva Om Kolsum.

At the same time, Choueka's social milieu and his studies at the French Lycée Français opened the world of French history, culture, literature, philosophy and science to him, and in particular the French insistence on clarity, precision and elegance of thought. It is there that he discovered his affinity for mathematical thinking and there that his talents were sharpened and honed.

After the Sinai campaign, in January 1957, Choueka and his relatives followed in the footsteps of other family members who had already left Egypt for Israel.

In October 1957, Choueka started his studies at the Department of Mathematics at the Hebrew University in Jerusalem, where he studied numerous mathematical subjects sitting at the feet of masters of international fame. He found himself, however, mostly attracted to the areas of foundations of mathematics, of mathematical logic and of computability, as sharpened by the use of precise mathematical tools. In 1962, Choueka received his M.Sc. (with distinction), submitting a thesis, supervised by Michael Rabin, on "Ultra-products and non-Standard Analysis", and in 1971 he received his Ph.D., submitting a thesis, also supervised by Michael Rabin, on "Finite Automata on Finite and Infinite Structures".

From the summer of 1962 until the end of 1964, Choueka did his military service in the Israel Defense Forces, ultimately attaining the rank of Captain. During the course of his service, he attended the first course on programming ever given in Israel and wrote programs in Assembler Language on the first and only computer (the "Philco") then operating in Israel (first, except for an innovative scientific computer – the WEIZAC – built by the Weizmann Institute of Science). In the summer of 1965, he married Sarah Shweka, and together they were blessed with eight children and (at this writing) 20 grandchildren; they hope to celebrate their golden wedding anniversary in a couple of years.

---

[1] Based on material provided by, and discussions with, Yaacov Choueka.

N. Dershowitz and E. Nissan (Eds.): Choueka Festschrift, Part I, LNCS 8001, pp. 19–36, 2014.
© Springer-Verlag Berlin Heidelberg 2014

In October 1964, Choueka joined the Department of Mathematics at Bar-Ilan University, attaining the rank of Full Professor and joining the University Senate in 1990. With the establishment of the Department of Computer Science at Bar Ilan in 2002 (for the creation of which he had struggled hard and stubbornly since the late 1970s), Choucka joined it, remaining there until his retirement, in 2005, as Professor Emeritus of Computer Science.

In the forty years of his academic career, Choueka balanced – in his unique way, which reflects well his personality and his profile – the various aspects of such a career: research, publications, conferences, teaching, guiding students, and academic and public activities. "Cultivating a brilliant student is most certainly more important than publishing a couple of papers which oftentimes have only a short-lived impact", he frequently claimed. Choueka supervised sixteen students in their M.Sc. and Ph.D. studies and theses.

During his early years at Bar-Ilan University, Choueka taught a large variety of subjects in mathematics and computer science, including calculus, set theory, number systems, classical analysis, complex functions, differential equations, linear spaces, and more, concentrating, from the mid-eighties, both in lectures and in research seminars, on mathematical logic, computability theory and automata and formal languages, and, somewhat later, on information retrieval, text algorithms and, finally, on natural language processing.

Until the late eighties, Choueka also taught at several other institutions of higher learning in Israel, offering, for example, a graduate course on automata theory at the Weizmann Institute of Science and a course in computing at the Hebrew University, as well as teaching part-time for a number of years at the Jerusalem College of Technology and at the Jerusalem College for Women. One of his aims in these varied teaching posts was to attract brilliant students to these subjects and encourage them to continue their graduate studies in these domains. Indeed, this is how some of his former star students, now researchers of international fame, started their career.

In the mid-sixties, Choueka joined the Responsa Project, a research project in full-text information retrieval systems, initiated a couple of years earlier by Aviezri Fraenkel of the Weizmann Institute of Science. This proved to be a crucial step, one which profoundly influenced Choueka's academic activities, since he became heavily involved in that project and remained involved in it for twenty years. Soon after joining this joint project of the Weizmann Institute and Bar Ilan University, Choueka became the *de facto* leader of the Bar-Ilan team (1967-1974), and in the summer of 1974, when it was decided to transfer the project to the sole trusteeship of Bar-Ilan University, he was appointed Head of the project, a position he held for twelve years.

The Responsa System, a highly successful and sophisticated full-text system for Rabbinic literature, whose corpus spans more than a thousand years of responsa and other works of Jewish heritage, is the first such system ever developed in Israel and one of the very first to be developed for humanities corpora worldwide. With its unique embedded linguistic component, developed by Choueka in the early seventies (!) and never changed or even touched since then, it is still the most influential and most widely-used system of its kind in Israel.

In September 1998, the Responsa Project was selected, along with 49 additional projects, to receive the "Quality Initiative Citation" in a contest for creative, high-quality and visionary projects, in celebration of the 50th anniversary of the establishment of the State of Israel. In 2007, it won the most prestigious prize awarded in Israel, the Israel Prize.

In order to stabilize the Project's activities, and to give it an adequate academic and administrative home, Choueka, with the approval of the University Senate, in 1974, created the Institute of Information Retrieval and Computational Linguistics (two quite novel domains at that time), and chaired it for thirty years, until his retirement in 2005. In the Institute, housed in the framework of the Faculty of Exact Sciences, Choueka initiated and built, in the mid-eighties, *Maba'* ("Bar-Ilan corpus of Modern Hebrew"), a large structured corpus of various strata of Modern Hebrew, a necessary tool for the computerized research of modern Hebrew.

At the height of the Responsa Project activities, a Center for Computers and Jewish Heritage was established at Bar-Ilan, which Choueka also chaired for three years (1983–1986).

Choueka's research interests, which shifted over the years, and the many publications that resulted, detailed in the annexed list of publications, are well represented by the three sabbatical years he spent outside of Israel. His first sabbatical (1974-1975) was at the Department of Mathematics of the University of Illinois at Urbana-Champaign, where he worked and published mainly on automata theory and formal languages. His second sabbatical (1979-1980) was at the Department of Computer Science and the *Institut d'études Médiévales* of the University of Montreal, to which he was invited by the Committee of the Program for Distinguished Visitors. His time there was spent working and publishing on information retrieval and full-text systems (architecture, compression, feedback and linguistic components). His third sabbatical (1986-1987) was at the Bell Communications Research (Bellcore) Laboratories in Morristown, NJ, where he worked and thereafter published on natural language processing (computerized lexicography, dictionaries and grammars; morphology, lemmatization and tagging; word-sense disambiguation; collocation discovery and extraction; corpus linguistics), a year that was followed by two summer visits to that same research laboratory.

Finally, shortly after his retirement, Choueka was asked to head a complex project for the digitization of the large, unique and critically important Cairo Genizah collection of more than 300,000 Jewish manuscripts, and since then, his research and publications shifted to the area of automatic processing of large collections of historical manuscripts and the computer analysis of digital images of such manuscripts.

Three international trips, the first two taken by Choueka in the early stages of his career and all sponsored by relevant organizations, are worth mentioning.

In the summer of 1975, as a preparatory step for his assumption of the position of Head of the Responsa Project, Choueka made a tour of all the major full-text systems in the Unites States and Canada, educating himself in the advanced experimental hardware and software that was being developed in this field and establishing professional contacts with all the major players in this - then novel - technology.

In 1980, the Council of Higher Learning in Israel was examining ways for advancing the status of Israel's university libraries in the digital sphere, and Choueka was asked to visit all the libraries in the United States and Europe in which digitized library systems were being installed (there were about ten of them) and present his recommendations. In his report, Choueka detailed the functioning of the various systems, pointed out their grave deficiencies, and recommended against adopting any of them, suggesting instead the fostering of a then-small Israeli company that was developing a library system by the name of Aleph. His recommendation was endorsed, and today, more than thirty years later, Aleph is the implemented system in all Israeli universities, and is, by far, the most common computerized system of library files in Western university and public libraries.

In the summer of 1990, Choueka was invited by the USSR Academy of Sciences for a two-week visit to Moscow and Leningrad (now St-Petersburg), to lecture at, and exchange information with the researchers of, VINITI, the USSR National Information Retrieval Institute in Moscow. The main task of this institute, housed in a gigantic twelve-story building, was to summarize and translate all scientific and technical publications of the West, disseminating them throughout the USSR scientific and technical communities, producing along the way more than a *million* abstracts a year, and yet not one operational projector could be found there to assist Choueka in his lectures. These were the tumultuous final years of the strict communist regime, still holding tight a few short months before the fall of the Berlin Wall. Choueka's visit was colored with events, adventures, and ways of life that imprinted unforgettable images and sensations on his mind and much affected some of his later attitudes in the scientific, cultural and personal spheres.

Starting in the mid-seventies, Choueka was heavily involved in international and national conference activities, contributing papers, chairing sessions, participating in panels or serving as a member of the organizing or program committees. In fact, many of his contributions, including some of the most frequently cited ones (such as item [43] in the list of publications appearing at the end of this chapter), appeared in conference proceedings and were not subsequently published in journals.

In particular, Choueka organized two international conferences and one national one, all in Jerusalem: the Fifteenth International Conference of the Association for Literary and Linguistic Computing (ALLC, 1988), which he chaired and at which he gave the opening address, the Second International Conference of the Association Internationale Bible et Informatique (AIBI, 1988), and the Eighteenth National Conference of the Information Processing Association of Israel (IPA, 1983), which he also chaired. The ALLC conference, in particular, was distinguished by three "firsts": it was the first conference in computing and the humanities at which free email was available to all attendants, the first at which remote access was available so that speakers could connect to their systems at home and display them at the conference, and the first time a special panel was organized on "Corpus Linguistics", then an emerging discipline.

A selected list of conferences to which Choueka was invited to give a keynote speech or a plenary talk is included at the end of this chapter.

Two remarkable incidents – probably unique in the world of conferences and speakers - from this quite active conference career are worth mentioning here.

In 1977, Choueka was invited by the organizers of ICCH 3 -- The Third International Conference on Computers and the Humanities (Waterloo, Canada) -- to give an opening plenary lecture on the Responsa Project, one of the first examples at that time of the application of computer technologies to Humanities' domains (incidentally, the other plenary speaker was the Iranian Ambassador to Canada…). While he was in the middle of his talk, Serge Lusignan, one of the conference organizers, came running through the lecture hall, approached the podium, asked Choueka to stop for a minute, and announced through the microphone: "I just got a telephone call from Jerusalem that Choueka's wife, Sarah, gave birth twenty minutes ago to a Choueka boy! Mother and child are feeling well". The standing ovation of the audience (really intended to applaud Sarah) was the last thing Choueka heard at that conference, since he hurried immediately after the announcement to catch the first plane back to Tel-Aviv.…

In 1982 Choueka was invited by the Norwegian Research Center for Computers and Law of the University of Oslo, to spend two weeks in Oslo, visiting the Center and giving a talk at the Faculty of Law Auditorium on the Responsa Project, as a prototype of a computerized system for storing and searching legal precedents.

Choueka visited the Center for a couple of days, after which he went touring in Norway with his wife, returning to Oslo to find that the Oslo media was in a frenzy about his planned lecture. Not being able to read Norwegian, he asked the then Chief Rabbi of Norway, Michael Melkior, to explain the situation to him and to keep him updated daily about any developments. These were the days of the Lebanon war, with Arik Sharon as Minster of Defense and Menachem Begin as Prime Minister, and the newspapers were full of vicious allegations about the Israeli Defense Forces committing war crimes against civilians in Lebanon. Journalists were writing vehemently against the planned talk, questioning how the university could invite a scholar from Israel under such circumstances, demanding that the university cancel the talk, and urging the guest to return immediately to his country. Others wrote that politics should not be mixed with science, that the visit had been arranged a long time ago, that the guest had, personally, nothing to do with what was happening in Lebanon, etc. The balance shifted when the University Students' Organization took sides and sent a formal letter to the university asking it to immediately cancel the talk, threatening the organization of large protests and the use of force, if necessary, to prevent anyone from attending the lecture. Violence was in the air, and Choueka was asked by the university if he would prefer to cancel his talk. Despite the advice of the Israel embassy officials that he should indeed cancel the talk, given the delicate situation, and the fact that they could not provide him with the necessary security measures, he told the university that he would give the lecture, unless the university itself cancelled it.

A few minutes before the talk was to start, he went to the Center offices, from where he was escorted, hands tightly coupled with those of the Center Head, for a ten-minute walk to the auditorium through a very narrow, empty, strip in the midst of a tumultuous sea of thousands of students shouting and branding their menacing fists and barricading the entry to the lecture hall. Somehow they got through the door, and there they found a completely empty lecture hall, but for the dean of the university, who had come directly from his office and was waiting on the presidential platform.

The three men waited the customary fifteen minutes, but, faithful to their warning, the students didn't allow anyone to enter the hall. The Center Head asked Choueka if he would like, nonetheless, to give the talk to an empty audience, and Choueka said: certainly, that was why he had come to Oslo. The dean then stood up, arranged his tie, and in a solemn voice congratulated "our distinguished visitor from Israel, etc.", then translated his words into Norwegian, and finally invited Choueka to the podium. Using the projector and his colorful transparencies, Choueka gave an enthusiastic one-hour talk to a large and splendid empty hall, at the end of which the dean stood up and asked if there were any questions, and there being none, since no one was there to ask, and after some hand-clapping, he grabbed Choueka by the elbow, hurried him through a back door and dark corridors to the rear exit of the university, where a taxi was waiting for him, engine running, which took him at full speed to the airport....

A striking feature of Choueka's many-faceted academic activities is his talent at initializing, heading, steering and implementing large and complex projects, both in the academic and the national or public spheres, projects that involve a delicate blend of research, technology and applications, on the one hand, and, on the other, require a solid grip on computer technologies, on the subject-matter (texts, Jewish heritage, linguistics) and on project management in general (leadership, budgets and timetables). One such project has to do with his long involvement with Hebrew computerized processing, which began in 1964 when he developed a fully operational, accurate, and complete morphological analyzer for Hebrew, one of the very first for any language. In the early seventies, he developed the linguistic Hebrew/Aramaic component embedded in the Responsa system mentioned above, a component that is still operational today and is still unique among all operational Jewish heritage full-text systems. In 1989, Choueka initiated and acted as Director and Principal Investigator (1989–1997) of *Rav-Milim*, a broad, robust, comprehensive and integrated computerized infrastructure, with the tools and technologies for the advanced processing of contemporary Hebrew texts, at the Center for Educational Technology in Ramat-Aviv. The outcome of this project consisted of several modules, the most important ones being the following: *Milim*, a complete and accurate morphological analyzer for Modern Hebrew (1989), which is still the only such program fully operational and currently embedded in many major governmental, intelligence and commercial full-text systems in Israel (the spelling-checker derived from *Milim* was chosen by Microsoft to be the standard Hebrew spelling-checker for Word); *Nakdan*, a computerized program for the automatic vocalization of Hebrew words, quite a daunting task, and its companion *Nakdan-text* for vocalizing running Hebrew texts, using a large assortment of word-disambiguation techniques; and *Rav-Milim*, a new dictionary of Modern Hebrew (6 vols., CET, Steimatzky and Miskal, 1997), which introduced new and revolutionary ideas and standards in Hebrew dictionary-making and was the first dictionary to adapt and embed the modern international approach and methodologies in dictionary-making inspired by the computerized processing of textual corpora. *Rav-Milim* was also the first dictionary of Hebrew with an online electronic version enriched with a number of sophisticated grammatical and other modules, available and continuously updated on the Internet (www.melingo.com). *Nakdan-text* won Choueka and the Rav-Milim team the Israel Prime Minister Prize for Computing in 1997, and, earlier, the 1992 Annual Prize of the Information Processing Association of Israel.

Additional projects that Choueka headed and brought to completion, as well as consulting positions of importance that he held, are detailed at the end of this chapter. Those projects that were developed at Bar-Ilan were covered by some 15 grants received from competitive international, as well as national, funding agencies.

The active participation of Choueka in international meetings was accompanied by international and binational activities, of which we will mention here his position as a member of the Advisory Committee of Domestic, a joint Israeli-German project for full-text retrieval systems with mini-computers; his participation by invitation in the crucial meeting of the Text Encoding Initiative (TEI) that took place at Vassar College (Poughkeepsie, NY) in 1987, an initiative meant to set-up standards for the international exchange of tagged text-corpora, which ultimately gave birth to the XML (and many other xML) languages; his being a member, and then a co-chairman, of the Joint Committee for France-Israel Cooperation in Computer Science Research Projects, established by the Ministry of Science and Technology (1989-1999); and finally his participation by invitation in the NEH-sponsored meeting that took place in Princeton, NJ (1990) on the future of the Princeton-Rutgers National Center for Machine-Readable Texts.

From the early eighties and throughout his career, Choueka was noticeably involved in academic and public activities related to the framework of higher learning in Israel, on one hand, and to computer-related education in the Israeli educational system on the other.

In the sphere of higher education, he served as a member or chairman of the following bodies, all appointed by the Council for Higher Learning in Israel: the Universities' Computing Resources Committee (1983–1986), the High Committee for Appointment of Associate and Full Professors in Colleges in Israel (1985–2013), the Super-Computing Resources Committee (1988–1991), the Committee for Accrediting Haifa University for a Master of Science program in Computer Science (2001–2002), and later (2005) Status Reviewer of this program, the Committee for Accrediting Colleges in Israel for First Degree (B.Sc.) Programs in Computer Science and Software Engineering (2003-2005), and recently (2013), the Committee for the Evaluation of the Associate/Full Adjunct Professor Degrees in the Institutes of Higher learning in Israel and of the title of Assistant Professor at the Technion.

At the other tip of the educational scale, Choueka played a key role, from the early seventies and until the early nineties, in the design, planning and implementation of the Ministry of Education's preliminary plans to introduce computer studies in all elementary and high schools in Israel. He was a co-organizer and the main lecturer of a first-of-a-kind program in Israel to help teachers of mathematics in schools adapt to teaching computers. These were the days of IBM punch-cards, when programs had to be punched on these cards and fed into the computer, and responses were sometimes received only a week later, and the days of Newton, a small hand-held "computer" with 32K (!) of memory, designed exclusively for writing simple programs in BASIC.

His activities in this domain included being a member or chairman of the following bodies, all appointed by the Ministry of Education: the Committee on Computer Education in the Israeli Educational System (1975–1985), the Curriculum Committee for Courses in Computing in the Intermediate and High Schools in Israel (1983–1986), the National Steering Committee for Telematics (Computers and Communications) and chairman of its sub-committee on Computers and Education (1983-1986), the Steering Committee for Computers in Education (1990–1992), the National Planning Committee for Science and Technology in the Educational System in Israel ("Tomorrow 2000") and chairman of its sub-committee on Computers and Education (1990-1992), and a position on the Board of Directors of the Centre for Science and Technology Education and of its sub-committee for Grants (1994-2000).

Additionally, Choueka was a member of the following academic or national bodies: the National Council for Information and Communications (1989-1990); the National Broadcasting Authority (1980-1984) and the Committee on Regulating Advertising in Cable Television (Ministry of Communications, 1992); the Committee for Landau Research Prizes of the National Lottery Organization (1989-1992); the Committee for "Chlore" Prizes (1995-1996); the National Committee for Infrastructures in Information Technologies (Ministry of Science and Technology, 1999-2002); and the Advisory Board for Equal Opportunities for Digital Access - *Lehava* (Ministry of Finances, 2002). Choueka also served on the Board of Trustees of *Mivhar,* the College for Science Education, in Bnei-Brak.

The mid-sixties were the beginning years of computer activities in Israel, preparing the ground for the creation of the Information Processing Association (IPA) of Israel, and for Choueka's close involvement with its operation. Choueka was Chairman of its Working Group on Computational Linguistics (1966-1973), a member of its Executive Board of Directors (1975), a member of its General Council (1975-1988, with some short interruptions), Chairman of its Committee for Annual Awards in Computer Science and Data Processing Applications (1982), the Organizer and Chairman of its Eighteenth National Conference (1983), the Chairman of its Committee for Grants to graduate students in Computer Science (1989), and presented papers at its Annual National Conferences in 1966, 1969, 1972, 1981, 1990, and 1995.

In 1981, Choueka was the recipient (with Paul Bratley from Montreal) of the IPA Annual Award for the Best Research Paper in Computer Science (item [14] in the List of Publications), and he (together with Yoni Neeman and the *Rav-Milim* team) was awarded its Annual Prize for the Best Scientific and Technological Applications of Computers in 1992. In 1990, on the occasion of the 25th anniversary of the IPA, he was awarded a recognition certificate as one of the veterans of computing in Israel, and in 1992, his many services to the Association were recognized by a special award.

In terms of public activities, a mention should be made of his participation in the activities of the World Center for Aleppo Jewish Heritage (the Aleppo Jewish Community being one of the oldest Jewish communities in the world, with written records more than a thousand years old). Choueka served as a member of the Board of Directors and Chairman of its Research Committee for thirty years (1985–2005). He initiated and supervised, among others, the publication of a comprehensive bibliography of all published books authored by Aleppo rabbis (numbering about 400), designing each book description as a double spread: a page of biographical and bibliographical information, accompanied by an image of the book's frontispiece (such a written monument apparently has never been erected for any other Jewish community), and of a lavishly-published Pentateuch with the popular and time-honored translation to Arabic (the *Sharh)*, a translation that any Aleppine child (boy or girl) was supposed to learn and know by heart. For his many contributions to preserve Aleppine Jewish heritage he was awarded a special recognition plaque in 2004.

To celebrate Choueka's 35 years of teaching and research, the Seventh International Symposium on the Foundations of Artificial Intelligence (BISFAI) was convened in his honor (Ramat Gan, 2001), and then on the occasion of his retirement, the Annual Meeting of the Israeli Society of Computational Linguistics (ISCOL) was convened in his honor (Ramat Gan, 2004).

Major Projects and Consulting Positions

1962-1965: Development of the first operational **Morphological Analyzer** of Hebrew – see above.

1965–1986: The **Responsa** Project – see above.

1968-1975: Chief Advisor for the computerization of the activities of a large **Intelligence Agency**, in particular the development of a sophisticated system for names matching and retrieval. The basics algorithms, considered then to be among the best in the world, were still operational in 2006.

1977–1980: Chief Advisor for the computerization of the comprehensive **Arabic-Hebrew Dictionary**, (A. Sharoni (Ed.) 3 vols., IDF Publishing House, 1987).

1982–1985: Chief Advisor for text processing, information retrieval and electronic publishing of the **Encyclopedia Hebraica**; responsible for the semi-automatic production and automatic publishing of the Encyclopedia Index volume, the first complex book ever to be published in Israel entirely by computerized technologies, with data transfer from the Encyclopedia offices to the printer's offices through regular telephone lines.

1988–1990: *Maba'* - Bar-Ilan Corpus of Modern Hebrew – see above.

1986–1989: Supervising the building (by a graduate student) of **Hyper-Talmud,** a hypertext system for the Babylonian Talmud, one of the first large ('non-toys') hypertext systems ever developed.

1988–1997: **Rav-Milim** – see above.

1997–2002: Chief Advisor to **Yedioth Ahronoth**, the largest daily newspaper in Israel, for "LateNews: a Full-Text and Images Knowledge Base for 60 years of Yedioth Ahronoth", a project in which the full one million pages of the newspaper (from 1939 on) were digitized and made available both as images and as full-text for search and retrieval needs.

1999: Responsible for one of the very first projects in Israel for data mining, data verification and data correction concerned with the largest insurance company in Israel databank of millions of data items.

2000–2005: Chief Scientist of Celebros, an Israeli start-up concerned with information retrieval, natural language processing and commercial entities.

2004–2005: Chief Advisor for the algorithmic aspects of the name-matching module of the Israel Borders Control System, currently the official operational system for controlling passengers' movements in all entry/exit points of Israel.

2006–2013: Head of the Cairo Genizah Computerization Project, part of the Friedberg Genizah Project. The related Genizah website the central user interface to the system, currently contains 450,000 (!) high-quality digital images covering all Genizah fragments collections in more than 60 libraries all over the world, about a million data items related to these fragments, and a rich, innovative and highly sophisticated set of tools for manipulating these images and metadata. This is most probably the largest and most advanced website currently operational for dealing with large collections of historical manuscripts.

2008–2013: Head of a research group (a cooperation between Tel Aviv University Faculty of Computer Science and the Friedberg Genizah Project) for computer analysis of digital images of historical manuscripts, that developed many innovative and world-first systems for such an analysis, systems that were presented (and published) in more than ten international conferences (winning the best paper award in one of them), which were inspired by - and then applied to - the Genizah case.

2012: Head of a project to build a computerized comprehensive corpus of Judeo-Arabic (basically a Jewish dialect of Arabic written in Hebrew characters), a language of critical importance to the study of Jewish history and culture of the Middle Ages, equipped with a full-text research software, and intended to help scholars better understand the language and its structure, and designed so as to apply on it the newest techniques of natural language processing to reveal the various inter-relationships of words and expressions in this language.

2012: Head of the Friedberg Talmud Bavli Variants Project, whose aim is to create a website in which will be displayed high-quality digital images of all Talmud manuscripts and first printings all over the world, together with their accurate transcriptions and a novel, very flexible and dynamic way of displaying the variant readings of any Talmudic text, by presenting a synopsis that can be locally tailored to the needs of every user.

Topical List of Publications of Yaacov Choueka

A - Automata and Computability Theories

1. Choueka, Y.: Bounded Sets of Nodes in Transfinite Trees, Israel. J. of Mathematics 11, 254–257 (1972)
2. Choueka, Y.: Structure-automata. IEEE Trans. on Computers C-23, 1218–1227 (1974)
3. Choueka, Y.: Theories of Automata on ω-tapes – a Simplified Approach. J. of Computer and Systems Sciences 8, 117–141 (1974)
4. Loeckx, J.C.: Book Review of "Computability and Decidability". Lecture Notes in Economics and Mathematical Systems, vol. 68. Springer (1972), Choueka, Y.: Philosophia 4, 213–215 (1974)
5. Choueka, Y.: Finite Automata, Definable Sets and Regular Expressions over ω^n tapes. J. of Computer and Systems Sciences 12, 81–97 (1978)
6. Amir, A., Choueka, Y.: Loop-programs and Polynomially Computable Functions. Int. J. of Computer Mathematics 9, 195–205 (1981)
7. Choueka, Y., Peleg, D.: An Essentially Finite Characterization of omega-regular Languages. Bulletin of the European Assoc. of Theoretical Computer Science (EATCS) 21, 21–24 (1983)
8. Amir, A., Choueka, Y.: Polynomial Computations in Non-deterministic Loop-programs and PL-programs. Int. J. of Computer Mathematics 4, 209–221 (1983)
9. Amir, A., Choueka, Y.: A Syntactical Definition of the P=NP Problem. Int. J. of Computer Mathematics 17, 217–228 (1985)

B - Full-Text Systems and Information Retrieval

10. Choueka, Y.: Itur Piskei-din beShitat haText haMale (Retrieval of Precedents by the Full-text Method), Institute of Criminology Publications, No. 18, pp. 39–44. The Hebrew University, Jerusalem (1971) (Hebrew)
11. Attar, R., Choueka, Y., Schindler, D., Fraenkel, A.: Leshoniyim beMa'arakhot liDlyat Meida' (Linguistic Files in Document Retrieval Systems). In: Moneita, Y. (ed.) Proc. of the 8th National Conf. of the Information Processing Assoc. of Israel (IPA) (Tel-Aviv, 1972), pp. 218–247. Information Processing Assoc. of Israel, Jerusalem (1972) (Hebrew)
12. Attar, R., Choueka, Y., Dershowitz, N., Fraenkel, A.S.: KEDMA - Linguistic Tools in Retrieval Systems. J. of ACM 25, 52–66 (1978)
13. Choueka, Y.: Computerized Full-text Systems and Research in the Humanities. Computers and the Humanities 14, 153–169 (1980)
14. Bratley, P., Choueka, Y.: Processing Truncated Terms in Document Retrieval Systems. Information Processing and Management 18, 257–266 (1982); A preliminary version appeared in Attar, E., Amit, A. (eds.): Proc. of the 16th National Conf. of the Information Processing Assoc. of Israel (IPA), pp. 67–93. The Information Processing Assoc. of Israel, Jerusalem (1982)
15. Choueka, Y.: Linguistic and Word-manipulation Components in Textual Information Systems. In: Keren, C., Perlmutter, L. (eds.) The Application of Mini- and Micro-Computers in Information, Documentation and Libraries, pp. 405–417. Elsevier, Amsterdam (1983)

16. Choueka, Y.: Conversationnel ou Concordances Imprimées: Le Problème de l'Exploitation d'un Gros Corpus, Informatique et Sciences Humaines, Institut des Sciences Humaines Appliquées, Université Paris-Sorbonne, no. 61-62, 93–105 (1984) (French)
17. Choueka, Y.: Statique et Dynamique dans le Traitement Automatique des Banques Textuelles. In: Hamesse, J. (ed.) Proc. of the 11th Int. Conf. of the Assoc. for Literary and Linguistic Computing (ALLC), Louvain-La-Neuve, Editions Slatkine, Geneva, pp. 115–120 (1984, 1985)
18. Choueka, Y., Fraenkel, A.S., Klein, S.T., Segal, E.: Improved Techniques for Processing Queries in Full-text Systems. In: Yu, C.T., van Rijsbergen, C.J. (eds.) Proc. of the 10th Annual Int. ACM-SIGIR Conf. on Research and Development in Information Retrieval, New Orleans, pp. 306–315. Assoc. Computing Machinery, New York (1987)
19. Choueka, Y., Aviad, A.: Yissum Hypertext Ivri beTahanat Avodah (Hypertalmud - A Hypertext System [for the Talmud] on a Workstation). In: Proc. of the 25th National Conf. of the Information Processing Assoc. of Israel (IPA), pp. 281–290. The Information Processing Assoc. of Israel, Jerusalem (1990) (Hebrew)
20. Choueka, Y., Dershowitz, N., Tal, L.: Matching with a hierarchical ontology. In: Dershowitz, N., Nissan, E. (eds.) Choueka Festschrift, Part I. LNCS, vol. 8001, pp. 395–398. Springer, Heidelberg (2014)

C - The Responsa Project

21. Choueka, Y., Cohen, M., Dueck, J., Fraenkel, A.S., Slae, M.: Full-text Document Retrieval: Hebrew Legal Texts (Report on the First phase of the Responsa Retrieval Project). In: Minker, M., Rosenfeld, S. (eds.) Proc. of the ACM Symposium on Information Storage and Retrieval, Maryland, pp. 61–79. Assoc. Computing Machinery, New York (1971)
22. Choueka, Y., Cohen, M., Dueck, J., Fraenkel, A.S., Slae, M.: (a solicited expanded form of the preceding paper) Full-text Law Retrieval - The Responsa Project, Pamphlet No. 3, Working Papers on Legal Information Processing Series. J. Schweitzer Verlag, Berlin, 64 p. (1972)
23. Choueka, Y.: The Responsa Project: A Status Report, Newsletter of Medieval Data Processing, Institut d'Etudes Médiévales, Université de Montréal, Montréal, vol. VII, pp. 35–42 (1977)
24. Choueka, Y., Slae, M., Spero, S.: The Responsa Project - Revisited. In: Proc. of the Assoc. of the Orthodox Jewish Scientists, vol. 5, pp. 19–66. Feldheim Publications, New York (1979)
25. Choueka, Y.: Proyect haShe'elot heHatshuvot (The Responsa Project). Mavo leTikhnut ulHaqarat haMahshev (An Introduction to Programming and Computers), The Open University 4, 64–69 (1979) (Hebrew)
26. Choueka, Y., Slae, M., Schreiber, A.: The Responsa Project: Computerization of Traditional Jewish Law. In: Erez, B. (ed.) Legal and Legislative Information Processing, ch. 18, pp. 261–286. Greenwood Press (1980)
27. Choueka, Y.: RESPONSA: An Operational Full-Text Retrieval System with Linguistic Components for Large Corpora, Law in Multicultural Societies. In: Cuomo, E.I. (ed.) Proc. of the Int. Assoc. of Law Libraries (IALL) Meeting, Jerusalem, pp. 47–82. The Hebrew University, Jerusalem (1985, 1989)
28. Choueka, Y.: Responsa, A Full-Text Retrieval System with Linguistic Processing for a 65 million-word Corpus of Jewish Heritage in Hebrew. Data Engineering (Special Issue on non-English Interfaces to Databases) 12(4), 22–31 (1989)

29. Choueka, Y.: RESPONSA - A Full-Text System with Linguistic Components for Large Corpora. In: Quemada, B., Zampolli, A. (eds.) Computational Lexicology and Lexicography, Giardini Editions, Pisa, pp. 181–217 (1990)
30. Choueka, Y.: RESPONSA - A Full-Text System with Linguistic Components for Large Corpora. In: Choueka, Y. (ed.) Proc. of the 15th Int. Conf. of the Assoc. for Literary and Linguistic Computing (ALLC), Champion-Slatkine, Paris-Geneve, pp. 51–92 (1989, 1990)

D - Text and File Compression

31. Choueka, Y.: Tekhnikot Mehirot le'Itur uShlifa bcMilon ubeKonkordanzia be'Ivrit (Fast Searching and Retrieval Techniques for Large Dictionaries and Concordances in Hebrew). In: Hebrew Computational Linguistics, Bar-Ilan University, Ramat-Gan, vol. 6, pp. 12–32 (1972) (Hebrew, English abstract p. E-33)
32. Choueka, Y., Fraenkel, A., Perl, Y.: Polynomial Construction of Optimal Prefix Tables for Text Compression. In: Proc. of the 19th Allerton Conf. on Communication, Control and Computing, vol. 1981, pp. 762–768. Allerton House, Monticello (1981)
33. Choueka, Y., Klein, S.T., Perl, Y.: Efficient Variants of Huffman Codes in High- level Languages. In: Proc. of 8th Annual Int. ACM-SIGIR Conf. on Research and Development in Information Retrieval, Montreal, pp. 122–130. Assoc. Computing Machinery, New York (1985)
34. Choueka, Y., Fraenkel, A., Klein, S.T., Segal, E.: Improved Hierarchical Bit-vector Compression in Document Retrieval Systems. In: Rabitti, F. (ed.) Proc. of the 9th Annual Int. ACM-SIGIR Conf. on Research and Development in Information Retrieval, Pisa, pp. 88–96. Assoc. Computing Machinery, New York (1986)
35. Choueka, Y., Fraenkel, A.S., Klein, S.T.: Compression of Concordances in Full-text Retrieval Systems. In: Chiramiella, Y. (ed.) Proc. of the 11th Annual Int. ACM-SIGIR Conf. on Research and Development in Information Retrieval, Grenoble, pp. 597–612. Presses Universitaires, Grenoble (1988)

E – Computational Linguistics and Natural Language Processing

36. Choueka, Y., Kasher, A. (eds.): Balshanut Hishuvit (Computational Linguistics), Proc. of the Conf. of the Information Processing Assoc. of Israel (IPA) Working Group on Computational Linguistics (Ramat-Gan, 1969), IPA Publications, Jerusalem, Vol. 2, 1969 (Hebrew).
37. Choueka, Y.: Balshanut Hishuvit - haYisumim (Computational Linguistics -The Applications). In: Choueka, Y., Kasher, A. (eds.) Computational Linguistics, vol. 2, pp. 93–115. IPA Publications, Jerusalem (1969) (Hebrew)
38. Choueka, Y.: Kvuzat hA'avoda le'Balshanut Hushuvit – Seker Pe'ilut – Razuy uMazuy (The [IPA] Working Group on Computational Linguistics - a Report). Hebrew Computational Linguistics, Bar-Ilan University, Ramat-Gan, no. 1, 55–58 (1969) (Hebrew)
39. Choueka, Y., Dreizin, F.: Mechanical Resolution of Lexical Ambiguity in a Coherent Text. In: Proc. of the Int. Conf. on Computational Linguistics - COLING 1976, paper no. 4, Ottawa (1976)
40. Choueka, Y., Goldberg, D.: Mechanical Resolution of Lexical Ambiguity - A Combinatorial Approach. In: Malachi, Z. (ed.) Proc. of the Int. Conf. on Literary and Linguistic Computing (Tel-Aviv, 1979), pp. 149–165. Tel Aviv University, Tel-Aviv (1979)

41. Choueka, Y., Klein, S.T., Neuwitz, E.: Automatic Retrieval of Frequent Idiomatic and Collocational Expressions in a Large Corpus. ALLC J. 4, 34–38 (1983)
42. Choueka, Y., Lusignan, S.: Disambiguation by Short Contexts. Computers and the Humanities 19, 147–157 (1985)
43. Choueka, Y.: Looking for Needles in a Haystack or: Locating Interesting Expressions in Large Textual Databases. In: Proc. of the Int. Conf. on User-Oriented Content-Based Text and Image Handling (RIAO), Cambridge, Mass, pp. 609–623 (1988)
44. Choueka, Y. (ed.): Literary and Linguistic Computing: Proc. of the Fifteenth Annual Int. Conf. of the Assoc. for Literary and Linguistics Computing (ALLC), Jerusalem, Editions Champion-Slatkine, Paris-Geneve (1988, 1990)
45. Gur, E., Choueka, Y.: A Natural Language Interface in Hebrew for Relational Databases. In: Proc. of the 30th National Conf. of the Information Processing Assoc. of Israel, Jerusalem. The Information Processing Assoc. of Israel, Jerusalem (1995)
46. Choueka, Y., Conley, E., Dagan, I.: A Comprehensive Bilingual Word Alignment System: Application to Disparate Languages - Hebrew and English. In: Veronis, J. (ed.) Parallel Text Processing, pp. 69–96. Kluwer Publications (2000)
47. Choueka, Y.: Natural Language Processing: Challenges, Achievements and Problems - A Sober Personal Perspective. In: Dershowitz, N., Nissan, E. (eds.) Choueka Festschrift, Part III. LNCS, vol. 8003, pp. 1–13. Springer, Heidelberg (2014)

F – Hebrew Linguistics and Computational Linguistics

48. Choueka, Y., Shapiro, M.: Nitu'ah Mekhanografi shel haMorphologia ha'Ivrit: Efsharouyot veHesegim (Machine Analysis of Hebrew Morphology: Potentialities and Achievements). Lěšonénu (A Journal for the Study of the Hebrew Language and Cognate Subjects) 26-27, 354–372 (1964)
49. Choueka, Y., Shapiro, M.: Machine Analysis of Hebrew Morphology: Potentialities and Achievements. The Finite String 3(5) (1966)
50. Choueka, Y.: Mahshevim veDikduk: Nituah Mekhani shel haPo'al ha'Ivri (Automatic Grammatical Analysis of the Hebrew Verb). In: Kasher, A. (ed.) Proc. of the 2nd National Conf. of the Information Processing Assoc. of Israel (IPA), Rehovot, pp. 49–67. Information Processing Assoc. of Israel, Jerusalem (1966) (Hebrew)
51. Choueka, Y.: Automatic Grammatical Analysis of the Hebrew Verb. The Finite String 4(4) (1967)
52. Choueka, Y.: Automatic Derivation and Inflection in Hebrew Morphology, vol. IV (11). Newsletter of ICRH – Institute for Computer Research in the Humanities, New York University (1969)
53. Choueka, Y.: Balshanut Hishuvit Ivrit – Lamma veKeizad (Hebrew Computational Linguistics, Why and How?). In: Computational Linguistics, Proc. Conf. of the IPA Working Group on Computational Linguistics, Ramat-Gan, vol. 2, pp. 133–138. IPA Publications, Jerusalem (1969)
54. Choueka, Y.: Dikduk Yezira Formali laMila haShemanit be'Ivrit (A Formal Generative Grammar for Hebrew Noun-words). In: Bar-Ilan Decennial, pp. 106–128. Bar-Ilan University Press, Ramat-Gan (1969) (Hebrew)
55. Choueka, Y.: Hipalgut haZurot lefi haOrekh – Ba'ya beBalshanut Statistit (Length-distribution of Words in Modern Hebrew – a Problem in Statistical Linguistics). In: Hebrew Computational Linguistics, Bar-Ilan University, Ramat-Gan, no. 1, pp. 33–34 (1969) (Hebrew)

56. Choueka, Y., Yeshurun, S.: Prakim beBalshanut Statistit Ivrit (Statistical Aspects of Modern Hebrew Prose). In: Kasher, A., Schild, U. (eds.) Proc. of the 5th National Conf. of the Information Processing Assoc. of Israel (IPA), Jerusalem. The Information Processing Assoc. of Israel (1969)

57. Choueka, Y.: Milhemet haMilon haMilhamti (The War about the "War Dictionary" [of Isaiah]), Maase Hoshev (Bulletin of the Information Processing Assoc. of Israel, - IPA) 2, 25–26 (1972) (Hebrew)

58. Choueka, Y. (ed.): Hebrew Computational Linguistics, Bar-Ilan University, no. 5 and no. 6 (1971, 1972)

59. Choueka, Y.: An Exhaustive Computerized Thesaurus of the Hebrew Language. In: Abstracts of the Sixth World Congress of Jewish Studies, Jerusalem, The Int. Assoc. of Jewish Studies, Jerusalem (1973), abstract E-1

60. Choueka, Y.: Milim – Ma'arekhet leNituah Dikduki Male, Meduyak uMekhuvan laMorfologia shel ha'Ivrit bat-Zemanenu (Milim, a System for the Complete, Accurate and On-line Analysis of the Morphology of Current Hebrew). In: Abstracts of the 7th Conf. for Computers in Education, Ramat-Gan, p. 62. The Israeli Assoc. for Computers in Education (1990)

61. Choueka, Y.: Rav-Milim, Ma'aerkhet Kolelet leMihshuv Ha'ivrit veHora'atah (Rav-Milim, a Comprehensive System for Hebrew Computerization and its Teaching). In: Abstracts of the 10th Conf. for Computers in Education, Tel Aviv, p. 116. The Israeli Assoc. for Computers in Education (1993)

62. Choueka, Y. (Chief Editor): Rav-Milim Hatza'ir Young Rav-Milim [A Dictionary of Contemporary Hebrew for the Young], Steimatzki, C.E.T. and Miskal, Tel-Aviv, 2 vols (1996)

63. Choueka, Y. (Chief Editor): Rav-Milim – haMilon haShalem la'Ivrit haHadasha (Rav-Milim - the Complete Dictionary of Contemporary Hebrew), Steimatzki, C.E.T. and Miskal, Tel-Aviv, 6 vols (1997)

64. Choueka, Y.: Rav Milim – A Modern Dictionary for an Ancient but Thriving Language, 27–31. Kernerman Dictionary News (July 2004)

65. Cohen, H., Choueka, Y.: Hebrew Lexicography. In: Brown, K. (ed.) Encyclopedia of Languages and Linguistics, 2nd edn. Elsevier, Oxford (2006)

G – The Cairo Genizah, Image Processing of Historical Manuscripts

66. Wolf, L., Littman, R., Mayer, N., German, T., Dershowitz, N., Shweka, R., Choueka, Y.: Automatically Identifying Join Candidates in the Cairo Genizah. Int. Journal of Computer Vision 94(1), 118–135 (2011); Extended abstract in Proc. of IEEE Workshop on eHeritage and Digital Art Preservation, 2009, in conjunction with ICCV 2009 Tokyo, Japan, Best Paper Award (2009)

67. Shweka, R., Choueka, Y., Wolf, L., Dershowitz, N.: Veqarev otam Ehad el Ehad": Zihuy Ktav-yad veZeruf Kit'ei haGenizah be'Emtsa'ut Mahshev (Identifying Handwriting and Joining Genizah Fragments by Computer). Ginzei Qedem (Genizah Research Annual) 7, 171–207 (2011)

68. Wolf, L., Dershowitz, N., Potikha, L., German, T., Shweka, R., Choueka, Y.: Automatic Palaeographic Exploration of Genizah Manuscripts. In: Fischer, F., Fritze, C., Vogeler, G. (eds.) Codicology and Palaeography in the Digital Age 2, Demand, Norderstedt, Germany, vol. 2, pp. 157–179 (2011)

69. Wolf, L., Dershowitz, N., Potikha, L., Shweka, R., Choueka, Y.: Computerized Paleography: Tools for Historical Manuscript. In: Macq, B., Schelkens, P. (eds.) Proc. of the 18th IEEE Int. Conf. on Image Processing (ICIP 2011), Brussels, Belgium, 3545–3548 (2011)

70. Wolf, L., Litwak, L., Dershowitz, N., Shweka, R., Choueka, Y.: Active Clustering of Document Fragments using Information Derived from Both Images and Catalogs. In: Metaxas, D.N., Quan, L., Sanfeliu, A., Van Gool, L.J. (eds.) Proc. Int. Conf. on Computer Vision (ICCV), Barcelona, Spain, pp. 1661–1667 (2011)

71. Choueka, Y.: Computerizing the Cairo Genizah: Aims, Methodologies and Achievements. Ginzei Qedem (Genizah Research Annual) 8, 9–30 (2012)

72. Shweka, R., Choueka, Y., Wolf, L., Dershowitz, N., Zeldin, M.: Automatic Extraction of Catalog Data from Genizah Fragments' Images, Literary and Linguistic Computing (LLC). Journal, Special issue on Digital Humanities (2013); (Extended abstract in Proc. of the Digital Humanities Conf. (DH 2011), Palo Alto, CA, 2011)

73. Choueka, Y.: miSimta'ot Qahir laInternet haMahir: Genizat Qahir uMihshuvah (From the Alleys of Cairo to the Internet Highway: The Cairo Genizah and its Computerization). In: Rimon, O. (ed.) Matmonim uGenizot KeParashyot baHistoria, Hecht Museum, Haifa University, Haifa (2013)

74. Choueka, Y.: 1,000-year Manuscripts meet Computer Technology the Cairo Genizah Case. To Appear in the Bulletin of the Israeli Academic Center in Cairo 28 (2013)

H – Judaica

75. Choueka, Y.: al haFormalism shel Hayahdut haHilkhtit (On the Formalism of Halakhic Judaism), Deoth 21, 12–28, (1962) (Hebrew)

76. Choueka, Y., Sabato, H. (eds.): Minhat Aharon, a collection of essays in memory of Rabbi Aharon Choueka, Jerusalem, 357 p. (1980) (Hebrew)

77. Choueka, Y.: Pirkei Haym. In: Choueka, Y., Sabato, H. (eds.) Minhat Aharon, Jerusalem, pp. 15–32 (1980) (Hebrew)

78. Choueka, Y.: ha'Ona'ah Shtut, in Sefer Higayon, Studies in Rabbinical Logic. In: Koppel, M., Merzbach, E. (eds.) Zomet Institute, Alon Shevut, pp. 153–163 (1995) (Hebrew)

79. Choueka, Y., Sabato, M.: Beit Arba'a Qabbin - leHeshbonah shel Mishna AhatbeMassekhet Baba Batra bidei Mefaresheiha, Sidra (to appear, 2013) (Hebrew)

I – Other

80. Choueka, Y.: haMahshevim baUniversit'aot beIsrael – Skira (Computers in the Universities in Israel - a Survey). In: Kasher, A. (ed.) Proc. of the 2nd National Conf. of the Information Processing Assoc. of Israel (IPA), Jerusalem, pp. 93–115 (1966) (Hebrew)

81. Choueka, Y., Rahaman, G.: Nitzul haMahshev beMehkarim Hilkhatiim ubeMehkarim beMada'ei hRruah (The Use of Computers in Halakhic and Humanistic Research), M.T.T., no. 9-10, 151–154 (1971) (Hebrew)

82. Choueka, Y.: Law in the Age of Electronic Computers - Technological Aspects, Institute of Criminology Publications, no. 18, pp. 3–8. The Hebrew University, Jerusalem (1971) (Hebrew)

83. Choueka, Y.: The Multi-faceted Contributions of Aviezri Fraenkel to Information Retrieval and the Related Areas. The Electronic Journal of Combinatorics, 8(2), paper # I4 (2001)

84. Choueka, Y.: From the Alleys of Cairo to the Internet Highways, An Intellectual Journey: Languages, Information and Intelligence. In: Dershowitz, N., Nissan, E. (eds.) Choueka Festschrift, Part I. LNCS, vol. 8001, pp. 1–18. Springer, Heidelberg (2014)

J – Unpublished (Circulated)

85. Choueka, Y.: On Regressive Functions and a Problem of Erdos and Hajnal, 17 p. (1967)
86. Choueka, Y.: Structure Automata (selected sections appeared in Item 2), 54 p. (1972)
87. Choueka, Y.: The Responsa Project – What, How and Why, 1976–1981 – a Status Report, Institute for Information Retrieval and Computational Linguistics, Bar Ilan University, Ramat-Gan, 59 p. (1981)
88. Choueka, Y.: Le Traitement Automatique du Gros Corpus: Méthodologie et Techniques, Invited talk, 9eme Colloque sur l'Ordinateur et le Texte Médiéval, Institut d'Etudes Médiévales, Université de Montréal, Montréal (1982) (French)
89. Choueka, Y.: Two Conferences on Optical Storage: An Informal Report and Some Reflections, Technical Memorandum TM-ARH-008691, Bell Communications Research, Morristown, NJ, 16 p. (1987)
90. Choueka, Y., Neeman, Y.: Nakdan-Text, an In-Context Text-Vocalizer for Modern Hebrew. In: The Fourth Bar-Ilan Symposium on Foundations of Artificial Intelligence (BISFAI 1995), Ramat-Gan (1995)

Invited Talks

- The Third International Conference on Computing in the Humanities (ICCH 3) (Waterloo, Canada, 1977)
- International Colloquium on the Logic Analysis of Tense and Quantifiers (Stuttgart, 1979)
- Ninth colloquium of the *Institut d'Etudes médiévales* (University of Montreal) on The Computer and the Medieval Text (Montreal, 1982)
- International Conference on the Application of Mini- and Micro- Computers in Information, Documentation, and Libraries (Tel-Aviv, 1983)
- National Seminar of the Information Processing Association of Israel (IPA) on Computers and Natural Languages (Tel-Aviv, 1984)
- Eleventh International Conference of the Association for Literary and Linguistic Computing (ALLC) (Louvain-La-Neuve, 1984)
- Second Congress of the International Association of Law Libraries (IALL) on Law in Multi-Cultural Societies (Jerusalem, 1985)
- International Conference on Value of Research Data for Government and Business (IFDO/ASSISST) (Jerusalem, 1989)
- National Seminar on Hebrew Computational Linguistics (Tel-Aviv, 1989)
- Eighth National Conference of the Israeli Association for Computers and Education (Tel-Aviv, 1990)
- The Sixth National Annual Meeting on Information (INFO 91), Seminar on Full-text Systems (Tel-Aviv, 1991)
- The Seventh National Annual Meeting on Information (INFO 92), Seminar on Full-text Systems (Tel-Aviv 1992)
- International Conference on Cultural Resources in the Electronic Era (Tel-Aviv, 1995)
- Third Mediterranean Exhibition of Technological Innovation (MEDITERINTEC III) (Naples, 1998)

- International Symposium on Semitic Linguistics (Tel-Aviv, 1999)
- Seventh Bar-Ilan International Symposium on the Foundations of Artificial Intelligence (BISFAI 07) (Ramat-Gan, 2001)
- Arabida International Seminar on Complexity (Lisbon, 2004)
- Judaeo-Arabic Culture and Arabic Speaking World: Linguistic, Textual and social Crosspollination (Society for Judaeo-Arabic Studies Conference) (Cambridge, 2011)
- International Colloquium on Written Arabic, Writing Arabic; Corpora and Lexica – WAWA 3 (Roma 2012)

Integrating and Rejuvenating Old and New Gems

Aviezri S. Fraenkel

Department of Computer Science and Applied Mathematics
Weizmann Institute of Science
Rehovot 76100, Israel

**Banquet talk, delivered at the BISFAI festive banquet in
honor of Professor Yaacov Choueka, Jerusalem, June 2001;
adapted to the Choueka Jubilee Volume, March 2008.**

1   Introduction

Ladies and Gentlemen; friends; organizers and participants of BISFAI, the Bar-Ilan International Symposium on the Foundations of Artificial Intelligence; the Choueka clan and its distinguished Chieftain, Professor Ya'acov Choueka. I feel privileged and pleased to have been invited by Prof. Nachum Dershowitz, Program Committee Chair of BISFAI, to pay tribute to our guest of honor, Ya'acov Choueka.

Although I have known Ya'acov for over 35 years, I always had some uncanny feeling that I don't really know him fully. I have therefore secured the Ya'acov Choueka files form the Shin Bet, the Secret Service of the State of Israel, under the pretext of the Free Information Disclosure Act. These files are very extensive, and they confirmed my suspicion that there is more to Prof. Choueka than meets the eye. I cannot hope to relate all the contents of these voluminous files in an after-dinner talk. Nevertheless, I'll try to share with you the essence of their main points.

Incidentally, I told the Shin Bet chief , upon his request, that I would transcribe some of the files onto a computer, in order to read it off on the occasion of a banquet honoring Ya'acov, and that this would actually be the first time ever, that I would read a lecture from a written record. The chief told me that, interestingly enough, also Ya'acov was planning to do so for the first time during his keynote address. As you all heard earlier today, this indeed happened.

Since the life of Ya'acov is intimately intertwined with the Hebrew language, I'll intersperse a few sentences in Hebrew from time to time, and then translate their gist into English. My dear wife Shaula, who has been supporting my efforts for over 45 years, did these translations. Obscurities, if any, are due to my editing of the translation.

2   The Beginning

Fig. 1 depicts the lead page of the first book of Moses, published in Vilna in 1922, fourteen years before the birth of Ya'acov. Fig. 2 shows the successor of the lead page, with a written entry in a special script called "Chatzi Kulmus", which translates

N. Dershowitz and E. Nissan (Eds.): Choueka Festschrift, Part I, LNCS 8001, pp. 37–49, 2014.

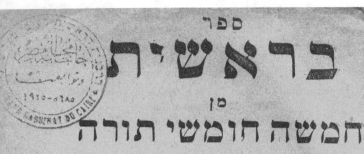

ספר

בראשית

מן

חמשה חומשי תורה

עם

תרגום אונקלוס, ופירש"י ז"ל, ושפתי חכמים, ובעל הטורים

ופירוש יקר נקרא בשם

התורה והמצוה

בנוי על שלשה יסודות קבועים:

א) מפרש דברי אלהים באופן שלא ימצא בשום מקום כפל ענין במלות שונות:

ב) שכל מלה הבאה במאמר, מוכרחת לבא במאמר ההוא, על פי כללי הלשון והבדלי הנרדפים:

ג) שלא נמצא מאמר ריק מרעיון נשגב:

מאת

הרב הגאון האמתי המפורסם בכל קצוי ארץ, כליל החכמה והמדעים, כקש"ת

מהר"ר מאיר ליבוש מלבי"ם זצלל"ה:

בעל המחבר פירוש מקראי קדש על נביאים וכתובים, ופירוש התורה והמצוה על תורת כהנים, ספר ארצות החיים על שו"ע או"ח, וספר ארצות השלום, ועוד כמה ספרים יקרים:

ווילנא

בדפוס והוצאות האלמנה והאחים ראם

שנת תרפ"ג לפ"ק

Fig. 1.

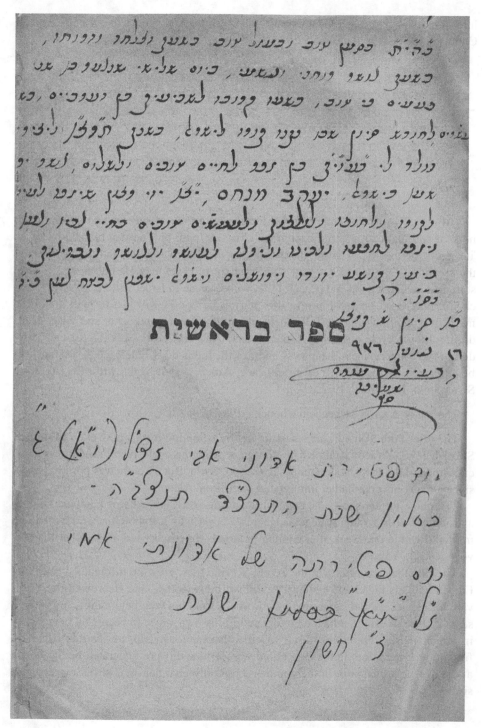

Fig. 2.

into something like "reed-pen writing" in English. And thus wrote Rabbi Aharon Choueka, the leading Rabbi of Cairo:

בסמן טוב ובמזל טוב, בשעת הצלחה והרווחה, בשעת אושר רוחני וגשמי, ביום שלישי שנאמר בו שני פעמים כי טוב, בשעה קרובה לשביעית בין הערביים, בששה ועשרים לחודש סיון שבו נתנה תורה לישראל, בשנת תרצו ליצירה, נולד לי בעהי"ת בן זכר לחיים טובים ולשלום, אשר ייקרא שמו בישראל יעקב מנחם יצ"ו. יהי רצון שיזכה לתורה ולחופה ולמצוות ולמעשים טובים בחיי אביו ואמו, ויזכה לחכמה ולבינה וליראה, לעושר ולאושר ולבריאות. בימיו תושע יהודה וירושלים, וישראל ישכון לבטח, אמן כי"ר. כו סיון, ש' תרצו; 16 גוניו 1936.
הצעיר אהרן מנחם שוויכה, ס"ט.

"At a lucky hour and time of good fortune, at a time of success and solace, at an hour of spiritual and material happiness, close to 7p.m. on Tuesday blessed by twice 'it's good', on the 26th of Sivan, the month that the Law was given, in the year 5696 to the creation of the world, I begot, with the help of G-od may He be blessed, a male son, may he live a good and peaceful life, whose name in Israel will be Ya'acov M'na-cheim, may G-od preserve him to life. May it be G-od's will that he will attain the merit of Torah, matrimony, fulfillment of religious commandments and good deeds during the life cycle of his father and mother. And may he possess intelligence, wis-dom, reverence, richness, happiness and health. In his days Judea and Jerusalem will be redeemed, and Israel will dwell in peace. Amen, may it be the will of G-od. 26-th Sivan 5696, 16-th June, 1936.

The junior Aharon Menachem Choueka, Pure S'phardi."

The title "Pure S'phardi" attests to the family sprouting from a pure and old stem of Spanish Jews. Ya'acov's immediate lineage is from the exclusive blue-blooded patri-cian stock of the Jewish community in Aleppo, Syria. But Ya'acov was born in Egypt, since already his grandfather immigrated there from Aleppo.

The photo further shows the dates of the demise of Rabbi Aharon Choueka's father and mother. It is written in regular Hebrew script, which Rabbi Aharon learned and mastered within one week after coming to Israel. His teacher was none other than his youngest son Ya'acov.

The little boy, according to the Secret Service files, grew up trilingually, speaking French with his father and siblings, Arabic with his mother, and Hebrew at the Y'shi-vah, his school. At the same time he absorbed, from his very beginnings, Jewish and secular cultural values, which he integrated in his own ways, to become a personality in which these cultures are fused together harmoniously, in a way that's hard to find in our generation. In the next photo we see how this pre-integrated being looked at the age of 2, in Cairo, in the company, possibly guardianship, of his more senior sisters.

Fig. 3.

The one on the right is the mother of the Sabato Rabbis. In the next photo we see him together with his classmates in the "Ahavah court" of Grammar School in Cairo, in a junior year. Ya'acov is the tiniest, sitting on the extreme right. The fifth person from the right is his late uncle, Rabbi Avraham Choueka, assistant Chief Rabbi of

Fig. 4.

Egypt, who had considerable influence on the development of Ya'acov, constituting a living example of a very fruitful and satisfying integration of Jewish scholarship with mathematics. The secret service files also contained, naturally, the encounter of Ya'acov with the late Prof. Avraham Halevi Fraenkel. The chief even told me that in his keynote address today, Ya'acov would claim that I don't know about this encounter. As you heard, Ya'acov indeed did so earlier today, very brazenly. Little did he know! Moreover, the files also informed me that there was a classmate of Ya'acov to whom Fraenkel also raised his eyes, telling him that he never saw him before, and that therefore he won't get a signature for taking the math exam. This student went to the end of the line, and at his second encounter with Fraenkel, was again denied permission to take the test, because of the same reason. After a few more rounds, Fraenkel already recognized him and signed.

Ya'acov immigrated to Israel in 1957, at the age of 21.

3   The Family Man, The Poet

The birth inscriptions in the Pentateuch suggest closely knit family ties in the Choueka clan, which Ya'acov inherited, embraced and amplified. In fact, he gave a personal example, by marrying his own niece Sarah, the daughter of his oldest brother Avraham, in August, 1965. See the photo.

Fig. 5.

He is very close to his family and has a fruitful formative influence on his children. Some of these attributes are reflected in the beautiful and moving speeches at the Bar-Mitzvah festivities of his sons, which exude a spirit of reverence and culture and a strong commitment to transmit these values to his children, a task in which he excels. On the death of his father, he organized and edited the striking and distinctive book "Minchat Aharon" to commemorate his father's legacy.

Ya'acov has a special love for poetry. His nephew Rabbi Chayim Sabato teaches at a Y'shiva, a Rabbinical College. In a recent article in the literary supplement of a newspaper, Rabbi Sabato related, inter alia, how he once visited his uncle Jacquot, as Ya'acov is known in the Choueka family, while uncle Jacquot was studying mathematics at the Hebrew University, and saw there a book on Jewish poetry. Ya'acov opened it "accidentally" on a certain page, containing a poem about the famous Bible Commentator Rashi. The boy Chayim, who had just learned to read the special Rashi script, drank it up, and this encounter made Sabato an addict to poetry. It is thus to Ya'acov's credit that Chayim

Sabato became one of the leading novelists of Israel, if not the greatest, though writing novels is only a secondary occupation, perhaps just a hobby, of Rabbi Sabato.

Not only does Ya'acov love poetry, he also engages in writing it. Here is an example of a "brindizi" piece, so called "real-time", or "on-the-fly" poetry, which the scholars of Aleppo and their descendents engage in with relish in arguing with each other at festive and other occasions, exhibiting their command of Jewish and secular knowledge. Ya'acov wrote it in September 1990, at a small gathering at the Math Department of Bar-Ilan University, when I retired from there.

מכם רבותי וידידי ומחתן המסיבה אבקש רשות
ולנפשי אומר במעמד זה חרוזיך שזרי
ושאי ברכה והוקרה עם שמץ של התרגשות
לידיד ותיק, ובאחזור מידע הוא מורי
שבשעת חסד הגה רעיון ויצק בו ממשות
לפתוח שערי מחשוב וחיפוש בכל טקסט עברי
לא נרתע ממכשולים והתמיד בעיקשות
ולא ויתר גם אם סבל מכך מחולי ומררי
ובניגוד לכולם אמר זו הדרך, אף אם אין זה פשוט
והמריץ להגביר בזה חיל ולהתגבר כארי
לעשות אזניים לדברי רבותינו, וללמוד בהתחדשות
תוך ניצול כל פועל ה' למענהו מהמצאות דורי
ומה אאריך לשון והלא כולכם יודעים את מפעל השו"ת
ואת השם הנרדף לו זה עשרים שנה הוא פרנקל אביעזרי
שא ברכה ותודה אביעזרי מריעים ותלמידים, ובליבנו אתה תמיד בראשות
להמשך פעילות וחיים ובריאות, ועד דור עשירי

Guests of honor, friends and participants,
Permit me at this gathering to compose my rhymes.
And albeit a little nervous,
to bless and honor an old friend,
my mentor in Information Retrieval,
who conceived an idea and realized it,
to open computer gates for searching any Hebrew text.
He overcame obstacles and persisted unyieldingly,
didn't give up in spite of opponents and hardships.
Alone, facing opposition, showed the right way,
and encouraged us to work hard and persist;
to expose the teachings of our sages, renew and regenerate,
harness modern new inventions and tools
for the benefit of Judaism.
Well, in brief, you all know about the Responsa Project,
And its synonym, for decades now, Aviezri Fraenkel.
Your friends and disciples bless and thank you,
for us you are always at the lead.
Wishing you an active healthy life until 120 years.

The following photo shows the Choueka family at the marriage of Rony,

Fig. 6.

Center, Ya'acov and Sarah's eldest, in June 2007 (the bride, Hanna, is absent, as she was preparing herself for the ceremony). The next depicts another   family gathering. Both reflect again the happy family relationships in the Choueka clan.

Fig. 7.

4   Scientific Activities

My scientific collaboration with Ya'acov began after I noticed the pioneering work of his with Meir Shapira, published in Hebrew in 1964, on the automatic analysis of Hebrew words, which I read with interest in connection with the then emerging Responsa Project, the idea of which I conceived in January 1963, in a conversation with the late Mr. Irving Kutoff of Minneapolis, MN. I told Ya'acov that I thought that in addition to the **analysis** of Hebrew words, which constituted his work with Shapira, we would also need an automatic **synthesis** tool. We produced such a tool under the leadership of Ya'acov, and the collaboration of a few eager students of computer science and linguists, including my former M.Sc. student Meir Cohen who wrote the first collection of programs for the Responsa system, and my Ph.D. student Dr. Rony Attar. Dr. Yair Halevi, in his M.Sc. thesis under Choueka, and Elazar Segal from the Responsa team contributed towards getting the online system underway.

Rabbi M'nacheim Slae, David Shindler and Joseph Dueck participated in the Responsa team, as well as the late Rabbi Yitzchak Pechenik. The late Professor Aharon Schreiber initiated and got us several grants from the NEH, on whose subproject he was Principal Investigator.   Incidentally, many senior computer scientists made their first steps in research with the Project, including prominent David Harel, past Dean of the Faculty of Mathematics and Computer Science at the Weizmann Institute, Nachum Dershowitz, Professor of Computer Science at Tel Aviv University, who also participated in the early linguistic efforts, my former Ph.D. students Prof. Shmuel Tomi Klein and the late Dr. Moshe Mor; Prof. Uri Schild, and many more. Professor Tzvi Arad, as rector, helped to sustain the Project in various ways. For the past few years, Rabbi Ya'acov Weinberger has been managing the Project wisely, together with a skeleton team, which includes Shim'on Goldschmidt, Sh'muel Levi and others. I apologize to those whose names I have forgotten to mention.

In 1975 Ya'acov replaced me at the helm of the Project, and it was then that he began to do research in the area of information retrieval, though his main love remained Hebrew computational linguistics. But even before he became formally the head of the Project, he participated in all of its phases and gave me considerable support and assistance, which were crucial to maintaining the shaky existence of the Project at Bar-Ilan. One of the major assets of Ya'acov, in addition to producing new ideas, is his persistent efforts in seeing things through. This was of utmost importance for the eventual success of the Responsa Project. Related to this is his talent to "market" and "sell" his achievements, getting grants and landing extra jobs. Among the extra jobs I'll just mention two:

1.   Important contributions to the defense establishment of Israel. Incidentally, Ya'acov served as an officer in the Israel defense forces during 1962-65. For proof, see the next photo.
2.   Consulting to industry and other institutions, mainly in the area of Hebrew computational linguistics.

Fig. 8.

A major undertaking that Ya'acov initiated and saw through is the Hebrew-Hebrew dictionary "Rav-Millim", roughly "words-chest" in English, though this translation doesn't do justice to all the connotations Ya'acov may or may not have had in mind for the Hebrew name. It is a monumental multi-volume new concept in dictionary construction, which of course, has also a computerized version, and a special youth edition. His work and experience on the Responsa system were crucial to accomplishing the "words-chest".

From Ya'acov's introduction to his "words-chest": "Basic questions, such as the mission and aim of a dictionary, what it should contain and how to edit it, have recently been radically re-evaluated. New concepts about dictionaries stem from an intensive research activity which ensued in the US and Europe (especially in England, Italy and Holland) since the beginning of the 1970s. This activity deals with the formal and computerized analysis of natural languages. The new dictionary concepts have since yielded many dictionaries (in several languages), but none in Hebrew."

Ya'acov has set out to rectify this situation. A spin-off of the dictionary project was an automatic punctuating tool for Hebrew, for which Ya'acov received the Prime Minister's prize in September, 1997. At a ceremony in the Knesset, Israel's Parliament, in the Prime Minister's presence, Ya'acov delivered a beautiful accomplished talk of thanks in the name of all the prize laureates.

The "words-chest" is an orchestra of many musicians, but Ya'acov was the maestro, fusing it together into a most harmonious and beautiful symphony. At the end of the introduction to the youth edition of the "words-chest", Ya'acov wrote the following:

ברכות שמיים לרעייתי ונוות ביתי, משוש ליבי ומאור עיני, שרה, שותפתי הנאמנה בניהולו של פרוייקט 'רב מלים' כמעט מאז ייסודו. בתחילת 1992 היא הציעה את פיתוחו של מילון זה, ואף צפתה את תבניתו ותכניתו. מאז ועד היום היא עמלה וטרחה, קראה והעירה, ניפתה וביררה וגם ליוותה את כל שלבי ההכנה, העריכה וההפקה של המילון באנרגיה בלתי נדלית, ומתוך חדוות יצירה ומעורבות רגשית עמוקה. ברוך טעמה וברוכות ידיה.

"Heaven's blessings to my wife and spouse Sarah, the joy of my heart and the light of my eyes, my loyal partner in managing the 'words-chest' project, almost from the start. At the beginning of 1992 she suggested the construction of this dictionary, and even foresaw its structure and plan. All these years she has toiled, read, remarked, sifted, purified and accompanied all stages of preparing, editing and realizing this dictionary. She invested endless energy, was deeply involved emotionally, and enjoyed the delight of creation. Blessed be her good taste and clever deeds."

These words, as well as the composition of this diverse and august gathering tonight at this banquet honoring Professor Choueka, once again attest to the blessed integration within Ya'acov's personality of the family man, the poet, the scientist, the Jewish scholar and the practical man, whose two feet are rooted deeply on this piece of land called Israel, a fusion that yields new gems and rejuvenates old ones.

(Paragraph added in 2007.) Talking about rejuvenation, I often tell my contemporaries that we have to keep exercising our gray cells, red cells and white cells. If you neglect to use but one of them, especially the gray ones, all three are bound to wither rapidly. As they say, "Use it or Lose it". A very good example for all of us is provided by Yaacov: Recently, about 5 years after retirement, he took upon himself, at the invitation of Professors Menachem Ben-Sasson and Haggai Ben Shammai, to lead the computerization of the Friedberg *Genizah* Project. Building on his expertise and experience of processing Jewish texts by computer, he has begun creating very high-quality digital images of all *Genizah* fragments, scattered in many places world-wide, aimed at cataloging and permitting access and retrieval of *Genizah* information. Also here his talent to "market" and "sell" his achievements is of big help to the success of this innovative venture. I am sure that under his direction, this project will flourish and come to a successful fruition. (תהלים צב טו) עוֹד יְנוּבוּן בְּשֵׂיבָה דְּשֵׁנִים וְרַעֲנַנִּים יִהְיוּ 'They will still be fruitful in old age, vigorous and fresh they will be" (Psalms 92 15). I believe that this verse is conditional, and that its true interpretation is that as long as a person stays spiritually fruitful in old age, he will indeed remain vigorous and fresh also physically. Yaacov Choueka is a living example demonstrating this interpretation.

In this week's portion of the Bible, "chukat", the tribes of Israel composed a brief piece of poetry commemorating the help of G-od in overcoming their many enemies. It is our prayer that in these difficult times G-od will once again redeem us from the difficult situation we are in. People such as the Choueka clan and their chieftain, Professor Ya'acov Choueka, have the potential of realizing the prayer quoted at the beginning, by Rabbi Aharon M'nachem Choueka: "In his days Judea and Jerusalem will be redeemed, and Israel will dwell in peace. Amen, may it be the will of G-od."

At the successful conclusion of the first five Bar Mitzvahs, it remains only to wish Ya'acov at least five more, in ever increasing creativity and joy amidst his wonderful and remarkable family.

Topological Complexity of Context-Free ω-Languages: A Survey

Olivier Finkel

Equipe de Logique Mathématique
Institut de Mathématiques de Jussieu - Paris Rive Gauche UMR7586
CNRS et Université Paris Diderot Paris 7
Bâtiment Sophie Germain Case 7012
75205 Paris Cedex 13, France
finkel@math.univ-paris-diderot.fr

Abstract. We survey recent results on the topological complexity of context-free ω-languages which form the second level of the Chomsky hierarchy of languages of infinite words. In particular, we consider the Borel hierarchy and the Wadge hierarchy of non-deterministic or deterministic context-free ω-languages. We study also decision problems, the links with the notions of ambiguity and of degrees of ambiguity, and the special case of ω-powers.

Keywords: Infinite words, pushdown automata, context-free (ω)-languages, ω-powers, Cantor topology, topological complexity, Borel hierarchy, Wadge hierarchy, complete sets, decision problems.

1 Introduction

The Chomsky hierarchy of formal languages of finite words over a finite alphabet is now well known, [49]. The class of regular languages accepted by finite automata forms the first level of this hierarchy and the class of context-free languages accepted by pushdown automata or generated by context-free grammars forms its second level [3]. The third and the fourth levels are formed by the class of context-sensitive languages accepted by linear-bounded automata or generated by Type-1 grammars and the class of recursively enumerable languages accepted by Turing machines or generated by Type-0 grammars [15]. In particular, context-free languages, firstly introduced by Chomsky to analyse the syntax of natural languages, have been very useful in Computer Science, in particular in the domain of programming languages, for the construction of compilers used to verify correctness of programs, [48].

There is a hierarchy of languages of infinite words which is analogous to the Chomsky hierarchy but where the languages are formed by infinite words over a finite alphabet. The first level of this hierarchy is formed by the class of regular ω-languages accepted by finite automata. They were first studied by Büchi in order to study decision problems for logical theories. In particular, Büchi proved that the monadic second order theory of one successor over the integers is decidable, using finite automata equipped with a certain acceptance condition for infinite words, now called the Büchi acceptance condition. Well known pioneers in this research area are named Muller, Mc Naughton,

N. Dershowitz and E. Nissan (Eds.): Choueka Festschrift, Part I, LNCS 8001, pp. 50–77, 2014.

Rabin, Landweber, Choueka, [61, 62, 68, 52, 16]. The theory of regular ω-languages is now well established and has found many applications for specification and verification of non-terminating systems; see [81, 78, 67] for many results and references. The second level of the hierarchy is formed by the class of context-free ω-languages. As in the case of languages of finite words it turned out that an ω-language is accepted by a (non-deterministic) pushdown automaton (with Büchi acceptance condition) if and only if it is generated by a context-free grammar where infinite derivations are considered. Context-free languages of infinite words were first studied by Cohen and Gold, [19, 20], Linna, [56–58], Boasson, Nivat, [64, 63, 7, 8], Beauquier, [4], see the survey [78]. Notice that in the case of infinite words Type-1 grammars and Type-0 grammars accept the same ω-languages which are also the ω-languages accepted by Turing machines with a Büchi acceptance condition [21, 78], see also the fundamental study of Engelfriet and Hoogeboom on **X**-automata, i.e. finite automata equipped with a storage type **X**, accepting infinite words,[29].

Context-free ω-languages have occurred recently in the works on games played on infinite pushdown graphs, following the fundamental study of Walukiewicz, [85, 82] [74, 40].

Since the set X^ω of infinite words over a finite alphabet X is naturally equipped with the Cantor topology, a way to study the complexity of ω-languages is to study their topological complexity. The first task is to locate ω-languages with regard to the Borel and the projective hierarchies, and next to the Wadge hierarchy which is a great refinement of the Borel hierarchy. It is then natural to ask for decidability properties and to study decision problems like : is there an effective procedure to determine the Borel rank or the Wadge degree of any context-free ω-language ? Such questions were asked by Lescow and Thomas in [55]. In this paper we survey some recent results on the topological complexity of context-free ω-languages. Some of them were very surprising as the two following ones:

1. there is a 1-counter finitary language L such that L^ω is analytic but not Borel, [35].
2. The Wadge hierarchy, hence also the Borel hierarchy, of ω-languages accepted by real time 1-counter Büchi automata is the same as the Wadge hierarchy of ω-languages accepted by Büchi Turing machines, [41].

The Borel and Wadge hierarchies of *non deterministic* context-free ω-languages are not effective. One can neither decide whether a given context-free ω-language is a Borel set nor whether it is in a given Borel class $\mathbf{\Sigma}^0_\alpha$ or $\mathbf{\Pi}^0_\alpha$. On the other hand *deterministic* context-free ω-languages are located at a low level of the Borel hierarchy: they are all $\mathbf{\Delta}^0_3$-sets. They enjoy some decidability properties although some important questions in this area are still open. We consider also the links with the notions of ambiguity and of degrees of ambiguity, and the special case of ω-powers, i.e. of ω-languages in the form V^ω, where V is a (context-free) finitary language. Finally we state some perspectives and give a list of some questions which remain open for further study.

The paper is organized as follows. In Section 2 we recall the notions of context-free ω-languages accepted by Büchi or Muller pushdown automata. Topological notions and Borel and Wadge hierarchies are recalled in Section 3. In Section 4 is studied the case of non-deterministic context-free ω-languages while deterministic context-free ω-languages are considered in Section 5. Links with notions of ambiguity in context free languages are studied in Section 6. Section 7 is devoted to the special case of ω-powers. Perspectives and some open questions are presented in last Section 8.

2 Context-Free ω-Languages

We assume the reader to be familiar with the theory of formal (ω)-languages [81, 78]. We shall use usual notations of formal language theory.

When X is a finite alphabet, a *non-empty finite word* over X is any sequence $x = a_1 \ldots a_k$, where $a_i \in X$ for $i = 1, \ldots, k$, and k is an integer ≥ 1. The *length* of x is k, denoted by $|x|$. The *empty word* has no letters and is denoted by λ; its length is 0. For $x = a_1 \ldots a_k$, we write $x(i) = a_i$ and $x[i] = x(1) \ldots x(i)$ for $i \leq k$ and $x[0] = \lambda$. $X^\star$ is the *set of finite words* (including the empty word) over X.

For $V \subseteq X^\star$, the complement of V (in $X^\star$) is $X^\star - V$ denoted V^-.

The *first infinite ordinal* is ω. An ω-*word* over X is an ω-sequence $a_1 \ldots a_n \ldots$, where for all integers $i \geq 1$, $a_i \in X$. When σ is an ω-word over X, we write $\sigma = \sigma(1)\sigma(2) \ldots \sigma(n) \ldots$, where for all i, $\sigma(i) \in X$, and $\sigma[n] = \sigma(1)\sigma(2) \ldots \sigma(n)$ for all $n \geq 1$ and $\sigma[0] = \lambda$.

The usual concatenation product of two finite words u and v is denoted $u.v$ (and sometimes just uv). This product is extended to the product of a finite word u and an ω-word v: the infinite word $u.v$ is then the ω-word such that:

$(u.v)(k) = u(k)$ if $k \leq |u|$, and $(u.v)(k) = v(k - |u|)$ if $k > |u|$.

The *prefix relation* is denoted $\sqsubseteq$: a finite word u is a *prefix* of a finite word v (respectively, an infinite word v), denoted $u \sqsubseteq v$, if and only if there exists a finite word w (respectively, an infinite word w), such that $v = u.w$. The *set of ω-words* over the alphabet X is denoted by X^ω. An ω-*language* over an alphabet X is a subset of X^ω. The complement (in X^ω) of an ω-language $V \subseteq X^\omega$ is $X^\omega - V$, denoted V^-.

For $V \subseteq X^\star$, the ω-power of V is :

$$V^\omega = \{\sigma = u_1 \ldots u_n \ldots \in X^\omega \mid \forall i \geq 1 \ u_i \in V\}.$$

We now define pushdown machines and the class of ω-context-free languages.

Definition 1. *A pushdown machine (PDM) is a 6-tuple $M = (K, X, \Gamma, \delta, q_0, Z_0)$, where K is a finite set of states, X is a finite input alphabet, Γ is a finite pushdown alphabet, $q_0 \in K$ is the initial state, $Z_0 \in \Gamma$ is the start symbol, and δ is a mapping from $K \times (X \cup \{\lambda\}) \times \Gamma$ to finite subsets of $K \times \Gamma^\star$.*

If $\gamma \in \Gamma^+$ describes the pushdown store content, the leftmost symbol will be assumed to be on "top" of the store. A configuration of a PDM is a pair (q, γ) where $q \in K$ and $\gamma \in \Gamma^\star$.

For $a \in X \cup \{\lambda\}$, $\beta, \gamma \in \Gamma^\star$ and $Z \in \Gamma$, if (p, β) is in $\delta(q, a, Z)$, then we write $a : (q, Z\gamma) \mapsto_M (p, \beta\gamma)$.

$\mapsto_M^\star$ *is the transitive and reflexive closure of $\mapsto_M$. (The subscript M will be omitted whenever the meaning remains clear).*

Let $\sigma = a_1 a_2 \ldots a_n \ldots$ be an ω-word over X. An infinite sequence of configurations $r = (q_i, \gamma_i)_{i \geq 1}$ is called a complete run of M on σ, starting in configuration (p, γ), iff:

1. $(q_1, \gamma_1) = (p, \gamma)$
2. *for each $i \geq 1$, there exists $b_i \in X \cup \{\lambda\}$ satisfying $b_i : (q_i, \gamma_i) \mapsto_M (q_{i+1}, \gamma_{i+1})$ such that $a_1 a_2 \ldots a_n \ldots = b_1 b_2 \ldots b_n \ldots$*

For every such run, $In(r)$ is the set of all states entered infinitely often during run r.

A complete run r of M on σ, starting in configuration (q_0, Z_0), will be simply called "a run of M on σ".

Definition 2. *A Büchi pushdown automaton is a 7-tuple $M = (K, X, \Gamma, \delta, q_0, Z_0, F)$ where $M' = (K, X, \Gamma, \delta, q_0, Z_0)$ is a PDM and $F \subseteq K$ is the set of final states. The ω-language accepted by M is*

$$L(M) = \{\sigma \in X^{\omega} \mid \text{there exists a complete run } r \text{ of } M \text{ on } \sigma \text{ such that } In(r) \cap F \neq \emptyset\}$$

Definition 3. *A Muller pushdown automaton is a 7-tuple $M = (K, X, \Gamma, \delta, q_0, Z_0, \mathcal{F})$ where $M' = (K, X, \Gamma, \delta, q_0, Z_0)$ is a PDM and $\mathcal{F} \subseteq 2^K$ is the collection of designated state sets. The ω-language accepted by M is*

$$L(M) = \{\sigma \in X^{\omega} \mid \text{there exists a complete run } r \text{ of } M \text{ on } \sigma \text{ such that } In(r) \in \mathcal{F}\}$$

Remark 4. *We consider here two acceptance conditions for ω-words, the Büchi and the Muller acceptance conditions, respectively denoted 2-acceptance and 3-acceptance in [52] and in [20] and $(inf, \sqcap)$ and $(inf, =)$ in [78]. We refer the reader to [19, 20, 78, 29] for consideration of weaker acceptance conditions, and to [46, 67] for the definitions of other usual ones like Rabin, Street, or parity acceptance conditions. Notice however that it seems that the latter ones have not been much considered in the study of context-free ω-languages but they are often involved in constructions concerning finite automata reading infinite words.*

Notation. In the sequel we shall often abbreviate "Muller pushdown automaton" by MPDA and "Büchi pushdown automaton" by BPDA.

Cohen and Gold and independently Linna established a characterization theorem for ω-languages accepted by Büchi or Muller pushdown automata. We shall need the notion of "ω-Kleene closure" which we now firstly define:

Definition 5. *For any family $\mathcal{L}$ of finitary languages, the ω-Kleene closure of $\mathcal{L}$ is :*

$$\omega\text{-}KC(\mathcal{L}) = \{\cup_{i=1}^{n} U_i . V_i^{\omega} \mid \forall i \in [1, n] \;\; U_i, V_i \in \mathcal{L}\}$$

Theorem 6 (Linna [56], Cohen and Gold [19]). *Let CFL be the class of context-free (finitary) languages. Then for any ω-language L the following three conditions are equivalent:*

1. *$L \in \omega\text{-}KC(CFL)$.*
2. *There exists a $BPDA$ that accepts L.*
3. *There exists a $MPDA$ that accepts L.*

In [19] are also studied ω-languages generated by ω-context-free grammars and it is shown that each of the conditions 1), 2), and 3) of the above Theorem is also equivalent to: 4) L is generated by a context-free grammar G by leftmost derivations. These grammars are also studied by Nivat in [63, 64]. Then we can let the following definition:

Definition 7. *An* ω-*language is a context-free* ω-*language iff it satisfies one of the conditions of the above Theorem. The class of context-free* ω-*languages will be denoted by* CFL_ω.

If we omit the pushdown store in the above Theorem we obtain the characterization of languages accepted by classical Muller automata (MA) or Büchi automata (BA) :

Theorem 8. *For any* ω-*language* L, *the following conditions are equivalent:*

1. L *belongs to* ω−$KC(REG)$,
   where REG *is the class of finitary regular languages.*
2. *There exists a MA that accepts* L.
3. *There exists a BA that accepts* L.

An ω-*language* L *satisfying one of the conditions of the above Theorem is called a regular* ω-*language. The class of regular* ω-*languages will be denoted by* REG_ω.

It follows from Mc Naughton's Theorem that the expressive power of deterministic MA (DMA) is equal to the expressive power of non deterministic MA, i.e. that every regular ω-language is accepted by a deterministic Muller automaton, [62, 67]. Notice that Choueka gave a simplified proof of Mc Naughton's Theorem in [16]. Another variant was given by Rabin in [68]. Unlike the case of finite automata, deterministic $MPDA$ do not define the same class of ω-languages as non deterministic $MPDA$. Let us now define deterministic pushdown machines.

Definition 9. *A PDM* $M = (K, X, \Gamma, \delta, q_0, Z_0)$ *is said to be deterministic iff for each* $q \in K, Z \in \Gamma$, *and* $a \in X$:

1. $\delta(q, a, Z)$ *contains at most one element,*
2. $\delta(q, \lambda, Z)$ *contains at most one element, and*
3. *if* $\delta(q, \lambda, Z)$ *is non empty, then* $\delta(q, a, Z)$ *is empty for all* $a \in X$.

It turned out that the class of ω-languages accepted by deterministic $BPDA$ is strictly included into the class of ω-languages accepted by deterministic $MPDA$. This latest class is the class $DCFL_\omega$ of deterministic context-free ω-languages. We denote $DCFL$ the class of deterministic context-free (finitary) languages.

Proposition 10 ([20])

1. $DCFL_\omega$ *is closed under complementation, but is neither closed under union, nor under intersection.*
2. $DCFL_\omega \subsetneq \omega−KC(DCFL) \subsetneq CFL_\omega$ *(these inclusions are strict).*

3   Topology

3.1   Borel Hierarchy and Analytic Sets

We assume the reader to be familiar with basic notions of topology which may be found in [60, 55, 50, 78, 67]. There is a natural metric on the set X^ω of infinite words over a finite alphabet X containing at least two letters which is called the *prefix metric* and defined as follows. For $u, v \in X^\omega$ and $u \neq v$ let $\delta(u, v) = 2^{-l_{\text{pref}(u,v)}}$ where $l_{\text{pref}(u,v)}$ is the first integer n such that $u(n+1)$ is different from $v(n+1)$. This metric induces on X^ω the usual Cantor topology for which *open subsets* of X^ω are in the form $W.X^\omega$, where $W \subseteq X^\star$. A set $L \subseteq X^\omega$ is a *closed set* iff its complement $X^\omega - L$ is an open set. Define now the *Borel Hierarchy* of subsets of X^ω:

Definition 11. *For a non-null countable ordinal α, the classes Σ_α^0 and Π_α^0 of the Borel Hierarchy on the topological space X^ω are defined as follows:*
Σ_1^0 *is the class of open subsets of X^ω, Π_1^0 is the class of closed subsets of X^ω, and for any countable ordinal $\alpha \geq 2$:*
Σ_α^0 *is the class of countable unions of subsets of X^ω in $\bigcup_{\gamma < \alpha} \Pi_\gamma^0$.*
Π_α^0 *is the class of countable intersections of subsets of X^ω in $\bigcup_{\gamma < \alpha} \Sigma_\gamma^0$.*

Recall some basic results about these classes :

Proposition 12

(a) $\Sigma_\alpha^0 \cup \Pi_\alpha^0 \subsetneq \Sigma_{\alpha+1}^0 \cap \Pi_{\alpha+1}^0$, *for each countable ordinal $\alpha \geq 1$.*
(b) $\bigcup_{\gamma < \alpha} \Sigma_\gamma^0 = \bigcup_{\gamma < \alpha} \Pi_\gamma^0 \subsetneq \Sigma_\alpha^0 \cap \Pi_\alpha^0$, *for each countable limit ordinal α.*
(c) *A set $W \subseteq X^\omega$ is in the class Σ_α^0 iff its complement is in the class Π_α^0.*
(d) $\Sigma_\alpha^0 - \Pi_\alpha^0 \neq \emptyset$ *and* $\Pi_\alpha^0 - \Sigma_\alpha^0 \neq \emptyset$ *hold for every countable ordinal $\alpha \geq 1$.*

For a countable ordinal α, a subset of X^ω is a Borel set of *rank* α iff it is in $\Sigma_\alpha^0 \cup \Pi_\alpha^0$ but not in $\bigcup_{\gamma < \alpha}(\Sigma_\gamma^0 \cup \Pi_\gamma^0)$.

There are also some subsets of X^ω which are not Borel. Indeed there exists another hierarchy beyond the Borel hierarchy, which is called the projective hierarchy and which is obtained from the Borel hierarchy by successive applications of operations of projection and complementation. The first level of the projective hierarchy is formed by the class of *analytic sets* and the class of *co-analytic sets* which are complements of analytic sets. In particular the class of Borel subsets of X^ω is strictly included into the class Σ_1^1 of *analytic sets* which are obtained by projection of Borel sets.

Definition 13. *A subset A of X^ω is in the class Σ_1^1 of* **analytic** *sets iff there exist a finite alphabet Y and a Borel subset B of $(X \times Y)^\omega$ such that $x \in A \leftrightarrow \exists y \in Y^\omega$ such that $(x, y) \in B$, where (x, y) is the infinite word over the alphabet $X \times Y$ such that $(x, y)(i) = (x(i), y(i))$ for each integer $i \geq 1$.*

Remark 14. *In the above definition we could take B in the class Π_2^0. Moreover analytic subsets of X^ω are the projections of Π_1^0-subsets of $X^\omega \times \omega^\omega$, where ω^ω is the Baire space, [60].*

We now define completeness with regard to reduction by continuous functions. For a countable ordinal $\alpha \geq 1$, a set $F \subseteq X^\omega$ is said to be a Σ_α^0 (respectively, Π_α^0, Σ_1^1)-*complete set* iff for any set $E \subseteq Y^\omega$ (with Y a finite alphabet): $E \in \Sigma_\alpha^0$ (respectively, $E \in \Pi_\alpha^0$, $E \in \Sigma_1^1$) iff there exists a continuous function $f : Y^\omega \to X^\omega$ such that $E = f^{-1}(F)$. Σ_n^0 (respectively Π_n^0)-complete sets, with n an integer ≥ 1, are thoroughly characterized in [76].

In particular $\mathcal{R} = (0^*.1)^\omega$ is a well known example of Π_2^0-complete subset of $\{0,1\}^\omega$. It is the set of ω-words over $\{0,1\}$ having infinitely many occurrences of the letter 1. Its complement $\{0,1\}^\omega - (0^*.1)^\omega$ is a Σ_2^0-complete subset of $\{0,1\}^\omega$.

We recall now the definition of the arithmetical hierarchy of ω-languages which form the effective analogue to the hierarchy of Borel sets of finite rank.

Let X be a finite alphabet. An ω-language $L \subseteq X^\omega$ belongs to the class Σ_n if and only if there exists a recursive relation $R_L \subseteq (\mathbb{N})^{n-1} \times X^*$ such that

$$L = \{\sigma \in X^\omega \mid Q_1 a_1 Q_2 a_2 \ldots Q_n a_n \quad (a_1, \ldots, a_{n-1}, \sigma[a_n + 1]) \in R_L\}$$

where Q_1 is the existential quantifier $\exists$, and every other Q_i, for $2 \leq i \leq n$, is one of the quantifiers $\forall$ or $\exists$ (not necessarily in an alternating order). An ω-language $L \subseteq X^\omega$ belongs to the class Π_n if and only if its complement $X^\omega - L$ belongs to the class Σ_n. The inclusion relations that hold between the classes Σ_n and Π_n are the same as for the corresponding classes of the Borel hierarchy. The classes Σ_n and Π_n are included in the respective classes Σ_n^0 and Σ_n^0 of the Borel hierarchy, and cardinality arguments suffice to show that these inclusions are strict.

As in the case of the Borel hierarchy, projections of arithmetical sets (of the second Π-class) lead beyond the arithmetical hierarchy, to the analytical hierarchy of ω-languages. The first class of this hierarchy is the class Σ_1^1 of *effective analytic sets* which are obtained by projection of arithmetical sets. An ω-language $L \subseteq X^\omega$ belongs to the class Σ_1^1 if and only if there exists a recursive relation $R_L \subseteq \mathbb{N} \times \{0,1\}^* \times X^*$ such that:

$$L = \{\sigma \in X^\omega \mid \exists \tau (\tau \in \{0,1\}^\omega \wedge \forall n \exists m ((n, \tau[m], \sigma[m]) \in R_L))\}$$

Then an ω-language $L \subseteq X^\omega$ is in the class Σ_1^1 iff it is the projection of an ω-language over the alphabet $X \times \{0,1\}$ which is in the class Π_2. The class Π_1^1 of *effective co-analytic sets* is simply the class of complements of effective analytic sets. We denote as usual $\Delta_1^1 = \Sigma_1^1 \cap \Pi_1^1$.

Recall that an ω-language $L \subseteq X^\omega$ is in the class Σ_1^1 iff it is accepted by a non deterministic Turing machine (reading ω-words) with a Büchi or Muller acceptance condition [78].

The Borel ranks of Δ_1^1 sets are the (recursive) ordinals $\gamma < \omega_1^{CK}$, where ω_1^{CK} is the first non-recursive ordinal, usually called the Church-Kleene ordinal. Moreover, for every non null ordinal $\alpha < \omega_1^{CK}$, there exist some Σ_α^0-complete and some Π_α^0-complete sets in the class Δ_1^1.

On the other hand, Kechris, Marker and Sami proved in [51] that the supremum of the set of Borel ranks of (effective) Σ_1^1-sets is the ordinal γ_2^1. This ordinal is proved to be strictly greater than the ordinal δ_2^1 which is the first non Δ_2^1 ordinal. In particular, the ordinal γ_2^1 is strictly greater than the ordinal ω_1^{CK}. Remark that the exact value of the ordinal γ_2^1 may depend on axioms of set theory, see [51, 41] for more details. Notice also that it seems still unknown whether *every* non null ordinal $\gamma < \gamma_2^1$ is the Borel rank of a Σ_1^1-set.

3.2 Wadge Hierarchy

We now introduce the Wadge hierarchy, which is a great refinement of the Borel hierarchy defined via reductions by continuous functions, [23, 83].

Definition 15 (Wadge [83]). *Let X, Y be two finite alphabets. For $L \subseteq X^\omega$ and $L' \subseteq Y^\omega$, L is said to be Wadge reducible to L' ($L \leq_W L'$) iff there exists a continuous function $f : X^\omega \rightarrow Y^\omega$, such that $L = f^{-1}(L')$.*

L and L' are Wadge equivalent iff $L \leq_W L'$ and $L' \leq_W L$. This will be denoted by $L \equiv_W L'$. And we shall say that $L <_W L'$ iff $L \leq_W L'$ but not $L' \leq_W L$.

A set $L \subseteq X^\omega$ is said to be self dual iff $L \equiv_W L^-$, and otherwise it is said to be non self dual.

The relation $\leq_W$ is reflexive and transitive, and $\equiv_W$ is an equivalence relation.

The *equivalence classes* of $\equiv_W$ are called *Wadge degrees*.

The Wadge hierarchy WH is the class of Borel subsets of a set X^ω, where X is a finite set, equipped with $\leq_W$ and with $\equiv_W$.

For $L \subseteq X^\omega$ and $L' \subseteq Y^\omega$, if $L \leq_W L'$ and $L = f^{-1}(L')$ where f is a continuous function from X^ω into Y^ω, then f is called a continuous reduction of L to L'. Intuitively it means that L is less complicated than L' because to check whether $x \in L$ it suffices to check whether $f(x) \in L'$ where f is a continuous function. Hence the Wadge degree of an ω-language is a measure of its topological complexity.

Notice that in the above definition, we consider that a subset $L \subseteq X^\omega$ is given together with the alphabet X. This is important as it is shown by the following simple example. Let $L_1 = \{0,1\}^\omega \subseteq \{0,1\}^\omega$ and $L_2 = \{0,1\}^\omega \subseteq \{0,1,2\}^\omega$. So the languages L_1 and L_2 are equal but considered over the different alphabets $X_1 = \{0,1\}$ and $X_2 = \{0,1,2\}$. It turns out that $L_1 <_W L_2$. In fact L_1 is open *and* closed in X_1^ω while L_2 is closed but non open in X_2^ω.

We can now define the *Wadge class* of a set L:

Definition 16. *Let L be a subset of X^ω. The Wadge class of L is :*

$$[L] = \{L' \mid L' \subseteq Y^\omega \text{ for a finite alphabet } Y \text{ and } L' \leq_W L\}.$$

Recall that each *Borel class* Σ_α^0 and Π_α^0 is a *Wadge class*.

A set $L \subseteq X^\omega$ is a Σ_α^0 (respectively Π_α^0)-*complete set* iff for any set $L' \subseteq Y^\omega$, L' is in Σ_α^0 (respectively Π_α^0) iff $L' \leq_W L$. It follows from the study of the Wadge hierarchy that a set $L \subseteq X^\omega$ is a Σ_α^0 (respectively, Π_α^0)-*complete set* iff it is in Σ_α^0 but not in Π_α^0 (respectively, in Π_α^0 but not in Σ_α^0).

There is a close relationship between Wadge reducibility and games which we now introduce.

Definition 17. *Let $L \subseteq X^\omega$ and $L' \subseteq Y^\omega$. The Wadge game $W(L, L')$ is a game with perfect information between two players, player 1 who is in charge of L and player 2 who is in charge of L'.*

Player 1 first writes a letter $a_1 \in X$, then player 2 writes a letter $b_1 \in Y$, then player 1 writes a letter $a_2 \in X$, and so on.

The two players alternatively write letters a_n of X for player 1 and b_n of Y for player 2.

After ω steps, player 1 has written an ω-word $a \in X^\omega$ and player 2 has written an ω-word $b \in Y^\omega$. Player 2 is allowed to skip, even infinitely often, provided he really writes an ω-word in ω steps.

Player 2 wins the play iff $[a \in L \leftrightarrow b \in L']$, i.e. iff :

$$[(a \in L \text{ and } b \in L') \text{ or } (a \notin L \text{ and } b \notin L' \text{ and } b \text{ is infinite})].$$

Recall that a strategy for player 1 is a function $\sigma : (Y \cup \{s\})^\star \to X$. And a strategy for player 2 is a function $f : X^+ \to Y \cup \{s\}$.

σ is a winning stategy for player 1 iff he always wins a play when he uses the strategy σ, i.e. when the nth letter he writes is given by $a_n = \sigma(b_1 \ldots b_{n-1})$, where b_i is the letter written by player 2 at step i and $b_i = s$ if player 2 skips at step i.

A winning strategy for player 2 is defined in a similar manner.

Martin's Theorem states that every Gale-Stewart Game $G(B)$, with B a Borel set, is determined, i.e. that one of the two players has a winning strategy in the game $G(B)$, see [50]. This implies the following determinacy result :

Theorem 18 (Wadge). *Let $L \subseteq X^\omega$ and $L' \subseteq Y^\omega$ be two Borel sets, where X and Y are finite alphabets. Then the Wadge game $W(L, L')$ is determined : one of the two players has a winning strategy. And $L \leq_W L'$ iff player 2 has a winning strategy in the game $W(L, L')$.*

Theorem 19 (Wadge). *Up to the complement and $\equiv_W$, the class of Borel subsets of X^ω, for a finite alphabet X, is a well ordered hierarchy. There is an ordinal $|WH|$, called the length of the hierarchy, and a map d^0_W from WH onto $|WH| - \{0\}$, such that for all $L, L' \subseteq X^\omega$:*
$d^0_W L < d^0_W L' \leftrightarrow L <_W L'$ and
$d^0_W L = d^0_W L' \leftrightarrow [L \equiv_W L' \text{ or } L \equiv_W L'^-]$.

The Wadge hierarchy of Borel sets of *finite rank* has length $^1\varepsilon_0$ where $^1\varepsilon_0$ is the limit of the ordinals α_n defined by $\alpha_1 = \omega_1$ and $\alpha_{n+1} = \omega_1^{\alpha_n}$ for n a non negative integer, ω_1 being the first non countable ordinal. Then $^1\varepsilon_0$ is the first fixed point of the ordinal exponentiation of base ω_1. The length of the Wadge hierarchy of Borel sets in $\mathbf{\Delta}^0_\omega = \mathbf{\Sigma}^0_\omega \cap \mathbf{\Pi}^0_\omega$ is the ω_1^{th} fixed point of the ordinal exponentiation of base ω_1, which is a much larger ordinal. The length of the whole Wadge hierarchy of Borel sets is a huge ordinal, with regard to the ω_1^{th} fixed point of the ordinal exponentiation of base ω_1. It is described in [83, 23] by the use of the Veblen functions.

4   Topological Complexity of Context-Free ω-Languages

We recall first results about the topological complexity of regular ω-languages. Topological properties of regular ω-languages were first studied by L. H. Landweber in [52] where he characterized regular ω-languages in a given Borel class. It turned out that a regular ω-language is a $\mathbf{\Pi}^0_2$-set iff it is accepted by a deterministic Büchi automaton.

On the other hand Mc Naughton's Theorem implies that regular ω-languages, accepted by deterministic Muller automata, are boolean combinations of regular ω-languages accepted by deterministic Büchi automata. Thus they are boolean combinations of $\mathbf{\Pi}_2^0$-sets hence $\mathbf{\Delta}_3^0$-sets. Moreover Landweber proved that one can effectively determine the exact level of a given regular ω-language with regard to the Borel hierarchy.

A great improvement of these results was obtained by Wagner who determined in an effective way, using the notions of chains and superchains, the Wadge hierarchy of the class REG_ω, [84]. This hierarchy has length ω^ω and is now called the Wagner hierarchy, [69, 71, 72, 70, 78]. Wilke and Yoo proved in [86] that one can compute in polynomial time the Wadge degree of a regular ω-language. Later Carton and Perrin gave a presentation of the Wagner hierarchy using algebraic notions of ω-semigroups, [14, 13, 67]. This work was completed by Duparc and Riss in [27].

Context-free ω-languages beyond the class $\mathbf{\Delta}_3^0$ have been constructed for the first time in [32]. The construction used an operation of exponentiation of sets of finite or infinite words introduced by Duparc in his study of the Wadge hierarchy [23]. We are going now to recall these constructions although some stronger results on the topological complexity of context-free ω-languages were obtained later in [38, 41] by other methods. However the methods of [32] using Duparc's operation of exponentiation are also interesting and it gave other results on ambiguity and on ω-powers of context-free languages we can not (yet ?) get by other methods, see Sections 6 and 7 below.

Wadge gave a description of the Wadge hierarchy of Borel sets in [83]. Duparc recently got a new proof of Wadge's results and gave in [22, 23] a normal form of Borel sets in the class $\mathbf{\Delta}_\omega^0$, i.e. an inductive construction of a Borel set of every given degree smaller than the ω_1^{th} fixed point of the ordinal exponentiation of base ω_1. The construction relies on set theoretic operations which are the counterpart of arithmetical operations over ordinals needed to compute the Wadge degrees.

Actually Duparc studied the Wadge hierarchy via the study of the conciliating hierarchy. Conciliating sets are sets of finite _or_ infinite words over an alphabet X, i.e. subsets of $X^\star \cup X^\omega = X^{\leq\omega}$. It turned out that the conciliating hierarchy is isomorphic to the Wadge hierarchy of non-self-dual Borel sets, via the correspondence $A \to A^d$ we recall now:

For a word $x \in (X \cup \{d\})^{\leq\omega}$ we denote by $x(/d)$ the sequence obtained from x by removing every occurrence of the letter d. Then for $A \subseteq X^{\leq\omega}$ and d a letter not in X, A^d is the ω-language over $X \cup \{d\}$ which is defined by :

$$A^d = \{x \in (X \cup \{d\})^\omega \mid x(/d) \in A\}.$$

We are going now to introduce the operation of exponentiation of conciliating sets.

Definition 20 (Duparc [23]). *Let X be a finite alphabet, $\leftarrow \notin X$, and let x be a finite or infinite word over the alphabet $Y = X \cup \{\leftarrow\}$.*
Then $x^{\leftarrow}$ is inductively defined by:
$\lambda^{\leftarrow} = \lambda$,
and for a finite word $u \in (X \cup \{\leftarrow\})^\star$:
$(u.a)^{\leftarrow} = u^{\leftarrow}.a$, *if $a \in X$,*
$(u.\leftarrow)^{\leftarrow} = u^{\leftarrow}(1).u^{\leftarrow}(2)\ldots u^{\leftarrow}(|u^{\leftarrow}|-1)$ *if $|u^{\leftarrow}| > 0$,*
$(u.\leftarrow)^{\leftarrow} = \lambda$ *if $|u^{\leftarrow}| = 0$,*

and for u infinite:
$(u)^{\leftarrow} = \lim_{n\in\omega}(u[n])^{\leftarrow}$, *where, given* β_n *and* v *in* $X^\star$,
$v \sqsubseteq \lim_{n\in\omega}\beta_n \leftrightarrow \exists n\forall p \geq n \quad \beta_p[|v|] = v$.
(The finite or infinite word $\lim_{n\in\omega}\beta_n$ *is determined by the set of its (finite) prefixes).*

Remark 21. *For* $x \in Y^{\leq\omega}$, $x^{\leftarrow}$ *denotes the string* x, *once every* $\leftarrow$ *occuring in* x *has been "evaluated" to the back space operation, proceeding from left to right inside* x. *In other words* $x^{\leftarrow} = x$ *from which every interval of the form "$a \leftarrow$ " ($a \in X$) is removed.*

For example if $u = (a \leftarrow)^n$, for n an integer ≥ 1, or $u = (a \leftarrow)^\omega$, or $u = (a \leftarrow\leftarrow)^\omega$, then $(u)^{\leftarrow} = \lambda$. If $u = (ab \leftarrow)^\omega$ then $(u)^{\leftarrow} = a^\omega$ and if $u = bb(\leftarrow a)^\omega$ then $(u)^{\leftarrow} = b$.

Let us notice that in Definition 20 the limit is not defined in the usual way:

for example if $u = bb(\leftarrow a)^\omega$ the finite word $u[n]^{\leftarrow}$ is alternatively equal to b or to ba: more precisely $u[2n + 1]^{\leftarrow} = b$ and $u[2n + 2]^{\leftarrow} = ba$ for every integer $n \geq 1$ (it holds also that $u[1]^{\leftarrow} = b$ and $u[2]^{\leftarrow} = bb$). Thus Definition 20 implies that $\lim_{n\in\omega}(u[n])^{\leftarrow} = b$ so $u^{\leftarrow} = b$.

We can now define the operation $A \to A^\sim$ of *exponentiation of conciliating sets*:

Definition 22 (Duparc [23]). *For* $A \subseteq X^{\leq\omega}$ *and* $\leftarrow\notin X$, *let*

$$A^\sim =_{df} \{x \in (X \cup \{\leftarrow\})^{\leq\omega} \mid x^{\leftarrow} \in A\}.$$

The operation $\sim$ is monotone with regard to the Wadge ordering and produces some sets of higher complexity.

Theorem 23 (Duparc [23]). *Let* $A \subseteq X^{\leq\omega}$ *and* $n \geq 1$. *if* $A^d \subseteq (X \cup \{d\})^\omega$ *is a* Σ^0_n-complete (respectively, Π^0_n-complete) set, then $(A^\sim)^d$ is a Σ^0_{n+1}-complete (respectively, Π^0_{n+1}-complete) set.*

It was proved in [32] that the class of context-free infinitary languages (which are unions of a context-free finitary language and of a context-free ω-language) is closed under the operation $A \to A^\sim$. On the other hand $A \to A^d$ is an operation from the class of context-free infinitary languages into the class of context-free ω-languages. This implies that, for each integer $n \geq 1$, there exist some context-free ω-languages which are Σ^0_n-complete and some others which are Π^0_n-complete.

Theorem 24 ([32]). *For each non negative integer* $n \geq 1$, *there exist* Σ^0_n-complete *context-free* ω-languages A_n *and* Π^0_n-complete *context-free* ω-languages B_n.

Proof. For $n = 1$ consider the Σ^0_1-complete regular ω-language
$A_1 = \{\alpha \in \{0,1\}^\omega \mid \exists i \quad \alpha(i) = 1\}$
and the Π^0_1-complete regular ω-language
$B_1 = \{\alpha \in \{0,1\}^\omega \mid \forall i \quad \alpha(i) = 0\}$.
These languages are context-free ω-languages because $REG_\omega \subseteq CFL_\omega$.
Now consider the Σ^0_2-complete regular ω-language
$A_2 = \{\alpha \in \{0,1\}^\omega \mid \exists^{<\omega} i \quad \alpha(i) = 1\}$
and the Π^0_2-complete regular ω-language
$B_2 = \{\alpha \in \{0,1\}^\omega \mid \exists^\omega i \quad \alpha(i) = 0\}$,

where $\exists^{<\omega}i$ means: " there exist only finitely many i such that . . ." , and
$\exists^{\omega}i$ means: " there exist infinitely many i such that . . .".
A_2 and B_2 are context-free ω-languages because they are regular ω-languages.

To obtain context-free ω-languages of greater Borel ranks, consider now O_1 (respectively, C_1) subsets of $\{0,1\}^{\leq\omega}$ such that $(O_1)^d$ (respectively, $(C_1)^d$) are Σ_1^0-complete (respectively Π_1^0-complete) .
  For example $O_1 = \{x \in \{0,1\}^{\leq\omega} \mid \exists i\, x(i) = 1\}$ and $C_1 = \{\lambda\}$.
  We can apply $n \geq 1$ times the operation of exponentiation of sets.
  More precisely, we define, for a set $A \subseteq X^{\leq\omega}$:
$A^{\sim\cdot0} = A$
$A^{\sim\cdot1} = A^{\sim}$ and
$A^{\sim\cdot(n+1)} = (A^{\sim\cdot n})^{\sim}$.

Now apply n times (for an integer $n \geq 1$) the operation $\sim$ (with different new letters $\leftarrow_1, \leftarrow_2, \leftarrow_3, \ldots, \leftarrow_n$) to O_1 and C_1.
  By Theorem 23, it holds that for an integer $n \geq 1$:
$(O_1^{\sim\cdot n})^d$ is a Σ_{n+1}^0-complete subset of $\{0,1,\leftarrow_1,\ldots,\leftarrow_n,d\}^{\omega}$.
$(C_1^{\sim\cdot n})^d$ is a Π_{n+1}^0-complete subset of $\{0,1,\leftarrow_1,\ldots,\leftarrow_n,d\}^{\omega}$.

And it is easy to see that O_1 and C_1 are in the form $E \cup F$ where E is a finitary context-free language and F is a context-free ω-language. Then the ω-languages $(O_1^{\sim\cdot n})^d$ and $(C_1^{\sim\cdot n})^d$ are context-free. Hence the class CFL_ω exhausts the finite ranks of the Borel hierarchy: we obtain the context-free ω-languages $A_n = (O_1^{\sim\cdot(n-1)})^d$ and $B_n = (C_1^{\sim\cdot(n-1)})^d$, for $n \geq 3$. $\qquad\square$

This gave a partial answer to questions of Thomas and Lescow [55] about the hierarchy of context-free ω-languages.
  A natural question now arose: Do the decidability results of [52] extend to context-free ω-languages? Unfortunately the answer is no. Cohen and Gold proved that one cannot decide whether a given context-free ω-language is in the class Π_1^0, Σ_1^0, or Π_2^0, [19]. This result was first extended to all classes Σ_n^0 and Π_n^0, for n an integer ≥ 1, using the undecidability of the Post Correspondence Problem, [32].
  Later, the coding of an infinite number of erasers $\leftarrow_n$, $n \geq 1$, and an iteration of the operation of exponentiation were used to prove that there exist some context-free ω-languages which are Borel of infinite rank, [36].
  Using the correspondences between the operation of exponentiation of sets and the ordinal exponentiation of base ω_1, and between the Wadge's operation of sum of sets, [83, 23], and the ordinal sum, it was proved in [33] that the length of the Wadge hierarchy of the class CFL_ω is at least ε_0, the first fixed point of the ordinal exponentiation of base ω. Next were constructed some Δ_ω^0 context-free ω-languages in ε_ω Wadge degrees, where ε_ω is the ωth fixed point of the ordinal exponentiation of base ω, and also some Σ_ω^0-complete context-free ω-languages, [31, 39]. Notice that the Wadge hierarchy of non-deterministic context-free ω-languages is not effective, [33].

The question of the existence of non-Borel context-free ω-languages was solved by Finkel and Ressayre. Using a coding of infinite binary trees labeled in a finite alphabet X, it was proved that there exist some non-Borel, and even Σ_1^1-complete, context-free ω-languages, and that one cannot decide whether a given context-free ω-language is a Borel set, [35]. Amazingly there is a simple finitary language V accepted by a 1-counter automaton such that V^ω is Σ_1^1-complete; we shall recall it in Section 7 below on ω-powers.

But a complete and very surprising result was obtained in [38, 41], which extended previous results. A simulation of multicounter automata by 1-counter automata was used in [38, 41]. We firstly recall now the definition of these automata, in order to sketch the constructions involved in these simulations.

Definition 25. *Let k be an integer ≥ 1. A k-counter machine (k-CM) is a 4-tuple $\mathcal{M}=(K, X, \Delta, q_0)$, where K is a finite set of states, X is a finite input alphabet, $q_0 \in K$ is the initial state, and $\Delta \subseteq K \times (X \cup \{\lambda\}) \times \{0, 1\}^k \times K \times \{0, 1, -1\}^k$ is the transition relation. The k-counter machine $\mathcal{M}$ is said to be real time iff: $\Delta \subseteq K \times X \times \{0, 1\}^k \times K \times \{0, 1, -1\}^k$, i.e. iff there are not any λ-transitions.*

If the machine $\mathcal{M}$ is in state q and $c_i \in \mathbf{N}$ is the content of the ith counter C_i then the configuration (or global state) of $\mathcal{M}$ is the $(k+1)$-tuple $(q, c_1, \ldots, c_k)$.

For $a \in X \cup \{\lambda\}$, $q, q' \in K$ and $(c_1, \ldots, c_k) \in \mathbf{N}^k$ such that $c_j = 0$ for $j \in E \subseteq \{1, \ldots, k\}$ and $c_j > 0$ for $j \notin E$, if $(q, a, i_1, \ldots, i_k, q', j_1, \ldots, j_k) \in \Delta$ where $i_j = 0$ for $j \in E$ and $i_j = 1$ for $j \notin E$, then we write:

$$a : (q, c_1, \ldots, c_k) \mapsto_\mathcal{M} (q', c_1 + j_1, \ldots, c_k + j_k)$$

Thus we see that the transition relation must satisfy:
if $(q, a, i_1, \ldots, i_k, q', j_1, \ldots, j_k) \in \Delta$ and $i_m = 0$ for some $m \in \{1, \ldots, k\}$, then $j_m = 0$ or $j_m = 1$ (but j_m cannot be equal to -1).

Let $\sigma = a_1 a_2 \ldots a_n \ldots$ be an ω-word over X. An ω-sequence of configurations $r = (q_i, c_1^i, \ldots c_k^i)_{i \geq 1}$ is called a run of $\mathcal{M}$ on σ, starting in configuration $(p, c_1, \ldots, c_k)$, iff:

(1) $(q_1, c_1^1, \ldots c_k^1) = (p, c_1, \ldots, c_k)$
(2) for each $i \geq 1$, there exists $b_i \in X \cup \{\lambda\}$ such that $b_i : (q_i, c_1^i, \ldots c_k^i) \mapsto_\mathcal{M} (q_{i+1}, c_1^{i+1}, \ldots c_k^{i+1})$ such that either $a_1 a_2 \ldots a_n \ldots = b_1 b_2 \ldots b_n \ldots$ or $b_1 b_2 \ldots b_n \ldots$ is a finite prefix of $a_1 a_2 \ldots a_n \ldots$

The run r is said to be complete when $a_1 a_2 \ldots a_n \ldots = b_1 b_2 \ldots b_n \ldots$
For every such run, $\mathrm{In}(r)$ is the set of all states entered infinitely often during run r.

A complete run r of M on σ, starting in configuration $(q_0, 0, \ldots, 0)$, will be simply called "a run of M on σ".

Definition 26. *A Büchi k-counter automaton is a 5-tuple $\mathcal{M}=(K, X, \Delta, q_0, F)$, where $\mathcal{M}'=(K, X, \Delta, q_0)$ is a k-counter machine and $F \subseteq K$ is the set of accepting states. The ω-language accepted by $\mathcal{M}$ is*

$$L(\mathcal{M}) = \{\sigma \in X^\omega \mid there\ exists\ a\ run\ r\ of\ \mathcal{M}\ on\ \sigma\ such\ that\ \mathrm{In}(r) \cap F \neq \emptyset\}$$

The notion of Muller k-counter automaton is defined in a similar way. One can see that an ω-language is accepted by a (real time) Büchi k-counter automaton iff it is accepted by a (real time) Muller k-counter automaton [29]. Notice that this result is no longer true in the deterministic case.

We denote $\mathbf{BC}(k)$ (respectively, $\mathbf{r\text{-}BC}(k)$) the class of Büchi k-counter automata (respectively, of real time Büchi k-counter automata.

We denote $\mathbf{BCL}(k)_\omega$ (respectively, $\mathbf{r\text{-}BCL}(k)_\omega$) the class of ω-languages accepted by Büchi k-counter automata (respectively, by real time Büchi k-counter automata).

Remark that 1-counter automata introduced above are equivalent to pushdown automata whose stack alphabet is in the form $\{Z_0, A\}$ where Z_0 is the bottom symbol which always remains at the bottom of the stack and appears only there and A is another stack symbol. The pushdown stack may be seen like a counter whose content is the integer N if the stack content is the word $A^N.Z_0$.

In the model introduced here the counter value cannot be increased by more than 1 during a single transition. However this does not change the class of ω-languages accepted by such automata. So the class $\mathbf{BCL}(1)_\omega$ is equal to the class $\mathbf{1\text{-}ICL}_\omega$, introduced in [33], and it is a strict subclass of the class $\mathbf{CFL}_\omega$ of context-free ω-languages accepted by Büchi pushdown automata.

We state now the surprising result proved in [41], using multicounter-automata.

Theorem 27 ([41]). *The Wadge hierarchy of the class $\mathbf{r\text{-}BCL}(1)_\omega$, hence also of the class $\mathbf{CFL}_\omega$, or of every class $\mathcal{C}$ such that $\mathbf{r\text{-}BCL}(1)_\omega \subseteq \mathcal{C} \subseteq \Sigma_1^1$, is the Wadge hierarchy of the class Σ_1^1 of ω-languages accepted by Turing machines with a Büchi acceptance condition.*

We now sketch the proof of this result. It is well known that every Turing machine can be simulated by a (non real time) 2-counter automaton, see [49]. Thus the Wadge hierarchy of the class $\mathbf{BCL}(2)_\omega$ is also the Wadge hierarchy of the class of ω-languages accepted by Büchi Turing machines.

One can then find, from an ω-language $L \subseteq X^\omega$ in $\mathbf{BCL}(2)_\omega$, another ω-language $\theta_S(L)$ which will be of the same topological complexity but accepted by a *real-time* 8-counter Büchi automaton. The idea is to add firstly a storage type called a queue to a 2-counter Büchi automaton in order to read ω-words in real-time. Then the queue can be simulated by two pushdown stacks or by four counters. This simulation is not done in real-time but a crucial fact is that one can bound the number of transitions needed to simulate the queue. This allows to pad the strings in L with enough extra letters so that the new words will be read in real-time by a 8-counter Büchi automaton. The padding is obtained via the function θ_S which we define now.

Let X be an alphabet having at least two letters, E be a new letter not in X, S be an integer ≥ 1, and $\theta_S : X^\omega \to (X \cup \{E\})^\omega$ be the function defined, for all $x \in X^\omega$, by:

$$\theta_S(x) = x(1).E^S.x(2).E^{S^2}.x(3).E^{S^3}.x(4)\ldots x(n).E^{S^n}.x(n+1).E^{S^{n+1}}\ldots$$

It turns out that if $L \subseteq X^\omega$ is in $\mathbf{BCL}(2)_\omega$ then there exists an integer $S \geq 1$ such that $\theta_S(L)$ is in the class $\mathbf{r\text{-}BCL}(8)_\omega$, and, except for some special few cases, $\theta_S(L) \equiv_W L$.

The next step is to simulate a *real-time* 8-counter Büchi automaton, using only a *real-time* 1-counter Büchi automaton.

Consider the product of the eight first prime numbers:

$$K = 2 \times 3 \times 5 \times 7 \times 11 \times 13 \times 17 \times 19 = 9699690$$

Then an ω-word $x \in X^\omega$ can be coded by the ω-word

$$h(x) = A.0^K.x(1).B.0^{K^2}.A.0^{K^2}.x(2).B.0^{K^3}.A.0^{K^3}.x(3).B \ldots B.0^{K^n}.A.0^{K^n}.x(n).B \ldots$$

where A, B and 0 are new letters not in X. The mapping $h : X^\omega \to (X \cup \{A, B, 0\})^\omega$ is continuous. It is easy to see that the ω-language $h(X^\omega)^-$ is an open subset of $(X \cup \{A, B, 0\})^\omega$ and that it is in the class $\mathbf{r\text{-}BCL}(1)_\omega$.

If $L(\mathcal{A}) \subseteq X^\omega$ is accepted by a real time 8-counter Büchi automaton $\mathcal{A}$, then one can construct effectively from $\mathcal{A}$ a 1-counter Büchi automaton $\mathcal{B}$, reading words over the alphabet $X \cup \{A, B, 0\}$, such that $L(\mathcal{A}) = h^{-1}(L(\mathcal{B}))$, i.e.

$$\forall x \in X^\omega \quad h(x) \in L(\mathcal{B}) \longleftrightarrow x \in L(\mathcal{A})$$

In fact, the simulation, during the reading of $h(x)$ by the 1-counter Büchi automaton $\mathcal{B}$, of the behaviour of the real time 8-counter Büchi automaton $\mathcal{A}$ reading x, can be achieved, using the coding of the content $(c_1, c_2, \ldots, c_8)$ of eight counters by the product $2^{c_1} \times 3^{c_2} \times \ldots \times (17)^{c_7} \times (19)^{c_8}$, and the **special shape** of ω-words in $h(X^\omega)$ which allows the propagation of the value of the counters of $\mathcal{A}$. A crucial fact here is that $h(X^\omega)^-$ is in the class $\mathbf{r\text{-}BCL}(1)_\omega$. Thus the ω-language

$$h(L(\mathcal{A})) \cup h(X^\omega)^- = L(\mathcal{B}) \cup h(X^\omega)^-$$

is in the class $\mathbf{BCL}(1)_\omega$ and it has the same topological complexity as the ω-language $L(\mathcal{A})$, (except the special few cases where $d_W(L(\mathcal{A})) \leq \omega$).

One can see, from the construction of $\mathcal{B}$, that at most $(K - 1)$ consecutive λ-transitions can occur during the reading of an ω-word x by $\mathcal{B}$. It is then easy to see that the ω-language $\phi(h(L(\mathcal{A})) \cup h(X^\omega)^-)$ is an ω-language in the class $\mathbf{r\text{-}BCL}(1)_\omega$ which has the same topological complexity as the ω-language $L(\mathcal{A})$, where ϕ is the mapping from $(X \cup \{A, B, 0\})^\omega$ into $(X \cup \{A, B, F, 0\})^\omega$, with F a new letter, which is defined by:

$$\phi(x) = F^{K-1}.x(1).F^{K-1}.x(2).F^{K-1}.x(3) \ldots F^{K-1}.x(n).F^{K-1}.x(n+1).F^{K-1} \ldots$$

Altogether these constructions are used in [41] to prove Theorem 27. As the Wadge hierarchy is a refinement of the Borel hierarchy and, for any countable ordinal α, Σ_α^0-complete sets (respectively, Π_α^0-complete sets) form a single Wadge degree, this implies also the following result.

Theorem 28. *Let $\mathcal{C}$ be a class of ω-languages such that:*

$$\mathbf{r\text{-}BCL}(1)_\omega \subseteq \mathcal{C} \subseteq \Sigma_1^1.$$

(a) The Borel hierarchy of the class $\mathcal{C}$ is equal to the Borel hierarchy of the class Σ_1^1.
(b) $\gamma_2^1 = Sup \ \{\alpha \mid \exists L \in \mathcal{C} \ such \ that \ L \ is \ a \ Borel \ set \ of \ rank \ \alpha\}$.

(c) *For every non null ordinal* $\alpha < \omega_1^{CK}$, *there exists some* Σ_α^0-*complete and some* Π_α^0-*complete* ω-*languages in the class* $\mathcal{C}$.

Notice that similar methods have next be used to get another surprising result: the Wadge hierarchy, hence also the Borel hierarchy, of infinitary rational relations accepted by 2-tape Büchi automata is equal to the Wadge hierarchy of the class $\mathbf{r}$-$\mathbf{BCL}(1)_\omega$ or of the class Σ_1^1, [42, 43].

5 Topological Complexity of Deterministic Context-Free ω-Languages

We have seen in the previous section that all *non-deterministic* finite machines accept ω-languages of the same topological complexity, as soon as they can simulate a real time 1-counter automaton.

This result is still true in the *deterministic* case if we consider only the Borel hierarchy. Recall that regular ω-languages accepted by Büchi automata are Π_2^0-sets and ω-languages accepted by Muller automata are boolean combinations of Π_2^0-sets hence Δ_3^0-sets. Engelfriet and Hoogeboom proved that this result holds also for all ω-languages accepted by *deterministic* $\mathbf{X}$-automata, i.e. automata equipped with a storage type $\mathbf{X}$, including the cases of k-counter automata, pushdown automata, Petri nets, Turing machines. In particular, ω-languages accepted by deterministic Büchi Turing machines are Π_2^0-sets and ω-languages accepted by deterministic Muller Turing machines are Δ_3^0-sets.

It turned out that this is no longer true if we consider the much finer Wadge hierarchy to measure the complexity of ω-languages. The Wadge hierarchy is suitable to distinguish the accepting power of deterministic finite machines reading infinite words. Recall that the Wadge hierarchy of regular ω-languages, now called the Wagner hierarchy, has been effectively determined by Wagner; it has length ω^ω [84, 69, 70].

Its extension to *deterministic* context-free ω-languages has been determined by Duparc, its length is $\omega^{(\omega^2)}$ [26, 24]. To determine the Wadge hierarchy of the class $DCFL_\omega$, Duparc first defined operations on DMPDA which correspond to ordinal operations of sum, multiplication by ω, and multiplication by ω_1, over Wadge degrees. In this way are constructed some DMPDA accepting ω-languages of every Wadge degree in the form :

$$d_W^0(A) = \omega_1^{n_j}.\delta_j + \omega_1^{n_{j-1}}.\delta_{j-1} + \ldots + \omega_1^{n_1}.\delta_1$$

where $j > 0$ is an integer, $n_j > n_{j-1} > \ldots > n_1$ are integers ≥ 0, and $\delta_j, \delta_{j-1}, \ldots, \delta_1$ are non null ordinals $< \omega^\omega$.

On the other hand it is known that the Wadge degree α of a boolean combination of Π_2^0-sets is smaller than the ordinal ω_1^ω thus it has a Cantor normal form :

$$\alpha = \omega_1^{n_j}.\delta_j + \omega_1^{n_{j-1}}.\delta_{j-1} + \ldots + \omega_1^{n_1}.\delta_1$$

where $j > 0$ is an integer, $n_j > n_{j-1} > \ldots > n_1$ are integers ≥ 0, and $\delta_j, \delta_{j-1}, \ldots, \delta_1$ are non null ordinals $< \omega_1$, i.e. non null countable ordinals. In a second step it is proved in [24], using infinite multi-player games, that if such an ordinal α is the Wadge degree of a deterministic context-free ω-language, then all the ordinals $\delta_j, \delta_{j-1}, \ldots, \delta_1$

appearing in its Cantor normal form are smaller than the ordinal $< \omega^\omega$. Thus the Wadge hierarchy of the class $DCFL_\omega$ is completely determined.

Theorem 29 (Duparc [24]). *The Wadge degrees of deterministic context-free ω-languages are exactly the ordinals in the form :*

$$\alpha = \omega_1^{n_j}.\delta_j + \omega_1^{n_{j-1}}.\delta_{j-1} + \ldots + \omega_1^{n_1}.\delta_1$$

where $j > 0$ is an integer, $n_j > n_{j-1} > \ldots > n_1$ are integers ≥ 0, and $\delta_j, \delta_{j-1}, \ldots, \delta_1$ are non null ordinals $< \omega^\omega$.

The length of the Wadge hierarchy of the class $DCFL_\omega$ is the ordinal $(\omega^\omega)^\omega = \omega^{(\omega^2)}$.

Notice that theWadge hierarchy of $DCFL_\omega$ is not determined in an effective way in [24]. The question of the decidability of problems like: "given two DMPDA $\mathcal{A}$ and $\mathcal{B}$, does $L(\mathcal{A}) \leq_W L(\mathcal{B})$ hold ?" or "given a DMPDA $\mathcal{A}$ can we compute $d_W^0(L(\mathcal{A}))$?" naturally arises.

Cohen and Gold proved that one can decide whether an effectively given ω-language in $DCFL_\omega$ is an open or a closed set [19]. Linna characterized the ω-languages accepted by DBPDA as the $\mathbf{\Pi}_2^0$-sets in $DCFL_\omega$ and proved in [58] that one can decide whether an effectively given ω-language accepted by a DMPDA is a $\mathbf{\Pi}_2^0$-set or a $\mathbf{\Sigma}_2^0$-set.

Using a recent result of Walukiewicz on infinite games played on pushdown graphs, [85], these decidability results were extended in [32] where it was proved that one can decide whether a *deterministic* context-free ω-language accepted by a given DMPDA is in a given Borel class $\mathbf{\Sigma}_1^0$, $\mathbf{\Pi}_1^0$, $\mathbf{\Sigma}_2^0$, or $\mathbf{\Pi}_2^0$ or even in the wadge class $[L]$ given by any regular ω-language L.

An effective extension of the Wagner hierarchy to ω-languages accepted by Muller *deterministic* real time blind (i. e. without zero-test) 1-counter automata has been determined in [30]. Recall that blind 1-counter automata form a subclass of 1-counter automata hence also of pushdown automata. A blind 1-counter Muller automaton is just a Muller pushdown automaton $M = (K, X, \Gamma, \delta, q_0, Z_0, \mathcal{F})$ such that $\Gamma = \{Z_0, I\}$ where Z_0 is the bottom symbol and always remains at the bottom of the store. Moreover every transition which is enabled at zero level is also enabled at non zero level, i.e. if $\delta(q, a, Z_0) = (p, I^n Z_0)$, for some $p, q \in K$, $a \in X$ and $n \geq 0$, then $\delta(q, a, I) = (p, I^{n+1})$. But the converse may not be true, i.e. some transition may be enabled at non zero level but not at zero level. Notice that blind 1-counter automata are sometimes called partially blind 1-counter automata as in [47].

The Wadge hierarchy of blind counter ω-languages, accepted by deterministic Muller real time blind 1-counter automata (MBCA), is studied in [30] in a similar way as Wagner studied the Wadge hierarchy of regular ω-languages in [84]. Chains and superchains for MBCA are defined as Wagner did for Muller automata. The essential difference between the two hierarchies relies on the existence of superchains of transfinite length $\alpha < \omega^2$ for MBCA when in the case of Muller automata the superchains have only finite lengths. The hierarchy of ω-languages accepted by MBCA is effective and leads to effective winning strategies in Wadge games between two players in charge of ω-languages accepted by MBCA. Concerning the length of the Wadge hierarchy of MBCA the following result is proved :

Theorem 30 (Finkel [30])

(a) *The length of the Wadge hierarchy of blind counter ω-languages in Δ_2^0 is ω^2.*

(b) *The length of the Wadge hierarchy of blind counter ω-languages is the ordinal ω^ω*
(hence it is equal to the length of the Wagner hierarchy).

Notice that the length of the Wadge hierarchy of blind counter ω-languages is equal to
the length of the Wagner hierarchy although it is actually a strict extension of the Wagner hierarchy, as shown already in item (a) of the above theorem. The Wadge degrees
of blind counter ω-languages are the ordinals in the form :

$$\alpha = \omega_1^{n_j}.\delta_j + \omega_1^{n_{j-1}}.\delta_{j-1} + \ldots + \omega_1^{n_1}.\delta_1$$

where $j > 0$ is an integer, $n_j > n_{j-1} > \ldots > n_1$ are integers ≥ 0, and $\delta_j, \delta_{j-1}, \ldots, \delta_1$
are non null ordinals $< \omega^2$. Recall that in the case of Muller automata, the ordinals
$\delta_j, \delta_{j-1}, \ldots, \delta_1$ are non-negative integers, i.e. non null ordinals $< \omega$.

Notice that Selivanov has recently determined the Wadge hierarchy of ω-languages
accepted by *deterministic* Turing machines; its length is $(\omega_1^{CK})^\omega$ [72, 71]. The ω-
languages accepted by deterministic Muller Turing machines or equivalently which are
boolean combinations of arithmetical Π_2^0-sets have Wadge degrees in the form :

$$\alpha = \omega_1^{n_j}.\delta_j + \omega_1^{n_{j-1}}.\delta_{j-1} + \ldots + \omega_1^{n_1}.\delta_1$$

where $j > 0$ is an integer, $n_j > n_{j-1} > \ldots > n_1$ are integers ≥ 0, and $\delta_j, \delta_{j-1}, \ldots, \delta_1$
are non null ordinals $< \omega_1^{CK}$.

6   Topology and Ambiguity in Context-Free ω-Languages

The notions of ambiguity and of degrees of ambiguity are well known and important in
the study of context-free languages. These notions have been extended to context-free
ω-languages accepted by Büchi or Muller pushdown automata in [34]. Notice that it
is proved in [34] that these notions are independent of the Büchi or Muller acceptance
condition. So in the sequel we shall only consider the Büchi acceptance condition.

We now firstly introduce a slight modification in the definition of a run of a Büchi
pushdown automaton, which will be used in this section.

Definition 31. *Let $\mathcal{A} = (K, X, \Gamma, \delta, q_0, Z_0, F)$ be a Büchi pushdown automaton.*
Let $\sigma = a_1 a_2 \ldots a_n \ldots$ be an ω-word over X. A run of $\mathcal{A}$ on σ is an infinite sequence
$r = (q_i, \gamma_i, \varepsilon_i)_{i \geq 1}$ where $(q_i, \gamma_i)_{i \geq 1}$ is an infinite sequence of configurations of $\mathcal{A}$ and,
for all $i \geq 1$, $\varepsilon_i \in \{0, 1\}$ and:

1. $(q_1, \gamma_1) = (q_0, Z_0)$
2. for each $i \geq 1$, there exists $b_i \in X \cup \{\lambda\}$ satisfying
   $b_i : (q_i, \gamma_i) \mapsto_{\mathcal{A}} (q_{i+1}, \gamma_{i+1})$
   and ($\varepsilon_i = 0$ iff $b_i = \lambda$)
   and such that $a_1 a_2 \ldots a_n \ldots = b_1 b_2 \ldots b_n \ldots$

As before the ω-*language accepted by* $\mathcal{A}$ *is*

$$L(\mathcal{A}) = \{\sigma \in X^\omega \mid \text{ there exists a run } r \text{ of } \mathcal{A} \text{ on } \sigma \text{ such that } In(r) \cap F \neq \emptyset\}$$

Notice that the numbers $\varepsilon_i \in \{0, 1\}$ are introduced in the above definition in order to distinguish runs of a BPDA which go through the same infinite sequence of configurations but for which λ-transitions do not occur at the same steps of the computations.

As usual the cardinal of ω is denoted $\aleph_0$ and the cardinal of the continuum is denoted $2^{\aleph_0}$. The latter is also the cardinal of the set of real numbers or of the set X^ω for every finite alphabet X having at least two letters.

We are now ready to define degrees of ambiguity for BPDA and for context-free ω-languages.

Definition 32. *Let* $\mathcal{A}$ *be a BPDA reading infinite words over the alphabet* X. *For* $x \in X^\omega$ *let* $\alpha_{\mathcal{A}}(x)$ *be the cardinal of the set of accepting runs of* $\mathcal{A}$ *on* x.

Lemma 33 ([34]). *Let* $\mathcal{A}$ *be a BPDA reading infinite words over the alphabet* X. *Then for all* $x \in X^\omega$ *it holds that* $\alpha_{\mathcal{A}}(x) \in \mathbb{N} \cup \{\aleph_0, 2^{\aleph_0}\}$.

Definition 34. *Let* $\mathcal{A}$ *be a BPDA reading infinite words over the alphabet* X.

(a) *If* $\sup\{\alpha_{\mathcal{A}}(x) \mid x \in X^\omega\} \in \mathbb{N} \cup \{2^{\aleph_0}\}$, *then* $\alpha_{\mathcal{A}} = \sup\{\alpha_{\mathcal{A}}(x) \mid x \in X^\omega\}$.
(b) *If* $\sup\{\alpha_{\mathcal{A}}(x) \mid x \in X^\omega\} = \aleph_0$ *and there is no word* $x \in X^\omega$ *such that* $\alpha_{\mathcal{A}}(x) = \aleph_0$, *then* $\alpha_{\mathcal{A}} = \aleph_0^-$.
  ($\aleph_0^-$ *does not represent a cardinal but is a new symbol that is introduced here to conveniently speak of this situation).*
(c) *If* $\sup\{\alpha_{\mathcal{A}}(x) \mid x \in X^\omega\} = \aleph_0$ *and there exists (at least) one word* $x \in X^\omega$ *such that* $\alpha_{\mathcal{A}}(x) = \aleph_0$, *then* $\alpha_{\mathcal{A}} = \aleph_0$

Notice that for a BPDA $\mathcal{A}$, $\alpha_{\mathcal{A}} = 0$ iff $\mathcal{A}$ does not accept any ω-word.

We shall consider below that $\mathbb{N} \cup \{\aleph_0^-, \aleph_0, 2^{\aleph_0}\}$ is linearly ordered by the relation $<$, which is defined by : $\forall k \in \mathbb{N}, k < k + 1 < \aleph_0^- < \aleph_0 < 2^{\aleph_0}$.

Definition 35. *For* $k \in \mathbb{N} \cup \{\aleph_0^-, \aleph_0, 2^{\aleph_0}\}$ *let*
$CFL_\omega(\alpha \leq k) = \{L(\mathcal{A}) \mid \mathcal{A} \text{ is a BPDA with } \alpha_{\mathcal{A}} \leq k\}$
$CFL_\omega(\alpha < k) = \{L(\mathcal{A}) \mid \mathcal{A} \text{ is a BPDA with } \alpha_{\mathcal{A}} < k\}$
$NA{-}CFL_\omega = CFL_\omega(\alpha \leq 1)$ *is the class of non ambiguous context-free* ω-*languages.*
For every integer k *such that* $k \geq 2$, *or* $k \in \{\aleph_0^-, \aleph_0, 2^{\aleph_0}\}$,
$A(k) - CFL_\omega = CFL_\omega(\alpha \leq k) - CFL_\omega(\alpha < k)$
If $L \in A(k) - CFL_\omega$ *with* $k \in \mathbb{N}, k \geq 2$, *or* $k \in \{\aleph_0^-, \aleph_0, 2^{\aleph_0}\}$, *then* L *is said to be inherently ambiguous of degree* k.

Notice that one can define in a similar way the degree of ambiguity of a finitary context-free language. If M is a pushdown automaton accepting finite words by final states (or by final states and topmost stack letter) then $\alpha_M \in \mathbb{N}$ or $\alpha_M = \aleph_0^-$ or $\alpha_M = \aleph_0$. However every context-free language is accepted by a pushdown automaton M with $\alpha_M \leq \aleph_0^-$, [3]. We denote the class of non ambiguous context-free languages by $NA{-}CFL$ and the class of inherently ambiguous context-free languages by $A{-}CFL$. Then one can state the following result.

Theorem 36 ([34])

$$NA-CFL_\omega \subsetneq \omega-KC(NA-CFL)$$

$$A-CFL_\omega \nsubseteq \omega-KC(A-CFL)$$

We now come to the study of links between topology and ambiguity in context-free ω-languages [34, 45].

Using a Theorem of Lusin and Novikov, and another theorem of descriptive set theory, see [50, page 123], Simonnet proved the following strong result which shows that non-Borel context-free ω-languages have a maximum degree of ambiguity.

Theorem 37 (Simonnet [45]). *Let $L(\mathcal{A})$ be a context-free ω-language accepted by a BPDA $\mathcal{A}$ such that $L(\mathcal{A})$ is an analytic but non Borel set. The set of ω-words, which have $2^{\aleph_0}$ accepting runs by $\mathcal{A}$, has cardinality $2^{\aleph_0}$.*

On the other hand, it turned out that, informally speaking, the operation $A \to A^\sim$ conserves globally the degrees of ambiguity of infinitary context-free languages (which are unions of a finitary context-free language and of a context-free ω-language). Then, starting from known examples of finitary context-free languages of a given degree of ambiguity, are constructed in [34] some context-free ω-languages of any finite Borel rank and which are non-ambiguous or of any finite degree of ambiguity or of degree $\aleph_0^-$.

Theorem 38

1. *For each non negative integer $n \geq 1$, there exist Σ_n^0-complete non ambiguous context-free ω-languages A_n and Π_n^0-complete non ambiguous context-free ω-languages B_n.*
2. *Let k be an integer ≥ 2 or $k = \aleph_0^-$. Then for each integer $n \geq 1$, there exist Σ_n^0-complete context-free ω-languages $E_n(k)$ and Π_n^0-complete context-free ω-languages $F_n(k)$ which are in $A(k) - CFL_\omega$, i.e. which are inherently ambiguous of degree k.*

Notice that the ω-languages A_n and B_n are simply those which were constructed in the proof of Theorem 24. On the other hand it is easy to see that the BPDA accepting the context-free ω-language which is Borel of infinite rank, constructed in [36] using an iteration of the operation $A \to A^\sim$, has an infinite degree of ambiguity. And 1-counter Büchi automata accepting context-free ω-languages of any Borel rank of an effective analytic set, constructed via simulation of multicounter automata, may also have a great degree of ambiguity. So this left open some questions we shall detail in the last section.

We indicate now a new result which follows easily from the proof of Theorem 27 sketched in Section 4 above, see [41]. Consider an ω-language L accepted by a **deterministic** Muller Turing machine or equivalently by a **deterministic** 2-counter Muller automaton. We get first an ω-language $\theta_S(L) \subseteq X^\omega$ which has the same topological complexity (except for finite Wadge degrees), and which is accepted by a **deterministic** real time 8-counter Muller automaton $\mathcal{A}$.

Then one can construct from $\mathcal{A}$ a 1-counter Muller automaton $\mathcal{B}$, reading words over the alphabet $X \cup \{A, B, 0\}$, such that $h(L(\mathcal{A})) \cup h(X^\omega)^- = L(\mathcal{B}) \cup h(X^\omega)^-$, where

$h : X^\omega \rightarrow (X \cup \{A, B, 0\})^\omega$ is the mapping defined in Section 4. Notice that the 1-counter Muller automaton $\mathcal{B}$ which is constructed is now also **deterministic**.

On the other hand it is easy to see, from the decomposition given in [41, Proof of Lemma 5.3], that the ω-language $h(X^\omega)^-$ is accepted by a 1-counter Büchi automaton which has degree of ambiguity 2 and the ω-language $L(\mathcal{B})$ is in $NA - CFL_\omega = CFL_\omega(\alpha \leq 1)$ because it is accepted by a **deterministic** 1-counter Muller automaton. Then we can easily infer, using [34, Theorem 5.16 (c)] that the ω-language $h(L(\mathcal{A})) \cup h(X^\omega)^- = L(\mathcal{B}) \cup h(X^\omega)^-$ is in $CFL_\omega(\alpha \leq 3)$. And this ω-language has the same complexity as $L(\mathcal{A})$ Thus we can state the following result.

Theorem 39. *For each ω-language L accepted by a **deterministic** Muller Turing machine there is an ω-language $L' \in CFL_\omega(\alpha \leq 3)$, accepted by a 1-counter Muller automaton $\mathcal{D}$ with $\alpha_\mathcal{D} \leq 3$, such that $L \equiv_W L'$.*

7 ω-Powers of Context-Free Languages

The ω-powers of finitary languages are ω-languages in the form V^ω, where V is a finitary language over a finite alphabet X. They appear very naturally in the characterization of the class REG_ω of regular ω-languages (respectively, of the class CFL_ω of context-free ω-languages) as the ω-Kleene closure of the family REG of regular finitary languages (respectively, of the family CF of context-free finitary languages) .

The question of the topological complexity of ω-powers naturally arises and was raised by Niwinski [66], Simonnet [75], and Staiger [79].

An ω-power of a finitary language is always an analytic set because it is either the continuous image of a compact set $\{0, 1, \ldots, n\}^\omega$ for $n \geq 0$ or of the Baire space ω^ω.

The first example of finitary language L such that L^ω is analytic but not Borel, and even Σ_1^1-complete, was obtained in [35]. Amazingly the language L was very simple and even accepted by a 1-counter automaton. It was obtained via a coding of infinite labelled binary trees.

We now give a simple construction of this language L using the notion of substitution which we now recall. A *substitution* is defined by a mapping $f : X \rightarrow \mathcal{P}(\Gamma^\star)$, where $X = \{a_1, \ldots, a_n\}$ and Γ are two finite alphabets, $f : a_i \rightarrow L_i$ where for all integers $i \in [1; n]$, $f(a_i) = L_i$ is a finitary language over the alphabet Γ.

Now this mapping is extended in the usual manner to finite words: $f(a_{i_1} \ldots a_{i_n}) = L_{i_1} \ldots L_{i_n}$, and to finitary languages $L \subseteq X^\star$: $f(L) = \cup_{x \in L} f(x)$. If for each integer $i \in [1; n]$ the language L_i does not contain the empty word, then the mapping f may be extended to ω-words: $f(x(1) \ldots x(n) \ldots) = \{u_1 \ldots u_n \ldots \mid \forall i \geq 1 \quad u_i \in f(x(i))\}$ and to ω-languages $L \subseteq X^\omega$ by setting $f(L) = \cup_{x \in L} f(x)$.

Let now $X = \{0, 1\}$ and d be a new letter not in X and

$$D = \{u.d.v \mid u, v \in X^\star \ and \ (|v| = 2|u|) \ or \ (|v| = 2|u| + 1) \}$$

$D \subseteq (X \cup \{d\})^\star$ is a context-free language accepted by a 1-counter automaton. Let $g : X \rightarrow \mathcal{P}((X \cup \{d\})^\star)$ be the substitution defined by $g(a) = a.D$. As $W = 0^\star 1$ is regular, $L = g(W)$ is a context-free language and it is accepted by a 1-counter automaton. Moreover one can prove that $(g(W))^\omega$ is Σ_1^1-complete, hence a non Borel set. This is done by reducing to this ω-language a well-known example of Σ_1^1-complete set : the set of infinite binary trees labelled in the alphabet $\{0,1\}$ which have an infinite branch in the Π_2^0-complete set $(0^\star.1)^\omega$, see [35] for more details.

Remark 40. *The ω-language $(g(W))^\omega$ is context-free. By Theorem 37 every BPDA accepting $(g(W))^\omega$ has the maximum ambiguity and $(g(W))^\omega \in A(2^{\aleph_0}) - CFL_\omega$. On the other hand we can prove that $g(W)$ is a non ambiguous context-free language. This is used in [45] to prove that neither unambiguity nor ambiguity of context-free languages are preserved under the operation $V \to V^\omega$.*

Concerning Borel ω-powers, it has been proved in [32] that for each integer $n \geq 1$, there exist some ω-powers of context-free languages which are Π_n^0-complete Borel sets. These results were obtained by the use of a new operation $V \to V^\approx$ over ω-languages, which is a slight modification of the operation $V \to V^\sim$. The new operation $V \to V^\approx$ preserves ω-powers and context-freeness. More precisely if $V = W^\omega$ for some context-free language W, then $V^\approx = T^\omega$ for some context-free language T which is obtained from W by application of a given context-free substitution. And it follows easily from [23] that if $V \subseteq X^\omega$ is a Π_n^0-complete set, for some integer $n \geq 2$, then $V^\approx$ is a Π_{n+1}^0-complete set. Then, starting from the Π_2^0-complete set $(0^\star.1)^\omega$, we get some Π_n^0-complete ω-powers of context-free languages for each integer $n \geq 3$.

An iteration of the operation $V \to V^\approx$ was used in [37] to prove that there exists a finitary language V such that V^ω is a Borel set of infinite rank. The language V was a simple recursive language but it was not context-free. Later, with a modification of the construction, using a coding of an infinity of erasers previously defined in [36], Finkel and Duparc got a context-free language V such that V^ω is a Borel set above the class Δ_ω^0, [25].

The question of the Borel hierarchy of ω-powers of finitary languages has been solved very recently by Finkel and Lecomte in [44], where a very surprising result is proved, showing that actually ω-powers exhibit a great topological complexity. For every non-null countable ordinal α there exist some Σ_α^0-complete ω-powers and also some Π_α^0-complete ω-powers. But the ω-powers constructed in [44] are not ω-powers of context-free languages, except for the case of a Σ_2^0-complete set. Notice also that an example of a regular language L such that L^ω is Σ_1^0-complete was given by Simonnet in [75], see also [54] .

8   Perspectives and Open Questions

We give below a list of some open questions which arise naturally. The problems listed here seem important for a better comprehension of context-free ω-languages but the list is not exhaustive.

8.1   Effective Results

In the *non-deterministic* case, the Borel and Wadge hierarchies of context-free ω-langua ges are not effective, [32, 35, 33]. This is not surprising since most decision problems on context-free languages are undecidable. On the other hand we can expect some decidability results in the case of *deterministic* context-free ω-languages. We have already cited some of them : we can decide whether a deterministic context-free ω-language is in a given Borel class or even in the Wadge class $[L]$ of a given regular ω-language L. The most challenging question in this area would be to find an effecive procedure to determine the Wadge degree of an ω-language in the class $DCFL_\omega$.

Recall that the Wadge hierarchy of the class $DCFL_\omega$ is determined in a non-effective way in [24]. On the other hand the Wadge hierarchy of the class of blind counter ω-languages is determined in an effective way, using notions of chains and superchains, in [30]. There is a gap between the two hierarchies because (blind) 1-counter automata are much less expressive than pushdown automata. One could try to extend the methods of [30] to the study of *deterministic* pushdown automata.

Another question concerns the complexity of decidable problems. A first question would be the following one. Could we extend the results of Wilke and Yoo to the class of blind counter ω-languages, i.e. is the Wadge degree of a blind counter ω-language computable in polynomial time ? Otherwise what is the complexity of this problem ? Of course the question may be further asked for classes of ω-languages which are located between the classes of blind counter ω-languages and of deterministic context-free ω-languages.

Another interesting question would be to determine the Wadge hierarchy of ω-languages accepted by deterministic higher order pushdown automata (even firstly in a non effective way), [28, 11].

8.2 Topology and Ambiguity

Simonnet's Theorem 37 states that non-Borel context-free ω-languages have a maximum degree of ambiguity, i.e. are in the class $A(2^{\aleph_0}) - CFL_\omega$. On the other hand, there exist some non-ambiguous context-free ω-languages of every finite Borel rank. The question naturally arises whether there exist some non-ambiguous context-free ω-languages which are Wadge equivalent to any given **Borel** context-free ω-language (or equivalently to any **Borel** Σ_1^1-set, by Theorem 28). This may be connected to a result of Arnold who proved in [2] that every Borel subset of X^ω, for a finite alphabet X, is accepted by a *non-ambiguous* finitely branching transition system with Büchi acceptance condition. By Theorem 38, if k is an integer ≥ 2 or $k = \aleph_0^-$, then for each integer $n \geq 1$, there exist Σ_n^0-complete context-free ω-languages $E_n(k)$ and Π_n^0-complete context-free ω-languages $F_n(k)$ which are in $A(k) - CFL_\omega$, i.e. which are inherently ambiguous of degree k. More generally the question arises : determine the Borel ranks and the Wadge degrees of context-free ω-languages in classes $CFL_\omega(\alpha \leq k)$ or $A(k) - CFL_\omega$ where $k \in \mathbb{N} \cup \{\aleph_0^-, \aleph_0, 2^{\aleph_0}\}$ ($k \geq 2$ in the case of $A(k) - CFL_\omega$). A ·first result in this direction is Theorem 39 stated in Section 6.

8.3 ω-Powers

The results of [32, 35, 37, 44] show that ω-powers of finitary languages have actually a great topological complexity. Concerning ω-powers of context-free languages we do not know yet what are all their infinite Borel ranks. However the results of [41] suggest that ω-powers of context-free languages or even of languages accepted by 1-counter automata exhibit also a great topological complexity.

Indeed Theorem 28 states that there are ω-languages accepted by Büchi 1-counter automata of every Borel rank (and even of every Wadge degree) of an effective analytic set. On the other hand each ω-language accepted by a Büchi 1-counter automaton can be written as a finite union $L = \bigcup_{1 \leq i \leq n} U_i.V_i^\omega$, where for each integer i, U_i and V_i are finitary languages accepted by 1-counter automata. Then we can conjecture that there exist some ω-powers of languages accepted by 1-counter automata which have Borel ranks up to the ordinal γ_2^1, although these languages are located at the very low level in the complexity hierarchy of finitary languages.

Recall that a finitary language L is a code (respectively, an ω-code) if every word of L^+ (respectively, every ω-word of L^ω) has a unique decomposition in words of L, [6]. It is proved in [45] that if V is a context-free language such that V^ω is a non Borel set then there are $2^{\aleph_0}$ ω-words of V^ω which have $2^{\aleph_0}$ decompositions in words of V; in particular, V is really not an ω-code although it is proved in [45] that V may be a code (see the example V=g(W) given in Section 7). The following question about **Borel** ω-powers now arises : are there some context-free codes (respectively, ω-codes) V such that V^ω is Σ_α^0-complete or Π_α^0-complete for a given countable ordinal $\alpha < \gamma_2^1$?

References

1. Andretta, A., Camerlo, R.: The use of complexity hierarchies in descriptive set theory and automata theory. Task Quarterly 9(3), 337–356 (2005)
2. Arnold, A.: Topological characterizations of infinite behaviours of transition systems. In: Díaz, J. (ed.) ICALP 1983. LNCS, vol. 154, pp. 28–38. Springer, Heidelberg (1983)
3. Autebert, J.-M., Berstel, J., Boasson, L.: Context free languages and pushdown automata. In: Handbook of Formal Languages, vol. 1. Springer (1996)
4. Beauquier, D.: Some results about finite and infinite behaviours of a pushdown automaton. In: Paredaens, J. (ed.) ICALP 1984. LNCS, vol. 172, pp. 187–195. Springer, Heidelberg (1984)
5. Berstel, J.: Transductions and context free languages. Teubner Studienbücher Informatik (1979)
6. Berstel, J., Perrin, D.: Theory of codes. Academic Press (1985)
7. Boasson, L.: Context-free sets of infinite words. In: Weihrauch, K. (ed.) GI-TCS 1979. LNCS, vol. 67, pp. 1–9. Springer, Heidelberg (1979)
8. Boasson, L., Nivat, M.: Adherences of languages. Journal of Computer and System Science 20(3), 285–309 (1980)
9. Cachat, T.: Symbolic strategy synthesis for games on pushdown graphs. In: Widmayer, P., Triguero, F., Morales, R., Hennessy, M., Eidenbenz, S., Conejo, R. (eds.) ICALP 2002. LNCS, vol. 2380, pp. 704–715. Springer, Heidelberg (2002)
10. Cachat, T., Duparc, J., Thomas, W.: Solving pushdown games with a Σ_3 winning condition. In: Bradfield, J.C. (ed.) CSL 2002 and EACSL 2002. LNCS, vol. 2471, pp. 322–336. Springer, Heidelberg (2002)
11. Cachat, T., Walukiewicz, I.: The complexity of games on higher order pushdown automata (May 2007), http://fr.arxiv.org/abs/0705.0262
12. Cagnard, B., Simonnet, P.: Baire and automata. Discrete Mathematics and Theoretical Computer Science 9(2), 255–296 (2007)

13. Carton, O., Perrin, D.: Chains and superchains for ω-rational sets, automata and semigroups. International Journal of Algebra and Computation 7(7), 673–695 (1997)
14. Carton, O., Perrin, D.: The Wagner hierarchy of ω-rational sets. International Journal of Algebra and Computation 9(5), 597–620 (1999)
15. Chomshy, N.: Three models for the description of language. IRE Transactions on Information Theory 2(3), 113–124 (1956)
16. Choueka, Y.: Theories of automata on omega-tapes: A simplified approach. Journal of Computer and System Science 8(2), 117–141 (1974)
17. Choueka, Y.: Finite automata, definable sets, and regular expressions over ω^n-tapes. Journal of Computer and System Science 17(1), 81–97 (1978)
18. Choueka, Y., Peleg, D.: A note of omega-regular languages. Bulletin of the EATCS 21, 21–23 (1983)
19. Cohen, R.S., Gold, A.Y.: Theory of ω-languages, parts one and two. Journal of Computer and System Science 15, 169–208 (1977)
20. Cohen, R.S., Gold, A.Y.: ω-computations on deterministic pushdown machines. Journal of Computer and System Science 16, 275–300 (1978)
21. Cohen, R.S., Gold, A.Y.: ω-computations on Turing machines. Theoretical Computer Science 6, 1–23 (1978)
22. Duparc, J.: La forme Normale des Boréliens de rang finis. PhD thesis, Université Paris VII (1995)
23. Duparc, J.: Wadge hierarchy and Veblen hierarchy: Part 1: Borel sets of finite rank. Journal of Symbolic Logic 66(1), 56–86 (2001)
24. Duparc, J.: A hierarchy of deterministic context free ω-languages. Theoretical Computer Science 290(3), 1253–1300 (2003)
25. Duparc, J., Finkel, O.: An ω-power of a context free language which is Borel above Δ_ω^0. In: Proceedings of the International Conference Foundations of the Formal Sciences V: Infinite Games, Bonn, Germany, November 26-29. Studies in Logic, vol. 11, pp. 109–122. College Publications at King's College (2007)
26. Duparc, J., Finkel, O., Ressayre, J.-P.: Computer science and the fine structure of Borel sets. Theoretical Computer Science 257(1-2), 85–105 (2001)
27. Duparc, J., Riss, M.: The missing link for ω-rational sets, automata, and semigroups. To Appear in International Journal of Algebra and Computation (2005)
28. Engelfriet, J.: Iterated pushdown automata and complexity classes. In: Proceedings of the Fifteenth Annual ACM Symposium on Theory of Computing, Boston, Massachusetts, USA, April 25-27, pp. 365–373. ACM Press (1983)
29. Engelfriet, J., Hoogeboom, H.J.: X-automata on ω-words. Theoretical Computer Science 110(1), 1–51 (1993)
30. Finkel, O.: An effective extension of the wagner hierarchy to blind counter automata. In: Fribourg, L. (ed.) CSL 2001 and EACSL 2001. LNCS, vol. 2142, pp. 369–383. Springer, Heidelberg (2001)
31. Finkel, O.: On the Wadge hierarchy of omega context free languages. In: Proceedings of the International Workshop on Logic and Complexity in Computer Science, held in Honor of Anatol Slissenko for his 60th Birthday, Créteil, France, pp. 69–79 (2001)
32. Finkel, O.: Topological properties of omega context free languages. Theoretical Computer Science 262(1-2), 669–697 (2001)
33. Finkel, O.: Wadge hierarchy of omega context free languages. Theoretical Computer Science 269(1-2), 283–315 (2001)
34. Finkel, O.: Ambiguity in omega context free languages. Theoretical Computer Science 301(1-3), 217–270 (2003)
35. Finkel, O.: Borel hierarchy and omega context free languages. Theoretical Computer Science 290(3), 1385–1405 (2003)

36. Finkel, O.: On omega context free languages which are Borel sets of infinite rank. Theoretical Computer Science 299(1-3), 327–346 (2003)
37. Finkel, O.: An omega-power of a finitary language which is a Borel set of infinite rank. Fundamenta Informaticae 62(3-4), 333–342 (2004)
38. Finkel, O.: Borel ranks and Wadge degrees of context free ω-languages. In: Cooper, S.B., Löwe, B., Torenvliet, L. (eds.) CiE 2005. LNCS, vol. 3526, pp. 129–138. Springer, Heidelberg (2005)
39. Finkel, O.: On the length of the Wadge hierarchy of ω-context free languages. Journal of Automata, Languages and Combinatorics 10(4), 439–464 (2005)
40. Finkel, O.: On winning conditions of high Borel complexity in pushdown games. Fundamenta Informaticae 66(3), 277–298 (2005)
41. Finkel, O.: Borel ranks and Wadge degrees of omega context free languages. Mathematical Structures in Computer Science 16(5), 813–840 (2006)
42. Finkel, O.: On the accepting power of 2-tape büchi automata. In: Durand, B., Thomas, W. (eds.) STACS 2006. LNCS, vol. 3884, pp. 301–312. Springer, Heidelberg (2006)
43. Finkel, O.: Wadge degrees of infinitary rational relations. Special Issue on Intensional Programming and Semantics in honour of Bill Wadge on the occasion of his 60th cycle, Mathematics in Computer Science 2(1), 85–102 (2008)
44. Finkel, O., Lecomte, D.: There exist some ω-powers of any borel rank. In: Duparc, J., Henzinger, T.A. (eds.) CSL 2007. LNCS, vol. 4646, pp. 115–129. Springer, Heidelberg (2007)
45. Finkel, O., Simonnet, P.: Topology and ambiguity in omega context free languages. Bulletin of the Belgian Mathematical Society 10(5), 707–722 (2003)
46. Grädel, E., Thomas, W., Wilke, T. (eds.): Automata, Logics, and Infinite Games. LNCS, vol. 2500. Springer, Heidelberg (2002)
47. Greibach, S.A.: Remarks on blind and partially blind one way multicounter machines. Theoretical Computer Science 7, 311–324 (1978)
48. Hopcroft, J.E., Motwani, R., Ullman, J.D.: Introduction to automata theory, languages, and computation. Addison-Wesley Series in Computer Science. Addison-Wesley Publishing Co., Reading (2001)
49. Hopcroft, J.E., Ullman, J.D.: Introduction to automata theory, languages, and computation. Addison-Wesley Series in Computer Science. Addison-Wesley Publishing Co., Reading (1979)
50. Kechris, A.S.: Classical descriptive set theory. Springer, New York (1995)
51. Kechris, A.S., Marker, D., Sami, R.L.: Π_1^1 Borel sets. Journal of Symbolic Logic 54(3), 915–920 (1989)
52. Landweber, L.H.: Decision problems for ω-automata. Mathematical Systems Theory 3(4), 376–384 (1969)
53. Lecomte, D.: Sur les ensembles de phrases infinies constructibles a partir d'un dictionnaire sur un alphabet fini. In: Séminaire d'Initiation a l'Analyse, Université Paris 6, vol. 1 (2001-2002)
54. Lecomte, D.: Omega-powers and descriptive set theory. Journal of Symbolic Logic 70(4), 1210–1232 (2005)
55. Lescow, H., Thomas, W.: Logical specifications of infinite computations. In: de Bakker, J.W., de Roever, W.-P., Rozenberg, G. (eds.) REX 1993. LNCS, vol. 803, pp. 583–621. Springer, Heidelberg (1994)
56. Linna, M.: On ω-words and ω-computations. Ann. Univ. Turku. Ser A I 168, 53 (1975)
57. Linna, M.: On omega-sets associated with context-free languages. Information and Control 31(3), 272–293 (1976)
58. Linna, M.: A decidability result for deterministic ω-context-free languages. Theoretical Computer Science 4, 83–98 (1977)

59. Mihoubi, D.: Characterization and closure properties of linear omega-languages. Theoretical Computer Science 191(1-2), 79–95 (1998)

60. Moschovakis, Y.N.: Descriptive set theory. North-Holland Publishing Co., Amsterdam (1980)

61. Muller, D.E.: Infinite sequences and finite machines. In: Proceedings of the Fourth Annual Symposium on Switching Circuit Theory and Logical Design, Chicago, Illinois, USA, October 28-30, pp. 3–16. IEEE (1963)

62. Mac Naughton, R.: Testing and generating infinite sequences by a finite automaton. Information and Control 9, 521–530 (1966)

63. Nivat, M.: Mots infinis engendrés par une grammaire algébrique. RAIRO Informatique Théorique et Applications 11, 311–327 (1977)

64. Nivat, M.: Sur les ensembles de mots infinis engendrés par une grammaire algébrique. RAIRO Informatique Théorique et Applications 12(3), 259–278 (1978)

65. Niwinski, D.: Fixed-point characterization of context-free ∞-languages. Information and Control 61(3), 247–276 (1984)

66. Niwinski, D.: A problem on ω-powers. In: 1990 Workshop on Logics and Recognizable Sets, University of Kiel (1990)

67. Perrin, D., Pin, J.-E.: Infinite words, automata, semigroups, logic and games. Pure and Applied Mathematics, vol. 141. Elsevier (2004)

68. Rabin, M.O.: Decidability of second-order theories and automata on infinite trees. Transactions of the American Mathematical Society 141, 1–35 (1969)

69. Selivanov, V.L.: Fine hierarchy of regular ω-languages. In: Mosses, P.D., Nielsen, M. (eds.) CAAP 1995, FASE 1995, and TAPSOFT 1995. LNCS, vol. 915, pp. 277–287. Springer, Heidelberg (1995)

70. Selivanov, V.L.: Fine hierarchy of regular ω-languages. Theoretical Computer Science 191, 37–59 (1998)

71. Selivanov, V.L.: Wadge degrees of ω-languages of deterministic Turing machines. RAIRO-Theoretical Informatics and Applications 37(1), 67–83 (2003)

72. Selivanov, V.L.: Wadge degrees of ω-languages of deterministic Turing machines. In: Alt, H., Habib, M. (eds.) STACS 2003. LNCS, vol. 2607, pp. 97–108. Springer, Heidelberg (2003)

73. Serre, O.: Contribution à l'étude des jeux sur des graphes de processus à pile. PhD thesis, Université Paris VII (2004)

74. Serre, O.: Games with winning conditions of high borel complexity. In: Díaz, J., Karhumäki, J., Lepistö, A., Sannella, D. (eds.) ICALP 2004. LNCS, vol. 3142, pp. 1150–1162. Springer, Heidelberg (2004)

75. Simonnet, P.: Automates et théorie descriptive. PhD thesis, Université Paris VII (1992)

76. Staiger, L.: Hierarchies of recursive ω-languages. Elektronische Informationsverarbeitung und Kybernetik 22(5-6), 219–241 (1986)

77. Staiger, L.: Research in the theory of ω-languages. Journal of Information Processing and Cybernetics 23(8-9), 415–439 (1987), Mathematical aspects of informatics (Mägdesprung, 1986)

78. Staiger, L.: ω-languages. In: Handbook of Formal Languages, vol. 3, pp. 339–387. Springer, Berlin (1997)

79. Staiger, L.: On ω-power languages. In: Păun, G., Salomaa, A. (eds.) New Trends in Formal Languages. LNCS, vol. 1218, pp. 377–393. Springer, Heidelberg (1997)

80. Staiger, L., Wagner, K.: Automatentheoretische und automatenfreie Charakterisierungen topologischer Klassen regulärer Folgenmengen. Elektron. Informationsverarbeit. Kybernetik 10, 379–392 (1974)

81. Thomas, W.: Automata on infinite objects. In: van Leeuwen, J. (ed.) Handbook of Theoretical Computer Science. Formal models and semantics, vol. B, pp. 135–191. Elsevier (1990)

82. Thomas, W.: Infinite games and verification (extended abstract of a tutorial). In: Brinksma, E., Larsen, K.G. (eds.) CAV 2002. LNCS, vol. 2404, pp. 58–64. Springer, Heidelberg (2002)
83. Wadge, W.: Reducibility and determinateness in the Baire space. PhD thesis, University of California, Berkeley (1983)
84. Wagner, K.: On ω-regular sets. Information and Control 43(2), 123–177 (1979)
85. Walukiewicz, I.: Pushdown processes: games and model checking. Information and Computation 157, 234–263 (2000)
86. Wilke, T., Yoo, H.: Computing the Wadge degree, the Lifschitz degree, and the Rabin index of a regular language of infinite words in polynomial time. In: Mosses, P.D., Nielsen, M. (eds.) CAAP 1995, FASE 1995, and TAPSOFT 1995. LNCS, vol. 915, pp. 288–302. Springer, Heidelberg (1995)

From Löwenheim to PSL and SVA*

Moshe Y. Vardi**

Rice University, Department of Computer Science, Rice University,
Houston, TX 77005-1892, U.S.A.
vardi@cs.rice.edu
http://www.cs.rice.edu/~vardi

Two major themes of my research have been mathematical logic and the automata theoretic approach. I learned both subjects from Ya'akov Choueka, who taught me automata theory as an undergraduate student and mathematical logic as a graduate student. Little did I know then that these courses would have such a profound impact on my future research.

Abstract. One of the surprising developments in the area of program verification is how ideas introduced by logicians in the early part of the 20th Century ended up yielding by the 21 Century industrial-standard property-specification languages. This development was enabled by the equally unlikely transformation of the mathematical machinery of automata on infinite words, introduced in the early 1960s for second-order logic, into effective algorithms for model-checking tools. This paper attempts to trace the tangled threads of this development.

1 Thread I: Classical Logic of Time

1.1 Monadic Logic

In 1902, Russell send a letter to Frege in which he pointed out that Frege's logical system was inconsistent. This inconsistency has become known as *Russell's Paradox*. Russell, together with Whitehead, published *Principia Mathematica* in an attempt to resolve the inconsistency, but the monumental effort did not convince mathematicians that mathematics is indeed free of contradictions. This has become know as the "Foundational Crisis." In response to that Hilbert launched what has become known as "Hilbert's Program." (See [1].)

One of the main points in Hilbert's program was the decidability of mathematic. In 1928, Hilbert and Ackermann published "Principles of Mathematical Logic", in which they posed the question of the *Decision Problem* for first-order logic. This problem was shown to be unsolvable by Church and Turing, independently, in 1936; see [2]. In response to that, logicians started the project of classifying the decidable fragments of first-order logic [2, 3]. The earliest decidability result for such a fragment is for the

---

* A earlier version of this paper, under the title "From Church and Prior to PSL", appeared in the *Proc. 2006 Workshop on 25 Years of Model Checking, Lecture Notes in Computer Science*, *Springer.*

** Supported in part by NSF grants CCR-9988322, CCR-0124077, CCR-0311326, and ANI-0216467, by BSF grant 9800096, and by a gift from the Intel Corporation.

N. Dershowitz and E. Nissan (Eds.): Choueka Festschrift, Part I, LNCS 8001, pp. 78–102, 2014.
© Springer-Verlag Berlin Heidelberg 2014

Monadic Class, which is the fragment of first-order predicate logic where all predicates, with the exception of the equality predicate, are required to be monadic. This fragment can express the classical sylogisms. For example the formula

$$((\forall x)(H(x) \rightarrow M(x)) \wedge (\forall x)(G(x) \rightarrow H(x))) \rightarrow (\forall x)(G(x) \rightarrow M(x))$$

expresses the inference of: "if all humans are mortal and all Greeks are human, then all Greeks are mortal."

In 1915 Löwenheim showed that the Monadic Class is decidable [4]. His proof technique was based on the *bounded-model property*, proving that a monadic sentence is satisfiable if it is satisfiable in a model of bounded size. This enables the reduction of satisfiability testing to searching for a model of bounded size. L"owenheim's tecchnique was extended by Skolem in 1919 to *Monadic Second Order Logic*, in which one can also quantify over monadic predicates, in addition to quantifying over domain elements [5]. Skolem also used the bounded-model property. To prove this property, he introduced the technique of *quantifier elimination*, which is a key technique in mathematical logic [2].

Recall, that the only binary predicate in Skolem's monadic second-order logic is the equality predicate. One may wonder what happens if we also allow inequality predicates. Such an extension is the subject of the next section.

1.2 Logic and Automata

Classical logic views logic as a declarative formalism, aimed at the specification of properties of mathematical objects. For example, the sentence

$$(\forall x, y, x)(mult(x, y, z) \leftrightarrow mult(y, x, z))$$

expressed the commutativity of multiplication. Starting in the 1930s, a different branch of logic focused on formalisms for describing computations, starting with the introduction of Turing machines in the 1930s, and continuing with the development of the theory of finite-state machines in the 1950s. A surprising, intimate, connection between these two paradigms of logic emerged in the late 1950s.

A *nondeterministic finite automaton on words* (NFW) $A = (\Sigma, S, S_0, \rho, F)$ consists of a finite input alphabet Σ, a finite state set S, an initial state set $S_0 \subseteq S$, a transition relation $\rho \subseteq S \times \Sigma \times S$, and an accepting state set $F \subseteq S$. An NFW runs over an finite input word $w = a_0, \ldots, a_{n-1} \in \Sigma^*$. A *run* of A on w is a finite sequence $r = s_0, \ldots, s_n$ of states in S such that $s_0 \in S_0$, and $(s_i, a_i, s_{i+1}) \in \rho$, for $0 \leq i < n$. The run r is *accepting* if $s_n \in F$. The word w is *accepted* by A if A has an accepting run on w. The *language* of A, denoted $L(A)$, is the set of words accepted by A. The class of languages accepted by NFWs forms the class of *regular* languages, which are defined in terms of regular expressions. This class is extremely robust and has numerous equivalent representations [6].

Example 1. We describe graphically below an NFW that accepts all words over the alphabet $\{0, 1\}$ that end with an occurrence of 1. The arrow on the left designates the initial state, and the circle on the right designates an accepting state.

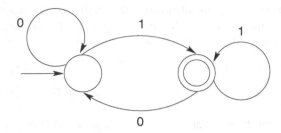

We now view a finite word $w = a_0, \ldots, a_{n-1}$ over an alphabet Σ as a relational structure M_w, with the domain of $0, \ldots, n-1$ ordered by the binary relation $<$, and the unary relations $\{P_a : a \in \Sigma\}$, with the interpretation that $P_a(i)$ holds precisely when $a_i = a$. We refer to such structures as *word structures*. We now use first-order logic (FO) to talk about such words. For example, the sentence

$$(\exists x)((\forall y)(\neg(x < y)) \wedge P_a(x))$$

says that the last letter of the word is a. We say that such a sentence is over the alphabet Σ.

Going beyond FO, we obtain *monadic second-order logic* (MSO), in which we can have monadic second-order quantifiers of the form $\exists Q$, ranging over subsets of the domain, and giving rise to new atomic formulas of the form $Q(x)$. Given a sentence φ in MSO, its set of models models(φ) is a set of words. Note that this logic extends Skolem's logic with the addition of the linear order $<$.

The fundamental connection between logic and automata is now given by the following theorem, discovered independently by Büchi, Elgot, and Trakhtenbrot.

Theorem 1. [7–12] *Given an MSO sentence φ over alphabet Σ, one can construct an NFW A_φ with alphabet Σ such that a word w in Σ^* is accepted by A_φ iff φ holds in the word structure M_w. Conversely, given an NFW A with alphabet Σ, one can construct an MSO sentence φ_A over Σ such that φ_A holds in a word structure M_w iff w is accepted by A.*

Thus, the class of languages defined by MSO sentences is precisely the class of regular languages.

To decide whether a sentence φ is *satisfiable*, that is, whether models(φ) $\neq \emptyset$, we need to check that $L(A_\varphi) \neq \emptyset$. This turns out to be an easy problem. Let $A = (\Sigma, S, S_0, \rho, F)$ be an NFW. Construct a directed graph $G_A = (S, E_A)$, with S as the set of nodes, and $E_A = \{(s, t) : (s, a, t) \in \rho \text{ for some } a \in \Sigma\}$. The following lemma is implicit in [7–10] and more explicit in [13].

Lemma 1. $L(A) \neq \emptyset$ *iff there are states $s_0 \in S_0$ and $t \in F$ such that in G_A there is a path from s_0 to t.*

We thus obtain an algorithm for the SATISFIABILITY problem of MSO over word structures: given an MSO sentence φ, construct the NFW A_φ and check whether $L(A) \neq \emptyset$ by finding a path from an initial state to an accepting state. This approach to satisfiability

checking is referred to as the *automata-theoretic approach*, since the decision procedure proceeds by first going from logic to automata, and then searching for a path in the
constructed automaton.

There was little interest in the 1950s in analyzing the computational complexity
of the SATISFIABILITY problem. That had to wait until 1974. Define the function
$exp(k, n)$ inductively as follows: $exp(0, n) = n$ and $exp(k+1, n) = 2^{exp(k,n)}$. We say
that a problem is *nonelementary* if it can not be solved by an algorithm whose running
time is bounded by $exp(k, n)$ for some fixed $k \geq 0$; that is, the running time cannot be
bounded by a tower of exponentials of a fixed height. It is not too difficult to observe
that the construction of the automaton A_φ in [7–10] involves a blow-up of $exp(n, n)$,
where n is the length of the MSO sentence being decided. It was shown in [14, 15] that
the SATISFIABILITY problem for MSO is nonelementary. In fact, the problem is already
nonelementary for FO [15].

1.3   Reasoning about Sequential Circuits

The field of hardware verification seems to have been started in a little known 1957
paper by Church, in which he described the use of logic to specify *sequential circuits*
[16]. A sequential circuit is a switching circuit whose output depends not only upon its
input, but also on what its input has been in the past. A sequential circuit is a particular
type of finite-state machine, which became a subject of study in mathematical logic and
computer science in the 1950s.

Formally, a sequential circuit $C = (I, O, R, f, g, \mathbf{r}_0)$ consists of a finite set I of
Boolean input signals, a finite set O of Boolean output signals, a finite set R of Boolean
sequential elements, a transition function $f : 2^I \times 2^R \to 2^R$, an output function $g :$
$2^R \to 2^O$, and an initial state $\mathbf{r}_0 \in 2^R$. (We refer to elements of $I \cup O \cup R$ as *circuit
elements*, and assume that I, O, and R are disjoint.) Intuitively, a state of the circuit is a
Boolean assignment to the sequential elements. The initial state is $\mathbf{r}_0$. In a state $\mathbf{r} \in 2^R$,
the Boolean assignment to the output signals is $g(\mathbf{r})$. When the circuit is in state $\mathbf{r} \in 2^R$
and it reads an input assignment $\mathbf{i} \in 2^I$, it changes its state to $f(\mathbf{i}, \mathbf{r})$.

A *trace* over a set V of Boolean variables is an infinite word over the alphabet 2^V,
i.e., an element of $(2^V)^\omega$. A trace of the sequential circuit C is a trace over $I \cup O \cup R$
that satisfies some conditions. Specifically, a sequence $\tau = (\mathbf{i}_0, \mathbf{r}_0, \mathbf{o}_0), (\mathbf{i}_1, \mathbf{r}_1, \mathbf{o}_1), \ldots$,
where $\mathbf{i}_j \in 2^I$, $\mathbf{o}_j \in 2^O$, and $\mathbf{r}_j \in 2^R$, is a trace of C if $\mathbf{r}_{j+1} = f(\mathbf{i}_j, \mathbf{r}_j)$ and $\mathbf{o}_j =$
$g(\mathbf{r}_j)$, for $j \geq 0$. Thus, in modern terminology, Church was following the *linear-time*
approach [17] (see discussion in Section 2.1). The set of traces of C is denoted by
traces(C).

We saw earlier how to associate relational structures with words. We can similarly
associate with an infinite word $w = a_0, a_1, \ldots$ over an alphabet 2^V, a relational structure $M_w = (\mathbf{N}, \leq, V)$, with the naturals $\mathbf{N}$ as the domain, ordered by $<$, and extended
by the set V of unary predicates, where $j \in p$, for $p \in V$, precisely when p *holds* (i.e.,
is assigned 1) in a_i.[1] We refer to such structures as *infinite word structures*. When we

---

[1] We overload notation here and treat p as both a Boolean variable and a predicate.

refer to the *vocabulary* of such a structure, we refer explicitly only to V, taking $<$ for granted.

We can now specify traces using First-Order Logic (FO) sentences constructed from atomic formulas of the form $x = y$, $x < y$, and $p(x)$ for $p \in V = I \cup R \cup O$.[2] For example, the FO sentence

$$(\forall x)(\exists y)(x < y \wedge p(y))$$

says that p holds infinitely often in the trace. In a follow-up paper in 1963 [18], Church considered also specifying traces using monadic second-order logic (MSO), where in addition to first-order quantifiers, which range over the elements of $\mathbf{N}$, we allow also monadic second-order quantifiers, ranging over subsets of $\mathbf{N}$, and atomic formulas of the form $Q(x)$, where Q is a monadic predicate variable. (This logic is also called *S1S*, the "second-order theory of one successor function".) For example, the MSO sentence,

$$(\exists P)(\forall x)(\forall y)((((P(x) \wedge y = x + 1) \rightarrow (\neg P(y)))\wedge$$
$$(((\neg P(x)) \wedge y = x + 1) \rightarrow P(y)))\wedge$$
$$(x = 0 \rightarrow P(x)) \wedge (P(x) \rightarrow q(x))),$$

where $x = 0$ is an abbrevaition for $(\neg(\exists z)(z < x))$ and $y = x + 1$ is an abbreviation for $(y > x \wedge \neg(\exists z)(x < z \wedge z < y))$, says that q holds at every even point on the trace. In effect, Church was proposing to use classical logic (FO or MSO) as a logic of time, by focusing on infinite word structures. The set of infinite models of an FO or MSO sentence φ is denoted by $\mathrm{models}_\omega(\varphi)$.

Church posed two problems related to sequential circuits [16]:

- The DECISION problem: Given circuit C and a sentence φ, does φ hold in all traces of C? That is, does $\mathrm{traces}(C) \subseteq \mathrm{models}(\varphi)$ hold?
- The SYNTHESIS problem: Given sets I and O of input and output signals, and a sentence φ over the vocabulary $I \cup O$, construct, if possible, a sequential circuit C with input signals I and output signals O such that φ holds in all traces of C. That is, construct C such that $\mathrm{traces}(C) \subseteq \mathrm{models}(\varphi)$ holds.

In modern terminology, Church's DECISION problem is the MODEL-CHECKING problem in the linear-time approach (see Section 2.2). This problem did not receive much attention after [16, 18], until the introduction of model checking in the early 1980s. In contrast, the SYNTHESIS problem has remained a subject of ongoing research; see [19–23]. One reason that the DECISION problem did not remain a subject of study, is the easy observation in [18] that the DECISION problem can be reduced to the VA-LIDITY problem in the underlying logic (FO or MSO). Given a sequential circuit C, we can easily generate an FO sentence α_C that holds in precisely all structures associated with traces of C. Intuitively, the sentence α_C simply has to encode the transition and output functions of C, which are Boolean functions. Then φ holds in all traces of C precisely when $\alpha_C \rightarrow \varphi$ holds in all word structures (of the appropriate vocabulary). Thus, to solve the DECISION problem we need to solve the VALIDITY problem over word structures. As we see next, this problem was solved in 1962.

---

[2] We overload notation here and treat p as both a circuit element and a predicate symbol.

1.4 Reasoning about Infinite Words

Church's DECISION problem was essentially solved in 1962 by Büchi who showed that the VALIDITY problem over infinite word structures is decidable [24]. Actually, Büchi showed the decidability of the dual problem, which is the SATISFIABILITY problem for MSO over infinite word structures. Büchi's approach consisted of extending the automata-theoretic approach, see Theorem 1, which was introduced a few years earlier for word structures, to infinite word structures. To that end, Büchi extended automata theory to automata on infinite words. For a nice introduction to the theory of automata on infinite words, see [25].

A *nondeterministic Büchi automaton on words* (NBW) $A = (\Sigma, S, S_0, \rho, F)$ consists of a finite input alphabet Σ, a finite state set S, an initial state set $S_0 \subseteq S$, a transition relation $\rho \subseteq S \times \Sigma \times S$, and an accepting state set $F \subseteq S$. An NBW runs over an infinite input word $w = a_0, a_1, \ldots \in \Sigma^\omega$. A *run* of A on w is an infinite sequence $r = s_0, s_1, \ldots$ of states in S such that $s_0 \in S_0$, and $(s_i, a_i, s_{i+1}) \in \rho$, for $i \geq 0$. The run r is *accepting* if F is visited by r infinitely often; that is, $s_i \in F$ for infinitely many i's. The word w is *accepted* by A if A has an accepting run on w. The *infinitary language* of A, denoted $L_\omega(A)$, is the set of infinite words accepted by A. The class of languages accepted by NBWs forms the class of ω-*regular* languages, which are defined in terms of regular expressions augmented with the ω-power operator (e^ω denotes an infinitary iteration of e) [24].

Example 2. We describe graphically an NBW that accepts all words over the alphabet $\{0, 1\}$ that contain infinitely many occurrences of 1. The arrow on the left designates the initial state, and the circle on the right designates an accepting state. Note that this NBW looks exactly like the NFW in Example 1. The only difference is that in Example 1 we considered finite input words and here we are considering infinite input words.

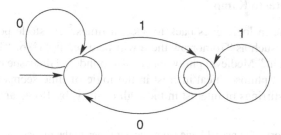

As we saw earlier, the paradigmatic idea of the automata-theoretic approach is that we can compile high-level logical specifications into an equivalent low-level finite-state formalism.

Theorem 2. [24] *Given an MSO sentence φ with vocabulary V, one can construct an NBW A_φ with alphabet 2^V such that a word w in $(2^V)^\omega$ is accepted by A_φ iff φ holds in the word structure M_w. Conversely, given an NBW A with alphabet 2^V, one can construct an MSO sentence φ_A with vocabulary V such that φ_A holds in an infinite word structure M_w iff w is accepted by A.*

Thus, the class of languages defined by MSO sentences is precisely the class of ω-regular languages.

To decide whether sentence φ is satisfiable over infinite words, that is, whether $models_\omega(\varphi) \neq \emptyset$, we need to check that $L_\omega(A_\varphi) \neq \emptyset$. Let $A = (\Sigma, S, S_0, \rho, F)$ be an NBW. As with NFWs, construct a directed graph $G_A = (S, E_A)$, with S as the set of nodes, and $E_A = \{(s, t) : (s, a, t) \in \rho \text{ for some } a \in \Sigma\}$. The following lemma is implicit in [24] and more explicit in [26].

Lemma 2. $L_\omega(A) \neq \emptyset$ iff there are states $s_0 \in S^0$ and $t \in F$ such that in G_A there is a path from s_0 to t and a path from t to itself.

We thus obtain an algorithm for the SATISFIABILITY problem of MSO over infinite word structures: given an MSO sentence φ, construct the NBW A_φ and check whether $L_\omega(A) \neq \emptyset$ by finding a path from an initial state to an accepting state and a cycle through that accepting state. Since the DECISION problem can be reduced to the SAT-ISFIABILITY problem, this also solves the DECISION problem.

Neither Büchi nor Church analyzed the complexity of the DECISION problem. The non-elementary lower bound mentioned earlier for MSO over words can be easily extended to infinite words. The upper bound here is a bit more subtle. For both finite and infinite words, the construction of A_φ proceeds by induction on the structure of φ, with complementation being the difficult step. For NFW, complementation uses the *subset construction*, which involves a blow-up of 2^n [13, 27]. Complementation for NBW is significantly more involved, see [28]. The blow-up of complementation is $2^{\Theta(n \log n)}$ [29, 30]. This yields a blow-up of $exp(n, n \log n)$ for the translation from MSO to NBW.

2 Thread II: Temporal Logic

2.1 From Aristotle to Kamp

The history of time in logic goes back to ancient times.[3] Aristotle pondered how to interpret sentences such as "Tomorrow there will be a sea fight," or "Tomorrow there will not be a sea fight." Medieval philosophers also pondered the issue of time.[4] By the Renaissance period, philosophical interest in the logic of time seems to have waned. There were some stirrings of interest in the 19th century, by Boole and Peirce. Peirce wrote:

---

[3] For a detailed history of temporal logic from ancient times to the modern period, see [31].

[4] For example, William of Ockham, 1288–1348, wrote (rather obscurely for the modern reader): "Wherefore the difference between present tense propositions and past and future tense propositions is that the predicate in a present tense proposition stands in the same way as the subject, unless something added to it stops this; but in a past tense and a future tense proposition it varies, for the predicate does not merely stand for those things concerning which it is truly predicated in the past and future tense propositions, because in order for such a proposition to be true, it is not sufficient that that thing of which the predicate is truly predicated (whether by a verb in the present tense or in the future tense) is that which the subject denotes, although it is required that the very same predicate is truly predicated of that which the subject denotes, by means of what is asserted by such a proposition."

"Time has usually been considered by logicians to be what is called 'extralogical' matter. I have never shared this opinion. But I have thought that logic had not yet reached the state of development at which the introduction of temporal modifications of its forms would not result in great confusion; and I am much of that way of thinking yet."

There were also some stirrings of interest in the first half of the 20th century, but the birth of modern temporal logic is unquestionably credited to Prior. Prior was a philosopher, who was interested in theological and ethical issues. His own religious path was somewhat convoluted; he was born a Methodist, converted to Presbytarianism, became an atheist, and ended up an agnostic. In 1949, he published a book titled "*Logic and The Basis of Ethics*". He was particularly interested in the conflict between the assumption of *free will* ("the future is to some extent, even if it is only a very small extent, something we can make for ourselves"), *foredestination* ("of what will be, it has now been the case that it will be"), and *foreknowledge* ("there is a deity who infallibly knows the entire future"). He was also interested in modal logic [32]. This confluence of interests led Prior to the development of *temporal logic*. [5] His wife, Mary Prior, recalled after his death:

"I remember his waking me one night [in 1953], coming and sitting on my bed, ..., and saying he thought one could make a formalised tense logic."

Prior lectured on his new work when he was the John Locke Lecturer at the University of Oxford in 1955–6, and published his book "*Time and Modality*" in 1957 [34].[6] In this book, he presented a temporal logic that is propositional logic extended with two temporal connectives, F and P, corresponding to "sometime in the future" and "sometime in the past". A crucial feature of this logic is that it has an implicit notion of "now", which is treated as an *indexical*, that is, it depends on the context of utterance for its meaning. Both future and past are defined with respect to this implicit "now".

It is interesting to note that the *linear* vs. *branching* time dichotomy, which has been a subject of some controversy in the computer science literature since 1980 (see [35]), has been present from the very beginning of temporal-logic development. In Prior's early work on temporal logic, he assumed that time was linear. In 1958, he received a letter from Kripke,[7] who wrote

"In an indetermined system, we perhaps should not regard time as a linear series, as you have done. Given the present moment, there are several possibilities for what the next moment may be like – and for each possible next moment, there are several possibilities for the moment after that. Thus the situation takes the form, not of a linear sequence, but of a 'tree'."

---

[5] An earlier term was *tense logic*; the term *temporal logic* was introduced in [33]. The technical distinction between the two terms seems fuzzy.

[6] Due to the arcane infix notation of the time, the book may not be too accessible to modern readers, who may have difficulties parsing formulas such as $CKMpMqAMKpMqMKqMp$.

[7] Kripke was a high-school student, not quite 18, in Omaha, Nebraska. Kripke's interest in modal logic was inspired by a paper by Prior on this subject [36]. Prior turned out to be the referee of Kripke's first paper [37].

Prior immediately saw the merit of Kripke's suggestion: "the determinist sees time as a line, and the indeterminist sees times as a system of forking paths." He went on to develop two theories of branching time, which he called "Ockhamist" and "Peircean". (Prior did not use path quantifiers; those were introduced later, in the 1980s. See Section 3.2.)

While the introduction of branching time seems quite reasonable in the context of trying to formalize free will, it is far from being simple philosophically. Prior argued that the nature of the course of time is branching, while the nature of a course of events is linear [38]. In contrast, it was argued in [33] that the nature of time is linear, but the nature of the course of events is branching: "We have 'branching *in* time,' not 'branching *of* time'."[8]

During the 1960s, the development of temporal logic continued through both the linear-time approach and the branching-time approach. There was little connection, however, between research on temporal logic and research on classical logics, as described in Section 1. That changed in 1968, when Kamp tied together the two threads in his doctoral dissertation.

Theorem 3. [39] *Linear temporal logic with past and binary temporal connectives ("strict until" and "strict since") has precisely the expressive power of FO over the ordered naturals (with monadic vocabularies).*

It should be noted that Kamp's Theorem is actually more general and asserts expressive equivalence of FO and temporal logic over all "Dedekind-closed orders". The introduction of binary temporal connectives by Kamp was necessary for reaching the expressive power of FO; *unary* linear temporal logic, which has only unary temporal connectives, is weaker than FO [40]. The theorem refers to FO formulas with one free variable, which are satisfied at an element of a structure, analogously to temporal logic formulas, which are satisfied at a point of time.

It should be noted that one direction of Kamp's Theorem, the translation from temporal logic to FO, is quite straightforward; the hard direction is the translation from FO to temporal logic. Both directions are algorithmically effective; translating from temporal logic to FO involves a linear blowup, but translation in the other direction involves a nonelementary blowup.

If we focus on FO sentences rather than FO formulas, then they define sets of traces (a sentence φ defines models(φ)). A characterization of of the expressiveness of FO sentences over the naturals, in terms of their ability to define sets of traces, was obtained in 1979.

Theorem 4. [41] *FO sentences over naturals have the expressive power of $*$-free ω-regular expressions.*

Recall that MSO defines the class of ω-regular languages. It was already shown in [42] that FO over the naturals is weaker expressively than MSO over the naturals. Theorem 4 was inspired by an analogous theorem in [43] for finite words.

---

[8] One is reminded of St. Augustin, who said in his *Confessions*: "What, then, is time? If no one asks me, I know; but if I wish to explain it to some who should ask me, I do not know."

2.2   The Temporal Logic of Programs

There were some early observations that temporal logic can be applied to programs. Prior stated: "There are practical gains to be had from this study too, for example, in the representation of time-delay in computer circuits" [38]. Also, a discussion of the application of temporal logic to processes, which are defined as "programmed sequences of states, deterministic or stochastic" appeared in [33].

The "big bang" for the application of temporal logic to program correctness occurred with Pnueli's 1977 paper [44]. In this paper, Pnueli, inspired by [33], advocated using future linear temporal logic (LTL) as a logic for the specification of non-terminating programs; see overview in [45].

LTL is a temporal logic with two temporal connectives, "next" and "until".[9] In LTL, formulas are constructed from a set $Prop$ of atomic propositions using the usual Boolean connectives as well as the unary temporal connective X ("next"), and the binary temporal connective U ("until"). Additional unary temporal connectives F ("eventually"), and G ("always") can be defined in terms of U. Note that all temporal connectives refer to the future here, in contrast to Kamp's "strict since" operator, which refers to the past. Thus, LTL is a *future temporal logic*. For extensions with past temporal connectives, see [46–48].

LTL is interpreted over traces over the set $Prop$ of atomic propositions. For a trace τ and a point $i \in \mathbb{N}$, the notation $\tau, i \models \varphi$ indicates that the formula φ holds at the point i of the trace τ. Thus, the point i is the implicit "now" with respect to which the formula is interpreted. We have that

- $\tau, i \models p$ if p holds at $\tau(i)$,
- $\tau, i \models X\varphi$ if $\tau, i + 1 \models \varphi$, and
- $\tau, i \models \varphi U \psi$ if for some $j \geq i$, we have $\tau, j \models \psi$ and for all k, $i \leq k < j$, we have $\tau, k \models \varphi$.

The temporal connectives F and G can be defined in terms of the temporal connective U; $F\varphi$ is defined as $\mathbf{true}\ U\varphi$, and $G\varphi$ is defined as $\neg F \neg \varphi$. We say that τ *satisfies* a formula φ, denoted $\tau \models \varphi$, iff $\tau, 0 \models \varphi$. We denote by models(φ) the set of traces satisfying φ.

As an example, the LTL formula $G(request \rightarrow F\ grant)$, which refers to the atomic propositions *request* and *grant*, is true in a trace precisely when every state in the trace in which *request* holds is followed by some state in the (non-strict) future in which *grant* holds. Also, the LTL formula $G(request \rightarrow (request\ U\ grant))$ is true in a trace precisely if, whenever *request* holds in a state of the trace, it holds until a state in which *grant* holds is reached.

The focus on satisfaction at 0, called *initial semantics*, is motivated by the desire to specify computations at their starting point. It enables an alternative version of Kamp's Theorem, which does not require past temporal connectives, but focuses on initial semantics.

---

[9] Unlike Kamp's "strict until" ("p strict until q" requires q to hold in the strict future), Pnueli's "until" is not strict ("p until q" can be satisfied by q holding now), which is why the "next" connective is required.

Theorem 5. [49] *LTL has precisely the expressive power of FO over the ordered naturals (with monadic vocabularies) with respect to initial semantics.*

As we saw earlier, FO has the expressive power of star-free ω-regular expressions over the naturals. Thus, LTL has the expressive power of star-free ω-regular expressions (see [50]), and is strictly weaker than MSO. An interesting outcome of the above theorem is that it lead to the following assertion regarding LTL [51]: "The corollary due to Meyer – I have to get in my controversial remark – is that that [Theorem 5] makes it theoretically uninteresting." Developments since 1980 have proven this assertion to be overly pessimistic on the merits of LTL.

Pnueli also discussed the analog of Church's DECISION problem: given a finite-state program P and an LTL formula φ, decide if φ holds in all traces of P. Just like Church, Pnueli observed that this problem can be solved by reduction to MSO. Rather than focus on sequential circuits, Pnueli focused on programs, modeled as (labeled) *transition systems* [52]. A transition system $M = (W, W_0, R, V)$ consists of a set W of states that the system can be in, a set $W_0 \subseteq W$ of initial states, a transition relation $R \subseteq W^2$ that indicates the allowable state transitions of the system, and an assignment $V : W \rightarrow 2^{Prop}$ of truth values to the atomic propositions in each state of the system. (A transition system is essentially a Kripke structure [53].) A *path* in M that *starts at* u is a possible infinite behavior of the system starting at u, i.e., it is an infinite sequence $u_0, u_1 \ldots$ of states in W such that $u_0 = u$, and $(u_i, u_{i+1}) \in R$ for all $i \geq 0$. The sequence $V(u_0), V(u_1) \ldots$ is a *trace* of M that *starts at* u. It is the sequence of truth assignments visited by the path. The *language* of M, denoted $L(M)$, consists of all traces of M that start at a state in W_0. Note that $L(M)$ is a language of infinite words over the alphabet 2^{Prop}. The language $L(M)$ can be viewed as an abstract description of the system M, describing all possible traces. We say that M *satisfies* an LTL formula φ if all traces in $L(M)$ satisfy φ, that is, if $L(M) \subseteq \text{models}(\varphi)$. When W is finite, we have a finite-state system, and can apply algorithmic techniques.

What about the complexity of LTL reasoning? Recall from Section 1 that satisfiability of FO over trace structures is nonelementary. In contrast, it was shown in [54–60] that LTL SATISFIABILITY is elementary; in fact, it is PSPACE-complete. It was also shown that the DECISION problem for LTL with respect to finite transition systems is PSPACE-complete [56–58]. The basic technique for proving these elementary upper bounds is the *tableau* technique, which was adapted from *dynamic logics* [61] (see Section 3.1). Thus, even though FO and LTL are expressively equivalent, they have dramatically different computational properties, as LTL reasoning is in PSPACE, while FO reasoning is nonelementary.

The second "big bang" in the application of temporal logic to program correctness was the introduction of *model checking* by Clarke and Emerson [62] and by Queille and Sifakis [63]. The two papers used two different branching-time logics. Clarke and Emerson used CTL (inspired by the branching-time logic UB of [64]), which extends LTL with existential and universal path quantifiers E and A. Queille and Sifakis used a logic introduced by Leslie Lamport [17], which extends propositional logic with the temporal connectives POT (which corresponds to the CTL operator EF) and $INEV$ (which corresponds to the CTL operator AF). The focus in both papers was on model checking, which is essentially what Church called the DECISION problem: does a given finite-state program, viewed as a finite transition system, satisfy its given temporal specification. In particular, Clarke and Emerson showed that model checking transition systems of size m with respect to formulas of size n can be done in time polynomial in m and n. This was refined later to $O(mn)$ (even in the presence of *fairness* constraints, which restrict attention to certain infinite paths in the underlying transition system) [65, 66]. We drop the term "DECISION problem" from now on, and replace it with the term "MODEL-CHECKING problem".[10]

It should be noted that the linear complexity of model checking refers to the size of the transition system, rather than the size of the program that gave rise to that system. For sequential circuits, transition-system size is essentially exponential in the size of the description of the circuit (say, in some Hardware Description Language). This is referred to as the "state-explosion problem" [68]. In spite of the state-explosion problem, in the first few years after the publication of the first model-checking papers in 1981-2, Clarke and his students demonstrated that model checking is a highly successful technique for automated program verification [69, 70]. By the late 1980s, automated verification had become a recognized research area. Also by the late 1980s, *symbolic* model checking was developed [71, 72], and the SMV tool, developed at CMU by McMillan [73], was starting to have an industrial impact. See [74] for more details.

The detailed complexity analysis in [65] inspired a similar detailed analysis of linear time model checking. It was shown in [75] that model checking transition systems of size m with respect to LTL formulas of size n can be done in time $m2^{O(n)}$. (This again was shown using a tableau-based technique.) While the bound here is exponential in n, the argument was that n is typically rather small, and therefore an exponential bound is acceptable.

2.3 Back to Automata

Since LTL can be translated to FO, and FO can be translated to NBW, it is clear that LTL can be translated to NBW. Going through FO, however, would incur, in general, a nonelementary blowup. In 1983, Wolper, Sistla, and I showed that this nonelementary blowup can be avoided.

Theorem 6. [76, 77] *Given an LTL formula φ of size n, one can construct an NBW A_φ of size $2^{O(n)}$ such that a trace σ satisfies φ if and only if σ is accepted by A_φ.*

It now follows that we can obtain a PSPACE algorithm for LTL SATISFIABILITY: given an LTL formula φ, we construct A_φ and check that $A_\varphi \neq \emptyset$ using the graph-theoretic approach described earlier. We can avoid using exponential space, by constructing the automaton *on the fly* [76, 77].

What about model checking? We know that a transition system M satisfies an LTL formula φ if $L(M) \subseteq \text{models}(\varphi)$. It was then observed in [78] that the following are equivalent:

---

[10] The model-checking problem is analogous to database query evaluation, where we check the truth of a logical formula, representing a query, with respect to a database, viewed as a finite relational structure. Interestingly, the study of the complexity of database query evaluation started about the same time as that of model checking [67].

- M satisfies φ
- $L(M) \subseteq \text{models}(\varphi)$
- $L(M) \subseteq L(A_\varphi)$
- $L(M) \cap ((2^{Prop})^\omega - L(A_\varphi)) = \emptyset$
- $L(M) \cap L(A_{\neg\varphi}) = \emptyset$
- $L(M \times A_{\neg\varphi}) = \emptyset$

Thus, rather than complementing A_φ using an exponential complementation construction [24, 79, 80], we complement the LTL property using logical negation. It is easy to see that we can now get the same bound as in [75]: model checking programs of size m with respect to LTL formulas of size n can be done in time $m2^{O(n)}$. Thus, the optimal bounds for LTL satisfiability and model checking can be obtained without resorting to ad-hoc tableau-based techniques; the key is the exponential translation of LTL to NBW.

One may wonder whether this theory is practical. Reduction to practice took over a decade of further research, which saw the development of

- an optimized search algorithm for explicit-state model checking [81, 82],
- a symbolic, BDD-based[11] algorithm for NBW nonemptiness [71, 72, 84],
- symbolic algorithms for LTL to NBW translation [71, 72, 85], and
- an optimized explicit algorithm for LTL to NBW translation [86].

By 1995, there were two model-checking tools that implemented LTL model checking via the automata-theoretic approach: Spin [87] is an explicit-state LTL model checker, and Cadence's SMV is a symbolic LTL model checker.[12] See [88] for a description of algorithmic developments since the mid 1990s. Additional tools today are *VIS* [89], *NuSMV* [90], and *SPOT* [91].

It should be noted that Kurshan developed the automata-theoretic approach independently, also going back to the 1980s [92–94]. In his approach (as also in [95, 77]), one uses automata to represent both the system and its specification [96].[13] The first implementation of COSPAN, a model-checking tool that is based on this approach [97], also goes back to the 1980s; see [98].

2.4 Enhancing Expressiveness

Can the development of LTL model checking [75, 78] be viewed as a satisfactory solution to Church's DECISION problem? Almost, but not quite, since, as we observed earlier, LTL is not as expressive as MSO, which means that LTL is expressively weaker than NBW. Why do we need the expressive power of NBWs? First, note that once we add fairness to transitions systems (sse [65, 66]), they can be viewed as variants of NBWs. Second, there are good reasons to expect the specification language to be as expressive as the underlying model of programs [99]. Thus, achieving the expressive

---

[11] To be precise, one should use the acronym ROBDD, for Reduced Ordered Binary Decision Diagrams [83].

[12] Cadence's SMV is also a CTL model checker. See
www.cadence.com/webforms/cbl_software/index.aspx

[13] The connection to automata is somewhat difficult to discern in the early papers [92, 93].

power of NBWs, which we refer to as ω-*regularity*, is a desirable goal. This motivated efforts since the early 1980s to extend LTL.

The first attempt along this line was made by Wolper [59, 60], who defined ETL (for *Extended Temporal Logic*), which is LTL extended with grammar operators. He showed that ETL is more expressive than LTL, while its SATISFIABILITY problem can still be solved in exponential time (and even PSPACE [56–58]). Then, Sistla, Wolper and I showed how to extend LTL with automata connectives, reaching ω-regularity, without losing the PSPACE upper bound for the SATISFIABILITY problem [76, 77]. Actually, three syntactical variations, denoted ETL_f, ETL_l, and ETL_r were shown to be expressively equivalent and have these properties [76, 77].

Two other ways to achieve ω-regularity were discovered in the 1980s. The first is to enhance LTL with monadic second-order quantifiers as in MSO, which yields a logic, QPTL, with a nonelementary SATISFIABILITY problem [100, 80]. The second is to enhance LTL with least and greatest fixpoints [101, 102], which yields a logic, μLTL, that achieves ω-regularity, and has a PSPACE upper bound on its SATISFIABILITY and MODEL-CHECKING problems [102]. For example, the (not too readable) formula

$$(\nu P)(\mu Q)(P \wedge X(p \vee Q)),$$

where ν and μ denote greatest and least fixpoint operators, respectively, is equivalent to the LTL formula GFp, which says that p holds infinitely often.

3   Thread III: Dynamic and Branching-Time Logics

3.1   Dynamic Logics

In 1976, a year before Pnueli proposed using LTL to specify programs, Pratt proposed using *dynamic logic*, an extension of modal logic, to specify programs [103].[14] In modal logic $\Box \varphi$ means that φ holds in all worlds that are possible with respect to the current world [53]. Thus, $\Box \varphi$ can be taken to mean that φ holds after an execution of a program step, taking the transition relation of the program to be the possibility relation of a Kripke structure. Pratt proposed the addition of dynamic modalities $[e]\varphi$, where e is a program, which asserts that φ holds in all states reachable by an execution of the program e. Dynamic logic can then be viewed as an extension of Hoare logic, since $\psi \rightarrow [e]\varphi$ corresponds to the Hoare triple $\{\psi\}e\{\varphi\}$ (see [109]). See [108] for an extensive coverage of dynamic logic.

In 1977, a propositional version of Pratt's dynamic logic, called PDL, was proposed, in which programs are regular expressions over atomic programs [110, 111]. It was shown there that the SATISFIABILITY problem for PDL is in NEXPTIME and EXPTIME-hard. Pratt then proved an EXPTIME upper bound, adapting tableau techniques from modal logic [112, 61]. (We saw earlier that Wolper then adapted these techniques to linear-time logic.)

Pratt's dynamic logic was designed for terminating programs, while Pnueli was interested in nonterminating programs. This motivated various extensions of dynamic logic

---

[14] See discussion of precursor and related developments, such as [104–107], in [108].

to nonterminating programs [113–116]. Nevertheless, these logics are much less natural for the specification of ongoing behavior than temporal logic. They inspired, however, the introduction of the (*modal*) μ-*calculus* by Kozen [117, 118]. The μ-calculus is an extension of modal logic with least and greatest fixpoints. It subsumes expressively essentially all dynamic and temporal logics [119]. Kozen's paper was inspired by previous papers that showed the usefulness of fixpoints in characterizing correctness properties of programs [120, 121] (see also [122]). In turn, the μ-calculus inspired the introduction of μLTL, mentioned earlier. The μ-calculus also played an important role in the development of symbolic model checking [71, 72, 84].

3.2 Branching-Time Logics

Dynamic logic provided a branching-time approach to reasoning about programs, in contrast to Pnueli's linear-time approach. Lamport was the first to study the dichotomy between linear and branching time in the context of program correctness [17]. This was followed by the introduction of the branching-time logic UB, which extends unary LTL (LTL without the temporal connective "until") with the existential and universal path quantifiers, E and A [64]. Path quantifiers enable us to quantify over different future behavior of the system. By adapting Pratt's tableau-based method for PDL to UB, it was shown that its SATISFIABILITY problem is in EXPTIME [64]. Clarke and Emerson then added the temporal conncetive "until" to UB and obtained CTL [62]. (They did not focus on the SATISFIABILITY problem for CTL, but, as we saw earlier, on its MODEL-CHECKING problem; the SATISFIABILITY problem was shown later to be solvable in EXPTIME [123].) Finally, it was shown that LTL and CTL have incomparable expressive power, leading to the introduction of the branching-time logic CTL*, which unifies LTL and CTL [124, 125].

The key feature of branching-time logics in the 1980s was the introduction of explicit path quantifiers in [64]. This was an idea that was not discovered by Prior and his followers in the 1960s and 1970s. Most likely, Prior would have found CTL* satisfactory for his philosophical applications and would have seen no need to introduce the "Ockhamist" and "Peircean" approaches.

3.3 Combining Dynamic and Temporal Logics

By the early 1980s it became clear that temporal logics and dynamic logics provide two distinct perspectives for specifying programs: the first is *state* based, while the second is *action* based. Various efforts have been made to combine the two approaches. These include the introduction of *Process Logic* [126] (branching time), *Yet Another Process Logic* [127] (branching time), *Regular Process Logic* [128] (linear time), *Dynamic LTL* [129] (linear time), and *RCTL* [130] (branching time), which ultimately evolved into *Sugar* [131]. RCTL/Sugar is unique among these logics in that it did not attempt to borrow the action-based part of dynamic logic. It is a state-based branching-time logic with no notion of actions. Rather, what it borrowed from dynamic logic was the use of regular-expression-based dynamic modalities. Unlike dynamic logic, which uses regular expressions over program statements, RCTL/Sugar uses regular expressions over state predicates, analogously to the automata of ETL [76, 77], which run over sequences of formulas.

4   Thread IV: From LTL to ForSpec, PSL, and SVA

In the late 1990s and early 2000s, model checking was having an increasing industrial impact. That led to the development of three industrial temporal logics based on
LTL: *ForSpec*, developed by Intel, and *PSL* and *SVA*, developed by industrial standards
committees.

4.1   From LTL to ForSpec

Intel's involvement with model checking started in 1990, when Kurshan, spending a
sabbatical year in Israel, conducted a successful feasibility study at the Intel Design
Center (IDC) in Haifa, using COSPAN, which at that point was a prototype tool; see
[98]. In 1992, IDC started a pilot project using SMV. By 1995, model checking was used
by several design projects at Intel, using an internally developed model checker based
on SMV. Intel users have found CTL to be lacking in expressive power and the Design
Technology group at Intel developed its own specification language, FSL. The FSL
language was a linear-time logic, and it was model checked using the automata-theoretic
approach, but its design was rather ad-hoc, and its expressive power was unclear; see
[132].

In 1997, Intel's Design Technology group at IDC embarked on the development of
a second-generation model-checking technology. The goal was to develop a model-
checking engine from scratch, as well as a new specification language. A BDD-based
model checker was released in 1999 [133], and a SAT-based model checker was released
in 2000 [134].

I got involved in the design of the second-generation specification language in 1997.
That language, ForSpec, was released in 2000 [135]. The first issue to be decided was
whether the language should be linear or branching. This led to an in-depth examination
of this issue [35][15] and the decision was to pursue a linear-time language. An obvious
candidate was LTL; we saw that by the mid 1990s there were both explicit-state and
symbolic model checkers for LTL, so there was no question of feasibility. I had numerous conversations with L. Fix, M. Hadash, Y. Kesten, and M. Sananes on this issue. The
conclusion was that LTL is not expressive enough for industrial usage. In particular,
many properties that are expressible in FSL are not expressible in LTL. Thus, it turned
out that the theoretical considerations regarding the expressiveness of LTL, i.e., its lack
of ω-regularity, had practical significance. I offered two extensions of LTL; as we saw
earlier both ETL and μLTL achieve ω-regularity and have the same complexity as LTL.
Neither of these proposals was accepted, due to the perceived difficulty of usage of
such logics by Intel validation engineers, who typically have only basic familiarity with
automata theory and logic.

These conversations continued in 1998, now with A. Landver. Avner also argued
that Intel validation engineers would not be receptive to the automata-based formalism
of ETL. Being familiar with RCTL/Sugar and its dynamic modalities [131, 130], he
asked me about regular expressions, and my answer was that regular expressions are
equivalent to automata [6], so the automata of ETL_f, which extends LTL with automata

---

[15] See [136] for another study of this issue.

on *finite* words, can be replaced by regular expressions over state predicates. This lead to the development of *RELTL*, which is LTL augmented by the dynamic regular modalities of dynamic logic (interpreted linearly, as in ETL). Instead of the dynamic-logic notation $[e]\varphi$, ForSpec uses the more readable (to engineers) (e triggers φ), where e is a regular expression over state predicates (e.g., $(p \vee q)^*$, $(p \wedge q)$), and φ is a formula. Semantically, $\tau, i \models (e$ triggers $\varphi)$ if, for all $j \geq i$, if $\tau[i, j]$ (that is, the finite word $\tau(i), \ldots, \tau(j)$) "matches" e (in the intuitive formal sense), then $\tau, j \models \varphi$; see [137]. Using the ω-regularity of ETL_f, it is now easy to show that RELTL also achieves ω-regularity [135].

While the addition of dynamic modalities to LTL is sufficient to achieve ω-regularity, we decided to also offer direct support to two specification modes often used by verification engineers at Intel: *clocks* and *resets*. Both clocks and resets are features that are needed to address the fact that modern semiconductor designs consist of interacting parallel modules. While clocks and resets have a simple underlying intuition, defining their semantics formally is quite nontrivial. ForSpec is essentially RELTL, augmented with features corresponding to clocks and resets, as we now explain.

Today's semiconductor designs are still dominated by synchronous circuits. In synchronous circuits, clock signals synchronize the sequential logic, providing the designer with a simple operational model. While the asynchronous approach holds the promise of greater speed (see [138]), designing asynchronous circuits is significantly harder than designing synchronous circuits. Current design methodology attempts to strike a compromise between the two approaches by using multiple clocks. This results in architectures that are globally asynchronous but locally synchronous. The temporal-logic literature mostly ignores the issue of explicitly supporting clocks. ForSpec supports multiple clocks via the notion of *current clock*. Specifically, ForSpec has a construct change_on $c\,\varphi$, which states that the temporal formula φ is to be evaluated with respect to the clock c; that is, the formula φ is to be evaluated in the trace defined by the high phases of the clock c. The key feature of clocks in ForSpec is that each subformula may advance according to a different clock [135].

Another feature of modern designs' consisting of interacting parallel modules is the fact that a process running on one module can be reset by a signal coming from another module. As noted in [139], reset control has long been a critical aspect of embedded control design. ForSpec directly supports reset signals. The formula accept_on $a\,\varphi$ states that the property φ should be checked only until the arrival of the reset signal a, at which point the check is considered to have *succeeded*. In contrast, reject_on $r\,\varphi$ states that the property φ should be checked only until the arrival of the reset signal r, at which point the check is considered to have *failed*. The key feature of resets in ForSpec is that each subformula may be reset (positively or negatively) by a different reset signal; for a longer discussion see [135].

ForSpec is an industrial property-specification language that supports hardware-oriented constructs as well as uniform semantics for formal and dynamic validation, while at the same time it has a well understood expressiveness (ω-regularity) and computational complexity (SATISFIABILITY and MODEL-CHECKING problems have the same complexity for ForSpec as for LTL) [135]. The design effort strove to find an acceptable compromise, with trade-offs clarified by theory, between conflicting demands, such as expressiveness, usability, and implementability. Clocks and resets, both important to hardware designers, have a clear intuitive semantics, but formalizing this semantics is nontrivial. The rigorous semantics, however, not only enabled mechanical verification of various theorems about the language, but also served as a reference document for the implementors. The implementation of model checking for ForSpec followed the automata-theoretic approach, using *alternating* automata as advocated in [140] (see [141]).

4.2 From ForSpec to PSL and SVA

In 2000, the Electronic Design Automation Association instituted a standardization body called *Accellera*.[16] Accellera's mission is to drive worldwide development and use of standards required by systems, semiconductor and design tools companies. Accellera decided that the development of a standard specification language is a requirement for formal verification to become an industrial reality (see [98]). Since the focus was on specifying properties of designs rather than designs themselves, the chosen term was "property specification language" (PSL). The PSL standard committee solicited industrial contributions and received four language contributions: *CBV*, from Motorola, ForSpec, from Intel, *Temporal e*, from Verisity [142], and Sugar, from IBM.

The committee's discussions were quite fierce.[17] Ultimately, it became clear that while technical considerations play an important role, industrial committees' decisions are ultimately made for business considerations. In that contention, IBM had the upper hand, and Accellera chose Sugar as the base language for PSL in 2003. At the same time, the technical merits of ForSpec were accepted and PSL adopted all the main features of ForSpec. In essence, PSL (the current version 1.1) is LTL, extended with dynamic modalities (referred to as the *regular layer*), clocks, and resets (called *aborts*). PSL did inherit the syntax of Sugar, and does include a branching-time extension as an acknowledgment to Sugar.[18]

There was some evolution of PSL with respect to ForSpec. After some debate on the proper way to define resets [144], ForSpec's approach was essentially accepted after some reformulation [145]. ForSpec's fundamental approach to clocks, which is semantic, was accepted, but modified in some important details [146]. In addition to the dynamic modalities, borrowed from dynamic logic, PSL also has weak dynamic modalities [147], which are reminiscent of "looping" modalities in dynamic logic [113, 148]. Today PSL 1.1 is an IEEE Standard 1850–2005, and continues to be refined by the IEEE P1850 PSL Working Group.[19]

Practical use of ForSpec and PSL has shown that the regular layer (that is, the dynamic modalities), is highly popular with verification engineers. Another standardized property specification language, called *SVA* (for SystemVerilog Assertions), is based, in essence, on that regular layer [149]. Today SystemVerilog is an IEEE Standard 1800-2005.

---

[16] See http://www.accellera.org/

[17] See http://www.eda-stds.org/vfv/

[18] See [143] and language reference manual at http://www.eda.org/vfv/docs/ PSL-v1.1.pdf

[19] See http://www.eda.org/ieee-1850/

5 Contemplation

This evolution of ideas, from Löwenheim and Skolem to PSL and SVA, seems to me to be an amazing development. It reminds me of the medieval period, when building a cathedral spanned more than a mason's lifetime. Many masons spend their whole lives working on a cathedral, never seeing it to completion. We are fortunate to see the completion of this particular "cathedral". Just like the medieval masons, our contributions are often smaller than we'd like to consider them, but even small contributions can have a major impact. Unlike the medieval cathedrals, the scientific cathedral has no architect; the construction is driven by a complex process, whose outcome is unpredictable. Much that has been discovered is forgotten and has to be rediscovered. It is hard to fathom what our particular "cathedral" will look like in 50 years.

Acknowledgments. I am grateful to E. Clarke, A. Emerson, R. Goldblatt, A. Pnueli, P. Sistla, P. Wolper for helping me trace the many threads of this story, to D. Fisman, C. Eisner, J. Halpern, D. Harel and T. Wilke for their many useful comments on earlier drafts of this paper, and to S. Nain, K. Rozier, and D. Tabakov for proofreading earlier drafts. I'd also like to thank K. Rozier for her help with graphics.

References

1. Davis, M.: Engines of Logic: Mathematicians and the Origin of the Computer. Norton (2001)
2. Börger, E., Grädel, E., Gurevich, Y.: The Classical Decision Problem. Springer (1996)
3. Dreben, D., Goldfarb, W.D.: The Decision Problem: Solvable Classes of Quantificational Formulas. Addison-Wesley (1979)
4. Löwenheim, L.: Über Möglichkeiten im Relativkalküll (On possibilities in the claculus of relations). Math. Ann. 76, 447–470 (1915) (Translated in From Frege to Gödel, van Heijenoort, Harvard Univ. Press, 1971)
5. Skolem, T.: Untersuchung über Axiome des Klassenkalküls und über Produktations- und Summationsprobleme, welche gewisse Klassen von Aussagen betreffen (Investigations of the axioms of the calculus of classes and on product and sum problems that are connected with certain class of statements). Videnskabsakademiet i Kristiania, Skrifter I 3 (1919); Translated in Selected Works in Logic by T. Skolem, J.E. Fenstak, Scand. Univ. Books, Universitetsforlaget, Oslo, 67–101 (1970)
6. Hopcroft, J., Ullman, J.: Introduction to Automata Theory, Languages, and Computation. Addison-Wesley (1979)
7. Büchi, J.: Weak second-order arithmetic and finite automata. Zeit. Math. Logik und Grundl. Math. 6, 66–92 (1960)
8. Büchi, J., Elgot, C., Wright, J.: The non-existence of certain algorithms for finite automata theory (abstract). Notices Amer. Math. Soc. 5, 98 (1958)
9. Elgot, C.: Decision problems of finite-automata design and related arithmetics. Trans. Amer. Math. Soc. 98, 21–51 (1961)
10. Trakhtenbrot, B.: The synthesis of logical nets whose operators are described in terms of one-place predicate calculus. Doklady Akad. Nauk SSSR 118(4), 646–649 (1958)
11. Trakhtenbrot, B.: Certain constructions in the logic of one-place predicates. Doklady Akad. Nauk SSSR 138, 320–321 (1961)
12. Trakhtenbrot, B.: Finite automata and monadic second order logic. Siberian Math 59, 101–131 (1962) (Russian), English translation in: AMS Transl. 59, 23–55 (1966)

13. Rabin, M., Scott, D.: Finite automata and their decision problems. IBM Journal of Research and Development 3, 115–125 (1959)
14. Meyer, A.R.: Weak monadic second order theory of successor is not elementary recursive. In: Proc. Logic Colloquium. Lecture Notes in Mathematics, vol. 453, pp. 132–154. Springer, Heidelberg (1975)
15. Stockmeyer, L.: The complexity of decision procedures in Automata Theory and Logic. PhD thesis, MIT, Project MAC Technical Report TR-133 (1974)
16. Church, A.: Applicaton of recursive arithmetics to the problem of circuit synthesis. Summaries of Talks Presented at The Summer Institute for Symbolic Logic, Communications Research Division, Institute for Defense Analysis, 3–50 (1957)
17. Lamport, L.: "Sometimes" is sometimes "not never" - on the temporal logic of programs. In: Proc. 7th ACM Symp. on Principles of Programming Languages, pp. 174–185 (1980)
18. Church, A.: Logic, arithmetics, and automata. In: Proc. Int. Congress of Mathematicians, Institut Mittag-Leffler, pp. 23–35 (1962, 1963)
19. Büchi, J., Landweber, L.: Solving sequential conditions by finite-state strategies. Trans. AMS 138, 295–311 (1969)
20. Kupferman, O., Piterman, N., Vardi, M.: Safraless compositional synthesis. In: Ball, T., Jones, R.B. (eds.) CAV 2006. LNCS, vol. 4144, pp. 31–44. Springer, Heidelberg (2006)
21. Kupferman, O., Vardi, M.: Safraless decision procedures. In: Proc. 46th IEEE Symp. on Foundations of Computer Science, pp. 531–540 (2005)
22. Rabin, M.: Automata on infinite objects and Church's problem. Amer. Mathematical Society (1972)
23. Thomas, W.: On the synthesis of strategies in infinite games. In: Mayr, E.W., Puech, C. (eds.) STACS 1995. LNCS, vol. 900, pp. 1–13. Springer, Heidelberg (1995)
24. Büchi, J.: On a decision method in restricted second order arithmetic. In: Proc. Int. Congress on Logic, Method, and Philosophy of Science, pp. 1–12. Stanford University Press (1960, 1962)
25. Choueka, Y.: Theories of automata on ω-tapes: A simplified approach. Journal of Computer and Systems Science 8, 117–141 (1974)
26. Trakhtenbrot, B., Barzdin, Y.: Finite Automata. North Holland (1973)
27. Sakoda, W., Sipser, M.: Non-determinism and the size of two-way automata. In: Proc. 10th ACM Symp. on Theory of Computing, pp. 275–286 (1978)
28. Vardi, M.Y.: The Büchi complementation saga. In: Thomas, W., Weil, P. (eds.) STACS 2007. LNCS, vol. 4393, pp. 12–22. Springer, Heidelberg (2007)
29. Schewe, S.: Büchi complementation made tight. In: Proc. 26th Int'l Symp. on Theoretical Aspects of Computer Science. Dagstuhl Seminar Proceedings, vol. 09001, pp. 661–672. Schloss Dagstuhl (2009)
30. Yan, Q.: Lower bounds for complementation of ω-automata via the full automata technique. In: Bugliesi, M., Preneel, B., Sassone, V., Wegener, I. (eds.) ICALP 2006. LNCS, vol. 4052, pp. 589–600. Springer, Heidelberg (2006)
31. Øhrstrøm, P., Hasle, P.: Temporal Logic: from Ancient Times to Artificial Intelligence, vol. 57. Studies in Linguistics and Philosophy. Kluwer (1995)
32. Prior, A.: Modality de dicto and modality de re. Theoria 18, 174–180 (1952)
33. Rescher, N.,, A.U.: Temporal Logic. Springer (1971)
34. Prior, A.: Time and Modality. Oxford University Press (1957)
35. Vardi, M.Y.: Branching vs. Linear time: Final showdown. In: Margaria, T., Yi, W. (eds.) TACAS 2001. LNCS, vol. 2031, pp. 1–22. Springer, Heidelberg (2001)
36. Prior, A.: Modality and quantification in s5. J. Symbolic Logic 21, 60–62 (1956)
37. Kripke, S.: A completeness theorem in modal logic. Journal of Symbolic Logic 24, 1–14 (1959)
38. Prior, A.: Past, Present, and Future. Clarendon Press (1967)

39. Kamp, J.: Tense Logic and the Theory of Order. PhD thesis, UCLA (1968)
40. Etessami, K., Vardi, M., Wilke, T.: First-order logic with two variables and unary temporal logic. Inf. Comput. 179(2), 279–295 (2002)
41. Thomas, W.: Star-free regular sets of ω-sequences. Information and Control 42(2), 148–156 (1979)
42. Elgot, C., Wright, J.: Quantifier elimination in a problem of logical design. Michigan Math. J. 6, 65–69 (1959)
43. McNaughton, R., Papert, S.: Counter-Free Automata. MIT Pres (1971)
44. Pnueli, A.: The temporal logic of programs. In: Proc. 18th IEEE Symp. on Foundations of Computer Science, pp. 46–57 (1977)
45. Goldblatt, R.: Logic of time and computation. Technical report, CSLI Lecture Notes, no.7, Stanford University (1987)
46. Lichtenstein, O., Pnueli, A., Zuck, L.: The glory of the past. In: Parikh, R. (ed.) Logic of Programs 1985. LNCS, vol. 193, pp. 196–218. Springer, Heidelberg (1985)
47. Markey, N.: Temporal logic with past is exponentially more succinct. EATCS Bulletin 79, 122–128 (2003)
48. Vardi, M.: A temporal fixpoint calculus. In: Proc. 15th ACM Symp. on Principles of Programming Languages, pp. 250–259 (1988)
49. Gabbay, D., Pnueli, A., Shelah, S., Stavi, J.: On the temporal analysis of fairness. In: Proc. 7th ACM Symp. on Principles of Programming Languages, pp. 163–173 (1980)
50. Pnueli, A., Zuck, L.: In and out of temporal logic. In: Proc. 8th IEEE Symp. on Logic in Computer Science, pp. 124–135 (1993)
51. Meyer, A.: Ten thousand and one logics of programming. Technical report, MIT, MIT-LCS-TM-150 (1980)
52. Keller, R.: Formal verification of parallel programs. Communications of the ACM 19, 371–384 (1976)
53. Blackburn, P., de Rijke, M., Venema, Y.: Modal Logic. Cambridge University Press (2002)
54. Halpern, J., Reif, J.: The propositional dynamic logic of deterministic, well-structured programs (extended abstract). In: Proc. 22nd IEEE Symp. on Foundations of Computer Science, 322–334 (1981)
55. Halpern, J., Reif, J.: The propositional dynamic logic of deterministic, well-structured programs. Theor. Comput. Sci. 27, 127–165 (1983)
56. Sistla, A.: Theoretical issues in the design of distributed and concurrent systems. PhD thesis, Harvard University (1983)
57. Sistla, A., Clarke, E.: The complexity of propositional linear temporal logics. In: Proc. 14th Annual ACM Symposium on Theory of Computing, pp. 159–168 (1982)
58. Sistla, A., Clarke, E.: The complexity of propositional linear temporal logic. Journal of the ACM 32, 733–749 (1985)
59. Wolper, P.: Temporal logic can be more expressive. In: Proc. 22nd IEEE Symp. on Foundations of Computer Science, pp. 340–348 (1981)
60. Wolper, P.: Temporal logic can be more expressive. Information and Control 56(1-2), 72–99 (1983)
61. Pratt, V.: A near-optimal method for reasoning about action. Journal of Computer and Systems Science 20(2), 231–254 (1980)
62. Clarke, E., Emerson, E.: Design and synthesis of synchronization skeletons using branching time temporal logic. In: Kozen, D. (ed.) Logic of Programs 1981. LNCS, vol. 131, pp. 52–71. Springer, Heidelberg (1982)
63. Queille, J., Sifakis, J.: Specification and verification of concurrent systems in Cesar. In: Dezani-Ciancaglini, M., Montanari, U. (eds.) Programming 1982. LNCS, vol. 137, pp. 337–351. Springer, Heidelberg (1982)
64. Ben-Ari, M., Manna, Z., Pnueli, A.: The logic of nexttime. In: Proc. 8th ACM Symp. on Principles of Programming Languages, pp. 164–176 (1981)

65. Clarke, E., Emerson, E., Sistla, A.: Automatic verification of finite state concurrent systems using temporal logic specifications: A practical approach. In: Proc. 10th ACM Symp. on Principles of Programming Languages, pp. 117–126 (1983)
66. Clarke, E., Emerson, E., Sistla, A.: Automatic verification of finite-state concurrent systems using temporal logic specifications. ACM Transactions on Programming Languagues and Systems 8(2), 244–263 (1986)
67. Vardi, M.: The complexity of relational query languages. In: Proc. 14th ACM Symp. on Theory of Computing, pp. 137–146 (1982)
68. Clarke, E., Grumberg, O.: Avoiding the state explosion problem in temporal logic model-checking algorithms. In: Proc. 16th ACM Symp. on Principles of Distributed Computing, pp. 294–303 (1987)
69. Browne, M., Clarke, E., Dill, D., Mishra, B.: Automatic verification of sequential circuits using temporal logic. IEEE Transactions on Computing C-35, 1035–1044 (1986)
70. Clarke, E., Mishra, B.: Hierarchical verification of asynchronous circuits using temporal logic. Theoretical Computer Science 38, 269–291 (1985)
71. Burch, J., Clarke, E., McMillan, K., Dill, D., Hwang, L.: Symbolic model checking: 10^{20} states and beyond. In: Proc. 5th IEEE Symp. on Logic in Computer Science, pp. 428–439 (1990)
72. Burch, J., Clarke, E., McMillan, K., Dill, D., Hwang, L.: Symbolic model checking: 10^{20} states and beyond. Information and Computation 98(2), 142–170 (1992)
73. McMillan, K.: Symbolic Model Checking. Kluwer Academic Publishers (1993)
74. Clarke, E.M.: The Birth of Model Checking. In: Grumberg, O., Veith, H. (eds.) 25 Years of Model Checking. LNCS, vol. 5000, pp. 1–26. Springer, Heidelberg (2008)
75. Lichtenstein, O., Pnueli, A.: Checking that finite state concurrent programs satisfy their linear specification. In: Proc. 12th ACM Symp. on Principles of Programming Languages, pp. 97–107 (1985)
76. Vardi, M., Wolper, P.: Reasoning about infinite computations. Information and Computation 115(1), 1–37 (1994)
77. Wolper, P., Vardi, M., Sistla, A.: Reasoning about infinite computation paths. In: Proc. 24th IEEE Symp. on Foundations of Computer Science, pp. 185–194 (1983)
78. Vardi, M., Wolper, P.: An automata-theoretic approach to automatic program verification. In: Proc. 1st IEEE Symp. on Logic in Computer Science, pp. 332–344 (1986)
79. Kupferman, O., Vardi, M.: Weak alternating automata are not that weak. ACM Transactions on Computational Logic 2(2), 408–429 (2001)
80. Sistla, A., Vardi, M., Wolper, P.: The complementation problem for Büchi automata with applications to temporal logic. Theoretical Computer Science 49, 217–237 (1987)
81. Courcoubetis, C., Vardi, M., Wolper, P., Yannakakis, M.: Memory efficient algorithms for the verification of temporal properties. In: Clarke, E., Kurshan, R.P. (eds.) CAV 1990. LNCS, vol. 531, pp. 233–242. Springer, Heidelberg (1991)
82. Courcoubetis, C., Vardi, M., Wolper, P., Yannakakis, M.: Memory efficient algorithms for the verification of temporal properties. Formal Methods in System Design 1, 275–288 (1992)
83. Bryant, R.: Graph-based algorithms for Boolean-function manipulation. IEEE Transactions on Computing C-35(8), 677–691 (1986)
84. Emerson, E., Lei, C.L.: Efficient model checking in fragments of the propositional μ-calculus. In: Proc. 1st IEEE Symp. on Logic in Computer Science, pp. 267–278 (1986)
85. Clarke, E., Grumberg, O., Hamaguchi, K.: Another look at LTL model checking. In: Dill, D.L. (ed.) CAV 1994. LNCS, vol. 818, pp. 415–427. Springer, Heidelberg (1994)
86. Gerth, R., Peled, D., Vardi, M., Wolper, P.: Simple on-the-fly automatic verification of linear temporal logic. In: Dembiski, P., Sredniawa, M. (eds.) Protocol Specification, Testing, and Verification, pp. 3–18. Chapman & Hall (1995)

87. Holzmann, G.: The model checker SPIN. IEEE Transactions on Software Engineering 23(5), 279–295 (1997)
88. Vardi, M.: Automata-theoretic model checking revisited. In: Cook, B., Podelski, A. (eds.) VMCAI 2007. LNCS, vol. 4349, pp. 137–150. Springer, Heidelberg (2007)
89. Brayton, R., Hachtel, G., Sangiovanni-Vincentelli, A., Somenzi, F., Aziz, A., Cheng, S.T., Edwards, S., Khatri, S., Kukimoto, T., Pardo, A., Qadeer, S., Ranjan, R., Sarwary, S., Shiple, T., Swamy, G., Villa, T.: VIS: a system for verification and synthesis. In: Alur, R., Henzinger, T.A. (eds.) CAV 1996. LNCS, vol. 1102, pp. 428–432. Springer, Heidelberg (1996)
90. Cimatti, A., Clarke, E., Giunchiglia, E., Giunchiglia, F., Pistore, M., Roveri, M., Sebastiani, R., Tacchella, A.: Nusmv 2: An opensource tool for symbolic model checking. In: Brinksma, E., Larsen, K.G. (eds.) CAV 2002. LNCS, vol. 2404, pp. 359–364. Springer, Heidelberg (2002)
91. Duret-Lutz, A., Poitrenaud, D.: SPOT: An extensible model checking library using transition-based generalized büchi automata. In: Proc. 12th Int'l Workshop on Modeling, Analysis, and Simulation of Computer and Telecommunication Systems, pp. 76–83. IEEE Computer Society (2004)
92. Aggarwal, S., Kurshan, R.: Automated implementation from formal specification. In: Proc. 4th Int'l Workshop on Protocol Specification, Testing and Verification, pp. 127–136. North-Holland (1984)
93. Aggarwal, S., Kurshan, R., Sharma, D.: A language for the specification and analysis of protocols. In: Proc. 3rd Int'l Workshop on Protocol Specification, Testing, and Verification, pp. 35–50. North-Holland (1983)
94. Kurshan, R.: Analysis of discrete event coordination. In: de Bakker, J.W., de Roever, W.-P., Rozenberg, G. (eds.) REX 1989. LNCS, vol. 430, pp. 414–453. Springer, Heidelberg (1990)
95. Sabnani, K., Wolper, P., Lapone, A.: An algorithmic technique for protocol verification. In: Proc. Globecom 1985 (1985)
96. Kurshan, R.: Computer Aided Verification of Coordinating Processes. Princeton Univ. Press (1994)
97. Hardin, R., Har'el, Z., Kurshan, R.: COSPAN. In: Alur, R., Henzinger, T.A. (eds.) CAV 1996. LNCS, vol. 1102, pp. 423–427. Springer, Heidelberg (1996)
98. Kurshan, R.P.: Verification technology transfer. In: Grumberg, O., Veith, H. (eds.) 25 Years of Model Checking. LNCS, vol. 5000, pp. 46–64. Springer, Heidelberg (2008)
99. Pnueli, A.: Linear and branching structures in the semantics and logics of reactive systems. In: Brauer, W. (ed.) ICALP 1985. LNCS, vol. 194, pp. 15–32. Springer, Heidelberg (1985)
100. Sistla, A., Vardi, M., Wolper, P.: The complementation problem for Büchi automata with applications to temporal logic. In: Brauer, W. (ed.) ICALP 1985. LNCS, vol. 194, pp. 465–474. Springer, Heidelberg (1985)
101. Banieqbal, B., Barringer, H.: Temporal logic with fixed points. In: Banieqbal, B., Pnueli, A., Barringer, H. (eds.) Temporal Logic in Specification. LNCS, vol. 398, pp. 62–74. Springer, Heidelberg (1989)
102. Vardi, M.: Unified verification theory. In: Banieqbal, B., Pnueli, A., Barringer, H. (eds.) Temporal Logic in Specification. LNCS, vol. 398, pp. 202–212. Springer, Heidelberg (1989)
103. Pratt, V.: Semantical considerations on Floyd-Hoare logic. In: Proc. 17th IEEE Symp. on Foundations of Computer Science, pp. 109–121 (1976)
104. Burstall, R.: Program proving as hand simulation with a little induction. In: Information Processing. IFIP, vol. 74, pp. 308–312. North-Holland (1974)
105. Constable, R.: On the theory of programming logics. In: Proc. 9th ACM Symp. on Theory of Computing, pp. 269–285 (1977)
106. Engeler, E.: Algorithmic properties of structures. Math. Syst. Theory 1, 183–195 (1967)

107. Salwicki, A.: Algorithmic logic: a tool for investigations of programs. In: Butts, R., Hintikka, J. (eds.) Logic Foundations of Mathematics and Computability Theory, pp. 281–295. Reidel (1977)
108. Harel, D., Kozen, D., Tiuryn, J.: Dynamic Logic. MIT Press (2000)
109. Apt, K., Olderog, E.: Verification of Sequential and Concurrent Programs. Springer (2006)
110. Fischer, M., Ladner, R.: Propositional modal logic of programs (extended abstract). In: Proc. 9th ACM Symp. on Theory of Computing, pp. 286–294 (1977)
111. Fischer, M., Ladner, R.: Propositional dynamic logic of regular programs. Journal of Computer and Systems Science 18, 194–211 (1979)
112. Pratt, V.: A practical decision method for propositional dynamic logic: Preliminary report. In: Proc. 10th Annual ACM Symposium on Theory of Computing, pp. 326–337 (1978)
113. Harel, D., Sherman, R.: Looping vs. repeating in dynamic logic. Inf. Comput. 55(1-3), 175–192 (1982)
114. Streett, R.: A propositional dynamic logic for reasoning about program divergence. PhD thesis, M.Sc. Thesis, MIT (1980)
115. Street, R.: Propositional dynamic logic of looping and converse. In: Proc. 13th ACM Symp. on Theory of Computing, pp. 375–383 (1981)
116. Streett, R.: Propositional dynamic logic of looping and converse. Information and Control 54, 121–141 (1982)
117. Kozen, D.: Results on the propositional μ-calculus. In: Nielsen, M., Schmidt, E.M. (eds.) ICALP 1982. LNCS, vol. 140, pp. 348–359. Springer, Heidelberg (1982)
118. Kozen, D.: Results on the propositional μ-calculus. Theoretical Computer Science 27, 333–354 (1983)
119. Bradfield, J., Stirling, C.: PDL and modal μ-calculus. In: Blackburn, P., van Benthem, J., Wolter, F. (eds.) Handbook of Modal Logic. Elsevier (2006)
120. Emerson, E., Clarke, E.: Characterizing correctness properties of parallel programs using fixpoints. In: de Bakker, J.W., van Leeuwen, J. (eds.) ICALP 1980. LNCS, vol. 85, pp. 169–181. Springer, Heidelberg (1980)
121. Park, D.: Finiteness is μ-ineffable. Theoretical Computer Science 3, 173–181 (1976)
122. Pratt, V.: A decidable μ-calculus: preliminary report. In: Proc. 22nd IEEE Symp. on Foundations of Computer Science, pp. 421–427 (1981)
123. Emerson, E., Halpern, J.: Decision procedures and expressiveness in the temporal logic of branching time. Journal of Computer and Systems Science 30, 1–24 (1985)
124. Emerson, E., Halpern, J.: "Sometimes" and "not never" revisited: On branching versus linear time. In: Proc. 10th ACM Symp. on Principles of Programming Languages, pp. 127–140 (1983)
125. Emerson, E., Halpern, J.: Sometimes and not never revisited: On branching versus linear time. Journal of the ACM 33(1), 151–178 (1986)
126. Harel, D., Kozen, D., Parikh, R.: Process logic: Expressiveness, decidability, completeness. J. Comput. Syst. Sci. 25(2), 144–170 (1982)
127. Vardi, M., Wolper, P.: Yet another process logic. In: Clarke, E., Kozen, D. (eds.) Logic of Programs 1983. LNCS, vol. 164, pp. 501–512. Springer, Heidelberg (1984)
128. Harel, D., Peleg, D.: Process logic with regular formulas. Theoreti. Comp. Sci. 38(2–3), 307–322 (1985)
129. Hafer, T., Thomas, W.: Computation tree logic CTL* and path quantifiers in the monadic theory of the binary tree. In: Ottmann, T. (ed.) ICALP 1987. LNCS, vol. 267, pp. 269–279. Springer, Heidelberg (1987)
130. Beer, I., Ben-David, S., Landver, A.: On-the-fly model checking of RCTL formulas. In: Vardi, M.Y. (ed.) CAV 1998. LNCS, vol. 1427, pp. 184–194. Springer, Heidelberg (1998)
131. Beer, I., Ben-David, S., Eisner, C., Fisman, D., Gringauze, A., Rodeh, Y.: The temporal logic sugar. In: Berry, G., Comon, H., Finkel, A. (eds.) CAV 2001. LNCS, vol. 2102, pp. 363–367. Springer, Heidelberg (2001)

132. Fix, L.: Fifteen years of formal property verification in Intel. In: Grumberg, O., Veith, H. (eds.) 25 Years of Model Checking. LNCS, vol. 5000, pp. 139–144. Springer, Heidelberg (2008)

133. Fix, L., Kamhi, G.: Adaptive variable reordering for symbolic model checking. In: Proc. ACM/IEEE Int'l Conf. on Computer Aided Design, pp. 359–365 (1998)

134. Copty, F., Fix, L., Fraer, R., Giunchiglia, E., Kamhi, G., Tacchella, A., Vardi, M.: Benefits of bounded model checking at an industrial setting. In: Berry, G., Comon, H., Finkel, A. (eds.) CAV 2001. LNCS, vol. 2102, pp. 436–453. Springer, Heidelberg (2001)

135. Armoni, R., et al.: The forSpec temporal logic: A new temporal property-specification language. In: Katoen, J.-P., Stevens, P. (eds.) TACAS 2002. LNCS, vol. 2280, pp. 296–311. Springer, Heidelberg (2002)

136. Nain, S., Vardi, M.Y.: Branching vs. Linear time: Semantical perspective. In: Namjoshi, K.S., Yoneda, T., Higashino, T., Okamura, Y. (eds.) ATVA 2007. LNCS, vol. 4762, pp. 19–34. Springer, Heidelberg (2007)

137. Bustan, D., Flaisher, A., Grumberg, O., Kupferman, O., Vardi, M.: Regular vacuity. In: Borrione, D., Paul, W. (eds.) CHARME 2005. LNCS, vol. 3725, pp. 191–206. Springer, Heidelberg (2005)

138. van Berkel, C.H., Josephs, M.B., Nowick, S.M.: Applications of asynchronous circuits. Proceedings of the IEEE 87(2), 223–233 (1999)

139. A comparison of reset control methods: Application note 11. Summit Microelectronics, Inc. (1999),
    http://www.metatech.com.hk/appnote/summit/pdf/note11.htm

140. Vardi, M.: Nontraditional applications of automata theory. In: Hagiya, M., Mitchell, J.C. (eds.) TACS 1994. LNCS, vol. 789, pp. 575–597. Springer, Heidelberg (1994)

141. Gastin, P., Oddoux, D.: Fast LTL to büchi automata translation. In: Berry, G., Comon, H., Finkel, A. (eds.) CAV 2001. LNCS, vol. 2102, pp. 53–65. Springer, Heidelberg (2001)

142. Morley, M.: Semantics of temporal e. In: Melham, T.F., Moller, F., (eds.): Banff'99 Higher Order Workshop (Formal Methods in Computation), University of Glasgow, Department of Computing Science Technical Report (1999)

143. Eisner, C., Fisman, D.: A Practical Introduction to PSL. Springer (2006)

144. Armoni, R., Bustan, D., Kupferman, O., Vardi, M.: Resets vs. aborts in linear temporal logic. In: Garavel, H., Hatcliff, J. (eds.) TACAS 2003. LNCS, vol. 2619, pp. 65–80. Springer, Heidelberg (2003)

145. Eisner, C., Fisman, D., Havlicek, J., Lustig, Y., McIsaac, A., Van Campenhout, D.: Reasoning with temporal logic on truncated paths. In: Hunt Jr., W.A., Somenzi, F. (eds.) CAV 2003. LNCS, vol. 2725, pp. 27–39. Springer, Heidelberg (2003)

146. Eisner, C., Fisman, D., Havlicek, J., McIsaac, A., Van Campenhout, D.: The definition of a temporal clock operator. In: Baeten, J.C.M., Lenstra, J.K., Parrow, J., Woeginger, G.J. (eds.) ICALP 2003. LNCS, vol. 2719, pp. 857–870. Springer, Heidelberg (2003)

147. Eisner, C., Fisman, D., Havlicek, J.: A topological characterization of weakness. In: Proc. 24th ACM Symp. on Principles of Distributed Computing, pp. 1–8 (2005)

148. Harel, D., Peleg, D.: More on looping vs. repeating in dynamic logic. Inf. Process. Lett. 20(2), 87–90 (1985)

149. Vijayaraghavan, S., Ramanathan, M.: A Practical Guide for SystemVerilog Assertions. Springer (2005)

Reactivity and Grammars: An Exploration

Howard Barringer[1], David Rydeheard[1], and Dov Gabbay[2]

[1] School of Computer Science, University of Manchester, Oxford Road, Manchester,
M13 9PL, UK
{Howard.Barringer,David.Rydeheard}@manchester.ac.uk
[2] Bar Ilan University, Ramat-Gan, 52900, Israel
Department of Informatics, King's College London, Strand, London, WC2R 2LS, UK
University of Luxembourg, Luxembourg, Belgium
School of Computer Science, University of Manchester, Oxford Road, Manchester,
M13 9PL, UK
Dov.Gabbay@kcl.ac.uk

Abstract. We consider the relationship between grammars and formal languages, exploring the following idea: Normally, in the process of deriving a word in a language using a grammar, all structures remain fixed except for the intermediate strings which are changed only by the replacement of substrings. By introducing a more dynamic view of this process, we may allow the grammar to change in various ways as the derivation proceeds, or we may change the notion of application of a rule to a string, or the intermediate strings may be modified between application of rules. We call these more dynamic approaches to language generation 'reactive grammars' and explore, in this paper a range of such reactivities. Some of these are related to previously introduced notions of generative grammars, others appear to be new. We consider the expressivity of various reactive grammars and also their relationship to each other and to other formalisms including modal logic and deontic logic. Reactivity of computational structures has been explored in other areas, e.g. in Kripke structures and in the general areas of evolvable and adaptive systems.

1 Background and Motivation

A standard approach to defining models of computation is to introduce fixed structures over which computation may take place. Such structures include graphs, relations, algebras, grammars, automata, etc. An alternative is to allow the structures themselves to change as computation proceeds. Such computational systems are called 'evolutionary', 'adaptive' or (the term we shall use) 'reactive'. The advantages of this additional flexibility are several: (1) they allow us to model desirable aspects of computation in dynamic settings where we require systems which may reconfigure themselves during computation, (2) they allow us to model the influence of external activity under which computation may have to adapt by changing computational structure, (3) they allow us to re-examine the relationship of a computational model with its semantics and

N. Dershowitz and E. Nissan (Eds.): Choueka Festschrift, Part I, LNCS 8001, pp. 103–155, 2014.
© Springer-Verlag Berlin Heidelberg 2014

(4) reactive systems allow us to establish relationships with other formalisms for dynamic change such as modal and deontic logics. The semantics may be a function computed, or a language generated or recognised, or a logical expression satisfied (e.g. for modal logics and Kripke models). The extra degree of freedom that reactivity introduces allows us additional mechanisms for generating a required semantics. It is this feature of reactive systems that we consider in this paper, where we explore ideas of reactivity in grammars and the relationship of these with the generation of formal languages.

For grammars, reactivity is realised through transformations that interact with the derivation steps by which a grammar generates a word in a language. The interaction may for example, at each step of a derivation, control which grammar rules may be applied, or change the notion of application of a rule to a string, or modify rules as they are used, or transform the intermediate strings as they are generated in a derivation. Introducing such reactive elements into the definitions of grammars allows us to re-examine the mathematical structures involved in language recognition and generation, to relate languages according to their reactive structure as well as their production rules, and to model more dynamically changing computational systems.

Before exploring reactivity in grammars, we briefly consider reactivity in the context of Kripke structures and automata. This is related to some of the forms of reactivity in grammars that we introduce later and has already been studied in [10]. Examples drawn from this study illustrate how different forms of reactivity interact with the semantics of these structures.

A Kripke structure has the form (S, R, a), where S is a non-empty set of worlds, $R \subseteq S \times S$ is the accessibility relation and $a \in S$ is the actual world. The semantic evaluation of a formula φ in a world $t \in S$ is inductively defined and involves values of its subformulas in other worlds s related to t. For example, we have:

$$t \models \Box\varphi \text{ iff in all accessible worlds } s \text{ (i.e. such that } tRs) \text{ we have } s \models \varphi.$$

The above is a static view, not a reactive one. The structure does not change as we evaluate. If we take a dynamic view of the evaluation process, we imagine the structure as a graph with a directed relation R (so aRb is viewed as a directed connection $a \longrightarrow b$). When we stand at point t and we want to evaluate $\Box\varphi$, we view this as an invitation to stroll along the arrows (accessibility relation R), go to the accessible worlds and check φ there. If φ holds in all of these worlds we report that $\Box\varphi$ holds at t. Now this point of view allows us to say that the model can change as we stroll through it from world to world. This is the idea of reactivity.

We adopt a similar point of view for automata. An automaton can be viewed either as a mathematical table M which, when given a state t and a letter σ can move to another state s chosen from $s \in M(t, \sigma)$. A more reactive view is to see the automaton as having some internal "will" and it can change its table M as it reacts to input. So for example if $\{s\} = M(t, \sigma)$ and the automaton gets the input σ three times, then s may become 'exhausted' and the automaton changes to a state $s' \neq s$ when getting the fourth σ. This means that $M(t,\sigma) = \{s'\}$ if σ is a fourth occurrence in the input. See [7].

We have a similar situation with grammars and also with proofs. We use a rule to make a step in a derivation or a proof and the use of this rule may then change the current state of the system. A simple example of such a change is where the rule deactivates itself on use and is then no longer available unless re-activated later.

Note that the reactive change is in response to the history of use and is not a meta-level (possibly time-dependent) intervention. When the changes involve switching rules/arrows on or off, we represent these graphically by double(-headed) arrows, reserving single(-headed) arrows for the transitions, as in the figure below.

State s

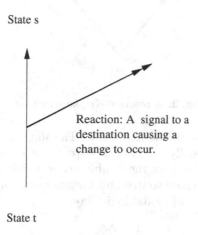

Reaction: A signal to a
destination causing a
change to occur.

State t

Fig. 1. Transition and reaction arrows

Reactivity may be perceived differently from system to system. In some systems, reactivity is perceived as a fault. Consider a washing machine which is continuously being used on the same cycle. If it changes and this overused cycle is no longer available, we see it is as a fault. In some other areas, the reactive point of view is new and offers its own meaning. In normative agent-based systems, the double arrow which changes the system can be viewed as immediate object-level punishment or response to an agent making a forbidden move. With grammars, reactivity is a formal notion. The grammar rules may, for example, get switched 'on' and 'off' depending on which rules are used. This means that the current rules available at any point depend on the history of which rules have been used up to that point. This is not an unusual point of view for grammars and indeed in the early years of automata and grammar investigations, many new grammars were introduced, adopting a computational point of view yielding variations and generalisations. In this paper, using the general theme of reactivity and of computational variation, we explore a range of reactive grammars, some of which have been considered before; others appear to be new.

Example 1 (Kripke semantics). Figure 2 is an example of a Kripke modal logic model.

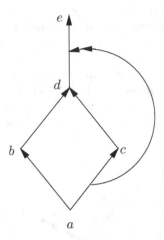

Fig. 2. A reactive Kripke structure

For the moment, ignore the double arrow. The single arrows indicate accessibility. Described traditionally, we have $S = \{a, b, c, d, e\}$ and $R = \{(a, c), (a, b), (b, d), (c, d), (d, e)\}$. We also have the double arrow which is really $R' = \{((a, c), (d, e))\}$, i.e. is an arrow whose source and targets are both arrows.

Now consider a formula of modal logic, say

$$A = \Diamond\Diamond\Box\bot.$$

The evaluation process at node a of the model runs as follows:

$$a \vDash \Diamond\Diamond\Box\bot \text{ iff } \exists x \exists y (aRx \wedge xRy \wedge \forall z(yRz \rightarrow z \vDash \bot))$$
$$\text{iff } \exists x \exists y (aRx \wedge xRy \wedge \sim \exists z(yRz)).$$

This is a static way of looking at the definition. It is a mathematical definition of satisfaction.

Let us adopt a dynamic point of view. We stand at node a and want to check whether $\Diamond\Diamond\Box\bot$ holds at a. We send messages from a to b and from a to c and give them the task to check and report whether $\Diamond\Box\bot$ holds. These messengers in turn send additional messages to d asking whether $\Box\bot$ holds and the people at d send messengers to e to ask whether $\bot$ holds.

The information is passed backwards in the chain and a final decision is made at node a.

Looking at the evaluation process in this way allows for several modifications and practical questions:

1. Are the messengers running in parallel or under any coordination or can one person do the job sequentially?
2. How long does it take to go to the various nodes?
3. How much does it cost to
   (a) move from node to node
   (b) get a value at a node
4. How can things change or go wrong?

The Kripke model is *reactive* if things can change as we traverse the model. The double arrows indicate how things change.

So a double arrow from $(a \rightarrow c)$ to $(d \rightarrow e)$ can indicate that when a messenger moves from a to c then a signal is sent to disconnect the arrow from d to e. So the accessible points that a messenger sees standing at point d depend on the path by which the point was reached. If the journey was via b then e is accessible. If the journey was via c, then the connection $d \rightarrow e$ is cancelled and the step from d to e is not available. Thus in model $\mathbf{m} = (S, R \cup R', a)$, we do have $a \vDash \Diamond\Diamond\Box\bot$, because there is a way to get to d (via c) and in this case $d \vDash \Box\bot$.

The model $\mathbf{m}$ is equivalent to the model depicted in Figure 3.

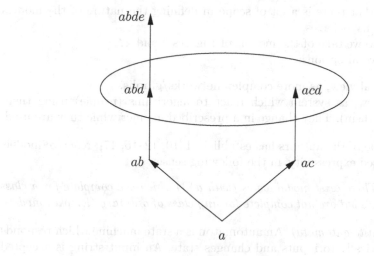

Fig. 3.

The nodes indicate the paths. The circle around abd and acd indicates they are really the same point (i.e. for any atomic q, $abd \vDash q$ iff $acd \vDash q$). Such models (with double arrows) are called *reactive models*.

Figure 4 is a more complicated example of a reactive model. We add in Figure 4 to the double arrow $((a,c),(d,e))$, $R_3 = \{((a,b),((a,c),(d,e)))\}$.

In this model, timing of the movements of the messengers is important. So if the messenger from a to b sets out before the messenger from a to c, then the

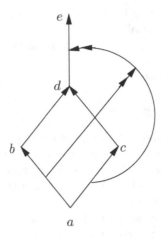

Fig. 4.

double arrow $(a, c) \to (d, e)$ will be cancelled and when the messenger from a to c sets out to c, nothing will happen to the connection $d \to e$.

We see here that there is a lot of scope in defining the nature of the models and how reactivity behaves.

What view do we take of the models of Figures 2 and 4?

There are several options:

1. Mathematical view, as more complex networks/graphs.
2. Reactive view, as system which react to algorithms (people) using them (traversing them). They change in a prescribed manner while they are used.

In fact, as one of the authors has established [10, 12–15, 17], reactive models have an increased expressivity, in the following sense:

Theorem 1. *There exist modal logics (with a $\square$) which are complete for a class of reactive models but are not complete for any class of ordinary (Kripke) models.*

Example 2 (Finite automata). An automaton is a state machine which responds non-deterministically to inputs and changes state. An input string is accepted by the automaton at its initial state, if after responding to the string as input it ends up in a terminal state.

An automaton can be represented by a multimodal Kripke model. Figure 5 is an example of such an automaton with two letter inputs $\{1, 2\}$ and states $\{a, b\}$.

The initial state is a the final state b. Let q be an atom and let q hold only at the final state. The model of Figure 5 has two relations $R_1 = \{(a, a), (a, b)\}$ and $R_2 = \{(b, a)\}$. For any sequence of numbers from $\{1, 2\}$ of the form $x_1, \ldots, x_n$ we can check whether the model satisfies $a \vDash \Diamond_{x_1} \Diamond_{x_2} \ldots \Diamond_{x_n} q$. It accepts words of the form $1^{m_1} 2 1^{m_2} 2 \ldots 1^{m_{k-1}} 2 1^{m_k}$ with $m_1, \ldots, m_k \geq 1$.

If we transfer the reactive idea to automata through the correspondence above, we get that a reactive automaton can change with every move into a

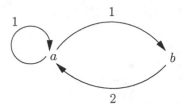

Fig. 5. A simple automaton

new automaton. So given automaton $\mathcal{A}$ at state s, it changes when seeing word σ into a new automaton $\mathcal{A}'$ at state s'.

One conclusion is immediate, any reactive finite automaton is equivalent to another non-reactive ordinary automaton.

We do gain something though:

Theorem 2 ([7]). *Every ordinary automaton with n states $n = p_1 \times \ldots \times p_k$ is equivalent to a reactive automaton with m states, $m = p_1 + \ldots + p_k$.*

Thus, the idea of reactivity of this kind does not allow automata to recognise more sets of words but it does allow us to economize on states.

Example 3 (An infinite state reactive automaton). The Kripke model point of view of automata does allow for a uniform presentation of automata. Consider an (infinite state) automaton for recognising all words of the form $0^n 1^n, n = 0, 1, 2, \ldots$ ($n = 0$ is the empty word). We need some infinity here, that of a stack getting fuller and fuller and then emptier. We can construct this as a reactive model as in Figure 6. The thicker (red) arrows are the transitions of the model; the thinner (blue) arrows are reactivities. Furthermore, all arrows are, by default, self-cancelling, i.e. whenever we traverse an arrow, the arrow is automatically de-activated. Initially, we assume all arrows are off apart from the first upward red arrow from X_0 to X_1. We start walking up from X_0 to X_1. The blue arrows activate the next upward arrow and the return downwards.

Let $q = \Box \bot$. Let X_0 be both the starting point and the terminal point. Then we have that exactly wffs of the form $\Diamond_1^n \Diamond_2^n \Box \bot$ hold at X_0.

Example 4 (An infinite state, with infinite branching, automaton). Consider the model of Figure 7. This corresponds to an infinite reactive automaton which accepts (or generates) $0^n 1^n 2^n \ldots (2k+1)^n, n = 0, 1, 2, \ldots, k = 0, 1, 2, \ldots$.

There are states X_i for $i = 0, 1, \ldots$ and the associated towers of the thicker (red) arrows accept (or generate) the symbols $0, 1, 2, \ldots$, i.e. traversal of the bottom leftmost red arrow from X_0 to X_1 will accept (or generate) a 0, whereas traversal of the red arrow from X_0 to X_1 in the column above 2 will accept (or generate) a 2. State X_0 is the final state. The thinner (blue) arrows are reactivities that flip the activation status of both red and blue arrows. First note that all arrows are self-cancelling, i.e. as an arrow is traversed its activation

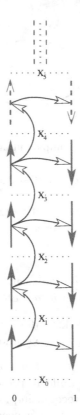

Fig. 6. Reactive model for $0^n 1^n$

status is switched off (and an arrow can only be traversed if its activation status is on). Also, for ease of presentation, we have used a convention that a blue arrow flipping the activation of a red arrow will also flip the activation of all of its associated blue arrows. Thus, for example, the blue arrow labelled (1) will flip the activation of the arrow $X_1 \to X_0$ in the 1 column. Blue arrows are also used to flip the activation status of other blue arrows as, for example, is the case for the arrow labelled (2). Thus, when the red arrow from X_2 to X_1 is traversed in column 1, the arrow labelled (2) flips the activation status of the blue arrow labelled (3). The activation status of all the arrows is off apart from the $X_0 \to X_1$ arrow in column 0 and its three blue reactivity arrows. The automaton then has the following operational behaviour. It can initially traverse the red $X_0 \to X_1$ arrow accepting 0. As a consequence the red arrows $X_1 \to X_2$ in column 0 and $X_1 \to X_0$ in column 1 are switched on. In addition, the blue arrow from $(X_0, X_1) \to (X_1, X_2)$ is switched on. The automaton is then able to either accept a further 0, moving one place up the leftmost tower, or accept a 1 by moving across and down in the second column (labelled 1). The automaton is thus able to accept, say, a sequence of n 0s. Without loss of generality let $n = 4$ and

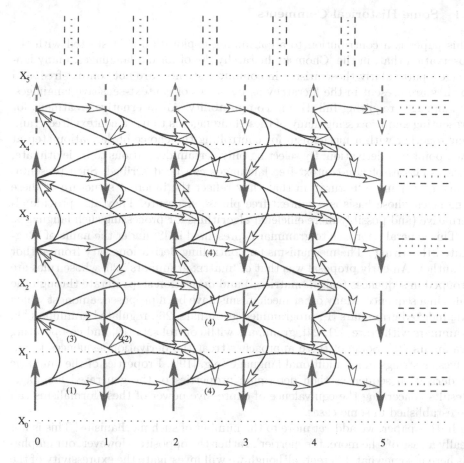

Fig. 7. Infinite reactive automaton for $0^n 1^n 2^n 3^n \ldots (2k+1)^n$

assume that the next symbol accepted is a 1. The machine thus starts moving down the second column labelled 1. However, in order to accept only words of the form $0^4 1^4 2^4 3^4 \ldots$ it must remember the turnaround point. This is encoded by disabling the reactivity $(X_3, X_4) \to (X_4, X_5)$ in the column labelled 2. Note, of course, that similar switching occurred for all lower transitions, however, as we progress down the 1 tower, those reactivities are switched back again with the effect that the automaton will be able to switch, sequentially, the correct number of up going red arrows in the third column. Note also that all the reactivities labelled (4) will have also been switched so that when the red arrows in the third column are traversed the option of immediately descending in the fourth column is removed up to the turnaround point when the machine is back in state X_4. We thus claim this infinite reactive automaton accepts

$$0^n 1^n 2^n \ldots (2k+1)^n, n = 0, 1, 2, \ldots, k = 0, 1, 2, \ldots$$

1.1 Some Historical Comments

This paper is a contribution to a continuing exploration that started with the observation that, in the 'Chomsky hierarchy' [6] of formal languages, many languages, particularly those arising in computer science, are not context-free, and so they are present in the hierarchy as instances of context-sensitive languages, or languages requiring full Turing computability. An alternative treatment for presenting and processing many of these languages is to use a context-free grammar together with a mechanism for controlling the choice of derivation step at each point in a derivation. By selecting only certain derivations to be legitimate, various classes of non-context-free languages can be described. Such presentations appear more 'natural' in that they reflect the inherent structure of these languages whose basis is a context-free phrase structure. They also provide alternative (and possibly more efficient) algorithms for processing such languages.

This general approach to grammar is presented in [8] under the name of 'Regulated Rewriting'. The mechanisms for controlling derivations vary from author to author. An early proposal was that of 'matrix grammars' [20] whose rules are grouped in sequences (called 'matrices') and derivation steps iterate through the rules in a sequence. Many other mechanisms have been proposed, amongst which are: indexed grammars [1], programmed grammars [26], regulated grammars [9], grammars with state [21, 24], grammars with control sets [19] and co-operating grammars [23]. Some of these approaches treat the derivation sequences themselves as strings in an additional language (e.g. [19]). Properties of the language of derivation sequences then determine properties of the generated language. Results concerning the equivalence of expressive power of these formalisms can be established in some cases.

In this paper, we add yet more to the number of such mechanisms! This is not really a case of 'the more, the merrier', rather the opposite. However, our emphasis here is somewhat different, although we will investigate the expressivity of the reactive grammars that we consider. We are interested in the general notion of reactivity in computational systems that may change their behaviour and evolve as computation progresses. There is an increasing focus on the development and analysis of computational systems that exhibit 'evolutionary' behaviour, that is, systems that may either compute normally or may invoke evolutionary changes which can modify the structure of the system itself. For various models of computation, these evolutionary changes take very different forms. For automata consisting of (labelled) transition systems, we have already seen some forms of evolutionary change in examples above. As well as changing the transition relation (i.e. the connectivity of nodes), we may change the labelling, or, if data is stored at nodes, change this data. As a counterpart to reactive automata, we here investigate reactive grammars.

In grammars, normal computation is the process of replacing non-terminals or substrings using the rules of a grammar. The evolutionary steps are the 'reactive elements' which may be introduced into the generation process at various points in the derivation. Reactivity may be present so that (1) at each step of a derivation, we may control which grammar rules may be applied (and this control itself can be of various forms, including additional 'reaction rules' which determine the availability of rules), or (2) we may change the notion of application of a rule to a string, or (3) we may modify rules as they are used, or (4) we may transform intermediate strings as they are generated in a derivation, before applying further rules. We consider some of these cases in this paper. Some of these are equivalent to already introduced forms of grammar, others appear to be new. We also consider examples of what we call 'embedded reactivity' in which substrings of a string can themselves determine changes in either the grammar, the current string or the derivation steps allowed. The extra degree of freedom that reactivity adds allows us to re-examine the mathematical structures involved in language recognition and generation, and to relate languages according to their reactive structure as well as their production rules. We have yet to explore the latter idea.

Reactive grammars have already appeared in applications other than language recognition and generation. For example, in runtime verification of computational systems, reactive rule-based systems arise naturally as in RULER [4] (see also the related EAGLE [3] and METATEM[2] systems). Other non-linguistic areas where non-context-free grammars appear include graph-based problems [25] and modelling biological systems [22].

Our exposition is driven by example – the examples indicate the complex structure of language generation when production rules of grammars are combined with notions of reactivity. We first consider 'switching grammars' and 'switch reactive grammars' in which the use of a grammar rule determines which rules are available for the next derivation step. We then consider 'string transformer grammars' in which each production rule of the grammar has an associated string transformer - a transformation of the string resulting from application of the rule. This is a powerful notion of reactivity and we will show that it can be used to model arbitrary derivation strategies in grammars. Finally, we consider several examples of 'embedded reactivity' in which substrings of a string may determine reactivity. This is all very much an initial exploration of the space of possibilities in this area.

2   Switching Grammars

We begin with a standard definition of grammar:

Definition 1. *A grammar, G, is a four-tuple consisting of a set of non-terminal symbols, N, a set of terminal symbols, Σ, a set of (production) rules, with each rule of the form $\alpha A \beta \to \gamma$ for $A \in N$, $\alpha, \beta, \gamma \in (N \cup \Sigma)^*$, and an initial non-terminal symbol $S \in N$.*

Recall that a grammar is *context-free* if all the production rules are of the form $A \to \gamma$ where $A \in N$ and $\gamma \in (N \cup \Sigma)^*$, and a grammar is *right regular* if all production rules are of the form $A \to wX$ or $A \to w$ with $w \in \Sigma^*$ and $A, X \in N$. A grammar is *linear* when, for each rule, γ contains at most one non-terminal. A grammar is said to be *ϵ-free* (where ϵ is the empty string) when all production rules have $\gamma \in (N \cup \Sigma)^+$.

To begin the exploration of reactivity in grammars, we introduce a very simple form of reactivity in, what we call, *switching grammars*. Here the application of a production rule can switch production rules of the grammar on or off. These are a special case of programmed grammars [26] where only 'success sets' are associated with production rules. The ϵ-free switching grammars are, effectively, an alternative presentation of (ϵ-free) state grammars [21, 24]. This simple form of reactivity is considered here to illustrate some of the issues which arise in reactive grammars and because it is related to other forms of reactivity that we consider, includig 'switch reactive grammars' and 'string transformer grammars'.

Definition 2. *A switching grammar is a tuple consisting of a finite set of non-terminal symbols, N, a finite set of terminal symbols, Σ, a set of rule labels, R, a set of R-labelled production rules P, each rule being of the form $r : \alpha A \beta \to \gamma, \rho$; for $r \in R$, $A \in N$, $\alpha, \beta, \gamma \in (N \cup \Sigma)^*$, $\rho \subseteq R$, together with an initial non-terminal symbol $S \in N$ and an initial rule set $\rho_0 \subseteq R$. A switching grammar is ϵ-free if its production rules have $\gamma \in (N \cup \Sigma)^+$.*

Definition 3. *Let $G = \langle N, \Sigma, R, P, S, \rho_0 \rangle$ be a switching grammar. G derives the string $s\gamma t$ from $s\alpha A\beta t$ and switches from ρ_i to ρ_j in one step (written as $\langle s\alpha A\beta t, \rho_i \rangle \Rightarrow \langle s\gamma t, \rho_j \rangle$) iff for some $r \in \rho_i$, $r : \alpha A\beta \to \gamma, \rho_j \subseteq P$. A word $w \in \Sigma^*$ is derived in G iff there is a sequence of single step derivations $\langle w_0, \rho_0 \rangle \Rightarrow \langle w_1, \rho_1 \rangle \Rightarrow \ldots \Rightarrow \langle w_n, \rho_n \rangle$ such that $w_k \in N \cup \Sigma^*$ and $\rho_k \subseteq R$, for $k \in 0..n$, and $S = w_0$ and $w = w_n$. The language generated by G is the set of its derivable words w.*

Let us look at an example of a switching grammar.

Example 5 (A right regular switching grammar). Consider a switching grammar G where $N = \{A\}$, $\Sigma = \{a, b\}$, $R = \{r_0, r_1, r_2, r_3\}$, the production rule set is

$$\{ \ r_0 : A \to a, \{r_2, r_3\},$$
$$r_1 : A \to aA, \{r_2, r_3\},$$
$$r_2 : A \to b, \{r_0, r_1\},$$
$$r_3 : A \to bA, \{r_0, r_1\}\}$$

with initial non-terminal $S = A$ and initial rule set $\{r_0, r_1\}$. G generates the language $(ab)^*a \cup (ab)^*$.

Note, (a) this is a right regular grammar, and (b) this grammar generates the same language as the (non-switching) right regular grammar $\langle \{A, B\}, \{a, b\}, \{A \to a, A \to aB, B \to b, B \to bA\}, A \rangle$.

The comment in this example suggests the following result.

Theorem 3. *A language is generated by a switching right regular grammar iff it is a regular language.*

Proof. Clearly any right regular grammar can be put as a switching regular grammar. Simply form a production rule set P_R by uniquely labelling each production rule of the regular grammar with a label from R and then make R the initial rule set.

The other direction is established as follows. Let $G = \langle N, \Sigma, R, P, S, \rho_0 \rangle$. Create a new set of non-terminal symbols $N_R = \{n_r \mid n \in N \text{ and } r \in R\} \cup \{S_R\}$. Create a new production rule set

$$Q_R = \{A_r \to u \mid (r : A \to u, \rho) \in P \text{ for } u \in \Sigma^*\} \cup$$
$$\{A_r \to vB_s \mid (r : A \to vB, \rho) \in P \text{ for } v \in \Sigma^* \text{ and } s \in \rho\} \cup$$
$$\{S_R \to S_{r_0} \mid r_0 \in \rho_0\}.$$

By construction, the grammar $G_R = \langle N_R, \Sigma, Q_R, S_R \rangle$ is regular. Furthermore, G_R generates exactly the same set of words as G.

More illustrative of the expressivity of switching grammars is the following example which generates the language $\{a^n b^n c^n \mid n \geq 1\}$. This language is a standard example of a language that cannot be generated by unrestricted rule application in a context-free grammar. There are however simple context-sensitive grammars for this language and, as we shall show below, a range of reactive context-free grammars of various forms which also generate the language. As an example of a context-sensitive grammar for this language, consider the following (non-switching) grammar,

$$S \to aSBC$$
$$S \to aBC$$
$$CB \to BC$$
$$aB \to ab$$
$$bB \to bb$$
$$bC \to bc$$
$$cC \to cc$$

with initial symbol S. Notice that because of the interchange steps (between B's and C's), generating the word $a^n b^n c^n$ requires $O(n^2)$ derivation steps.

Example 6 (The language $\{a^n b^n c^n \mid n \geq 1\}$). Consider a switching context-free grammar generating this language:

$$G = \langle \{A, B, C\}, \{a, b, c\}, \{r_0, r_1, r_2, r_3, r_4\}, P, A, \{r_0\} \rangle$$

where

$$P = \begin{cases} r_0 : A \to BC, \{r_1, r_2\} \\ r_1 : B \to ab, \{r_3\} \\ r_2 : B \to aBb, \{r_4\} \\ r_3 : C \to c, \{\} \\ r_4 : C \to cC, \{r_1, r_2\} \end{cases}$$

The following is an example derivation:

$$A, \{r_0\} \Rightarrow BC, \{r_1, r_2\} \Rightarrow aBbC, \{r_4\} \Rightarrow$$
$$aBbcC, \{r_1, r_2\} \Rightarrow aabbcC, \{r_3\} \Rightarrow aabbcc, \{\}$$

After the first step replacing A by BC, the grammar reacts by only allowing rules which replace B to be applied. The second step replaces B by aBb and then only allows the rule that expands C by cC. And so on. Thus the language generated is $\{a^n b^n c^n \mid n \geq 1\}$.

Theorem 4. *The class of ϵ-free switching context-free grammars is identical to the (ϵ-free) state context-free grammars and hence correspond to the class of context-sensitive languages.*

See Kasai [21] for the relation between state and context-sensitive grammars. The identity of ϵ-free switching context-free grammars and (ϵ-free) context-free state grammars is trivial.

3   Switch Reactive Grammars

In switch reactive Kripke models, the accessibility of one state from another may be turned 'on' and 'off'. In traversing such a structure only the accessibilities currently 'on' or activated are available. Accessibilities are changed according to additional arcs which determine the reactivity. Such reactive arcs may themselves be turned on and off according to other reactive arcs. This produces a typed hierarchy of arcs, the base arcs being the accessibilities between states.

We now turn to grammars which have an analogous reactivity, extending that of switching grammars. We call these *switch reactive grammars*. It turns out that there is a range of possibilities which we explore here.

The idea is that associated with each production rule in a grammar is a set of 'reaction rules' which determine what rules (production rules and reaction rules) are active (or 'available') at the next step. Reaction rules may themselves have associated reaction rules.

The possibilities here are generated by the following issues:

1. Base rules and reaction rules. We may wish to distinguish the way that rules operate according to whether they are

- base rules, which include the production rules of the grammar, but also may include additional rules for the presentation of grammars,
- reaction rules, whose role is the activation and de-activation of other rules, including reaction rules.

Thus a grammar consists, in general, of a base grammar and a collection of reaction rules.

2. Transient and persistent rules. What happens to an active rule when it is used (or 'fired')? It may

- become de-activated – this is the case of *transient* rules,
- remain activated – this is the case of *persistent* rules.

The transience or persistency of rules may vary either (a) by allowing both forms in a grammar (defining the nature of each rule), or (b) by distinguishing base rules from reaction rules.

3. Operation of reaction rules. There are various possibilities as to how the reaction rules operate: They may

- switch (or 'flip') the activation status of the target rule when the source rule fires – turning on rules that are off, and turning off rules that are on.
- act only 'positively' i.e. turn on target rules that are off and leave target rules on that are on (these may then be turned off by firing, if they are transient).

Let us now look at example of these various cases.

Example 7 (Transient base rules, persistent reactivity and switching reaction rules). Consider a grammar for the language $\{a^n b^n \mid n \geq 1\}$. It has production rules:

$$c_0 : S \rightarrow AB$$
$$c_1 : A \rightarrow a$$
$$c_2 : A \rightarrow aA$$
$$c_3 : B \rightarrow b$$
$$c_4 : B \rightarrow bB$$

The reaction rules are:

$$r_0 : c_0 \rightarrow c_1, c_2$$
$$r_1 : c_1 \rightarrow c_2, c_3$$
$$r_2 : c_2 \rightarrow c_1, c_4$$
$$r_3 : c_4 \rightarrow c_1, c_2$$

Let the rules that are initially 'on' be c_0 together with all the reaction rules. Let the base rules be transient and the reaction rules be persistent. Finally, let the reaction rules operate by switching: flipping the on/off status.

Initially, rule c_0 fires (and becomes de-activated). The reaction rule for c_0 is r_0, which thus flips the status of c_1 and c_2, turning both on. At the next step, if c_1 is fired (and is then de-activated), rule c_2 is switched off and rule c_3 switched on, to generate the string ab. Alternatively, if c_2 is fired (and is then de-activated), rule c_1 is switched off and rule c_4 switched on, to generate the string $aAbB$. Then c_1 and c_2 are activated to continue the derivation.

This scheme may be extended to generate the non-context-free language $\{a^n b^n c^n \mid n \geq 1\}$.

The above grammar is directly equivalent to (has the same derivations as) the standard switching grammar:

$$c_0 : S \rightarrow AB, \ \{c_0, c_1\}$$
$$c_1 : A \rightarrow a, \ \{c_3\}$$
$$c_2 : A \rightarrow aA, \ \{c_4\}$$
$$c_3 : B \rightarrow b, \ \{\}$$
$$c_4 : B \rightarrow bB, \ \{c_1, c_2\}$$

Notice however, that the reaction mechanisms are different. In the case of the switching grammar, at each step, all rules are turned off and only then is the set of rules for the next step turned on.

In this example then, introducing reaction rules does not result in anything more than standard switching grammars.

Let us now consider an example of a different form.

Example 8 (All rules persistent, switching reaction rules). Here, all rules are persistent and reaction works by 'flipping' the activation state of its target arrow.

$$c_0 : S_0 \to aS_1$$
$$c_1 : S_1 \to bS_2$$
$$c_2 : S_2 \to dS_2$$
$$c_3 : S_2 \to c$$

The reaction rule is:

$$r : c_2 \to c_3$$

Let all the rules be 'on' initially. Then rule c_3 is 'on' only after an even number of firings of rule c_2. So the language generated is $\{abd^{2n}c \,|\, n \geq 0\}$.

This reactive grammar is directly equivalent to (i.e. has the same derivations as) the normal grammar:

$$c_0 : S_0 \to aS_1$$
$$c_1 : S_1 \to bS_2$$
$$c_2 : S_2 \to dS_2'$$
$$c_2 : S_2' \to dS_2$$
$$c_3 : S_2 \to c$$

In fact, for this form of reactivity, even for higher-order reactivity (when reaction rules act on reaction rules), it appears that the grammar is equivalent, by an expansion and copying technique, to a normal (non-reactive) grammar.

Let us consider another form of switch reactive grammar. In this case, all rules are transient.

Example 9 (All rules transient, switching reaction rules). Let us consider again the language of Example 1, $\{a^n b^n \,|\, n \geq 1\}$. The base rules are the same:

$$c_0 : S \to AB$$
$$c_1 : A \to a$$
$$c_2 : A \to aA$$
$$c_3 : B \to b$$
$$c_4 : B \to bB$$

with c_0 initially 'on'. Let us see how to add transient reaction rules so that this grammar is restricted to generate the required language. Consider, for example, the rule c_2. Part of its reaction is to switch rule c_4 together with all its reaction rules. But the latter reaction rules include a rule to switch rule c_2 and all its reaction rules...

So far, we have labelled the reaction rules with *rule names*, but they have not been used. Now, in order to describe this dependency of reaction rules on others, the names are crucial and allow us to define this via mutual recursion, as follows:

$$r_0 : c_0 \rightarrow c_1, c_2, r_1, r_2$$
$$r_1 : c_1 \rightarrow c_2, c_3, r_2$$
$$r_2 : c_2 \rightarrow c_1, c_4, r_1, r_4$$
$$r_3 :$$
$$r_4 : c_4 \rightarrow c_1, c_2, r_1, r_2$$

The rule name r_3 labels an empty rule. Notice that r_2 changes the activation of r_4 and vice versa. Initially r_0 is active. A derivation proceeds by firing c_0, which then activates c_1 and c_2 via reaction rule r_0. If c_1 then fires, c_2 is turned off and c_3 turned on via reaction rule r_1, etc.

Notice, that *if no rule names are introduced for the reaction rules* and instead we use a hierarchical assembly of 'reactions' of the form $c_0 \rightarrow c_1, c_2$, then the mutual recursion can only be expressed through infinite rules or an infinite set of rules.

In fact, grammars of the form in Example 3 are equivalent to switching grammars, as we now show.

Example 10 (Example 3 continued). First notice that switching grammars specify only which rules are to be active at the next step, instead of the 'flipping' reactivity used in Example 3. However, we can convert Example 3 to this positive form of reaction, in which case the grammar is:

$$c_0 : S \rightarrow AB$$
$$c_1 : A \rightarrow a$$
$$c_2 : A \rightarrow aA$$
$$c_3 : B \rightarrow b$$
$$c_4 : B \rightarrow bB$$

$$r_0 : c_0 \rightarrow c_1, c_2, r_1, r_2$$
$$r_1 : c_1 \rightarrow c_3$$
$$r_2 : c_2 \rightarrow c_4, r_4$$
$$r_3 :$$
$$r_4 : c_4 \rightarrow c_1, c_2, r_1, r_2$$

From this combination of base rules and the reaction rules, we construct a switching grammar whose labels are derived from those of the base and reaction rules as follows:

$$c_{0r_0} : S \rightarrow AB, \{c_{1r_1}, c_{2r_2}\}$$
$$c_{1r_1} : A \rightarrow a, \{c_{3r_3}\}$$
$$c_{2r_2} : A \rightarrow aA, \{c_{4r_4}\}$$
$$c_{3r_3} : B \rightarrow b, \{\}$$
$$c_{4r_4} : B \rightarrow bB, \{c_{1r_1}, c_{2r_2}\}$$

In summary, we have explored various types of switch reactive grammars and shown their equivalence to normal non-reactive grammars or to switching grammars. Some of these conversions are economical (do not lead to a great expansion of the grammar). Others (e.g. Example 2) are less so.

4   A Reduction Result

We present a result showing how, using switch reactive grammars, a linear grammar may be reduced, in terms of the number of non-terminal symbols, to a reactive linear grammar generating the same language. In fact, we establish a 'simulation' between a grammar and its reduction. The reduction in the number of non-terminal symbols is considerable: from k^n to kn. The form of switch reactive grammars used is that all rules are transient (or self-cancelling), i.e. as soon as a rule is fired its activation status is switched off. Reaction rules are switching, i.e. change the activation status of their targets.

Theorem 5. *A linear grammar G with k^n non-terminal symbols can be simulated by a linear switch reactive grammar $\mathbb{T}(G)$ with kn non-terminal symbols.*

Proof outline. Suppose G is a linear grammar with k^n non-terminal symbols – i.e. the non-terminals are in an n-dimensional cube of k-entries in each dimension, so each non-terminal symbol may be represented as an n-tuple of symbols from k sets.

Let $[a^i_j]$ be a matrix of distinct elements for $i = 1, \ldots, n$ and $j = 1, \ldots, k$. Let $x = (x_1, \ldots, x_n)$ be a vector such that $x_i \in \{a^i_1, \ldots, a^i_k\}$. There are exactly k^n such vectors.

We construct a reactive grammar $\mathbb{T}(G)$ with non-terminals $[a^i_j]$ which simulates G.

Let us show how it is done for the case $k = 3$, $n = 5$ (these numbers are chosen simply to allow us to draw the appropriate figures).

The aim is to simulate the effect of the rule of G

$$x \to w_1 y w_2$$

where w_1 and w_2 are terminal letters. (For regular grammars, consider rules of the form $x \to y w_2$ instead.)

Let $x = (x_1, \ldots, x_n)$ and $y = (y_1, \ldots, y_n)$. The construction is illustrated in Figure 8. The arrows in this diagram are grouped into various types:

Group 1. These are the (red) vertical arrows $(x_i, x_{i+1}) : x_i \to x_{i+1}$, $i = 1, 2, 3, 4$ and $(y_j, y_{j+1}) : y_j \to y_{j+1}$, $j = 1, 2, 3, 4$. They can be either on or off. Each chain of such arrows forms the basis of the encoding of a non-terminal from the original grammar.

Group 2. The possibly multi-targetted (blue) arrows are reactivity arrows. The source is an arrow and the target is a set of arrows, e.g. $(\alpha, \{\beta_1, \beta_2, \ldots, \beta_m\})$. This reads as follows: if you use the rule α then flip on or off the activation status of the target rules $\beta_1, \ldots, \beta_m$, e.g. if β_1 is on, flip to off, or if it is off, flip it to on.

Group 3. Other arrows connect arrows of any group to those of any group. For example the multi-targetted (green) bold-face arrow in the diagram marked (3) denotes the grammar rule $x_5 \to w_1 y_1 w_2$.

Note the following: The vector $x = (x_1, x_2, x_3, x_4, x_5)$ is a non-terminal of G. This is represented in the diagram by the left-hand side, with the vertical

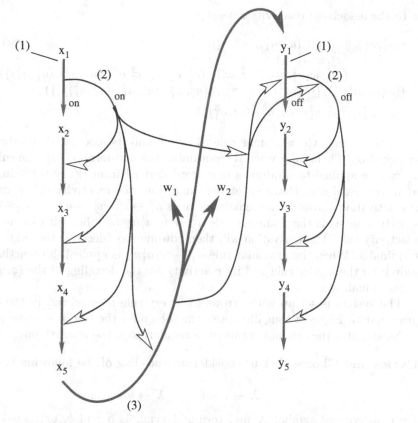

Fig. 8. An example of the construction for a rule of G

arrows, and the hierarchy of curved arrows between them. The last curved arrow, to $(x_4 \to x_5)$, contains all the information of the vector x. So from this arrow, we send arrows to activate y and all its arrows.

How do we simulate $x \to w_1 y w_2$? As an example, let the non-terminal x be encoded by the vector $(a_1^1, a_1^2, a_2^3, a_1^4, a_3^5)$ of non-terminals from the reduced grammar and y encoded by the vector $(a_1^1, a_2^2, a_1^3, a_1^4, a_1^5)$. Thus the original grammar rule $x \to w_1 y w_2$ is transformed to the following collection of grammar rules

$$a_1^1 \to a_1^2$$
$$a_1^2 \to a_2^3$$
$$a_2^3 \to a_1^4$$
$$a_1^4 \to a_3^5$$
$$a_3^5 \to w_1 a_1^1 w_2$$
$$a_1^1 \to a_2^2$$
$$a_2^2 \to a_1^3$$
$$a_1^3 \to a_1^4$$
$$a_1^4 \to a_1^5$$

with the associated reactivity rules

$$((a_1^1, a_1^2), \{(a_1^2, a_2^3), (a_2^3, a_1^4), (a_1^4, a_3^5),$$
$$(a_3^5, w_1 a_1^1 w_2),$$
$$((a_3^5, w_1 a_1^1 w_2), \{(a_1^1, a_2^2), ((a_1^1, a_2^2), \{(a_2^2, a_1^3), (a_1^3, a_1^4), (a_1^4, a_1^5)\})\})\})\})$$
$$((a_3^5, w_1 a_1^1 w_2), \{(a_1^1, a_2^2), ((a_1^1, a_2^2), \{(a_2^2, a_1^3), (a_1^3, a_1^4), (a_1^4, a_1^5)\})\})$$
$$((a_1^1, a_2^2), \{(a_2^2, a_1^3), (a_1^3, a_1^4), (a_1^4, a_1^5)\})$$

We start with the grammar rule $a_1^1 \to a_1^2$ and its associated reactivity rule switched on. Then, for a word W containing the non-terminal a_1^1, the rule $a_1^1 \to a_1^2$ can be applied to produce a new word derived from W by replacing a_1^1 by a_1^2 in the usual way. However, at the same time, the reactivity rule is fired and the activation status of the remaining rules $a_1^2 \to a_2^3$, $a_2^3 \to a_1^4$ and $a_1^4 \to a_3^5$ are switched on, as is the grammar rule $a_3^5 \to w_1 a_1^1 w_2$ together with its associated reactivity rule. The derivation will then continue to "decode" the original non-terminal x. When the grammar rule $a_3^5 \to w_1 a_1^1 w_2$ is applied, its reactivity will switch on the header rule and its reactivity for the decoding of the (original) y nonterminal.

The system is set up with arrows for every rule $u \to w_1' v w_2'$ in the original grammar G. Figure 8 thus illustrates the set-up for the rule $x \to w_1 y w_2$.

Note that if the original grammar is regular, so is the reactive one.

Cycles and Choice. Let us consider an encoding of the following two linear rules

$$X \to a \qquad\qquad X \to bX$$

for non-terminal symbol X and terminal symbols a and b, extracted from a grammar with 5^4 non-terminals. The reactive grammar will encode the non-terminals of the grammar as vectors of length 4.

For ease of initial presentation, we label each grammar and reactivity rule for the reactive linear (sub)grammar depicted in Figure 9.

Grammar rules

$$g_1 : x_1 \to x_2$$
$$g_2 : x_2 \to x_3$$
$$g_3 : x_3 \to x_4$$
$$g_4 : x_4 \to b$$
$$g_5 : x_4 \to ax_1$$

Reactivities

$$r_1 : (g_1, \{g_2, g_3, g_4, r_4, g_5, r_5\})$$
$$r_4 : (g_4, \{g_5, r_5\})$$
$$r_5 : (g_5, \{g_4, r_4, g_1, r_1\})$$

A rule can be named by its source and target, e.g. g_1 by (x_1, x_2), hence, the above can be represented by labelling just one rule, as below.

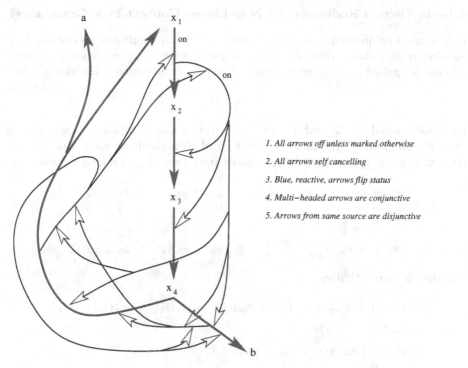

1. All arrows off unless marked otherwise

2. All arrows self cancelling

3. Blue, reactive, arrows flip status

4. Multi-headed arrows are conjunctive

5. Arrows from same source are disjunctive

Fig. 9. Cycle and choice

Grammar rules

$$x_1 \rightarrow x_2$$
$$x_2 \rightarrow x_3$$
$$x_3 \rightarrow x_4$$
$$x_4 \rightarrow b$$
$$x_4 \rightarrow ax_1$$

Reactivities

$$((x_1, x_2), \{ (x_2, x_3), (x_3, x_4),$$
$$(x_4, b), ((x_4, b), \{(x_4, ax_1), r_5\}),$$
$$(x_4, ax_1), r_5\})$$
$$r_5 : ((x_4, ax_1), \{ (x_4, b), ((x_4, b), \{(x_4, ax_1), r_5\}),$$
$$(x_1, x_2), ((x_1, x_2), \{ (x_2, x_3), (x_3, x_4),$$
$$(x_4, b), ((x_4, b), \{(x_4, ax_1), r_5\}),$$
$$(x_4, ax_1), r_5\})\})$$

Whilst the above example encodings indicate how a linear grammar with k^n non-terminals can be represented by a reactive linear grammar with kn non-terminals, it is clear there may be a very large number of reactivity rules. Furthermore, the reactivities will be mutually recursive as soon as there are non-terminal cycles in the original grammar, as illustrated in the above example.

4.1   Is There a Reduction for Non-Linear Context-Free Grammars?

It is natural to question whether a similar reduction result can be obtained for non-linear grammars. Here we briefly explore what happens when the above scheme is applied to non-linear context-free production rules. Consider a rule

$$X \rightarrow YZ$$

for non-terminals X, Y and Z. Let the vector of non-terminals $(x_1, x_2, \ldots, x_n)$ from the simulating grammar encode X, and then similarly for Y and Z. The context-free rule would then be translated into a set of grammar rules such as

$$
\begin{array}{llll}
x_1 \rightarrow x_2 & x_n \rightarrow y_1 z_2 & y_1 \rightarrow y_2 & z_1 \rightarrow z_2 \\
x_2 \rightarrow x_3 & & y_2 \rightarrow y_3 & z_2 \rightarrow z_3 \\
\vdots & & \vdots & \vdots \\
x_{n-1} \rightarrow x_n & & y_{n-1} \rightarrow y_n & z_{n-1} \rightarrow z_n
\end{array}
$$

together with reactivities

$$((x_1, x_2), \{(x_2, x_3), \ldots (x_{n-1}, x_n), (x_n, y_1 z_1), ((x_n, y_1 z_1), \{\ldots\})\})$$
$$((x_n, y_1 z_1), \{\ldots\})$$
$$((y_1, y_2), \{(y_2, y_3), \ldots (y_{n-1}, y_n), \ldots\})$$
$$((z_1, z_2), \{(z_2, z_3), \ldots (z_{n-1}, z_n), \ldots\})$$

Superficially this seems adequate. Unfortunately, there are problems. Firstly it is important to remember that, for any given i, the non-terminals denoted by x_i, y_i and z_i are not necessarily disjoint (of course, those from different levels in the encoding chain are necessarily disjoint). Since the non-terminals Y and Z are jointly active, there may be conflict between their respective encoding chains. For example, if $y_1 = z_1 = a_1^1$ and $y_2 = z_2 = a_3^2$ then the application of the rule $y_1 \rightarrow y_2$ to the derived word $y_1 z_1$ will deactivate itself (all rules are self cancelling) with the consequence that the rule $z_1 \rightarrow z_2$ is deactivated. Thus the Z non-terminal will not get "decoded" and applied.

The above reduction result works for linear grammars because there is only one non-terminal present (i.e. active) in a derived word. This therefore suggests that perhaps the context-free case can be made to work by encoding, for example, a leftmost derivation strategy in which only the leftmost non-terminal in a derived word is allowed to be active. This would require a mechanism to ensure that the decoding rules and reactivities associated with non-leftmost non-terminals are disabled until the leftmost non-terminal has been fully expanded. Consider again the rule $X \rightarrow YZ$ in the original grammar. For the situation where the sets of non-terminals derived from Y and Z are always disjoint, then this is possible. However, in general, there may be dependencies between the Y and Z non-terminals, as in Figure 10 which then require a stack in order to determine when a derivation from a non-terminal has been completed.

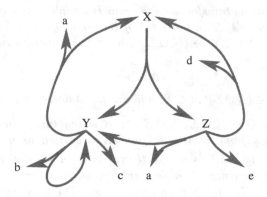

Fig. 10. Non-terminal Graph

5 String Transformer Grammars

We now consider a quite different example of reactivity in grammars in which each string produced by the application of a rule may undergo a transformation before further rules may be applied. Such transformations may be thought of as 'mutations' of a string in which case their occurrence is spontaneous and unpredictable, or as a form of 'corruption' caused by, say, noise or other forms of degradation, in which case transformations of each string may be 'small' but unavoidable.

In fact, we consider a general formulation of such grammars which covers various interpretations of the string transformations. To do so we introduce a set of string transformers and define *string transformer grammars* in terms of rules where each rule has an associated string transformer. After application of the rule, the string undergoes the associated transformation before application of further rules. Special cases are standard grammars where no transformation takes place (i.e. allowing only the identity transformation), the case when transformations are independent of the rules used, and the case where string transformations may apply optionally. We concentrate our attention on certain forms of string transformations – those induced by actions on the non-terminal symbols in a string, which therefore interact directly with the application of rules.

Introducing this form of reactivity into grammars may considerably extend the expressivity of grammars. We begin to explore the classification of string transformer grammars. Moreover, this reactivity introduces an additional 'degree of freedom' into grammars and we consider how varying the string transformations affects the language generated.

Definition 4. *A string transformer grammar is a tuple consisting of a finite set of non-terminal symbols, N, a finite set of terminal symbols, Σ, a set of string transformers, $T \subseteq (N \cup \Sigma)^* \to (N \cup \Sigma)^*$, a set of production rules P with each rule of the form*

$$\alpha A \beta \xrightarrow{t} \gamma$$

for $A \in N$, $\alpha, \beta, \gamma \in (N \cup \Sigma)^*$, $t \in T$, and an initial non-terminal symbol $S \in N$.

Definition 5. *Let $G = \langle N, \Sigma, T, P, S \rangle$ be a string transformer grammar. G derives the string s from $u\alpha A\beta v$ in one step (written as $u\alpha A\beta v \Rightarrow s$) for $u, v, s \in (N \cup \Sigma)^*$ iff $\alpha A \beta \xrightarrow{t} \gamma$ and $t(u\gamma v) = s$. A word $w \in \Sigma^*$ is derived in G iff there is a sequence of single step derivations $s_0 \Rightarrow \ldots s_k \Rightarrow \ldots \Rightarrow s_n$ such that $s_k \in (N \cup \Sigma)^*$ and $S = s_0$ and $w = s_n$. The language generated by G is the set of its derivable words w.*

Note that the strings resulting from the application of string transformers need not be (and will not be, in general) strings generated from the underlying grammar. The definition is very general in terms of the string transformers that are considered, allowing any function from the set of strings of terminals and non-terminal symbols to itself. As a consequence, if we wish to consider ϵ-freeness in this context, we need a modified definition. Restricted forms of string transformations are of particular interest. One such restriction is to limit string transformations to those that are induced by functions $f : N \to N$ from non-terminal symbols to non-terminal symbols. Such a function induces a string transformation by replacing each non-terminal symbol X in a string with the non-terminal symbol $f(X)$. Notice that interchanging non-terminal symbols in this way interacts with the application of production rules. It is in this interaction that we find new forms of expressivity of grammars. Often the form of the functions on non-terminal symbols that we consider may be succinctly expressed in terms of labelled symbols, that is the non-terminal symbols are of the form $\langle X, l \rangle$ with n a symbol and l a label from a label set Λ. A label transformer $f : \Lambda \to \Lambda$ defines a function f^* on these non-terminal symbols in an obvious way $f^*\langle X, l \rangle = \langle X, f(l) \rangle$.

Let us look at a few examples of string transformer grammars to show how words are generated and illustrate the power of these grammars.

First consider a right regular grammar written with labelled non-terminal symbols:

Example 11 (Odds and Evens). Consider the following string transformer grammar with labelled non-terminal symbols

$$G = \langle \{S\} \times \{even, odd\}, \{a\}, \{t_1, t_2, t_3\}, P, \langle S, even \rangle \rangle$$

where the set of production rules P is

$$\langle S, even \rangle \xrightarrow{t} a\langle S, odd \rangle$$
$$\langle S, odd \rangle \xrightarrow{t} a$$
$$\langle S, odd \rangle \xrightarrow{t} a\langle S, even \rangle$$

Notice that, for this example, all the rules have the same associated string transformer. When t is the identity function it is easy to see that G generates the language $\{a^{2n} \mid n > 0\}$. What do we get for non-identity transformers? Defining the transformers as functions on the label set, there are three other transformations to consider:

1. When $t = \{even \mapsto even, odd \mapsto even\}$, the first rule application yields the string $a\langle S, even\rangle$ since the generated label of S is odd which is then transformed under t to $even$. No finite word can therefore be generated and the language generated is thus empty.
2. $t = \{even \mapsto odd, odd \mapsto even\}$ also generates the empty language for the same reason.
3. $t = \{even \mapsto odd, odd \mapsto odd\}$ generates the language $\{a^{n+1} \mid n > 0\}$.

We may associate different string transformers with each production rule, as in the next example. Consider the above production rules, but with differing string transformers:

$$\langle S, even\rangle \xrightarrow{t_1} a\langle S, odd\rangle$$
$$\langle S, odd\rangle \xrightarrow{t_2} a$$
$$\langle S, odd\rangle \xrightarrow{t_3} a\langle S, even\rangle$$

where the string transformers are defined by the following functions on labels:

$$t_1 : \quad \{even \mapsto even, odd \mapsto even\}$$
$$t_2 : \quad \{even \mapsto odd, odd \mapsto even\}$$
$$t_3 : \quad \{even \mapsto odd, odd \mapsto odd\}.$$

The grammar generates the set of words $\{a^n \mid n > 0\}$.

Notice that, in these examples, each right regular grammar generates a regular language. This is, in fact, a general result.

Theorem 6. *The class of languages generated by right regular string transformer grammars whose transformers are defined by functions on non-terminal symbols coincides with regular languages.*

Theorem 7. *Given two right regular grammars G_1 and G_2 that generate languages $\mathcal{L}_1$ and $\mathcal{L}_2$ respectively, there is a right regular string transformer grammar G with an identity string transformer which generates $\mathcal{L}_1$ and for which a different string transformer t makes G generate the language $\mathcal{L}_2$, moreover t is induced by a function on non-terminal symbols.*

Proof. Without loss of generality we assume that the regular grammars G_1 and G_2 have disjoint non-terminal sets apart from their initial non-terminal symbol S. Let $G_i = \langle N_i, \Sigma_i, P_i, S\rangle$ for $i = 1, 2$. Construct a string transformer grammar $G_l = \langle N_1 \cup N_2, \{1, 2\}, \Sigma_1 \cup \Sigma_2, \{\iota\}, S_l, 1\rangle$ where the production rules in P are given by the set

$$\{\langle S_l, 1\rangle \xrightarrow{\iota} \langle S, 1\rangle\} \cup$$
$$\{\langle X, 1\rangle \xrightarrow{\iota} \alpha[\langle Y, 1\rangle] \mid X \rightarrow \alpha(Y) \in P_1, \; X, Y \in N_1\} \cup$$
$$\{\langle X, 2\rangle \xrightarrow{\iota} \alpha[\langle Y, 2\rangle] \mid X \rightarrow \alpha(Y) \in P_2, \; X, Y \in N_2\}$$

and ι is the identity string transformer. It is easy to see that G_l will generate the language of G_1.

Now replace the transformation ι by that defined by the relabelling $\{1 \mapsto 2, 2 \mapsto 2\}$. This revised grammar now generates the language of G_2.

It is not the case that any standard grammar that generates a regular language also generates a regular language when extended with string transformers, even those defined by functions on non-terminal symbols.

We illustrate this with an example which also shows that a very simple grammar with simple string transformers can generate fairly complex languages. Indeed, our experience is that even in simple cases of string transformer grammars it is often very difficult to determine what the language generated is.

Example 12 (A simple grammar for a complex language). The context-free grammar

$$G = \langle \{S, A, B\}, \{a, b\}, P, S \rangle$$

where P is the set of production rules

$$S \to AB$$
$$A \to aA$$
$$A \to a$$
$$B \to b$$

generates the regular language $\{a^n b \mid n > 0\}$. A regular grammar for the same language is straightforward to define, for example:

$$S \to aS$$
$$S \to b$$

with S as the only non-terminal symbol and hence initial symbol. As an example of a string transformer grammar consider associating with each rule the string transformer induced by the function $\{A \mapsto B, B \mapsto A\}$ on non-terminal symbols. Different derivation strategies give rise to different languages. The language generated by just leftmost derivations is $\{bb\}$ for we have only one derivation, namely:

$$S \Rightarrow BA \Rightarrow bB \Rightarrow bb$$

Note that $S \Rightarrow BA$ since $S \to AB$ and the transformation then yields the string BA. Similarly, $BA \Rightarrow bB$ as $B \to b$ and hence BA produces the bA which is then transformed to the string bB. The language generated by just rightmost derivations is $\{aa, aba, bab\}$, for we have

$$S \Rightarrow BA \Rightarrow Aa \Rightarrow aa$$
$$S \Rightarrow BA \Rightarrow Aa \Rightarrow aBa \Rightarrow aba$$
$$S \Rightarrow BA \Rightarrow AaB \Rightarrow Bab \Rightarrow bab$$

Note that both the above are regular languages. Consider now, however, the language generated through the unrestricted use of production rules. Here is an exhaustive list of derivations beginning with the initial symbol S.

$$S \Rightarrow BA \Rightarrow bB \Rightarrow bb$$
$$S \Rightarrow BA \Rightarrow Aa \Rightarrow aa$$
$$S \Rightarrow BA \Rightarrow Aa \Rightarrow aBa \Rightarrow aba$$
$$S \Rightarrow BA \Rightarrow AaB \Rightarrow aaA \Rightarrow aaa$$
$$S \Rightarrow BA \Rightarrow AaB \Rightarrow aaA \Rightarrow aaaB \Rightarrow aaab$$
$$S \Rightarrow BA \Rightarrow AaB \Rightarrow aBaA \ldots$$
$$S \Rightarrow BA \Rightarrow AaB \Rightarrow Bab \Rightarrow bab$$

All bar the sixth branch are complete derivations. The partial derivation given by the sixth branch has been stopped at a point at which it recurses. The above set is sufficient for us to obtain a description of the generated language in a closed form. Before doing so, let us continue the derivation from $aBaA$ for one more unfolding of the derivation tree to $aaBaaA$.

$$\ldots aBaA \Rightarrow abaB \Rightarrow abab$$
$$\ldots aBaA \Rightarrow aAaa \Rightarrow aaaa$$
$$\ldots aBaA \Rightarrow aAaa \Rightarrow aaBaa \Rightarrow aabaa$$
$$\ldots aBaA \Rightarrow aAaaB \Rightarrow aaaaA \Rightarrow aaaaa$$
$$\ldots aBaA \Rightarrow aAaaB \Rightarrow aaaaA \Rightarrow aaaaaB \Rightarrow aaaaab$$
$$\ldots aBaA \Rightarrow aAaaB \Rightarrow aaBaaA \ldots$$
$$\ldots aBaA \Rightarrow aAaaB \Rightarrow aBaab \Rightarrow abaab$$

If we examine the form of this recursion, we find that the language (of finite words) generated may be expressed in the following closed form:

$$\{a^n ba^n b \cup aaa^n \cup a^{n+1}ba^{n+1} \cup aaa(aa)^n b \cup a^n ba^{n+1}b \mid n \geq 0\}$$

The first term specifies the words derivable via the the first branch; the second term covers words derivable via the second and fourth branches; the third term covers those words derivable via the third branch; the fourth term for the fifth branch; and finally the fifth term covers those words derivable via the seventh branch. Note that the terms denote disjoint sets of finite words. The pumping lemma for regular languages can be used to show that the language is not regular.

In Example 6, we saw that switching context-free grammars can define languages beyond context-free, using the example of $a^n b^n c^n$. We now revisit this language showing how it may be defined using a context-free string transformer grammar. In fact, there are many ways of generating this language using simple string transformer languages, each corresponding to a restricted derivation strategy. This suggest a general result which we present later and which relates derivation strategies to string transformer grammars.

Example 13 (The language $\{a^n b^n c^n \mid n \geq 1\}$ again). In this example, we show how the labelling and associated transformers can be used to control the derivation and therefore restrict the language associated with a grammar. The context-free grammar $G = \langle \{A, B, C, S\}, \{a, b, c\}, P, S \rangle$ where P is the set of production rules

$$
\begin{aligned}
1 &: \quad S \rightarrow ABC \\
2 &: \quad A \rightarrow a \\
3 &: \quad A \rightarrow aA \\
4 &: \quad B \rightarrow b \\
5 &: \quad B \rightarrow bB \\
6 &: \quad C \rightarrow c \\
7 &: \quad C \rightarrow cC
\end{aligned}
$$

generates the language $a^n b^m c^l$ for $n, m, l \in \mathbb{N}$. Let us now consider a labelled version of this in which functions on the labels are used to ensure that the production rules numbered 3, 5 and 7 are always applied in that sequential order and, similarly, the rules numbered 2, 4 and 6 are applied sequentially. These constraints ensure that the only words generated are those for which $n = m = l$ holds.

More formally, define the string transformer grammar

$$
G = \langle \{A, B, C, S\} \times \{0, 1, 2, 3, 4\}, \{a, b, c\}, \{t_1, t_2, t_3\}, P, S, 0 \rangle
$$

where P is the set of production rules

$$
\begin{aligned}
1 &: \quad \langle S, 0 \rangle \xrightarrow{t_1} \langle A, 1 \rangle \langle B, 0 \rangle \langle C, 2 \rangle \\
2 &: \quad \langle A, 2 \rangle \xrightarrow{t_2} a \\
3 &: \quad \langle A, 2 \rangle \xrightarrow{t_1} a \langle A, 2 \rangle \\
4 &: \quad \langle B, 3 \rangle \xrightarrow{t_3} b \\
5 &: \quad \langle B, 2 \rangle \xrightarrow{t_1} b \langle B, 2 \rangle \\
6 &: \quad \langle C, 4 \rangle \xrightarrow{t_3} c \\
7 &: \quad \langle C, 2 \rangle \xrightarrow{t_1} c \langle C, 2 \rangle
\end{aligned}
$$

and the functions on non-terminal symbols are defined the following label transformers:

$$
\begin{aligned}
&t_1 \text{ is } +1 \text{ modulo } 3 \\
&t_2 \text{ is the constant function } 3 \\
&t_3 \text{ is } +1
\end{aligned}
$$

This grammar has derivations

$$
\begin{aligned}
\langle S, 0 \rangle &\Rightarrow \langle A, 2 \rangle \langle B, 1 \rangle \langle C, 0 \rangle \\
&\Rightarrow a \langle A, 0 \rangle \langle B, 2 \rangle \langle C, 1 \rangle \Rightarrow a \langle A, 1 \rangle b \langle B, 0 \rangle \langle C, 2 \rangle \Rightarrow a \langle A, 2 \rangle b \langle B, 1 \rangle c \langle C, 0 \rangle \\
&\vdots \\
&\Rightarrow a^{n-1} \langle A, 2 \rangle b^{n-1} \langle B, 1 \rangle c^{n-1} \langle C, 0 \rangle \\
&\Rightarrow a^n b^{n-1} \langle B, 3 \rangle c^{n-1} \langle C, 3 \rangle \Rightarrow a^n b^n c^{n-1} \langle C, 4 \rangle \Rightarrow a^n b^n c^n
\end{aligned}
$$

and thus generates the language $\{a^n b^n c^n \mid n \geq 1\}$.

As a final example, illustrating again the complexity of derivation in string transformer grammars even when the rules are simple and so are the string transformers, consider a variant of Example 12.

Example 14 (Another simple grammar for a complex language). Consider the grammar $G = \langle \{S, A, B\}, \{a, b\}, P, S \rangle$ where the production rule set P is

$$S \to AB$$
$$A \to aA$$
$$A \to a$$
$$B \to bB$$
$$B \to b$$

This generates the regular language $\{a^n b^m \mid n, m > 0\}$. Now associate with each rule the same string transformer defined by the function interchanging non-terminal symbol symbols $\{A \mapsto B, B \mapsto A\}$.

What language is now generated?

For leftmost derivations, we obtain the following prefixes of derivation paths.

$$S \Rightarrow BA \Rightarrow bB \ldots$$
$$S \Rightarrow BA \Rightarrow bAB \Rightarrow baA \ldots$$
$$S \Rightarrow BA \Rightarrow bAB \Rightarrow baBA \ldots$$

Given that B generates the language $(ba)^* b \cup (ba)^+$ and A generates the language $(ab)^* a \cup (ab)^+$, the leftmost derivation language will be

$$(ba)^* (b((ba)^* b \cup (ba)^+) \cup ba((ab)^* a \cup (ab)^+)).$$

For rightmost derivations, we obtain the prefixes

$$S \Rightarrow BA \Rightarrow Aa \ldots$$
$$S \Rightarrow BA \Rightarrow AaB \Rightarrow Bab \ldots$$
$$S \Rightarrow BA \Rightarrow AaB \Rightarrow BabA \ldots$$

Because of the third sequence, it is slightly trickier to derive the closed form. We have the recursion

$$Z(\mu) \Rightarrow A\mu a$$
$$Z(\mu) \Rightarrow B\mu ab$$
$$Z(\mu) \Rightarrow Z(\mu ab)$$

where $S \Rightarrow Z(\epsilon)$. The general form for μ is therefore $(ab)^*$ and hence the rightmost derivations generate the language

$$((ab)^* a \cup (ab)^+)(ab)^* a \cup ((ba)^* b \cup (ba)^+)(ab)^+$$

or more simply

$$(ab)^* a (ab)^* a \cup (ab)^+ a \cup (ba)^+ b \cup (ba)^+ (ab)^+.$$

Now consider the case of unrestricted rule application. Let us again give some of the prefixes of derivation paths.

$$1 \; S \Rightarrow BA \Rightarrow bB \ldots$$
$$2 \; S \Rightarrow BA \Rightarrow bAB \ldots$$
$$3 \; S \Rightarrow BA \Rightarrow AaB \ldots$$
$$4 \; S \Rightarrow BA \Rightarrow Aa \ldots$$

Branches 1 and 4 are easy to close off. The first will yield words $b(ba)^*b \cup b(ba)^+$. Similarly, the fourth generates finite words $(ab)^*aa \cup (ab)^+a$.

What happens with the second and third branches? Let us expand the second branch.

$$2.1\ bAB \Rightarrow baA\ldots$$
$$2.2\ bAB \Rightarrow baBA\ldots$$
$$2.3\ bAB \Rightarrow bBbA\ldots$$
$$2.4\ bAB \Rightarrow bBb\ldots$$

Again, we know what will happen with the first and fourth branches — as we had above apart from being prefixed by the letter b. The branch (2.2) now recurses having generated prefix ba. Thus it will generate a set of finite words that are prefixed by $(ba)^*$. But what follows the prefix? More interestingly, consider branch 2.3. There is recursion again, however, the letter b is both prefixed and placed between the non-terminal symbol B and A — if one iterated just using this branch, then words of the form $b^n B b^n A$ are derived. Let us expand the third branch (3) of the derivation.

$$3.1\ AaB \Rightarrow aaA\ldots$$
$$3.2\ AaB \Rightarrow aBaA\ldots$$
$$3.3\ AaB \Rightarrow BabA\ldots$$
$$3.4\ AaB \Rightarrow Bab\ldots$$

The first and fourth branches are straightforward. The second and third branches maintain the presence of non-terminal symbols A and B but switched in order, as in the case above.

It is instructive to see what happens with this string transformer grammar if we re-present it as a standard grammar using parameterised production rules. The new grammar will be directly constructed from the derivation tree, the beginnings of which we've written out above.

$$S \to Z(\epsilon)$$

$$Z(\mu) \to b\mu B$$
$$Z(\mu) \to ba\mu A$$
$$Z(\mu) \to baZ(\mu)$$
$$Z(\mu) \to bZ(\mu b)$$
$$Z(\mu) \to bB\mu b$$
$$Z(\mu) \to a\mu aA$$
$$Z(\mu) \to aZ(\mu a)$$
$$Z(\mu) \to Z(\mu ab)$$
$$Z(\mu) \to B\mu ab$$
$$Z(\mu) \to A\mu a$$

$$B \to b$$
$$B \to bA$$
$$A \to a$$
$$A \to aB$$

The non-terminal symbol Z is parameterised by a terminal string μ; $Z(\mu)$ represents derived words of the form $B\mu A$. The initial production S fires Z with an empty string, i.e. denoting the non-terminal pairing BA, the result of the first production application (after transformation) in the original grammar.

First of all, note the non-terminal symbol B yields the set of words $(ba)^*b \cup (ba)^+$. Similarly, A yields the set of words $(ab)^+ \cup (ab)^*a$. Thus, we can easily compute the words generated from the non-recursive rules for $Z(\mu)$. The other recursive cases are more interesting! A general pattern for words after a number of iterations from $Z(\mu)$ is as follows

$$((ba)^* b^{n_p} a^{m_p})^p Z(\mu \, ((ab)^* b^{n_p} a^{m_p})^p)$$

Note that we have the same indices occurring in the prefix substring as in the μ extension. We can thus substitute in the words generated through no further recursion of Z, obtaining the set of words

$\{((ba)^* b^{n_p} a^{m_p})^p \, b \, ((ab)^* b^{n_p} a^{m_p})^p \, ((ba)^* b \cup (ba)^+) \mid p, n_1, \ldots, n_p, m_1, \ldots, m_p \in \mathbb{N}\}$
$\cup$
$\{((ba)^* b^{n_p} a^{m_p})^p \, ba \, ((ab)^* b^{n_p} a^{m_p})^p \, ((ab)^+ \cup (ab)^* a) \mid p, n_1, \ldots, n_p, m_1, \ldots, m_p \in \mathbb{N}\}$
$\cup$
$\{((ba)^* b^{n_p} a^{m_p})^p \, b \, ((ba)^* b \cup (ba)^+) \, ((ab)^* b^{n_p} a^{m_p})^p \, b \mid p, n_1, \ldots, n_p, m_1, \ldots, m_p \in \mathbb{N}\}$
$\cup$
$\{((ba)^* b^{n_p} a^{m_p})^p \, a \, ((ab)^* b^{n_p} a^{m_p})^p \, a \, ((ab)^+ \cup (ab)^* a) \mid p, n_1, \ldots, n_p, m_1, \ldots, m_p \in \mathbb{N}\}$
$\cup$
$\{((ba)^* b^{n_p} a^{m_p})^p \, ((ba)^* b \cup (ba)^+) \, ((ab)^* b^{n_p} a^{m_p})^p \, ab \mid p, n_1, \ldots, n_p, m_1, \ldots, m_p \in \mathbb{N}\}$
$\cup$
$\{((ba)^* b^{n_p} a^{m_p})^p \, ((ab)^+ \cup (ab)^* a) \, ((ab)^* b^{n_p} a^{m_p})^p \, a \mid p, n_1, \ldots, n_p, m_1, \ldots, m_p \in \mathbb{N}\}$

Thus we see that a simple context-free grammar with a simple string transformer has given rise to a very complex language indeed.

We have already shown that context-free string transformer grammars may generate non-context-free languages. Thus, we are led to ask: what is the expressivity of context-free string transformer grammars?

Theorem 8. *A deterministic Turing machine (TM) can be simulated by a context-free string transformer grammar.*

Proof. The essence of the simulation is to represent the tape of the TM by the currently derived word and the finite control of the TM is represented by the context-free grammar. Tape head movements are simulated by the string transformers. The non-terminal symbols of the regular grammar are triples formed from the state of the TM with the content of a tape cell and a marker 0 or 1 denoting whether the cell is under the head. The string transformers representing tape head movement may change the state component of a non-terminal symbol that is to come under the tape head following a left or right move.

The form of the string transformers here is, in fact, replacement of non-terminal symbols with non-terminal symbols but is not defined in terms of a function on the set of non-terminal symbols, as the determination of which symbol will replace a given one depends on its context in the string. This is the mechanism by which tape head movement is encoded.

In more detail, given a Turing Machine $TM = \langle Q, \Sigma, V, R, q_0, F \rangle$ where Q are the states of the finite control, Σ is the input alphabet, V is an alphabet, $R \subseteq (Q \times ((\Sigma \cup V) \times (\Sigma \cup V) \times \{L, R\}) \times Q)$ is the transition relation, and $F \in Q$ is the distinguished halt state, and q_0 is an starting state of the finite control. We assume an initial finitely populated tape $\sigma = \#_b \sigma_1 \ldots \sigma_n \#_e$ where $\#_b$ and $\#_e$ are beginning and end markers on the tape and $\sigma_i \in \Sigma$. We further assume that the tape head is positioned under σ_n.

We construct a context-free string transformer grammar with labelled non-terminal symbols

$$G = \langle N_{(\Sigma \cup V \cup \{\#_b, \#_e\}) \cup \{S\}, Q \times \{0,1\}}, \Sigma, T(\{L, R\} \times Q), P, S \rangle$$

where $N(\Sigma \cup V \cup \{\#_b, \#_e\})$ is a set of non-terminal symbols corresponding to the tape symbols of the Turing machine, i.e. the set $\{N_x \mid x \in (\Sigma \cup V \cup \{\#_b, \#_e\})\}$; S is a unique initial non-terminal symbol; the non-terminal labelling is drawn from $Q \times \{0, 1\}$, i.e. the states of the Turing machine paired with a 0 or 1 marker to denote whether the tape symbol corresponding to the non-terminal symbol is under the tape head; $T_{(\{L,R\} \times Q)}$ is a set of string transformers defined in terms of functions on labels, each one corresponding to either a left or right tape head movement into state $q \in Q$. Finally P is a set of context-free production rules related to the transitions of the Turing machine and is defined as follows.

1. The initial production for S generates the initial tape, i.e.

$$S \to \langle \sigma_1, q_0, 0 \rangle \ldots \langle \sigma_n, q_0, 1 \rangle$$

For ease of notation, in the labelled non-terminal symbol, we let σ_1 stand for non-terminal symbol N_{σ_1}.

2. For each TM rule of the form $q \xrightarrow{x,y,L} q'$ for $q \neq F$ and $x \neq \#_b$, we have the production rule

$$\langle x, q, 1 \rangle \xrightarrow{t_{Lq'}} \langle y, q, 1 \rangle$$

3. For each TM rule of the form $q \xrightarrow{x,y,R} q'$ for $q \neq F$ and $x \neq \#_e$, we have the production rule

$$\langle x, q, 1 \rangle \xrightarrow{t_{Rq'}} \langle y, q, 1 \rangle$$

4. For each TM rule of the form $q \xrightarrow{\#_b,y,L} q'$ for $q \neq F$, we have the production rule

$$\langle \#_b, q, 1 \rangle \xrightarrow{t_{Lq'}} \langle \#_b, q, 0 \rangle \langle y, q, 1 \rangle$$

5. For each TM rule of the form $q \xrightarrow{\#_e,y,R} q'$ for $q \neq F$, we have the production rule

$$\langle \#_e, q, 1 \rangle \xrightarrow{t_{Rq'}} \langle y, q, 1 \rangle \langle \#_e, q, 0 \rangle$$

6. Three termination rules that rewrite the non-terminal symbols to their corresponding terminal letter (tape symbol).

$$\langle x, F, p \rangle \to x \quad \text{for } x \neq \#_b, \#_e$$
$$\langle \#_b, F, p \rangle \to \epsilon$$
$$\langle \#_e, F, p \rangle \to \epsilon$$

The label sequence transformation functions are defined as below.

$$t_{Lq} : (Q \times \{0,1\})^* \to (Q \times \{0,1\})^*$$
$$t_{Lq}^1 : (Q \times \{0,1\})^+ \to (Q \times \{0,1\})^+$$

$$t_{Rq} : (Q \times \{0,1\})^* \to (Q \times \{0,1\})^*$$
$$t_{Rq}^1 : (Q \times \{0,1\})^+ \to (Q \times \{0,1\})^+$$

$$t_{Lq}(\langle \rangle) = \langle \rangle$$
$$t_{Lq}(\sigma :: \langle s, 0 \rangle) = t_{Lq}(\sigma) :: \langle q, 0 \rangle$$
$$t_{Lq}(\sigma :: \langle s, 1 \rangle) = t_{Lq}^1(\sigma) :: \langle q, 0 \rangle$$
$$t_{Lq}^1(\langle \langle s, 0 \rangle \rangle) = \langle \langle q, 1 \rangle \rangle$$
$$t_{Lq}^1(\sigma :: \langle s, 0 \rangle) = t_{Lq}(\sigma) :: \langle q, 1 \rangle$$

$$t_{Rq}(\langle \rangle) = \langle \rangle$$
$$t_{Rq}(\langle s, 0 \rangle :: \sigma) = \langle q, 0 \rangle :: t_{Rq}(\sigma)$$
$$t_{Rq}(\langle s, 1 \rangle :: \sigma) = \langle q, 0 \rangle :: t_{Rq}^1(\sigma)$$
$$t_{Rq}^1(\langle \langle s, 0 \rangle \rangle) = \langle \langle q, 1 \rangle \rangle$$
$$t_{Rq}^1(\langle s, 0 \rangle :: \sigma) = \langle q, 1 \rangle :: t_{Rq}(\sigma)$$

We now claim that the string transformer grammar generates a word w if and only the Turing machine halts with tape contents $\#_b w \#_e$. The proof can be given by showing a bisimulation between the Turing machine and the string transformer grammar. We leave the details as an exercise for the interested reader.

6   Reactivity and Derivation Strategies

We note from some of the previous examples that we may use the labelling and associated transformations of string transformer grammars to mimic derivation strategies. Can all derivation strategies be encoded this way? We answer this positively by first defining a suitable general notion of derivation strategy, then encoding through labels and relabelling functions a general scheme for constructing string transformer grammars.

Given a context-free grammar, let us uniquely name each of its production rules by, say, R_i, for $i \in \mathbb{N}$. For a given derivation sequence

$$S \Rightarrow \alpha_1 \Rightarrow \dots \alpha_i \Rightarrow \dots s$$

each derivation step can be labelled by the rule name applied at that step and the non-terminal position (amongst the non-terminal symbols of the currently derived string) at which the application took place. For example, given $G = \langle \{S, A, B\}, \{a, b\}, P, S \rangle$ with P the set of named production rules:

$$R_0 : S \to AB$$
$$R_1 : A \to a$$
$$R_2 : A \to aA$$
$$R_3 : B \to b$$
$$R_4 : B \to bB$$

This generates $\{a^m b^n \mid m, n \geq 1\}$. Here is an example of a (labelled) derivation sequence:

$$S \overset{R_0,1}{\Rightarrow} AB \overset{R_1,1}{\Rightarrow} aB \overset{R_3,1}{\Rightarrow} ab.$$

A leftmost derivation sequence is clearly a derivation sequence for which the non-terminal position is always 1, as above. Indeed, we can define a leftmost derivation strategy as one which only allows derivation sequences where the non-terminal position is always 1.

Of course, there are many other derivation strategies of interest. To move towards the more general situation let us consider a strategy for generating words of the form $a^{2n} b^n$ for $n \geq 1$ using the above production rules. An example of such a strategy is alternating the generation of 2 a's with 1 b, and so on. We can write this strategy explicitly in terms of derivation sequences, using only the last two rules used (at most). We can write this strategy as a function σ which takes a current derivation sequence and yields the set of rules which may be used next together with the position of the occurrence in the current string of the non-terminal symbol at which the rule is used. In the following definition of the function σ, let δ be an arbitrary derivation sequence, a dot denotes the concatenation of an item onto a derivation sequence, and ϵ is the empty sequence.

$$\sigma(\epsilon) = \{(R_0, 1)\}$$
$$\sigma((R_0, 1)) = \{(R_2, 2)\}$$
$$\sigma(\delta.(R_2, 1).(R_2, 1)) = \{(R_4, 2)\}$$
$$\sigma(\delta.(R, j).(R_2, 1)) = \{(R_1, 1), (R_2, 1)\} \qquad \text{for } R \neq R_2$$
$$\sigma(\delta.(R_1, 1)) = \{(R_3, 2)\}$$
$$\sigma(\delta.(R_4, 2)) = \{(R_2, 1)\}$$

For all other sequences the result is the empty set.

We are now in a position to introduce the general notion of a *derivation strategy* in a derivation tree of a context-free grammar.

Definition 6. *Consider a context-free grammar G with uniquely named production rules (with Rule the set of rule names in G). A derivation strategy (or simply a strategy) of G is a function*

$$\sigma : (Rule \times \mathbb{N}_1)^* \rightarrow \mathcal{P}_f(Rule \times \mathbb{N}_1).$$

Here $\mathcal{P}_f$ is the finite powerset function and $\mathbb{N}_1$ the positive integers. The argument to the strategy σ is a derivation sequence — the history of the derivation so far – recording the (possibly empty) sequence of named rules and the non-terminal positions in the strings at which the rule is applied. Given a derivation sequence, a strategy yields a (possibly empty) finite set of pairs (R, i) consisting of a rule name R and a non-terminal position i in the current string. For such a pair (R, i), a possible next step in the derivation is to apply the rule named R to the non-terminal at position i.

A derivation sequence δ is said to be a derivation in strategy σ if, at any position j in δ, $(0 \leq j \leq n)$, we have $\delta_j \in \sigma(\delta|_{j-1})$, where δ_j is the j-th step in δ and $\delta|_{j-1}$ is the initial segment of δ up to the $(j-1)$-th entry.

A strategy σ of grammar G is said to generate a word w if there is a derivation of w in σ. The language generated by a strategy is the set of all its generated words.

As in games, strategies may depend on only certain aspects of the history of a derivation (e.g. on the number of rule applications, as in the examples above) or, in fact, may be *history-free*, in which case they do not depend on the history of a derivation at all but only on the current string. In these cases, the strategy, as a function, is constant over certain collections of inputs.

Example 15 (History-free strategies). A *leftmost* derivation strategy σ for a context-free grammar G (with uniquely named rules) is history-free, and $(R, i) \in \sigma(s)$ for derived string s iff $i = 1$ and R is the name of a rule of G for rewriting the non-terminal at position 1 in s.

A *leftish* derivation strategy σ for a context-free grammar G (with uniquely named rules) is history-free, and $(R, i) \in \sigma(s)$ for derived string s iff for all j, $j < i$, there are no rules in G for rewriting the non-terminal at position j, and R is the name of a rule for rewriting the i-th non-terminal symbol.

This notion of a derivation strategy is *general* in the following sense.

Theorem 9. *For a context-free grammar, any set Δ of (finite or infinite) derivation sequences defines a strategy σ such that $\delta \in \Delta$ iff δ is a derivation sequence in σ.*

We now turn to the main result of this section, showing that any strategy for deriving words in a context-free grammar corresponds exactly to a string transformer grammar with unrestricted use of production rules. This result both shows the expressivity of string transformer grammars and also provides a general construction of such grammars for various languages.

Theorem 10. *Let G be a context-free grammar with a finite set of uniquely named production rules and σ a derivation strategy of G. Then there is a context-free string transformer grammar (possibly with an infinite set of rules) whose unrestricted rule application generates the language of σ. In fact, we may construct the context-free string transformer grammar so as to exactly simulate the strategy σ (in the sense of derivation steps being in 1-1 correspondence).*

Proof. The key to the proof is the construction of a context-free string transformer grammar G' using labelled non-terminal symbols, where the labels code the current history together with a non-terminal position. We then ensure that G' has a rule for a particular labelled non-terminal just when the strategy σ allows that rule to be applied. This, together with suitable label transformations, ensures that the derivations of G' correspond exactly to those of the strategy σ of grammar G.

Thus, the non-terminal symbols of G' consist of the non-terminal symbols of G labelled with a pair (δ, i) where δ is a derivation sequence of σ and i a position of a non-terminal in the string derived by δ. This may produce a finite or an infinite set of labelled non-terminal symbols depending whether there is a finite or infinite number of derivation sequences of σ.

For the rules of G', consider a derivation sequence δ in strategy σ. For each $(R, i) \in \sigma(\delta)$ with rule $X \to s$ in G named by R, we create the rule of G',

$$\langle X, (\delta, i) \rangle \xrightarrow{t} \tilde{s}$$

where $\tilde{s}$ consists of the string s with each non-terminal labelled by the derivation δ and its non-terminal position in s. The transformation t acts on labels by 'advancing the history' and adding the current position of the non-terminal, that is, for the non-terminal at position j in the current string,

$$t(\delta, \_) = (\delta.(R, i), j).$$

The initial symbol of G' is $\langle S, (\epsilon, 1) \rangle$ where S is the initial symbol of G and ϵ is the empty derivation sequence.

It is straightforward to verify that, for each word w, there is a bijection between derivation sequences in strategy σ of word w and unrestricted derivations in G' of word w.

Whilst, in general, this construction of a string transformer grammar may yield a grammar with an infinite set of rules, we shall see that for many natural strategies for generating languages, not only is the resulting grammar finite, but it is a succinct and useful presentation of the language. In other cases, the infinite set of rules is presented as a finite set of rule schema (i.e. parameterised rules).

We give examples of both these cases, constructing string transformer grammars from strategies in context-free grammars.

Example 16 (An alternation strategy as a string transformer grammar). We revisit the strategy described above for the language $\{a^{2n}b^n \mid n \geq 1\}$. The strategy is one of strict alternation between generating pairs of a's and single b's. This strategy depends only on the last two (at most) rules used, and so we can label the non-terminal symbols in the constructed string transformer grammar with the necessary one or two previous rules:

$$\langle S, (\epsilon, 1) \rangle \xrightarrow{t_0} \langle A, (\epsilon, 1) \rangle \langle B, (\epsilon, 2) \rangle$$
$$\langle A, ((R_0, 1), 1) \rangle \xrightarrow{t_1} a \langle A, ((R_0, 1), 1) \rangle$$
$$\langle B, ((R_2, 1).(R_2, 1), 2) \rangle \xrightarrow{t_2} b \langle B, ((R_2, 1).(R_2, 1), 2) \rangle$$
$$\langle A, ((R, j).(R_2, 1), 1) \rangle \xrightarrow{t_3} a \qquad R \neq R_2$$
$$\langle A, ((R, j).(R_2, 1), 1) \rangle \xrightarrow{t_4} a \langle A, ((R, j).(R_2, 1), 1) \rangle \qquad R \neq R_2$$
$$\langle B, ((R_1, 1), 2) \rangle \xrightarrow{t_5} b$$
$$\langle A, ((R_4, 2), 1) \rangle \xrightarrow{t_6} a \langle A, ((R_4, 2), 1) \rangle$$

with label transformations:

$$t_0(\epsilon, \_) = ((R_0, 1), j)$$
$$t_1((R_0, 1), \_) = ((R_0, 1).(R_2, 1), j)$$
$$t_2((R_2, 1).(R_2, 1), \_) = ((R_4, 2), j)$$
$$t_3((R, j)(R_2, 1), \_) = ((R_1, 1), j)$$
$$t_4((R, j)(R_2, 1), \_) = ((R_2, 1).(R_2, 1), j)$$
$$t_5((R_1, 1), \_) = ((R_3, 2), j)$$
$$t_6((R_4, 2), \_) = ((R_4, 2).(R_2, 1), j)$$

with $j = 1$ for non-terminal symbol A and $j = 2$ for B.

Simplifying the labels reduces this grammar to the set of rules:

$$S \rightarrow \langle A, 0 \rangle \langle B, 0 \rangle$$
$$\langle A, 0 \rangle \xrightarrow{t_0} a \langle A, 0 \rangle$$
$$\langle B, 22 \rangle \xrightarrow{t_1} b \langle B, 22 \rangle$$
$$\langle A, 2 \rangle \xrightarrow{t_2} a$$
$$\langle A, 2 \rangle \xrightarrow{t_3} a \langle A, 2 \rangle$$
$$\langle B, 1 \rangle \xrightarrow{t_4} b$$
$$\langle A, 4 \rangle \xrightarrow{t_5} a \langle A, 4 \rangle$$

with label transformations: $t_0(0) = 2, t_1(22) = 4, t_2(2) = 1, t_3(2) = 22, t_4(1) = 3$, $t_5(4) = 2$.

What about other strategies for the same language $\{a^{2n}b^n \mid n \geq 1\}$ using the same grammar?

Example 17 (Another string transformer construction). As another strategy for the language $\{a^{2n}b^n \mid n \geq 1\}$, we could allow arbitrary interleaved generation of a's and b's but allow termination only when the correct number of a'a and b's are generated. This again provides a derivation strategy which, using the above construction, produces the following equivalent string transformer grammar.

$$\langle S, ([0, 0, 0, 0, 0], 1) \rangle \xrightarrow{t_0} \langle A, ([0, 0, 0, 0, 0], 1) \rangle \langle B, ([0, 0, 0, 0, 0], 1) \rangle$$
$$\langle A, ([1, 0, m, 0, n], 1) \rangle \xrightarrow{t_1} a \langle A, ([1, 0, m, 0, n], 1) \rangle \qquad m, n \geq 0$$
$$\langle B, ([1, 0, m, 0, n], 2) \rangle \xrightarrow{t_2} b \langle B, ([1, 0, m, 0, n], 2) \rangle \qquad m, n \geq 0$$
$$\langle A, ([1, 0, 2n - 1, 0, n - 1], 1) \rangle \xrightarrow{t_3} a \qquad n \geq 1$$
$$\langle B, ([1, 0, 2n - 1, 0, n - 1], 2) \rangle \xrightarrow{t_4} b \qquad n \geq 1$$
$$\langle B, ([1, 1, m, 0, n], 1) \rangle \xrightarrow{t_5} b$$
$$\langle A, ([1, 0, m, 1, n], 1) \rangle \xrightarrow{t_6} a$$

Here the arrays encode information about the derivation so far: The $i - th$ entry records the number of application of rule R_i of the grammar at the beginning of this section. The transformations of labels extend the count according to which rule has just been used:

$$t_0([0,0,0,0,0], \_) = ([1,0,0,0,0], j)$$
$$t_1([1,0,m,0,n], \_) = ([1,0,m+1,0,n], j)$$
$$t_2([1,0,m,0,n], \_) = ([1,0,m,0,n+1], j)$$
$$t_3([1,0,2n-1,0,n-1], \_) = ([1,1,2n-1,0,n-1], j)$$
$$t_4([1,0,2n-1,0,n-1], \_) = ([1,0,2n-1,1,n-1], j)$$
$$t_5([1,1,2n-1,0,n-1], \_) = ([1,1,2n-1,1,n-1], j)$$
$$t_6([1,0,2n-1,1,n-1], \_) = ([1,1,2n-1,1,n-1], j)$$

with $j = 1$ for non-terminal symbol A and $j = 2$ for B.

Note that this is a context-free string transformer grammar with a set of *parameterised* rules, i.e. a finite schema for an infinite set of rules, one for each valid m and n.

We now turn to another example – the running example of a non-context-free language: $\{a^n b^n c^n \mid n \geq 1\}$.

Example 18 ($a^n b^n c^n$ yet again). Consider the context-free grammar G with named rules:

$$R_0 : S \to AC$$
$$R_1 : A \to aAb$$
$$R_2 : A \to ab$$
$$R_3 : C \to cC$$
$$R_4 : C \to c$$

A strategy for generating the language $\{a^n b^n c^n \mid n \geq 1\}$ is to alternate use of rules R_1 and R_3. This derivation strategy σ of G is defined as follows. For any derivation sequence δ:

$$\sigma(\epsilon) = \{(R_0, 1)\}$$
$$\sigma((R_0, 1)) = \{(R_1, 1), (R_2, 1)\}$$
$$\sigma(\delta.(R_1, 1)) = \{(R_3, 2)\}$$
$$\sigma(\delta.(R_2, 1)) = \{(R_4, 2)\}$$
$$\sigma(\delta.(R_3, 2)) = \{(R_1, 1), (R_2, 1)\}$$

This strategy generates the language $\{a^n b^n c^n \mid n > 0\}$.

Notice that this strategy depends only on the previous rule applied, thus we may simplify the labelling of non-terminal symbols using the previously applied rule in place of the entire derivation history. Thus, labels consist of a rule name and the non-terminal position of its application, together with the current position of the non-terminal symbol.

Following the construction in the proof above, we construct a string transformer grammar G' with labelled non-terminal symbols which mimics this strategy to generate the same language. The rules of G' are:

$$\langle S, (\epsilon, 1)\rangle \xrightarrow{t_0} \langle A, (\epsilon, 1)\rangle \langle C, (\epsilon, 1)\rangle$$
$$\langle A, ((R_0, 1), 1)\rangle \xrightarrow{t_1} a\langle A, ((R_0, 1), 1)\rangle b$$
$$\langle A, ((R_0, 1), 1)\rangle \xrightarrow{t_2} ab$$
$$\langle C, ((R_1, 1), 2)\rangle \xrightarrow{t_3} c\langle C, ((R_1, 1), 1)\rangle$$
$$\langle C, ((R_2, 1), 2)\rangle \xrightarrow{t_4} c$$
$$\langle A, ((R_3, 2), 1)\rangle \xrightarrow{t_5} a\langle A, ((R_3, 2), 1)\rangle b$$
$$\langle A, ((R_3, 2), 1)\rangle \xrightarrow{t_6} ab$$

The string transformations t_m act on the labels of non-terminal symbols as follows, for the j-th non-terminal symbol in a string:

$$t_0(\epsilon, \_) = ((R_0, 1), j)$$
$$t_1((R_0, 1), \_) = ((R_1, 1), j)$$
$$t_2((R_0, 1), \_) = ((R_2, 1), j)$$
$$t_3((R_1, 1), \_) = ((R_3, 2), j)$$
$$t_4((R_1, 1), \_) = ((R_4, 2), j)$$
$$t_5((R_3, 2), \_) = ((R_1, 1), j)$$
$$t_6((R_3, 2), \_) = ((R_2, 1), j)$$

By observing the pattern of the non-terminal labels in the rules of this grammar, we may simplify it considerably, using rule numbers as labels:

$$S \to \langle A, 0\rangle\langle C, 0\rangle$$
$$\langle A, 0\rangle \xrightarrow{t_1} a\langle A, 0\rangle b$$
$$\langle A, 0\rangle \xrightarrow{t_2} ab$$
$$\langle C, 1\rangle \xrightarrow{t_3} c\langle C, 1\rangle$$
$$\langle C, 2\rangle \xrightarrow{t_4} c$$
$$\langle A, 3\rangle \xrightarrow{t_5} a\langle A, 3\rangle b$$
$$\langle A, 3\rangle \xrightarrow{t_6} ab$$

with transformations $t_1(0) = 1, t_2(0) = 2, t_3(1) = 3, t_4(1) = 4, t_5(3) = 1, t_6(3) = 2$.

Example 19 (A context-sensitive grammar). In [26], Rosenkrantz uses the following context-sensitive language to demonstrate a programmed context-free grammar with both success and failure continuation rule sets:

$$\{\text{bin}(n)ha^n \mid n \in \mathbb{N}\}$$

where $\text{bin}(n)$ is a binary representation (with, say, leftmost digit as the most significant) of the positive integer n. Let us first give an unrestricted grammar for this language. Take $G_u = \langle \{S, T, T', D, Z, F\}, \{1, 0, h, a\}, P, S\rangle$ with P the set of rules

$$S \to TZ$$
$$T \to 1T'aD$$
$$T \to 0T'D$$
$$T' \to 1T'aD$$
$$T' \to 0T'D$$
$$T' \to hF$$
$$Da \to aaD$$
$$DZ \to Z$$
$$Fa \to aF$$
$$FZ \to \epsilon$$

G_u thus has derivations such as:

$$S \Rightarrow TZ \Rightarrow 1T'aDZ \Rightarrow 11T'aDaDZ \Rightarrow 11T'aaaDDZ \Rightarrow 11hFaaaDDZ$$
$$\Rightarrow 11haFaaDDZ \Rightarrow 11haaFaDDZ \Rightarrow 11haaaFDDZ \Rightarrow 11haaaFDZ$$
$$\Rightarrow 11haaaFZ \Rightarrow 11haaa$$

Consider now the following context-free grammar with named rules

$$G_{cf} = \langle \{S, A\}, \{1, 0, h, a\}, \{r_0, r_1, r_2, r_3, r_4\}, P, S \rangle$$

with rules in P as

$$r_0 : S \to 1SA$$
$$r_1 : S \to 0S$$
$$r_2 : S \to h$$
$$r_3 : A \to AA$$
$$r_4 : A \to a$$

The language generated by this context-free grammar clearly contains the language of G_u. So by defining an appropriate strategy for G_{cf}, we can obtain the language of G_u.

6.1   Switching Grammars and String Transformers

We now consider the relationship between switching grammars, introduced earlier in the paper, and string transformer grammars.

Theorem 11. *Every context-free switching grammar can be exactly simulated by a context-free string transformer grammar i.e. there is a context-free string transformer grammar whose derivation steps correspond exactly to those of the switching grammar. In particular, the class of languages generated by context-free switching grammars is contained in that of context-free string transformer grammars.*

Proof. Let $G = \langle N, \Sigma, I, P, S, i_0 \rangle$ be a context-free switching grammar. For each $i \in I$, we form a set of string transformer rules $\tilde{P}_i$ as follows: For each rule $X \to \gamma, j$ in P_i form the rule $\langle X, i \rangle \xrightarrow{t} \tilde{\gamma}$ in $\tilde{P}_i$ where $\tilde{\gamma}$ is γ with each non-terminal symbol Y replaced by $\langle Y, i \rangle$, and the string transformer t is defined by the function on non-terminal symbols $t(\langle Y, k \rangle) = \langle Y, j \rangle$.

Now form the set of production rules of a string transformer grammar $\tilde{P} = \bigcup_{i \in I} \tilde{P}_i$. It is easy to verify that this string transformer grammar exactly simulates the original switching grammar.

We have shown that any derivation strategy may be represented (by an exact simulation) by a context-free string transformer grammar with unrestricted rule application. Context-free switching grammars have the same degree of expressivity for arbitrary derivation strategies but the encoding of strategies is different and the encoding in string transformer grammars does not factor through the construction for switching grammars. A difficulty in both cases is to identify the n-th non-terminal symbol (which is used in the definition of strategies) in a string after a substitution has taken place. With string transformers, we relabel the non-terminal symbols after a rule application, for switching grammars this option is not available and we have to code, within the labels, information about relative positions of the non-terminal symbols. Switching grammars as representations of strategies tend to be less succinct than string transformer grammars, partly because of this more elaborate labelling of non-terminal symbols.

Theorem 12. *Let G be a context-free grammar with uniquely named production rules and σ a derivation strategy of G. Then there is a context-free switching grammar with unrestricted rule application which exactly simulates σ.*

Proof. Consider a valid derivation δ of string s in strategy σ with non-empty $\sigma(\delta)$. We proceed by induction on the length of δ. Assume that there is a switching grammar with rule sets indexed by initial substrings of δ (not including δ) which exactly simulates the steps of δ to produce a string $\tilde{s}$. Form a set of rules P_δ as follows. For each $\langle l, n \rangle \in \sigma(\delta)$, let $X \to \gamma$ be the rule labelled l. Form switching rule $\langle X, \lambda \rangle \to \tilde{\gamma}, \delta'$ in P_δ where λ is the label of the n-th non-terminal symbol in $\tilde{s}$, $\tilde{\gamma}$ is γ with non-terminal symbol Y at the j position in γ replaced by $\langle Y, \lambda.j \rangle$ and $\delta' = \delta.\langle l, n \rangle$.

Then for all valid derivation sequences δ of σ, the indexed set of rule sets P_δ forms, together with initial symbol $\langle S, 0 \rangle$ where S is initial symbol of G, and initial set of rules $\sigma([])$, forms a switching grammar that exactly simulates the strategy σ of G.

Example 20 (The language $\{a^n b^n c^n \mid n \geq 1\}$). Consider the context-free grammar G with rules

$$
\begin{aligned}
1: & \quad S \to AX \\
2: & \quad X \to bXc \\
3: & \quad X \to bc \\
4: & \quad A \to AA \\
5: & \quad A \to a
\end{aligned}
$$

As a strategy σ for $a^n b^n c^n$, for $n \geq 1$, consider alternating between extending the A's and generating X's, then, when there are no X's, finally reducing A's to a's in an arbitrary order. Thus:

$$\sigma([]) = \{\langle 1,1 \rangle\}$$
$$\sigma([\langle 1,1 \rangle]) = \{\langle 4,1 \rangle, \langle 5,1 \rangle\}$$
$$\sigma(\delta.\langle 4,1 \rangle) = \{\langle 5, |\delta| + 1 \rangle\}$$
$$\sigma(\delta.\langle 5,i \rangle) = \{\langle 4,1 \rangle, \langle 3,i \rangle\}$$
$$\sigma(\delta.\langle 3,i \rangle) = \{\langle 5,j \rangle \mid 1 \le j \le |\delta|\}$$
$$\sigma(\delta.\langle 5,i \rangle) = \{\langle 5,j \rangle \mid 1 \le j \le k\}$$

where k is the number of A symbols in the string generated by $\delta.\langle 5,i \rangle$

We consider the first few steps of the construction using the derivation sequence $\delta = S \Rightarrow AX \Rightarrow AAX$. The initial set is

$$P_{[]} = \{\langle S,0 \rangle \to \langle A,0.1 \rangle\langle X,0.2 \rangle, [\langle 1,1 \rangle]\}.$$

The corresponding step in the switching grammar for $S \Rightarrow AX$ is therefore $\langle S,0 \rangle \Rightarrow \langle A,0.1 \rangle\langle X,0.2 \rangle$. For the next step, the strategy gives two rules, $A \to AA$ or $A \to a$. Thus, the ruleset for the switching grammar is

$$P_{[\langle 1,1 \rangle]} = \{ \langle A,0.1 \rangle \to \langle A,0.1.1 \rangle\langle A,0.1.2 \rangle, [\langle 1,1 \rangle, \langle 4,1 \rangle],$$
$$\langle A,0.1 \rangle \to a, [\langle 1,1 \rangle, \langle 5,1 \rangle]\}.$$

Then the derivation δ, represented in the switching grammar, yields the string $\langle A,0.1.1 \rangle\langle A,0.1.2 \rangle\langle X,0.2 \rangle$. Notice how the labels are used to code the tree of substitution positions so that the correct rules may be applied according to the form of the labelled non-terminal symbol.

7   Embedded Reactivity

We now turn to examples of reactive grammars where the reactivity, instead of being associated with rules of the grammar, is determined by the generated string or parts of the string. The presentation and formalisation of such grammars is not straightforward because what is meant by 'parts of a string' depends, in general, on the parsing of the string, i.e. on the derivation sequence used to generate it. Moreover, the effect of reactivity will depend again on the derivation sequence and how subtrees in a parse tree are related to each other.

Let us begin by looking at some examples of embedded reactivity.

Example 21 (Correction grammars). Consider the following example text:

'Tom likes playing basketball, sorry I mean football.'

Here, the phrase *'sorry I mean X'* is a reactive component of the text, that is, it describes a transformation to be performed on the text. In this case, the transformation is to replace the word *'basketball'* with *'football'* and remove the reactive component, resulting in the string:

'Tom likes playing football.'

Let us look at the process in more detail. How is the *'X'* in *'sorry I mean X'* matched to part of the remaining text? Clearly, it ought to have the same 'phrase type' which in this case is a noun phrase (indeed it is a noun). But there are two noun phrases in the text '*Tom likes playing basketball.*' Which to choose? Both semantics and proximity may have a role in determining the action to be associated with a reactive component.

Reactive components may interact. Consider the example text:

> '*Jack loves Mary. Mary rejected Jack, sorry I mean the man in blue, sorry I mean red, sorry I mean accepted.*'

Of course, as a natural language text, this is rather contrived, but as an example of an embedded reactivity, it illustrates the complex phenomena that may be involved. One possible resolution of this (i.e. determination of the actions associated with the reactive components) is the text:

> '*Jack loves Mary. Mary accepted the man in red.*'

Other resolutions are possible, for example:

> '*The man in red loves Mary. Mary accepted the man in red.*'

When a string has multiple derivations, i.e. ambiguity in parsing, then the reactivity may depend upon the derivation. For example:

> '*British left waffles on Falkland Islands, sorry I mean toast!*'

We are not proposing embedded reactive grammars as a technique for analysing such natural language phrases as in the example above. Rather, we are using the example to illustrate embedded reactivity and its analysis.

Example 22 (Spelling reform). A widely quoted text, purporting to be an incremental spelling reform, is:

> For example, in Year 1 that useless letter 'c' would be dropped to be replased either by 'k' or 's,' and likewise 'x' would no longer be part of the alphabet. The only kase in which 'c' would be retained would be the 'ch' formation, which will be dealt with later. Year 2 might reform 'w' spelling, so that 'which' and 'one' would take the same konsonant, wile Year 3 might well abolish 'y' replasing it with 'i' and Iear 4 might fiks the 'g/j' anomali wonse and for all. Jenerally, then, the improvement would kontinue iear bai iear with Iear 5 doing awai with useless double konsonants, and Iears 6-12 or so modifaiing vowlz and the rimeining voist and unvoist konsonants. Bai Iear 15 or sou, it wud fainali bi posibl tu meik ius ov thi ridandant letez 'c,' 'y' and 'x''—bai now jast a memori in the maindz ov ould doderez—tu riplais 'ch,' 'sh,' and 'th' rispektivli. Fainali, xen, aafte sam 20 iers ov orxogrefkl riform, wi wud hev a lojikl, kohirnt speling in ius xrewawt xe Ingliy-spiking werld.

The reactivity here is the replacement of letters, or letter combinations. Notice how the action associated with a reactive component may depend upon the phonetics as well as on letters and letter combinations. Notice also that, unlike the previous example where the action was retrospective and we are given the phrase before the action, here it is applied to subsequent text and we are given the result of the application. Again, reactive components are acted on by other reactive components.

Example 23 (Grammar and word order). Consider the example text:

> Tom loves Mary. From now on, subjects switch with objects. Pizza likes Jack. From now on, verbs switch with objects. Cat Mary loves.

Here again there are reactive components, now acting on word order according to phrase classes occupied by words. Like the previous example, this is forward action. Notice also that the reactive component '*verbs switch with objects*' is subject to the component '*subjects switch with objects*' and so the actual action is '*objects switch with verbs*', which, in this case, is the same action but, in general, would be different. Again, this brings out the complexity of embedded reactivity, where the reactivity can act on other reactive components, or indeed allows the possibility of two reactive components acting on each other.

7.1   Formalising Grammars with Embedded Reactivity

We begin the process of formalising a general notion of an *embedded reactive grammar*. To do so, we first formalise parse trees in terms of derivations.

We introduce a labelling of non-terminals in a derivation sequence using lists of numbers. For example, consider a derivation step

$$aAcB \to aaCAcB$$

which is the result of replacing A using a rule

$$r : A \to aCA.$$

If the original non-terminal symbol A is labelled p then the C in the result string is labelled $p.1$ and the A in the resultant string is labelled $p.2$; the label of B remains unchanged. The initial symbol is labelled with the empty sequence. Each derivation step is denoted by a pair (p, r) consisting of a non-terminal label p (the label of the non-terminal to be replaced) and a rule name r (the rule used).

Definition 7. *For derivation steps $\pi = (p, r)$ and $\pi' = (p', r')$, we say that (p', r') extends (p, r) iff sequence p is a prefix of p'.*

For a derivation sequence, $\delta = \pi_0, \ldots, \pi_n$ a subsequence $\pi_{i_0}, \ldots \pi_{i_k}$ is compatible iff (1) $\pi_{i_{j+1}}$ extends π_{i_j} for $0 \leq j \leq k - 1$, and (2) no intermediate derivations extend any of the elements of the subsequence.

In a derivation sequence δ of string s, the collection of compatible subsequences which are left closed (i.e. may not be extended leftwards) forms a tree (i.e. is prefix closed). This is the parse tree $\mathsf{parsetree}(\delta, s)$ determined by the derivation sequence. A path p in a parse tree (as a list of numbers) determines a subtree $\mathsf{subtree}(\delta, s, p)$. The set of paths in a parse tree, we denote by $\mathsf{paths}(\delta, s)$.

Definition 8 (Embedded reactive grammar). *An* embedded reactive grammar *consists of a set of non-terminal symbols N, an initial non-terminal $S \in N$, a set of terminal symbols Σ, a set of (production) rules P as in Definition 1, together with for each derivation sequence δ of string s a set of reactive components $R(\delta, s) \subseteq \mathsf{paths}(\delta, s)$. In addition, there is a transformation of strings T, which associates with each reactive component $p \in R(\delta, s)$ a transformed string $s' = T(p, \delta, s)$ together with a derivation sequence δ' of s'.*

The definition is fairly general. It allows reactive components to contain non-terminals (i.e. allows some forms of 'reactive patterns'). The transformations associated with a reactive component are unrestricted – any string may be the result of such a transformation. Note that the result of a transformation is not simply a string but a derivation sequence of a string. Thus, transformations associated with reactive components map derivation sequences to derivation sequences. However, the transformation is functional – a unique string and its derivation is determined by a reactive component in a derivation of a string. The recognition of reactive components is, in general, dependent upon the context, i.e. on the string in which it is embedded. For example, in the case of text correction, a phrase '*sorry I mean football*' may be considered not to be a reactive component if, for example, it appears in a direct quote.

In defining a grammar, it is usual to define what is meant by a derivation step. However, this is no longer a simple matter because embedded reactivities move us between derivation sequences. Several options are available which correspond to strategies for applying the actions associated with reactive components. One is to first generate a terminal string using the underlying grammar, then apply the actions of any reactive components (in any order, each time producing a new derivation sequence), to end possibly with a word with no reactive components (this will not always occur - it depends on the transformations). Another possibility is to interleave applications of production rules with reactive transformations. In either case, we need a new term to denote the combined processes of applying production rules and reactive transformations.

Definition 9. *A string s' with derivation δ' is a* single step result *from string s with derivation δ, written $(\delta, s) \rightarrow (\delta', s')$ in an embedded reactive grammar iff either (1) this is a single step derivation in the underlying grammar, or (2) (δ', s') is the result of a transformation associated with a reactive component of (δ, s).*

Chains of such single steps arise from various strategies for applying grammar productions and reactive transformations.

Let us now consider how one of the examples above is an embedded reactive grammar in this sense.

Example 24 (Correction grammars revisited). We revisit the example of correction grammars above (Example 21) and show how it is an example of an embedded reactive grammar.

The reactive components are of the form $\rho =$ '*sorry I mean w*' where w is a terminal word generated from a non-terminal X. In the tree $t = \mathsf{parsetree}(\Delta, s)$, the action of a subtree determining the reactive component ρ is the replacement of a suitably chosen subtree of t and the removal of subtree ρ from t. The resultant tree must itself be a parse tree in the underlying grammar i.e. have an associated derivation Δ'. Which subtree is replaced is a choice determined by our understanding of the notion of text correction.

This is one form of an embedded reactive grammar that describes the correction process. Notice that we only replace with terminal words. This is not always necessary (depending upon how trees are matched in the correction phase) and an alternative formulation would allow reactive components to be of the form '*sorry I mean s*' where $s \in (N \cup \Sigma)^*$.

Thus, in the case of correction grammars, we present the string before any actions of reactive components are undertaken, and then consider the result of these actions. For the other two examples above, the text presented is the result of applying the actions. An analysis of the text requires us to find a chain of single steps (consisting of applying grammar rules and reactive transformations) which result in the given text. Notice also that, in these cases, the reactive transformation leaves in place the reactive component (i.e. the instructions for modifying the text) instead of deleting it.

8   Reactivity and Contrary to Duty

The previous sections entertained the idea of reactive rules, namely when a certain rewrite rule r_1 is used then another rule r_2 gets activated (or de-activated) and is available (resp. no longer available) to use. This concept allows us to achieve two more goals:

1. Introduce the idea of contrary to duty rules into grammars.
2. Use the expanded types of grammars to provide proof theory to contrary to duty obligations in deontic logic.

Let us begin with an example.

Example 25 (A simple grammar). We introduce a simple grammar. Let the non-terminal letters be $\infty, 0, x_1, \neg x_1, x_2, \neg x_2$.

The letters "$\neg x$" are considered atomic. The significance of the prefix "$\neg$" will become apparent when we make a connection with deontic logic, see [18].

Consider the following rules:

$$
\begin{array}{ll}
r_{\infty,0}: & \infty \to 0 \\
r_{0,x_1}: & 0 \to x_1 \\
r_{0,\neg x_1}: & 0 \to \neg x_1 \\
r_{\neg x_1 x_2}: & \neg x_1 \to x_2 \\
r_{\neg x_1, \neg x_2}: & \neg x_1 \to \neg x_2.
\end{array}
$$

Assume our grammar has the starting letter as ∞ and has the rules $r_{0,\infty}$ and r_{∞,x_1} active and all the other rules not active and that this does not change during derivation. Our starting point is always ∞. We can derive in this grammar

$$\infty \to 0 \to x_1$$

and no more.

So the above reactive grammar is equivalent to the traditional context free grammar with the rules

$$\infty \to 0 \text{ and } 0 \to x_1.$$

We can ask ourselves what if we are naughty and decide to use rules which are not active and derive words using them?

Suppose we use the following derivation:

$$\infty \to 0 \to \neg x_1.$$

Having done that we can continue to illegitimately derive either $\neg x_1 \to x_2$ or $\neg x_1 \to \neg x_2$.

A contrary to duty approach might say that if the inactive rule $0 \to \neg x_1$ is used then activate the rule $\neg x_1 \to x_2$. So the way to understand this intuitively is as follows:

(a) From 0 you should go to x_1 not to $\neg x_1$.
(b) If however you do illegitimately go to $\neg x_1$ then at least be good and continue to x_2 and not to $\neg x_2$.

Let us write the reactive grammar for this:

1. ∞ starting point.
   $r_{\infty,0}, r_{\infty,x_1}$ active. All other rules inactive.
2. If $r_{0,\neg x_1}$ is used then activate rule $r_{\neg x_1, x_2}$.
   Note that (2) leaves rule $0 \to x_1$ still active and so it is possible also to derive x_1. We could have used (2*) instead of (2).
2*. If rule $r_{0 \neg x_1}$ is used then deactivate rule r_{0,x_1} and activate rule $r_{\neg x_1, x_2}$.

To see the connection with deontic logic, consider the next example.

Example 26 (Local housing estate). The following is a set of rules for a local housing estate.

1. It is obligatory to have a fence around your house. Formally

$$\bigcirc \text{Fence}$$

2. If you do not have a fence, you should have a dog. Formally

$$\neg \text{Fence} \to \bigcirc \text{Dog}$$

Deontic logic traditionally uses **SDL** (standard deontic logic) to model obligations. This is the modal logic **K** with the modal operator $\bigcirc$ and the axiom $\neg \bigcirc \perp$.

Obligation statements are written in this logic. Statement 2 above is a contrary to duty statement. You should have a fence but failing that (i.e. if you violate the fence obligation), then at least have a dog. It is not clear (open) whether once you have a dog, the obligation to have a fence is still in force. **SDL** has difficulties modelling contrary to duty obligations and one such famous difficulty is the Chisholm paradox set, see [5, 11].

C1:   You should go and help your neighbour:

$$\bigcirc \text{go}$$

C2:   If you go you ought to tell him you are coming

$$\text{go} \to \bigcirc \text{tell}$$

C3:   If you do not go you ought not to tell him you are coming:

$$\neg \text{go} \to \bigcirc \neg \text{tell}$$

C4:   Fact: you do not go.

$$\neg \text{go}$$

This is a set of logically independent clauses. It is difficult to model in **SDL** (i.e. find a uniform translation into **SDL** such that the four clauses are consistent, independent and closed under substitution) and many logic papers have been written about it. Gabbay [11] proposed a reactive solution. This is our point of contact with reactive grammars.

Remark 1. To show the connection of deontic logic with reactive grammars we need an intermediate language which can be read by both disciplines. We explain this by an example

Consider Figure 11

This figure has a set of nodes $S = \{\infty, 0, x_1, \neg x_1, x_2, \neg x_2\}$ and a binary relation $R \subseteq S \times S$ denoted by the arrows and another relation $\mathbb{R} \subseteq S^2 \times S^2$ denoted by the double arrows.

The figure can be read in two ways

(i) As a carrier figure for a denotic contrary to duty system.
(ii) As a carrier figure for some specialised reactive grammar.

Let us address (i) first. We read ∞ as home and 0 as office. $\infty \to 0$ means you go from home to office and thus your obligations begin. The double arrow

$$(\infty \to 0) \twoheadrightarrow (0 \to x_1)$$

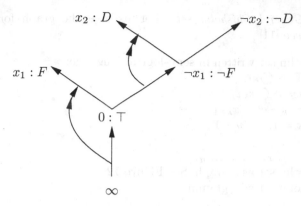

Fig. 11.

says your obligation is to continue to x_1 (i.e. $\bigcirc$Fence). If you go there then you are done. If you go to $\neg x_1 : \neg F$ you trigger a new obligation

$$(0 \rightarrow \neg x_1) \twoheadrightarrow (\neg x_1 \rightarrow x_2)$$

namely to go to $x_2 : D$

$$(\neg \text{Fence} \; \rightarrow \bigcirc \text{Dog}).$$

Formally our graph figure is a tree with root ∞, with 0 the only successor to ∞ and from each $y_1 \rightarrow y_2$ there exists at most one double arrow and this double arrow is of the form

$$(y_1 \rightarrow y_2) \twoheadrightarrow (y_2 \rightarrow z).$$

in which case we write $y_2 \rightarrow \bigcirc z$.

Let us address reading (ii) now. The graph nodes are the grammars non-terminals.

- ∞ is the starting point of the grammar.
- $\infty \rightarrow 0$ is active at the start. Everything else is nonactive.
- Whenever we have $x \rightarrow y$ in the graph this indicates a rule of grammar $x \rightarrow y$.
- whenever we use a rule $x \rightarrow y$ and in the graph we have

$$(x \rightarrow y) \twoheadrightarrow (y \rightarrow z)$$

then $(y \rightarrow z)$ gets activated and all other rules get deactivated.

We allow naughty illegitimate derivations as well (naughty meaning one uses rules even if they are not active) but record violations (a violation instance is the use of a rule even though it is not active).

The following are the only possible derivations in the grammar of Figure 11. 1 means legitimate move, 0 means illegitimate move:

$$\infty \rightarrow_1 0 \rightarrow_1 x_1$$
$$\infty \rightarrow_1 0 \rightarrow_0 \neg x_1 \rightarrow_1 x_2$$
$$\infty \rightarrow_1 0 \rightarrow_0 \neg x_1 \rightarrow_0 \neg x_2$$

Example 27 (General Chisholm set). Let us give the graph for the general Chisholm set, see [11].

1. The Chisholm set written in semi-logical language:

   C1: $\quad \top \to \bigcirc x_1$

   Ck: $\quad x_k \to \bigcirc x_{k+1}$

   $\qquad \neg x_k \to \bigcirc \neg x_{k+1}$

   $\qquad k = 1, \ldots, n-1.$

   Facts: $\quad \neg x_1, \pm x_2, \ldots, \pm x_n.$

2. The Chisholm set as a graph. See Figure 12

3. The Chisholm set as a grammar

$$\infty \to 0$$
$$0 \to x_1$$
$$0 \to \neg x_1$$
$$\vdots$$
$$x_k \to x_{k+1}$$
$$\neg x_k \to \neg x_{k+1}$$

   — ∞ the starting point
   — $\infty \to 0, 0 \to x_1$ active
   — All other rules not active
   — If we use $z \to \pm x_k$ then this makes $\pm x_k \to \pm x_{k+1}$ active and all other rules inactive.

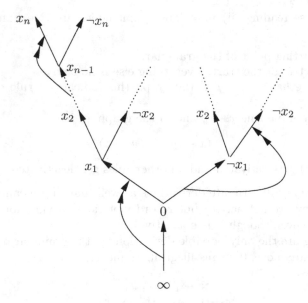

Fig. 12.

Definition 10. *1. A reactive grammar is said to be a linear-resource grammar (the word "linear" here comes from the resource logic known as "linear logic") if whenever a rule is used in a derivation it is permanently deactivated. So for example switch grammars are not a linear resource.*

2. A linear resource grammar is said to be Chisholm if it has only non-terminal letters and rules of the form $x \to y$ only, where x, y are single non terminals. We further have

   (a) Let ∞ be the starting point, then each point $y \neq \infty$ has a unique $x \neq y$ such that $x \to y$ is a rule.

   (b) Whenever rule $x \to y$ is used then maybe some rules $y \to z$ (same y) are activated and all other rules are deactivated.

   (c) Let $(\infty, x_1, x_2 \ldots)$ be a maximal path in the tree. (Such a path is called a complete contrary to duty run.) We annotate each connection $x_i \to x_{i+1}$ by 1 (legitimate) or 0 (not legitimate) as follows:

   c1. $\infty \to x_1$ is annotated 1 if active at start otherwise annotated 0.

   c2. Assume at x_i it is clear which rules are active or not. Then annotate $x_i \to x_{i+1}$ by 1 if active at x_i and by 0 if not active at x_i. Use clause (b) above to decide which rules $u \to v$ are active at x_{i+1}.

   c3. The annotated contrary to duty run (path) tells us about the "violations" of the derivation constructing the path.

3. A Chisholm linear resource grammar is said to be with a meta-level policy, if it has an associated algorithm for deciding, for each complete annotated contrary to duty run, whether it is acceptable or not (for example the meta-level policy not to accept any run with more than one violation).

The ideas behind the above definitions are very promising. They invite the systematic study of how to add logically "compensation/counter/retraction" to any evolving system with choice. This is a subject for further papers.

9 Conclusions

Reaction to movement is a pretty natural concept. If one considers the dynamic operation of an automaton, or state machine, there is movement as the automaton transits from one state to another as a symbol is accepted (or generated). Thus, it is natural to explore how automata, themselves, might be extended to react to such movement. Guided by prior work applying ideas of reactivity in automata and Kripke structures, we have made an initial exploration into how different forms of reactivity can be applied in the context of grammars. Given the considerable research that has been undertaken in the area of grammars over the past 40 years, it comes as little surprise that some of the reactivities we've considered coincide with various, well-known, extensions to grammar systems. Our interests, however, have been driven primarily by an investigation of principles, rather than finding ways to extend the expressiveness of particular forms of grammar rules. Our work in this area is preliminary and, although results are few, we believe that the range of reactivities explored is itself of considerable interest. One particular area that we have not explored in this paper and which we believe warrants further work is the use of reactive grammars in language processing, for example, parsing, with the intention of generating efficient algorithms for fairly complex languages which can, nevertheless, be expressed using simple reactive grammars.

Acknowledgments. The authors would like to thank Yanliang Jiang for his Masters work at the University of Manchester on investigating and implementing some forms of embedded reactive grammars.

References

1. Aho, A.V.: Indexed Grammars — An Extension of Context-Free Grammars. Journal of the ACM 15(4), 647–671 (1968)
2. Barringer, H., Fisher, M., Gabbay, D., Owens, R., Reynolds, M.: The Imperative Future: Principles of Executable Temporal Logic. Research Studies Press (1996)
3. Barringer, H., Goldberg, A., Havelund, K., Sen, K.: Rule-Based Runtime Verification. In: Steffen, B., Levi, G. (eds.) VMCAI 2004. LNCS, vol. 2937, pp. 44–57. Springer, Heidelberg (2004)
4. Barringer, H., Havelund, K., Rydeheard, D.: Rule systems for run-time monitoring: from Eagle to RuleR (extended version). Journal of Logic and Computation 20(3), 675–706 (2010)
5. Chisholm, R.M.: Contrary-to-duty imperatives and deontic logic. Analysis 24, 33–36 (1969)
6. Chomsky, N.: On Certain Formal Properties of Grammars. Information and Control 2, 137–167 (1959)
7. Crochemore, M., Gabbay, D.: Reactive Automata. Information and Computation 209(4), 692–704 (2011)
8. Dassow, J., Paun, G.: Regulated Rewriting in Formal Language Theory. EATCS Monographs on Theoretical Computer Science, vol. 18. Springer (1989)
9. Fernau, H.: Regulated grammars with leftmost derivation. In: Rovan, B. (ed.) SOFSEM 1998. LNCS, vol. 1521, pp. 322–331. Springer, Heidelberg (1998)
10. Gabbay, D.M.: Introducing Reactive Kripke Semantics and Arc Accessibility. In: Avron, A., Dershowitz, N., Rabinovich, A. (eds.) Pillars of Computer Science. LNCS, vol. 4800, pp. 292–341. Springer, Heidelberg (2008)
11. Gabbay, D.M.: Temporal deontic logic for the generalised Chisholm set of contrary to duty obligations. In: Ågotnes, T., Broersen, J., Elgesem, D. (eds.) DEON 2012. LNCS, vol. 7393, pp. 91–107. Springer, Heidelberg (2012)
12. Gabbay, D.: Overview on the connection between reactive Kripke models and argumentation networks. Annals of Mathematics and Artificial Intelligence, Special Issue: New Developments in Reactive Semantics 66(1-4), 1–5 (2012)
13. Gabbay, D.: Introducing reactive Kripke semantics and arc accessibility. Annals of Mathematics and Artificial Intelligence, Special Issue: New Developments in Reactive Semantics 66(1–4), 7–53 (2012)
14. Gabbay, D.: Introducing reactive modal tableaux. Annals of Mathematics and Artificial Intelligence, Special Issue: New Developments in Reactive Semantics 66(1–4), 55–79 (2012)
15. Gabbay, D.: Completeness theorems for reactive modal logics: Annals of Mathematics and Artificial Intelligence. Special Issue: New Developments in Reactive Semantics 66(1–4), 81–129 (2012)

16. Gabbay, D., Marcelino, S.: Modal logics of reactive frames. Studia Logica 93, 403–444 (2009)
17. Gabbay, D., Marcelino, S.: Global view on reactivity: switch graphs and their logics. Annals of Mathematics and Artificial Intelligence, Special Issue: New Developments in Reactive Semantics 66(1–4), 131–162 (2012)
18. Gabbay, D., Horty, J., van der Meyden, R., Parent, X., van der Torre, L. (eds.): Handbook of Deontic Logic and Normative Systems. College Publications (2013)
19. Ginsburg, S., Spanier, E.H.: Control Sets on Grammars. Mathematical Systems Theory 2(2), 159–177 (1968)
20. Ibarra, O.H.: Simple matrix languages. Information and Control 17, 359–394 (1970)
21. Kasai, T.: An Hierarchy between Context-Free and Context-Sensitive Languages. Journal of Computer and System Sciences 4, 492–508 (1970)
22. Lindenmayer, A.: Mathematical models for cellular interaction in development, I and II. Journal of Theoretical Biology 18, 280–315 (1968)
23. Meersman, R., Rozenberg, G.: Cooperating grammar systems. In: Winkowski, J. (ed.) MFCS 1978. LNCS, vol. 64, pp. 364–373. Springer, Heidelberg (1978)
24. Moriya, E.: Some remarks on State Grammars and Matrix Grammars. Information and Control 23, 48–57 (1973)
25. Paun, G.: The Generative Mechanisms of Some Economic Processes. Techn. Publ. House, Bucharest (1980)
26. Rosenkrantz, D.J.: Programmed grammars and classes of formal languages. Journal of the ACM 16(1), 107–131 (1969)

Modal Scenarios as Automata

David Harel and Amir Kantor

Faculty of Mathematics and Computer Science,
Weizmann Institute of Science, Rehovot, Israel
{dharel,amir.kantor}@weizmann.ac.il

Abstract. Scenario-based modeling in *live sequence charts* (LSC) involves specifying multi-modal inter-object scenarios, in which events can
be mandatory (hot) or possible (cold). In translating LSCs into automata
over infinite words, an intermediate step constructs a kind of transition
system that we call a *modal state structure* (MSS). Here we present MSSs
as abstract forms of modal scenarios (with both mandatory, possible and
forbidden behavior), which may encode more general patterns than those
inherent in LSC, such as loops, alternatives and breaks. MSSs are essentially automata, in which the notion of temperature is adopted from
LSCs, replacing traditional acceptance conditions.

Keywords: live sequence charts, scenario, multi-modal, automata, modal
state structures.

*Dedicated to Prof. Yaacov Choueka: scholar, teacher, researcher
— all of the very highest quality — and a true inspiration too.*

1 Introduction

Scenario-based specification and programming is an approach to the modeling
of reactive systems via inter-object interactions [5,14]. The components of the
system interact with each other and with the system's environment (including
the user). In this approach the inter-object interactions *define* the behavior of
the system. This is in contrast to the more traditional intra-object approach
(e.g. statecharts [10,11]), where a reactive system is defined through the behavior
of each of its components. The scenario-based approach considers what happens
between the components and the environment, with less emphasis put on the
separate behavior of each object.

Live sequence charts (LSC) [5,14] is a primary example of a visual scenario-
based formalism, which may be used for the specification and the programming
of reactive systems. The language extends classical message sequence charts
(MSC) [15], mainly by being *multi-modal*, i.e., distinguishing between behaviors that *may* happen in the system (cold) and those that *must* happen (hot).
LSCs can also naturally express a variety of flavors of behavior and constraints,
such as forbidden scenarios.

N. Dershowitz and E. Nissan (Eds.): Choueka Festschrift, Part I, LNCS 8001, pp. 156–167, 2014.

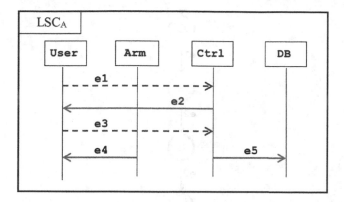

Fig. 1. An example: LSC$_A$

We consider here the UML2-compliant variant of the LSC language, defined in [13], which is slightly generalized and more uniform than the original. A chart contains objects arranged in vertical lifelines and the messages (events) that they send and receive drawn as horizontal arrows. Messages are either hot or cold (mandatory or possible, respectively). Since we are interested here purely in the inter-object dynamics of scenarios, we disregard conditions that constrain the state of the system. We do, however, allow trivial True/False conditions (either hot or cold), in order to specify synchronization points (using the condition True) and anti-scenarios (using hot False conditions).

The semantics of LSC may be presented via a translation into Büchi automata [16,13]. As an intermediate step, a process of 'unwinding' the chart results in a structure that is essentially a kind of modal transition system. This transition system, which we call a *modal state structure* (MSS), captures the modal scenario encoded in the chart.

In Sect. 2, we present an example of a live sequence chart and its underlying MSS. Section 3 provides a definition of modal state structures, and presents their semantics via Büchi automata. Section 4 extends the interpretation of MSS to express universality and a similar notion of iteration. A few patterns of scenarios that can be encoded naturally in MSS are considered in Sect. 5. Section 6 concludes with some shortcomings of MSS and future work.

2   MSS Underlying LSC

LSC$_A$, which appears in Fig. 1, is an example of a universal live sequence chart. It may correspond to an interaction of purchasing a product in a vending machine, and it captures the following modal scenario. If and when the User sends e_1 to Ctrl, the latter must respond with e_2. Then, if User sends e_3 to Ctrl, the mechanical Arm must respond with e_4 and Ctrl must update the database by sending e_5. There is no order dependency of e_4 and e_5.

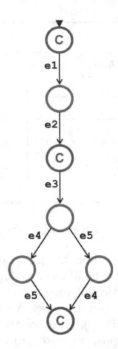

Fig. 2. MSS_A underlying LSC_A

In order to present trace-based semantics for LSCs, they may be translated into Büchi automata [16,13]. This involves 'unwinding' [16] each chart into states that correspond to cuts in the chart (which record progress along lifelines). This results in what we shall call a modal state structure (MSS), which captures the modal scenario encoded in the chart. MSS_A, which corresponds to LSC_A, is depicted in Fig. 2. Each state of MSS_A corresponds to a cut in LSC_A, and the initial state (drawn with a small incoming black triangle) is the minimal cut of LSC_A. The temperature of cuts, either cold or hot, is recorded by temperature of states (cold states are drawn marked with the letter 'C'). Outgoing transitions of each state correspond to enabled events in the corresponding LSC_A cut, each of which results in a change of cut. We regard an event as holding information about its source and target, e.g. $event = source!message?target$, so that this information is not lost in MSS_A.

In addition to the above, we also designate a set R of restricted events of MSS_A. These are not allowed to occur 'out of order' in MSS_A (i.e., when they are not enabled), and cause a violation if they do (see Sect. 3). There are few possible interpretations of LSCs with respect to this set of restricted events [16,14]. We may interpret LSC_A in the *strict* sense, meaning that the restricted events are exactly the events appearing in the chart, i.e., $R = \{e_1, e_2, \ldots, e_5\}$. When one of these events occurs out of order, it causes a violation. Other events may occur without causing such violation. Other interpretations, namely *immediate* and *tolerant* (or *weak*), are discussed in Sect. 3.

3   MSS and Büchi Automata

A *modal state structure* (MSS) $\mathcal{M}$ is defined by $\mathcal{M} = \langle \Sigma, S, s_0, \rightarrow, C, R \rangle$, where Σ is a finite alphabet of events, S is a finite set of states, $s_0 \in S$ is the initial state, $\rightarrow \subseteq S \times \Sigma \times S$ is a labeled transition relation, and $C \subseteq S$ are designated as *cold* states. All other states are *hot*. $R \subseteq \Sigma$ is a set of *restricted* events, which are roughly events that cause a *violation* if they appear 'out of order'.

For $s, s' \in S$ and $e \in \Sigma$, we write $s \xrightarrow{e} s'$ iff $\langle s, e, s' \rangle \in \rightarrow$. Moreover, for $s \in S$ and $e \in \Sigma$, $s \xrightarrow{e}$ denotes that there exists $s' \in S$ such that $s \xrightarrow{e} s'$.

Let $s \in S$ be any state. The set of *enabled* events in s, i.e., events on some transition outgoing from s, is defined by $\mathrm{E}(s) = \{e \in \Sigma : s \xrightarrow{e}\}$. We say that s is *dead-end* iff $\mathrm{E}(s) = \emptyset$. All other events, namely *disabled* events $\Sigma \setminus \mathrm{E}(s)$, are partitioned into two sets: *violating* events $\mathrm{V}(s)$ and *indifferent* events $\mathrm{I}(s)$. $\mathrm{V}(s)$ is the set of disabled events that are also restricted; or, in the case of a dead-end state, all disabled events. These are the events that cause a violation (either cold or hot). The rest of the disabled events do not cause a violation, and are indifferent in state s. More formally we define

$$\mathrm{V}(s) = \begin{cases} R \setminus \mathrm{E}(s) & \text{if } \mathrm{E}(s) \neq \emptyset \\ \Sigma & \text{if } \mathrm{E}(s) = \emptyset \end{cases}$$

$$\mathrm{I}(s) = \begin{cases} (\Sigma \setminus R) \setminus \mathrm{E}(s) & \text{if } \mathrm{E}(s) \neq \emptyset \\ \emptyset & \text{if } \mathrm{E}(s) = \emptyset \ . \end{cases}$$

Figure 2 is an example of an MSS, obtained from the LSC of Fig. 1.

$\mathcal{M}$ is interpreted as following. An infinite word $\alpha \in \Sigma^\omega$ denotes a chain of events, and may designate a trace of an infinite execution. It is accepted by $\mathcal{M}$ (i.e., it complies with $\mathcal{M}$) iff there is an accepting run of $\mathcal{M}$ on α. The *language* of $\mathcal{M}$, denoted $\mathcal{L}(\mathcal{M})$, is the set of $\alpha \in \Sigma^\omega$ that are accepted by $\mathcal{M}$. A cold state is stable, while a hot state is unstable and carries a commitment to arrive later at a cold state. Consider an event e occurring when a run of $\mathcal{M}$ is in some state s (initially in s_0). If e is enabled in s, it must lead to some $s' \in S$ such that $s \xrightarrow{e} s'$. If e is indifferent in s (i.e., $e \in \mathrm{I}(s)$) we must stay at state s. And if, however, e is violating in s (i.e., $e \in \mathrm{V}(s)$), a violation occurs. Such a violation is either hot or cold according to the temperature of s. A hot violation is regarded as invalid (since a hot state is unstable and carries a commitment to eventually reach a cold state), yielding a rejection of the run. On the other hand, a cold violation (also called *completion*) yields acceptance of the run. If no violation occurs during the run it is accepting iff every hot state is followed by a cold state; i.e., cold states occur infinitely often.

In order to present the semantics of $\mathcal{M}$, we translate it into a Büchi automaton over infinite words [21,4], which we denote by $\mathfrak{B}(\mathcal{M})$; see Fig. 3. Specifically, we let $\mathfrak{B}(\mathcal{M}) = \langle \Sigma, \overline{S}, s_0, \Delta, F \rangle$, where Σ is the alphabet of $\mathfrak{B}(\mathcal{M})$, $\overline{S} := S \dot\cup \{\top\}$ are

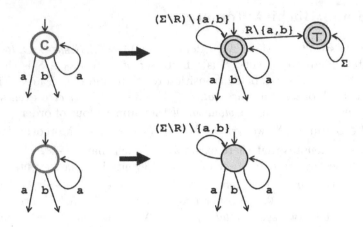

Fig. 3. Translation of an MSS into a Büchi automaton

its states, and s_0 is the initial state. $F := C \cup \{\top\}$ is the set of accepting states of $\mathfrak{B}(\mathcal{M})$, and its transition relation Δ is given by

$$\Delta := \ \rightarrow \ \cup \ \{\langle s, e, s \rangle : s \in S, \ e \in I(s)\}$$
$$\cup \ \{\langle s, e, \top \rangle : s \in C, \ e \in V(s)\}$$
$$\cup \ \{\langle \top, e, \top \rangle : e \in \Sigma\} \ .$$

The language of $\mathcal{M}$, denoted by $\mathcal{L}(\mathcal{M}) = \mathcal{L}(\mathfrak{B}(\mathcal{M})) \subseteq \Sigma^\omega$, is taken to be the language accepted by the automaton $\mathfrak{B}(\mathcal{M})$; i.e., consisting of the infinite words $\alpha \in \Sigma^\omega$ on which there exists an accepting run of $\mathfrak{B}(\mathcal{M})$. From this translation we see that runs that enter a cold (hot) dead-end state s are accepted (rejected). So these simple constructs are essentially 'accept' and 'reject', respectively. The result of translating MSS_A (originating from LSC_A) is depicted in Fig. 4.

The difference between MSS and Büchi automata lies in the semantics of disabled events. In MSS, if a disabled event occurs at state s, it is either indifferent or violating, and in the latter case it yields either acceptance or rejection of the run, according to the temperature of s. In contrast, in Büchi automata disabled events are always rejecting in both accepting and non-accepting states. We believe that the duality of hot and cold states in MSS, and the existence of indifferent events, is natural for specifying modal scenarios.

Different values of the set R of restricted events yield different semantical variants. When $R = \Sigma$, we term the MSS *immediate*, and any disabled event is violating, so transitions are to be taken immediately (if taken at all). If R is exactly the set of events appearing in the transition relation $\rightarrow$, the MSS is termed *strict* [16,14]. When $R = \emptyset$, no events are restricted, and the MSS is termed *tolerant*, or *weak* [16,14]. In this case, all disabled events are indifferent (unless the state is dead-end), and leave the scenario in the same state.

Given a Büchi automaton $\mathfrak{B}$ over alphabet Σ, we can translate it into an MSS $\mathcal{M}_\mathfrak{B}$ over Σ, in which the set R of restricted events is arbitrary. In this reverse translation we turn every accepting (resp. non-accepting) state q of $\mathfrak{B}$ into a

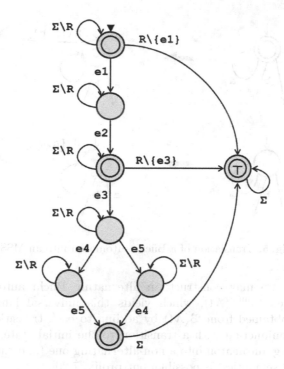

Fig. 4. Büchi automaton obtained from MSS_A

cold (resp. hot) state, and add transitions $\Sigma \setminus E(q)$ leading to a 'reject' state (an additional hot state with no outgoing transitions). This translation is depicted in Fig. 5. Note that $\mathcal{M_B}$ has no disabled events — all events at any state (except for the 'reject' state) are enabled — so $\mathcal{M_B}$ acts just like a Büchi automaton. From this we see that given a finite alphabet Σ and any set of restricted events $R \subseteq \Sigma$, MSSs over Σ and R are just as expressive as Büchi automata (i.e., they yield the ω-regular languages), and translations are simple. Immediate, strict and weak semantics are all equivalent in this general context of MSS.

4 Universality and Iteration

The semantics suggested for MSS is *initial*, in the sense that the prescribed behavior is checked to hold starting from the beginning of a trace (cf. [3,17]). The language defined above corresponds to this initial interpretation of $\mathcal{M}$, and is now denoted $\mathcal{L}^{init}(\mathcal{M}) = \mathcal{L}(\mathcal{M})$. However, scenarios prescribed by universal LSCs are usually interpreted as invariants. This means that in order for a trace $\alpha \in \Sigma^\omega$ to be accepted, it must conform to the scenario from *any* point on.

This *universal* semantics may be defined for MSS as follows. Denote by α/i the infinite word obtained from α with the first i letters truncated ($i \in \omega$). The universal language of MSS $\mathcal{M}$ is defined by

$$\mathcal{L}^{univ}(\mathcal{M}) = \{\, \alpha \in \Sigma^\omega : \forall i \in \omega,\ \alpha/i \in \mathcal{L}^{init}(\mathcal{M}) \,\} \; .$$

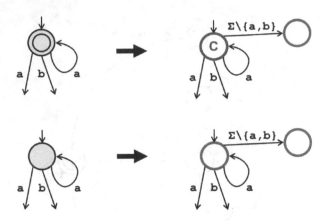

Fig. 5. Translation of a Büchi automaton into an MSS

Alternatively, we may construct an alternating Büchi automaton [20,18] from $\mathcal{M}$, denoted $\mathfrak{B}^{univ}(\mathcal{M})$, which yields this universal language directly (cf. [13]). It is obtained from $\mathfrak{B}(\mathcal{M})$ by adding to each transition leaving the initial state a conjunction with a transition to the initial state. A translation of this alternating automaton into a non-alternating one (and thus also into an MSS with initial semantics) is possible, but prolix [7,20].

A possible alternative to universality is an *iterative* semantics for MSS (cf. [3]). In this interpretation, similarly to initial semantics, we need only follow a single copy of the MSS at any point during the trace (except for non-deterministic transitions). However, if the scenario is completed (i.e., a cold violation occurs) the MSS starts over from its initial state, and needs to hold again from this point on. The event that caused the completion is not skipped; it is reconsidered at the initial state. Iterative semantics is more permissive than universal, as the scenario is checked to hold only from certain points on (the beginning, and points of completion). It is, however, more restrictive than initial semantics. More formally, $\mathcal{L}^{univ}(\mathcal{M}) \subseteq \mathcal{L}^{iter}(\mathcal{M}) \subseteq \mathcal{L}^{init}(\mathcal{M})$. When following a trace from the beginning, it may reside in any of the states of $\mathcal{M}$. In contrast to universality, there are no 'overlapping' configurations that correspond to different starting points of $\mathcal{M}$ along the trace. This suggests that iterative semantics may be easier to grasp and use in certain contexts. Moreover, in the context of LSC play-out [14] for instance, iterative semantics may yield more efficient executions, since only one copy of LSC is needed.

We present iterative semantics of $\mathcal{M}$ by translation into a Büchi automaton, denoted $\mathfrak{B}^{iter}(\mathcal{M})$; see Fig. 6. The automaton is defined by $\mathfrak{B}^{iter}(\mathcal{M}) = \langle \Sigma, S, s_0, \Delta, F \rangle$, where Σ is the alphabet of $\mathfrak{B}^{iter}(\mathcal{M})$, S are its states, and s_0 is the initial state. The set of accepting states is $F := C$, and the transition relation Δ is given by

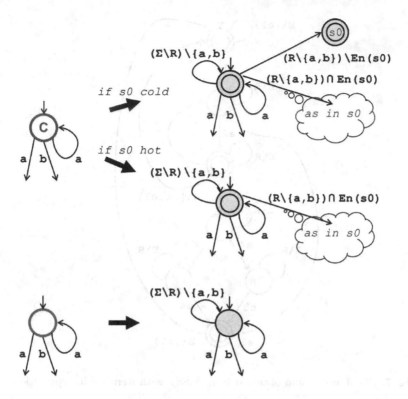

Fig. 6. Translation of an MSS with iterative interpretation into a Büchi automaton

$$\Delta := \;\rightarrow \cup \{\langle s,e,s\rangle : s \in S,\, e \in I(s)\}$$
$$\cup \{\langle s,e,q\rangle : s \in C,\, e \in V(s) \cap E(s_0),\, q \in S,\, s_0 \xrightarrow{e} q\}$$
$$\cup \{\langle s,e,s_0\rangle : s \in C,\, e \in V(s) \cap I(s_0)\}$$
$$\cup \{\langle s,e,s_0\rangle : s \in C,\, e \in V(s) \cap V(s_0),\, s_0 \in C\}^1 \;.$$

For M we define the iterative language $\mathcal{L}^{\text{iter}}(M) = \mathcal{L}(\mathfrak{B}^{\text{iter}}(M)) \subseteq \Sigma^\omega$, to be the language accepted by the automaton $\mathfrak{B}^{\text{iter}}(M)$. From the definition of $\mathfrak{B}^{\text{iter}}(M)$ we see that a hot dead-end state s is essentially 'reject', as all runs that enter it are rejected. Regarding a cold dead-end state s, it is equivalent in $\mathfrak{B}^{\text{iter}}(M)$ to the initial state (except possibly being accepting, as s_0 may be hot). This essentially means "accept and continue with the next iteration". The result of translating MSS_A with the iterative interpretation into a Büchi automaton is depicted in Fig. 7.

Any Büchi automaton may be translated into an MSS with iterative interpretation (in which the set R of restricted events is arbitrary). Actually, the same translation into initial MSS works here too. From this we see that given

---

[1] This part of Δ is empty if s_0 is hot.

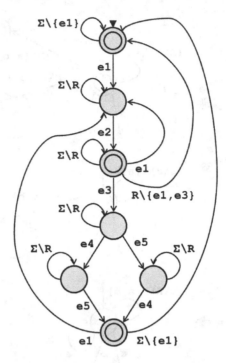

Fig. 7. Büchi automaton obtained from MSS$_A$ with iterative interpretation

a finite alphabet Σ and $R \subseteq \Sigma$ any set of restricted events, iterative MSS over Σ and R are just as expressive as Büchi automata over Σ; i.e., they yield the ω-regular languages. Immediate, strict and weak semantics are all equivalent in this context as well.

5   Patterns in MSS

Extended patterns are available in LSC through advanced constructs [13,14], which extend the syntax and the basic partial-order semantics of LSC. MSS allow the abstract specification of such patterns with only few primitive notions. Note that in the context of MSS we do not consider conditions or guards that constrain the state of the system.

Alternatives and *breaks* in the progress of modal scenarios are inherent in MSS through a multitude of transitions originating from a state, including non-deterministic ones. Unbounded *loops* are also easy to specify. Figure 8 shows a loop and a break escaping from it.

6   Shortcomings of MSS and Future Work

Bounded loops are not explicitly supported in MSS. They may be modeled by unraveling them into finite segments of the scenario. Additionally, in MSS one

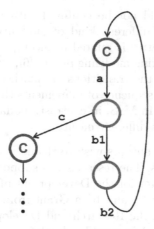

Fig. 8. Loop and break

needs to specify the transitions of each state separately. In many situations, however, taking a single transition should cause only a *partial* change in the required
behavior. Consider for instance the LSC of Fig. 1 after e_3 occurs. There are two
events that must take place — e_4 and e_5. After e_4 occurs, e_5 is still required to
occur, but e_4 is not. The required behavior changed, but only partially. In MSS
this needs to be specified accordingly in each state separately; see Fig. 2. This
independence of states in MSS yields additional expressive power, but it affects
the ease of use of this formalism in such cases.

In Petri nets [24,22] transitions cause only partial, local, change in the global
state. This principle traditionally suggests interpretations like concurrency and
distribution. In another piece of work [12], we consider a multi-modal extension
of Petri nets as a flexible and expressive means to specifying modal scenarios.
We introduce modalities into labeled Petri nets by assigning each transition a
temperature, either hot or cold. Now, a marking (i.e., the global state of the
net) is hot (unstable) if there is an enabled hot transition, and otherwise it is
cold (stable). Into this new setting we then incorporate other notions related to
temperature, such as hot and cold violations. Moreover, a unification principle is
introduced, through which firings of few enabled transitions, which are labeled
with the same event, are identified.

The definitions we presented for the semantics of MSS do not relate specifically to an interaction between an open system and its environment. In an open
system, the system and its environment are regarded as adversaries (see [23,9]).
This issue is treated in the context of LSC through the definition of its operational semantics (namely, play-out [14] and its extensions). Another treatment
appears in [2,1]; it involves not only distinguishing system events from environment events, but also expresses the semantics of LSC by dividing it into safety
and liveness. Extending the semantics of MSS to relate explicitly to open-systems
in a general and natural way is an interesting topic for future research. In this
context, one may discuss the execution of such abstract scenarios.

We note that MSS should not be confused with modal transition systems (MTS) [19], which carry a different kind of modality; essentially that of being partially defined. The latter is related to incomplete information about the transitions of the system during modeling phases [6], and to the analysis of properties [8]. Roughly, some of the transitions are marked as provisional, and may be retained or removed in a sequence of refinements that continues until no provisional transitions remain. In MSS, in contrast, modality is attached to states, and its interpretation is of a different nature.

Acknowledgements. The authors wish to thank Shahar Maoz and Itai Segall for many helpful discussions. The research was supported in part by The John von Neumann Minerva Center for the Development of Reactive Systems at the Weizmann Institute of Science, and by a Grant from the G.I.F., the German-Israeli Foundation for Scientific Research and Development. The research was also supported in part by an Advanced Research Grant to the first-listed author, from the European Research Council (ERC), under the European Community's Seventh Framework Programme (FP7/2007-2013).

References

1. Bontemps, Y.: Relating Inter-Agent and Intra-Agent Specifications (The Case of Live Sequence Charts). Ph.D. thesis, Facultés Universitaires Notre-Dame de la Paix, Institut d'Informatique (University of Namur, Computer Science Dept) (April 2005)
2. Bontemps, Y., Heymans, P., Schobbens, P.Y.: From live sequence charts to state machines and back: A guided tour. IEEE Trans. Software Eng. 31(12), 999–1014 (2005)
3. Brill, M., Damm, W., Klose, J., Westphal, B., Wittke, H.: Live Sequence Charts. In: Ehrig, H., Damm, W., Desel, J., Große-Rhode, M., Reif, W., Schnieder, E., Westkämper, E. (eds.) INT 2004. LNCS, vol. 3147, pp. 374–399. Springer, Heidelberg (2004)
4. Büchi, J.R.: On a decision method in restricted second order arithmetic. In: Proc. Internat. Congress on Logic Methodology and Philosophy of Science 1960, pp. 1–12. Stanford Univ. Press, Stanford (1962)
5. Damm, W., Harel, D.: LSCs: Breathing Life into Message Sequence Charts. J. on Formal Methods in System Design 19(1), 45–80 (2001); preliminary version in Ciancarini, P., Fantechi, A., Gorrieri, R. (eds.): Proc. 3rd IFIP Int. Conf. on Formal Methods for Open Object-Based Distributed Systems (FMOODS 1999), pp. 293–312. Kluwer Academic Publishers (1999)
6. D'Ippolito, N., Fischbein, D., Chechik, M., Uchitel, S.: MTSA: The Modal Transition System Analyser. In: Proceedings of the 23rd IEEE/ACM International Conference on Automated Software Engineering (ASE 2008), pp. 475–476. IEEE Computer Society, Washington, DC (2008)
7. Drusinsky, D., Harel, D.: On the power of bounded concurrency I: finite automata. J. ACM 41(3), 517–539 (1994)
8. Godefroid, P., Huth, M., Jagadeesan, R.: Abstraction-Based Model Checking Using Modal Transition Systems. In: Larsen, K.G., Nielsen, M. (eds.) CONCUR 2001. LNCS, vol. 2154, pp. 426–440. Springer, Heidelberg (2001)

9. Grädel, E., Thomas, W., Wilke, T. (eds.): Automata, Logics, and Infinite Games. LNCS, vol. 2500. Springer, Heidelberg (2002)

10. Harel, D.: Statecharts: A visual formalism for complex systems. Sci. Comput. Program. 8(3), 231–274 (1987)

11. Harel, D., Gery, E.: Executable object modeling with statecharts. IEEE Computer 30(7), 31–42 (1997)

12. Harel, D., Kantor, A.: Multi-modal scenarios revisited: A net-based representation. Theoretical Computer Science 429, 118–127 (2012)

13. Harel, D., Maoz, S.: Assert and Negate Revisited: Modal Semantics for UML Sequence Diagrams. Software and Systems Modeling (SoSyM) 7(2), 237–252 (2008), Preliminary version appeared in Proc. 5th Int. Workshop on Scenarios and State-Machines (SCESM 2006) at the 28th Int. Conf. on Soft. Eng (ICSE 2006), May 13-19, pp. 237–252. ACM Press (2008)

14. Harel, D., Marelly, R.: Come, Let's Play: Scenario-Based Programming Using LSCs and the Play-Engine. Springer (2003)

15. ITU: International Telecommunication Union Recommendation Z.120: Message Sequence Charts. Tech. rep. (1996)

16. Klose, J., Klose, H.: An Automata Based Interpretation of Live Sequence Charts. In: Margaria, T., Yi, W. (eds.) TACAS 2001. LNCS, vol. 2031, pp. 512–527. Springer, Heidelberg (2001)

17. Kugler, H., Harel, D., Pnueli, A., Lu, Y., Bontemps, Y.: Temporal Logic for Scenario-Based Specifications. In: Halbwachs, N., Zuck, L.D. (eds.) TACAS 2005. LNCS, vol. 3440, pp. 445–460. Springer, Heidelberg (2005)

18. Kupferman, O., Vardi, M.Y.: Weak alternating automata are not that weak. ACM Trans. Comput. Logic 2(3), 408–429 (2001)

19. Larsen, K.G., Thomsen, B.: A modal process logic. In: Proceedings of the Third Annual Symposium on Logic in Computer Science (LICS 1988), pp. 203–210. IEEE Computer Society Press (1988)

20. Miyano, S., Hayashi, T.: Alternating finite automata on ω-words. Theor. Comput. Sci. 32(3), 321–330 (1984)

21. Mukund, M.: Finite-state automata on infinite inputs. In: The 6th National Seminar on Theoretical Computer Science, Banasthali, Rajasthan, India (August 1996)

22. Peterson, J.L.: Petri nets. ACM Comput. Surv. 9(3), 223–252 (1977)

23. Pnueli, A., Rosner, R.: On the synthesis of a reactive module. In: Proceedings of the 16th ACM SIGPLAN-SIGACT Symposium on Principles of Programming Languages (POPL 1989), pp. 179–190. ACM, New York (1989)

24. Reisig, W.: Petri nets: an introduction. Springer, New York (1985)

Immunity against Local Influence

D. Peleg*

Department of Applied Mathematics and Computer Science,
The Weizmann Institute, Rehovot 76100, Israel
david.peleg@weizmann.ac.il

Abstract. This paper considers the question of the influence of a coalition of vertices, seeking to gain control (or majority) in local neighborhoods in a graph. A vertex v is said to be *controlled* by the coalition M if the majority of its neighbors are from M. Let $Ruled(G, M)$ denote the set of vertices controlled by M in G. Previous studies focused on constructions allowing small coalitions to control many vertices, and provided tight bounds for the maximum possible size of $Ruled(G, M)$ (as a function of $|M|$). This paper introduces the dual problem, concerning the existence and construction of graphs *immune* to the influence of small coalitions, i.e., graphs G for which $Ruled(G, M)$ is small (relative to $|M|$ again) for every coalition M. Upper and lower bounds are derived on the extent to which such immunity can be achieved.

1 Introduction

1.1 Background

Resolution of inconsistencies by majority voting is a commonly used tool in distributed computing [6, 7, 12, 17, 19–21, 32]. The idea is to overcome the damage caused by failures by maintaining redundant copies of important data, and performing a *voting* process among the participating processors whenever faults occur, adopting the values stored at the majority of the processors as the correct data. Assuming that in today's reliable technology the number of failures in the system at any given moment is small, the required level of replication can be rather limited.

A natural setting in which the majority voting method may be most useful is that of locally distributed data, where the replication of processor v's data, and the process of majority voting regarding processor v's data, are both restricted to processors in v's *local vicinity*. This is desirable due to obvious practical considerations, such as the cost and complexity of performing these operations.

A number of recent papers have concentrated on understanding one major aspect of local majority voting, namely, the extent to which the outcome can be affected by a small (but well-situated) coalition of (possibly failed or malicious)

---

* Supported in part by a grant from the Israel Science Foundation and by a grant from the Israel Ministry of Science and Art.

N. Dershowitz and E. Nissan (Eds.): Choueka Festschrift, Part I, LNCS 8001, pp. 168–179, 2014.

elements. This question may be relevant also in other contexts, e.g., in under-standing the power of small (but well-situated) coalitions in social networks or in media networks. Clearly, once the voting is performed over local subsets of the vertices, the influence of coalesced vertices becomes not only a function of their *number* but also a function of their *location* in the network.

Specifically, the following fundamental question was raised in [22]. A vertex v in a network $G(V, E)$ is said to be *controlled* by the vertex set M if the majority of its neighbors are in M. (Imagine that the vertex v regularly consults its neighbors and always adopts the opinion of the majority. In such a setting, if the vertices of M coalesce, they can fully control v's opinions.) What is the maximum number of vertices that a given set M can control (as a function of its size $|M|$)?

Since our focus is on obtaining asymptotic results, there are a number of slightly different definitions for the terms "neighborhood" and "majority" that we can use in the above definition, without affecting the results. For concreteness, let us define the *neighborhood* of v, denoted $\Gamma(v)$, as including the vertex v itself and all vertices adjacent to it, and for a set of vertices $W \subseteq V$, let $\Gamma(W) = \bigcup_{v \in W} \Gamma(v)$. Let us define *majority* as a non-strict one (including equality).

It turns out that as far as extremal behavior is concerned, the above question is easy to answer: control of virtually all vertex neighborhoods can be achieved by extremely small coalitions in certain graphs. For instance, in a complete bipartite graph with the set $M = \{a, b\}$ on one side and $V \setminus M$ on the other, M controls every vertex in $V \setminus M$.

Two special cases of the above problems were raised and studied in [4, 22]. They are based on the following notions. Call the set M a *monopoly* if it controls every vertex in the graph. Call the set M a *self-ignoring monopoly* if it controls every vertex in $V \setminus M$, namely, every vertex except its own.

Note that a self-ignoring monopoly M controls the rest of the world, but its own vertices may be controlled by others. Hence this notion is mainly relevant in contexts where the vertices of the coalition M are assumed to be faulty, malicious, or at least oblivious to the views of other vertices outside the coalition. Otherwise, to ensure control by M, one must require that M is a (full) monopoly, namely, that it also controls its own vertices. The questions addressed in [3, 4, 22] (see also [27]) involved deriving bounds on the size of monopolies and self-ignoring monopolies in a graph.

Let $Ruled(G, M)$ denote the set of vertices of G controlled by M. For every integer $1 \leq m \leq n$ and n-vertex graph G, let $\Psi_{Ruled}(G, m)$ denote the maximum number of vertices that can be controlled by an m-vertex coalition in G,

$$\Psi_{Ruled}(G, m) = \max_{M \subseteq V, \, |M|=m} \{|Ruled(G, M)|\}.$$

Dually, let $\Psi_{Mono}(G)$ (respectively, $\Psi_{Simon}(G)$) denote the minimum cardinality of a monopoly (resp., SI-monopoly) in G,

$$\Psi_{Mono}(G) = \min\{|M| \, : \, M \subseteq V, \, Ruled(G, M) = V\},$$
$$\Psi_{Simon}(G) = \min\{|M| \, : \, M \subseteq V, \, Ruled(G, M) = V \setminus M\}.$$

As discussed above, previous studies focused on constructions allowing small coalitions to control many vertices (namely, graphs with large $\Psi_{Ruled}(G,m)$ and small $\Psi_{Mono}(G)$ and $\Psi_{Simon}(G)$). In particular, it follows from the above example (see also [4, 22]) that there exist graphs G for which a constant size coalition can control a fraction of the graph, or even all the vertices of the graph except its own, thus forming a self-ignoring monopoly, namely, $\Psi_{Ruled}(G, O(1)) = \Omega(n)$ and $\Psi_{Simon}(G) = O(1)$. Perhaps more surprisingly, it is shown therein that there exist graphs G for which there are rather small (full) monopolies, and specifically $\Psi_{Mono}(G) = O(\sqrt{n})$, although this is the smallest example possible, namely, $\Psi_{Mono}(G) = \Omega(\sqrt{n})$ for every graph G. (As one may imagine, for such a small coalition to be a monopoly, its members must be densely connected among themselves, whereas all other vertices of the graph must be nearly isolated, with links only to members of the monopoly.)

In contrast, this paper introduces the dual problem, concerning the existence of graphs *immune* to the influence of small coalitions. These are graphs G for which $Ruled(G, M)$ is small (relative to $|M|$ again) for *every* coalition M, or in other words, $\Psi_{Ruled}(G, m)$ is small, and hence also $\Psi_{Mono}(G)$ and $\Psi_{Simon}(G)$ are large. This question may be of considerable interest from a practical point of view, since these immune graphs are precisely the ones most suitable for use in applications where fault-tolerance is achieved through local majority voting.

In what follows, upper and lower bounds are derived on the extent to which such immunity can be achieved. As may perhaps be expected, the main practical lesson is that in order to prevent small coalitions from gaining too much control, it is necessary to ensure that the graph vertices have uniformly high connectivity and that they are connected in a diversified manner, rather than to the same "core".

1.2 Results

To formally discuss the immunity level of a given graph, let us present the following definitions.

Definition 1. *A graph G is (α, β)-immune if $\Psi_{Ruled}(G, m) \leq \alpha m$ for every $1 \leq m \leq \beta n$.*

Definition 2. *A graph G is an (a, b)-expander if $\Gamma(W) \geq a|W|$ for every subset W of size $|W| \leq bn$.*

Definition 3. *A graph $G(V, E)$ is near-Δ-regular if $\Delta/2 \leq deg(v) \leq 2\Delta$ for every $v \in V$. Let $\mathcal{G}_{n,p}^{REG}$ denote the restriction of the probability distribution $\mathcal{G}_{n,p}$ to near-np-regular graphs.*

This paper establishes the following results. First, we observe that immunity is strongly related to expansion. In particular:

1. If a Δ-regular graph G is an (a, b)-expander for $a > \Delta/2$, then it is (α, β)-immune for $\alpha = \frac{1}{a - \Delta/2}$ and $\beta = (a - \Delta/2)b - \epsilon$ (for any $\epsilon > 0$).
2. If a Δ-regular graph G is (α, β)-immune, then it is an (a, b)-expander for $a = 1/\alpha$ and $b = \alpha\beta$.

As a consequence, for every sufficiently large constant integer Δ and for every $\epsilon > 0$, there exists some $\beta > 0$ such that for $\alpha = \frac{1}{\Delta/2 - 1 - \epsilon}$, a random Δ-regular graph is (α, β)-immune with high probability.

For non-constant degree bound Δ, we show that there exist constants $c_1, c_2, \beta > 0$ such that for every $c_1/n \leq p \leq 1$, every graph from $\mathcal{G}_{n,p}^{REG}$ is $(\frac{c_2 \log n}{np}, \beta)$-immune with high probability (i.e., $1 - 1/n$ or higher).

The above relationship provides us mainly with *existential* proofs. (In fact, as long as one insists on constructions within the *optimal* parameter range, the above relationship gives us *only* existential proofs). For $\Delta = \Omega(\sqrt{n})$, an *explicit* example of an (asymptotically optimal) immune graph is established constructively, by showing a Δ-regular $(\frac{4}{\Delta}, \beta'')$-immune graph for some constant β''. This example is based on using known constructions for symmetric block designs.

As direct corollaries of the above, we get that there exist (infinitely many) graphs G for which $\Psi_{Simon}(G) = \Omega(n)$ (hence also $\Psi_{Mono}(G) = \Omega(n)$).

In the other direction, we provide a complementing bound proving that the above results are tight up to a logarithmic factor. Specifically, we show that for every graph G of maximum degree Δ_{max} and every $m \geq 1$, $\Psi_{Ruled}(G, m) \geq \lfloor \frac{2m}{\Delta_{max} + 1} \rfloor$. (Hence there is a constant $3 > c_1 > 0$ such that for any $\beta \geq 1$, there does not exist a $(\frac{c_1}{\Delta_{max}}, \beta)$-immune graph G.)

1.3   Related Work

Questions concerning coalitions, monopolies and self-ignoring monopolies in graphs were studied in [3, 4, 22, 27]. Repetitive polling systems have been studied as well. In such systems, each of the vertices is colored, and the coloring changes dynamically in every round, with each vertex recoloring itself with the color of the majority of its neighbors. A variety of problems concerning the limit behavior of such systems in various models and types of graphs were studied in [28, 2, 8–10, 15, 16, 23].

Majority voting, in one form or another, is used in number of fault-tolerant algorithms in various contexts, including agreement and consensus problems (cf. [6, 7, 21]), quorum system applications (cf. [11, 12, 17, 32]), self-stabilization and local mending [19, 20], and more.

Certain *dynamic* variants of majority voting problems were studied in the literature, in the context of discrete time dynamical systems. These variants dealt with a setting in which the nodes of the system operate in discrete time steps, and at each step, each node computes the majority in its neighborhood, and adapts the resulting value as its own. Typical problems studied in this setting concern the behavior of the resulting sequence of global states (represented as a vector $\bar{x}^t = (x_1^t, \ldots, x_n^t)$, where x_i^t represents the value at node v_i after time step t). For instance, the fact that the period of such sequences is either one or two is proved (in various contexts) in [13, 29, 30]. The problem was studied further in [24–26]. Also, the applicability of majority voting as a tool for fault-local mending was investigated in [19, 20].

The relation between the expansion of a graph and properties similar to immunity has been implicitly observed before in the literature (see, e.g., Thm. 1 in [31]).

2   Basic Properties

Given a graph $G = (V, E)$, a vertex $v \in V$, and a set $M \subset V$, we denote by $\deg_G(v, M)$ the number of neighbors of v in G belonging to M, namely, $|\Gamma(v) \cap M|$. (We omit the parameter M when it is the entire vertex set of G; we omit the subscript G when it is clear from the context.)

We use the following definitions. Let Δ_{max} and Δ_{min} denote the maximum and minimum vertex degrees in the graph G, respectively. The *influence* of a coalition $M \subset V$ on a vertex v in the graph G is defined as $\mathcal{I}_G(M, v) = |M \cap \Gamma(v)|$. (We omit the subscript G whenever clear from the context.) More generally, the influence of the coalition M on the set S is $\mathcal{I}_G(M, S) = \sum_{v \in S} \mathcal{I}_G(M, v)$. Note that a node in M may contribute more than 1 to $\mathcal{I}_G(M, S)$, and in particular, the contribution of each node w in M will be $|S \cap \Gamma(w)|$.

We start with the basic observation that a vertex v of degree $\deg(v)$ can be controlled by a coalition M only if v has more than $\deg(v)/2$ neighbors in M. Hence in a graph G with minimum degree Δ_{min}, a coalition of cardinality $1 \leq m \leq \Delta_{min}/2$ can rule nobody, hence $\Psi_{Ruled}(G, m) = 0$ in that range, and the problem becomes interesting only for $m > \Delta_{min}/2$.

More generally, let us characterize the spectrum of degrees in the graph G by defining $h_G(k)$ as the number of vertices v whose degree in G is at most k, $h_G(k) = |\{v \mid \deg(v) \leq k\}|$. Then we have

Claim. $\Psi_{Ruled}(G, m) \leq h_G(2m)$ for every $m \geq 1$.   ∎

Furthermore, we have

Claim. For every graph $G(V, E)$,

1. $\Psi_{Ruled}(G, m) \leq 2m\Delta_{max}/\Delta_{min}$ for every $m \geq 1$, and
2. $\Psi_{Mono}(G) \geq |E|/\Delta_{max}$.

Proof: Note that

$$\mathcal{I}_G(M, Ruled(G, M)) \geq \sum_{v \in Ruled(G,M)} \deg(v)/2.$$

On the other hand, $\mathcal{I}_G(M, Ruled(G, M)) \leq |M| \cdot \Delta_{max}$, since each $v \in M$ can contribute at most Δ_{max} to the influence. Put together, we get that

$$|M| \cdot \Delta_{max} \geq \sum_{v \in Ruled(G,M)} \deg(v)/2. \tag{1}$$

As $\deg(v) \geq \Delta_{min}$ for every v, we get that $|Ruled(G, M)| \leq 2|M|\Delta_{max}/\Delta_{min}$, and the first claim follows. The second claim also follows from inequality (1), since for a monopoly, $Ruled(G, M) = V$ and hence $\sum_{v \in Ruled(G,M)} \deg(v)/2 = |E|$. ∎

Indeed, the constructions described in [22, 4, 3] for small coalitions controlling large sets of vertices are all based on large degree gaps, and utilize sets M of high-degree vertices ruling many low-degree vertices. The last claim clearly implies that in a near-regular graphs, an m-vertex coalition can rule no more than $O(m)$ vertices, hence we have the following corollary.

Corollary 1. *For every near-Δ-regular or bounded-degree graph G, $\Psi_{Ruled}(G, m) = O(m)$ and $\Psi_{Mono}(G), \Psi_{Simon}(G) = \Omega(n)$.*

The main goal of this paper is to establish the existence of near-Δ-regular graphs G for which the power of small coalitions is even more limited than that; essentially, these graphs guarantee $\Psi_{Ruled}(G, m) = O(m/\Delta)$. This is the best one can hope for, as indicated by the following lemma, providing a bound on the possible level of immunity one can expect from a graph.

Lemma 1. *For every graph G and every $m \geq 1$, $\Psi_{Ruled}(G, m) \geq \lfloor \frac{2m}{\Delta_{max}+1} \rfloor$.*

Proof. Given a graph G with $\Delta = \Delta_{max}$ and an integer $m \geq 1$, let $\ell = \lfloor 2m/(\Delta + 1) \rfloor$. If $\ell = 0$ then the lemma is satisfied vacuously, so suppose $\ell \geq 1$. Pick ℓ arbitrary vertices $v_1, \ldots, v_\ell$ in G, with neighborhoods Γ_i for $1 \leq i \leq \ell$. Select the coalition M by taking $\lceil |\Gamma_i|/2 \rceil$ arbitrary vertices from each neighborhood Γ_i. Clearly, the chosen coalition controls each of the vertices v_i, hence $|Ruled(G, M)| \geq \ell$. Also, M is of cardinality at most $\ell \cdot (\Delta + 1)/2 \leq m$, and the lemma follows. ∎

Corollary 2. *There is a constant $3 > c_1 > 0$ such that for any $\beta \geq 1$, there does not exist a $(\frac{c_1}{\Delta_{max}}, \beta)$-immune graph G.*

3   Existential Results

In what follows, we concentrate on regular or near-regular graphs (with Δ_{max} and Δ_{min} within a ratio of up to 4 of each other), and prove the existence of graphs with immunity level close to that indicated by the last corollary. To do that, we first derive close connections between immune graphs and expanders.

Lemma 2.   *1. If a Δ-regular graph G is an (a, b)-expander for $a > \Delta/2$, then it is (α, β)-immune for $\alpha = \frac{1}{a - \Delta/2}$ and $\beta = (a - \Delta/2)b - \epsilon$ (for any $\epsilon > 0$).*
   2. If a Δ-regular graph G is (α, β)-immune, then it is an (a, b)-expander for $a = 1/\alpha$ and $b = \alpha\beta$.

Proof. Let G be a Δ-regular (a, b)-expander with $a > 1/2$. Consider a coalition M of size

$$m = |M| \leq \beta n < (a - \Delta/2)bn \tag{2}$$

attaining $\Psi_{Ruled}(G, M)$. Letting $R = Ruled(G, M)$, set $k = \min\{|R|, bn\}$ and let X be an arbitrary size k subset of R, $X = \{v_1, \ldots, v_k\} \subseteq R$. By choice of k, X satisfies $|\Gamma(X)| \geq ak$. For every $1 \leq i \leq k$, let $M_i = M \cap \Gamma(v_i)$ and $\bar{M}_i = \Gamma(v_i) \setminus M_i$. Since M controls X, we have $|M_i| \geq |\Gamma(v_i)|/2 = \Delta/2$, or $|\bar{M}_i| < \Delta/2$, for every $1 \leq i \leq k$, and hence $|\bigcup_i \bar{M}_i| < k\Delta/2$. Noting that

$$\bigcup_i M_i = \bigcup_i (\Gamma(v_i) \setminus \bar{M}_i) \supseteq \Gamma(X) \setminus \bigcup_i \bar{M}_i,$$

it follows that

$$m \geq |\bigcup_i M_i| \geq |\Gamma(X)| - |\bigcup_i \bar{M}_i| \geq ak - \Delta k/2 = (a - \Delta/2)k. \quad (3)$$

Combining inequalities (2) and (3) we conclude that $k < bn$, implying by choice of k that $k = |R|$. Hence by inequality (3) again we get that $m \geq (a - \Delta/2)|R|$, or $|R| \leq \alpha m$, proving the first part of the lemma.

For the opposite direction, let G be a Δ-regular (α, β)-immune graph. Consider a vertex set W of size $k = |W| \leq bn$, and let $M = \Gamma(W)$. The proof that $|M| \geq a|W|$ is derived by contradiction. Suppose, to the contrary, that

$$|M| < ak \leq bn/\alpha = \beta n. \quad (4)$$

By the assumption that G is immune, the set $R = Ruled(G, M)$ satisfies $|R| \leq \alpha|M|$. As $M = \Gamma(W)$, the vertices of W are controlled by M, hence $W \subseteq R$ and we get, relying on inequality (4), that

$$k = |W| \leq |R| \leq \alpha|M| < \alpha ak = k,$$

contradiction. The second part of the lemma follows. ∎

The following is known concerning the existence of strong expanders.

Proposition 1. [18] *For every sufficiently large constant integer Δ and for every $a < \Delta - 1$, there exists some $0 < b < 1/a$ such that a random Δ-regular graph is an (a, b)-expander with high probability.* ∎

Consequently, by Part 1 of Lemma 2 we get

Corollary 3. *For every sufficiently large constant integer Δ and for every $\alpha > \frac{1}{\Delta/2 - 1}$, there exists some $\beta > 0$ such that a random Δ-regular graph is (α, β)-immune with high probability.*

For non-constant degree bound Δ, such strong expansion is generally unavailable, but it is still possible to prove the following somewhat weaker result.

Proposition 2. *There exist constants $c_1, c_2, \beta > 0$ such that for every $c_1/n \leq p \leq 1$, every graph from $\mathcal{G}_{n,p}^{REG}$ is $(\frac{c_2 \log n}{np}, \beta)$-immune with probability at least $1 - 1/n$.*

Proof. Consider a graph from the probability distribution $\mathcal{G}_{n,p}$. For a vertex v and an m-vertex set $M \subseteq V$ in this graph, the degree $\deg(v, M)$ is a random variable with expectation $\mathbb{E}(\deg(v, M)) = mp$. Define a bernoulli random variable $s_{v,M}$ whose value is 1 if $\deg(v, M) \geq np/4$ and 0 otherwise, and denote $q_{v,M} = \mathbb{P}(s_{v,M} = 1)$. Using Chernoff bound (cf. [1]) with $\epsilon = n/4m - 1$, we conclude that

$$q_{v,M} = \mathbb{P}(\deg(v, M) \geq (1 + \epsilon)mp) < \left(\frac{e}{1+\epsilon}\right)^{(1+\epsilon)mp} = \left(\frac{4em}{n}\right)^{np/4}.$$

(Here we assume that $\epsilon > 0$, which requires $m < n/4$ and thus necessitates $\beta < 1/4$.)

Next define for an m-vertex set $M \subseteq V$ a random variable $Z_M = \sum_{v \in V} s_{v,M}$, whose expectation is

$$\mathbb{E}(Z_M) = \sum_{v \in V} q_{v,M} < n \cdot \left(\frac{4em}{n}\right)^{np/4}.$$

We next estimate the probability that $Z_M \geq c_2 m \log n / np$. Fixing ϵ to satisfy $(1 + \epsilon)\mathbb{E}(Z_M) = c_2 m \log n / np$ and applying Chernoff's bound again, we get that

$$\mathbb{P}\left(Z_M \geq \frac{c_2 m \log n}{np}\right) < \left(\frac{e}{1+\epsilon}\right)^{(1+\epsilon)\mathbb{E}(Z_M)} \leq \left(\frac{e}{1+\epsilon}\right)^{\frac{c_2 m \log n}{np}}$$

$$\leq \left(\frac{epn^2 \left(\frac{4em}{n}\right)^{np/4}}{c_2 m \log n}\right)^{\frac{c_2 m \log n}{np}}.$$

(Here, to ensure that $\epsilon > 0$ we require $p > 64/n$ and $m < n/8e$, necessitating $c_1 > 64$ and $\beta < 1/8e$.)

We are interested in the event

$$\mathcal{A} = \text{``} \exists M \subseteq V, |M| \leq \beta n, \text{ such that } Z_M \geq \frac{c_2 m \log n}{np} \text{''}.$$

Letting $\mathcal{P} = \mathbb{P}(\mathcal{A})$, we have

$$\mathcal{P} < \sum_{m=1}^{\beta n} \binom{n}{m} \left(\frac{epn^2 \left(\frac{4em}{n}\right)^{np/4}}{c_2 m \log n}\right)^{\frac{c_2 m \log n}{np}}.$$

Fixing $p = c/n$ and $\sigma = c_2 \log n$, we get that

$$\mathcal{P} < \sum_{m=1}^{\beta n} n^m \left(\frac{ecn}{c_2 m \log n} \left(\frac{4em}{n}\right)^{np/4}\right)^{\frac{c_2 m \log n}{np}}$$

$$= \sum_{m=1}^{\beta n} \left(n^{1+\sigma/c-\sigma/4} \cdot 4^{\sigma/4} \cdot e^{\sigma/c+\sigma/4} \cdot c^{\sigma/c} \cdot \sigma^{-\sigma/c} \cdot m^{\sigma/4-\sigma/c}\right)^m.$$

Since $c \geq c_1 > 64$, it follows that $\sigma/4 - \sigma/c > 0$, and therefore

$$\mathcal{P} < \beta n \left(n^{1+\sigma/c-\sigma/4} \cdot 4^{\sigma/4} \cdot e^{\sigma/c+\sigma/4} \cdot c^{\sigma/c} \cdot \sigma^{-\sigma/c} \cdot (\beta n)^{\sigma/4-\sigma/c} \right)^1$$
$$< n^2 \cdot 4^{\sigma/4} \cdot e^{\sigma/c+\sigma/4} \cdot c^{\sigma/c} \cdot \sigma^{-\sigma/c} \cdot \beta^{\sigma/4-\sigma/c+1}.$$

Relying on the fact that $c > 64$ (and hence also $\ln c < c$) it is possible to write this bound as

$$\mathcal{P} < \exp(d_1 \ln n - (d_2 \ln n \ln \ln n)/c + d_3 \ln \beta \ln n) < \exp(d_1 \ln n + d_3 \ln \beta \ln n),$$
$$(5)$$

where d_1, d_2, d_3 are constants depending only on c_2. Hence for a sufficiently small constant β, $\mathcal{P} < \exp(-2 \ln n) = \frac{1}{n^2} < \frac{1}{2n}$.

Let $\mathcal{R}$ denote the event that the graph at hand is near-np-regular. It is easy to verify that $\mathbb{P}(\mathcal{R}) \gg 1/2$ for p in the said range (cf. [5]). Hence the probability of the event $\mathcal{A}$ conditioned on the graph being near-np-regular is bounded by

$$\mathbb{P}(\mathcal{A} \mid \mathcal{R}) = \frac{\mathbb{P}(\mathcal{A} \cap \mathcal{R})}{\mathbb{P}(\mathcal{R})} \leq \frac{\mathbb{P}(\mathcal{A})}{1/2} = 2\mathcal{P} < \frac{1}{n}.$$

Finally, the claim follows upon noting that in a near-np-regular graph G, in order for a coalition M to control a vertex v it must contain at least $\deg(v)/2 \geq np/4$ of its neighbors, and hence the event

$$\mathcal{A}' = \text{“} \exists M \subseteq V, \ |M| \leq \beta n, \ \text{such that } |Ruled(G,M)| \geq \frac{c_2 m \log n}{np} \text{”}$$

is a subset of the event $\mathcal{A}$, so $\mathbb{P}(\mathcal{A}' \mid \mathcal{R}) \leq \mathbb{P}(\mathcal{A} \mid \mathcal{R}) < 1/n$. ∎

Corollary 4. *1. There exists a constant $c_1 > 0$ such that for every $c_1 \log n/n \leq p \leq 1$, every graph from $\mathcal{G}_{n,p}^{REG}$ satisfies $\Psi_{Simon}(G) = \Omega(n)$ (hence also $\Psi_{Mono}(G) = \Omega(n)$) with probability at least $1 - 1/n$.*
2. There exist constants $c_1, c_2 > 0$ such that for every $c_1/n \leq p \leq c_2 \log n/n$, every graph from $\mathcal{G}_{n,p}^{REG}$ satisfies $\Psi_{Simon}(G) = \Omega(n^2 p/\log n)$ (hence also $\Psi_{Mono}(G) = \Omega(n^2 p/\log n)$) with probability at least $1 - 1/n$.

4   Explicit Constructions

In this section we present some explicit constructions of (asymptotically optimal) immune graphs, using symmetric block designs. A *symmetric block design* $\mathcal{B}(n, \Delta, \lambda)$ is a collection of n *blocks*, $\mathcal{B} = \{B_1, \ldots, B_n\}$, where each block is a size Δ subset of an n-element universe $U = \{u_1, \ldots, u_n\}$, each element u_i occurs in exactly Δ blocks, every two blocks B_i and B_j have precisely λ elements in common, and every two elements u_i and u_j occur together in precisely λ blocks. The order q finite projective plane $FPP(q)$ is an example for a symmetric block design with $n = q^2 + q + 1$, $\Delta = q + 1$ and $\lambda = 1$. A comprehensive coverage of block designs, their properties and methods for constructing them can be found in [14].

One simple property of symmetric block designs that will be needed later on is that

$$\Delta(\Delta - 1) = \lambda n. \tag{6}$$

Given a block design $\mathcal{B} = \mathcal{B}(n, \Delta, \lambda)$, we construct an immune bipartite graph $G(\mathcal{B})$ as follows. Let $G(\mathcal{B}) = (V, W, E)$, where $V = \{v_1, \ldots, v_n\}$, $W = \{w_1, \ldots, w_n\}$, and $(v_i, w_j) \in E$ iff the element u_i occurs in the block B_j in $\mathcal{B}$.

Note that a coalition M in this graph can be decomposed into $M_V = M \cap V$ and $M_W = M \cap W$, and their influence is restricted to the other bipartition, namely, $R = Ruled(G, M)$ can be decomposed into $R_V = R \cap V$ and $R_W = R \cap W$ where $R_V = Ruled(G, M_W)$ and $R_W = Ruled(G, M_V)$. Therefore it suffices to concentrate on coalitions restricted to one bipartition. Henceforth, our coalition M will be restricted to V, and the controlled set $Ruled(G, M)$ will thus be a subset of W.

Lemma 3. *For every graph $G(\mathcal{B})$ as above, and for every m-vertex coalition $M \subseteq V$ where $m < n/8$, $\Psi_{Ruled}(G(\mathcal{B}), m) = O(m/\Delta)$.*

Proof. Consider a graph $G(\mathcal{B})$ as above, and an m-vertex coalition $M \subseteq V$ where $m < n/8$. Let $\ell = \min\{|Ruled(G, M)|, (n-1)/2(\Delta - 1)\}$ and consider a size ℓ subset X of $Ruled(G, M)$, $X = \{x_1, \ldots, x_\ell\}$. For every $1 \leq i \leq \ell$, let M_i denote the set of M vertices neighboring x_i, $M_i = M \cap \Gamma(x_i)$. Let $Z = \bigcup_{1 \leq i \leq \ell} M_i \subseteq M$ and $z = |Z| \leq m$. For every $1 \leq i < j \leq \ell$, the two sets M_i and M_j satisfy $M_i \subseteq B_i$ and $M_j \subseteq B_j$, and therefore $|M_i \cap M_j| \leq |B_i \cap B_j| = \lambda$. Also, since M_i controls x_i we have $|M_i| \geq \Delta/2$. By the inclusion-exclusion theorem we have that

$$z \geq \sum_{1 \leq i \leq \ell} |M_i| - \sum_{1 \leq i < j \leq \ell} |M_i \cap M_j| \geq \ell \Delta/2 - \binom{\ell}{2} \lambda \geq \ell(\Delta - \ell\lambda)/2. \tag{7}$$

By the choice of ℓ we have that $\ell \leq (n-1)/2(\Delta - 1)$. Combining that with Eq. (6), we get that $\ell\lambda \leq \Delta/2$ and hence by inequality (7) we have

$$m \geq z \geq \ell\Delta/4. \tag{8}$$

By assumption, $m < n/8 < (n-1)\Delta/8(\Delta-1)$ (the latter inequality follows from the fact that $\Delta < n$). Hence $(n-1)\Delta/8(\Delta-1) > \ell\Delta/4$, or $\ell < (n-1)/2(\Delta-1)$. By the choice of ℓ, this implies that $\ell = |Ruled(G, M)|$, hence by inequality (8) we have $m \geq |Ruled(G, M)|\Delta/4$, or $|Ruled(G, M)| \leq 4m/\Delta$. The lemma follows. ∎

In particular, using a finite projective plane of order q yields an asymptotically optimally immune regular graph of degree $\Delta = \Theta(\sqrt{n})$. Symmetric block designs with $\lambda > 1$ can be used to derive asymptotically optimally immune regular graphs of degrees higher than $\sqrt{n}$.

We remark that an alternate explicit construction applicable for many values of Δ can be based on Ramanujan graphs (see [1]).

5   Future Research Directions

It would be interesting to construct asymptotically optimally immune regular graphs of degrees higher than $\sqrt{n}$.

The results presented herein concern immunity against a "static" type of influence. It would be interesting to explore dynamic variants of the notion of influence, such as the types studied in repetitive polling systems (cf. [28, 2, 8–10, 15, 16, 23]), and analyze the graph properties providing immunity against such influences.

References

1. Alon, N., Spencer, J.H.: The Probabilistic Method. John Wiley & Sons, NY (1992)
2. Berger, E.: Dynamic Monopolies of Constant Size. J. Comb. Theory, Ser. B 83, 191–200 (2001)
3. Bermond, J.-C., Bond, J., Peleg, D., Perennes, S.: Tight bounds on the size of 2-monopolies. In: Proc. 3rd Colloq. on Structural Information & Communication Complexity, pp. 170–179 (1996)
4. Bermond, J.-C., Peleg, D.: The Power of Small Coalitions in Graphs. In: Proc. 2nd Colloq. on Structural Information & Communication Complexity, pp. 173–184 (1995)
5. Bollobás, B.: Random Graphs. Academic Press (1975)
6. Bracha, G.: An $o(\log n)$ expected rounds randomized Byzantine generals algorithm. J. ACM 34, 910–920 (1987)
7. Dwork, C., Peleg, D., Pippenger, N., Upfal, E.: Fault tolerance in networks of bounded degree. SIAM J. Computing 17, 975–988 (1988)
8. Flocchini, P., Geurts, F., Santoro, N.: Optimal irreversible dynamos in chordal rings. Discrete Applied Mathematics 113, 23–42 (2001)
9. Flocchini, P., Kralovic, R., Ruzicka, P., Roncato, A., Santoro, N.: On time versus size for monotone dynamic monopolies in regular topologies. J. Discrete Algorithms 1, 129–150 (2003)
10. Flocchini, P., Lodi, E., Luccio, F., Pagli, L., Santoro, N.: Dynamic monopolies in tori. Discrete Applied Mathematics 137, 197–212 (2004)
11. Garcia-Molina, H., Barbara, D.: How to assign votes in a distributed system. J. ACM 32, 841–860 (1985)
12. Gifford, D.K.: Weighted voting for replicated data. In: Proc. 7th Symp. Oper. Sys. Princip., pp. 150–159 (1979)
13. Goles, E., Olivos, J.: Periodic behaviour of generalized threshold functions. Discrete Mathematics 30, 187–189 (1980)
14. Hall, M.: Combinatorial Theory. John Wiley & Sons, Chichester (1986)
15. Hassin, Y., Peleg, D.: Extremal Bounds for Proabilistic Polling in Graphs. In: Proc. 7th Colloq. on Structural Information & Communication Complexity, pp. 167–180 (2000)
16. Hassin, Y., Peleg, D.: Distributed probabilistic polling and applications to proportionate agreement. Information and Computation 171, 248–268 (2001)
17. Jalote, P., Rangarajan, S., Tripathi, S.K.: Capacity of voting systems. Technical Report UMIACS-TR-91-118, University of Maryland (1991)
18. Kahale, N.: Eigenvalues and expansion of regular graphs. J. ACM 42, 1091–1106 (1995)

19. Kutten, S., Peleg, D.: Fault-local distributed mending. J. of Algorithms 30, 144–165 (1999)
20. Kutten, S., Peleg, D.: Tight fault-locality. SIAM J. on Computing 30, 247–268 (2000)
21. Lamport, L., Shostak, R., Pease, M.: The Byzantine generals problem. ACM Trans. Programming Languages and Systems 4, 382–401 (1982)
22. Linial, N., Peleg, D., Rabinovich, Y., Saks, M.: Sphere packing and local majorities in graphs. In: Proc. 2nd ISTCS, pp. 141–149. IEEE (1993)
23. Luccio, F., Pagli, L., Santoro, N.: Network decontamination in Presence of Local Immunity. Int. J. Found. Comput. Sci. 18, 457–474 (2007)
24. Moran, G.: On the period-two-property of the majority operator in infinite graphs. Trans. American Math. Society 347, 1649–1667 (1995)
25. Moran, G.: Parametrization for stationary patterns of the r-majority operators on 0-1 sequences. Discrete Mathematics 132, 175–195 (1994)
26. Moran, G.: The r-majority vote action on 0-1 sequences. Discrete Mathematics 132, 145–174 (1994)
27. Peleg, D.: Local Majorities, Coalitions and Monopolies in Graphs: A Review. Theoretical Computer Science 282, 231–257 (2002)
28. Peleg, D.: Size Bounds for Dynamic Monopolies. Discrete Applied Mathematics 86, 263–273 (1998)
29. Poljak, S., Sura, M.: On periodical behaviour in societies with symmetric influences. Combinatorica 3, 119–121 (1983)
30. Poljak, S., Turzik, D.: On an application of convexity to discrete systems. Discrete Applied Mathematics 13, 27–32 (1986)
31. Sipser, M., Spielman, D.: Expander codes. In: 35th IEEE Symp. on Foundations of Computer Science, pp. 566–576 (1994)
32. Spasojevic, M., Berman, P.: Voting as the optimal static pessimistic scheme for managing replicated data. IEEE Trans. Parallel & Distr. Systems 5, 64–73 (1994)

The Development of the Strategic Behavior of Peer Designed Agents*

Efrat Manistersky[1], Raz Lin[1], and Sarit Kraus[1,2]

[1] Department of Computer Science
Bar-Ilan University
Ramat-Gan, Israel 52900
{linraz,sarit}@cs.biu.ac.il
[2] Institute for Advanced Computer Studies
University of Maryland
College Park, MD 20742 USA

Abstract. As computerized agents have become more and more common, e-commerce has become a major candidate for incorporation of automated agents. Thus, it is vital to understand how people design agents for online markets and how their design changes over time. This, in turn, will enable a better design of agents for these environments. We focus on the design of trading agents for bilateral negotiations with unenforceable agreements. In order to simulate this environment we conducted an experiment with human subjects who were asked to design agents for a resource allocation game. The subjects' agents participated in several tournaments against each other and were given the opportunity to improve their agents based on their performance in previous tournaments. Our results show that, indeed, most subjects modified their agents' strategic behavior with the prospect of improving the performance of their agents. However, their average score significantly decreased throughout the tournaments and became closer to the equilibrium agents' score. In particular, the subjects modified their agents to break more agreements throughout the tournaments, while also increasing their means of protection against deceiving agents.

1 Introduction

With the growth and accessibility of the internet and the web, e-commerce has become widely used [13]. As trading in many markets (e.g. NASDAQ) has now become fully electronic [8], designing automated trading agents has received growing attention. Instead of personally trading online, the trader can now use a computerized agent which trades on her behalf and makes the decisions for her. For example, a person who desires to purchase an item can be represented

---

* This research is based upon work supported in part by ERC grant #267523, the Google Inter-university center for Electronic Markets and Auctions, MURI grant number W911NF-08-1-0144 and ARO grants W911NF0910206 and W911NF1110344.

by a software agent. This agent negotiates for the item on behalf of the person and can eventually purchase the item for her when all conditions are met [21]. Thus, there is growing importance in understanding how people develop agents for these environments. Indeed, examining the ways in which people design their agents has been established as a key goal in several AI studies [10,25,26].

Apparently, we could have applied game theory considerations to predict the strategies of these kinds of agents. However, extensive research conducted in behavioral economics and psychology has shown that people play differently from the game theoretic predictions [9,20]. Beyond the rational utility maximization, humans are also motivated by social factors such as equality, reciprocity, and fairness [6]. Preliminary research on how computer agents are designed by humans has shown that people design agents differently from the way they play. Moreover, they do not use game theory or equilibrium considerations in their design [10].

In this paper we present a novel research, which further enhances the understanding of strategic behavior of agents designed by humans. More specifically, we investigate the change in the agents design over time. We focus on the design of trading agents for bilateral negotiations with unenforceable agreements (e.g., as in eBay). We term these agents Peer Designed Agents (PDAs). In this context, it is important to understand how people modify the strategy behavior of their agents, based on performance in the past, as automated agents are, by nature, used in recurring events and transactions. Thus, in this respect our work provides a significant contribution.

In order to simulate a common real-life bilateral negotiation environment we used the domain of a resource allocation game [17]. In the resource allocation game, two sides are given an initial set of resources and a goal. Both sides negotiate the exchange of resources with each other in order for each to achieve her goal. The player's negotiation policy is always accompanied by the decision whether to send the resources which she has agreed upon. If the number of interactions between the players is finite, the equilibrium strategy requires that no exchanges are made. The strategy space in the resource allocation game is richer and larger than most models previously studied in economic research [1,5,11,18,19]. Moreover, this game supplies a general negotiation platform which is more similar to real-life negotiations than typical economic games.

We ran experiments in which two groups of graduate students were instructed to design agents that play the resource allocation game. Each student was responsible for designing her own agent. Each group received a different version of the resource allocation game. Each version was governed by different dependencies between the players (that is, the resources the player needs and its dependency on the other player to supply those resources). Each group was involved in several tournaments where each subject's agent played against all other agents in her group, including itself. After each tournament, subjects were permitted to improve their agents based on the feedback they received about their agent's performance in previous tournaments.

The line of research most similar to this work includes studies that explore human strategies using a strategy method[1], where people are able to revise their strategies based on their performance in the past [18,23]. Similar to developing agents, using the strategy method requires subjects to specify their choices for all information sets of the game and not only the ones that occur during the course of a play of a game. Despite the similarity, asking subjects to design and program agents is different from the strategy method. Developing agents enables subjects to implement much more complex strategies (e.g., using heuristics, learning algorithms, etc.). Moreover the strategy method is usually used to elicit subjects' strategies in games that are relatively simple (e.g. public goods, generations games [14,18]). Our work, on the other hand, involves a richer and more complex strategy space.

Our results show that the subjects fundamentally modified their agents' strategic behavior throughout the tournaments. Surprisingly, though, the agents' average score significantly decreased throughout the tournaments, while in the last tournament the agents' average score was closer to the equilibrium agent's score than in the first tournament. However, even in the last tournament most subjects did not develop agents that adhere to the equilibrium strategy in this game (see Sect. 3.2 for an analysis of the equilibrium strategy). Thus, the decrease in the agents' average scores warrant an explanation. One explanation can be given by analyzing the agents' strategies. More agents were less cooperative and their reliability level decreased (i.e., agents did not live up to their promises) throughout the tournaments.

Despite the decrease in the agents' reliability throughout the tournaments, even in the final tournament there were still subjects whose agents were reliable. Among these subjects and others, we observed an interesting behavior pattern: subjects learned from their agents' experiments in the previous tournaments and increased their agents' means of protection against deceiving agents (that is, agents that promise a transfer of resources but do not carry it out). For example, some subjects developed agents that do not send any resources to an agent whose behavior in the negotiation is suspicious (e.g., agents that are too generous and offer to send all their extra resources in exchange for the resources they need).

This paper contributes to research on agents' designs in several ways. First, it provides insight into the considerations people take into account when designing agents. Second, the results of these experiments provide information about the changes in agents' behavior throughout the tournaments. These findings can help better understand the agents' behavior over time. These results suggest that the number of tournaments has a substantial effect on the market and on agent design.

The rest of this paper is organized as follows. We begin by reviewing related work in Sect. 2. Then we continue with a description of our trading framework in Sect. 3. The experiment design is provided in Sect. 4 and the results in Sect. 5. In Sect. 6 we discuss our results, and finally we conclude and discuss future work in Sect. 7.

---

[1] A strategy method is a known economic experimental methodology which requires people to elicit their actions in every decision node in the game.

2   Related Work

In this paper we explore the strategic behavior of Peer Designed Agents. A very known competition which has shed light on automated trading agents' strategies is the Trading Agent Competition (TAC) [16,25,26]. In this competition entrants develop travel agents that need to arrange itineraries for a group of clients who want to fly from one city to another within a certain time period. Most of the papers describe the strategy of a single TAC agent (e.g., [4,12]). However, some of these papers describe the strategies of trading agents that were developed for a certain competition. In addition, there are several fundamental differences between the TAC competition and our work. First, our trading domain is different from the TAC as we focus on bilateral negotiations with unenforceable agreements, while TAC focuses on agents' bidding strategies for complementary and substitutable goods. Second, the TAC is a competition in which the agent's target is to win (i.e. to attain the highest number of points/money), while in our work, as in many real life domains, the goal is to accumulate as many points as possible, regardless of the other agents' performance.

Another known tournament is the Prisoner's Dilemma [19]. In the Prisoner's Dilemma the "cooperation" option can be compared to the decision whether to send the promised resources in our domain and similarly the "defect" option is comparative to choosing not to send. In the finite repeated Prisoner's Dilemma problem the equilibrium strategy is to always defect. Likewise, in our setting, if the number of interactions between the players is finite, the equilibrium is that no exchange will occur. However, it has been shown in the Prisoner's Dilemma that if the game is repeated many times cooperation between players can transpire [2,3]. Actually the winner's strategy in Axelrod's tournament was the *Tit-for-Tat* strategy. According to this strategy, the player cooperates on the first move, and then does whatever her opponent does. In our setting this is equivalent to sending the promised resources in the first agreement and then imitating the other player (that is, sending the promised resource according to the agreement, if the other player fulfills her previous agreement). Nevertheless, in our work we consider situations, where the number of resources that each player needs from the other player is relatively small and consequently the number of iterations is relatively very small. Accordingly, the Tit-for-Tat strategy is not necessarily recommended for our setting, as the number of interactions between players is too small in order for trust to emerge.

Some research in economics has explored the strategic behavior when people are able to revise their strategies based on their performance in the past [24]. Most of them used a strategy method[2]. The strategy method was first proposed by Selten [22]. Similar to developing agents, using the strategy method requires subjects to specify their choices for all information sets of the game and not only the ones that occur during the course of a play of a game. Strategy method has been applied in many experimental settings. In addition, in some of these works,

---

[2] A strategy method is a known economic experimental methodology which requires people to elicit their actions in every decision node in the game.

similar to ours, subjects have the opportunity to revise their strategies based on the feedback received [15,23]. For example, Selten *et al.* [23] investigate subjects' strategies for playing any 2-person 3x3 games with integer payoffs between 0 and 99. The authors examine the subject's strategic behavior throughout five tournaments. They found that the frequency of the play of pure strategy equilibrium increases throughout the tournaments. Keser and Gardner [15] examine the strategic behavior of experienced subjects throughout three tournaments in a common pool resource game. The authors' main result showed that, even though at the aggregate level the sub-game perfect equilibrium organizes the data fairly well, fewer than 5% of the subjects behave according to the game equilibrium prediction. Despite the similarity, asking subjects to design and program agents is different from the strategy method. Developing agents enables subjects to implement much more complex strategies like using heuristics, learning algorithms, etc. Moreover the strategy method is usually used to elicit subjects' strategies in games that are relatively simple (e.g. public goods, Prisoner's Dilemma, ultimatum game and generation game) in contrast to our game which has a richer strategy space and is much more complicated.

The resource allocation game is a simple version of the CT game that was designed by Kraus and Grosz to investigate properties of decision making strategies in multi agent situations [10]. The authors compare the behavior of subjects that play the game online with Peer Designed Agents' that were developed by the same population. The authors show that people design agents that are less cooperative and their strategies are closer to the equilibrium strategies. In contrast to our work, in the CT game subjects design their agents only once and do not have the opportunity to modify them. We on the other hand investigate agents' strategic behavior over time. By doing so our model resembles real life situations, where people can see how their agents perform and modify them according to their performance.

3   The Trading Framework

In order to simulate a general trading framework we have designed the resource allocation game, used as a test-bed to represent various situations in real economic markets [17].

We begin by describing the environment and we continue by analyzing the different strategies in our framework.

3.1   Environment Description

Each player $i \in \{1, 2\}$, is allocated an initial pool of resources R_i^{init}, which are attributed to several types. The goal of the game is to possess a specified set of resources G_i, which includes a certain quantity (zero or more) of each resource type. There are enough resources for both players to satisfy their goals, i.e. $G_1 \cup G_2 \subseteq R_1^{init} \cup R_2^{init}$. However, some of the resources needed by one player may be in the possession of the other. The negotiation protocol consists of a finite number of rounds n. In each round a different agent proposes an offer, while the other agent can respond to it. Each round $0 \le l \le n$ is comprised of two phases: a negotiation phase and an exchange phase. In the negotiation phase one of the players makes an offer to exchange resources, $O^l = (Ogive_i^l, Ogive_j^l)$, in which the proposer (player i) promises to send $Ogive_i^l$ resources to the receiver (player j) and in return requests that player j send $Ogive_j^l$ back to her. Player j should inform player i whether she accepts or rejects the offer. Next, there is an exchange phase, in which the two players, players i and j, send a set of resources S_i^l and S_j^l, respectively, to the other player. Since agreements are not enforced, i.e. each player can break agreements, thus S_i^l and S_j^l can differ from $Ogive_i^l$ and $Ogive_j^l$, respectively. The exchange is executed simultaneously, so the players cannot know in advance whether the opponent will keep her promise. The performance of each player is determined by her score at the end of the game. The score of a player takes into account both the number of resources she possesses, as well as whether or not she has reached the goal. For each resource the player possesses at the end of the game, she will receive a score of $Score_{Res}$. In addition, if she holds her whole target set, she will receive an additional score of $Score_{goal}$. Formally

$$
score_i = \begin{cases} Score_{goal} + |R_i^{end}|Score_{Res} & G_i \subseteq R_i^{end} \\ |R_i^{end}|Score_{Res} & \text{otherwise} \end{cases}
$$

In our experiment we used $n = 10$, $Score_{goal} = 200$, $Score_{Res} = 10$, $|G_i| = 3$ and $|R_{init}^i| = 8$. Thus, obtaining the target set becomes the most important component of the scoring function.

To generalize and strengthen our results, we used two distinct configurations: the one independent player configuration (OIP) and the asymmetric depth configuration (AD). In the OIP configuration, while one player is *independent* and initially obtains all resources needed for her to reach the goal, the other player lacks two specific resources, and she is *dependent* on the other player's resources. Both players also have some extra available resources, which they do not need to attain their respective goals, and can be used for negotiation purposes. This configuration enables an examination of situations in which the equilibrium strategy is not Pareto-optimal, and cooperation between the players yields better results for both parties: the dependent player can obtain the resources she needs to complete the target set, and the independent player can increase the number of resources she possesses. This setting enables the examination of situations, where one side might gain substantially more from the transaction than the other side. These situations are very common in real life. Consider, for instance, a researcher who crucially needs to buy some books for an important research. While the seller of the books will gain some money from the transaction, the researcher, might gain much more from this deal.

In the AD configuration each of the players needs at least one resource from the other player in order to complete her target set. However, the needs of these players are asymmetric. The first player, the *2-resources player*, needs two resources from the second player, while the second player, the *1-resource player*, needs only one resource from the other player in order to complete her target set. Again cooperation between the players yields better results for both parties: both players can obtain the resources they need in order to complete the target set. This setting enables the examination of a very common situation, where each of the traders significantly gains from the exchange of resources, yet one side is more dependent than the other. Consider, for instance, two researchers, each possesses books that the other needs for her research, while each of them needs a different amount of books from the other. In this case both can gain from the exchange.

In the following subsection we analyze the different strategies in both configurations.

3.2   Strategies Analysis

The agent's strategy includes offers, responses and decisions regarding which resource to send. These decisions are not separate from one another. Consider an agent that does not send any resources. In such a case this agent can proffer attractive offers (e.g. give all its extra resources in return for the resources it needs to complete its target set) as it does not send the promised resources.

Using a backward induction we can deduce that the equilibrium strategy of an agent (in both roles and configurations) is to send nothing. In fact any agent that does not send any resources is an equilibrium agent, regardless of her negotiation policy. Indeed, not sending any resources is an equilibrium strategy but it is not a dominant strategy (like the "always defect strategy" is not a dominant strategy in the finitely repeated Prisoner's Dilemma [7]). To explain this, consider the OIP configuration and assume agent i plays against agent j. Assume that agent j's strategy is to negotiate one resource at a time. In addition this agent will fulfill its agreement until it has been deceived. Once agent j has been deceived, it stops sending resources. This implies that if agent i is an equilibrium agent, agent i will never complete its target set (as agent j will send agent i only one resource; after sending this resource it will stop sending resources as it has been deceived by agent i). Nevertheless if player i is not an equilibrium agent and sends the promised resources according to the agreement it will complete its target set (as agent j will fulfill its agreement with reference to the second resource).

Similar to the finitely repeated Prisoner's Dilemma, the resource allocation game has a dominant strategy in the final round of the game. In this round the dominant strategy of both players is not to send any resources, since breaking an agreement in this round can only increase the player's score.

In the following section we describe the experiment's design and methodology.

4   Experiment Design

The experiments involved 32 different agents developed by 32 computer science graduate students. The students were divided into two groups of size 15 and 17. All subjects were instructed to design an agent that plays the resource allocation game, which was explained in class. The experiment was identical for the two groups, except each group received a different configuration, as described earlier. Subjects were explained that their agent would play in a tournament against all the other subjects' agents, including their own agent, in both roles. We kept the identity of all agents anonymous so that agents would not be able to treat any other agent based on its history.

A skeleton of the agent and a support environment were provided to the students. In addition to programming the agents, the subjects were instructed to submit documentation explaining their strategies.

After a given tournament each of the subjects received feedback about her agent's performance during the tournament. More specifically, each of the subjects received a log file for each game that her agent played, which included the course of the game (that is, the offers that were proposed, the responses to these offers, and the resources that each of the players sent in each round of the game). Then, subjects had the opportunity to revise their agents and resubmit them for the next tournament. We repeated this process three times; thus each of the agents participated in four tournaments.

The subjects were motivated to perform well by receiving a course grade. We emphasized that the grade would be based only upon the subject's own score, and not upon other subjects' scores. This is similar to real negotiation environments, where traders gain money only according to their own agents' performance.

To motivate the subjects to put forth effort also in the later tournaments, we explained that their grade would be calculated according to the score obtained by their agents accumulated over all tournaments, whereby later tournaments would receive much larger weights. Moreover, in order to ensure that in each tournament each of the subjects would do their best and would not count on future tournaments to improve their agents, we did not reveal to them in advance whether there would be additional tournaments or not. In this manner the subjects tended to believe that each tournament was their final one.

5   Experimental Results

The agents participated in four tournaments, enumerated 1-4. To analyze the performance of the agents we used two benchmark scores. The first benchmark was the score obtained by equilibrium agents. As these agents do not send any resources, their final scores are equal to their initial scores. More specifically, given the OIP configuration, the equilibrium agent's score when it plays the dependent role, denoted by sc_{dep}, equals 80 (8 resources multiplied only by $Score_{Res}$, as it does not complete its target set). The equilibrium agent's scores when it plays both roles in the AD configuration, denoted sc_{2Res} and sc_{1Res}, also equal 80, based on the same considerations. On the other hand, the equilibrium agent's score when it plays the independent role, denoted sc_{ind}, equals 280 (it receives $Score_{Goal}$ as it completes its target set, with an additional score of the resources it has, that is 8 resources multiplied by $Score_{Res}$).

The second benchmark was supplied by agents that achieve a Pareto-optimal solution which is mutually beneficial. In other words, both agents' score at the end of the game is higher than the score they began with at the start of the game. Moreover, no agent can increase its score at the end of the game without decreasing the other agent's score. More specifically, in the OIP configuration the dependent agent will complete its target set at the end of the game and the independent player will increase the number of the resources it obtains (it will possess more than 8 resources at the end of the game). This means that the independent player's score will be greater than 280 (as it will possess more than 8 resources at the end of the game), while the dependent score will be greater than 230 (as it will possess at least the three resources that comprise its target set at the end the game). As both players at the end of the game complete their target set and together obtain 16 resources (the only change during the game is the distribution of the resources between the players) the total score of the agents playing both roles at the end of the game equals 560, and thus $sc_{dep} = 560 - sc_{ind}$. This implies that the average score, denoted sc_{OIPAvg}, that an agent obtains when it plays both roles equals 280. Similar to the OIP configuration, in the AD configuration both players possess at least the three resources that they need to complete their goal, which implies that both players' score is greater than 230. As both agents complete their target set at the end of the game, it follows that $sc_{2Res} + sc_{1Res} = 560$ and the average score, denoted sc_{ADAvg}, that the agent obtains when it plays both roles equals 280. However, in contrast to the OIP configuration, any distribution of the resources between the agents in which each of the agents possesses its target set at the end of the game is possible. Table 1 summarizes these benchmark agents' scores.

Table 1. Benchmark agents' score

Agent		Equilibrium	Pareto-optimal
OIP Configuration	sc_{ind}	280	$280 \leq sc_{ind} \leq 330$
	sc_{dep}	80	$560 - sc_{ind}$
	sc_{OIPAvg}	80	140
AD Configuration	sc_{2Res}	80	$230 \leq sc_{2Res} \leq 330$
	sc_{1Res}	80	$560 - sc_{2Res}$
	sc_{ADAvg}	40	140

First we will examine the change in the agents' average score for all the tournaments, as depicted in Figures 1(a) and (b). When comparing the scores to the benchmarks we can see that on average the PDA's obtained higher scores than those of the equilibrium agents. On the other hand, this score is lower than that of the Pareto-optimal agents. Moreover, the PDA's average score decreases with the tournaments and in the last tournament the agent's average score is closer to that of the equilibrium agents' score than in the first tournament. This decrease can be explained by the percentage of agents that complete the target set.

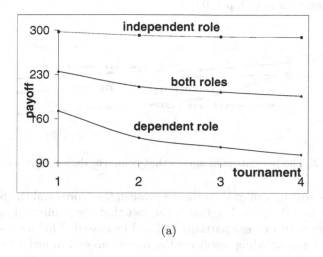

(a)

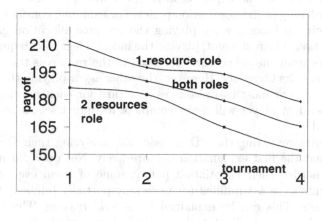

(b)

Fig. 1. The agents' average score in the different tournaments (a) in the OIP configuration (b) in the AD configuration

Figure 2 presents the percentage of agents (not including agents playing the independent role) that completed their target set. We can see that in all considered roles the percentage of agents that completed their target set monotonously decreases over the tournaments. We observe a significant decrease in the percentage of the dependent agents that completed their target set from the first (55%) to the second tournament (30%) (χ^2, $p < 0.01$). In addition, for all the considered agents, a significant decrease in the percentage of agents that completed their target set can be observed from the first tournament to the third tournament (χ^2, $p < 0.05$). This decrease is more pronounced when comparing the first tournament to the fourth tournament (χ^2, $p < 0.01$).

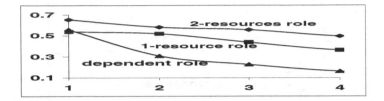

Fig. 2. The percentage of agents that complete their target set

Two possible reasons can explain the decrease in the scores and the percentage of agents that reach the goal. The first is the fact that the number of agreements that were not fulfilled or were partially fulfilled increased. This means that less resources were sent, including resources the agents needed in order to complete their target set. The second explanation is that fewer agreements were reached due to the hardening of the negotiation policy. For example, consider two agents that fulfill their agreements when playing the resource allocation game in the OIP configuration. The first agent, playing the independent role, requires at least three resources from the other agent for each of the resources the other agent needs to complete its target set. However, the other agent playing the dependent role agrees to give at most two in return for each resource it needs. Thus the dependent player will never complete its target set as no agreement will be reached.

However, after reviewing the PDAs code and analyzing their strategies, we can deduce that the first explanation is more likely. Not only did most of the subjects not harden their negotiation policy, some of them even softened it. Still, agreements were not fulfilled (or were only partially fulfilled) throughout the tournaments. This can be explained by several reasons. The first can be attributed to the agents' reliability level which decreased throughout the tournaments. Thus, the agent broke more agreements regardless of the other agent's reliability (i.e., the agents did not fulfill their agreements even if the other agents sent all the resources that were agreed upon). We discuss this strategy in detail in section 6.1. The second reason is that agents tended to break more agreements in order to protect themselves against deceivers (i.e., the agents broke their agreements as a result of the other agents' behavior). This preventive behavior is based on deducing the nature of the opponent from previous rounds. We elaborate on this behavior in Sect. 6.2.

6   Discussion

In this section we present a list of the possible reasons for our results based on an analysis of the subjects' codes.

6.1   Agents' Strategies for Sending Resources

It is interesting to unveil the reasons for the decrease in the agents' average scores. We investigated the agents' strategies for sending resources (i.e., deciding whether to send resources and if so how many) by reviewing the agents' codes. We observed that about 50% of the subjects decreased their agents' reliability throughout the tournaments in both configurations. An additional observation can be made if we also divide the agents into two types: (a) agents that never send the other agent all the required resources it needs to complete its target set (note that a special subset of these agents are equilibrium agents), denoted NSRR (Never Send Required Resources), and (b) the complementary set of NSRR, denoted cNSSR. That is, agents for which there are scenarios where they send all the resources that the other agent needs to complete its target set. As Table 2 shows the number of NSSR agents increases slightly throughout the tournaments in the AD configuration, and it increases more significantly in the OIP configuration. Although the agents' strategies in the last tournament are closer to the equilibrium strategies than in the first tournament, most of the agents in the last tournament are not equilibrium agents.

Our findings indicate that subjects develop agents that deceive more and break more agreements throughout the tournaments although their strategies even in the last tournament are still different from the equilibrium strategies. As a matter of fact in both groups about 33% of the agents usually do not deceive without being deceived first (some of the subjects even explicitly wrote that they do not wish to deceive).

6.2   Detection and Protection Against Dishonest Agents

We also observed that subjects increased their means of protection against deceivers. When we analyzed the modifications the subjects had implemented in their code, we were able to classify this type of behavior into four sub-categories:

1. Punishing the other agents based on their behavior in previous rounds (e.g., the agents cease to send any resources to agents that have priorly deceived them).
2. Limiting the number of resources which they agree to negotiate per round. Using this protection method allows the agent to minimize the risk of playing against deceivers by avoiding sending all the resources required while not receiving any resources in return.
3. Postponing sending the resources the agent has committed to send during round r to the following round $r + 1$, after being assured it has acquired the promised resources from the other agent.

Table 2. The change in agents' types throughout the tournaments

Agent's type	AD configuration	
	first tournament	last tournament
NSSR (EQ)	5 (0)	6 (1)
cNSSR	12	11

Agent's type	OIP Configuration	
	first tournament	last tournament
NSSR (EQ)	3 (2)	9 (6)
cNSSR	12	6

4. Trying to characterize the other player as a deceiver based on its suspicious negotiation policy (e.g., the agents will not send resources to agents that are too generous and offer to send all their extra resources in exchange for the resources they need).

Subjects were able to make these modifications thanks to the large and rich game strategy space that our game introduces. In particular, 33% and 64% of the subjects in the OIP game and the AD game, respectively, improved their agents' protection level using the means of protections detailed above.

6.3 Does Modifying the Agent Ensure Improvement?

The final issue we investigated is whether the modifications made by the subjects in their agents actually yielded agents that performed better. In other words for each agent A_j we checked which agent version, after tournament T_i, would receive a higher score, the older version of the agent, which was submitted for tournament T_i, or the newer version, which was submitted for tournament T_{i+1}, when competing against the same agents that participated in tournament T_i.

Despite the fact that the average agents' score decreases over tournaments (as illustrated in Figure 1) this does not necessarily imply that subjects made their agents worse. This is because the new agent's version can increase its score at the expense of the other older version of agents by being less cooperative. As a result the new agent (the agent that was sent to tournament T_{i+1}) will achieve a better score when it plays against the old version of agents (all the other agents that were sent to tournament T_i). However, when the new version agents compete against each other, since they are less cooperative, the total score of all agents decreases. This phenomenon is similar to the Prisoner's Dilemma [19]. Assume that all the agents' original strategy in the Prisoner's Dilemma is always to cooperate. Given this, each agent that will modify its strategy to always defect will increase its score (since the other agents' strategies are always

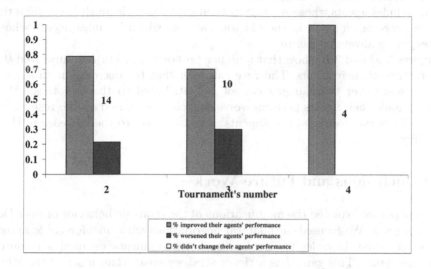

(a)

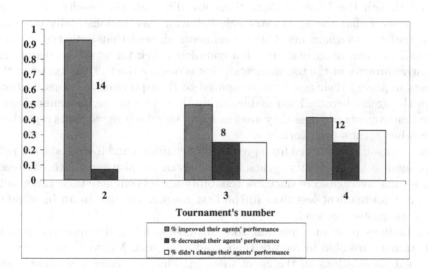

(b)

Fig. 3. Changes in agents' performance in (a) the OIP configuration (b) the AD configuration among modified agents with respect to the original agents. The numbers near the bar represent the number of subjects who modified their agents.

to cooperate, when this agent plays against all the other agents it will achieve a better score). However, the average score of an agent in the new tournament, which includes agents whose strategy is to always defect, is much lower than the average score of an agent in the old tournament, which includes agents whose strategy is to always cooperate.

Figures 3(a) and 3(b) show that a higher proportion of subjects improved the performance of their agents. Thus, we can infer that the decrease in an agent's average score over tournaments cannot be attributed to the hypothesis that humans made their agents perform worse. Instead, and based on the results, we can attribute the decrease in the agents' average scores to the decrease in their reliability.

7   Conclusions and Future Work

In this paper we explored the modifications of the strategic behavior of Peer Designed Agents. We focused on bilateral negotiations with unenforceable agreements over time. In order to simulate such environments we used a resource allocation game. This game has a richer strategy space than most of the standard economic games [1,5,11,18,19]. We tested two different configurations of this game reflecting real life and common situations, which differ from each other by the number of resources each player needs and each player's dependency on the other player.

Even though the basic configurations are different, the results of our experiment show that the agents strategic behavior was fundamentally modified throughout the tournaments. Our experiments showed that both the average score and the percentage of agents that completed their target set decreased significantly throughout the tournaments. This is despite the fact that most of the subjects improved their agents as compared to their previous versions. In both groups the agents become less reliable during the course of the tournaments and as the tournaments progress they are less likely keep their agreements regardless of the other agent's behavior.

Moreover subjects learned from previous tournaments and increased their protection against low reliability agents. This behavior can also explain the decrease in the agents' average score since low reliability agents complete their target sets in the last tournament less than in the first tournament due to an increase in the agents' protection level.

Our findings play an important role in understanding dynamic markets in which traders are able to modify their trading agents. Moreover these results have great implications on the agent's design. Thus we recommend that agent designers take the tournament number into account when designing agents for this type of market.

In future work we will investigate how people develop agents in more complex games as well as the behaviors that emerge in online games.

References

1. Andreoni, J.: Why free-ride? strategies and learning in public goods experiments. Journal of Public Economics 37, 291–304 (1988)
2. Axelrod, R.: The evolution of cooperation. Basic Books (1984)
3. Axelrod, R., Hamilton, W.: The evolution of cooperation. Science 211, 1390–1396 (1981)
4. Benisch, M., Andrews, J., Sadeh, N.: Pricing for customers with probabilistic valuations as a continuous knapsack problem. In: Eighth International Conference on Electronic Commerce, pp. 128–134 (2006)
5. Camerer, C.F., Fehr, E.: Foundations of Human Sociality, chapter Measuring Social Norms and Preferences using Experimental Games: A Guide for Social Scientists. Oxford University Press (2004)
6. Camerer, C.F., Fehr, E.: Measuring Social Norms and Preferences using Experimental Games: A Guide for Social Scientists. Foundations of human sociality: Economic experiments and ethnographic evidence from fifteen small-scale societies. Oxford University Press, New York (2004)
7. Chellapilla, K., Fogel, D.: Evolution, neural networks, games, and intelligence. Proc. IEEE 87(9), 1471–1496 (1999)
8. Da-Jun, C., Liang-Xian, X.: A negotiation model of incomplete information under time constraints. In: AAMAS 2002, pp. 128–134 (2002)
9. Erev, I., Roth, A.: Predicting how people play games: Reinforcement learning in experimental games with unique, mixed strategy equilibrium. American Economic Review 88(4), 848–881 (1998)
10. Grosz, B., Kraus, S., Talman, S., Stossel, B., Havlin, M.: The influence of social dependencies on decision-making: Initial investigations with a new game. In: AAMAS 2004, pp. 782–789 (2004)
11. Guth, W., Damme, E.: Information, strategic behavior and fairness in ultimatum bargaining: An experimental study. Journal of Mathematical Psychology 42(2), 227–247 (1998)
12. He, M., Rogers, A., Luo, X., Jennings, N.R.: Designing a successful trading agent for supply chain management. In: AAMAS 2006, pp. 1159–1166 (2006)
13. Ishihara, Y., Huang, R., Ma, J.: A real trading model based price negotiation agents. In: AINA, pp. 597–604 (2006)
14. Keser, C.: Strategically planned behavior in public goods experiments. Working Paper, Scientific Series 2000s-35, CIRANO, Montreal, Canada (2000)
15. Keser, C., Gardner, R.: Strategic behavior of experienced subjects in a common pool resource game. International Journal of Game Theory 28, 241–252 (1999)
16. Lanzi, P.L., Strada, A.: Analysis of the trading agent competition 2001. SIGecom 3(2), 1–8 (2002)
17. Manisterski, E., Katz, R., Kraus, S.: Providing a recommended trading agent to a population: a novel approach. In: IJCAI 2007, pp. 1408–1414 (2007)
18. Offerman, T., Potters, J., Verbon, H.A.A.: Cooperation in an overlapping generations experiment. Games and Economic Behavior 36(2), 264–275 (2001)
19. O'Riordan, C.: Iterated prisoner's dilemma: A review. Technical report, Department of Information Technology, NUI, Galway (2001)
20. Roth, A.: Bargaining Experiments. In: Kagel, H., Roth, A.E. (eds.) The Handbook of Experimental Economics. Princeton University Press (1995)
21. Schnizler, B., Luckner, S., Weinhardt, C.: Automated trading across e-market boundaries. In: Group Decision and Negotiation, pp. 199–201 (June 2006)

22. Selten, R.: Die strategiemethode zur erforschung des eingeschränkt rationalen verhaltens im rahmen eines oligopolexperiments. Beiträge zur experimentellen Wirtschaftsforschung 1, 136–168 (1967)
23. Selten, R., Abbink, K., Buchta, J., Sadrieh, A.: How to play (3x3)-games: A strategy method experiment. Games and Economic Behavior 45(1), 19–37 (2003)
24. Selten, R., Mitzkewitz, M., Uhlich, G.R.: Duopoly strategies programmed by experienced players. Econometrica 65, 517–555 (1997)
25. Stone, P., Greenwald, A.: The first international trading agent competition: autonomous bidding agents. Electronic Commerce Research 5(2), 65–229 (2005)
26. Wellman, M.P., Greenwald, A., Stone, P., Wurman, P.R.: The 2001 trading agent competition. Electronic Markets 13(1), 4–12 (2003)

A New Approach to Alphabet Extension
for Improving Static Compression Schemes

Shmuel T. Klein

Department of Computer Science
Bar Ilan University, Ramat-Gan 52900, Israel
tomi@cs.biu.ac.il

Abstract. The performance of data compression on a large static text
may be improved if certain variable-length strings are included in the
character set for which a code is generated. A new method for extending
the alphabet is presented, based on a reduction to a graph-theoretic
problem. A related optimization problem is shown to be NP-complete, a
fast heuristic is suggested, and experimental results are presented.

1 Introduction and Background

Compression methods may be classified according to various criteria, such as
compression efficiency, speed, necessary space in RAM, etc. (see [32] or [6] for an
overview). The present work focuses on a static compression scheme, for which
we assume that the time restrictions on the encoding and decoding processes are
not symmetrical: we shall put no constraint on compression time, but require
very fast decompression. The corresponding scenario is that of a large full-text
information retrieval (IR) system, for which compression is usually performed
only once or periodically (but rarely), but which may be accessed frequently, so
that (possibly many) small parts of it need to be decompressed while the user
is waiting for responses to a query. The text of the IR system may be static,
like for the Encyclopædia Britannica, the *Trésor de la Langue Française* [11],
the *Responsa Retrieval Project* (RRP) [16,14], etc., or it might be dynamically
increasing over time, like collections of news wire messages, newspapers, and
ultimately, the whole World Wide Web. The RRP mentioned above, one of the
oldest IR systems, was headed by Prof. Yaacov Choueka for many years and was
a major incentive for the present, as well as many related works.

Statistical compression methods, like Huffman or arithmetic coding, assume
that the text at hand is a sequence of data items, that will be encoded according
to their occurrence frequencies. These data items are generally single characters,
but sometimes more sophisticated models are used for which a character pair, a
word, or more generally, certain character strings, are considered to be an item.
Dictionary compression methods work by replacing the occurrence of certain
strings in the text by (shorter) pointers to some dictionary, which again may
be either static, fixed in advance (e.g., the most frequent words in English),
or dynamically adapted to the given text, like the various Lempel-Ziv methods

N. Dershowitz and E. Nissan (Eds.): Choueka Festschrift, Part I, LNCS 8001, pp. 197–212, 2014.

and their variants. The statistical methods working only on single characters are often inferior to the dictionary methods from the compression point of view. Nevertheless, they may be the preferred choice in IR applications, as they do not require a sequential scan of the compressed file.

To improve the performance of the statistical methods, much larger alphabets could be defined, as in the *Huffword* variant [17], in which every word, rather than every character, is considered as an atomic element to be encoded. Another line of investigation suggested to trade a part of the compression efficiency against better processing abilities, including faster decoding and the possibility to search directly in the compressed text [28,12,24]. Using large alphabets, the reduction in compression is only a few percent, but decoding and searches are much faster.

The focus in this paper is again the compression ratio of statistical methods, and we shall follow the approach in [9] and [10], and construct a *meta-alphabet*, which extends the standard alphabet by including also frequent variable-length strings. The idea is that even if we assume a quite involved model for the text generation process, there will always be strings deviating from this model. One may thus improve the accuracy of the model by including such strings as indivisible items, called below *meta-characters*, into the extended alphabet.

Obviously, the larger the meta-alphabet, the better compression we may expect. The problem then is that of an optimal exploitation of a given amount of RAM, which puts a bound on the size of the dictionary. We shall assume that this resource is limited, so that decompression at least should be possible even on very weak machines. In addition, there is a problem with the selection of the set of meta-characters, because the potential strings are overlapping. A similar problem has been shown to be NP-complete under certain constraints [18]. Several efficient greedy heuristics have been suggested in [3,4]. They are based on iteratively choosing the most promising string, and substituting all its non-overlapping occurrences, except one, by a new meta-character. Other works addressing the problem of compressing using a fixed alphabet can be found in [26,13,8].

Our approach concentrates on the meta-alphabet itself, rather than on the individual occurrences of its elements in the text. This enables a clean separation of the modeling (definition of the meta-alphabet) from the actual encoding (choice of encoding and parsing methods), as advocated by [7]. Such a separation allows the evaluation of the contribution of each part independently from the other, by fixing the model and varying the encoding, or alternatively, by using a given encoding scheme and applying it to various models. We strive in this work to optimize the model or at least to make sound decisions in successive approximations of such an optimum.

The paper is organized as follows: in the next section, we present a novel approach to alphabet extension and show that a related optimization problem is NP-complete. Section 3 deals with implementation issues and refinements and suggests a fast heuristic, and Section 4 mentions some possible extensions. Finally, we bring some experimental results in Section 5.

2 Definition of Meta-alphabet

The criterion for including a string of characters as a new meta-character into the meta-alphabet is the expected savings we would incur by its inclusion. The exact value is hard to evaluate, since the savings depend ultimately on the encoding method, and for Huffman codes, say, the length of each codeword may depend on all the others. Assume for simplicity in a first stage, that we shall use a fixed length code to refer to any element of the meta-alphabet $\mathcal{A}$, which contains both single characters and the meta-characters. If $|\mathcal{A}| = D$, any element can be encoded by $\lceil \log_2(D) \rceil$ bits.

Our approach starts by a reduction to a graph-theoretic problem in the following way. There will be a vertex for every possible character string in the text, and vertices are connected by an edge if the corresponding strings are overlapping. Both vertices and edges are assigned weights. The weight $w(x)$ of a vertex x will be the *savings*, measured in number of characters, obtained by including x in $\mathcal{A}$. The weight $w(x, y)$ of an edge (x, y) will be the *loss* of such savings due to the overlap between x and y. We are thus interested in a subset V' of the vertices, not larger than some predetermined constant K, which maximizes the overall savings

$$\sum_{x \in V'} w(x) - \sum_{x, y \in V'} w(x, y). \tag{1}$$

Formally, we are given a text $T = t_1 t_2 \cdots t_n$, where each t_i belongs to a finite alphabet Σ; define a directed graph $G = (V, E)$, where V is the set of all the substrings of T, i.e., the strings $t_i \cdots t_j$ for $1 \le i \le j \le n$, and there is a directed edge from $x = x_1 \cdots x_k$ to $y = y_1 \cdots y_\ell$ if some suffix of x is a prefix of y, i.e., there is a $t \ge 1$ such that $x_{k-t+j} = y_j$ for all $1 \le j \le t$. For example, there will be a directed edge from the string element to mention, corresponding to $t = 4$. The weight of a vertex x is defined as

$$w(x) = freq(x)(|x| - 1),$$

where $freq(x)$ is the number of occurrences of the string x in T, $|a|$ denotes the length (number of characters) of a string a, and the -1 accounts for the fact that if the string x is selected as a meta-character, then for each occurrence of x, $|x|$ characters are saved, but one meta-character will be used, so we save only $|x| - 1$ characters (recall that we assume a fixed-length code, so that the characters and meta-characters are encoded by the same number of bits).

For strings x and y like above, define the super-string, denoted $\overline{xy}$, as the (shortest) concatenation of x with y, but without repeating the overlapping part, i.e., $\overline{xy} = x_1 \cdots x_k y_{t+1} \cdots y_\ell$, where t has been chosen as largest among all possible t's. For example, if x is element and y is mention, then $\overline{xy}$ is elemention. The weight of the directed edge from x to y is defined as

$$w(x, y) = freq(\overline{xy})(|y| - 1).$$

The reason for this definition is that if the text will be parsed by a greedy method, it may happen that $freq(\overline{xy})$ of the $freq(y)$ occurrences of y will not be detected, because for these occurrences, the first few characters of y will be parsed as part of x.

In fact, assuming that the parsing of $\overline{xy}$ will always start with x in a greedy method is an approximation. For it may happen that certain occurrences of x will stay undetected because of another preceding string z, that has a non-empty suffix overlapping with a prefix of x. To continue the example, suppose z is `steel`, then $\overline{z\overline{xy}}$ is `steelemention`, which could be parsed as zey. Moreover, when the overlapping part itself has a prefix which is also a suffix, then choosing the *shortest* concatenation in the definition of $\overline{xy}$ does not always correspond to the only possible sequence of characters in the text. For example, if x is `managing` and y is `ginger`, $\overline{xy}$ would be `managinger`, but the text could include a string like `managinginger`. We shall however ignore such cases and keep the above definition of $w(x, y)$.

A first simplification results from the fact that we seek the subgraph induced by the set of vertices V', so that either both directed edges (x, y) and (y, x) will be included, if they both exist, or none of them. We can therefore consider an equivalent undirected graph, defining the label on the (undirected) edge (x, y) as

$$w(x, y) \;=\; freq(\overline{xy})(|y| - 1) \;+\; freq(\overline{yx})(|x| - 1).$$

For a text of n characters, the resulting graph has $\Theta(n^2)$ vertices, and may thus have $\Theta(n^4)$ edges, which is prohibitive, even for small n. We shall thus try to exclude a priori strings that will probably not be chosen as meta-characters. The excluded strings are:

1. a string of length 1 (they are included anyway in $\mathcal{A}$);
2. a string that appears only once in the text (no savings can result from these).

For example, consider the text

> `the-car-on-the-left-hit-the-car-i-left-on-the-road`.

Using the above criteria reduces the set of potential strings to: {`the-car-`, `-on-the-`, `-left-`}, and all their substrings of length > 1. If this seems still too large, we might wish to exclude also

3. a string x that always appears as a substring of the same string y.

This would then purge the proper substrings from the above set, except the string `the-`, which appears as substring of *different* strings. The rationale for this last criterion is that it is generally preferable to include the longer string y into the extended alphabet. This is, however, not always true, because a longer string has potentially more overlaps with other strings, which might result in an overall loss, as will be shown below.

Figure 1 depicts the graph of the above example, but to which we have added `on-the-` as fifth string to the alphabet (in spite of it appearing always as substring of `-on-the-`) because it will yield an example showing a deficiency of criterion 3. Edges with weight 0 have been omitted, so there is no edge between `-left-` and `the-car-`, or between `on-the-` and `the-car-`, because the super-strings `the-car-left-` and `on-the-car-` do not appear; similarly,

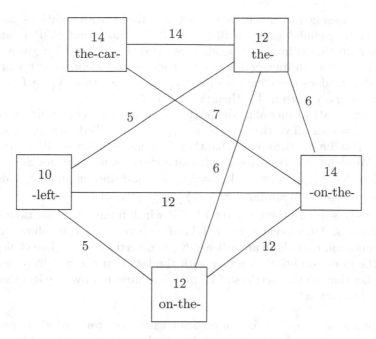

Fig. 1. Graph for text
`the-car-on-the-left-hit-the-car-i-left-on-the-road`

there is no self-loop on the vertex x =`-left-`: even though the super-string $\overline{xx}$ =`-left-left-` is defined, its frequency is zero. If we are looking for a set of 3 meta-characters, the best of the $\binom{5}{3} = 10$ triplets is `the-car-`, `-left-`, `on-the-`, yielding savings of $14 + 10 + 12 - 5 = 31$ characters. Indeed, replacing all occurrences of the meta-characters in the text reduces the number of elements in the parsing from 50 to 19, of which 14 are single characters and 5 are meta-characters. However, one can see here that the criterion of excluding a string x if it always appears as substring of y, does not assure optimality: if we would choose the string `on-the` instead of `on-the-` as fifth vertex, the text could be parsed as 16 instead of 19 elements.

There is, however, still a problem with the complexity of the algorithm. A similar problem has been shown to be NP-complete in [30], but we bring here a direct proof:

Theorem 1. *The problem of finding a subgraph maximizing (1) is NP-complete.*

Proof: One actually has to deal with the corresponding decision problem, which we denote SDP (Substring Dictionary Problem). Given a graph $G = (V, E)$, with weights on both vertices and edges, and 3 non-negative constants K_1, K_2 and K_3, is there a subset of vertices $V' \subseteq V$, such that $|V'| \leq K_1$, $\sum_{x \in V'} w(x) \geq K_2$ and $\sum_{x,y \in V'} w(x, y) \leq K_3$?

Once a guessing module finds the set V', the other conditions are easily checked in polynomial time, so SDP $\in$ NP. To show that SDP is also NP-hard, the reduction is from Independent Set (IS) [19], defined by: given a graph $G_1 = (V_1, E_1)$ and an integer L, does G_1 contain an independent set of size at least L, that is, does there exist a subset $V_1' \subseteq V_1$, such that $|V_1'| \geq L$, and such that if x and y are both in V_1', then $(x, y) \notin E_1$?

Given a general instance of IS, define the following instance of SDP: let $G = G_1$, define $w(x) = 1$ for all vertices $x \in V$, $w(x, y) = 1$ for all edges $(x, y) \in E$, $K_1 = |V|, K_2 = L$ and $K_3 = 0$. Suppose that there is an independent set V_1' of size at least L in G_1. We claim that the same set also satisfies the constraints for SDP. Indeed, $|V_1'| = L \leq K_1$, $\sum_{x \in V_1'} w(x) = |V_1'| = L \geq K_2$, and since in an independent set, there are no edges between the vertices, $\sum_{x,y \in V_1'} w(x, y) = 0 \leq K_3$.

Conversely, suppose there is a set $V' \subseteq V$ which fulfills the conditions of SDP in the graph G. Then because the weight of each vertex is 1, it follows from the second condition that there are at least $K_2 = L$ vertices in V'. The choice of K_3 as 0 in the third condition, together with the fact that the weight of each edge is 1, implies that no two vertices of V' may be connected by an edge, that is, V' is an independent set.   ∎

Two problems have therefore to be dealt with: first, we need a fast procedure for the construction of the graph, and second we seek a reasonable heuristic, running fast enough to yield a practical algorithm, and still making better choices than discarding any strings that overlap with one previously chosen.

3   Implementation Details

3.1   Graph Construction

Since we are looking for a special set of substrings of the given input text T, a *position-tree* or *suffix-tree* [5,31] may be the data structure of choice for our application, as it is in similar algorithms like, e.g., in [4]. The strings occurring at least twice correspond to the internal nodes of the tree. As to condition 3. above, if a string x occurs always as a prefix of y, the node corresponding to x has only one child in the position tree, and will therefore not appear as a node in the *compacted* form of the tree. Seeking the longest re-occurring strings, these correspond, for each branch of the tree, to the lowest level of the internal nodes, i.e., the parent nodes of the leaves. The other internal nodes of the compacted tree correspond to strings that are prefixes of at least two different strings. However, the set of strings corresponding to the internal nodes of the compacted position tree might include more strings than those defined by conditions 1.–3., e.g., a string x that always appears as *suffix* of some other string y. Such strings could be purged by using an auxiliary position tree, built for the reversed input string, but empirical tests have shown that this may not be worth the effort.

The advantage of defining the set of vertices as corresponding to the internal nodes of the position tree is that we get n, the length of the text, as immediate bound for the number of vertices. Indeed, the branching factor of every internal node in the compacted position tree is at least 2 (and for many nodes much larger than that), so in the worst case, we have a full binary tree with n leaves, and therefore $n-1$ internal nodes. Figure 2 shows a part of the compacted position tree for our example, where the black vertices correspond to the four strings left after applying conditions 1.–3. above.

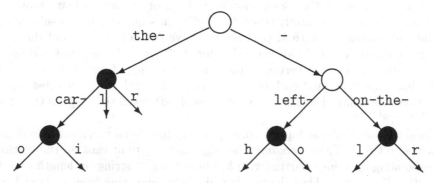

Fig. 2. Part of the compacted position tree

Compacted position trees can be constructed in time linear in the length of the input text T. Also in linear time one could add to each vertex in the tree, the number of times the corresponding string occurs in T [2]. Thus, the set of vertices V and their labels can be constructed in time $O(n)$.

As to the edges, it suffices to check for each string x corresponding to a vertex v_x whether there should be a directed edge from it to a vertex corresponding to a string y. This will be the case if and only if the super-string $\overline{xy}$ exists. We have thus to search the position tree for each of the $|x|-1$ proper suffixes of x. If the path in the position tree corresponding to one of these proper suffixes leads to an internal node t, there will be an edge from v_x to each of the vertices in the subtree rooted by t.

If there is an upper limit K, independent of the size n of the text, on the length of a string corresponding to a vertex, the number of edges in the graph G will be linear. Indeed, a proper suffix of length i of x can be extended to at most $|\Sigma|^{K-i}$ strings y such that $\overline{xy}$ exists, therefore the outdegree of x is bounded by $|\Sigma|^K$, which is a constant relative to n. Assuming the existence of such an upper bound K is not unrealistic for real-life applications, where most re-occurring strings will tend to be words or short phrases. Even if some long strings re-occur, e.g., runs of zeros or blanks, it will often be the case that a bound K exists for the lengths of all except a few strings, which will still yield a linear number of edges. The following Theorem shows that such a linear bound on the number of edges can not always be found.

Theorem 2. *There are input texts T for which the corresponding graph $G = (V, E)$ satisfies $|E| = \Theta(|V|^2)$.*

Proof: Recall that a DeBruijn sequence of order k is a binary string B_k of length 2^k, such that each binary string of length k occurs exactly once in B_k, when B_k is considered as a circular string (see [15, Section 1.4]). For example, B_3 could be 00111010.

Consider the text $T = CB_k$, where C is the suffix of length $k-1$ of B_k. Each of the 2^k possible binary strings of length k appears exactly once in CB_k, so no string of length longer than k appears more than once. Every binary sequence of length $k-1$ appears exactly twice in a DeBruijn sequence, and as sub-strings of different strings of length k, thus there is a vertex in G for each of the 2^{k-1} strings of length $k-1$. More generally, for $2 \leq i < k$ (recall that strings of length 1 do not generate vertices), there are 2^i strings of length i that occur more than once in T, and each of these strings of length $< k$ is a substring of more than one string of length k. The number of vertices in the graph is therefore $\sum_{i=2}^{k-1} 2^i = 2^k - 4$.

Consider one of the strings x, corresponding to a vertex v_x, and denote its rightmost bit by b. Then there must be edges from v_x to at least all the vertices corresponding to strings starting with b. There are 2^{i-1} strings of length i starting with b, $2 \leq i < k$. Thus the number of edges emanating from v_x is at least $\sum_{i=2}^{k-1} 2^{i-1} = 2^{k-1} - 2$. Therefore the total number of edges in the graph is at least $(2^k - 4)(2^{k-1} - 2)$, which is quadratic in the number of vertices.   ∎

3.2   Heuristics for Finding a Good Sub-graph

The optimization problem has been shown above to be NP-complete, so there is probably no algorithm to find an optimal solution in reasonable time. A family of simple greedy heuristics that have previously been used (see, e.g., [11]) includes the following steps:

1.	Decide on a set S of potential strings and calculate their weights $w(x)$ for $x \in S$
2.	Sort the set S by decreasing values of $w(x)$
3.	Build the set $\mathcal{A}$ of the strings forming the meta-alphabet by
3.1	start with $\mathcal{A}$ empty
3.2	repeat until $|\mathcal{A}|$ is large enough or S is exhausted
3.2.1	$x \longleftarrow$ next string of sorted sequence S
3.2.2	if x does not overlap with any string in $\mathcal{A}$, add it to $\mathcal{A}$

The set S could be chosen as the set of all sub-strings of the text of length up to some fixed constant k, or it might be generated iteratively, e.g., starting with character pairs, purging the overlaps, extending the remaining pairs to triplets, purging overlaps again, etc. Such a strategy of not allowing any overlaps corresponds in our approach above to choosing an independent set of vertices.

To extend this greedy heuristic to include also overlapping strings, we have to update the weights constantly. It is therefore not possible to sort the strings by weight beforehand, and the data structure to be used is a *heap*. This will give us at any stage access in time $O(1)$ to the element x with largest weight $W(x)$, which should represent the expected additional savings we incur by adding x to the set $\mathcal{A}$, the currently defined meta-alphabet. $W(x)$ is therefore $w(x)$ if none of the neighbors of x belongs to $\mathcal{A}$, and it is more generally $w(x) - \sum_{y \in \mathcal{A}} w(x, y)$. The proposed heuristic is thus as follows:

1.   Define the set S as strings corresponding to the
                     internal nodes of the compacted position tree
2.   for each $x \in S$ define $W(x) \longleftarrow w(x)$
3.   build heap of elements $W(x)$, with root pointing to maximal element
4.   Build the set $\mathcal{A}$ of the strings forming the meta-alphabet by
4.1   start with $\mathcal{A}$ empty
4.2   repeat until $|\mathcal{A}|$ is large enough or heap is empty
4.2.1 $x \longleftarrow$ string with weight at root of heap
4.2.2   add x to $\mathcal{A}$ and remove $W(x)$ from heap
4.2.3   repeat for all neighbors y of x in graph
4.2.3.1 $W(y) \longleftarrow W(y) - w(x, y)$
4.2.3.2   if $\quad W(y) \leq 0 \quad$ remove $W(y)$ from heap
4.2.3.3   else   relocate $W(y)$ in heap

Note that $W(x)$ may indeed become negative, as can be seen when working through the example of Figure 1. This would mean that the potential gain obtained from including x in $\mathcal{A}$ might be canceled because of the overlaps.

The complexity of the heuristic can be evaluated as follows: step 1. can be done in time linear in the size n of the text as explained above. Let $m = |S|$ be the number of vertices. Steps 2. and 3. are $O(m)$. Step 4.2.1 is $O(1)$ and step 4.2.2 is $O(\log m)$. Any edge (x, y) of the graph is inspected at most once in the loop of 4.2.3, and for each such edge, a value $W(y)$ is either removed or relocated in the heap in time $O(\log m)$. Thus the total time of step 4. is $O(|E| \log m)$. As we saw in Theorem 2, $|E|$ could be quadratic in m. But when $W(y)$ is updated, it may only decrease, so that its relocation in the heap can only be to a lower level. The total number of updates for any $W(y)$ is therefore bounded by the depth of the heap, which implies that the complexity of step 4. is only $O(m \log m)$.

The Off-line heuristic of [4] has some similarities with the latter procedure, but differs in various aspects. It also successively chooses new meta-characters to be substituted, but it considers at each stage non-overlapping *occurrences* of a given meta-character within the text, whereas the new heuristic above considers overlaps between different meta-characters rather than between their occurrences. That is, Off-line works directly on the text itself, while the new heuristic tries to extract the meta-alphabet from the given graph, which models the text. The advantage of Off-line is then the fact that its decisions are based on real data and not on estimates, which yields very good compression performance, as reported in [4]. The advantage of the present approach, on the other hand, is in its focus on the model alone; this allows an independent subsequent application of different encoding schemes.

4   Extensions

4.1   Variable Length Encodings

In our above description, we have made various simplifying assumptions. In a more precise analysis, we shall try in a second stage to adapt the general strategy to more complex — and more realistic — settings.

When defining the graph, we assumed that the elements of the meta-alphabet are encoded by a fixed length code. Such a code will, however, be optimal only if the occurrence distribution of the elements is close to uniform. Otherwise, variable-length codes such as Huffman or arithmetic codes should be used. The problem is then one of the correct definition of the graph weights, but the generalization of the above method is not straightforward. We look for a set of strings which are selected on the basis of the lengths of their encodings; the lengths depend on their probabilities; these in turn are a function of the full set of strings, which is the set we wish to define.

A possible solution to this chicken and egg problem is as follows. We first estimate the average length, $\hat{\ell}$, of the strings $s_1, s_2, \ldots$ that will ultimately be selected. This can be done by some rough rule of thumb or by applying the heuristic iteratively. Clearly, if $n = |T|$ is the length of the text and N is the number of the selected strings, we have

$$n = \sum_{i=1}^{N} |s_i| freq(s_i).$$

Replacing now all $|s_i|$ by their estimated average value $\hat{\ell}$, we get

$$n = \hat{\ell} \sum_{i=1}^{N} freq(s_i),$$

from which an estimate for the total frequency, $W = \sum_{i=1}^{N} freq(s_i)$, of the selected elements can be derived as

$$W = \frac{n}{\hat{\ell}}.$$

Hence, when defining the probabilities in the weights of the vertices and edges, we shall use as approximation the frequency of a string divided by W, even though this is not a real probability distribution, as the selected values will not necessarily add up to 1. But the estimation bias is alleviated by the fact that the probabilities are only needed to determine the lengths of the codewords. We shall use $-\log_2 p$ as approximation for the length of a codeword that appears with probability p. This is exact for arithmetic coding, and generally close for Huffman coding [27].

The new weights are not measured in number of characters, but in number of bits. For a string $x = x_1 \cdots x_r$, the weight of the corresponding vertex will be

$$w(x) = freq(x) \left(-\sum_{i=1}^{r} \log_2 \frac{freq(x_i)}{W} + \log_2 \frac{freq(x)}{W} \right),$$

where $freq(x_i)$ are the frequencies of the individual characters making up the string, and similarly for the weights $w(x, y)$ of the edges. This is again an approximation, as we compare the cost of using the string as a single element versus the cost of using the constituent characters individually. So the string the would be compared with the characters t, h and e, whereas in fact the alternative to the could be using one of the *substrings* th or he. Once the set of meta-characters $\mathcal{A}$ is determined by the heuristic, we can update our estimate for the average length $\hat{\ell}$, and repeat the process iteratively. Even without a convergence guarantee, this will be useful for the elimination of bad strings.

4.2   Markov Process

Many authors have commented on the importance of source modeling for good compression (see, e.g., [29]). We shall thus try to adapt the above techniques also to more involved models. The model suggested in [9] is based on extending first the alphabet, and then considering the sequence of meta-characters as generated by a first-order Markov process; each element in the sequence is then Huffman encoded according to its predecessor. The large overhead of the Markov process can be dealt with by clustering [10] and by using canonical Huffman codes [22]. This approach yields, on large textual test files, compression factors that compete well, and sometimes even beat, those of the best popular compression methods such as gzip or PPM, even though only very simple heuristics have been used for alphabet extension.

The problem in applying a Markov process to the definition of our graph is that the weights of the vertices are not fixed any more, and can not even be approached as done above for the variable length encoding, because the expected savings at any vertex now depend on the edge through which the vertex is accessed. The extension of our graph-based approach to deal with a Markov model will be deferred to future work, but we bring in the experimental section results of applying Markov based Huffman codes on the set of meta-characters generated by the previous methods.

4.3   Non-greedy Parsing

A similar problem to the latter is encountered when we abandon the assumption that, once the meta-alphabet $\mathcal{A}$ is given, the text will be parsed greedily, i.e., by trying at each point to match the longest possible prefix of the remaining text with one of the meta-characters. If the weights are known beforehand, an optimal parsing can be found by a reduction to a shortest path problem [23].

Here again, we took a practical approach: instead of trying to generate a set $\mathcal{A}$ which should be optimal under the constraint of optimal parsing, the processes of alphabet construction and of the actual compression are separated. Once the set $\mathcal{A}$ is obtained by the above methods and the length of the encoding of each element can be evaluated, $\mathcal{A}$ is considered as *fixed*, and the optimal parsing for the *given* weights is generated.

5   Experimental Results

Papers suggesting new compression methods often present comparative performance charts on a large set of "standard" files like the Calgary or Canterbury corpora [1]. Since the purpose of this work is not the presentation of a specific heuristic, but rather of a general method for the improvement of static compression schemes, we restrict the experiments to only a few representative examples. Three texts of varying lengths and different languages were chosen for the tests: the King James version of the *Bible* in English, a French text by Voltaire called *Dictionaire philosophique* and a lisp program *progl* from the Calgary corpus. Table 1 lists the full sizes of these files in Mbytes, as well as the number of vertices in the graph, as percentage of the number of leaves of the compacted position tree.

Table 1. Test file statistics

	Bible	Voltaire	progl
Full size	3.32	0.53	0.068
# vertices	55%	53%	64%

It should be noted that the final heuristic is a product of several layers of approximations: the vertices of the graph do not cover all possible substrings, the weights describe the gains and losses only under certain constraints, and the heuristic does not necessarily find an optimal subset. It therefore made sense to relax the requirements at various stages of the construction, and for example not invest too much effort in the construction of the exact set of vertices, as many of them are ultimately discarded anyway.

As mentioned earlier, the separation of the model for the construction of the extended alphabet from the actual encoding applied to the elements of this alphabet, allows an independent evaluation of the performance of the different models. In the first set of experiments, we considered the weights in the graph corresponding to fixed length encodings and generated the set of meta-characters according to the second heuristic of Section 3.2. The meta-alphabet consisted of the basic 256 ASCII characters, to which 256 more strings have been adjoined, so that any meta-character could be encoded by 9 bits. The first line of Table 2 gives the sizes of these fixed-length encoded files, yielding a reduction of 40–60%.

The meta-alphabet used to produce the next line of the table is based on the weights for the variable-length codewords of Section 4.1, but on which fixed-length encoding was applied. As expected, the compression results are inferior to those of the previous meta-alphabet.

To compare our method also with some simple techniques that are often used, we produced, for each file, a list of the most frequent words, as well as a list of the most frequent character bigrams. Each of these in turn were used to define a new set of meta-characters, again extending the basic 256 elements by 256 more. The last two lines of Table 2 refer to these meta-alphabets, which gave lower savings.

Table 2. Compression results for fixed-length encoding

Fixed length	Bible	Voltaire	progl
Best strings for fixed	1.97	0.29	0.031
Best strings for variable	2.20	0.32	0.034
Most frequent words	2.39	0.40	0.048
Most frequent pairs	2.02	0.31	0.042

Table 3. Compression results with Huffman coding

Variable length	Bible	Voltaire	progl
Best strings for fixed	1.48	0.23	0.0214
Best strings for variable	1.47	0.22	0.0212
Most frequent words	1.50	0.24	0.028
Most frequent pairs	1.73	0.26	0.036

Table 3 are the corresponding results when Huffman coding is applied instead of fixed length coding. Obviously, all the values are smaller than those in the corresponding positions in Table 2. It can be seen that among the alternatives tested, the meta-characters produced by the heuristic on the graph with the weights corresponding to fixed length encoding indeed achieve the best compression by fixed length encodings, while the meta-characters produced with the weights of the variable length encoding are best when Huffman coding is applied. It is noteworthy that when passing from the fixed length to the variable length weights, the number of meta-characters in the parsing increases (this number is proportional to the size, since fixed length encoding is used), and nevertheless, the size of the corresponding Huffman encoded file is smaller. This is due to the fact that the distribution of frequencies in the latter case is much skewer than in the former, resulting in the overall gain. We also see that the differences between the different methods are smaller than for Table 2, as Huffman coding tends to partially correct the deficiencies of a bad choice of elements to be encoded.

The figures in Tables 2 and 3 are still far from the compression that can be achieved with adaptive dictionary methods. For instance, the Bible file can be reduced by LZW to 1.203 MB, by gzip to 1.022 MB, and by bzip to merely 0.74 MB. But recall that we are looking for a *static* method, which will allow random and not only sequential access to the compressed file, so that these dynamic methods are ruled out. On the other hand, using Huffman coding in combination with a first order Markov model as in Section 4.2, may achieve compression factors that can sometimes beat some of the dynamic methods.

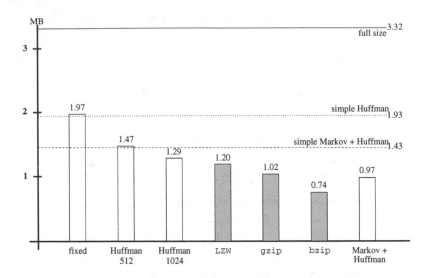

Fig. 3. Comparative chart of the compression of the Bible file

Figure 3 schematically compares the various techniques on the Bible file. The upper horizontal line corresponds to the full size, and the dotted and dashed lines are produced by applying simple Huffman coding, and Huffman coding based on a first order Markov model, respectively, on a standard 256 character alphabet. The white histogram bars give the sizes of the compressed files when alphabet extension is used, and the grey bars bring the values of the dynamic methods. The leftmost two bars correspond to the values in Tables 1 and 2. By using a larger extended alphabet, these can be improved: with 1024 meta-characters (including the 256 basic ones), simple Huffman coding yields 1.29MB, which is only 8% more than for `LZW`. But with a Markov model, one can get even below one MB, which is better than `gzip` but still far from `bzip`; the value was obtained with an extended alphabet of 512 meta-characters, and includes 60K of overhead for the description of the model.

6   Concluding Remarks and Future Work

Alphabet extension is not new to data compression. However, the decision about the inclusion into the alphabet of various strings, such as frequent words, phrases or word fragments, has often been guided by some *ad-hoc* heuristic. The present work aims at making this decision in a systematic, theoretically justifiable way.

There are still many more details to be taken care of, in particular, devising more precise rules wherever approximations have been used. We have throughout applied greedy decisions to simplify processing. Though such greedy heuristics seem to give good results for the type of problem we consider here [20], we shall try in another line of investigation to adapt other approximation schemes to our case. The Independent Set optimization problem has been extensively studied, and some good heuristics exist (see [21]). In particular, we can use the fact that our graph has a low average vertex degree, and is of bounded vertex degree if we put some constraints on the lengths of the strings we consider. Another problem similar to ours, with edge weights but without weights on the vertices, has been approximated in [25].

Acknowledgement. As mentioned in the introduction, this research, as well as many other related ones, has been influenced by a long lasting connection with the Responsa Project, which has been headed for many years by Prof. Yaacov Choueka. I would like to take this opportunity of a volume in his honor to thank him for his help and guidance, which no doubt had a major impact on my research.

References

1. Arnold, R., Bell, T.: A corpus for the evaluation of lossless compression algorithms. In: Proc. Data Compression Conference DCC 1997, Snowbird, Utah, pp. 201–210 (1997)
2. Apostolico, A.: The myriad virtues of subword trees, Combinatorial Algorithms on Words. NATO ASI Series, vol. F12, pp. 85–96. Springer, Berlin (1985)
3. Apostolico, A., Lonardi, S.: Some theory and practice of greedy off-line textual substitution. In: Proc. Data Compression Conference DCC 1998, Snowbird, Utah, pp. 119–128 (1998)
4. Apostolico, A., Lonardi, S.: Off-line compression by greedy textual substitution. Proc. of the IEEE 88, 1733–1744 (2000)
5. Aho, A.V., Hopcroft, J.E., Ullman, J.D.: The Design and Analysis of Computer Algorithms. Addison-Wesley, Reading (1974)
6. Bell, T.C., Cleary, J.G., Witten, I.A.: Text Compression. Prentice Hall, Englewood Cliffs (1990)
7. Bell, T., Witten, I.H., Cleary, J.G.: Modeling for Text Compression. ACM Computing Surveys 21, 557–591 (1989)
8. Bentley, J., McIlroy, D.: Data compression using long common strings. In: Proc. Data Compression Conference, DCC 1999, Snowbird, Utah, pp. 287–295 (1999)
9. Bookstein, A., Klein, S.T.: Compression, Information Theory and Grammars: A Unified Approach. ACM Trans. on Information Systems 8, 27–49 (1990)
10. Bookstein, A., Klein, S.T., Raita, T.: An overhead reduction technique for mega-state compression schemes. Information Processing & Management 33, 745–760 (1997)
11. Bookstein, A., Klein, S.T., Ziff, D.A.: A systematic approach to compressing a full text retrieval system. Information Processing & Management 28, 795–806 (1992)
12. Brisaboa, N.R., Fariña, A., Navarro, G., Esteller, M.F. (S,C)-Dense Coding: An Optimized Compression Code for Natural Language Text Databases. In: Nascimento, M.A., de Moura, E.S., Oliveira, A.L. (eds.) SPIRE 2003. LNCS, vol. 2857, pp. 122–136. Springer, Heidelberg (2003)
13. Cannane, A., Williams, H.E.: General-purpose compression for efficient retrieval. Journal of the ASIS 52(5), 430–437 (2001)
14. Choueka, Y.: Responsa: A full-text retrieval system with linguistic processing for a 65-million word corpus of jewish heritage in Hebrew. IEEE Data Eng. Bull. 14(4), 22–31 (1989)

15. Even, S.: Graph Algorithms. Computer Science Press (1979)
16. Fraenkel, A.S.: All about the Responsa Retrieval Project you always wanted to know but were afraid to ask. Expanded Summary, Jurimetrics J. 16, 149–156 (1976)
17. Moffat, A.: Word-based text compression. Software – Practice & Experience 19, 185–198 (1989)
18. Fraenkel, A.S., Mor, M., Perl, Y.: Is text compression by prefixes and suffixes practical? Acta Informatica 20, 371–389 (1983)
19. Garey, M.R., Johnson, D.S.: Computers and Intractability: A Guide to the Theory of NP-Completeness. W.H. Freeman, San Francisco (1979)
20. Halldorsson, M.M., Radhakrishnan, J.: Greed is good: approximating independent sets in sparse and bounded degree graphs. In: Proc. 26th ACM-STOC, pp. 439–448 (1994)
21. Hochbaum, D.S.: Approximation Algorithms for NP-Hard Problems. PWS Publishing Company, Boston (1997)
22. Klein, S.T.: Skeleton trees for the efficient decoding of Huffman encoded texts. The Special issue on Compression and Efficiency in Information Retrieval of the Kluwer Journal of Information Retrieval 3, 7–23 (2000)
23. Klein, S.T.: Efficient optimal recompression. The Computer Journal 40, 117–126 (1997)
24. Klein, S.T., Kopel Ben-Nissan, M.: On the Usefulness of Fibonacci Compression Codes. The Computer Journal 53, 701–716 (2010)
25. Kortsarz, G., Peleg, D.: On choosing dense subgraphs. In: Proc. 34th FOCS, Palo-Alto, CA, pp. 692–701 (1993)
26. Larson, N.J., Moffat, A.: Offline dicionary based compression. Proceedings of the IEEE 88(11), 1722–1732 (2000)
27. Longo, G., Galasso, G.: An application of informational divergence to Huffman codes. IEEE Trans. on Inf. Th. IT–28, 36–43 (1982)
28. de Moura, E.S., Navarro, G., Ziviani, N., Baeza-Yates, R.: Fast and flexible word searching on compressed text. ACM Trans. on Information Systems 18, 113–139 (2000)
29. Rissanen, J., Langdon, G.G.: Universal modeling and coding. IEEE Trans. on Inf. Th. IT–27, 12–23 (1981)
30. Storer, J.A., Szymanski, T.G.: Data compression via textual substitution. J. ACM 29, 928–951 (1982)
31. Ukkonen, E.: On-line construction of suffix trees. Algorithmica 14(3), 249–260 (1995)
32. Witten, I.H., Moffat, A., Bell, T.C.: Managing Gigabytes: Compressing and Indexing Documents and Images. Van Nostrand Reinhold, New York (1994)

Four Apt Elementary Examples of Recursion

Edward M. Reingold

Department of Computer Science, Illinois Institute of Technology, 10 West 31st
Street, Chicago, Illinois 60616-2987, USA
`reingold@iit.edu`

Abstract. We give four elementary examples of recursion that are real-
life, non-trivial, more natural than the corresponding iterative approach,
and do not involve any sophisticated algorithms, data structures, or
mathematical problems. The examples are two forms of writing numbers
in words, coalescing page references for an index, and finding unclosed
begin blocks.

> My New Zoo, McGrew Zoo, will make people talk.
> My New Zoo, McGrew Zoo, will make people gawk
> At the strangest odd creatures that ever did walk.
> I'll get, for my zoo, a new sort-of-a-hen
> Who roosts in another hen's topknot, and *then*
> *Another* one roosts in the topknot of his,
> And another in *his,* and another in HIS,
> And so forth and upward and onward, gee whiz!
> —Dr. Seuss: *If I Ran the Zoo*

1 Introduction

Teaching recursion in elementary programming courses is a critical, but always
difficult task. Students have not quite mastered iteration, know no sophisticated
algorithms, have not been exposed to advanced data structures, and do not have
much feel for the process of turning an inchoate idea of an algorithm into a
working program. The most common examples used to illustrate recursion in
introductory courses are badly flawed; here are some illustrative examples taken
from introductory programming texts:[1]

- Factorials. This is more naturally done by iteration and seems pointless
  anyway—why would anybody want to compute them? Given integer size
  limitations, one can only compute a few values any way.
- Fibonacci numbers. Another seemingly pointless computation. Worse still,
  the naïve recursive approach leads to exponential computation time.
- Input character/digit reversal. Cute, but of no particular use.
- Towers of Hanoi. An interesting puzzle, but not connected to real life.
- How many ways to make change. A beautiful example of dynamic programming, but who cares how many ways there are to make change for a dollar?

---

[1] For obvious reasons we do not give citations!

N. Dershowitz and E. Nissan (Eds.): Choueka Festschrift, Part I, LNCS 8001, pp. 213–224, 2014.
© Springer-Verlag Berlin Heidelberg 2014

When only examples like these are given, the concept of recursion is marginalized. Students come away from such examples with the view (often encouraged by inadequate instructors!) that in addition to being difficult to master, recursion is applicable only to puzzles or peculiar mathematical problems, pointless in real life, and likely to lead to inefficient algorithms. This misguided view is exacerbated when instructors introduce important theoretical examples such as Ackermann's function [1], [2], McCarthy's "91 function" [3], [4], or Takeuchi's function [3], [5].

One can, of course, cite many deep, natural, and important uses of recursion, but such examples cannot be presented without substantial algorithmic background or sophisticated data structures. Tree traversals, [6] for instance, are certainly worthy examples of recursive techniques, but to discuss them one needs to have introduced trees; even then, the application of traversals to real problems is beyond the reach of a neophyte programmer. Depth-first search of a graph [7], for another example, is a fundamental technique, enormously important and more natural recursively than iteratively, but it involves a sophisticated data structure (graphs, usually represented as an adjacency structure) and does not seem useful until one has embroidered it in clever ways to determine—in linear time—complex graph properties like connectivity, biconnectivity, triconnectivity, Eulerian paths, and planarity. Recursive descent parsing [8, sec. 4.4], is yet another powerful, beautiful, and useful example of recursion that is too advanced for introductory courses.

In this note we present four examples of recursion that are perfect for elementary programming courses because they involve learning no extraneous material, are difficult to do iteratively but relatively straightforward recursively, and efficiently perform algorithmic tasks of obvious utility. The four examples are two versions of writing numbers in words, coalescing index page references, and finding unclosed `begin` blocks. Our examples are written in a functional style, presented in C-like notation, but without adherence to the syntax of any particular programming language. We assume that arbitrarily large integers can be manipulated.

2 Writing Numbers in Words—Naïve Version

We want to write a function that prints positive integers digit by digit, with each digit expressed as a word; that is, for the integer 60203 we want to produce the output "six zero two zero three". Such a function might be used by the telephone company for an automated information service in which the requested phone number is read digit by digit to the customer. Doing this iteratively is difficult because we need the most significant digit first. Recursively it is simple: We begin with a function that prints (speaks) a single digit:

```
1  printDigit (integer n) {
2  // Write the name of a number n, 0 <= n < 10.
3
```

```
4    case (n) {
5      0: print("zero");
6      1: print("one");
7      2: print("two");
8      3: print("three");
9      4: print("four");
10     5: print("five");
11     6: print("six");
12     7: print("seven");
13     8: print("eight");
14     9: print("nine");
15     else: error("Digit too large");
16     }
17   }
```

where `print` is the basic system print command. Now with integer (truncated) division `div` and modulus `mod` we write

```
1    printDigits (integer n) {
2    // Write n digit by digit in words.
3
4      if (n < 10)
5        printDigit(n);
6      else {
7        printDigits(n div 10);
8        print(" ");
9        printDigit(n mod 10);
10     }
11   }
```

3   Writing Numbers in Words—Sophisticated Version

The way we wrote numbers in words in the previous section is inadequate for some purposes. Suppose instead that we want to write a number as it would be spoken; that is, we want the number 8018018851 to be written in words as "eight billion eighteen million eighteen thousand eight hundred fifty one" (Conway and Guy [9, p. 15] call this "Knuth's number", the first prime number in the alphabetic ordering of the natural numbers [10, p. 4]). English speakers do this more or less automatically, at least for numbers below one billion, but expressing this algorithmically is subtle. Such an algorithm would be needed for a check-writing program to protect against alteration of the digits in the amount paid. We assume American English nomenclature [11, pp. 12 and 22–24], [12, p. 1549], but the method here is easily adapted to the British English nomenclature, or that of other languages. The imaginative nomenclatures of [9, pp. 14–15] or [13, pp. 311–312] are also easy to accommodate with the ideas presented here.

Our approach, which covers the full range of American English, $(-10^{66}, 10^{66})$, is based on [14]; [10, p. 6] has a similar method.

Numbers less than twenty are idiosyncratic, so we handle them with a case statement:

```
1   printSmallNumber (integer n) {
2   // Write the name of a number < 20.
3
4      case (n) {
5        1: printString("one");
6        2: printString("two");
7        3: printString("three");
8        4: printString("four");
9        5: printString("five");
10       6: printString("six");
11       7: printString("seven");
12       8: printString("eight");
13       9: printString("nine");
14      10: printString("ten");
15      11: printString("eleven");
16      12: printString("twelve");
17      13: printString("thirteen");
18      14: printString("fourteen");
19      15: printString("fifteen");
20      16: printString("sixteen");
21      17: printString("seventeen");
22      18: printString("eighteen");
23      19: printString("nineteen");
24      else
25      error("Small number too large");
26      }
27  }
```

All output is centralized in the procedure printString because it allows us to add spaces, commas, and hyphens between words, as is conventional; we ignore these issues for the moment. We use printMediumNumber to handle numbers less than 1000:

```
1   printMediumNumber(integer n) {
2   // Write the name of a number < 1000.
3
4      if (n > 99) {
5        printSmallNumber(n/100);
6        printString("hundred");
7        n = n mod 100;
8      }
9      if (n > 19) {
```

```
10      printDecade(n/10);
11      n = n mod 10;
12   }
13   if (n > 0)
14      printSmallNumber(n);
15 }
```

where the "decade" is written by

```
1  printDecade (integer n) {
2  // Write the name of a multiple of 10.
3
4     case (n) {
5       2: printString("twenty");
6       3: printString("thirty");
7       4: printString("forty");
8       5: printString("fifty");
9       6: printString("sixty");
10      7: printString("seventy");
11      8: printString("eighty");
12      9: printString("ninety");
13    else
14      error("Decade too large");
15    }
16 }
```

Numbers with four or more digits are handled recursively. To express $n \times 1000^i$ in words, we

express $\lfloor n/1000 \rfloor \times 1000^{i+1}$ in words,
express $n \bmod 1000$ in words, and
write the name of 1000^i in words.

The last step, writing the name of 1000^i, is done with

```
1  printMillenary (integer n) {
2  // Write the name of the power of a 1000.
3
4     case (n) {
5       1: printString("thousand");
6       2: printString("million");
7       3: printString("billion");
8       4: printString("trillion");
9       5: printString("quadrillion");
10      6: printString("quintillion");
11      7: printString("sextillion");
12      8: printString("septillion");
13      9: printString("octillion");
```

```
14      10: printString("nonillion");
15      11: printString("decillion");
16      12: printString("undecillion");
17      13: printString("duodecillion");
18      14: printString("tredecillion");
19      15: printString("quattuordecillion");
20      16: printString("quindecillion");
21      17: printString("sexdecillion");
22      18: printString("septendecillion");
23      19: printString("octodecillion");
24      20: printString("novemdecillion");
25      21: printString("vigintillion");
26      else
27        error("Millenary too large");
28      }
29    }
```

A "vigintillion" (10^{63}) is as high as American nomenclature goes. With printMillenary we translate our recursive structure into

```
1    printBigNumber(integer n, integer i) {
2    // Write the name of a number n * 1000^i, n > 0, i >= 0.
3
4      if (n > 0) {
5        printBigNumber(n/1000, i+1);
6        if ((n mod 1000) != 0) {
7          printMediumNumber(n mod 1000);
8          printMillenary(i);
9        }
10     }
11   }
```

Calling printBigNumber(n, i) writes $n \times 1000^i$ in words, so the initial call to printBigNumber should have a second parameter of zero. Thus we would write the publicly available code as

```
1    printNumber(integer n) {
2    //  Write a number in English words according to
3    //  the American nomenclature.
4
5      printBigNumber(n, 0);
6    }
```

with printString being simply

```
1    printString (string s) {
2    // Write a string
3
4      print(s);
5    }
```

However, as the code now stands, a call such as printNumber(1234) would produce the output "onethousandtwohundredthirtyfour" because no spaces are introduced between words. To do this properly, we cannot simply write a space after a word (it might be the only word), nor can we simply write a space before each word (it might be the first word). We use a global variable of state (the only acceptable type of global variable!) to tell us whether a space is needed. Similarly, commas and hyphens may be needed in certain contexts. The use of global variables can be avoided by passing the values as parameters to all functions, but because there are many functions here, and several values needed, we illustrate the use of global values as a means of communication across all levels of recursion.

Thus we rewrite printNumber as

```
1  printNumber(integer n) {
2  //  Write a number in English words according to
3  //  the American nomenclature.
4
5     global needBlank = false;
6     printBigNumber(n, 0);
7  }
```

and printString as

```
1  printString (string s) {
2  // Write a string, preceded by a blank if needed
3
4     if (needBlank) then print(" ");
5     print(s);
6     needBlank = true;
7  }
```

Ordinarily in English we would write commas after the words "thousand", "million", "billion", and so on. The above code can be adapted to add such commas with a global variable needComma that is set to false initially in printNumber and is set to true at the end of printMillenary; if the value is true in printString, a space followed by a comma is printed before the argument is printed, after which the value is reset to false. Similarly, some usages require a hyphen between the decade value and the units value (that is, "forty-five", not "forty five"). Again, we introduce a global variable needHyphen that is set to false initially in printNumber, is set to true in printMediumNumber after the decade is printed, and is reset to false at the end of printMediumNumber. If the value is true in printString, a hyphen (and no space) is printed before the argument is printed.

We can similarly capitalize the first word by introducing a global variable firstWord, setting to true initially in printNumber, modifying printString to capitalize its argument when the value is true, and resetting it to false as soon as the first word is written. With all of these fillips we can now write

$$2^{219} = 842498333348457493583344221469363458551160763204392890034487820288$$

in words as

> Eight hundred forty-two vigintillion, four hundred ninety-eight
> novemdecillion, three hundred thirty-three octodecillion, three hundred
> forty-eight septendecillion, four hundred fifty-seven sexdecillion, four
> hundred ninety-three quindecillion, five hundred eighty-three
> quattuordecillion, three hundred forty-four tredecillion, two hundred
> twenty-one duodecillion, four hundred sixty-nine undecillion, three
> hundred sixty-three decillion, four hundred fifty-eight nonillion, five
> hundred fifty-one octillion, one hundred sixty septillion, seven hundred
> sixty-three sextillion, two hundred four quintillion, three hundred
> ninety-two quadrillion, eight hundred ninety trillion, thirty-four billion,
> four hundred eighty-seven million, eight hundred twenty thousand, two
> hundred eighty-eight .

Some usage requires the word "and" after the word "hundred", especially
for the rightmost three digits of a number ("one hundred *and* twenty"); this
would require another global variable **needAnd** and a slight modification of
printMediumNumber. Other easy modifications could handle zero and negative
numbers properly.

4   Indexing Page Numbers

Suppose that we need to convert a sorted sequence of page numbers into an
index entry for a book. For example, if a term occurs on pages 1, 3, 4, 6, 7, 8, 9,
12, and 13, the index entry would be

1, 3, 4, 6–9, 12, 13

We want to write a function that produces this list of pages from the sorted
sequence of page numbers. We assume a function **nextPage** that provides the
input sequence of page numbers, one by one, in increasing order; the sequence
is ended with the page number −1.

To begin, notice that each index entry except the last is followed by a comma.
We could use the same technique we used to get blank spaces in the right places
when writing numbers in words—a global variable **needComma** that is true when
the previous index entry needs to be followed by a comma before we print the
next entry. However in this case, because all printing is done in one place, it is
cleaner to include this value as a boolean parameter. The function to write a
single index entry spanning pages **first** to **last** is

```
1   printIndexEntry
2         (integer first, integer last, boolean needComma) {
3   // Print the range of pages first-last as an index entry,
4   // preceded by a comma if needed
5
```

```
6    if (needComma)
7      print(", ");
8    if (first == last)         // one-page run
9      print(first);
10   else if (first+1 == last) // two-page run
11     print(first, ", ", last);
12   else                       // run of 3 or more pages
13     print(first, "-", last);
14 }
```

This function is the basis for our scanning a list of pages and printing the index entries; we must call printIndexEntry for each run of pages that we find in the list. We scan the list accumulating pages in a single run of pages until the run ends; when the run ends, we call printIndexEntry.

As we scan the list, we can represent the current run of pages by its starting and ending page. If the current run stretches from first to last, then the value of the next page in the list tells us whether to extend the current run or to end it. When the current run ends, we write it with a call to printIndexEntry and then, if it was not the final run, use the next page to begin a new run. Thus there are three cases

1. The last run has ended; this happens when there are no more pages in the list, that is, when nextPage returns the dummy value −1.
2. The current run needs to be extended by one page; this happens when the next page in the list is one more than the last page.
3. The current run has ended, but there are more pages in the list; this happens when the next page is *not* one more than the last page and we are not at the end of the list.

Putting this into code we have

```
1    printIndexList
2        (integer first, integer last, boolean needComma) {
3    // Print a list of index entries, preceded by the run
4    // first-last; runs of three or more pages are coalesced
5    // into one hyphenated entry.
6
7    integer page = nextPage();
8    if (page == -1)                       // end of final run
9      printIndexEntry(first, last, needComma);
10   else if (last+1 == page)              // extend current run
11     printIndexList(first, last+1, needComma);
12   else {                                // end current run
13     printIndexEntry(first, last, needComma);
14     printIndexList(page, page, true); // start new run
15   }
16 }
```

Notice that we start a new run (of one page) by making the starting and ending pages equal to the new value given by nextPage.

The function as seen by the outside world must initiate `printIndexList` properly with the first index entry becoming the current run. It is here that we must initialize the value of `needComma`; the initial value must be `false` since no comma is needed before we print the first index entry:

```
1   IndexList () {
2   // Print a list of index entries with runs of three or
3   // more pages coalesced into one hyphenated entry.
4
5     integer page = nextPage();
6     printIndexList(page, page, false);
7   }
```

5   Finding Unclosed Begins

When editing programs in a block-structured language, one often needs to close the last open block. For example, in LaTeX there are blocks of text that are enclosed in matched, parameterized **begin-end** statements. A LaTeX file might look something like

```
\documentclass{article}

\begin{document}
...
\begin{abstract}
...
\end{abstract}
...
\begin{center}
\begin{itemize}
...
\begin{code}
...
\end{code}
...
\begin{enumerate}
...
\end{enumerate}
\end{itemize}
\end{center}
...
\begin{quote}
...
\end{quote}
...
\end{document}
```

When editing such a file it is convenient to have an editing command that closes that last unclosed **begin** by adding the appropriate **end** at the current point in the file; for example GNU Emacs [15, sec. 22.9.2] has such a command. But how does the editor find the last unclosed block in a complicated nested arrangement? You cannot search backward for the last **begin**, because that may already have a matching **end**. No, you must search backward for an *unmatched* **begin**.

We assume for simplicity that we have a boolean function `searchBackward` that searches backward from the present location in the file (called the *point*) returning **true** if the search was successful and **false** otherwise, together with a boolean function `lookingAt` that tells us what the text begins at the point. Moreover, we assume that when we call the function that does the search, it changes the point to the start of string found that caused the search to end successfully, but that if the search ends unsuccessfully, the point is unchanged. Here, then, is how we find the last unclosed **begin**:

```
1   findLastUnendedBegin () returns boolean {
2   // Leave point at the beginning of the last unended begin
3     while (searchBackward("begin" or "end"))
4       do
5         if (lookingAt("begin")) then
6           return true
7         else  // looking at "end", so find matching "begin"
8           return findLastUnendedBegin()
9       // could not find earlier "begin" or "end"
10    return false
11  }
```

The idea here, which is quite difficult to express or explain iteratively, is that we search backward from the present location until we find either a **begin** or an **end**. If we have found a **begin**, the search ends the current recursive call successfully—if that call was the top level, we have found the last unended begin; if it was not the top level, we have found the matching **begin** for the **end** that prompted this recursive call. On the other hand, if the search has found an **end**, we search backward one level deeper in the recursion for *that* matching **begin**. The search ends unsuccessfully if the search backward fails to find either a **begin** or an **end**.

Acknowledgments. The author is grateful to the editors of this volume, Nachum Dershowitz and Ephraim Nissan, for helpful corrections and suggestions.

References

1. Ackermann, W.: Zum hilbertschen aufbau der reellen zahlen. Mathematische An-nalen 99, 118–133 (1928)
2. Wichmann, B.A.: Ackermann's function in ada. Ada Lett. VI, 65–70 (1986)

3. Knuth, D.E.: Textbook examples of recursion. In: Artificial Intelligence and Mathematical Theory of Computation: Papers in Honor of John McCarthy, pp. 207–229. Academic Press Professional, Inc., San Diego (1991)
4. Manna, Z.: Mathematical Theory of Computation. McGraw-Hill, New York (1974)
5. Takeuchi, I.: On a recursive function that does almost recursion only. Technical report, Musahino Electrical Communication Laboratory, Nippon Telephone and Telegraph Company, Tokyo, Japan (1978)
6. Knuth, D.E.: The Art of Computer Programming, Volume 1: Fundamental Algorithms, 3rd edn. Addison Wesley Longman Publishing Co., Inc., Redwood City (1997)
7. Tarjan, R.E.: Depth-first search and linear graph algorithms. SIAM Journal on Computing 1(2), 146–160 (1972)
8. Aho, A.V., Sethi, R., Ullman, J.D.: Compilers—Principles, Techniques, and Tools. Addison-Wesley Publishing Co., Inc., Reading (1986)
9. Conway, J.H., Guy, R.: The Book of Numbers. Springer, New York (1996)
10. Knuth, D.E., Miller, A.A.: A programming and problem-solving seminar. Technical Report STAN-CS-81-863, Department of Computer Science, Stanford University, Stanford, CA, USA (1981)
11. Davis, P.J.: The Lore of Large Numbers. Yale University Press, New Haven (1961)
12. Gove, P.B.: Webster's Third New International Dictionary of the English Language. G. & C. Merriam Co., Springfield (1961)
13. Knuth, D.E.: Supernatural numbers. In: Klarner, D.A. (ed.) The Mathematical Gardner, pp. 310–325. Wadsworth, Boston (1981)
14. Reingold, E.M.: Writing numbers in words in TeX. TUGboat 28(2), 256–259 (2007)
15. Stallman, R.: GNU Emacs Manual, 16th edn. Free Software Foundation, Boston (2007)

Integrating a Lightweight Information Agent with the Cyc Knowledge Base

Kendall Lister and Leon Sterling

Faculty of Information and Communication Technologies
Swinburne University of Technology
Melbourne, Australia
lsterling@swin.edu.au
http://www.ict.swin.edu.au/ictstaff/lsterling

Abstract. In this paper we present details of our experience of integrating a lightweight information agent, designed to retrieve sports match results from web sites, with Cyc, a huge knowledge base and reasoning engine. Placing an information agent into a large ontology requires careful planning and non-trivial overhead. Once integrated, however, a synergy occurs as the existing knowledge in the ontology is brought to bear on the new information provided. We explore the effects of moving knowledge from the heuristic-based information agent into the massive Cyc knowledge base, with the goal of providing Cyc the means of generating new information agents to retrieve new information as required.

Keywords: Information agent, knowledge, ontology, Cyc.

1   Introduction

The history of research in Artificial Intelligence has shown the importance of building on large stores of knowledge in order to achieve general intelligent behaviour. Also, research has shown the need for interpreting knowledge in context, and that some applications can reason effectively with local knowledge. This paper describes experience in trying to integrate a large knowledge base with small programs that depend on lightweight context. We describe several stages of progress toward a general framework for building and eventually automatically generating software agents to supplement the Cyc knowledge base with information from external sources.

An information agent called SportsReporter is the basis for this exploration. The task of finding sports results from Web pages has been used as an example for over ten years within the Intelligent Agents Lab at the University of Melbourne. It is a task where a little knowledge can be used effectively, but a task of sufficient complexity to illustrate issues of context and the value of lightweight reasoning. SportsReporter is described undergoing several significant re-factorings during the exploration.

As general ontologies and knowledge bases grow in number and size, the issue of when certain statements or assertions are true and relevant and when they

N. Dershowitz and E. Nissan (Eds.): Choueka Festschrift, Part I, LNCS 8001, pp. 225–251, 2014.
© Springer-Verlag Berlin Heidelberg 2014

are not becomes more important. Legg gives examples of simple statements that require extra information in order to determine their truth or meaning by identifying logically contradictory statements that might be encountered while reading books, newspapers or web pages [7]: the assertion "New Orleans escaped major hurricane damage" could be stated truly prior to August 31st, 2005 but not after, demonstrating the need to consider the temporal context of an assertion. The pair of statements, "John Brown was born in 1945" and "John Brown was born in 1967", cannot both be true unless the entities indicated by the textual sign 'John Brown' are different. Context, in the form of a definitive identification of which particular entity is relevant, is essential to resolving the apparent inconsistency of the statements.

Other forms of context are also important in determining the truth of a statement. For example, the statement that vampires exist would generally be considered untrue in the context of contemporary Western culture, yet this culture also contains a widely-known genre of fictional stories in which creatures known as vampires are very real to the readers. The recent bestselling Twilight series of books by Stephenie Meyer is a reminder. Although considered to be obviously fictional by almost everybody who lives in contemporary Western culture, such a statement about vampires could easily be encountered by a machine perusing the Semantic Web, and thus such a machine will require the ability to contextualise in order to avoid confusion.

In general, statements can mean different things in different contexts. Most evaluations of information inevitably depend on subjective criteria such as importance, relevance, urgency or reliability. Software systems will increasingly be expected to deal with ordinary, unstructured information as we ask them to assist us with more and more everyday tasks. If knowledge models and ontology-based applications are to be widely usable by large numbers of people and software agents then it is necessary to accommodate subjectivity.

Given the difficulty of modelling and representing knowledge and reasoning in the first place, it is not clear how to extend the models and representations to deal with subjectivity. The idea usually employed as an aid in approaches to extending models is that of context, that the meaning of a word or text is determined by the texts and statements that surround it. Additionally, context incorporates the circumstances or setting in which an event occurs. For example, if a news report includes a local temperature forecast of 25 degrees, it is reasonable to act on that knowledge and choose clothing or make plans accordingly; but if the report was generated in a foreign country, it would no longer be sensible to base your choices on the information that it contains. Although the statement "it will be 25 degrees tomorrow" is bound to be true for certain people in certain places, it is most unlikely, barring coincidence, to be true for us. The question of whether the forecast temperature has been given in degrees Celsius or Fahrenheit is also an example of the importance of context for correctly interpreting information. Without some extra information, such as the country of origin of the forecast and which scale of temperature is generally used there, it is very difficult to decide whether tomorrow will be quite warm or very cold. Although this might seem trite, exactly this sort of contextualising information is often omitted when information is recorded in software systems. One simple example is the Mars Climate Orbiter spacecraft, which was lost in 1999 due to one component of the control system passing data in imperial units and another component treating the data as though it was metric [13]. Another example is the tendency of stores to publish prices for items on their web site, but fail to indicate the currency.

The example of a temperature forecast needing a context to be meaningful bears examination with a view to what exactly it is that renders a single piece of information relevant or irrelevant, useful or useless. In the case of the weather report, it is the presence in the surrounding information, or context, of a fact that indicates that the report originated in a place sufficiently removed from your current location that the contents of the report are not applicable to you. A key observation from this example is that rather than asking about the meaning of an assertion, we could ask about its relevance to us, in our current situation, given our current activities and goals. The relationship between meaning and relevance is not completely clear; it can be difficult to say whether the meaning or the relevance of an assertion is more valuable. Arguably, the meaning is useless without some consideration of the relevance, while relevance would seem to be difficult to determine without an idea of the meaning. In the above example of a weather report, the interests of the recipient of the report viewer are served equally well by judging the forecast irrelevant based on its context as they are by considering its meaning in light of the origin of the report - if the former can be done quickly, it seems unnecessary to perform the latter.

In many situations, context extends beyond the contents of a particular information source or report. Motivation, immediate and future goals, attitude and available resources all tend to influence the interpretation of both the truth and the relevance of information. In general, the meaning and the relevance of a piece of information are bound to be dependent on not just the obvious context - the extra information surrounding a particular piece of data - but also whatever facts are already known or believed. Even if a weather forecast is judged to be applicable to your neighbourhood, if you have no intention of going outside at all, then the report has little relevance. In group environments, individuals will interpret information differently according to the roles they are playing and the tasks they are performing. For example, to the commander of an entire theatre of war, the particular formation of a group of enemy aircraft may not be at all relevant - what matters is their apparent destination. However, to the pilots tasked to engage the enemy aircraft, the formation may be a crucial factor in choosing which tactics to employ. Similarly, to the average person it is true that it is impossible for something to jump instantly from one place to another; simple Newtonian physics and their everyday experiences rule out anything else. But to a physicist, quantum theory reverses that truth. Likewise, software agents in multi-agent systems increasingly have to deal with different interpretations and viewpoints, as theories based on ideas such as joint intentions, dynamic groups and hierarchies, collaborative planning and heterogeneous communities are becoming increasingly popular, as can been seen by the number of conferences, workshops and tracks that cover these topics, e.g. AAMAS, the International Conference on Autonomous Agents and Multiagent Systems, AAWSE, the International Workshop on Agents for Autonomic Web-Service Environments, ASAMI,the Symposium on Artificial Societies for Ambient Intelligence, EUMAS, the European Workshop On Multi-Agent Systems, IASB, the Society for the Study of Artificial Intelligence and the Simulation of Behaviour, IDC, the International Symposium on Intelligent Distributed Computing, IWEA, the IEEE International Workshop on e-Activity, and KR, the International Conference on Principles of Knowledge Representation and Reasoning.

The Cyc project is one of the longest running projects in the field of artificial intelligence, and its handling of context in determining meaning makes a good starting point for our discussion. In this paper we explore the role of context and meaning in enabling the performance of tasks through a simple software agent built to answer the question, important to many, did my sporting team win on the weekend? The core of the paper is a presentation of efforts to integrate the lightweight, task-oriented software agent with the massive, general-purpose Cyc knowledge base, and the issues that arose while trying to fit a domain- specific ontology into a larger global ontology while retaining meaning. Further, the roles of the lightweight software agent and the massive knowledge base are then reversed as the heuristic knowledge embodied in the agent is transferred to Cyc, with the eventual goal of providing Cyc with the ability to generate new forms of the information agent on demand to answer different questions in other domains.

2 The Cyc Project

The long-standing, highly visible Cyc project is a useful study in the practical implementation of context in a functioning ontology-based system [2, 6]. Cyc is interesting because its knowledge base/ontology is huge and general - it attempts to be completely objective in the hope of being understandable and reusable by anyone. The Cyc project is a very large, multi-contextual knowledge base and inference engine, currently containing more than 300,000 concepts and 3 million assertions [2]. Concepts can be marked as specialisations of other concepts, creating a tree-like structure of inheritance relationships that allow existing assertions to be applied to new knowledge without being specifically defined. Cyc knowledge is represented via a predicate logic language called CycL, and Cyc itself is implemented in a variant of Common Lisp called SubL. Note that we have adopted Cyc's notation in this paper. Cyc can also contain meta-facts such as functions that extend itself by processing other facts and rules, as well as functions that allow it to interact with external systems.

A project has existed within Cycorp for several years to connect the Cyc knowledge base to external data sources, although it has so far been primarily concerned with structured databases rather than semi-structured and unstructured information sources such as agents and web sites. This effort, known as the

Semantic Knowledge Source Integration project (SKSI[1]) [11, 12], has provided Cyc with the ability to query external databases, web sites, and other applications, translating the information contained within them into atoms and predicates that can then be reasoned about alongside Cyc's own hand-crafted and inferred knowledge. The SKSI project aimed to go beyond manual translations and wrappings of databases to describe the structure of an external information source in Cyc, so that Cyc itself could consider the knowledge within the source and decide how best to integrate it with its own knowledge.

The primary motivation for the project is to make the myriad tiny facts stored in databases and other record stores available to Cyc, without requiring a person to laboriously enter their minutiae. It would be valuable for Cyc to know the daily recorded temperatures for major cities or the daily index values of major stockmarkets, but to add all these facts into Cyc would require either manually asserting every value, which is almost certainly never going to be undertaken, or creating a customised importing script or program to dump the records as at a particular time and generate Cyc assertions for each value, which is neither elegant nor efficient. Such an approach to interaction between two information systems would be at a much lower level than most software engineers would consider appropriate, but worse is the fact that the resulting information would immediately be out of date, as new records are created every day. Thus, the approach taken by the SKSI project is to provide Cyc with the mechanisms to query databases and other information sources, and the knowledge to reason about how to interpret the resulting data.

The information agent that is presented in this chapter was implemented via the SKSI API, in a fashion similar to several other extension modules implemented by Cyc engineers to demonstrate the SKSI project, as discussed in personal communication between the first author and Cyc developers. One notable difference is that the information agent was constructed from an agent-oriented, heuristic-based viewpoint with a view to re-usability and multi-applicability, whereas the internally developed extension modules are wrappers and scrapers designed directly for a particular source. More details of the SKSI project and framework are covered in later sections.

3   Context in Cyc

During the Cyc project several approaches have been taken to representing and incorporating context. The initial direction of the Cyc project was to amass the vast collection of facts that form general knowledge and common sense by explicit specification, in essence compiling the contents of an encyclopaedia. When that endeavour appeared unlikely to be sufficient for intelligence to emerge, the Cyc direction expanded to specifying the larger body of knowledge that surrounds and informs our understanding of the facts in the encyclopaedia, without which

---

[1] It seems that the SKSI project was originally titled Structured Knowledge Source Integration but more recent references to the project call it Semantic Knowledge Source Integration.

we are left struggling to communicate in a sea of knowledge; as Brian Smith put it, "everything we know, but have never needed to write down" [15]. In other words, the daily experiences and mundane common knowledge that permits us to function in the world and to understand the information we read in the encyclopaedia. The purpose of this section is not to critique the Cyc project or its goals, but instead to observe its experiences with the implementation of context-sensitive knowledge manipulation to provide a background discussion for the research presented in this paper.

For the first half dozen years of its life Cyc contained no explicit consideration of context [8, 15]. From 1989 to 1991, contextualisation was added to the various attributes or characteristics that concepts and assertions possess in Cyc. Contexts were defined and said to have assumptions and contents, assertions could be imported from one context by another, and contexts were actual first-class terms in the Cyc representation language that were partially ordered by specialisation. Unsatisfied with this, Doug Lenat, the initiator and leader of the Cyc project, listed the primary drawbacks as:

- the expense of importing assertions from one context to another,
- the burden on the ontology builders of explicating the assumptions of each context,
- and the cost of placing every assertion into the proper context [8].

Two things can be learnt from this episode in the life of Cyc: first, that some direct consideration of context is necessary for a large ontology-based system, and second, that representing context as just another piece of knowledge is not an effective way to capture the particular effects that context has on information. Cyc now has a more sophisticated mechanism for explicating and manipulating context using *microtheories* (in the Cyc glossary, the entry for the term context says "often used interchangeably with microtheory" [3]).

Microtheories are based on the idea that context is a multi-dimensional space [8]. The dimensions of this space reflect the attributes of an assertion that define under what conditions it is valid. The twelve dimensions of context space proposed for Cyc by Lenat in [8] are:

- absolute time,
- type of time,
- absolute place,
- type of place,
- culture,
- sophistication/security,
- topic/usage,
- granularity,
- modality/disposition/epistemology,
- argument preferences,
- justification, and
- *lets.*

By specifying segments along the axes of some or all of these dimensions, regions of the context space are carved and a context is defined. Assertions in the Cyc knowledge-base can have the appropriate region of context space specified for them, and queries can be restricted to certain regions of the context space, thus limiting the set of assertions that can be referenced when Cyc tries to supply an answer. Specified regions of context space can be reified within the Cyc knowledge base and then re-used for a set of assertions - these are the actual microtheories.

In practice, microtheories are used as grouping devices that tie together a number of assertions under a label [6]. Those assertions must be true in the context referenced by the label of the microtheory. Thus, each assertion, or truth, in the Cyc ontology is tagged with the microtheory, or context, in which it is true. This opens the way not only for the inclusion of assertions that are apparently contradictory when taken out of context (e.g. using microtheories it should be possible to add to Cyc the two assertions *"Jesus Christ was the son of God"* and *"Jesus Christ was an ordinary man who was a wise teacher"*, which cannot both be true in the same context), but also for a calculus of microtheories, allowing various manipulations of not just assertions but whole contexts at a time. Importantly, queries to Cyc are also tagged with a microtheory, effectively adding to the questions an attempt to specify the context in which each question is being asked. As a hypothetical example, when asking the question *"Was Jesus Christ the son of God?"*, one could specify the microtheory *AtheistDoctrineMt* and be told by Cyc *"No, Jesus Christ was not the son of God"*. If, however, the microtheory label provided with the query was *ChristianDoctrineMt*, the answer would be *"Yes, definitely"*.

Similarly, the roster of teams competing in the F.A. Premier League changes each year due to relegations and promotions, yet it would be useful to be able to assert facts about the teams in the league, and so microtheories could be used to contextualise such assertions. Microtheories could be created to represent each iteration of the league, such as *FAPremierLeague2005-06*, *FAPremierLeague2006-07* and so on (the Premier League doesn't follow the calendar year). Following this, assertions such as *(winner FAPremierLeague ArsenalFC)* could be contextualised by specifying a microtheory of *FAPremierLeague1997-98*, and similarly general queries could be disambiguated in the same way: *(winner FAPremier-League ?)* in the context of *FAPremierLeague2004-05* could return *ChelseaFC*.

A more flexible, although potentially more complicated, way to specify a temporal context would be to use appropriate units to precisely select the desired period, such as the following for the F.A. Premier League season 2004-05:

```
(TimeIntervalInclusiveFn (MonthFn August (YearFn 2004))
                         (MonthFn May (YearFn 2005)))
(winnerInConflict FAPremierLeague ArsenalFC)
```

The implementation of microtheories in Cyc permits hierarchies of microtheories, with inheritance of properties from parent contexts to specialising child contexts, as well as providing for relations to assume default and inherited contexts. A stated aim of the framework is to, by breaking the huge Cyc knowledge base into contexts, speed both knowledge entry and inference. The need is removed for the knowledge engineer to specify myriad assumptions on which each truth that they enter hinges. Additionally, opportunities are provided for an inferencing engine to efficiently remove large chunks of the knowledge base from consideration based on what is known about, for example, the context of a query. To paraphrase Lenat, when asking if, given that it is raining, should one take an umbrella, it is not worth considering the number of legs on a spider or the birth date of Julius Caesar [8].

The Cyc approach to handling and exploiting context as just discussed produces effective demonstrations. However it is by no means clear whether it can achieve the goals desired. Lenat has explained the choice of twelve dimensions, but is not certain that his choices will be comfortable or even comprehensible for others who wish to use Cyc. He admitted that there is no real limit to the number of dimensions of context space that could be identified and that each dimension is almost certainly continuous rather than discrete, which further complicates the bounding of context spaces by requiring hard delineations. More problematic, though, is the question of how many actual contexts are enough. Although they seem to greatly simplify and reduce the number of assertions required to resolve complex questions of meaning and truth, already Cyc has thousands of microtheories. There seems to be a clear preference, based on our personal observations, on the part of people adding to the Cyc knowledge base to name their contexts and work with them as labels, rather than specifying in detail the location of each assertion in context space. This significantly reduces the ability of the Cyc engine to reason about contexts, one of the driving motivations for the approach in the first place.

To illustrate the problem, consider that Cyc knows that geological changes take place over millennia and are generally not observable from decade to decade and century to century. If Cyc is also told that an assertion that a certain mountain exists is true in a microtheory defined as the time period from 1700 AD to 1799 AD, then it can infer that the mountain's existence will also be true in any microtheories defined for the periods from 1600 to 1699 and 1800 to 1899. On the other hand, if Cyc had been told that the assertion that the mountain exists was true in the microtheory *The18thCentury*, with no further definition provided for that microtheory, Cyc will be unable to infer that the mountain should still exist in *The17thCentury* or *The19thCentury*. Unlike humans, who readily parse and interpret labels and infer properties from their names, Cyc cannot and doesn't know anything about *The18thCentury* until it is defined as a region of context space.

It seems likely that the number of microtheories will continue to grow rapidly, particularly as the Cyc knowledge base specialises. As a small example of the degree of granularity that can be expected to be required, the ACM Computing Classification System [1] classifies technical papers in the area of computing into 1474 topics, in a hierarchy four levels deep. Perhaps Cyc's general knowledge will make it unnecessary to specify all of these contexts, but even starting from such a specialised area as *Computing*, it takes a further four levels to specify *Object-oriented languages* (see Figure 1) and that doesn't seem like an over-specialisation for the context of a query. When other fields are considered, such as medicine, science, engineering and folklore, the number of contexts appears to grow without limit.

1. General Literature
2. Hardware
3. Software
   (a) GENERAL
   (b) PROGRAMMING TECHNIQUES
   (c) SOFTWARE ENGINEERING
   (d) PROGRAMMING LANGUAGES
      i. General
      ii. Formal Definitions and Theory
      iii. Language Classifications
         − Applicative (functional) languages
         − Concurrent, distributed, and parallel languages
         − ...
         − **Object-oriented languages**
      iv. Language Constructs and Features
   (e) OPERATING SYSTEMS
   (f) ...
4. Data
5. Mathematics of Computing
6. Information Systems
7. ...

Fig. 1. Extract from the ACM Computing Classification System hierarchy of topics [1]

4 The Task at Hand

In his exhaustive exploration of the world of 12-dimensional context space, Lenat made a significant remark that context enables people to, among other things, "ignore 99.999% of our knowledge so that we can focus on the task at hand" [8].

The problems associated with capturing complete knowledge have led many to limit their efforts to domain-specific approaches to ontology-based systems. Limited focus knowledge bases or ontologies have been referred to as purposive, a term that neatly expresses the goal of specifying all and only the knowledge required for a particular purpose or task. So when Lenat writes that context is some intangible thing that permits us to identify the set of our knowledge that is not relevant to our current purposeful activity, the conclusion can be drawn that context, practically considered, is defined as much by the purposive knowledge that has been included as relevant to the task at hand as by the knowledge that has been excluded. In other words, when trying to understand what makes some knowledge relevant to a task and what gives it specific meaning for that context, don't set aside the knowledge identified as necessary to the current purpose and look for the context in the vast remainder of our knowledge. Instead, look to the defining characteristics of the knowledge already deemed relevant and seek the context within it. If necessary, identify and make explicit any knowledge assumed or implied by the task definition itself.

In many ontology-based systems that perform information-oriented tasks, purposive knowledge bases or ontologies provide an efficient way to specify and represent the knowledge needed to successfully operate in the required environment. Lightweight techniques such as knowledge unit analysis [5, 17] attempt to explicitly model common sense knowledge for a strictly limited domain, without trying to use a general purpose formal knowledge representation technique such as description logic. The lightweight approach avoids the mysticism with which context sometimes seems to be viewed, by considering the context to be inherently captured as the purposively relevant domain knowledge units are specified. Put flippantly, if you have defined the task adequately that it can be successfully performed in the desired circumstances, you have surely defined the context sufficiently, or else how is the task being performed.

Even if it is not explicitly discernible, sufficient context can be determined to be present by considering whether the task is being performed correctly. Knowledge unit analysis works, to a degree, at the sub-concept level, by assuming that where there are knowledge units in a text, the concepts that the knowledge units represent are present, rather than trying to decide if the concepts themselves are present or not [17]. In this way, because concepts are not formally defined and generalised with theoretically complete assertion and axiom systems, the problem of formally locating those which are not concepts or assertions but elements of context is avoided. The context is explicated, but it is not discerned from the concepts and other elements that comprise domain knowledge. The close relationship between information and context is due primarily to the importance of the environment in defining and performing a task. The environment in which a task is to be performed plays a crucial part in the definition of the task, often implicitly. The crucial nature of the environment is true for tasks performed both by people and by information agents.

5   SportsReporter

For the rest of this paper, the role of a task-oriented information agent is filled by SportsReporter, the successor to a lightweight information agent developed in the Intelligent Agent Lab at the University of Melbourne called SportsFinder. SportsFinder was the result of an experiment to retrieve the results of a sporting match from a web page without having to be told exactly where and how the match result is reported [10, 16].

Developed in an evolutionary manner, SportsFinder showed not only significant success in assessing a given web page to interpret its contents and highlight the information about a certain team, but also remarkable adaptability. Developed to report the outcomes of soccer matches, it was adapted to a range of team sports including basketball, rugby and Australian Rules football. The SportsFinder agent was able to cope well with new information sources, and was able to incorporate new sports on the fly by the user filling out a simple template. Despite, or perhaps due to, the fact that it understood nothing about natural language, SportsFinder coped equally well with the Italian Serie A results as it did with the FA Premier League, and it was also adapted to report on the results of Chinese matches.[2] The knowledge units that SportsFinder dealt with included those in Figure 2.

Score format:	<number> - <number>
Team name:	(a sequence of) <capitalised string>
Winning team:	the team with the numerically greater score
Score correspondence:	the left-most team is given the left-most score, regardless of the ordering of actual score numbers and team names
Conceivable scores:	$0 \leq$ potential score ≤ 13
Irrelevance:	anything between parentheses, e.g. given the information *Inter Milan 2 (Baggio 12, Beresi 67) def Lazio 1 (Simone 34)*, SportsFinder does not report that Inter Milan lost to Baggio 12 goals to 2.

Fig. 2. Examples of knowledge units of the SportsFinder information retrieval agent

So where is the context? The point of describing the SportsFinder information agent is to show the success that a lightweight, purposive knowledge base or ontology gave, despite the clearly high dependency on context of the task of being able to identify which words and number on a sport results page are actually teams and scores, and which teams and scores together represent the outcome of an actual match. This example has clear relevance to the issue of having to rely on context to interpret a text - does the text '3' represent the number of goals scored by a team, the minute in which one goal was scored, the day or month of the fixture, the number of a player dismissed from the field for foul play, the minute in which he was sent off or the position on the league ladder one of the teams now occupies as a result of losing the match? Obviously the immediately surrounding text defines the meaning of the number. How much of the surrounding text is required? SportsFinder deliberately started with the

---

[2] The adaptation was performed in 1999 by Tiechuan Wang as a directed study project while studying in the Department of Computer Science and Software Engineering at the University of Melbourne.

minimum consideration necessary to solve the problem of reporting match results in one instance, and slowly grew in knowledge until it could handle a very wide range of soccer results represented in diverse information sources.

It is not, however, necessary to build up the required knowledge units slowly on an informed trial and error basis. The conversion of SportsFinder from English to Chinese match reports demonstrated that it is possible to efficiently identify the knowledge units for a new domain that will permit the agent to migrate with success. This is especially encouraging, as it implies that newly created agents could be informed from their beginning with the results of knowledge unit analysis of their intended domain and environment. We want to empha-sise that people can and do perform tasks in a corresponding manner to the behaviour exhibited by SportsFinder. The second author enjoys the challenge when travelling internationally of looking up sports scores in local newspapers. He is usually successful despite the wide variety of formats of the newspapers and the fact that he rarely understands the local languages. The task of locating the scores is made achievable by its context. For example, the assumption that the scores will be present explicitly in a certain part of the newspaper makes it possible to ignore large parts of knowledge, such as the format of particular newspapers and the syntax of foreign languages.

6   Meaning and Relevance

The knowledge units used by SportsFinder, and the heuristics by which they were generated, raise interesting issues concerning meaning and relevance. At first glance, it is satisfying to imagine that SportsFinder is at some level determining the meaning of individual elements of information, or knowledge units. Certainly, it seems appropriate to consider the information agent analysing a line that contains several numbers and deciding that one number is probably not a score and that another number most likely is. From this perspective, the meaning of the numbers has been determined and they have been ruled out as candidates for inclusion in the final answer to the user's question about how their team fared. But an alternative consideration could view the actions of SportsFinder as assessing the relevance of each knowledge unit to the original task. As elements of the web site being processed are deemed unlikely to warrant inclusion in the final response, they are removed. Domain-specific knowledge such as that content within parentheses is not a score is used in such processing. Only then is what is left interpreted and an answer formulated for the user, via other domain-specific knowledge such as that the leftmost team is given the leftmost score.

Literally, context is concerned with meaning. It describes the influence that related facts and assertions have on the meaning of a particular statement. But very often it is not clarification of meaning that we require, but an evaluation of relevance. In these cases it is not so much that context is used to fully determine the meaning of a text, but merely to determine that the meaning is not something that we are interested in - that whatever it means, it's not relevant. This goes to the core of Lenat's hope for Cyc that incorporating context into the huge knowledge base will greatly reduce the processing required to answer queries and infer new knowledge. It also provides a compelling reason to consider the specifics of a task or purpose as defining the context. As SportsFinder shows, the approach of defining the knowledge units required for a task can leverage context by excluding all other knowledge. Whether, theoretically, this is by determining the meaning via context or evaluating the relevance via context seems to be a point of semantics rather than practical concern.

The techniques demonstrated by SportsFinder have been employed in a number of other successful information agents within the Intelligent Agent Lab. These agents operate in a wide variety of domains, including CASA, for searching semi-structured real-estate classified advertisements [5], Justice, which uses the context of a legal case to report summary information about judgements and rulings [14], and CiFi, an agent that retrieves citations from the World Wide Web [9]. Each agent uses lightweight purposive knowledge that both defines the target information and bounds the context of the agent's task. Rather than dismissing these agents as *ad hoc*, they can be usefully viewed as exhibiting purposive knowledge as a feature.

7   Building a Lightweight Information Agent

Since the original SportsFinder had been successful at reporting match results for a variety of sports and leagues, we chose, somewhat arbitrarily, to focus on the F.A. Premier League in England. The home page of the Premier League web site was identified as a source for F.A. Premier League match results. Figure 3 gives a page retrieved on May 8th, 2007 from http://www.premierleague.com/ fapl.rac?command=forwardOnly & nextPage=homepage & tab=results.

Analysing this page revealed that heuristics similar to those used in Sports-Finder would be effective for this page, as described in Figure 4.

The Cyc architecture has been designed to allow for the implementation of reasoning techniques other than pure logical inference. This allows Cyc to be given more efficient ways to reason about certain types of knowledge for which logical inference would be inefficient. For instance, although Cyc could be taught to perform arithmetic by being told (plus 1 1 2), (plus 1 2 3), (plus 2 2 4) and so on, it is far more efficient to simply provide an external calculator module that can produce the appropriate result for any instance of the predicate plus with three arguments. These external modules are called *removal modules* [4], and this is the same framework that SportsReporter uses to provide Cyc with information from an external source.

The framework of removal modules that augment Cyc's inferencing ability is quite similar in practice to that of an interface in object-oriented programming. A predicate is defined within Cyc's knowledge-base, and a SubL function is inserted into Cyc to tell Cyc that whenever it encounters this new predicate it should not try to prove it but should pass it to an external function and wait for the result - the external function can be thought of as 'implementing'

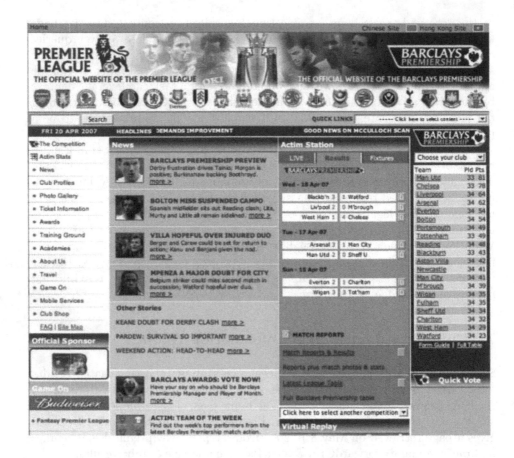

Fig. 3. Match results for the F.A. Premier League as published on the F.A. Premier League web site

the predicate. Cyc will then replace the original predicate and its arguments with the result of the external function, much as described above for the example of arithmetic addition, and further reasoning can occur. In the case of SportsReporter, the predicate defined within Cyc to be implemented was called `sksiSoccerMatchResult`[3], and when called with partially unbound arguments it would use the information retrieved by the SportsReporter agent to bind its arguments to elements of the relevant match result. In this way, when Cyc encounters the predicate with unbound variables, such as[4]:

---

[3] The prefix sksi indicates that this predicate will be processed via a removal module using the SKSI API, although this signification is only of use to people - other internal predicates are used to tell Cyc how to handle the predicate.

[4] Strictly, the Cyc atoms such as sksiSoccerMatchResult and SoccerTeamNamedFn should be prefaced with #$ to indicate that they are defined concepts. This prefix is omitted here to aid readability.

> **Soccer match report:** team name, soccer score, soccer score, team name
> **Team name:**   Arsenal, Blackburn, Chelsea, ...
> **Soccer score:** $0 \leq n \leq 15$

Fig. 4. Example heuristics used in the SportsReporter information retrieval agent

```
(sksiSoccerMatchResult (SoccerTeamNamedFn "ArsenalFC") ?TEAM2
?SCORE1 ?SCORE2)
```

it will call on the appropriate removal module to provide a more fully bound expression, such as:

```
(sksiSoccerMatchResult (SoccerTeamNamedFn "ArsenalFC")
                       (SoccerTeamNamedFn "EvertonFC") 0 1)
```

This predicate, once filled with information retrieved from the F.A. Premier League web page, allows Cyc to reason about the match result, and combine this information with the rest of its knowledge.

SportsReporter was thus designed as a lightweight, heuristic-driven information agent, implemented in SubL, that generates a predicate that can be used in queries of Cyc's knowledge-base. At this point, just like its predecessor, it contained hard-coded knowledge sufficient to parse a web page and identify a match report involving a particular team. These heuristics, implemented in SubL, looked like:

```
(define is-soccer-score? (string)
(pwhen
 (integer-string-p string)
  (clet ((score (string-to-integer string)))
   (ret (cand (>= score 0) (< score 15))))))
```

which expresses whether a string from a web page or other document can be considered to signify a soccer score, and:

```
(define is-fapl-team-name? (string)
  (clet ((fapl-team-names-hash (make-hash-table 30 #'equal)))
    (sethash "Arsenal" fapl-team-names-hash "Arsenal")
    (sethash "Aston Villa" fapl-team-names-hash "Aston Villa")
    (sethash "A Villa" fapl-team-names-hash "Aston Villa")
    (sethash "Birmingham" fapl-team-names-hash "Birmingham")
    (sethash "Blackburn" fapl-team-names-hash "Blackburn")
    (sethash "Black'bn" fapl-team-names-hash "Blackburn")
    ...
    (ret (gethash string fapl-team-names-hash))))
```

which expresses whether a string can be considered to represent an F.A. Premier League team.

8   Integrating SportsReporter into the Cyc Ontology

As with any ontology or knowledge base, in order to be useful to Cyc, new concepts and knowledge must be attached to existing concepts and relationships, to permit reasoning on a technical level, and to make sense on an ontological and semantic level - a lone concept with no relation to any other is arguably meaningless. Several assertions were added to the Cyc knowledge-base to provide some scaffolding to help Cyc understand the `sksiSoccerMatchResult` predicate:

```
(implies
    (sksiSoccerMatchResult (SoccerTeamNamedFn ?TEAM1) ?TEAM2 ?SCORE1 ?SCORE2))
    (and
        (competingAgents (MatchBetweenFn ?TEAM1 ?TEAM2) ?TEAM1)
        (competingAgents (MatchBetweenFn ?TEAM1 ?TEAM2) ?TEAM2)
        (scoreInAction ?TEAM1 (MatchBetweenFn ?TEAM1 ?TEAM2) ?SCORE1)
        (scoreInAction ?TEAM2 (MatchBetweenFn ?TEAM1 ?TEAM2) ?SCORE2)))
(implies
    (and
        (scoreInAction ?TEAM1 ?MATCH ?SCORE1)
        (scoreInAction?TEAM2?MATCH?SCORE2)
        (greaterThan ?SCORE1?SCORE2))
    (winnerInConflict?MATCH?TEAM1))
```

Here, `SoccerTeamNamedFn` is a function denoting a non-atomic term. It is important to note that it was not necessary to define the predicates `competingAgents`, `scoreInAction, greaterThan` and `winnerInConflict`, as these general predicates were already present in the Cyc knowledge base.

As can be seen in Figure 5, the predicate `winnerInConflict` can be applied to any pair of individuals in the Cyc knowledge base that are an instance of a `ConflictEvent` and an instance of an `Agent-Generic`, or any of their descendants. By telling Cyc that the result of the denoting function `SoccerTeamNamedFn` is a `SoccerTeam`:

`(resultIsa SoccerTeamNamedFn SoccerTeam)`

and then attaching the `SoccerTeam` collection to the appropriate place in Cyc's hierarchy of concepts(see Figures 6 and 7), individuals of the collection `SoccerTeam` can now be used with the predicate `winnerInConflict`. Making similar arrangements for the predicate `MatchBetweenFn`:

`(resultIsa MatchBetweenFn SportsMatch)`

means that the knowledge newly added to Cyc about the result of last weekend's F.A. Premier League match involving Arsenal can now be reasoned about via all the relevant pre-existing concepts and relationships in Cyc. This is a significant result because the ontological engineer who originally defined the winnerInConflict predicate did not have to foresee that it would be applied years later to a sporting match, let alone one sourced dynamically from a web page. Indeed, the Internet as we know it today barely existed when the Cyc project began.

Predicate : winnerInConflict

GAF Arg : 1

Mt : UniversalVocabularyMt
isa : ⌐ActorSlot

Mt : BookkeepingMt
quotedIsa : ⌐HasBeenReviewedInRolePredicateSweep

Mt : UniversalVocabularyMt
genlPreds : ⌐successfulForAgents
arity : ⌐2
arg1Isa : ⌐ConflictEvent
arg2Isa : ⌐Agent-Generic

Mt : AgentGMt
arg2Format : ⌐SetTheFormat
⌐(argFormat winnerInConflict 2 SetTheFormat)

Mt : UniversalVocabularyMt
⌐(argIsa winnerInConflict 2 Agent-Generic)
⌐(argIsa winnerInConflict 1 ConflictEvent)
comment : ⌐"(winnerInConflict CONFLICT VICTOR) means in the ConflictEvent
   CONFLICT, the #$Agent VICTOR was the winner."

Fig. 5. Predicate winnerInConflict as defined in Cyc

By crafting the scaffolding by which the SportsReporter agent is integrated
with the Cyc knowledge base carefully, unforeseen yet ontologically valid inferences and conclusions can be made based on the small pieces of information
provided by SportsReporter. For instance, another ontological engineer working on a completely separate area of Cyc's huge knowledge base - say, human
emotional reactions to events - might have used the winnerInConict predicate
to assert that:

```
(implies
    (winnerInConflict ?PERSON)
    (happy ?PERSON))
```

and now, with no extra effort, Cyc can infer that if Arsenal defeated Everton
then they should be happy about it. With a little more work, Cyc could be told
that any fans of Arsenal should also be happy, and without too much imagination
it is possible to see various distantly-related social and economic consequences
being predicted just from this simple match report. This is possible because of
the vast general knowledge already present in Cyc.

Collection : <u>SoccerTeam</u>

GAF Arg : 1

Mt : <u>UniversalVocabularyMt</u>
<u>isa</u> : ⬤<u>ExistingObjectType</u> ⬤<u>SportsTeamTypeBySport</u>

Mt : <u>IRExpansionRulesMt</u>
<u>isa</u> : ⬤<u>QAClarifyingCollectionType</u>

Mt : <u>UniversalVocabularyMt</u>
<u>genls</u> : ⬤<u>SportsTeam</u>
<u>comment</u> : ⬤"The collection of organizations of athletes who play soccer."

Mt : <u>SportsMt</u>
<u>conceptuallyRelated</u> : ⬤<u>SoccerPlayer</u> ⬤<u>Soccer</u>

Mt : <u>BaseKB</u>
<u>definingMt</u> : ⬤<u>SportsMt</u>
<u>focalTermTypeForInducedTemplateType</u> : ⬤<u>(FormulaTemplateInductionTopicTypeFn</u>
  <u>SoccerTeam)</u>

Mt : <u>UniversalVocabularyMt</u>
<u>rewriteOf</u> : ⬤<u>(SubcollectionOfWithRelationToFn</u> <u>SportsTeam</u> <u>focalActivityType</u>
  <u>(PlayingFn</u> <u>Soccer))</u>

Mt : <u>FrenchLexicalMt</u>
<u>termStrings</u> : ⬤"equipe de foot" ⬤"equipe de football"

Fig. 6. Soccer Team concept as defined in Cyc

9   Moving Task-Defining Heuristic Knowledge into Cyc

Because the knowledge used by SportsReporter to identify and interpret match results is at this point hard-coded into the agent, any changes require source-level modifications to be made. It was noted earlier that the design of SportsReporter's ancestors makes them both flexible in terms of applying them to other domains without modification, and also simple in that when their heuristics do need to be modified, adjusting their behaviour does not require any architectural or design consideration. However, there are degrees of simplicity, and modifying a program's source is certainly less than ideal. As described earlier, we envisage that in the future Cyc would be able to put together the information necessary to generate lightweight information agents on demand, providing them with the details required to find the answer to whichever question Cyc currently requires be answered.

Therefore, the next step of integrating the SportsReporter information agent with Cyc was to move the knowledge encoded within it into the Cyc knowledge base. This made the SportsReporter agent more pure in a design sense, but was

SoccerTeam

isa: ExistingObjectType, QAClarifyingCollectionType, SportsTeamTypeBySport
genls: SportsTeam
Context: Union of all contexts
Predicate: genls
Index: 2

Parameters updated at 21:28:32 on 05/20/2008

? **Change Hierarchy Browser Settings**

... *SportsOrganization
    *SportsTeam [UniversalVocabularyMt]
... *Team
    *SportsTeam [UniversalVocabularyMt]
SoccerTeam
[UniversalVocabularyMt] -> (*SportsTeam)]
    *IndoorSoccerTeam [UniversalVocabularyMt] <-

Fig. 7. Constant SoccerTeam in Cyc hierarchy of concepts

also a move toward providing Cyc with the means to generate new versions of the SportsReporter agent as needed to fulfill its information needs. This was not done to make the SportsReporter agent more elegant or lighter in its implementation, but to reduce Cyc's dependence on the heuristics hand-coded into the agent. Translating these heuristics into Cyc's knowledge base not enables Cyc to modify them as necessary to answer different questions, but also makes them available to other users of Cyc to co-opt for purposes we haven't imagined.

Constants were created within Cyc to represent the different concepts present in SportsReporter's heuristics. The definition of a valid soccer score became a unary predicate stating that:

```
(scoreInSoccerMatch (IntegerFromToFn 0 15))
```

Rather than simple strings for team names, the SoccerTeam concept was used as a collection, with individuals created for each team currently playing in the F.A. Premier League, such as ArsenalFC and ManchesterUnitedFC. Because not all soccer teams play in the F.A. Premier League, a new class of soccer team called FAPremierLeagueTeam was used.

```
(isa SoccerTeam FAPremierLeagueTeam)
```

However, using inheritance in this way is somewhat heavy-handed and could cause complications later (for instance when teams are relegated and promoted at the end of each season - this shouldn't change the nature of the team). Ontologically, inheritance is a fairly restricting relationship. Instead we opted to express membership in a league by a relation rather than as an existential property, so that a team is defined and described thus:

```
(isa ArsenalFC SoccerTeam)
(nameString ArsenalFC "Arsenal FC")
(nameString ArsenalFC "Arsenal")
(playsInLeague ArsenalFC FAPremierLeague)
```

Now that Cyc knows what a valid soccer score is and what teams play in the F.A. Premier League, it is possible to replace the hard-coded functions in the SportsReporter agent that contained these pieces of knowledge. Where the SportsReporter agent previously had the function:

```
(define is-soccer-score? (string)
  (pwhen
    (integer-string-p string)
      (clet ((score (string-to-integer string)))
        (ret (cand (>= score 0) (< score 15))))))
```

it can now call on Cyc to make this judgement:

```
(define is-soccer-score? (string)
  (pwhen
    (integer-string-p string)
    (clet ((score (string-to-integer string)))
      (pif (new-cyc-query
          '(#$admittedSentence (#$scoreInSoccerMatch ,score)) #$SportsMt)
        (ret T)
        (ret NIL))))))
```

The `admittedSentence` predicate is a way to ask Cyc if a fully-bound clause is acceptable given what Cyc knows. In this case, having already told Cyc that `scoreInSoccerMatch (IntegerFromToFn 0 15)`, the SportsReporter agent can then use the `admittedSentence` predicate to check the legitimacy of statements of the form `scoreInSoccerMatch x` - if x can be unified with `(IntegerFromToFn 0 15)` then Cyc will reply positively, and otherwise the reply will be negative.

Similarly, where knowledge about team names had previously been encoded into the SportReporter agent's source:

```
(define is-fapl-team-name? (string)
    (clet ((fapl-team-names-hash (make-hash-table 30 #'equal)))
      (sethash "Arsenal" fapl-team-names-hash "Arsenal")
      (sethash "Arsenal FC" fapl-team-names-hash "Arsenal")
      (sethash "Aston Villa" fapl-team-names-hash "Aston Villa")
      ...
```

the agent can now access all of this knowledge via a query to Cyc:

```
(define is-team-name? (string)
   (pif (new-cyc-query '(#$and (#$isa ?TEAM #$FAPremierLeagueTeam)
                               (#$nameString ?TEAM ,string)) #$SportsMt)
     (ret string)
     (ret nil)))
```

Thus around 50 repetitive lines of the SportsReporter agent's source code have been replaced with a single function call, but that is only an incidental benefit. This is a more extensible and re-usable approach, not only in the sense of programming and source code but more significantly in terms of functionality and meaning. Since the task-specific knowledge has been moved into Cyc, the SportsReporter agent requires fewer modifications in order to be applied to a new league or even a new sport; correspondingly, Cyc now knows about some English soccer teams and in which league they play, information that is now available for use in ways that might not have been considered, but that may be valuable in the future when they become the context to someone else's task.

Another piece of knowledge hard-coded into SportsReporter was the location of the web page that contains the match results that are wanted. This knowledge can also be moved into Cyc, creating `matchResultsWebPageURL`, a binary predicate that relates a web page to a sports league:

```
(matchResultsWebPageURL FAPremierLeague
     "http://www.premierleague.com/fapl.rac?command=forwardOnly&
     nextPage=homepage&tab=results")
```

This allows the replacement of another hard-coded constant in the SportsReporter agent, but it also makes it easy to change which web page is used to retrieve match results for the F.A. Premier League. As the concept of a league has already been defined within Cyc's knowledge base via the `FAPremierLeague` constant, another level of reasoning can be added here. Because a team identifier was provided when SportsReporter was originally invoked, it can query Cyc to find out which league that team plays in:

```
(clet (league
    (first
        (query-variable '?LEAGUE
         '(#$playsInLeague ,team ?LEAGUE) #$SportsMt))))
```

and then via another query it can find the URL for a web page that reports match results for that league:

```
(clet (results-page-url
    (first
        (query-variable '?URL '(#$matchResultsWebPageURL ,league ?URL)
                        #$SportsMt))))
```

The `query-variable` function is very similar to the new-cyc-query function, but instead of simply returning true or false it returns a list of values that Cyc was able to unify with the specified variable, in this case ?URL. The first result is taken for now, although the possibility exists to accept more than one.

10   Generalising the SportsReporter Heuristics

One significant piece of knowledge still encoded explicitly in the SportsReporter agent is how to actually identify a match report. We began with a heuristic adapted from the previous incarnations of SportsReporter:

> **Score format**: team name ... score ... score ... team name

A strong motivation for moving knowledge from SportsReporter into Cyc was to pave the way for the possibility of generating similar agents on demand. Although the heuristic for soccer match reporting given above has proven to be widely applicable, other formats are also used, one common example being:

> **Score format**: team name ... score ... team name ... score

which leads to the timeless driving joke of, when passing a sign that shows the distance to the upcoming suburbs in Melbourne, such as *Moorabbin 3, Mordialloc 5*, calling out *"That's a good win for Mordialloc!"*. The joke is easily adapted to other cities and countries.

Since Cyc has now been told about leagues that teams play in and web sites that report match results for leagues, it is appropriate to add information about how the elements of the match report might appear. Up until now, this was expressed in SportsReporter's source code by looking explicitly first for a team name and then a score, followed by a second score and then a second team name. To move this knowledge into Cyc, a `MatchReportFormat` collection was created as a specialisation of a `List`, from which a `SoccerMatchReportFormat` collection was extended. An individual member of that collection was then created called `FAPremierLeagueMatchReportFormat`.

As a `List`, the type of each element of `FAPremierLeagueMatchReportFormat` can be defined as follows:

```
(tupleMemberIndex FAPremierLeagueMatchReportFormat SoccerTeam 1).
(tupleMemberIndex FAPremierLeagueMatchReportFormat scoreInSoccerMatch 2).
(tupleMemberIndex FAPremierLeagueMatchReportFormat scoreInSoccerMatch 3).
(tupleMemberIndex FAPremierLeagueMatchReportFormat SoccerTeam 4).
```

This says that the first element of an `FAPremierLeagueMatchReportFormat` is a `SoccerTeam`, the second element is a `scoreInSoccerMatch`, and so on. The parts of SportsReporter that look for a match report in the contents of a web page were replaced with a general loop that adjusts to each of the elements of a provided `MatchReportFormat`, which has been retrieved from Cyc via a function call similar to those already introduced:

```
(clet (cyc-report-format-constant
        (first
          (query-variable '?FORMAT
          '(#$matchReportFormatForLeague ,league ?FORMAT)
          #$SportsMt))))
```

This only gives the Cyc constant that represents the match report format that needs to be used, not the elements of the format, which can be retrieved similarly:

```
(clet (next-report-element-type
        (first
          (query-variable '?X '(#$tupleMemberIndex
                    ,cyc-report-format-constant ?X
                    ,curr-pos-in-report-format) #$SportsMt))))
```

Having thus obtained the Cyc constant representing the type of the next element of the match report to look for, SportsReporter can then search through the web page and compare its elements. Because the 'type' of the match report element is a Cyc constant, the only way to compare anything to it is to ask Cyc again, so a final query is made, either

```
(new-cyc-query
  '(#$admittedSentence (,next-report-element-type ,web-page-element))
  #$SportsMt)
```

if the web page element is an integer, or

```
(new-cyc-query
  '(#$and (#$isa ?X ,next-report-element-type)
      (#$nameString ?X ,web-page-element))
  #$SportsMt)
```

if it is a string. The latter query involves two clauses because the string used to represent a Cyc constant in natural language is usually different the the name given to the constant; for example, the word 'Arsenal' is commonly used to signify the Arsenal Football Club, but ArsenalFC is a more appropriate name for the Cyc constant that represents the club, since Cyc might need to know about other things in the world that are also identified by the word 'arsenal'. The Cyc predicate nameString was used earlier to attach strings to Cyc constants; these are words or phrases that are known to be used to signify the constant in natural language expressions. A constant can have many such name strings. The query above simply asks if Cyc knows of a thing that is of the correct type and can be written as the current web page element in natural language.

With this last set of queries, almost all of the heuristic knowledge encoded in SportsReporter has now been transferred into Cyc, expressed in CycL assertions and relationships that can be used by both the SportsReporter agent and by any other user of Cyc, human or software.

Fig. 8. Match results for Italian Serie A League as published on Soccerstats

11   Conclusions

We have presented work toward a framework for building and eventually generating information agents designed to fulfill specific tasks, in this case augmenting the Cyc knowledge base with information from external sources such as web sites. We have illustrated through detailed explanations and examples how a lightweight, purposive information agent can maintain a symbiotic relationship with a huge, general knowledge base, and how the two can leverage each other's capabilities to produce unforeseen beneficial results.

We claim that the final work presented here is significantly more general and applicable than previous efforts of integration. To briefly illustrate, consider the prospect of adding knowledge to Cyc about the most recent match results from the Italian Serie A football competition. Through the SportsReporter agent, implemented as a removal module, Cyc has all of the infrastructure required. Aside from the creation of a concept for the league, perhaps ItalianSerieA, the first pieces of new knowledge needed would be the URL of a web page or other resource that contains the match result (such as in Figure 8[5]):

```
(matchResultsWebPageURL ItalianSerieA
"http://www.soccerstats.com/latest.asp?league=Italy")
```

and the format in which that page presents match results, in this case:

```
(tupleMemberIndex ItalianSerieAMatchReportFormat SoccerTeam 1).
(tupleMemberIndex ItalianSerieAMatchReportFormat scoreInSoccerMatch 2).
(tupleMemberIndex ItalianSerieAMatchReportFormat scoreInSoccerMatch 3).
(tupleMemberIndex ItalianSerieAMatchReportFormat SoccerTeam 4).
```

and so on for the other teams in the league.

At this point it might be observed that the match report format is the same as for the F.A. Premier League, and so an intermediary re-usable concept might be created, such as SoccerMatchReportFormatTeamScoreScoreTeam, although perhaps this is a little cumbersome. Regardless, Cyc would then need to be told about the teams that compete in the league:

```
(isa SampdoriaUC SoccerTeam)
(nameString SampdoriaUC "Sampdoria Unione Calcio")
(nameString SampdoriaUC "Sampdoria")
(playsInLeague SampdoriaUC ItalianSerieA)
```

At this point Cyc knows everything that is required to reason about match results from the Italian Serie A just as it can for the F.A. Premier League. When the `sksiSoccerMatchResult` removal module is passed a team it will ask which league that team plays. It will then use that information to query Cyc for the URL of the web page that contains match results for this league, as well as for the match report format, which it can then use to retrieve and parse the match results and return them to Cyc.

Because SportsReporter is intrinsically a web-based information retrieval agent, it would not be as simple to use it to retrieve information from a non-web source as it is to change the particular web source that it queries. However, the changes required to operate in a different medium would not be great. Modifying the underlying transfer method from HTTP to something else would be quite easy, and the only other significant effort required would be to help Cyc to under- stand that there is more than one way to find a match result, perhaps by creating a predicate like `sksiSoccerMatchResultBySOAP` and a couple of relationships to explain that `sksiSourceAccessMethod DeutscheBundesLiga SOAP`.

Of course, all of the content presented in this paper is in no way limited to soccer - `sksiSoccerMatchResult` could (indeed should) easily become `sksiMatchResultByHTTP`, with the creation of a rule that explains how to win a

---

[5] Retrieved from `http://www.soccerstats.com/latest.asp?league=Italy` on April 28th, 2008

non-soccer sports match. And a further hope is that it doesn't take much imagination to see that what has been described is really a flexible framework for enabling Cyc to build a lightweight module to answer any particular question that requires external information.

An ongoing effort within the Cyc development team is the processing of natural language expressions to populate Cyc with new knowledge - effectively providing Cyc with the ability to 'read' the World Wide Web. The framework we have described is effectively antithetical to this effort. We suggest augmenting Cyc by providing the means to construct and deploy purposive information agents to interoperate with external systems and information sources, allowing it to draw upon the oceans of data that is being interconnected as the Internet continues to reach into previously private or inaccessible data stores.

As this data is integrated with the Cyc ontology, it becomes semantically richer - to the extent that Cyc might serve as a *lingua franca* for interoperating information systems, served by lightweight, purposive information agents.

Acknowledgments. The work presented in this paper was performed at the University of Melbourne supported by the Australian Research Council Linkage Grant LP0454027 and Cycorp. Thanks to Dr Catherine Legg with whom we had initial discussions about integrating information agents with Cyc and who was responsible for the grant. Thanks also to the Cyc engineers who helped explain some of the issues with integration.

References

1. Association for Computing Machinery. The ACM Computing Classification System (1998 Version), http://www.acm.org/class/1998 (retrieved on September 22, 2005)
2. Cycorp, Inc., Cyc, http://www.cyc.com/ (retrieved on July 7, 2006)
3. Cycorp, Inc., Glossary of Common Cyc Terminology, http://www.cyc.com/cycdoc/ref/glossary.html (retrieved on May 20, 2008)
4. Cycorp, Inc., Ontological Engineer's Handbook, http://www.cyc.com/doc/handbook/oe/oe-handbook-toc-opencyc.html (retrieved on November 2, 2007)
5. Gao, S.X., Leon, S.: Semi-structured Data Extraction from Heterogeneous Sources. In: Schwartz, D., Divitini, M., Bratjevik, T. (eds.) Internet-based Knowledge Management and Organizational Memories, pp. 83–102. Idea Group Publishing (2000)
6. Legg, C.: Implementation of a Large-scale General Ontology at Cycorp, Departmental seminar, Department of Computer Science and Software Engineering, The University of Melbourne, Melbourne (2002)
7. Legg, C.: Ontologies on the Semantic Web. Annual Review of Information Science and Technology 41 (2007)
8. Lenat, D.: The Dimensions of Context-Space (2002), http://www.cyc.com/context-space.pdf (retrieved on July 1, 2003)
9. Loke, S.W., Sterling, L., Sonenberg, L., Kim, H.: ARIS: a shell for information agents that exploits web site structure. In: Proceedings of the 3rd International Conference on Practical Applications of Intelligent Agents and Agent Methodology, London, pp. 201–219 (1998)

10. Lu, H., Sterling, L., Wyatt, A.: Knowledge discovery in sportsFinder: An agent to extract sports results from the web. In: Zhong, N., Zhou, L. (eds.) PAKDD 1999. LNCS (LNAI), vol. 1574, pp. 469–473. Springer, Heidelberg (1999)
11. Masters, J., Gungordu, Z.: Semantic knowledge source integration: a progress report. In: Proceedings of the International Conference on the Integration of Knowledge Intensive Multi-Agent Systems, Boston, pp. 562–566 (2003)
12. Masters, J.: Structured Knowledge Source Integration and its applications to information fusion. In: Proceedings of the 5th International Conference on Information Fusion, Annapolis (2002)
13. National Aeronautics and Space Administration, Mars Climate Orbiter Team Finds Likely Cause of Loss, http://mars.jpl.nasa.gov/msp98/news/mco990930.html (retrieved on May 20, 2008)
14. Osborn, J., Sterling, L.: Automated Concept Identification within Legal Cases. Journal of Information, Law and Technology (JILT) 1 (1999)
15. Smith, B.: The owl and the electric encyclopaedia. Artificial Intelligence 47 (1991)
16. Sterling, L.: On Finding Needles in WWW Haystacks. In: Sattar, A. (ed.) Canadian AI 1997. LNCS (LNAI), vol. 1342, pp. 25–36. Springer, Heidelberg (1997)
17. Sterling, L.: Surveying and Reviewing Methods of Representing Scenarios, Technical Report, The Department of Computer Science and Software Engineering, The University of Melbourne, Melbourne (1998)

A Knowledge-Based Approach to Initial Population Generation in Evolutionary Algorithms: Application to the Protein Structure Prediction Problem

Erick Fredj[1,2] and Moshe Goldstein[2,3]

[1] Department of Computer Science, Jerusalem College of Technology, Jerusalem 91160, Israel
[2] Department of Environmental Science, Weizmann Institute, Rehovot 76100 Israel
[3] Department of Physical Chemistry and The Fritz Haber Research Center,
The Hebrew University of Jerusalem, Jerusalem 91904, Israel
erick@weizmann.ac.il, goldmosh@jct.ac.il

Abstract. In this study we introduce a new approach to generate the initial population of an Evolutionary Algorithm (EA), based on problem-specific knowledge. We discuss the key ingredients (knowledge and diversity) necessary to generate a good diverse initial random population, with particular application to the protein structure prediction problem. Two main components of our Initial Population Generation (IPG) algorithm are described: (a) one provides the bio-chemical problem-specific knowledge (Molecular Dynamics (MD) and Normal Mode Analysis (NMA)); (b) the second one is an algorithm which ensures population diversity by using the complete graph of the generated bio-molecular conformations. Results show that IPG is a promising algorithm for the creation of good diversity initial populations.

Keywords: Evolutionary Algorithm, Initial Population Generation, Molecular Dynamics, Normal Mode Analysis, Population Diversity, Complete Graph.

1 Introduction

Evolutionary Algorithms (EAs) [1-9] have been extensively used as heuristic tools for doing search in huge search spaces. EAs take their inspiration from Nature: species evolve according with the environment - the survival of the fittest. EAs can be used for solving a wide range of problems. In most cases, EAs do not exploit _problem-specific knowledge_, making them less efficient.

We consider global optimization problems of the following form

$$\text{Optimize} \quad f(x), x = (x_1, ..., x_n) \in R^n \tag{1}$$

In EAs, a candidate solution x is called an _individual_ and iterations are called _generations_. EAs are _generate-and-test_ iterative algorithms [10] (see Fig. 1); they deal with a set of individual solutions at-a-time - a _population_.

N. Dershowitz and E. Nissan (Eds.): Choueka Festschrift, Part I, LNCS 8001, pp. 252–262, 2014.
© Springer-Verlag Berlin Heidelberg 2014

```
1  def EA:
     p = create initial population p with random individuals from problem domain
     while (termination condition does not hold):
         new_p = generate(p)
         p = test(new_p)
     return p
2  def generate(p₀):
     parents = parentselection(p₀)
     offspring = crossover(pairs of parents)
     p₁ = p₀ + offspring
     p₂ = mutation(p₁)
     return p₂
3  def test(p):
     new_p = survivorselection(p)
     return new_p
```

Fig. 1. Python-like pseudo-code of a general Evolutionary Algorithm

As can be seen in Fig. 1, the first step in any kind of EA (Genetic Algorithms, Evolution Strategies, Evolutionary Programming, or others) is the generation of the *initial population* from which the iterative process starts. EAs apply the principles of evolution found in Nature to global optimization problems. The basic operators used in EAs to emulate evolution are called *genetic* operators: (a) parent and survivor *selection* operators, and (b) *variation* (*crossover/recombination*, and *mutation*) operators. In selection operators, individuals are selected according to some quality or fitness criterion. In crossover, the selected parents are crossbred to produce offspring; a variety of crossover operators can be found in the literature (see, for example [4, 5]). In mutation, individuals are altered according to random-based rules.

The *generate* step of the EA essentially is some combination of crossover and/or mutation. The *test* step of the EA essentially is the application of survivor selection on the set of individuals produced by the *generate* step of the EA; this *selection* operator selects individuals who survive and then are copied to the population of the next generation. A variety of genetic operators of all kinds can be found in the literature (see, for example [4, 5]).

Theoretical studies about EAs have involved genetic operators and the analysis of their effect in EAs performance, which is often considered significant [11]. However, until recently [12-16], there have been almost no formal studies on the role and effect of the initial population generation on EAs performance, and whether the initial population should be generated at random, as it is usually done. The disadvantage of a randomly generated initial population is that it may contain infeasible individuals, meaning that individuals in successive generations may remain infeasible too. Two commonly used ways to deal with infeasible individuals are (a) the penalty functions [2, 3, 17] approach and (b) the "death penalty" [2] approach. In the former, a specially designed "penalty" function is incorporated to the objective function. In the latter, infeasible individuals are simply rejected; they are not considered at all for the computation.

In Protein Structure Prediction (PSP), the goal is to find a good approximation of the 3D geometry of the native structure of a protein molecule, which is the global minimum of its Potential Energy Surface (PES) [18-23]). In PSP, infeasible individuals are those that are *physically* infeasible molecular structures which are far from bio-chemical reality and need to be rejected. For that, if we wish to solve the PSP problem by using an EA, the initial population *cannot* be generated simply at random but by a specially designed population generation algorithm based on a "death penalty" approach which takes into account physico-chemical characteristics of the molecule at hand. Such an algorithm has been designed by us and will be described in the rest of this paper.

A more general motivation underlies our presentation here, and it is to encourage researchers to pay more attention on how one should generate an initial population of feasible individuals vis-a-vis the characteristics of the *specific* problem at hand.

The rest of the paper is organized as follows: The following section states the basic idea of our Initial Population Generation (IPG) algorithm, based on two key ingredients necessary to generate a good initially diverse population: *problem-specific knowledge* and *population diversity*. We discuss the main components of our algorithm: (a) two of them provide the *bio-chemical problem-specific knowledge* (Molecular Dynamics (MD) [18,19] and Normal Mode Analysis (NMA) [18,19]); (b) the last one is an algorithm designed to ensure *population diversity* by using the complete graph of the generated bio-molecular conformations. Section 3 discusses run results. Section 4 concludes the paper.

2   Initial Population Generation

Population *diversity* [16] is a term which refers to how widely distributed are the generated individuals over the search space. We talk about good population diversity when the Euclidian distance between two individuals (protein conformations) is greater than some minimum distance $\Delta > 0$. A well distributed population is needed during the first iterations of an EA run. IPG is similar in its approach to the "Simple Sequential Inhibition Process" (SSI) algorithm proposed by H. Maaranen, K. Miettinen and A. Penttinen [12]. IPG creates an ensemble of local minima molecular conformations whose Root Mean Square Deviation (RMSD)[1] between them and a given initial unfolded molecular conformation, and among themselves, are at least 2.5 Å in the case of peptides of length less than 10 amino acids, or at least 4 Å in the case of peptides of length at least 10 amino acids. In order to ensure physical feasibility, IPG makes use of the physico-chemical knowledge provided by Molecular Dynamics (MD) [18,19] (see paragraph 2.1 below) and Normal Modes Analysis (NMA) [18,19] (see paragraph 2.2). Population diversity is achieved by a specially designed complete graph algorithm (see paragraph 2.3 below). Using that *chemical knowledge*, IPG generates an initial population of physically feasible conformations, with good *diversity* (see Fig. 2,), promoting the exploitation of a broad covering of the search space.

---

[1] The RMSD between a pair of molecular conformations represents the structural difference (or distance) between them.

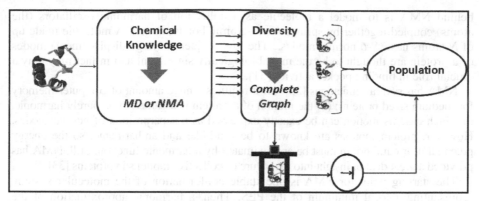

Fig. 2. A schematic representation of the IPG algorithm. From an initial molecular conformation, a population of molecular conformations is generated with a minimal RMSD $\Delta > 0$ among all of them.

2.1   Molecular Dynamics Simulations

MD simulations propagate an atomic system by solving Newton's equation of motion F = ma, updating atomic positions and velocities over a time step Δt. The Leapfrog [24, 25] method is a propagator which updates the positions and momenta by using a second order Taylor series discretization of Newton's equations.

$$\frac{dx}{dt} = M^{-1}\vec{p}, \frac{dp}{dt} = -\nabla U(\vec{x}) \tag{2}$$

Newtonian dynamics can be characterized more generally by Eq (2), where $U(\vec{x})$ is the Potential Energy Surface (PES) of the bio-molecular system, $\vec{x}$ is the vector of atomic positions, and $\vec{p}$ is the vector of atomic momenta. These vectors are of dimension *3N*, where *N* is the number of atoms in the system. Given an initial conformation, the entire system is thermalized at a desired temperature (*T*=800K). This is accomplished initializing the dynamics from that initial conformation by imparting random velocities selected from a Maxwell Boltzmann distribution [24, 26] corresponding to a mean kinetic energy *kT*. The total energy of the system is followed periodically to check conservation. The thermal equilibrium of the system is propagated in time for a period of 10-20 ps in its ground state potential energy surface. The thermally equilibrated system is then used as the initial state of the conformational space sampling promoted by the MD simulation. In IPG, candidate conformations for the initial population, are chosen equally spaced in simulated time; for example, a conformation snapshot every 1 ps. The MD's simulation was performed using TINKER's[27] *'dynamic'* program.

2.2   Normal Mode Analysis

MD simulations often become trapped at low temperature and, moreover, they poorly sample higher energy regions. Consequently, we developed a new approach based on NMA to provide sufficient sampling. NMA has been known for years to be applicable for the description of the movements of biological molecules [28-30]. The basic idea behind NMA is to model a molecule as a collection of harmonic oscillators (the atoms) coupled together by springs (inter-atomic bonds model). A molecule made up of N atoms has $3N-6$ normal modes. The low frequency (large displacement) modes of a protein are thought to be the most biologically significant and in fact may play a crucial role in binding pocket activity [31].

NMA has several limitations [32]: (a) it requires a huge amount of computer memory for medium sized proteins; (b) the motion of a protein is assumed to be purely harmonic, in which case its motion can be exactly expressed as a superposition of normal modes. However, protein motions are known to be fluid-like and an-harmonic, so the energy potential near equilibrium must be approximated by a harmonic function. Still, NMA has provided a great deal of insight into the nature of collective motions in proteins [33].

The starting point for NMA is one stable conformation of the molecular system, representing a local minimum of the PES. Then, a harmonic approximation of the potential well is constructed around this conformation. A harmonic potential well has the form described by Eq. (3)

$$U(\vec{x}) = \frac{1}{2}(\vec{x} - \vec{x}_{eq}) \cdot K(\vec{x}_{eq}) \cdot (\vec{x} - \vec{x}_{eq}) \tag{3}$$

where $\vec{x}_{eq}$ is an N-dimensional vector and N is the number of atoms describing the stable conformation at the center of the well and $\vec{x}$ is an N-dimensional vector representing the current conformation. The symmetric and positive semi-definite matrix K (the Hessian matrix) describes the shape of the potential well.

NMA is a suitable method for studying large amplitude deformational motions of bio-molecules [34]. In many cases it has been found that functionally important transition pathways of bio-molecules often follow the trajectories of one of the low frequency normal modes [35]. In IPG we have implemented and applied a new randomized vector normal mode (RVN) technique to generate conformational changes described by normal modes. Given a conformation, we generate a new conformation $\vec{x}_{Map}$ which is a perturbation from a first order approximation obtained using Eq (4).

$$\vec{x}_{Map} = \vec{x}_{eq} + \sum_{i=1}^{M} C_i v_i \tag{4}$$

The parameter M is the number of dominant normal modes (those chosen randomly from a Gaussian distribution over the low frequency normal modes, for example between 500 and 1300 cm^{-1}) which are used to generate the new conformation $\vec{x}_{Map}$, v_i corresponds to the normalized eigenvector of the Hessian matrix obtained from the equilibrium conformation $\vec{x}_{eq}$, C_i are the random normal mode coordinates obtained from a Gaussian distribution. The mapped structure $\vec{x}_{Map}$ will be accepted by IPG if the RMSD between it and the source structure is greater than some given $\Delta > 0$.

This NMA-based method has been implemented as part of our 'population' program, whose code is based on TINKER's 'vibrate' program [27] which is written in Fortran77.

2.3   IPG – Initial Population Generation Algorithm

IPG was designed to solve the problem of finding an initial population of *popsize* conformations with RMSD relative to the initial conformation, and among themselves, greater than a minimum structural distance $\Delta > 0$. A Python-like pseudo-code of the IPG algorithm is presented in Fig. 3.[2]

IPG starts with a given initial conformation. First, a loop of MD simulation runs is executed in order to produce an initial population containing a pool of the required *popsize* feasible conformations. At each iteration, the MD simulation randomly generates k feasible conformations. This pool of conformations, as a list object, is assigned to *genconfs*. All the conformations with RMSD smaller than Δ, relative to the initial conformation, and relative to all others in *genconfs*, are unacceptable; therefore, they are rejected by moving them to the list *rejectedconfs*; otherwise, they are accepted and moved to the list *acceptedconfs*. If the size of the *acceptedconfs* list is smaller than the required *popsize*, the loop of MD simulation runs continues until *maxMDruns* iterations are executed. If the size of the *acceptedconfs* list is at least *popsize*, IPG will stop. If those *maxMDruns* iterations of MD simulation runs were not enough to generate the required *popsize* conformations of the initial population, another iterative process is launched in which our RVN method is run at most *maxRVNruns* times in order to randomly generate an additional pool of conformations. Again, all the unacceptable conformations are rejected and therefore moved to the list *rejectedconfs*, and those accepted are moved to the list *acceptedconfs*. If at the end of this second iterative process, the size of the *acceptedconfs* list continues to be smaller than the required *popsize*, IPG will randomly select conformations from the set of rejected conformations found in the list *rejectedconfs*, and stop.

In order to decide if a conformation is acceptable or not, a (directed) complete graph [36,37], represented as a directed tree, represents the set of generated conformations, as shown in Fig. 4. The root a_0 of the tree represents the given initial conformation, the nodes $a_1, , a_n$ represent the generated conformations in the pool, and the weights assigned to the directed edges (a_i , a_j) are the RMSD between a_i and a_j. The idea of the acceptance algorithm is as follows: construct the complete graph; the tree is scanned in preorder; if a node a_i is unacceptable, its in-going edges and its out-going edges are deleted; the remaining connected sub-graph is that of the accepted conformations. As can be seen in Fig. 3, our implementation is simpler than that described procedure: for each node, only its in-going edges are generated and their RMSD values calculated; it is enough that one RMSD value will be smaller than Δ in order to reject that node. It is clear that for a set of k generated conformations, the worse-case complexity of the implemented version of the acceptance algorithm is $O(k^2)$. Thus, most, and hopefully all, the conformations of the resulting *acceptedconfs* list, will be a population of n conformations with RMSD $\geq \Delta$ among themselves and also relative to the initial conformation. This is represented by the connectivity matrix of the graph where the values are the pairwise RMSD distances between conformations; this matrix is used to evaluate the diversity of the population at every step of the algorithm; because of that we call it a *diversity matrix*. That is, we can expect to start the EA search with good initial population *diversity*. Finally, IPG

---

[2] All the variables referred to in the following paragraph, are from those used in the IPG algorithm's pseudo-code shown in Fig. 3.

locally minimizes all those accepted conformations, before returning the *acceptedconfs* list. That is done because DEEPSAM[38]'s search space is the set of all local minima of the PES.

```
1.  def accepted(initconf,acceptedconfs,newconf, Δ):
      treedges = [ ]
      treedges.append([initconf,newconf])
      for conf in acceptedconfs:
        treedges.append([conf, newconf])
      retval = True
      for edge in treedges:
        if  (RMSD(edge) < Δ):
          retval = False
          break
      return retval

2.  def IPG(initconf, maxMDruns, maxRVNruns, T, M, k, Δ, popsize):
      # initconf: initial conformation
      # maxMDruns: maximum times MDproc should be run
      # maxRVNruns: maximum times RVNproc should be run
      # Δ: minimum required structural distance between any two conformations
      # popsize: requested population size
      # MDproc: MD procedure at constant temperature T - generates k conformations
      # RVNproc: RVN procedure for M normal modes - generates k conformations
      # genproc: procedure to generate a set of k conformations
      genproc = MDproc
3.    acceptedconfs = [ ]
      rejectedconfs = [ ]
      nrofacceptedconfs = 0
      looptimes = maxMDruns
      while True:
4.      for i in range(looptimes):
5.        genconfs = genproc(k)
          foreach conf in genconfs:
            # selection from complete graph
            if  accepted(initconf, acceptedconfs, conf, Δ):
              acceptedconfs.append(conf)
              nrofacceptedconfs = nrofacceptedconfs + 1
              if  (nrofacceptedconfs >= popsize):
                # terminate
                return locallyminimized(acceptedconfs)
            else:
              rejectedconfs.append(conf)
        if  (genproc == RVNproc):
          missingconfs = randomly select missing confs from rejectedconfs
          acceptedconfs.append(missingconfs)
          # terminate
          return locallyminimized(acceptedconfs)
6.      else:
          genproc = RVNproc
          looptimes = maxRVNruns
```

Fig. 3. Python-like pseudo-code of the IPG algorithm

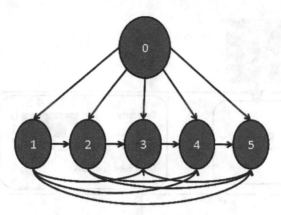

Fig. 4. Directed complete graph/tree representing a 5-conformation population

3   Discussion

Our IPG algorithm has been implemented as part of the DEEPSAM PSP algorithm. The IPG results that will be presented in this section were obtained using the MD-based component of IPG; the NMA-based component is still under quality control tests. Results using the NMA-based component will be presented elsewhere in the future.

For the presentation here, we took one of the five cyclic peptides used as the proof-of-concept of DEEPSAM. It is important to highlight the main reasons of this choice: (a) the amino acid sequences of those cyclic peptides were long enough to have a nontrivial number of local minima, and short enough to allow relatively short run times, and (b) the X-Ray Crystallography of the native structures of those cyclic peptides were well-known in the literature, allowing us to verify the predicted structures with the known experimental ones (see [39] for the case of the example cyclic peptide used here).

The example cyclic peptide presented here is composed by a sequence of six amino acids. According to the rule-of-thumb used in [40], two conformations of such a peptide are geometrically distant enough if the RMSD between them is at least 2.5Å The adopted Δ for our IPG algorithm was based on this rule-of-thumb as its population diversity criterion. As can be seen in Fig. 5, the IPG algorithm finds a set of conformations which is mostly in agreement with that rule-of-thumb.

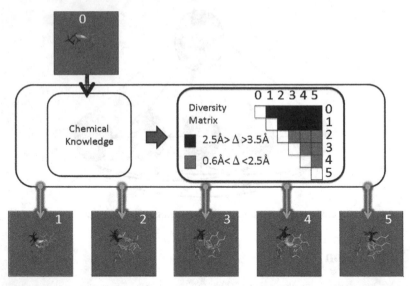

Fig. 5. Given an initial conformation (0) of Bamblik *cyclo*-(Gly-L-His-Gly-L-Ala-L-Tyr-Gly), a *mostly well* distributed population of 5 conformations is generated by the IPG algorithm. The *diversity matrix* represents the directed complete graph of the population. The pairwise RMSD values between conformations are the weights of the edges used by the IPG algorithm to accept (black) or possibly reject (grey) conformations with a threshold $\Delta = 2.5$ Angstrom.

4   Concluding Remarks and Future Work

In this paper we introduced a new way to generate an EA's initial population with good diversity, which integrates both, randomness and problem-specific knowledge. Our general framework to generate an initial population was applied to bio-molecular systems, combining randomness with knowledge from NMA and MD simulations, on top of a complete graph algorithm which fulfills the diversity criterion. The program implementing our IPG algorithm has been tried on small and large peptides, but it is important to note that it needs to be checked over a wider range of bio-molecular systems.

In the future we will consider the use of our new initial population generation strategy to other kinds of applications by appropriately adapting IPG's main components to the new specific endeavors.

Acknowledgements. Thanks to our colleagues at Prof. R. B. Gerber's research group, from the Fritz Haber Research Center of the Hebrew University of Jerusalem, for their insights and cooperation during the development of the ideas presented here.

References

1. Holland, J.: Adaptation in Natural and Artificial Systems. MIT Press, Cambridge (1992)
2. Michalewicz, Z., Fogel, D.B.: How to solve it: Modern Heuristics. Springer, Heidelberg (2000)

3. Eiben, A.E., Smith, J.E.: Introduction to Evolutionary Computing. Springer, Heidelberg (2007)
4. Back, T., Fogel, D.B., Michalewicz, T. (eds.): Evolutionary Computation 1: Basic Algorithms and Operators. IOP Publishing Ltd., Bristol (2000)
5. Back, T., Fogel, D.B., Michalewicz, T. (eds.): Evolutionary Computation 2: Advanced Algorithms and Operators. IOP Publishing Ltd., Bristol (2000)
6. Goldberg, D.E.: Genetic Algorithms in Search, Optimization and Machine Learning. Addison-Wesley Publ. Co., USA (1989)
7. Mitchell, M.: An Introduction to Genetic Algorithms. The MIT Press, Cambridge (1996)
8. De Jong, K.A.: Evolutionary Computation – A Unified Approach. The MIT Press, Cambridge (2006)
9. Fogel, D.B.: Evolutionary Computation – Toward a New Philosophy of Machine Intelligence. IEEE Press, Piscataway (2006)
10. Yao, X., Xu, Y.: Recent Advances in Evolutionary Computation. J. Comput. Sci. & Technol. 21, 1–18 (2006)
11. Spears, W.M.: Evolutionary Algorithms – The Role of Mutation and Recombination. Springer, Heidelberg (2000)
12. Maaranen, H., Miettinen, K., Penttinen, A.: On initial populations of a genetic algorithm for continuous optimization problems. J. Glob. Optim. 37, 405–436 (2007)
13. Hill, R.R.: A Monte Carlo Study of Genetic Algorithm Initial Population Generation Methods. In: Proc. of the 31st Winter Simulation Conference, pp. 543–547 (1999)
14. Rahnamayan, S., Tzihoosh, H.R., Salama, M.M.A.: A novel population initialization method for accelerating evolutionary algorithms. Computers and Mathematics with Applications 53, 1605–1614 (2007)
15. Morrison, R.W.: Dispersion-based Population Initialization. In: Cantú-Paz, E., et al. (eds.) GECCO 2003. LNCS, vol. 2723, pp. 1210–1221. Springer, Heidelberg (2003)
16. Ursem, R.K.: Diversity-guided evolutionary algorithms. In: Guervós, J.J.M., Adamidis, P.A., Beyer, H.-G., Fernández-Villacañas, J.-L., Schwefel, H.-P. (eds.) PPSN 2002. LNCS, vol. 2439, pp. 462–471. Springer, Heidelberg (2002)
17. Smith, A.E., Coit, D.W.: Penalty Functions. In: [5], pp. 41–48 (2000)
18. Leach, A.: Molecular Modelling - Principles and Applications, 2nd edn. Prentice-Hall, Pearson Education Ltd., Essex (2001)
19. Schlick, T.: Molecular Modeling and Simulation – An Interdisciplinary Guide. Springer, New York (2002)
20. Floudas, C.A., Klepeis, J.L., Pardalos, P.M.: Global Optimization Approaches in Protein Folding and Peptide Docking. In: Proc. of DYCOPS-5, pp. 167–178 (1998)
21. Straub, J.E.: Optimization Techniques with Applications to Proteins. In: Elber, R. (ed.) New Developments in Theoretical Studies of Proteins, pp. 137–196. World Scientific Publ., Singapore (1996)
22. Prentiss, M.C., Hardin, C., Eastwood, M.P., Zong, C., Wolynes, P.G.: Protein Structure Prediction: The Next Generation. J. Chem. Theory Comput. 2, 705–716 (2006)
23. Ponder, J.W., Case, D.A.: Force Fields for Protein Simulation. Adv. Protein Chem. 66, 27–85 (2003)
24. Allen, M.P., Tildesley, D.J.: Computer Simulation of Liquids. Clarendon Press, Oxford (1987)
25. Matthey, T., Cickovski, T., Hampton, S.S., Ko, A., Ma, Q., Nyerges, M., Raeder, T., Slabach, T.: Izaguirre, PROTOMOL: An object-oriented framework for prototyping novel algorithms for molecular dynamics. ACM Trans. Math. Softw. 30(3), 237–265 (2004)

26. Carter, A.H.: Classical and Statistical Thermodynamics. Printice Hall, Inc., New Jersey (2001)

27. Ponder, J.W.: TINKER - Software Tools for Molecular Design. Version 4.1, Washington University School of Medicine, St. Louis, MO (2003)

28. Brooks, B., Karplus, M.: Normal modes for specific motins of macromolecules: Application to the hinge-bending mode of lysozyme. Proc. Nat. Acad. Sci. USA 80, 6571–6575 (1983)

29. Goldstein, H.: Classical Mechanics. Addison Wesley, Reading (1980)

30. Elber, R., Karplus, M.: Multiple conformation states of proteins: A molecular dynamics analysis of myoglobin. Science 235, 318–321 (1987)

31. Tirion, M.M.: Analysis of domain motions by approximate normal mode calculations. Proteins 33, 417–429 (1998)

32. Wriggers, W., Schulten, K.: Protein domain movements: detection of rigid domains and visualization of hinges in comparisons of atomic coordinates. Proteins 29(1), 1–14 (1997)

33. Delarue, M., And Dumas, P.: Macromolecular structural models. PNAS 101(18), 6957–6972 (2004)

34. Lindahl, E., Azuara, C., Koehl, Delarue, M.: Refinement of macromolecular structures based on all-atom normal mode analysis. Nucleic Acids Res. 34, w52–w56 (2006)

35. Doruker, P., Bahar, I., Baysal, C., Erman, B.: Collective deformations in proteins determined by a mode analysis of molecular dynamics trajectories. Polymer 43, 431–439 (2002)

36. Diestel, R.: Graph Theory – Electronic Edition 2005. Springer, Heidelberg (2005)

37. Pfaltz, J.L.: Computer Data Structures. McGraw-Hill Inc., New York (1977)

38. Goldstein, M., Fredj, E., Gerber, R.B.: A New Hybrid Algorithm for Finding the Lowest Minima of Potential Surfaces: Approach and Application to Peptides. J. Comput. Chem. 32, 1785–1800 (2011)

39. Yang, C.-H., Brown, J.N., Kopple, K.D.: Crystal Structure and Solution Studies of the Molecular Conformation of the Cyclic Hexaqpeptide cyclo-(Gly-L-His-Gly-L-Ala-L-Tyr-Gly). J. Am. Chem. Soc. 103, 1715–1719 (1981)

40. Rayan, A., Senderowitz, H., Goldblum, A.: Exploring the conformational space of cyclic peptides by a stochastic search method. Journal of Molecular Graphics and Modelling 22, 319–333 (2004)

Nuclear In-core Fuel Reload Design:
The Trajectory of a Sequence of Projects

Ephraim Nissan

Department of Computing, Goldsmiths College, University of London,
25–27 St. James Street, New Cross, London SE14 6NW, England, U.K.
ephraim.nissan@hotmail.co.uk

Abstract. Between 1986 and 2000, I have been involved in a sequence
of projects, FUELCON and FUELGEN, applying artificial intelligence
techniques to an economically important problem in nuclear engineering: how to design refuellings, i.e., the replacement of spent fuel and
rearrangement of other fuel assemblies, inside the core of a nuclear reactor, so that power generation be efficient, and that the cycle be usefully
long. Design used to consist of a fuel manager manually reshuffling fuel
from given categories inside a grid representing a symmetrical slice of
a reactor core section. This process was automated by the FUELCON
expert system, by means of a ruleset. This was a breakthrough in in-
core fuel management. Then, after probing into the possibility of further automation in a hybrid architecture combining rulesets and neural
computing, a different direction was taken: in FUELGEN, evolutionary
computing was applied, and for a while, the results reported were at the
forefront. Since then, the application to refuellings of other techniques
from artificial intelligence has been reported. One derives the impression
that the industry is now relatively satisfied with efficiency levels, so we
no longer see the pioneering spirit of the 1990s, but nevertheless, there
appear several relevant papers for novel situations or contexts, or with
novel techniques or configurations of techniques, so the problem is still
not considered solved.

Keywords: Artificial intelligence, Heuristic problem-solving, Genetic
algorithms, Evolutionary computing, Allocation problem, Nuclear engineering, Nuclear reactor, In-core fuel management problem, Fuel reload
pattern design, refuelling, FUELCON, FUELGEN.

1 Introduction

In 1983–1989, I pursued a Ph.D. in Computer Science by developing a project
in computational linguistics which I had proposed myself. I was based at Ben-
Gurion University of the Negev in Beer-Sheva, Israel, but my doctoral project
was supervised by Prof. Yaacov Choueka, of Bar-Ilan University in Ramat-Gan.
One day in 1986, I received a visit in my office, by Alex Galperin, a professor of
nuclear engineering at Ben-Gurion University. When he introduced himself, he
explained that he wanted to develop an expert system for the design of how to
refuel nuclear reactors (he had discussed exploring the search space in [42]), and

N. Dershowitz and E. Nissan (Eds.): Choueka Festschrift, Part I, LNCS 8001, pp. 263–363, 2014.
© Springer-Verlag Berlin Heidelberg 2014

as he needed a collaborator whose area is artificial intelligence, he had turned to Prof. Martin Golumbic at Bar-Ilan University. Marty was not interested in taking part, but he signalled to Alex that I was working at his same university in Beer-Sheva. That was the beginning of my involvement with nuclear fuel realod pattern design, as a domain of application of artificial intelligence, during the nearly fifteen years that followed (cf. [104–106]). Alex and I designed, as early as 1986, a rule-based expert system, FUELCON [46] (cf. [47, 113, 48, 57, 107]). FUELCON as being an operational expert system was developed as a doctoral project in Nuclear Engineering [78] by Shuky (Yehoshua) Kimhi [53, 45, 52].

"The problem of optimizing refueling in a nuclear boiling water reactor is difficult since it concerns combinatorial optimization and it is NP-Complete. In order to solve this problem, many techniques have been applied, ranging from expert systems to genetic algorithms" [123]. In fact, the techniques used in our own sequence of projects has corresponded to the successive waves of paradigms within artificial intelligence.

With Hava Siegelmann, who in 1993/4 was my colleague at Bar-Ilan University, and who was researching artificial neural networks, I explored the possibility of developing a sequel to FUELCON, NeuroFUELCON, being a hybrid symbolic and subsymbolic tool (cf. [108]) that in addition to FUELCON's task, would also exhibit machine learning and would revise rules [114, 115, 55, 116, 149].

In the summer of 1994, I moved to London, and I brought with me the project of a sequel to FUELCON. The decision was taken in the team to adopt evolutionary computing, and eventually this became the doctoral project of Jun Zhao [176], who was also supervised by Alan Soper and Brian Knight, and who developed FUELGEN, a tool for fuel reload pattern design driven by a genetic meta-algorithm [177, 178, 117, 118, 179, 154, 119].

The structure of the present study is shown in Table 1.

Table 1. Table of contents of this article

1. Introduction
2. Nuclear Plants
3. The Geometry of a Core Section
4. The Preliminaries of Nuclear Fuel Reload Design
5. Batches of Fuel at End-of-Cycle
6. Factors Limiting Forecasting
7. The Nature of the Constraints
8. Reload-Design Automation:
    What the State of the Art Was Before FUELCON
9. Early Prototypes or Tools in the Same Category as FUELCON
10. The Contribution Made by FUELCON
11. How FUELCON Executes
12. A Sample Ruleset in FUELCON
13. Symbolic Rules, Coded as a Program Intended for
    Compilation by Symbolic-to-Neural Transformation
14. The Workings of FUELGEN

Table 1. (*Continued.*)

15. Macroevolution in FUELGEN
16. Interpretation of FUELCON and FUELGEN
     in Terms of Hyperrecursion and Hyperincursion
17. A Typology, and Typological Positioning
     of the Sequence of Architectures
18. Parameter Prediction: From Nodal Algorithms, to Neural
     Networks, with Considerations About Grid Geometry
19. Particle Swarm Optimization for Refuelling
20. Improved Fuel Bundle Design, and Combined Design
     of Fuel Assemblies and Core Configurations
21. Some Applications Which Genetic Algorithms
     Found in Nuclear Engineering
22. Further Advances in the Literature in the 2000s
23. Submarine Refuellings and Victor Raskin's
     Computational Linguistics Tool for
     Sensitive Document Declassification
24. Concluding Remarks

2   Nuclear Plants

Nuclear plants include one or more units, i.e. *reactors.* A reactor has a vessel, Each reactor has a *core,* where nuclear fuel generates energy through a process of *fission,* i.e. of splitting of the "heavy" atoms of uranium. Fig. 1 shows the scheme of a nuclear reactor. It is of a specific model, but gives a good idea about the structure of nuclear fission reactors in general. There exist pressurized water reactors (PWR), which are the kind with which we are concerned, as well as boiling water reactors (BWR).

> Pressurized water reactors (PWRs) comprise a majority of all western
> nuclear power plants and are one of two types of light water[1] reactor
> (LWR), the other type being boiling water reactors (BWRs). In a PWR
> the primary coolant (superheated water) is pumped under high pressure
> to the reactor core, then the heated water transfers thermal energy to a

---

[1] *Light water* is how normal water (i.e., H_2O) is called, as distinct from *heavy water* (i.e., deuterium oxide: D_2O. Also HDO, with one atom of hydrogen, one atom of deuterium, and one atom of oxygen, is called 'heavy water'). There also exist such nuclear reactors that use heavy water as both moderator (of the neutron reactions) and coolant. Heavy water has very low neutron absorption. *Heavy-water reactors* include *CANDU reactors* (i.e., *Canada deuterium uranium reactors*), and *SGHWR reactors* (the latter are also called *steam generating heavy water reactors*). CANDU reactors were developed and are widely used in Canada, and their fuel rods are made of pellets of natural (i.e., unenriched) uranium canned in Zircaloy tubes. Papers at the symposia of the Canadian Nuclear Society are typically concerned with CANDU reactors.

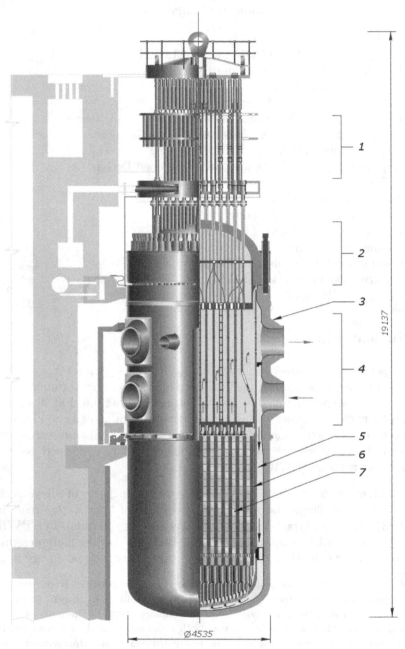

Fig. 1. A pressurized water reactor (PWR) of the Russian model WWER-1000 (ВВЭР-1000, Water-Water Energetic Reactor, 1000 megawatt electric power). Based on http://en.wikipedia.org/wiki/File:Wwer-1000-scheme.png (in colour, public domain). **Key List.** 1 - control rods; 2 - reactor cover; 3 - reactor chassis; 4 - inlet and outlet nozzles; 5 - reactor vessel; 6 - active reactor zone; 7 - fuel rods.

steam generator. In contrast to a boiling water reactor, pressure in the primary coolant loop prevents the water from boiling within the reactor. All LWRs use ordinary light water as both coolant and neutron moderator.[2] PWR's were originally designed to serve as nuclear submarine power plants and were used in the original design of the first commercial power plant at Shippingport Atomic Power Station.[3]

Fuel units, called *fuel-assemblies,* are assemblies of long rods. The assemblies (see Fig. 2, parts a, b) are packages, 350 cm long, of 200 to 250 cylindrical rods — made of uranium dioxide — whose diameter is 1 cm. An individual fuel rod is full of pellets of uranium oxide (or more rarely, uranium), and these pellets are stacked end to end inside the fuel rod.[4] The fuel assemblies are located inside the nuclear reactor *core,* which is the active area of the reactor where the nuclear reaction takes place.

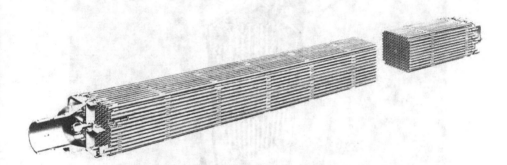

Fig. 2(a). A fuel assembly. This is the type in use on the cargo ship NS Savannah, and designed and built by the Babcock and Wilcox Company. The fuel assembly contains four bundles of 41 fuel rods. The uranium oxide is enriched to 4,2 and 4,6 percent of uranium-235. http://en.wikipedia.org/wiki/File:Nuclear_fuel_element.jpg https://voa.marad.dot.gov/programs/ns_sava This image, produced for the U.S. Maritime Administration, is in the public domain, because it is a work of the United States Federal Government under the terms of Title 17, Chapter 1, Section 105 of the U.S. Code.

---

[2] "A moderator needs to reduce the energy of neutrons without capturing many of them. In other words neutrons should react and change direction on colliding with a nucleus, releasing energy, but should not induce fission. Such nuclei have low molecular weight. Carbon, beryllium, water or heavy water are good moderators and can be either interspersed with the fuel or placed around the fuel elements" [170, p. 796].

[3] http://en.wikipedia.org/wiki/Pressurized_water_reactor

[4] One uranium fuel pellet has as much energy available as three barrels of oil of 42 gallons each, or one ton of coal, or one cord of wood (i.e, two tons and a half), or 17,000 cubic feet of natural gas.
http://www.iberdrolaingenieria.com/ibding/contenido/documentacion/06.pdf

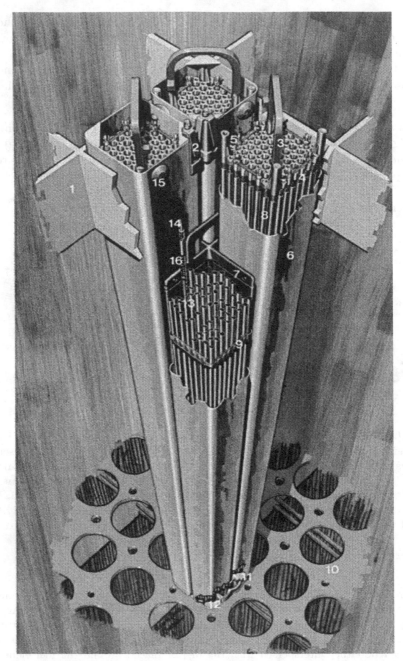

Fig. 2(b). A fuel assembly and its parts. This image is modified from an image from General Electric.

Key List: (1) top fuel guide; (2) channel fastener; (3) upper tie plate; (4) expansion spring; (5) locking tab; (6) channel; (7) control rod; (8) fuel rod; (9) spacer; (10) core plate assembly; (11) lower tie plate; (12) fuel support piece; (13) fuel pellets; (14) end plug; (15) channel spacer; (16) plenum spring.

Pressurized water reactor (PWR) fuel consists of cylindrical rods put into bundles. A uranium oxide ceramic is formed into pellets and inserted into Zircaloy tubes[5] that are bundled together. The Zircaloy tubes are about 1 cm in diameter, and the fuel cladding gap is filled with helium gas to improve the conduction of heat from the fuel to the cladding. There are about 179–264 fuel rods per fuel bundle and about 121 to 193 fuel bundles are loaded into a reactor core. Generally, the fuel bundles consist of fuel rods bundled 14×14 to 17×17. PWR fuel bundles are about 4 meters in length. In PWR fuel bundles, control rods are inserted through the top directly into the fuel bundle. The fuel bundles usually are enriched several percent in ^{235}U. The uranium oxide is dried before

---

[5] *Zircaloy* is a trade name "for an alloy of zirconium with small amounts of tin, iron and chromium, used to clad fuel elements in water reactors. There are two kinds commonly used, zircaloy-2 in boiling-water reactors and zircaloy-4 in pressurized-water reactors. The latter has less nickel in the alloy and is significantly less brittle after irradiation" [170, p. 1276, s.v.]. There exists a series of international symposia on Zirconium in the Nuclear Industry.

The design, manufacture and behaviour of nuclear fuel in pressurized-water reactrs (as well as in fast reactors) is the subject of a book edited by Bailly et al. [4]. After an introduction to nuclear fuel and fuel studies, the book has a chapter on fuel fabrication, cladding fabrication, fuel assembly fabrication component fabrication, and fuel rod fabrication. Then there is a chapter on in-reactor behaviour of fuel materials (heat production and removal, temperature effects, irradiation effects, fission product effects, oxide chemistry, as well as a section on advanced fuels for fast reactors), followed by a chapter on cladding and structural materials, and a chapter on fuel assemblies for pressurized water reactors: the support structure and the fuel rods are described, fuel management, reactor operating classes, the design of fuel assemblies and fuel rods, the in-reactor behaviour of fuel rods (e.g. the interaction between fuel pellets and cladding), and then models (fission gas release models, corrosion models, and PCI simulations, i.e., the mumerical simulation of pellet/cladding interaction), and a discussion of fuel behaviour under accidental conditions (accident classification with respect to reactor design, a discussion of extensively investigated accidents up to 1999, and the role of fuel in accident scenarios). The next chapter in the book is about fuel subassemblies for fast reactors, and then there is a chapter about absorber elements, beginning with a discussion of PWR control devices (control rod clusters, chemical control, and "poisons"); there is a section about absorber material selection criteria, a section on boron carbide, and sections about various kinds of absorbers.

The last chapter in the book is concerned with spent fuel management (the physical state and the radiochemical state of irradiated assemblies, the removal of fuel to a storage site, the unloading of the fuel, transport from one site to another, then a discussion of interim storage, either wet storage or dry storage, and then a section on various reprocessing processes, a section on reprocessing strategies, and final waste disposal). The book also comprises appendices on basic fuel elements calculations of the thermal behaviour and the mechanical behaviour, on post-irradiation examination (either destructive or non-destructive) or irradiated fuel rods and pins, and about equations used in fission gas release modelling (with subsections on gas migration due to atomic diffusion, and on gas bubble migration).

inserting into the tubes to try to eliminate moisture in the ceramic fuel that can lead to corrosion and hydrogen embrittlement. The Zircaloy tubes are pressurized with helium to try to minimize pellet cladding interaction (PCI) which can lead to fuel rod failure over long periods.[6]

The manufacturing of nuclear fuel is as follows [64, p. 30]:

In light water reactors it is necessary to increase the proportion of fissionable isotope ^{235}U (in nature only 0.711%) to 3–5% in the nuclear fuel. Such isotopic enrichment is based on separating the initial quantity of uranium hexafluoride in gaseous form into the enriched and the depleted streams using a slightly lowermass of the UF_6 molecule of ^{235}U then ^{238}U (uranium enrichment). The enrichment plant uses diffusion or centrifuge technology. Uranium hexafluoride also has very convenient properties for phase transformation. Easy transition between solid, gaseous and liquid phases enables simple and safe filling, handling and transportation of uranium hexafluoride. Finally, in the fabrication plant uranium hexafluoride is re-converted into UO_2. Fuel pellets are pressed from UO_2 powder, sintered, braced and stacked into fuel elements (zirconium tubes). The completed fuel (fresh fuel) assembly is an array of fuel elements fixed together via the top and bottom nozzle and several spacer grids.

Fig. 3 shows the vessel of a pressurized water reactor. Fuel assemblies have to each be inserted into a case in a *planar grid*, which is the surface or a section of the reactor core. It is by reasoning about such a grid, that engineers design refuellings. Positions inside the grid are such that one inserts into each of them either a fuel assembly, or, sometimes, a *control rod*,[7] whose function is to stop the nuclear fission chain reaction. Usually the control rods are placed vertically above the reactor cover, ready for being lowered into their respective position inside the grid. The reactor cover surmounts the reactor chassis, which encloses the reactor vessel, itself surrounding the reactor core, which is the active reactor zone. Fig. 4 shows a PWR vessel with control rods on top. Control rods are manufactured by filling them with pellets of substances that readily capture neutrons. Hafnium and cadmium are such substances. Those neutrons which the control rods absorb are no longer available for a chain reaction. Lifting the control rod enables more neutrons to strike the fissile fuel.

Among the fuel rods, liquid coolant, pumped from below the assembly, circulates. It usually is pressurized water. Pressure is needed to prevent the water from boiling. There are steam generators on the borders of the core: they act as heat exchangers. Just part of the thermal energy thus produced can be exploited as electric power: for example, about 3000 thermal megawatts would

---

[6] http://en.wikipedia.org/wiki/Nuclear_fuel

[7] Control rods are called *barres de contrôle* in French. Lengthening fuel cycles, which is what is done by means of the tools developed within the projects with which this paper is concerned, is not of interest for nuclear reactors in France, because in France there has long been a policy of having cycles of one year, for the sake of administrative simplicity, by lengthening the cycle.

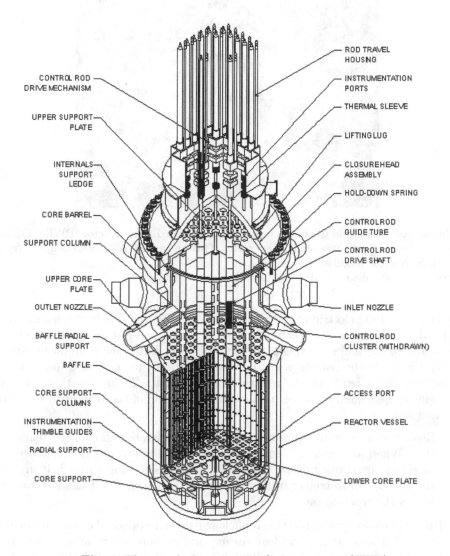

Fig. 3. The vessel of a pressurized water reactor (PWR)
http://www.eia.doe.gov/cneaf/nuclear/page/nuc_reactors/pwr.html
http://en.wikipedia.org/wiki/File:Reactorvessel.gif
(image in the public domain; U.S. Energy Information Agency).
Key List. 1 - control rods; 2 - reactor cover; 3 - reactor chassis; 4 - inlet and outlet nozzles; 5 - reactor vessel; 6 - active reactor zone; 7 - fuel rods.

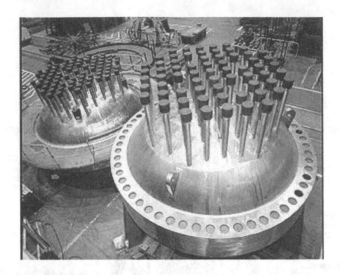

Fig. 4. Control rods on top of the vessel of a pressurized water reactor (PWR). Edited from a the public-domain original in colour. This image of PWR vessel heads is from the U.S. Nuclear Regulatory Commission.
http://en.wikipedia.org/wiki/File:Reactor_Vessel_head.jpg

yield about 1000 electric megawatts. Such is the power supply generated by a typical *pressurized-water reactor (PWR)*. A single fuel-rod generates about 80 kilowatts of thermal energy. One fuel-assembly generates about 20 megawatts.

Water inside the reactor vessel has two functions: to moderate the neutron reactions (for safety), and to remove the heat of the fission reaction, so that the energy generated could be used (to fulfil the goal of the reactor in terms of economics).

> Light water reactors use ordinary water to moderate and cool the reactors. When at operating temperature, if the temperature of the water increases, its density drops, and fewer neutrons passing through it are slowed enough to trigger further reactions. That negative feedback stabilizes the reaction rate[8]

Reactors whose type of reaction is nuclear *fission* (as opposed to the practically unattained desideratum of nuclear *fusion*, and as opposed to atomic batteries operated by exploiting passive radioactive decay, such as radioisotope thermoelectric generators), are either *thermal reactors*, which use slowed or thermal neutrons (almost all current reactors are of this type), or *fast neutron reactors* (these do not have a neutron moderator. They use less-moderating coolants. Some Russian naval propulsion units are fast reactors). We are only concerned with thermal reactors, in this article.

"Pressurized water reactors, like thermal reactor designs, require the fast fission neutrons to be slowed down (a process called moderation or thermalization)

---

[8] http://en.wikipedia.org/wiki/Nuclear_reactor_technology

in order to interact with the nuclear fuel and sustain the chain reaction."[9] An alternative to water-moderated reactors is graphite-moderated reactors. "Graphite and heavy water reactors tend to be more thoroughly thermalized than light water reactors. Due to the extra thermalization, these types can use natural uranium/unenriched fuel."[10] For example, the type of reactor (RBMK) involved in the Chernobyl disaster uses solid graphite for the neutron moderator, while using ordinary water for the coolant.[11] There also exists a British model, the advanced gas-cooled reactor, in which the coolant is carbon dioxide, and whose core is made of a graphite neutron moderator.

> Gas cooled reactors are cooled by a circulating inert gas, often helium in high-temperature designs, while carbon dioxide has been used in past British and French nuclear power plants. Nitrogen has also been used. Utilization of the heat varies, depending on the reactor. Some reactors run hot enough that the gas can directly power a gas turbine. Older designs usually run the gas through a heat exchanger to make steam for a steam turbine.[12]

In a pressurized water reactor, the nuclear fuel heats the water in the *primary coolant loop* by thermal conduction through the fuel cladding. *Power transfer* is therefore from the reactor core to the *primary coolant,* whose tubes are entirely

---

[9] http://en.wikipedia.org/wiki/Pressurized_water_reactor

[10] http://en.wikipedia.org/wiki/Nuclear_reactor_technology

[11] http://en.wikipedia.org/wiki/Pressurized_water_reactor explains that in pressurized water reactors, "the coolant water is used as a moderator by letting the neutrons undergo multiple collisions with light hydrogen atoms in the water, losing speed in the process. This 'moderating' of neutrons will happen more often when the water is denser (more collisions will occur). The use of water as a moderator is an important safety feature of PWRs, as any increase in temperature causes the water to expand and become less dense; thereby reducing the extent to which neutrons are slowed down and hence reducing the reactivity in the reactor. Therefore, if reactivity increases beyond normal, the reduced moderation of neutrons will cause the chain reaction to slow down, producing less heat. This property, known as the negative temperature coefficient of reactivity, makes PWR reactors very stable. In contrast, the RBMK reactor design used at Chernobyl, which uses graphite instead of water as the moderator and uses boiling water as the coolant, has a high positive coefficient of reactivity, that increases heat generation when coolant water temperatures increase. This makes the RBMK design less stable than pressurized water reactors. In addition to its property of slowing down neutrons when serving as a moderator, water also has a property of absorbing neutrons, albeit to a lesser degree. When the coolant water temperature increases, the boiling increases, which creates voids. Thus there is less water to absorb thermal neutrons that have already been slowed down by the graphite moderator, causing an increase in reactivity. This property is called the void coefficient of reactivity, and in an RBMK reactor like Chernobyl, the void coefficient is positive, and fairly large, causing rapid transients. This design characteristic of the RBMK reactor is generally seen as one of several causes of the Chernobyl accident."

[12] http://en.wikipedia.org/wiki/Nuclear_reactor_technology

inside the containment structure of the reactor (i.e., the building containing the reactor chassis and whatever it contains). The tubes of the primary coolant enter and exit the reactor vessel through the inlet and outlet nozzles (see in Fig. 1). To the tubes of the primary coolant, a *pressurizer* is applied. These tubes of the primary coolant loop pass through a *heat exchanger:* this is a *steam generator* containing *secondary coolant.*[13] Heat is transferred across a set of tubes to the lower-pressure secondary coolant, and the latter evaporates to pressurized steam. The steam generator is inside the containment structure of the reactor, but a tube at the top connects it to the top of a container placed outside the reactor containment structure, and inside that container there is a turbine. That turbine is connected to an electrical generator, driven by the turbine, and which in turn transfers power to the electric grid which distributes it. After passing through the turbine the secondary coolant is cooled down. As it cools, it becomes a water-steam mixture, and this in turn is condensed in a condenser. In fact, the bottom of the container in which the turbine is, is itself connected to the top of another structure which is a condenser: the condenser transforms the steam of the secondary coolant into liquid, which is then moved as *feedwater* to the bottom of the steam generator. See Fig. 5. The feedwater is sometimes preheated in order to minimize thermal shock.[14] As there are two coolant loops,

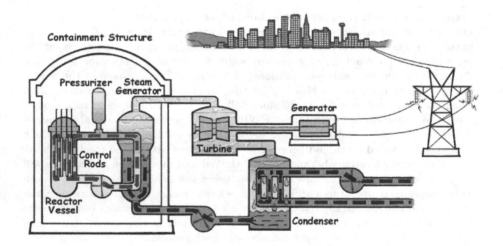

Fig. 5. A scheme of power transfer in a pressurized water reactor, with the primary and secondary coolant loops.
http://en.wikipedia.org/wiki/File:PressurizedWaterReactor.gif
http://www.nrc.gov/reading-rm/basic-ref/students/animated-pwr.html
(in the public domain; the original is an animated diagram in colour, from the U.S. Nuclear Regulatory Commission).

---

[13] In the European Pressurized Water Reactor, or EPR, heat exchangers are horizontal instead of vertical.

[14] http://en.wikipedia.org/wiki/Pressurized_water_reactor

the transfer of heat is accomplished without mixing the two fluids. In fact, this is a precaution dictated by safety considerations, since the primary coolant might become radioactive.

In a PWR, there are two separate coolant loops (primary and secondary), which are both filled with demineralized / deionized water. A boiling water reactor, by contrast, has only one coolant loop, while more exotic designs such as breeder reactors use substances other than water for coolant and moderator (e.g. sodium in its liquid state as coolant or graphite as a moderator). The pressure in the primary coolant loop is typically 15-16 megapascals (150-160 bar), which is notably higher than in other nuclear reactors, and nearly twice that of a boiling water reactor (BWR). As an effect of this, only localized boiling occurs and steam will recondense promptly in the bulk fluid. By contrast, in a boiling water reactor the primary coolant is designed to boil.[15]

Even though in this article we are going to concern ourself with pressurized water reactors, let us also say something about boiling water reactors (whose vessel is shown in Fig. 6, whereas their power transfer is shown in Fig. 7):

Steam exiting from the turbine flows into condensers located underneath the low pressure turbines where the steam is cooled and returned to the liquid state (condensate). The condensate is then pumped through feedwater heaters that raise its temperature using extraction steam from various turbine stages. Feedwater from the feedwater heaters enters the reactor pressure vessel (RPV) through nozzles high on the vessel, well above the top of the nuclear fuel assemblies (these nuclear fuel assemblies constitute the "core") but below the water level. The feedwater enters into the downcomer region and combines with water exiting the water separators. The feedwater subcools the saturated water from the steam separators. This water now flows down the downcomer region, which is separated from the core by a tall shroud. The water then goes through either jet pumps or internal recirculation pumps that provide additional pumping power (hydraulic head). The water now makes a 180 degree turn and moves up through the lower core plate into the nuclear core where the fuel elements heat the water. Water exiting the fuel channels at the top guide is about 12 to 15% saturated steam (by mass), typical core flow may be 45,000,000 kg/hr (100,000,000 lb/hr) with 6,500,000 kg/hr (14,500,000 lb/hr) steam flow.[16]

3 The Geometry of a Core Section

The *core geometry* of both PWRs and BWRs is schematized by the grid of positions hosting fuel assemblies or control rods, and this grid can be conceptualized as either a view from above, or (typically) a core section. See Figs. 7 and 8.

---

[15] http://en.wikipedia.org/wiki/Pressurized_water_reactor

[16] http://en.wikipedia.org/wiki/Boiling_water_reactor

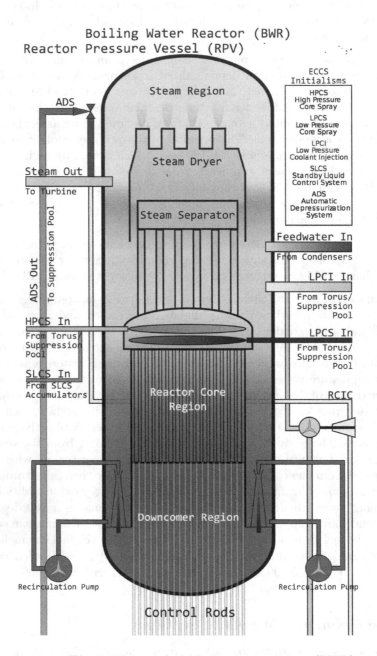

Fig. 6. The vessel of a boiling water reactor (BWR)
http://en.wikipedia.org/wiki/File:Bwr-rpv.svg   (an edited version of a colour image,
simplifying a diagram drawn by David C. Synnott).

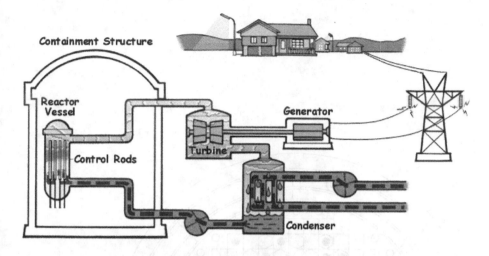

Fig. 7. A scheme of power transfer in a boiling water reactor
http://en.wikipedia.org/wiki/File:BoilingWaterReactor.gif
http://www.nrc.gov/reading-rm/basic-ref/students/animated-bwr.html
(in the public domain; the original is an animated diagram in colour, from the
U.S. Nuclear Regulatory Commission).

The core is symmetrical, so reasoning for the application with which we are
concerned in this article — namely, *fuel allocation* to the grid positions — is
done on just a one-eighth slice of the core schema.

Fuel assemblies (for our purposes, fuel units) are inserted vertically into the
core, which for the purposes of designing the refuelling can be viewed as a planar
horizontal section, as shown in Fig. 9. It is practically sufficient to reason on a
slice of the grid, in one-eighth (or, less often, one-quarter) symmetry; hence,
pos11 labels the core position at the center, but the rest of the labelling in
the same figure is in one-eight symmetry, for the purposes of just one slice (see
Fig. 10, parts a and b). The upper tip of the slice is the center of the core. In the
core geometry, important regions include the border of the core, the main axis,
the diagonal, as well as the core periphery. All of these are indicated in Fig. 9.

One fuel-unit is inserted by being lowered vertically into a given square position in the grid; all core positions are to contain one fuel unit. By "square", such
a position is intended that it has four and only four contiguous positions in the
same grid, unless the position is on the periphery of the core. (Actually, a different kind of core geometry is found in former-Soviet reactors, where contiguity is
between hexagonal positions in the grid. Moreover, in the Canadian deuterium
uranium (CANDU) reactors, fuel is inserted horizontally; but for that matter,
the kind of fuel reload design under discussion in this paper is not relevant for
CANDU reactors, because for one thing, there is no need to shut down the reactor in order to load there the fuel units: natural uranium is used as fuel, and
there is no need for downtime periods (at least, for the purposes of refuelling),
as replacement is on-line, i.e., continuous.

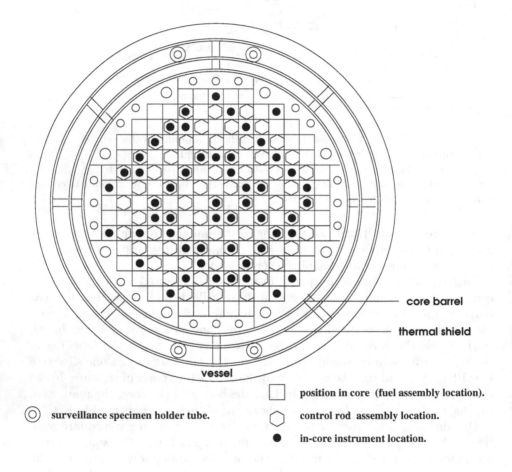

core barrel

thermal shield

vessel

☐ position in core (fuel assembly location).

◎ surveillance specimen holder tube.   ⬡ control rod assembly location.

● in-core instrument location.

Fig. 8. A planar horizontal section of a reactor core

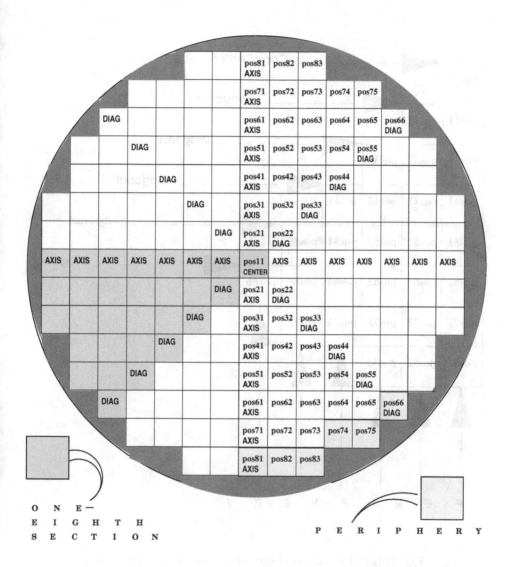

Fig. 9. Symmetry inside a horizontal section of a reactor core

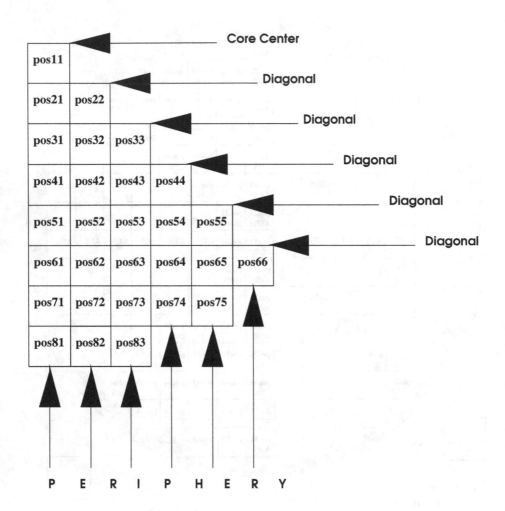

Fig. 10(a). A symmetrical slice of a section of a reactor core

pos81 AXIS	pos82	pos83					
pos71 AXIS	pos72	pos73	pos74	pos75			
pos61 AXIS	pos62	pos63	pos64	pos65	pos66 DIAG		
pos51 AXIS	pos52	pos53	pos54	pos55 DIAG			
pos41 AXIS	pos42	pos43	pos44 DIAG				
pos31 AXIS	pos32	pos33 DIAG					
pos21 AXIS	pos22 DIAG						
pos11 CENTER	AXIS	AXIS	AXIS	AXIS	AXIS	AXIS	AXIS

Fig. 10(b). The reactor core's diagonal vs. the axis of the core, in one quarter of a reactor core section

Let us go back to a conventional, PWR context. A typical PWR core generates, by means of 157 assemblies, about 3000 MW (megawatt) — these being thermal — from which about 1000 MW (electrical) are produced. A single fuel rod generates about 80 KW (kilowatt) of thermal energy. One fuel assembly, consisting of 200 to 250 rods, generates about 20 MW (megawatt).

A few of the positions in the reactor core are to house not only a fuel unit, but a control rod as well, which in turn is to be lowered into the position in order to stop the nuclear fission reaction and shut down the reactor. A reactor is to be stopped either for its regular shut-down period (as intended for refueling and maintenance), or because of an emergency. To avoid overheating, liquid coolant (such as pressurized water in the PWR kind of reactor) is necessary, among the fuel rods. In pressurized water reactors, pressure is intended to prevent the water from boiling. We also saw there also exist boiling water reactors, or BWR. "In a conventional pressurized-water reactor (PWR), like the ones at Three Mile Island, water flows through the core, where it is heated under pressure of 2200 pounds per square inch. The water flows through a steam generator, where it turns a second closed loop of water to steam. The steam powers turbines that drive the electric generators. A boiling-water reactor (BWR) operates in a similar way, except that water in the primary loop is only at 1000 pounds per square inch, and so itself turns to steam that is piped directly to the turbines" [36, p. 31].

The *nuclear fuel cycle* includes not only the positioning and depletion of the fuel inside the reactor, but, as well, those stages that take place upstream and downstream of the fuel burning inside the reactor core, from the extraction of the natural uranium ore, through enrichment and fuel assembly manufacturing, down to the disposal of the spent fuel once it is discharged from the reactor (unless it is recycled, where this is permitted: in 1977, the U.S. government banned fuel reprocessing and recycling). There are three parts in the nuclear fuel cycle. "The first part, called Front-End, covers all activities connected with fuel procurement and fabrication. The middle part of the cycle includes fuel reload design activities and the operation of the fuel in the reactor. Back-End comprises all activities ensuring safe separation of spent fuel and radioactive waste from the environment.[17] The individual stages of the fuel cycle are strongly interrelated.[18] Overall economic optimization is very difficult" [64, p. 30].

Importantly, the nuclear fuel cycle of the process is not coincident with periodical shutdown and refuelling (which is in the middle part of the nuclear fuel cycle): along with the three batches of fuel units (fresh, one-burnt, and twice-burnt) that are available for use in the design of the refuelling, there is just one batch (thrice-burnt fuel) that is to be discarded, apart from such fuel units that upon being inspected, are found to be damaged. The fuel units from the two other batches are simply to be repositioned, according to the suitability of their respective degree of depletion. For example, fresh fuel is not to be positioned at the centre of the grid, to avoid too high a localized power density, which could damage the fuel units (or, worse, result in a safety hazard).

The positions in the grid are typified by both (a) the geometry, and (b) other factors. E.g., a' : Is the position on a symmetry diagonal? a'' : How many positions separate the position considered from the center of the core? b' : Is a *control rod* (i.e. a device related to pressurization) located upon the given position?

The actions of mining, refining, purifying, using fissile fuel, and finally disposing of the spent fuel, together make up the *nuclear fuel cycle*. There is a

---

[17] The back-end of the nuclear fuel cycle, when fuel is disposed of, comes in two alternative basic strategies. One of these is *Open cycle:* "the spent fuel is stored in long-term storage and then disposed of in a deep geological repository" [64, p. 30]. The other strategy is *Closed cycle:* "the spent fuel is reprocessed (the nuclear material is separated from the construction material and the products of fission reaction, and is re-used in the new fuel), and only vitrified radioactive waste is disposed of in a deep geological repository (smaller in size than for open cycle)" [64, p. 30].

[18] Optimizing one part of the nuclear fuel cycle may come at a cost in another part. In fact, "optimal designs of fresh fuel have been developed for individual reactors with the aim of making maximum use of the fuel in the reactor. Progress in the alloys used for structural fuel materials has enabled this. However such optimized fuels achieve very high burn-up, and are subjected to very harsh conditions in the core over a long period of time. The number of fuel element failures and the release of radioactivity into the primary circuit coolant has been rising with increasing fuel burn-up. This leads to increased NPP [i.e., nuclear power plant] operational costs and to higher production of waste for treatment and disposal. Greater burn-up of spent fuel also means higher residual heat. Disposal containers must then be spaced further apart. This implies a larger geological repository and higher Back-End costs. Optimization only in one part of the nuclear fuel cycle can thus have an adverse effect on other parts of the fuel cycle" [64, p. 31].

different sense of the term, which is the cycle between two successive refuellings at a nuclear plants, when the reactors of that plant are shut down and the refuelling designed and carried out, and the chain reaction is restarted. That second sense is the sense with which we are concerned.

There are two areas in *fuel management,* within nuclear engineering: **(i)** the management of fuel as kept in store, and **(ii)** the allocation of fuel to be burned in the reactor core during a certain temporal interval between two *refueling points.* Area **(ii)** is the task of the *FUELCON* expert system developed in Beer-Sheva, Israel, in 1986–1990, and of the FUELGEN tool developed in London in in 1994–1996.

4   The Preliminaries of Nuclear Fuel Reload Design

The problem of how to replace depleted fuel assemblies and how to position, inside the reactor core, fresh fuel assemblies and partly depleted fuel assemblies, is the *in-core fuel management problem* (as opposed to the management of fuel kept in store). As energy is produced, fuel becomes depleted. The degree of depletion depends, among the other things, on whether the fuel units considered were entered as part of a fresh fuel batch, or were being reused, at the start of the relevant cycle. In fact, most nuclear plants operate by cycles, whose length is variable, but which are about one year long. A standard textbook on the nuclear fuel cycle has long been Cochran and Tsoulfanidis [22]. In the edition from 1990, Sec. 6 is the one most relevant to our present topic.

Most kinds of nuclear plants practice *annual reload:* the reactor is shut down for a few weeks, and, during this *downtime period,* the reactor is inspected, and a specialized engineer, called the *in-core fuel manager,* has to design a reallocation of fuel units into the core of the reactor. The new allocation is intended for effective power generation during the next *operation cycle.* Once the engineer has provided the design, it is validated: standard simulations are mandated by regulations, for *safety* purposes; moreover, quality is checked in terms of *effectiveness.* Upon approval, the design is implemented: actual refueling takes place [22]. The length of the annual operation cycles at plants, between shutdown periods for refuelling, is variable; so are requirements of power supply. Longer active periods are desirable, economically. Shortening the current downtime period — by making reload design quicker — can save millions of dollars.

5   Batches of Fuel at End-of-Cycle

As mentioned, most kinds of nuclear power reactors operate by discrete, successive power production cycles, and need to be shut down, periodically (more or less, once every year: at "end-of-cycle", or EOC), for inspection and to load a new configuration of fuel. Power production cycles are not standard. Every cycle is unique, and poses a new problem for design; it is typified by specific power demands, availability of fresh fuel, and cycle length (symbolized by K_{eff}) before shutdown. Only part of the new batch is fresh fuel. Typically, one third of all

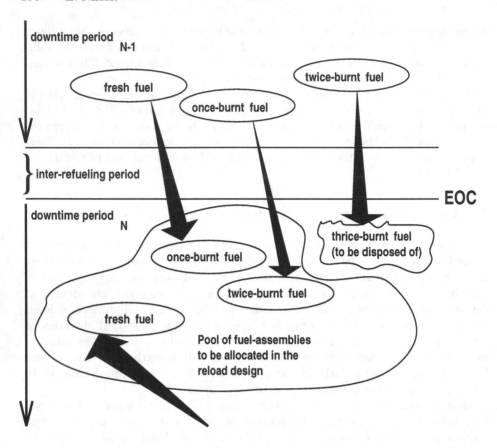

Fig. 11. Fuel assemblies (subdivided in classes of depletion degree), and their involvement in reuse and replenishment for the purposes of the next reload

fuel is replaced, at "beginning-of-cycle" (BOC). Instead, the rest of the fuel is retained from the previous EOC; it is partly depleted fuel (once or twice burnt fuel), and is being reused from the last one or two cycles before the current shutdown. See Fig. 11. The thrice burnt fuel is discharged at EOC, and replaced with fresh fuel. Discarding spent fuel (and, sometimes, reprocessing) is a domain by itself.

Twice burnt fuel has highest burnup degree, and therefore the lowest potency, among the fuel retained for the next cycle; i.e., twice burnt fuel is the kind of fuel assembly with the lowest power density. This constitutes an advantage in terms of manoeuvering, when designing the new arrangement of the contiguous fuel assemblies in the reactor: the spatial power density of the fuel as arranged, indeed, is the main design parameter considered by the fuel manager who has to produce the design.

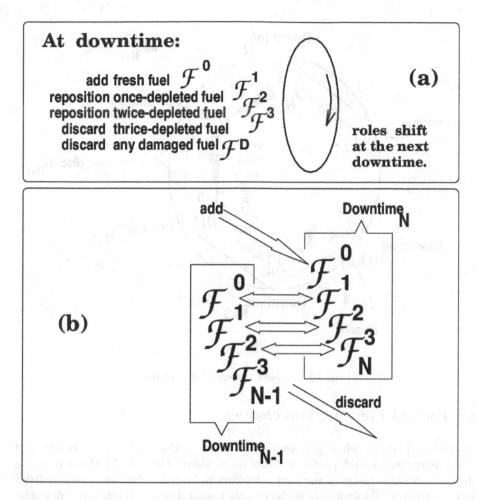

Fig. 12. A notation for batches of fuel, and their shifting role at the next downtime

Fig. 12(a) introduces a notation for the various batches of fuel, along with the operation which is respectively relevant. In order of recency of inclusion into the pool, it is the two batches at the extremes that are concerned by, respectively, addition into the pool, and removal from further use: see Fig. 12(b). At each given regular shut-down out of a sequence, the batches are more depleted, and move down in the sequence as shown in Fig. 12(b). Some fresh fuel is added, and some of the older fuel is discarded: see Fig. 13.

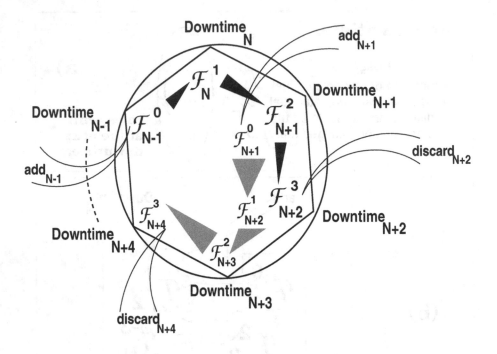

Fig. 13. Looping through types of fuel

6   Factors Limiting Forecasting

Downtime periods, when the reactor does not produce power, are costly, and plant managers would prefer to keep them short. One would think it to be desirable for the design of the next refuelling to be ready for the refuelling itself to be carried out immediately as the reactor is shut down; yet, this is not possible. There is an unavoidable bottleneck. Inspection is necessary, and then the design of a suitable fuel reload may take a few days to accomplish, because not just the design proper, but simulations as well must be carried out. In fact, once the new downtime period arrives, i.e., at end-of-cycle (EOC), the fuel manager could not possibly have a ready-made design for reload, i.e., a tailored, reasonably good configuration that assigns one fuel-assembly (of a given kind) to each single position in the core geometry.

To account for that, it is not enough to point out that each power production cycle is unique; it is, indeed, because of specific power demands, availability of fresh fuel, past cycle length as yielding certain cumulative burnup values for each fuel-assembly, and expected length of the next cycle. The impossibility to prepare the reload design beforehand, stems from the fact the actual situation at each EOC is *not predictable* to any useful degree of exactitude. During the cycle, the fuel becomes depleted, and tentative forecasts of future states are possible

— and simulations are indeed performed — but the final state of the fuel (and of the resulting power densities) is known accurately enough only at EOC, or a few weeks ahead. Uncertainties are such that they invalidate predictions of over two or three months ahead.

Were a design prepared for the next cycle of the particular reactor, as based on forecasts for the end of the current cycle, that solution would not be *robust* enough in front of unforeseen variations, to fit the actual situation at EOC. It is necessary to reach EOC (or, often, to be about to reach it), as an enablement for assessing EOC state and, thus, producing the design for the new cycle. This depends on sensitivity to variations such as irregularities in power supply (stops, or increases that had to be enacted hastily to satisfy sudden demand).

When a reactor is shut down, some fuel assembly may be damaged. Moreover, unforeseen supply requirements (e.g., because of the weather) during the cycle that has just ended may cause the depletion of the fuel, and the length of the cycle, to have been different than planned during the previous shutdown. See Figs. 14 and 15.

Forecasts are not robust enough for reload design to be reliably done and completed before shutdown. On the other hand, every week, or even day, the plant is shut down involves a major cost. If the company is contracted to supply electricity to the region, then it may find itself forced to buy supply from a competitor when unable to provide it itself. Anyway, the industry is characterized by one or a few operators per country, and possibly different regulations in this heavily regulated domain. The plant manager has the interest of designing such a refuelling that will exploit the fuel as efficiently as possible. Oftentimes, this also means getting a longer cycle before shutdown. Vertical integration in the industry, however, may mean that the industry is not really motivated to achieve such efficiency, when it also supplies fuel to the plants. This way, there is regional variation in the factors affecting the economics of refuelling.

Factors and their dependency as involved in the "noise" affecting predictions, may cause forecasts for the state of the reactor core at the next EOC, not to correspond to its actual state at EOC. Uncertainties include (but are not limited to) the following: *(a)* network requirements, depending on the availability of other functioning reactors ("units") in the same plant; *(b)* the availability of other plants (in face of possible technical problems); *(c)* climatic conditions that influence power consumption; and *(d)* the availability of reload-maintenance teams at EOC. The latter is a factor that may shift the reactor shut-down by some weeks.

Downtime periods at plants typically take a few weeks per years, and are costly, in terms of energy not supplied (and the need, for a company, to provide an alternative supply). Good fuel-allocation design strives for efficient peaking during the fuel cycle, and for as long a cycle as possible, but shortening downtime periods is also a goal. Cutting down inactivity periods by just planning ahead before reaching EOC is tentatively possible. Experienced engineers actually do it, but notwithstanding a flexibility window, such forecasting is not robust enough for a ready-made design to be applied to the problem at hand the way it results

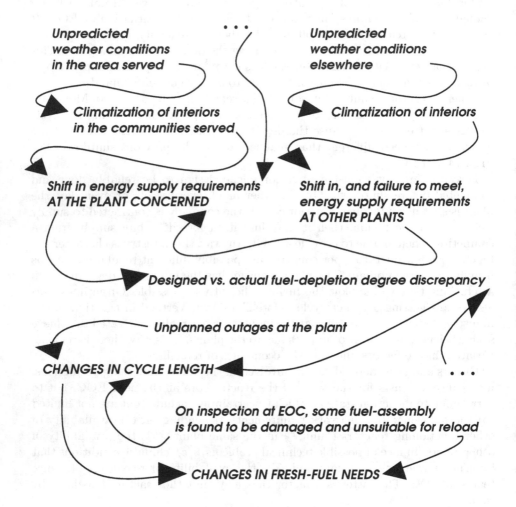

Fig. 14. Factors that contribute to make the state of a given reactor at end of cycle (EOC) not reliably predictable before EOC

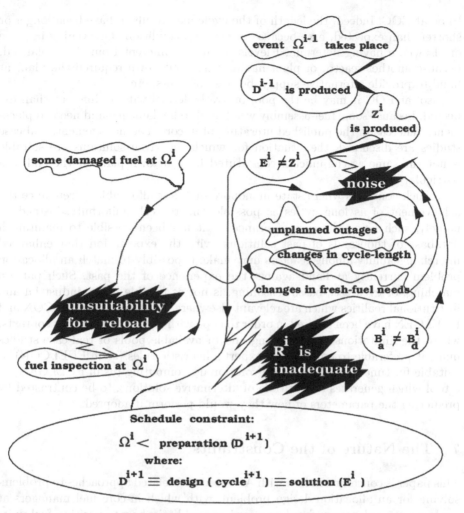

Fig. 15. Factors and their dependency as involved in the "noise" affecting predictions. Why cannot forecasts be robust, and therefore they cannot be finalized, before downtime periods?

Key List:

Ω^i is the end-of-cycle of the ith operation cycle at the given plant.

B_a^i is the actual fuel-burnup cumulated values at Ω^i.

B_d^i is the designed fuel-burnup cumulated values at Ω^i.

D^i is the design of the in-core fuel-allocation for the ith operation cycle.

E^i is the actual end-of-cycle of the reactor core once the ith operation cycle is completed.

Z^i is forecasts for the state of the reactor core at the end of the ith operation cycle at the given plant.

R^i is the robustness of solutions for the in-core fuel-management problem (i.e., of such fuel-configurations that may be designed for fuel-reload into the core) as devised for Z^i.

to be at EOC. Indeed, the length of the cycle may result to have been longer or shorter than expected, e.g., because of climatic conditions intervening in place or elsewhere having determined levels of supply different from those planned, because another reactor or plant having been shut down required the plant at hand to provide alternative supply, because of faults, etc.

Also, at EOC it may be the pool of available fuel will be different than expected, because some fuel-assembly was found to be damaged and needs replacement. Whereas in the published literature of in-core fuel management, real case studies are discussed, the situation for which the given solutions are suitable is not the same as the unicum constituted by your own plant at the end of a particular cycle.

In such countries where state monopoly makes it affordable to renounce the achievement of as long cycles as possible and to seek uniformity, instead — namely, such being the case of France — it has been possible to maintain a database of thousands of past solutions, with the expectation that enhanced interchangeability among reactors may make it possibly to match an allocation problem currently at hand against the experience of the past. Such pattern matching, or even case-based reasoning, is not as feasible in the industrial and institutional realities which are relevant elsewhere. Tools such as FUELCON and FUELGEN have been devised in order to cope with such heterogeneous contexts, where the limitations of forecasting and of available pools of real-case studies make it preferable to embody the expert's heuristic rules (as in FUELCON) or suitable finetuned parameters for evolutionary computing (as in FUELGEN) in a tool which generates a multitude of alternative solutions, to be contrasted by predicting the parameters of how they would perform if adopted.

7   The Nature of the Constraints

This paper is concerned indeed with AI-based and related approaches to problem-solving for an allocation design problem, with which in-core fuel managers at nuclear power plants are faced on a peri-annual basis: how to position fuel-units in the reactor core (whose planar section is a symmetrical grid), in order to achieve longer, and usually better performance during the operation period up to the next EOC point (end of cycle), when over a new downtime period the allocation problem will have to be solved again. We have seen that forecasting in this domain is not accurate enough to enable the preparation of robust solutions before the reactor has actually been shut down, and the depletion degree of the fuel-units, let alone their possibly damaged status, can be ascertained. Various approaches exist. Westinghouse's LPOP is based on backcalculation from a target power-distribution.

In contrast, the FUELCON expert system applies a heuristic ruleset and generates alternative candidate solutions by the hundreds, these being then simulated for parameter prediction, and visualized as "clouds" of dots in the plane of power peaking and cycle length. FUELCON's successor, FUELGEN, applies evolutionary computing.

During the operation cycle (other than at downtime periods), as there is no state observability for such variables which require direct inspection, current state estimates are based on those parameters which are observable instead, along with the forecast that was obtained by simulation at downtime, so that current state estimates partly depend on future states [119].

We have already seen that there exist different kinds of fuel, in terms of depletion. For the purposes of fuel reload pattern design, the relevant criterion of classification is how many times the fuel unit has already been used. This is reflected in a *cumulated burnup* degree. Once a reactor is shut down, not all of the fuel from the activity period just concluded is dumped. Just such fuel that has been used during three cycles is disposed of, and replaced with *fresh fuel*. Instead, fuel that was used once *(once-burnt)*, or twice *(twice-burnt)*, is put back into the *fuel inventory*, that also includes some fresh fuel. Fuel is costly. The assemblies in the inventory at the plant are the pool from which to pick one fuel-unit per position in the grid. This is one constraint, concerning resources, and is of an *economical* nature. The geometry of the core is a *structural* constraint; each reactor has its own individuality. There are *safety* constraints: e.g. fresh fuel must not be placed in the central region of the grid, lest overheating would make cooling ineffective. (Less dramatically than a disaster, local overheating in some region of the core could damage some fuel-unit, making it unfit for reuse.)

8   Reload-Design Automation: What the State of the Art Was Before FUELCON

In 1991, a team from Westinghouse Electric Corporation pointed out a need [18]:

> Pressurized water reactor core designs have become more complex and must meet a plethora of design constraints. Trends have been toward longer cycles with increased discharge burnup, increased burnable absorber (BA) number,[19] mixed BA types, reduced radial leakage, axially blanketed fuel, and multiple-batch feed fuel regions. Obtaining economical reload core loading patterns (LPs) that meet design criteria is a difficult task to do manually. Automated LP search tools are needed. An LP search tool cannot possibly perform an exhaustive search because of the sheer size of the combinatorial problem. On the other hand, evolving complexity of the design features and constraints often invalidates expert rules based on past design experiences.

The consecutive waves of methods from computing — linear programming from operations research; then, expert systems based on heuristic rulesets, and other knowledge-based systems from artificial intelligence; and then again, artificial neural networks; next, genetic algorithms, and finally, hybrid methods combining the above — had a major impact in nuclear engineering over the

---

[19] Burnable absorbers are burnable "poisons", which slow down the chain reaction. We are going to discuss burnable poisons later.

1980s and 1990s, and I was fortunate in that I was able to participate in these developments in computational methods for designing reactor refuellings.

Let us consider what the state of the art was, when it comes to applying computing to refuelling, before the FUELCON project. There existed tools for assisting the practitioner in designing fuel reload [131]. In 1992, Parks and Lewins [131] outlined three categories of computerized tools for in-core fuel management: *manual design packages* (the engineer's own expertise is applied, and software only assists with calculations for analyzing the reactor core physics, and for visualizing the data); *expert systems* (which, like FUELCON, have a ruleset prune the search space, seeking good configurations); and *optimization packages*. One such package is Westinghouse's LPOP, described in 1991 by Alsop et al. [2, 18], and whose conceptual structure we illustrate in Fig. 16. LPOP adopts an integer programming (near-)optimization procedure that starts from a target power distribution and calculates backwards how to obtain it, by matching the available fuel inventory. In 1991, Chao et al. [18] claimed:

> Westinghouse has developed a sophisticated loading pattern search methodology. This methodology is embodied in the LPOP code, which Westinghouse nuclear designers use extensively. The LPOP code generates a variety of LPs meeting design constraints and performs a two-cycle economic evaluation of the generated LPs [i.e., loading

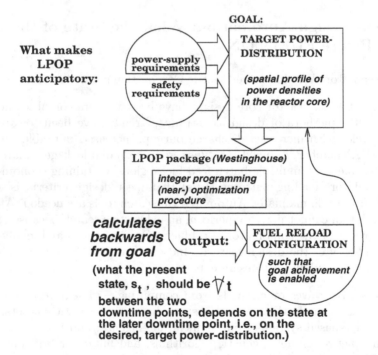

Fig. 16. The conceptual structure of Westinghouse's LPOP optimization package. A reload pattern is produced by backward calculation, from an input target power distribution, by matching input requirements and the available fuel inventory.

patterns]. The designer selects the most appropriate patterns for fine tuning and evaluation by the design codes.

There are tools that just help with either computations or graphics, to perform single steps in the design procedure, whereas the overall procedure is manual. Tools from another class embody some optimization method from operations research, as customized for the task. Algorithms adopted there, do not transparently reflect the intuitive rules of thumb of the human expert. *Observability* in the space of solutions is very reduced, so such tools just seek one solution that is admissible, and, if possible, locally optimal. Generally, one solution for the *in-core fuel management problem* is one full configuration of core-position/fuel-assembly allocation, for the entire core. It will be referred to as *configuration* for short.

There used to be computer programs that did not incorporate artificial intelligence techniques.[20] For fuel reload pattern design, there had been one or two attempts to apply AI, but these did not depart from the conception of manual design as seeking just one solution [141]. Typically, a given solution, known — e.g. from some published case-study — to have suited a different situation, was adapted to the new situation. This was done by means of a series of *shuffles*, i.e. by switching the positions of two (or more) fuel-assemblies. See Fig. 17. Adaptation can be by shuffling indeed, i.e., by swapping again and again the positions of two (or more) fuel assemblies in the one-eighth slice of the core, and evaluating by simulation whether the configuration obtained is safe, could keep the nuclear reaction going long enough, and is efficient. Conceptually, such a procedure is depth-first search, with shuffles constituting backtracking. Rules check whether the candidate shuffle is admissible. Thereafter, simulation has to check whether the new solution is admissible for the problem at hand, i.e. for the given reactor after a given operation cycle.

Bernard and Washio [8] surveyed ongoing projects applying expert system technology to nuclear engineering. For refuelling in particular, two kinds of tasks have had expert systems or prototypes deal with them:

- the repositioning of fuel-units based on the physical constraints of a crane having to take out, transfer and reinsert the unit in another position in the grid which represents the core,

---

[20] For example, while guest-editing a journal special issue in 1996 concerning intelligent technologies for nuclear and electric power systems, I had contacted Ben Rouben, of Atomic Energy of Canada Ltd. in Mississauga, Ontario, Canada, hoping to obtain a paper submission concerning a CANDU reactor. I received a reply (dated 4 December 1996) which among the other things stated: "I am Manager of Reactor Core Physics at AECL, and I'm afraid that up to now we have not really applied the methods you mention. I had, several years ago, produced a computer program to automatically select (or help the reactor operator select) fuel channels for the (on-line) refuelling of CANDU reactors, however this was a good old FORTRAN program, not one in the fancy new AI methods." In nuclear engineering in general, other than for refuelling, there had been applications of artificial intelligence (e.g., [104, 110, 105, 109]).

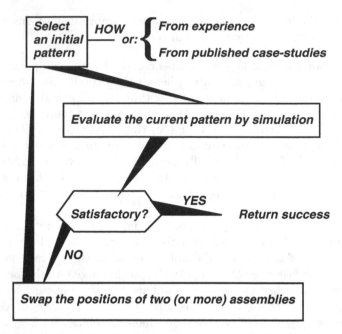

Fig. 17. The shuffling loop in the traditional practice of core reload design

- and designing such a reload of the fuel while deliberately ignoring such lo-
  gistics of the material operation, and while focusing on the benefits in terms
  of effective power peaking in the successive states of the reactor core, and
  of length of the period over which the nuclear fission can be usefully sustained (for example, one year and a half instead of just one year), as well as
  (of course) in terms of safety (the power peaking being sustained, yet not
  excessive).

A project in the former category was NUCLEXPERT, described by Jardon and
Dubois [72]. Quite possibly, an incentive for such a focus on the first version of
the task, instead of the second option, may have been grounded in an approach
to (or culture of) nuclear power as known from the French national context: the
state has a monopoly, and moreover the provision of fuel and the management
of nuclear power plants is integrated vertically, so that the national strategy is
to have reactors refuelled on a strictly annual basis, with no attempt to achieve
longer operation periods between successive shutdowns of the reactor. Whereas
vertical integration is also found in the United States, managers of the individual
plants there (as opposed to the company-level decision-making typical of the
United Kingdom) have the interest of increasing the temporal distance between
shutdowns, apart from the generalized requirement that downtime periods be
kept short (they usually take a few weeks).

This is not to say that in the United States there had been no attempt to devise expert systems that would approach refuelling from the perspective of planning crane movements. "Expert systems have also been developed to assist with scheduling the movements of fuel assemblies. One such system is CLEO, which was developed at Hanford for use in the Fast Flux Test Facility [152, 153]. Moreover, EPRI,[21] in conjunction with Intellicorp and the Virginia Electric Power Company, developed a prototype expert system [99, 100], which planned crane movements for the fuel insert shuffle of a PWR" [8, p. 41].[22] Joseph Naser, Robert Colley, John Gaiser, Thomas Brookmire, and Steven Engle [100] explained as follows the advantages of using their shuffling system, over manual design of fuel reload:

> The development of the fuel insert shuffle expert system [...] shows that the [widely recognized] potential benefits [of expert systems in the nuclear power industry] are realizable. Currently, the development of the insert shuffle plan requires three to four man-weeks of effort. Further modifications to this plan are sometimes required due to either changes in the desired core load pattern or damaged fuel assemblies or inserts. These changes generally require two to four man-days of effort and could be stressful if they are critical path items on the outage schedule. Lastly,

---

[21] EPRI is the Electric Power Research Institute in Palo Alto, California.

[22] To give an idea of the spectrum of applications of expert system technology at power plants and nuclear plants by 1987, consider that Naser et al. [99] appeared in the *Proceedings of the 1987 Conference on Expert-System Applications in Power Plants*, held in Boston, MA, May 27–29, 1987. That conference (http://www.gbv.de/dms/tib-ub-hannover/017148499.pdf) had sessions on applying expert systems to power plant operations, on applying them to fossil power plants, on applying them to power plant diagnostics, as well as on applying them to nuclear power plants (this being the fifth session).

The session on nuclear power plants comprised papers about "An Expert System for Technical Specifications", by G. Finn, F. Whittum, and R. Bone from Stone and Webster Engineering Co.; "A Fuel Insert Shuffle Planner Expert System" by J. Naser and R. Colley of EPRI (i.e., the Electric Power Research Institute, in Palo Alto, California), J. Gaiser of Intellicorp, T. Brookmire of the Virginia Electric Power Company, and S. Engle, of Expert-EASE Systems, Inc.

In that same session on nuclear power plants, the other papers were: "Expert System Application to Fault Diagnosis and Procedure Synthesis", by B. Hajek, S. Hashemi, R. Bhatnagar, D. Miller, and J. Stasenko, from the Ohio State University; "Realm: An Expert System for Classifying Emergencies", by R. Touchton and A. Gunter of Technology Applications, Inc., and D. Cain of EPRI; "TRIBES – A CPC/CEAC Trip Buffer Expert System", by R. Lang (of Middle South Utilities System Services); "A Production System for Computerized Emergency Procedures Tracking ", by W. Petrick, K. Ng, and C. Stuart (of Nuclear Software Services) and D. Cain (of EPRI); "CSRL Application to Nuclear Power Plant Diagnosis and Sensor Data Validation", by S. Hashemi, W. Punch and B. Hajek (Ohio State University); and "An Expert System Technology for Work Authorization Information Systems", by J. Munchausen, K. Glazer (Southern California Edison Company), the latter paper's application being to staff working at nuclear power plants.

the personnel that perform the plan development are often reassigned to other responsibilities, taking with them their experience and developed intuitive skills. It is anticipated that once the expert system is integrated into the current process, the entire process will take no more than a day. The expertise already captured will continue to be available and can be improved as more strategies are tried and the experience is encoded.

Samary Baranov, a formerly Soviet researcher who was a colleague of mine in Beer-Sheva, at one time "developed — for application at Soviet nuclear plants — a method by which a solution algorithm is converted into an optimized logic circuit design for incorporation into the hardware. (Baranov's conversion procedure is independent of the application domain, and was exemplified in several ways, in [a book of 1994 (see especially [5])] which however does not include the by now [in 1998] old, but as yet unpublished application to nuclear power plants)", I wrote in a survey [104].

9 Early Prototypes or Tools in the Same Category as FUELCON

With reference to the two categories of application of expert system technology to refuellings, as pointed out by Bernard and Washio [8] and which we mentioned in the previous section, arguably the earliest project in the second category — the one which tries to achieve good solutions in the plane whose two dimensions are power peaking and cycle length — were:

- FUELCON [46, 113, 78, 53, 45, 52, 48, 57, 107] (cf. [42]); as well as
- a prototype whose ongoing development had been reported in 1988 in Rothleder et al. [141], and previously (in 1986) in Poetschhat et al. [138], and by Faught in 1987 [34].

In 1991, Tahara [158] reported about an expert system for reshuffling, i.e., like the previous project but unlike FUELCON, emulating the way a human expert would try to generate an admissible and hopefully good fuel allocation into the positions of the grid representing the reactor core; FUELCON, instead, generates many candidate fuel-configurations at once and, which is what matters in the above respect, ex nihilo. Another tool for reload design is AUTOLOAD, described in 1994 by Li and Levine [86]; in AUTOLOAD, an expert system with heuristic rules is integrated with search by means of the SCAM-W algorithm.

As to our project FUELGEN, it is based on genetic algorithms — the viva for Jun Zhao's doctoral project was in 1996 [176] — it, too, came early, and in 1996 was at the forefront in terms of efficiency as reported. Other early attempts to apply genetic algorithms to refuelling include the ones reported by DeChaine and Feltus in 1995 and 1996 [23–25], by Poon briefly as early as 1990 [139] (cf. [140]), and (at the University of Cambridge) Parks in 1995 and 1996 [128, 129]. In 1992, Parks and Lewins had reported in one page [131] about the state of the art of in-core fuel management and optimization.

10   The Contribution Made by FUELCON

The expert system, FUELCON, in whose design I was fortunate to participate, was a major contribution to the application domain, where it got a good
reception. [53] is a detailed description oriented to an audience of scholars in
artificial intelligence. Ambitions, with FUELCON, were of global optimization.
FUELCON generates not one, but hundreds of alternative configurations per
session. A heuristic ruleset finds a good position for a given fuel-assembly, and
this is done recursively, until the entire core is filled with all of the available fuel
units. Basically, search is breadth-first. There is no backtracking. The output of
the generation module is fed to *NOXER,* a simulator using *nodal algorithms*
(NOXER was developed by Meir Segev, a professor who used to share with Alex
Galperin the same office).

The numeric results of NOXER are visualized. Each configuration is displayed
as a dot in the cartesian plane of two parameters: x is *boron concentration at
EOC* (i.e. at the *end of the cycle* concluded by the current downtime period),
and has to be maximized. As to y, it is *power peaking:* $y < \bar{y}$ defines the *admis-
sibility window,* whose "southwestern" corner is at the origin of the coordinates.
Instead, configurations above $\bar{y}$ are unsafe. As FUELCON produced hundreds of
alternative solutions, a "cloud" of solutions is displayed in the plane. Sometimes,
none is safe. Or, then, some are, but they are not satisfactory, because $x < \bar{x}$.
The interesting region is $y < \bar{y} \wedge x > \bar{x}$.

Whereas the practitioner may be satisfied with being able to pick one configuration that happens to be in a good region, the domain expert, when using
FUELCON, may wish to move the "cloud" of solutions into a "southeast" direction, in order to get several configurations that are both safe and very efficient.
S/he may wish to test new heuristics, or to concentrate search (by focusing:
zooming) on a cluster of interesting configurations, previously unknown to researchers in the domain. To do so, s/he manually revises the ruleset.

Once the domain expert takes notice of interesting solutions in the visualized
results of simulation, he or she will typically want to focus exploration during
the next iteration of FUELCON: in terms of how the results of both iterations
are going to be visualized, the new iteration is wanted to *zoom* on the restricted
region affected, in the search-space. This is done by revising the ruleset by making general rules more particular, or by having some rule exclude other regions.
More exactly, as mandatory rules remain the same (which does not mean we cannot insert some additional elimination rules that are not mandatory, to exclude
certain search-subspaces), it is the preference rules (including added elimination
rules) that actually typify the particular session, by defining the current sub-
space of possibilities to be searched. Whereas such delimitation does exclude the
rest of the total space, in FUELCON those regions of the space that are included

are searched *exhaustively* for solutions, to prevent missing interesting options [46, 53].[23]

In [57, Sec. 3], we pointed out that one of the advantages of FUELCON has to do with *isomorphism*. By "isomorphism", it is meant that in the model, mapping is element by element as in the same relationship. There is an advantage, with FUELCON, in that the allocation problem is solved similarly when the design specifications for solving the in-core fuel management problem for pressurized water reactors is with or without BP, i.e., with use being or not being made of the so-called *burnable poisons* (i.e., rods of neutron absorbers inserted in part of the fuel assemblies, to better control reactivity). In contrast, when using other such computer tools that handle both kinds, handling with and without burnable poisons is quite different, and the procedures look very much apart.

> To control large amounts of excess fuel reactivity without control rods, burnable poisons are loaded into the core. Burnable poisons are materials that have a high neutron absorption cross section that are converted into materials of relatively low absorption cross section as the result of neutron absorption. Due to the burn-up of the poison material, the negative reactivity of the burnable poison decreases over core life. Ideally, these poisons should decrease their negative reactivity at the same rate that the fuel's excess positive reactivity is depleted. Fixed burnable poisons are generally used in the form of compounds of boron or gadolinium that are shaped into separate lattice pins or plates, or introduced as additives to the fuel. Since they can usually be distributed more uniformly than control rods, these poisons are less disruptive to the core's power distribution. Fixed burnable poisons may also be discretely loaded in specific locations in the core in order to shape or control flux profiles to prevent excessive flux and power peaking near certain regions of the reactor. Current practice however is to use fixed non-burnable poisons in this service.[24]

Burnable poisons were discovered by Alvin Radkowsky, who was chief scientist at the U.S.'s Navy nuclear propulsion program (the chief scientist of the Nuclear Propulsion Division of the U.S. Bureau of Ships), then moved to Israel in 1972, and

---

[23] From the *ergonomical* viewpoint, i.e., of the way FUELCON is used by the human expert to develop new knowledge, there is some kinship with the so-called *expert critic* paradigm of expert systems. When in 1992 Silverman [150, 151] defined the paradigm, he pointed out that several extant expert systems embody the paradigm to some degree, without developers ever meaning it. This was the case of FUELCON, indeed; it was only upon completion of the project the way it has been described here, well after industrial demos have been given, that the system was reanalyzed in terms of the paradigm proposed by Silverman: see [53, Sec. 13]. Galperin and his doctoral student, Kimhi, carried out experiments on the data of published real-case studies, and a body of knowledge was developed not only about how to formulate good rules of thumb for generating reload configurations, but also about how to use the tool itself, FUELCON. A new ergonomical procedure had been developed, in which the human expert makes trials and has the tool validate or refute his expectations: this can be assimilated to a critic's role.

[24] http://en.wikipedia.org/wiki/Nuclear_poison

was Alex Galperin's doctoral supervisor.[25] Radkowsky was prized in 1964 for his invention of the burnable poison method, which made nuclear-powered submarines possible.[26]

---

[25] Alvin Radkowsky (1915–2002) was a student of Edward Teller before the Second World War. He supervised Alex Galperin doctoral project in Israel. I in turn learned whatever I know about the structure and the operation of nuclear reactors from Alex Galperin (or at any rate, whatever else I was able to learn was made possible by what I had learnt from him). At one point I declined his offer that apart from my doctorate in computer science, I also pursue a doctorate in nuclear engineering.

[26] Radkowsky was 82 in 1997, when *The Jerusalem Report* published an article about him, and his plans for thorium reactors that would eliminate plutonium as a byproduct of conventional fission reactors, as plutonium could become raw material for building nuclear bombs, and for nuclear terrorism. In Radkowsky's fuel assembly design for the core of his thorium reactors, the *seed fuel* — which when it breaks down, irradiates and transforms the *blanket fuel* surrounding it into materials that also provide energy — is enriched uranium, whereas the blanket is mainly thorium. Radkowsky mixed some uranium into the blanket, so that the isotopes produced cannot undergo fission, and therefore cannot be used for building a bomb. It was Edward Teller who urged Radkowsky to develop such a design that would provide an alternative to the usual designs of light-water reactors, which produce plutonium as a byproduct: it takes as little as four kilograms of plutonium to build a bomb big enough to blow up a small city. In the late 1990s, the nearly 400 light-water commercial reactors worldwide "annually produce roughly 70 tons of plutonium as a byproduct. Enough, that is, to produce approximately 17,500 of those 4-kilo bombs" [174, p. 24].

"The proliferation potential of the light water reactor fuel cycle may be significantly reduced by utilization of thorium as a fertile component of the nuclear fuel" [56, p. 265]. The concept of the Radkowsky Thorium Reactor (RTR) was presented in the paper [56], which in 1997 stated: "So far the concept has been applied to a Russian design of a 1,000 MWe pressurized water reactor, known as a VVER-1000, and designated as VVERT" [56, p. 265]. As intended for Russian reactors, which have a core geometry of adjacent hexagons, fuel assemblies have an hexagonal section. The seed is an inner hexagon inside the fuel assembly section, and it is surrounded by a wider hexagon, with the blanket fuel rods fitting between the two hexagons [56, Fig. 2 on p. 272]. "The amount of plutonium contained in the RTR spent fuel stockpile is reduced by 80 percent in comparison with a VVER of a current design" [56, p. 265]. "This barrier, in combination with existing safeguard measures and procedures is adequate to unambiguously disassociate civilian nuclear power from military nuclear power" [56, p. 265].

Radkowsky "spent 24 years designing propulsion systems for the U.S.'s Navy's first nuclear-powered submarines, aircraft carriers and ships. And he's drawn the blueprints for dozens of nuclear reactors, including the first commercial one in Shippingport, Pennsylvania, in the 1950s" [174, p. 24]. "Histories of the development of the U.S.'s first nuclear submarines, the Nautilus and the Seawolf, highlight the tough, domineering Admiral Hyman George Rickover, who directed the subs' construction. Radkowski, who served as the brains behind the project, doesn't even get a footnote" [174, p. 25].

The use of thorium in light water reactors is the subject of [137, 162, 97, 58, 59, 163]. Earlier on, in 1984, Galperin [41] was concerned with the use of thorium in light water reactors, and in 1986, Galperin [43] discussed the feasibility of using thorium as fuel in CANDU reactors.

(Incidentally, by *poison* it is not meant that it would poison humans — of course such stuff would — but it is rather meant that it is such material that could slow down or shut down a reactor; this is called *poisoning* the reactor. Poison is contaminating material which degrades performance as intended, or, mark this, is actually intended to degrade performance, in which case one speaks about a *deliberate poison*. In general, *poison* as meant in nuclear engineering and in physics is "Any contaminating material which, because of high-absorption cross-section, degrades intended performance, eg fission in a nuclear reactor, radiation from a phosphor" [170, p. 888, s.v.]. In chemistry, *catalytic poison* is "A substance which inhibits the activity of a catalyst. Also *anticatalyst*" [170, p. 180, s.v.]. Poisons are intended to either slow down fission, or to shut down a reactor. We have been concerned with gadolinium being used as a burnable poison. "Natural gadolinium has a high neutron capture cross-section of 49 000 barns and is expensive, but gadolinium oxide has been used as a *burnable poison* during the start-up of reactors and in nitrate form as a deliberate poison during the shutdown of *CANDU* reactors" [170, p. 488, s.v. *gadolinium*]. In physics, *barn* is defined as a "Unit of effective cross-sectional area of nucleus equal to 10^{-28}m^2. So called, because it was pointed out that although one barn is a very small unit of area, to an elementary particle the size of an atom which could capture it is 'as big as a barn door'" [170, p. 96, s.v.].).

The context is explained by Ladislav Havlíček [64, p. 30]:

As fissionable isotopes are gradually consumed in the reactor core, due to their depletion a chain reaction is not longer sustainable under safe conditions. Reactor operation must be halted. During outage the most depleted nuclear fuel is replaced by fresh fuel and the quantity of fissionable isotopes in the reactor (core reactivity) is increased again. In fact, the reactivity in the core must be excessive at the beginning of the cycle in order to enable 12 months or longer operation of the reactor. Such excessive reactivity must be compensated at the beginning of the reactor cycle by burnable absorbers integrated in the fuel (gadolinium or boron based), control clusters and boron acid concentration in the primary circuit. In case of a 12-month cycle between two refueling outages, 1/4-1/5 of the fuel inventory in the reactor core is changed. In the case of a 18-month cycle, roughly 1/3 of the fuel is reloaded, and in case of a 24-month cycle about 1/2 is changed. Partly used fuel remaining in the core is repositioned and / or rotated.

In particular [64, p. 31]:

Because there is an upper limit of 5% on the enrichment level used in fresh fuel (an administratively imposed limit aimed at preventing misuse of nuclear material for military purposes), the total theoretical reactivity in fresh fuel is limited. At the same time, there is another limit on the amount of reactivity loaded into reactor in fresh fuel during an outage, as the power distribution curve in the reactor core must fulfill certain conditions during the whole cycle. With the use of burnable absorbers reactivity can be temporarily suppressed but at an additional cost.

Whether burnable poisons are included or not, the problem-solving of the allocation problem is similar, when one uses FUELCON. This is just a reflection of the fact that in FUELCON, modelling is isomorphic with the rules of thumb of the human expert's professional cognition. Other approaches, instead, strive to achieve the goals of the expert by means of contrived procedures that refurbish optimization techniques from operations research. Or, then, knowledge-based systems that perform shuffling (binary swapping of core positions starting from an initial reload pattern), do replicate the human expert's procedure, but instead of rendering (like FUELCON) the operational knowledge of the expert fuel manager about the effect of given kinds of fuel in given regions of the core, they embody a step-by-step replica of those manual procedures that are dictated by the observational and calculational limitations of the human expert.

Another kind of isomorphism is achieved in the visualization of solutions as a cloud of dots plotted on the screen. When the expert user tries to improve on the cloud, by revising the "preference rules" in the ruleset, he conceives of that as aiming to move the cloud to a better region in the plane of the parameters predicted by the simulator for the solutions plotted. to involve substantial change in the size of the set of configurations. The cardinality of the set of configurations can be expected to remain about the same. If, instead, the improved version of the ruleset is meant to achieve "zooming", by focusing on a trend displayed by some preference rules, then, by definition, the family of generated configurations becomes smaller, or denser: a priori, the generated set of configurations converges on a smaller region of the search space, i.e., the generator looks for solutions that are less apart from each other. No identical configurations are generated inside the tree, because this is explicitly prevented by a suitable constraint in the tree-generation algorithm. However, when the ruleset is revised for zooming, the configurations in the output set will tend to be more similar: both in respect of the way fuel assemblies are positioned inside the core-geometry, and in respect of where the dots are going to be plotted in the bidimensional space of the simulation parameters being visualized. The spread of the configurations dotting that plane, i.e., how much they are apart, is reduced by zooming; moreover, two or more distinct configurations will be more likely to be visualized as one dot, or as a heap of overlapping dots. Far from being an inconvenient, this just reflects success at achieving zooming as a goal of ruleset revision.

11   How FUELCON Executes

The main part of the FUELCON expert system is a solution-space generator based on the beam-search algorithm, thus, a combination of the best-first and breadth-first methods. Solution space expansion is performed in a tree level by level, and, at each level, several best branches are developed — the rest of the branches being discarded, which makes backtracking impossible. In FUELCON, the algorithm is applied to the generation of a tree, where each level corresponds to one fuel assembly to be positioned in the reactor core (with different core cells corresponding to the various branches on the same level in the tree). The method is adequate for the application. Chronological backtrack, i.e., revoking the last placed assembly, would be ineffective with regard to improving the current configuration, and no alternative backtracking method was envisioned.

Two kinds of knowledge are resorted to: (a) basic knowledge in reactor physics and termal hydraulic principles; and (b) specific local heuristic knowledge, related to the positions in the core geometry, and to the degree of depletion of the fuel to be positioned there. This knowledge is represented, in FUELCON, in if-then rule format. There are two subsets within the ruleset: "elimination rules" (which are mandatory, and dictated by safety considerations), and "preference rules", which express a policy of design, and make one version of the ruleset peculiar with respect to other potential and permissible versions of the ruleset. The loading sequence of the fuel assemblies is given, and is dictated by heuristic considerations.

A set of predefined heuristic rules is executed recursively by FUELCON's control component: see Fig. 18(a). As mentioned, the ruleset of FUELCON comprises a few rules, *elimination rules,* which constitute mandatory avoidance constraints (to prevent too high local power densities in the reactor core), and a few more rules, *preference rules,* which vary according to the performance-seeking strategy to be

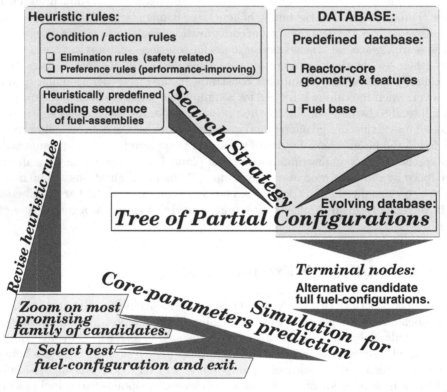

Fig. 18(a). How FUELCON executes. Structure and control of FUELCON.

adopted. Moreover, the loading sequence of the fuel assemblies is also heuristically predefined, and is a given, in the same way the rules are. Such heuristic knowledge is applied to the data in the stable database of the problem at hand (the geometric structure of the core's symmetric slice, the positions at which the control rods are located, the pool of available fuel assemblies). The ruleset is executed, determining which nodes to generate (or, instead, avoid generating) as, level by level, a tree is being built: see Fig. 18(b).

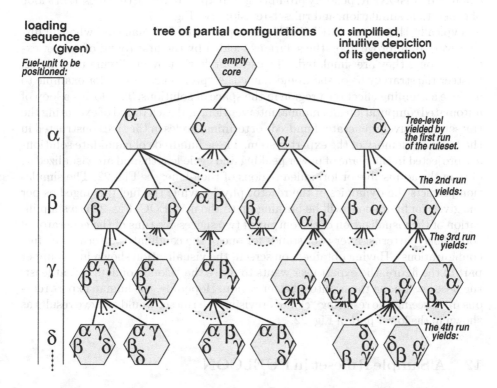

loading sequence (given)

Fuel-unit to be positioned:

tree of partial configurations

(a simplified, intuitive depiction of its generation)

Fig. 18(b). How FUELCON executes. Tree generation in FUELCON.

The tree levels correspond to a given fuel-unit out of the given loading sequence. The terminal nodes will be alternative fuel configurations (i.e., fuel reload patterns). Nonterminals are partial configurations. At any given level in the tree, the sibling nodes display the grid of the reactor core; those fuel-units corresponding to tree-levels which are upper than the current level, appear to be positioned as inherited, i.e., in the way selected for the relevant ancestor-nonterminal of the given node (i.e., each node inherits the partial configuration having been constructed along the path leading to the node itself). Moreover, the fuel-unit corresponding to the given tree-level is positioned differently in those nodes (of the same given level) whose immediate ancestor is the same. The solution-space generator is based on the beam-search algorithm, thus, we have there a combination of the best-first and breadth-first methods. Solution space expansion is performed in the tree, and, at each level, several best branches are developed; the rest of the branches are discarded, which makes backtracking impossible.

Fig. 19 relates the two parts of the ruleset (namely, the elimination rules and the preference rules) to the parts of the database of FUELCON, based on the overall flow of control. The ruleset being run, gradually fills the positions (see Fig. 20) in a growing set of alternative candidate configurations, that then are visualized and simulated by NOXER, possibly prompting the expert to revise the ruleset, in a loop of generation, simulation, and ruleset-revision (see Fig. 21).

Typically, the user of FUELCON is an experienced fuel manager, who will further want to improve upon the solutions yielded by the first round of ruleset execution, once they are simulated. The user can do that by modifying the ruleset: to steer the strategy he or she would refine the "preference rules", for example to achieve a zooming effect on a region in the space of solutions. This forms a loop of automated computation and manual intervention, and each round of executing the ruleset, recursively generates hundreds of terminal nodes in the tree constructed in the working memory of the expert system. These hundreds of candidate solutions are projected in the plane of power peaking and cycle length, and are visualized as dots in the admissible or forbidden regions of the plane; see Fig. 22. The simulation predicts the dynamics of the reactor physics while the fuel (arranged as per the given configuration) will be burning up to the next EOC. Fig. 22 is a simplification of the visualization of the output of two successive runs of the generator of core reload patterns. Every dot stands for one of the candidate patterns (i.e., fuel configurations). Having obtained, on screen, the visualization shown in the upper part of the figure, the expert user wants to move the "cloud" of dots (or, at least, the best few among them) into a better region. Hopefully, the human expert reckons upon seeing the resulting "cloud", revising the ruleset would achieve results as shown in the lower part of Fig. 22.

12   A Sample Ruleset in FUELCON

In the heuristics corresponding to the rules in the ruleset, much relevant knowledge is not made explicit. Actually, several of the configurations generated and retained by the generator can be expected to be found unsafe, or inefficient, or both, once the simulator will carry out reactor physics calculations and plot the dots for those configurations in the unsafe region, or with a short-cycle coordinate, in the plane of the two parameters predicted: power peaking and cycle length.

When the fuel manager approaches the task of designing a new arrangement for the fuel in the core, the solution procedure may be regarded as a multi-stage process with a series of design decisions taken successively. The main design parameter considered by the engineer is the spatial power density in the core, as resulting from the power density of each fuel assembly. Physical properties of different materials, which make up the reactor core and what it contains, are described by complicated functions of energy and space. An accurate evaluation of the spatial power distribution (as simulated, e.g., by NOXER) involves a series of complex and lengthy

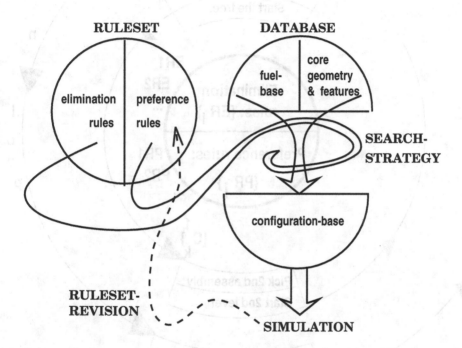

Fig. 19. The subcomponents of the ruleset and the database of FUELCON, and relationship between them within the control flow of FUELCON's execution

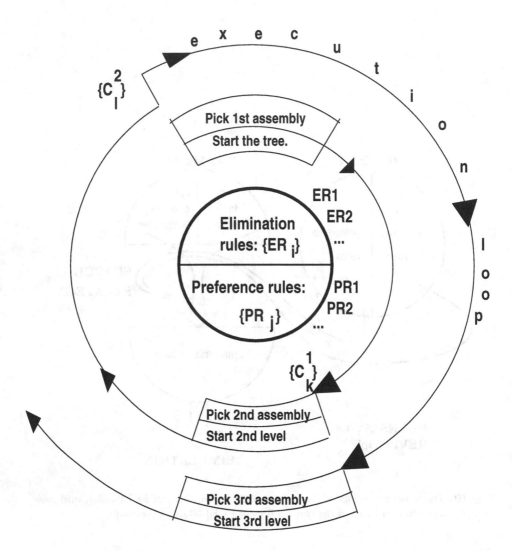

Fig. 20. The generator of configurations, in FUELCON, constructs a tree, one level per fuel assembly, by executing the ruleset for each level. Eventually, the leaves of the tree are generated, corresponding to full patterns of reload, that are alternative to each other. The figure shows the generation of the first three levels in the tree. The first run of the ruleset yields C_k^1, the set of the generated partial core-reload configurations with just one position filled in the one-eighth symmetry slice of the reactor-core geometry. The second run of the ruleset yields C_l^2, the set of partial configurations with two positions filled in the symmetric slice of the grid; and so forth.

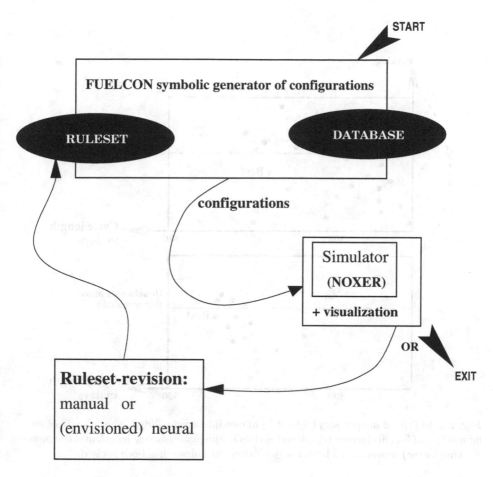

Fig. 21. Phases in the operation loop of the FUELCON expert system, with feedback for the human expert to possibly revise the ruleset

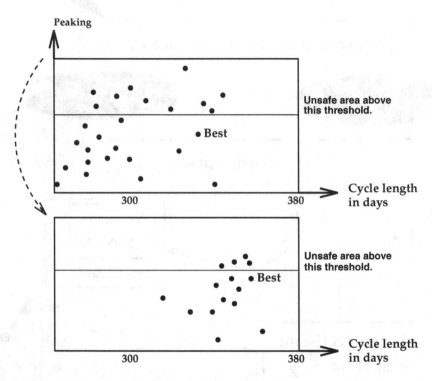

Fig. 22. Improved output sets ("clouds") of candidate refuellings. The "cloud" of configurations of fuel in the core (displayed as dots in the plane of cycle length and the power peaking factor) moves into a better region, after the ruleset has been revised.

calculations, solving a space-energy dependent Boltzmann equation. Local (or assembly averaged) power level basically depends on the assembly location inside the core, on the assembly physical characteristics (mainly, degree of burnup, this being zero for fresh fuel), and on the characteristics of neighbouring assemblies. An expert practitioner may predict roughly, without actually carrying out detailed calculations, a power profile across the core, and even local power spikes. It is this kind of rules of thumb that is embodied in the rules of FUELCON's ruleset.

The following ruleset is taken from one of our papers [53, pp. 404–405]. The rules in the ruleset were formulated by Alex Galperin. Actually this section is lifted from another paper of ours, [57]. Considering the specifics of the heuristic rules closely gives a good idea of what is involved in the human expert's considerations.

1) *Don't load any fresh fuel assembly in any such position that its distance from the center of the core is shorter that the distance of POS44 therefrom.* Refer to Fig. 10 in the present paper, to locate position POS44 in the grid symmetric slice. The distance is an integer number: the number of positions separating the given position from the center. This rule is meant to prevent the loading of fresh assemblies into the innermost region of the core, and is intended to make it less likely that such configurations are generated that would yield too high local power densities in the innermost region of the core. A more generic formulation of Rule 1 would be: *Don't load fresh fuel-assemblies in the innermost region of the core.* This rule is meant to prevent situations where local power increase in this region exceeds a certain upper bound, that is dictated by thermo-hydraulic considerations. Exceeding such an upper bound would impair the ability to satisfy the vital requirement of cooling the reactor core.

2) *Don't load a fresh assembly in such a position that is adjacent to another position where there is another assembly of the same kind, except when one of those two positions is in a corner position, i.e., except when one of those two positions is adjacent along two of its sides to the reflector* (i.e., the liquid coolant that surrounds the fuel assemblies in the core). This rule prevents placing two fresh assemblies side by side, and has the same motivation as Rule 1. Indeed, placing two fresh assemblies adjacently when none of them contains rods of burnable poison, would lead, in most cases, to an increase of local power density at BOC ("beginning of cycle"), i.e., soon after the reload, if the region considered is not on the periphery of the core.

Another version of this rule could be formulated as follows:

2') *Don't place two fresh fuel-assemblies in adjacent positions, except in such a situation when one of the two positions is on the periphery of the core.* This rule is meant to prevent the occurrence of excessive increases in local power distribution, in the internal regions of the core.

3) *Don't place any twice-burned assembly in any of the positions of the eighth row and of positions POS74, POS75, and POS66.* This rule, which prevents placing high-burnup assemblies in the outermost region of the core, fits into the general strategy adopted, which is "from the outside, inside" in principle, i.e., such that more power is expected to go on the periphery. That eventually allows to replace some fresh assemblies with low-burnup non-fresh assemblies. More generally,

the same rule could be expressed as follows: *Don't place two twice-burned fuel assemblies in adjacent positions in the core, if their distance from the center of the core exceeds a given upper bound.* This rule is meant to prevent "power dips", i.e., such locations where power is too low, in regions near the periphery of the core.

4) *Don't load a twice-burned assembly in such a position that is adjacent to another position where there is another twice-burned assembly, if the positions considered are comprised in rows 5 to 8 in the core.* This rule, that prevents placing high-burnup assemblies adjacently to each other, is intended to direct the process towards the generation of such reload configurations that fit into the category typified by a "checkerboard pattern" in respect of burnup levels. Burnup checkerboard configurations are such patterns where fresh and high-burnup fuel assemblies alternate in contiguous positions.[27]

5) *Don't load any such twice-burned assembly that has a very high value of cumulated burnup (over 20500 MWd/t), adjacently to a position containing a twice-burned assembly.* This rule is in line with Rule 4, and is meant to prevent the concentration of such assemblies that have a high burnup (correspondingly to a low value of K, the neutron multiplication factor) — this time (and in this it differs from Rule 4) in any region of the core, and this in order to prevent the formation of "hollows" in respect of power density.

6) *Don't load any twice-burned assembly in any position belonging to any of rows 2, 3, or 4, if more than one position adjacent thereto does contain a twice-burned assembly.* This rule is meant to prevent a concentration of high-K fuel in the innermost region of the core: this is an important region, in terms of neutron flow. Rule 6 is intended to prevent the formation of configurations where local power densities would exceed the threshold allowed. Moreover, Rule 6 encourages the generator to produce burnup checkboard configurations.

7) *If it is a twice-burned assembly that is currently being considered, then choose for it — from amongst those positions that were not forbidden by Rules 1 to 6 — that position whose distance from the center of the core is minimal.* (Cf. Rule 3.)

8) *If it is a once-burned assembly that is currently being considered, then choose for it — from amongst those positions that were not forbidden bu Rules 1 to 6 — that position whose distance from the center of the core is minimal.* Rule 8, along with Rule 7, and along with the input order of the loading list of fuel assemblies,

---

[27] Checkerboard reload patterns are a rather popular class of patterns in the practice of manual design of nuclear reactor core reload. It is possible to view such patterns — and other situations of adjacency (and adjacency-prevention) in the heuristic rules we have been considering — as particular cases of the more general combinatorial problems in *tiling.* This domain of discrete mathematics includes dominoes and polyominoes, i.e., respectively, pairs or more general patterns of same-type squares. "The *mistiling ratio* of the board is the proportion of squared covered by the worst tiling" [61]. For our own purposes, the quality of the tiling depends on how well the pool of available fuel is exploited: in the first place, we have to use the fuel-assemblies at hand, and secondly, we need to optimize the reactor-core performance parameters. To our best knowledge, this subject in nuclear engineering has not been considered, thus far, in this kind of perspective from discrete mathematics.

is intended to direct the generation process into producing such configurations that the lower the burnup value of the assembly, the more important for neutron flow the region is where that assembly's position has been selected.

Rules 1 to 6 are elimination rules, whereas Rules 7 and 8 are not mandatory from the physical viewpoint, but are "preference rules" — a strategy where alternatives would also be quite legitimate — intended to achieve pruning, and are enacted last. A constraint was imposed, that the size of the space of solutions must not exceed about one thousand solutions at any moment in the generation process. What this constraint affects most, is the possibility to optimize the way partly burned assemblies are reloaded. However, the influence, on the fuel cycle length, of how partly burned assemblies are ordered inside the core, is smaller than the influence of how the fresh assemblies are placed. FUELCON was coded in Lisp. The representation of the heuristic rules makes use of some standard functions, such as the following (which is from [53, p. 388]):

– The binary function

    (ADJACENT position1 position2)

is true iff the two positions are adjacent.
– The function

    (DISTANCE_FROM_CENTER position)

returns a number: the distance from the centre of the reactor core.
– The three-valued function

    (NUMBER_OF_REFLECTOR_SIDES position)

returns 2 if the argument is a "corner position" (like POS83, as shown in Fig. 10 in this paper), returns 1 if the argument is a "flat periphery position" (like POS73 in Fig. 10 in this paper), and returns zero if the argument is a "core inner position".
– The function

    (K_OF ID)

returns a certain parameter, the multiplication factor at BOC (beginning of cycle), of the fuel assembly indicated by ID.

The rule "It is FORBIDDEN to load fresh fuel assemblies in Core Internal Region" is amenable to a formulation in terms of a standard, reduced vocabulary, (POS11 stands for the position at the centre of the core). The following formula is from [53, p. 389]:

```
IF
    (BURNUP OF CURRENT_ASSEMBLY < 5000)
    AND
    (DISTANCE OF CURRENT_POSITION FROM POS11 < 5)
THEN
    CONFIGURATION_CONSIDERED IS FORBIDDEN
```

In Lisp, this was coded as follows:

```
(DEFUN EXAMPLE1_1 ( CURRENT_ASSEMBLY CURRENT_POSITION )
   (COND ( ( AND ( < ( BURNUP_OF CURRENT_ASSEMBLY ) 5000 )
            ( < ( DISTANCE_FROM CURRENT_POSITION
                              POS11
               )
             5
        ) )
        ( SETQ POS_FLAG 'PERMITTED )
  ) ) )
```

13   Symbolic Rules, Coded as a Program Intended for Compilation by Symbolic-to-Neural Transformation

In the sequel project in which neural revision of the ruleset was envisaged, a representation framework for the rules was developed, in which a rule would be coded at the symbolic level in a particular programming language (developed by Hava Siegelmann), and then transformed into a neural network. Consider this elimination rule:

2″)   *Don't load a fresh assembly in such a position that is adjacent to another position where there is another assembly of the same kind, except when one of those two positions is in a corner position.*

The following, which was formulated by Hava Siegelmann [116, 149], is the code for Rule 2″:

```
1.   Function  rule-2 (A, s): Boolean;
2.   var  p: Integer, flag: Boolean;
3.   Begin
4.      p=0 ;
5.      flag = Good-position ;
6.      If
7.        ((A.burnt = fresh) ∧ (¬ corner(s))
8.      then
9.        Repeat
10.           p = p + 1;
11.        If
12.        (neighbor(s,p) ∧ ¬ corner(p) ∧ kind (A) = kind(assembly (p)))
13.          then
14.               flag = Bad;
15.        Until
16.           (flag = Bad-position) ∨ (p = 20);
17.      rule-2 = flag
18. End;
```

This program scans all the the positions in the one-eight slice of the reactor core. An alternative version just checks adjacent positions. It was next shown how to translate this code into a network: into either a simple feedforward network that tests the 20 positions simultaneously, or into a recurrent network that tests them serially [116, 149].

Now, consider Rule 8, which is a "preference rule". Correspondingly, we have this code (taken from [149], and also written by Hava Siegelmann):

```
1.  Function  rule-8 (A): Integer;
2.  var  i, p, v: Integer;
3.  Begin
4.      v = ∞ ;
5.      p = 0 ;
6.      If
7.          A.burnt-once
8.      then
9.          For  i = 1 to 20  do
10.         If
11.             rule₁(A, i) ⋀ rule₂(A, i) ⋀ rule₃(A, i) ⋀ rule₄(A, i) ⋀
12.             rule₅(A, i) ⋀ rule₆(A, i) ⋀ (i.radius < v)
13.         then
14.             p = i;
15.             v = i.radius;
16.     rule-8 = p
17. End;
```

In contrast, in FUELGEN it is a genetic algorithm that generates the configurations, and there is no need for the ruleset to be applied, let alone revised, either by hand, or automatically.

14   The Workings of FUELGEN

In contrast to the transparency of FUELCON's ruleset, its functional replacement, FUELGEN, works like a black box, and is more suitable for such fuel managers who are not necessary as experienced as FUELCON's users. It would be an apt metaphor if we said that FUELCON is like a sports car, which does not suit everybody who wants to drive a car.

In FUELGEN, candidate pattern reload is represented as a set of genes. These correspond to the cells in the reactor core. The particular values (alleles) that each gene can take are the fuel assemblies.[28] The choice of such a minimal representation is deliberate, even though it restricts the possible crossover and mutation operators

---

[28] The following few paragraphs are based on the final section in [117]. The role, in the making of FUELGEN, of my colleague, Alan Soper, and of our doctoral student, Jun Zhao, cannot be overstressed. They deserve credit as my senior co-authors of the text of this section and the next one.

that can be constructed, because of the limits on information available to them. Nuclear physics dictates that our genes, which represent cells, will interact strongly, so that fitness variance of gene sets will be large (the power peak, being a local constraint, makes it easy to produce configurations with low fitness by giving the remainder of the genes appropriate alleles). The fact that adjacent assemblies interact most strongly, suggests a natural linkage for the core reload problem: Poon and Parks [139, 140, 128–130] used a bidimensional chromosome, with structure identical to the sector of the core represented, so that adjacent cells correspond to adjacent genes. However, there are no groups of linked genes, that are unlinked or weakly linked to others. The exchange of a linked set of genes cannot proceed without disruption to others. The local nature of the power peak measure implies that disruption will normally produce undesirable loading patterns with a high power peak and hence poor fitness.

The exchange of a linked set of genes will in most cases produce offspring containing more than one copy of an assembly. Adjustments need to be made to the offspring to restore the assembly set. This is further evidence against the existence of independent groups of linked genes suitable for recombination, since restoration will disrupt linked gene combinations. Because of these considerations, in FUELGEN it was considered preferable not use any additional structure defining linkage for recombination. Instead the minimal representation was used and appropriate mutation strategies defined. We used an assorting crossover. This kind of crossover is highly explorative, as it takes those genes that are common to both parents into the offspring and fills in the remaining genes randomly using all available allele values, rather than only those residing in the parents. In FUELGEN, it consists of these steps: given two selected parent loading maps, create two empty, child loading maps with no assemblies assigned to cells; copy the contents of all cells for which the parents have identical assemblies to the offspring; fill the rest of the cells in the children randomly from the available assemblies, subject to the symmetry restrictions. Since our search strategy is based on mutation, we use higher mutation rates, than are normally used with a recombining crossover (where the mutation operator traditionally plays a secondary role); this way, search is given a strong emphasis on hill climbing.

Population structure in FUELGEN (the project adopted the so-called Island Model), consists of many small subpopulations, each evolving under the action of a separate genetic algorithm, and exchanging individuals infrequently with other subpopulations. As to the selection operator, we used ranking selection. Our approach to the fitness function was to use a multiobjective strategy [129]. Here population members are placed in ranked groups according to whether they are dominated by other individuals. Ours is a strategy of gradually increasing the penalization of the fitness of solutions for violating the constraint as the search progresses. The initial stages of the search will be directed towards increasing cycle length while less hampered by the presence of local minima arising from the constraint on the power peak. As evolution progresses and the average fitness of the population increases, the search will be more directed to reducing the power peak.

15   Macroevolution in FUELGEN

FUELGEN adopts MacroGA, the "macro genetic algorithm" the London team developed, within the framework of what is known as macroevolution, in genetic algorithms research. In macroevolution, a number of species co-evolve. In FUEL-GEN, we chose not to have dominant species among these. Migration is controlled by a migration rate (or probability) determining when migration occurs, the number of migrants per migration (normally two), and a migration topology, such as the so-called ring or line topology. Migrants are the best individuals in the source species, and they will compete with all the individuals within the destination species for survival; the same number of least fit individuals will then be removed. Each species has a different crossover and mutation rate, which are generated from a mutation rate range and a crossover rate range. The ranking selection method is applied to all species. It is only as a particular case, that all species may happen to use the same crossover and mutation operators. Once in the macro genetic algorithm the parameters and a set of species are initialized, the probability of migration is set, and each species is initialized in terms of selection operator, crossover operator, mutation operator, population size, and crossover and mutation rates. Afterwards, all species evolve in parallel, and migrations take place at each generation.

As each generation is created, the fitness for each individual in the population is evaluated, and the best individual is recorded and checked; next, the genetic operators are applied, in order to create a next generation. Yet, if the current best individual is acceptable in terms of fitness (i.e., if a fuel-loading pattern has been found that is as good as we want it to be), then a termination message, "Stop", is distributed to all species, and the macroevolution process comes to an end. See Fig. 23. One of the advantages is that we have a set of weakly interacting species, allowing each species to concentrate on a separate area of the search space. The species can search their own regions aggressively (under high selection pressure) and hence quickly, without the risk of a premature loss of diversity. Moreover, as we allow the use of different crossover and mutation rates in the various species, we avoid the problem of having to determine effective values for these parameters.

FUELCON, and FUELGEN as well (because of its checks on populations), exhibit the advantage that when parameter-predicting simulation is carried out, it reckons with, and plots, hundreds of solutions instead of just one. Moreover, a major feature of both FUELCON and FUELGEN (a feature which sets them apart from other projects reported in the specialized literature) consists of the fact that the fuel reload pattern design is integrated with the inclusion of the so-called "burnable poisons" (BP),[29] instead of only incorporating these (and recalculating) downstream, at a later phase of the problem-solving process. This is a definite advantage, in that the fuel-allocation problem is solved similarly (and at the same go) when the

---

[29] Incidentally: Galperin [44] was concerned with a gadolinium burnable poison. Boron and gadolinium burnable poisons were discussed by Galperin, Segev and Radkowsky [50]; cf. [49]. Galperin, Grimm and Raizes [54] discussed the modelling and verification of designs of burnable poisons for pressurised water reactors. For use in district heating boiling water reactors, [51] were concerned with the so-called poison zoning technique for power peaking control.

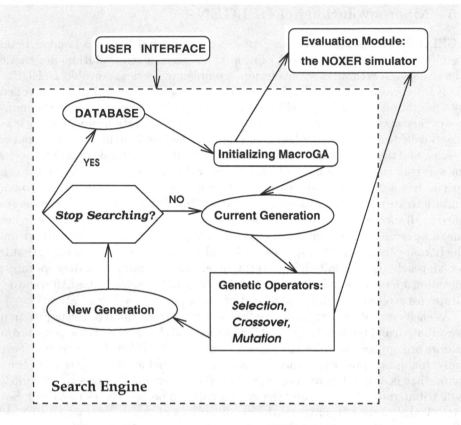

Fig. 23. The structure of control in FUELGEN [176, 179]

design specifications for solving the in-core fuel management problem for pressurized water reactors is with or without BPs. The latter are rods of neutron absorbers inserted in part of the fuel assemblies, to better control reactivity.

16   Interpretation of FUELCON and FUELGEN in Terms of Hyperrecursion and Hyperincursion

Like a few other parts of this paper, this section is based on what I wrote in [119], a paper which appeared in the *International Journal of Computing Anticipatory Systems* in Liège, Belgium. In this section, we interpret FUELCON and FUELGEN in terms of computing anticipatory systems indeed.

Hyperrecursion takes place when, generally speaking, multiple states are generated at an iteration of a recursive procedure, instead of merely one state being generated. See Fig. 24. Both FUELCON and FUELGEN are hyperrecursive indeed. Their unifying feature is that they generate several alternative candidate fuel-configurations, which are then simulated, visualized, and thus ostensibly contrasted as to their respective benefits. Multiple state generation at each recursive

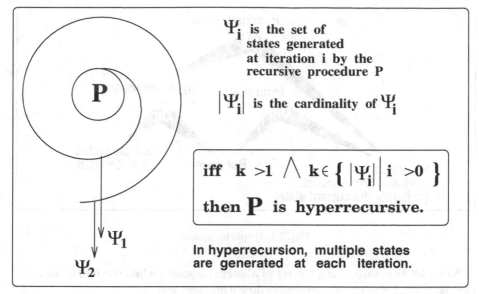

Ψ_i is the set of states generated at iteration i by the recursive procedure P

$|\Psi_i|$ is the cardinality of Ψ_i

iff $k > 1 \bigwedge k \in \left\{ |\Psi_i| \,\middle|\, i > 0 \right\}$

then **P** is hyperrecursive.

In hyperrecursion, multiple states are generated at each iteration.

Fig. 24. Hyperrecursion

state is, in that sense, one of the things which set FUELCON apart, as soon as it appeared, from extant tools for computer-assisted refuelling.

Anticipation permeates several tasks and functions in many a domain. In particular, in a computational anticipatory system, the current state estimate depends (also, or even: only) on future states. When anticipation co-occurs with hyperrecursion, we have *hyper-incursion,* as shown in Fig. 25. Refuellings being designed with future performance of the nuclear reactor in view, has much to do with forecasting, for all of this not being robust, as we saw in Sec. 5. Parameter prediction by means of simulation comes downstream of the generation of candidate fuel-configurations — this being the case in both FUELCON and FUELGEN. Moreover, state observability being much diminished (notwithstanding the monitoring of some parameters) while the fuel is burning, direct inspection is possible only at downtime periods. Unless the reactor is shut down, there are aspects of current state estimation which depend on the previous simulations of the operation cycle, and therefore (in part) on states which are still future. Arguably, FUELCON and FUELGEN are hyper-incursive.

What makes the two tools hyperincursive? Let us notate as $\mathcal{O}_\rho$ the set of observable states of reactor ρ, and as Π_ρ the set of parameters of the same reactor ρ. Let such parameters be indicated as $x(t) \in \Pi_\rho$. Only parameters that can be at least sometimes observed are included in Π_ρ, by our definition.

And then, let S_A be the set of (practically) possible observations (i.e., of observable states) of the parameters at the jth occurrence of a downtime period:

$$S_A \equiv \left\{ x(t_{\text{Downtime}_j}) \,\middle|\, x(t) \in \Pi_\rho \right\} \qquad \text{where:} \qquad S_A \subset \mathcal{O}_\rho.$$

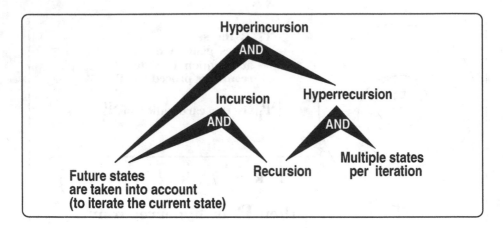

Fig. 25. Hyperincursion

Next, let as notate as S_B the set of observable states while the fuel is burning, that is to say, between two successive downtime periods:

$$S_B \equiv \left\{ x(t) \, \middle| \, \begin{array}{l} t_{\text{Downtime}_j} < t < t_{\text{Downtime}_{j+1}} , \\ x(t) \in \Sigma\rho(t) \, , \, \Sigma\rho(t) \subset \Pi_\rho \end{array} \right\}$$

where: $\qquad S_A \bigcup S_B = \mathcal{O}_\rho$.

The subset of reactor parameters that are observable even between two successive downtime periods is considerably smaller than the set of all parameters that can be observed at least sometimes:

$$16|\Sigma\rho(t)16| \ll 16|\Pi\rho(t)16|$$

Now, fuel reload pattern design is carried out and simulated at t_{Downtime_N} , for t such that

$$t_{\text{Downtime}_N} < t < t_{\text{Downtime}_{N+1}} .$$

S_C is that subset of the states of that simulation that are future with respect to any time t_K , such that

$$t_N < t_K < t_{\text{Downtime}_{N+1}} ,$$

when the team at the power plant is estimating the current state, $x(t_K)$, of the reactor ρ, based on S_A , S_B , and S_C .

Therefore, there is anticipation. Inasmuch as the fuel reload pattern design is carried out by using either FUELCON or FUELGEN, the process of making use of the tool is anticipatory. As we have already seen, FUELCON and FUELGEN are hyperrecursive, so we are also able to say that they display hyperincursion as well.

17   A Typology, and Typological Positioning of the Sequence of Architectures

The sequence of system architectures within our umbrella project corresponds to the historical sequence of waves within artificial intelligence: rule-based expert systems, then the neural networks wave, then the genetic algorithm wave. Fig. 26 is about typology, i.e., taxonomy. In Fig. 26(a), an AND/OR tree is shown, which represents various possible characteristics for a computer system for in-core fuel management, and which moreover introduces the elements for a compact notation as adopted in Fig. 26(b). In Fig. 26(a), "Nodal" refers to the technique of Meir Segev's NOXER simulation software for parameter prediction, which takes as input the output of FUELCON. Fig. 26(b) captures the architectural characteristics of the systems on which we have been working from 1986 to the late 1990s, and which appear in the figure from the left to the right, in chronological order.

To read Fig. 26(a), start from the left: the root of the tree is the box "in-core fuel management". It is customary to devise a tentative allocation (of fuel units, either recycled or fresh, on a symmetric slice of the grid which represents a planar section of the core of the reactor). The resulting reload pattern (or, the way we did it in our own systems: families of hundreds competing candidate reload-patterns) is then fed into a simulator, which performs parameter prediction. Therefore, in the AND/OR tree, it is an AND that we have between the two branches whose source is in the root. Let us start from the nonterminal on the second branch, i.e., "parameter prediction", which we symbolize by the hexagon on whose perimeter we position the values (i.e., the terminals on the periphery of the subtree) of three variables represented by the three nonterminals of the subtree considered.

First (to be noted under the hexagon), the simulator may be either ad hoc, or industrial. Meir Segev's NOXER ad hoc simulator provided the basis of all prototypes in the overall project, starting with the FUELCON generator of reload patterns. When licensing a system to an industrial plant, NOXER was replaced with the industrial simulator relevant for the given plant. Secondly (to be noted above the hexagon), the simulator may be a piece of software carrying on conventional symbolic manipulation (which is the case of NOXER), or, instead, a neural, much quicker simulator. Thirdly (to be noted on the right side of the hexagon), the reactor core dynamic simulation model embodied may be based on a nodal algorithm [22] (which is the case of NOXER), or otherwise.

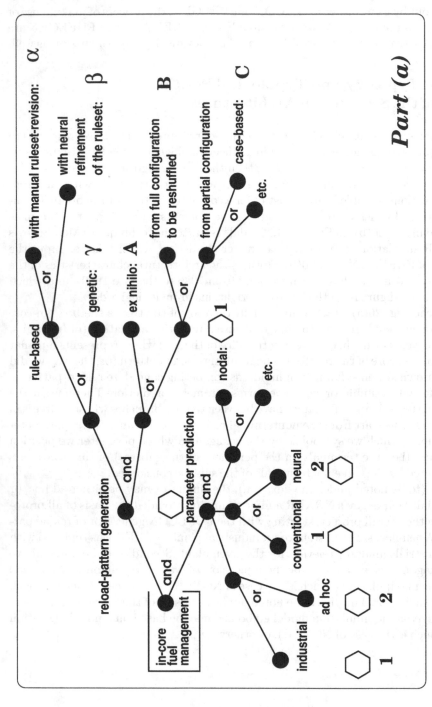

Fig. 26(a). A typology of options. An AND/OR tree of characteristics of computer tools for fuel reload pattern design.

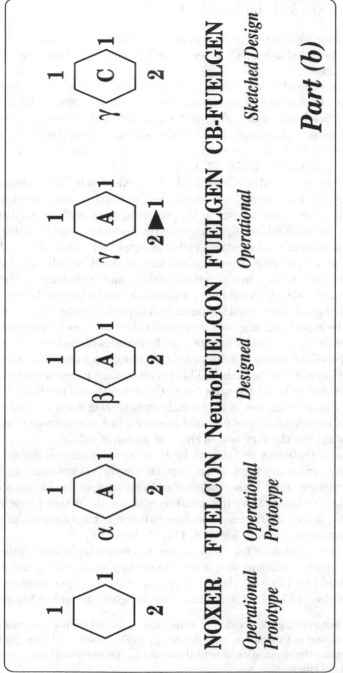

Fig. 26(b). A typology of options. The features of a sequence of architectures within our umbrella project.

Part (b)

Still referring to the same figure, let us shift our attention to the nonterminal labelled "reload-pattern generation". Here again, there are different aspects to consider (hence, the AND of the two outgoing branches):

– Which computation paradigm(s) is or are embodied in the respective tool? (the choice is to be noted as a Greek letter on the left side of the hexagon: see in part (b) of the figure).

α) An archetype of *rule-based* generation of fuel-configurations is the tool FUELCON, whose first prototype was developed in 1986–8 [46] and whose further development into a full-fledged operational prototype — tested for effectiveness and accuracy on several case studies from the published literature of the discipline — constituted the subject of Shuky Kimhi's doctoral project [78]. Cf. [53, 45, 52, 47, 113, 48, 57, 107].

The ergonomics of operating FUELCON effectively [53] can be conceived of in terms of a control loop, combining automated and manual stages: there is a pre-stored ruleset in the expert system, with mandatory rules (safety constraints), and optional rules (embodying a search strategy); once the generator of configurations yields as output a batch of (typically) hundreds reload patterns, these are fed into NOXER, which then visualizes them as dots in the plane of power-peaking and cycle-length. The "best" solution (peaking high but under a threshold, and a long cycle) can then be picked, if good enough and falling under the peaking safety threshold. However, the expert user may well decide to revise the ruleset, in order to either explore new strategies, or improve on the features of the few very best solutions (or of the family of solutions: by zooming on a region, or moving the "cloud" of dots in the plane). This revision stage is performed manually. This proved to be, at the same time, the strength and the limit of FUELCON: like a racing car, it is elatingly empowering for a user who is very knowledgeable of in-core fuel management, but the average practitioner cannot get out the very best of the tool, to put it mildly.

β) The early 1990s saw an attempt by Hava Siegelmann and myself to integrate a *neural* component in the loop, for the purposes of revising the ruleset automatically.[30] This remained at the design stage. This is a topic of considerable interest in principle, but whereas the design phase was carried out, at the London team we chose to invest in the following, practically more promising option. See [114, 115, 55, 116, 149].

γ) *Genetic* computation for the purposes of generating reload patterns was an emerging paradigm, with several teams reporting on ongoing projects, [139, 140, 128–130, 161, 160, 23–25] or known to be experimenting with it. We developed FUELGEN, a robust tool, which in the late 1990s entered an

---

[30] Historically, automating the revision of knowledge acquired from a human expert by resorting to neural networks was not unique. In 1997, Shouhong Wang published a paper [171] about the application of neural networks in generalizing expert knowledge, for an industrial engineering application.

Already in 1990, Parks et al. [132] reported about solving the PWR reload core optimization problem algorithmically.

industrial adoption phase, and which in 1996 yielded results better than those published and known to us [177, 178, 176, 117, 118, 179, 154, 119]. The simulator used with the prototype, NOXER, was replaced with an industrial simulator.

– What does the reload-pattern generation tool start from?

A) One possibility, adopted in both FUELCON and FUELGEN, is to produce reload patterns *ex nihilo,* i.e., starting from an empty core, and filling it gradually: each complete pattern is a terminal in a tree. Another possibility, adopted by others, is to look for only one reload patterns at a time, possibly *ex nihilo.*

B) In a fuel manager's manual practice, it was customary to select out of experience, the plant's record, or the literature, such a reload pattern that provided a suitable solution for a problem that looks similar to the one at hand, and then to make this initial solution admissible and hopefully convenient, by shuffling positions in the grid (i.e., performing binary or more complex exchanges).

There used to exist such tools which assist such a manual practice ([131] is of 1992), And in the late 1980s, there also existed also such tools which performed such a procedure automatically, by emulating shuffling as performed by humans [141, 158].

C) Different ways of starting from a partial configurations can be conceived of. In particular, we tried to preliminarily explore a variant of FUELGEN which would start from a database of precedents, and select one by means of *case-based reasoning.* This did not eventuate, in part in relation to discontinued employment circumstances. At any rate, it was a possibility of interest in principle, and was a renewed attempt at coping with the expert's heuristics directly (something avoided in FUELGEN, whose very advantage is in that it is a black box, as far as the user is concerned). On the other hand, when running FUELCON, the insertion of each fuel unit into the grid represents a generation in the tree of patterns being constructed. This, too, is a way of considering partial configurations.

18   Parameter Prediction: From Nodal Algorithms, to Neural Networks, with Considerations About Grid Geometry

We have seen that the output of both FUELCON and FUELGEN used to be fed as input to NOXER. Let us discuss the task of the latter tool, and available techniques that can be applied to that task. With a tool such as NOXER or its equivalents, which carry out detailed calculations, three steps have to be carried out: the generation of cross-section data, the generation of cross-section libraries, and the prediction of reactor parameters such as cycle length, power peak, reactivity, power distribution, fuel depletion, and so on. "Considered as an event, a neutron-nucleus collision is a stochastic phenomenon, i.e., there is a probability for the collision to take place, a probability given by a nuclear cross section. Once the collision takes place, its outcome is also another stochastic phenomenon" [22, p. 128].

In nuclear engineering, the simulation of the power production cycle of a power reactor is performed by a complicated calculational sequence, involving several codes and a large number of data files.[31] Calculations are performed by different code systems, from simple 2D (so-called *nodal* or *coarse mesh*) tools up to detailed 3D neutronic and thermal-hydraulic codes.

Choice of the calculational tool is guided by the accuracy and level of details required for the particular task performed. Thus, for a safety analysis report, a detailed and accurate calculation is required, whereas for an initial search of reload configuration, a fast method is needed to evaluate two core parameters only: cycle length (i.e., how long the plant will operate before the next shut-down and fuel-reload) — or, instead, core criticality at end-of-cycle (EOC) — and maximum power peaking factor (actually a power map at each time point). The availability of a *fast and reliable* method for evaluating these parameters is essential in *all* reload optimization methods and therefore has a potential of a large economic value.

In the 1990s (and perhaps still going strong today), most of the fast tools used have been employing so-called *nodal* methods, which reduce the time needed for cycle evaluation by one order of magnitude, as compared with methods based on *finite difference* (or *finite elements*) for solving the Boltzmann equation. The utilization of neural networks was expected to reduce the time by another two orders of magnitude and to provide a real breakthrough in the domain of nuclear fuel management. Several attempts were published in the open literature [76, 77].

Graphic visualization capabilities were developed for NOXER. They greatly enhanced the ergonomics of FUELCON, but the bottom line is that the development of NOXER was relatively low-cost — this being a provisional constraint — and its performance was relatively slow. The simulator remained the least innovative component within the FUELCON meta-architecture, in terms of keeping abreast with novel computation paradigms. In the history of the FUELCON project, a shift of hardware platforms considerably improved times of simulation, but improvements of about one further order of magnitude was expected to be yielded by a neural simulator.

Kim, Chang and Lee [76] described such a fast simulator, which by the way is apparently somewhat indebted to previous descriptions of FUELCON and NOXER for the organization of parameters, just as the rule-based component of FUEL-CON has clearly been a model of emulation (and is cited indeed). What was particularly novel about Kim et al. [76, 77] is in their going neural for the simulation, whereas their generator resorts to a fuzzy ruleset: their Optimal Fuel Shuffling System (OFSS) is "a hybrid system in which a rule-based system, fuzzy logic, and an artificial neural network (ANN) are connected with each other" [76]. "The rule-based system classifies loading patterns into two types by using several heuristic rules and a fuzzy rule. The fuzzy rule is introduced to achieve a more effective and faster search. Its membership function is automatically updated in accordance with the prediction results. The ANN predicts core parameters for the patterns generated from the rule-based system. A backpropagation network is used for fast prediction of the core parameters" [76]. Limitations with their simulation as reported,

---

[31] This section is based on part of [48].

we reckoned at the time, were mainly on two counts: the case analyzed was over-simplistic, and the choice of parameters did not prune out interdependence so as to avoid noise.

More in general, considering the state of the art of the simulation and the neural prediction of nuclear reactor performance parameters, Alex Galperin felt that the early neural attempts at parameter prediction were limited because basically, the prediction of the cycle length and of power peaking factors was not accurate enough to be of practical use.

This relative lack of success may be attributed to one of two sources. First, the net structure was not adequate, or, then, it is the learning algorithm that was not good enough. Secondly, the physical model on which the net is based, was not adequate. It should be noted that two output parameters are obtained: in the domain terminology, $Pmax$ (i.e. peaking) and K_{eff} (or cycle length). A separate net was constructed for each parameter. Input parameters were many (there were 21 of them). The loading pattern (i.e. each configuration produced by the generator) was converted into a numeric vector of 21 elements. These elements constituted a core model used in net training. To Galperin, this model was not satisfactory, at least for some examples he saw in the domain literature.

An additional factor is the method by which reload patterns are generated, namely, those patterns which are used to train the network. Kim et al. [76] claimed that patterns were generated randomly. Galperin considered this to be a wrong approach. This prompted us to envision a neural substitute for NOXER, replacing it in the FUELCON meta-architecture. First, a physical model of reactor core has to be developed, to be used in the neural-net training algorithm. Probably, aggregate pattern parameters should be used, in order to avoid "unimportant" input data. Secondly, the patterns on which the net is trained should be generated randomly, *but* within a predetermined (relatively) small part of the search space. Galperin did not believe that it was possible to train any network on such huge (1E+24 patterns) and "non-linear" search space. On the other hand, using the FUELCON system we may "curve out" a sub-space, which will be characterized by a common physical basis (set of rules). This subspace may be still very large (1E+12 patterns), but using an adequate learning model, the net may be successfully trained (or not). Third, we reckoned in the late 1990s, we had all the tools for generating patterns, testing solutions, and so on, so neural networks would have definitely been our paradigm of choice for the new simulator, intended to replace NOXER (cf. [122–124]). A distinction is to be made between such simulators whose calculations are in two dimensions, and such simulators that calculate the reactor core parameters in three dimensions: "Normally, the reactor simulator time depends on the kind of modeling, for example a 3D calculation has high precision, but it requires much more time than a 2D calculation" [122, p. 544].

We now turn to core geometry. Consider Fig. 27; let the grid shown there be part of the reactor core schema. Consider the power distribution in the case marked with X. We have to evaluate power distribution exactly, in case X, based on known distributions in a, b, c, d, p, q, r, s. In the 1990s, this was done by computationally very heavy software for solving systems of equations with 21 parameters, of which,

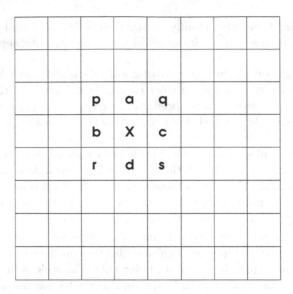

Fig. 27. Adjacencies in a region of the grid of a reactor core section. Evaluating power distributions is based on adjacent positions.

	1	2	3	4	5		
	16	p	a	q	6		
	15	b	X	c	7		
	14	r	d	s	8		
	13	12	11	10	9		

Fig. 28. An outer circle of adjacent positions is added

several are truly independent. It was a promising direction of research to try to do that, instead, by means of neural networks. One way to do that is as follows: first, we try an estimator for X based on just a, b, c, d, that is, face-to-face adjacency.

Then, once we get the function, we try again for a, b, c, d, p, q, r, s, that is, including diagonal contiguity. Then, we try to compare with one more function, which we get by considering an outer surrounding circle; see Fig. 28.

By using a symbolic-to-neural schema,[32] parts of the physical model are to be translated, and the rest is to be learned. Whereas the network would require a very long time to be trained to approximate the core, after training it may enable fast simulation. The physical idea that underlies the training phase is as follows. Assume we are to evaluate the power distribution in the case labeled X in the grid of Fig. 27, and standing for a position in the reactor core. As a first training phase, according to the steps outlined above, we would have the neural predictor calculate X based on a, b, c, d only, that is, as seen, the face-to-face adjacent positions encircling that position. We would then consider the second-order effects by measuring the diagonal contiguity p, q, r, s. Only later (cf. Fig. 28) the third order effects of positions 1 to 16 are to be accounted for in the network. Once this yields satisfactory results, no more data are to be fed to the network.

There is something more that could be said about adjacency in the grid of a nuclear reactor core's planar section. We have been considering grids with square cases. This is the most common situation. However, there exists a smaller, yet important class of reactors (from the former Soviet Union), in which core positions consist of adjacent hexagons instead of adjacent squares. In principle, prediction for reactor cores with hexagonal positions is also called for. Only, such reactors also happen to be part of the minority of reactor kinds that do not require to be shut down for refueling. Therefore, there is more to it than just redevising prediction for a different geometry.[33]

There exist, on the market, fuel assemblies for use in different types of reactors. The making of fuel assemblies is constrained, as to the geometry of their sections, by the way such fuel units are intended to be inserted inside the reactor core. Typically, the section of the latter is a grid, with rows and columns of adjacent square cells. Accordingly, the section of fuel assemblies is also square. Actually, however, the grid of adjacent cases sometimes has a different geometry, depending upon the structure of the single cases inside the grid. Cells, and, accordingly, fuel assemblies, in general have a polygonal section; a square section is just a particular cell. The requirement that cells be adjacent restricts admissible kinds of polygons: only hexagons would also do. [34]

---

[32] Possibly, the same adopted for the ruleset-revision module [114, 115, 55, 116, 149].

[33] Cho et al. [20] described in 1997 a nodal method for hexagonal geometry. Also a University of Illinois doctoral dissertation of 1995, by William Edward Fitzpatrick [37] (supervised by Abderrafi M. Ougouag), was concerned with nodal reactor analysis tools for hexagonal geometry. Fitzpatrick [37] described a new nodal method for the solution of multigroup multidimensional diffusion problems in hexagonal geometry. He developed solution techniques for the time-dependence of the diffusion equations; those techniques were coupled to spatial nodal algorithms. The so-called moment integral method for multidimensional nodal kinetic problems was introduced [37].

[34] Our present discussion does not take into account whether such extant reactors need or need not be shut down for refuelling. For example, CANDU reactors from Canada do not require to be shut down in order to replace fuel.

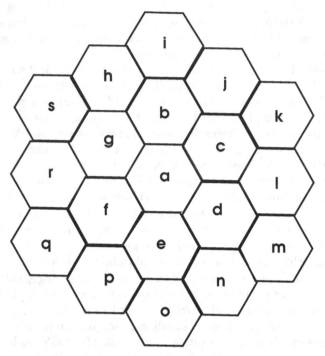

Fig. 29. A grid of hexagons, with a spiral of adjacent core-positions

One constraint that we left implicit is that cells in the grid are homogeneous: to simplify calculations, as well as to enable a better exploitment of available batches of fuel units, sections are polygons of the same kind. Squares and hexagons can be contiguous on all sides: on each, with another square, or, respectively, hexagon. Squares are convenient, with respect to hexagons, in that there is a simpler array structure with rows and columns. Also symmetries inside the grid are simpler. The advantage of hexagons over a square section is that power distribution with respect to the centre of the section is less different in different points of the periphery of the section: in this respect, the ideal is a circle, as the radius is constant, and there are no such discrepancies. In contrast, with a square section, there is a remarkable difference in power distribution with respect to the centre of the section, if it is measured at an angle of the square, as opposed to the centre of one of its edges.

Nevertheless, a circular section does not allow face-to-face adjacency. Two circumferences can only be tangent in one point. Second best, for the purposes of minimizing the difference between the radius of the inscribed circumference and the radius of the circumscribed circumference, are hexagons, which, as seen, are those polygons with the maximal number of edges that enable adjacency with polygons of the same type and size. Figs. 29 and 30 depict, respectively, a grid of hexagons, and distances inside polygons. In Fig. 29, a possible, spiralling here, alphabetical ordering is defined between contiguous hexagonal positions inside a grid.

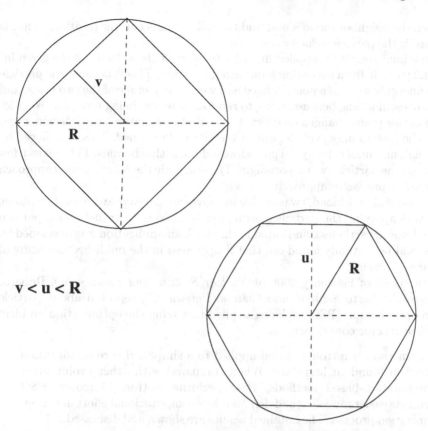

Fig. 30. The difference between the radius, R, of the circumscribed circumference, and the radius (v in a square, u in a hexagon) of the inscribed circumference, is smaller in a hexagon that in a square. The limit (infinite edges, zero difference) is reached in a circle, but no adjacency with no gaps is possible among circles. Therefore, hexagonal structure is optimal in respect of minimizing the difference between radiuses.

19   Particle Swarm Optimization for Refuelling

In the mid 2000s, I was convinced that it would be worthwhile to try and develop a new software tool for assisting fuel managers in the design of reload patterns, by appying techniques from *swarm intelligence* [74], and in particular, *particle swarm optimization* [74, Chs. 7 to 9], based on the metaphor of a swarm of flying particles. Swarm optimization is a loop which for each individual (i.e., individual particle) in the swarm, evaluates the fitness of that individual, in order to establish whether for each dimension in turn, the particular individual is best so far. Having completed the inner loop on the dimensions, the fitness of the particular individual is compared to the fitness of each neighbour, in order to find out who is the best performer in the neighbourhood. Then another inner loop is carried out on all dimensions in turn: change is in terms of velocity of the particle, and change is a function of the difference between the individual's previous best and current positions and the difference between the neighbourhood's best and the individual's current position. What is adjusted is the particle velocity and position.

A maximal velocity is applied, in order to prevent the velocity of the given individual particle from exceeding it on each dimension. This is because the particle cycles unevenly around a point defined as a weighted average of the two bests, and there are oscillations, because owing to random numbers being used, the exact location of this point changed on every iteration. As oscillations become wider and wider, the system may explode, unless velocity is dampened. This is achieved by imposing a maximal velocity, soi particles oscillate within bounds. There exist a few versions of the particle swarm paradigm. These include the *inertia weight* approach and *constriction factor* approach.

Because of his workload, I was unable to convince a colleague who had been doing some work applying the particle swarm paradigm, to nuclear fuel realod pattern design. I was nevertheless vindicated in that such an application was developed by others, and I eventually found out that it appeared in the published literature of nuclear engineering.

In the issue of February 2006 of *Nuclear Science and Engineering,* Roberto Domingos, Roberto Schirru, and Cláudio Pereira [27] reported about particle swarm optimization (PSO) as being applied to solving the optimization problem in nuclear reactor core design:

> The method is introduced and applied to a simplified core optimization problem found in literature. When compared with other evolutionary computation-based methods, PSO performs better. Moreover, PSO presents easier modeling and demands less computational effort in the optimization process. The obtained results are shown and discussed.

Concerning power distribution in a power system (independently of how power is generated), a team from Tiruchendur, in Tamilnadu, India, described in 2012 [1] a "particle swarm optimization algorithm (PSO) that performs feature and model selection simultaneously for the probabilistic neural network (PNN) classifier for power system disturbances" [1, p. 832]. "*Power quality* may be defined as the continuous availability of electric power that confirms [it should be: conforms] to accepted standards of phase, frequency, and voltage" [1, pp. 832–833]. Failures in this are *power system disturbances*. Detection of these, as well as detecting their location and types, are important, and data mining is suitable because of the huge mass of the data.

20   Improved Fuel Bundle Design, and Combined Design of Fuel Assemblies and Core Configurations

Daniel Rozon and Wei Shen's 2001 paper [145] is a parametric study, a tandem analysis, of the DUPIC fuel cycle, reflecting fuel management strategy for both pressurized water reactors (PWR) and a CANDU-6 reactor. ("A generic study of the DUPIC fuel cycle is carried out using the linear reactivity model for initial enrichments ranging from 3.2 to 4.5 wt% in a PWR" [145].) The direct use of the of spent PWR fuel in the two kinds of reactors was studied, and for that purpose, Rozon and Shen resorted to the DRAGON/DONJON chain of codes with the ENDF/B-V and ENDF/B-VI libraries. Their reference feed material is a 17×17 French standard 900-MW(electric) PWR fuel. "Because of the uneven power histories of the spent PWR assemblies, the spent PWR fuel composition is expected to differ from one assembly to the next" [145].

> The PWR spent-fuel composition is obtained from two-dimensional DRAGON assembly transport and depletion calculations. After a number of years of cooling, this defines the initial fuel nuclide field in the CANDU unit cell calculations in DRAGON, where it is further depleted with the same neutron group structure. The resulting macroscopic cross sections are condensed and tabulated to be used in a full-core model of a CANDU 6 reactor to find an optimized channel fueling rate distribution on a time-average basis. Assuming equilibrium refueling conditions and a particular refueling sequence, instantaneous full-core diffusion calculations are finally performed with the DONJON code, from which both the channel power peaking factors and local parameter effects are estimated.

In that same paper, Rozon and Shen [145] discussed reducing fuel composition uncertainties. In fact: "Uneven mixing of the powder during DUPIC fuel fabrication may lead to uncertainties in the composition of the fuel bundle and larger peaking factors in CANDU" [145].

In a paper of 2009, Wasim Raza and Kwang-Yong Kim [143] discussed how they carried out multiobjective shape optimization of the deisgn of a fuel-assembly (a 19-pin wire-wrapped fuel assembly), by using a hybrid multiobjective evolutionary approach. They sought a compromise between "two competing objectives, i.e., enhancement of heat transfer and reduction of friction loss" [143]. They chose as design variables "[t]wo nondimensional variables, wire-spacer diameter to fuel rod diameter ratio and wire-wrap pitch to fuel rod diameter ratio" [143]. They resorted to a technique known as the *response surface approximation method,* in order "to construct the surrogate with objective function values calculated by means of Reynolds-averaged Navier-Stokes analysis of the flow and heat transfer. The shear stress transport turbulence model is used as a turbulence closure". For robustness, they applied the Pareto-optimal method to the results of the optimization. Raza and Kim explained [143]:

> The Pareto-optimal solutions are obtained using a combination of the evolutionary algorithm NSGA-II and a local search method. The Pareto-optimal front for the wire-wrapped fuel assembly has been obtained. With an increase in the wire-spacer diameter, both heat transfer and friction loss in the assembly increase. The design with higher heat transfer on the Pareto-optimal curve shows not only a lower maximum temperature but also a more uniform temperature distribution on the cross section of the assembly in comparison with the other designs.

In the bulk of the present article, we have been concerned with how to optimize configurations of fuel assemblies inside a nuclear reactor core. Bear in mind however that the position of the fuel rods inside a cross section of a fresh fuel assembly is also designed, and this is done by the manufacturer. It is also interesting to combine the study of fresh fuel rods, the way they are positioned inside their bundle, with the study of configurations of fuel assemblies inside the core. In 2007, Matthew Jessee and David Kropaczek [73] discussed coupled bundle-core design using fuel rod optimization for boiling water reactors. "An optimization method has been developed to determine the optimal fresh fuel rod configurations, fresh streams, and fresh bundle design placements given a known exposed fuel loading pattern and operational strategy for boiling water reactors" [73]. A *simulated annealing* algorithm was used by Jessee and Kropaczek for optimization:[35]

> The optimization method is based on a first-order approximation of various core parameters, such as hot excess reactivity and critical power ratio, using fuel rod perturbations to the reference fresh bundle designs. A simulated annealing optimization algorithm is shown to produce fresh bundle designs, consisting of rods selected from a user-defined set of rod types that optimize the core design with respect to its design constraints.

As such calculations are costly, Jessee and Kropaczek resorted to a parallel computing system [73]:

> The method utilizes a linear superposition method based upon sensitivity coefficients to approximate core parameters. A parallel computing system was implemented to decrease wall clock time for the numerous lattice physics and core simulator calculations. A periodic update of the reference bundle design, without the computational burden of updating the sensitivity coefficients, was introduced and is shown to significantly improve the accuracy of the approximation model.

Jessee and Kropaczek found "that improved core designs are achieved when a many-fresh bundle design (i.e., stream) solution is considered as part of the design space" [73]. Combining bundle design and the design of positioning inside the core enables a kind of saving that was not previously possible: "Six-stream (and higher) core designs that increase fuel utilization while simultaneously reducing manufacturing costs through reduction of fuel rod types fabricated, previously unattainable with existing methodologies, are now possible" [73].

21   Some Applications Which Genetic Algorithms Found in Nuclear Engineering

In an article published in 1999 [164], a team from Russia and Japan — Vladimir Toshinsky, Hiroshi Sekimoto, and Georgy I. Toshinsky — reported about the application of genetic algorithms to multiobjective fuel management optimization

---

[35] Already in 1991, Kropaczek, Parks, Maldonado, and Turinsky [80] reported about the application of simulated annealing to in-core nuclear fuel management optimization. In 1995, Stephens, Smith, Rempe, and Downar [156] reported about the optimization of pressurized water reactor shuffling by simulated annealing with heuristics.

for the so called Self-Fuel-Providing LMFBR (SFPR), this being "a reactor that requires no plutonium reprocessing for itself, and provides high efficiency of natural uranium utilization" [164]. These are advantages of that kind of reactor. On the face of it, the design of that reactor came with a number of disadvantages: "Several design considerations were previously given to this reactor type which, however, suffer from some problems connected with insufficient power flattening, large reactivity swings during burnup cycles, and peak fuel burnup being significantly higher than recent technology experience" [164]. Nevertheless, it was understood that some remedy to such shortcomings could be obtained by good fuel management: "the mentioned core parameters demonstrate high sensitivity to the fuel management strategy selected for the reactor" [164]. For that purpose, genetic algorithms were applied.

The kinds of applications of genetic algorithms (GA) within nuclear engineering have been various [83, pp. 219–220]:

> The most common problem in nuclear engineering to which evolutionary computation has been applied is the nuclear core reload problem. DeChaine and Feltus (1995), Chapot et al. (1999)[36] have been using GA to face this problem. Alvarenga et al. (1997), Pereira et al. (1998)[37] have been investigating GA applications in transient classification problems. Few applications of GA can also be seen in the nuclear reactor design optimization (Pereira et al., 1999),[38] and surveillance and maintenance optimization (Muñoz et al., 1997).[39]

In an article [83] published in 2000, a team from Rio de Janeiro, Brazil — Celso Lapa, Cláudio Pereira, and Antônio Carlos Mol — described the application of a genetic algorithm to a task different from that of FUELGEN. Theirs is "a method for preventive maintenance scheduling optimization of standby systems, based on genetic algorithm and probabilistic safety analysis" [83, p. 219]. The aim of this is the maximization of a nuclear system availability: "to improve the average availability of the system through the optimization of the preventive maintenance policy" [83, p. 219]. One advantage is that the genetic modelling enables nonconstant intervals between times at which maintenance is scheduled. "The auxiliary feed-water system (AFWS) was chosen as a sample case due to its high importance as a safety system in a nuclear power plant" [83, p. 219]. The use of the AFWS is as follows [83, p. 220]:

---

[36] These are the papers [23, 19].

[37] These are the papers [3, 135]. In [135], a method in pattern recognition was proposed, "that uses genetic learning to get an optimized classification system. Each class is represented by several time series in a data base. The idea is to find clusters in the set of the training patterns of each class so that their centroids can distinguish the classes with a minimum of misclassifications. Due to the high level of difficulty found in this optimization problem and the poor prior knowledge about the patterns domain, a model based on genetic algorithm is proposed to extract this knowledge, searching for the minimum number of subclasses that leads to a maximum correctness [...]".

[38] The paper cited is [136]. Also see [146].

[39] That is, the paper [98].

According to Lapa (1996), Lapa and Frutuoso e Melo (1996), That is, the papers [82, 84]. The AFWS has two primary functions. The first is to guarantee the water feed to the steam generators (SGs) at the failure of the feed water system in order to provide the residual heat removal until the residual heat removal system starts. The other function is to maintain the water levels in the SGs in order to remove the heat generated by the reactor during shutdown. In other words, the AFWS must be ready to start during the time that the plant is operating and must start immediately after a trip occurrence.

That same article explains [83, p. 220]: This passage cites[63, 167, 32, 9, 98], in that order.

Maintenance scheduling optimization of standby systems has been of interest to many nuclear engineers and researchers. Harunuzzaman and Aldemir (1996) proposed the use of dynamic programing to minimize maintenance cost. Vaurio (1997) has also developed a method for economic optimization. According to Duthie et al. (1998), probabilistic safety analysis (PSA) techniques have been underutilized to establish preventive maintenance policy of safety systems. Billinton and Pan (1997), however, considered PSA in the maintenance policy optimization, but applied to simple engineering system. In practice, to establish a good maintenance policy is often a complex task, due to the large number of components that make up the industrial systems. Aiming to better face such complexity, Muñoz et al. (1997) proposed the use of genetic algorithm as the optimization tool. The approach presented in this work considers both the use of GA and PSA to optimize preventive maintenance policies of standby systems. Here, different from the method proposed by Muñoz et al. (1997), the genetic modeling is made in such a way that unconstrained optimization is performed, allowing the search for nonconstant intervals between maintenance that better adapt the aging parameter of a Weibull distribution, for each component.

In 2009, an Egyptian team — Mohamed El-Sayed Wahed, Wesam Zakaria Ibrahim and Ahmed Mostafa Effat — reported [169] about a genetic algorithm being used (with every target being considered as a separate objective to be optimized), in order to optimize the plate element of the second Egyptian Research Reactor, ET-RR-2, which went critical on November 27, 1997, and the responsibility for whose safety evaluation and assessment is of Egypt's National Center of Nuclear Safety and Radiation Control. "The fuel element plate is designed with a view to improve reliability and lifetime, and it is one of the most important elements during the shutdown" [169]. The team presented "a conceptual design approach for the fuel element plate, in conjunction with a genetic algorithm to obtain a fuel plate that maximizes a fitness value for optimizing the safety design of the fuel plate"[169].

In 2001, 2004, and 2009, Cecilia Martín-del-Campo and her colleagues — a team from Mexico — discussed the application of genetic algorithms to fuel reload design to in boiling water reactors (BWR) [93–95]. The paper [93] discussed

AXIAL, a system resorting to genetic algorithms, and whose task is axial optimization in boiling water reactors. Parameter prediction of the output reload configurations was done by "using the 3D steady state simulator code Core-Master-PRESTO (CM-PRESTO) to evaluate the objective function" [93]. Positioning of fuel assemblies (FA) on the two symmetrical axes of the reactor core was of special interest, in AXIAL: "The axial location of different fuel compositions is found in order to minimize the FA mean enrichment needed to obtain the cycle length under the safety constraints" [93]. At the end of the cycle, thermal limits were evaluated by using the Haling calculation, and

> the hot excess reactivity and the shutdown margin at the beginning of cycle are also evaluated. The implemented objective function is very flexible and complete, incorporating all the thermal and reactivity limits imposed during fuel design analysis; furthermore, additional constraints can be easily introduced in order to obtain an improved solution. The results show a small improvement in the FA average enrichment obtained with the system related to the reference case that has been studied. The results show that the system converges to an optimal solution, it is observed that the mean fuel enrichment decreases while all the constraints are satisfied.

In [94], the optimization method in a "computer program named Loading Pattern Optimization System based on Genetic Algorithms" combined genetic algorithms with expert knowledge coded in heuristics rules. The candidate fuel reload patterns selected by the genetic algorithm were evaluated by the core simulator code CM-PRESTO.

> A multi-objective function was built to maximize the cycle energy length while satisfying power and reactivity constraints used as BWR design parameters. Heuristic rules were applied to satisfy standard fuel management recommendations as the Control Cell Core and Low Leakage loading strategies, and octant symmetry. To test the system performance, an optimized cycle was designed and compared against an actual operating cycle of Laguna Verde Nuclear Power Plant, Unit I.

In [95], progress in the team's use of genetic algorithms was described:

> In order to avoid specific implementations of genetic operators and to obtain a more flexible treatment, a binary representation of the solution was implemented; this representation had to take into account that a little change in the genotype must correspond to a little change in the phenotype. An identifier number is assigned to each assembly by means of a Gray Code of 7 bits and the solution (the loading pattern) is represented by a binary chain of 777 bits of length.

In [95], another contribution discussed a device for integrating the genetic algorithm with heuristic knowledge from a human expert. Namely,

> the use of a *Fitness Function* which includes a *Heuristic Function* and an *Objective Function*. The *Heuristic Function* which is defined to give flexibility on the application of a set of positioning rules based on knowledge,

and the *Objective Function* that contains all the parameters which qualify
the neutronic and thermal hydraulic performances of each loading pattern.

In 2002, Jonathan Carter published a survey [16] of the applications of genetic
algorithm for in-core fuel management in nuclear reactors; his survey also covered
some other then recent developments in optimization in nuclear engineering. That
survey should be considered complementary to my present study.

22   Further Advances in the Literature in the 2000s

In 2009, Amir Hosein Fadaei, Saeed Setayeshi, and Shabnam Kia [35] described an
optimization method combining *cellular automata* (CA) and *simulated annealing*
(SA) for generating fuel reload patterns in a Russian reactor model, VVER-1000,
at the Bushehr power plant in Iran. "This method contains two principles that are
neighboring concept from CA and accepting each displacement basis on decreasing
of objective function and Boltzman distribution from SA that plays role of transition rule" [35]. Fadaei et al. [35] compared their own method to the "Hopfield neural
network procedure that was used for solving this problem and has been shown that
the result, velocity and qualification of new method are comparable with that" [35].

In 2009, Tong Kyu Park, Han Gyu Joo, Chang Hyo Kim, and Hyun Chul Lee
[127] described multiobjective loading pattern optimization (the two objectives being maximizing the cycle length, and minimizing the radial peaking factor), by resorting to simulated annealing, and employing a discontinuous penalty function
and a bidimensional screening technique. The application was to refuelling in a
pressurized water reactor. Parameter prediction was done by means of a three-
dimensional model. They explained:

> The problem of multiobjective fuel loading pattern (LP) optimization em-
> ploying high-fidelity three-dimensional (3-D) models is resolved by intro-
> ducing the concepts of discontinuous penalty function, dominance, and
> two-dimensional (2-D)-based screening into the simulated annealing (SA)
> algorithm. Each constraint and objective imposed on a reload LP design is
> transformed into a discontinuous penalty function that involves a jump to
> a quadratic variation at the point of the limiting value of the corresponding
> core characteristics parameter.

Park et al. [127] showed "that with this discontinuous form the sensitivity of the
penalty coefficients is quite weak compared to the stochastic effect of SA." Those
feasible loading patterns that are discovered during the update of the simulated
annealing, "update the set of candidate LPs through a dominance check that is done
by examining multiple objectives altogether" [127]. A screening technique in two
dimensions "uses a precalculated database of the 2-D solution errors and is shown
to be very effective in saving the SA computation time by avoiding 3-D evaluations
for the unfavorable LPs that are frequently encountered in SA" [127].

Castillo et al. [17] (the team included Martín-del-Campo, by whom we discussed
e.g. [95] in the previous section) discussed boiling water reactor (BWR) fuel reloads

design, by resorting to a Tabu search technique[40] (using such Tabu search ideas as random dynamic Tabu tenure, and frequency-based memory), along with the heuristic rules of Control Cell Core and Low Leakage. "These heuristic rules are a common practice in fuel management to maximize fuel assembly utilization and minimize core vessel damage, respectively" [17]. For parameter prediction, calculations in three dimensions were carried out: "The system uses the 3-D simulator code CM-PRESTO and it has as objective function to maximize the cycle length while satisfying the operational thermal limits and cold shutdown constraints" [17]. Comparisons were made to the energy cycle as obtained from loading patterns generated by a human expert of by genetic algorithms, and the numerical experiments showed that the system based on Tabu search had a relatively improved energy cycle.

In 2004, two scholars from the University of Granada (Spain), Juan José Ortiz and Ignacio Requena [124], reported about an order coding genetic algorithm to optimize the nuclear fuel reload in a boiling water reactor (BWR). They proposed an order coding for the chromosomes, and appropriate crossover and mutation operators. Therefore, it is of interest to compare this system to FUELGEN. Whereas in its academic setting, FUELGEN was used with NOXER (the latter being replaced when adoption in industry was considered), Ortiz and Requena's

---

[40] In 1999, Geoffrey Parks's team, too, reported about an application of tabu search to nuclear fuel reload design [7]. In contrast, another paper of 1999 from Park's team reported about simulated annealing being applied to PWR reload optimisation designs [133]. Already in 1991, Kropaczek, Parks, Maldonado, and Turinsky [80] reported about the application of simulated annealing to in-core nuclear fuel management optimization. Cf. [81], of 1994, by those same four authors (and cf. [132], of 1992). In 2002, Paul J. Turinsky and Geoffrey T. Parks published an article entitled "Advances in Nuclear Fuel Management for Light Water Reactors" [166].

Unlike Alex Galperin, who has always published within nuclear engineering, Geoffrey T. Parks of the University of Cambridge (the results of whose own research on the application of genetic algorithms to fuel reload design were, in the mid-1990s [128–130], competing with those of FUELGEN) has published not only within nuclear engineering (e.g., in 2010 [21]) — two papers of 2007 [65, 66] were about transmutation of nuclear waste — but in other engineering domains as well.

It is to those other engineering domains, that during the 2000s most efforts of Parks's team have been directed. The unifying thread is that they developed optimization methods for engineering. More precisely, within nuclear engineering, the Cambridge team has been concerned with in-core nuclear fuel management optimization (the subject of my present paper), and with the analysis and design of nuclear reactor systems, whereas in other fields within engineering that team has been concerned with the simulation and optimization of advanced cycles for engines and turbines.

Among the other things, Parks's team has published about adaptive parametrization in multi-objective Tabu search optimization [60]; cf. [70], and [79], the application being to design optimization for axial compressors. Parks's Cambridge team applied optimization by simulated annealing instead to the design of bicycle frames [157]. Another project of Parks's team was the application of simulated annealing in a scheduling algorithm for selecting reverse osmosis membrane cleaning schedules [147], this being an example of water software systems (software applied to water systems).

genetic system was used along with a neural simulator for parameter prediction. Ortiz and Requena [124] designed their fitness function

> so that the genetic algorithm creates fuel reloads that, on one hand, satisfy the constrictions for the radial power peaking factor, the minimum critical power ratio, and the maximum linear heat generation rate while optimizing the effective multiplication factor at the beginning and end of the cycle. To find the values of these variables, a neural network trained with the behavior of a reactor simulator was used to predict them. The computation time is therefore greatly decreased in the search process. We validated this method with data from five cycles of the Laguna Verde Nuclear Power Plant in Mexico.

Already in 2002, Ortiz and Requena [122] described their use of a Multi-State Recurrent Neural Network (MSRNN) for the purpose of optimizing the nuclear fuel reload in a boiling water reactor. By changing neuronal states, the MSRNN proposed different fuel reloads. Both safety aspects and cycle length were taken into account, as the energy function of each candidate fuel-reload was evaluated. Whereas the MSRNN proposed candidate reloads, the equivalent of what NOXER was for both FUELCON of FUELGEN was instead, in the architecture described by Ortiz and Requena [122], a parameter prediction system being a trained Back-Propagation Neural Network (BKPNN), instead of a conventional reactor simulator (of the kind which, like NOXER, uses some nodal algorithm). The MSRNN and the BKPNN, coupled together, form the system called RENOR. The validation of the MSRNN was using data from the same nuclear plant from Mexico as mentioned earlier. "The cycle length of the RENOR fuel reload is longer than the cycle length of the fuel reload of Laguna Verde Nuclear Power Plant (LVNPP) in Mexico for the selected cycle" [122, p. 549] (the Laguna Verde plant has two reactors). Ortiz and Requena conceded that it is desirable to maintain an eighth core symmetry. Nevertheless, they "maintained just a quarter core symmetry because with an eighth symmetry it would be possible that there were not enough" [fuel assemblies] with the same or similar [infinite multiplicative factor] value to be placed in symmetrical positions when it is expanded to a quarter or full core symmetry for a fuel reload" [122, p. 545].

In 2003, again Ortiz and Requena [123] discussed their using neural networks to predict core parameters in a boiling water reactor. In most procedures for optimizing refuelling, they pointed out, whereas techniques ranging from expert systems to genetic algorithms are used in order to select good candidate reload patterns, "nuclear reactor simulators are used, which require a longer computation time, to evaluate the goodness of the proposed solutions. As the processes are iterative, many evaluations with the simulator are necessary, and this makes the process extremely slow" [123]. Ortiz and Requena [123] proposed "the use of trained neural networks (NNs) [. . .] as an alternative to the simulator, and the results of the NN training are shown in order to predict some variables of interest in the optimization, such as the effective multiplication factor and some thermal limits, related to safety aspects" [123].

In 2007, Juan José Ortiz, Alejandro Castillo, José Luis Montes, and Raúl Perusquía [125] discussed their new system, OCOTH, for optimizing both control rod pattern and fuel-loading design in boiling water reactors. The techniques applied are genetic algorithms, neural networks, and ant colonies. The *ant colony* paradigm of optimization, a cooperative learning approach to the Travelling Salesman Problem [89, 33, 29, 28, 26, 90],[41] is also known as *distributed stigmergetic control*. Ant colony algorithms are based on the metaphor of a colony of ants (or termites), when individual members of the colony follow a route once they detect the olfactive trace of chemicals (*pheromones*) released by their companions that already passed by that route. The family of optimization algorithms known as ant colony optimization (ACO) is inspired by pheromone-based strategies of ant-foraging. "ACO algorithms were orignally conceived to find the shortest route in traveling salesman problems. In ACO several ants travel across the edges that connect the nodes of a graph while depositing virtual pheromones" [38, p. 527]. "Ants that travel on the shortest path will be able to make more return trips and deposit more pheromones in a given amount of time. Consequently, that path will attract more ants in a positive feedback loop" [38, pp. 527–528]. Ant colony algorithms "have been developed with variations that address the specificities of the problems to be solved", not only travelling salesman problems [38, p. 528]. There is a shortcoming to be remedied, in that if ants in nature have initially chosen a longer path,

---

[41] The paper [92] resulted from a collaboration between scholars in behavioural biology (entomologists: Anna Dornhaus and Nigel Franks), complex systems modelling (James Marshall), and computer science (Tim Kovacs). Other articles from Anna Dornhaus's team include [15, 12, 30, 39, 40]. There exists a discipline called *mathematical insect sociobiology,* and Dornhaus has become quite visible there, researching especially collective decision-making by ants or bees. It is not only about what computer scientists call the ant colony paradigm. Dornhaus researches ants and bees, and even just considering ants, there is more to model than what is captured by what in artificial intelligence and operations research goes metaphorically by the name *ant colony algorithms.* Moreover, bear in mind that articles in *functional ecology* are also replete with mathematical formulae.

Actually, in 2003, Marshall et al. [92] modelled computationally ant pheromone-trail not for foraging, but for the ant colony to find a nest:

When an ant colony needs to find a new nest, scouts are sent out to evaluate the suitability of potential sites, particularly their size. It has been suggested that ant scouts of *Leptothorax albipennis* use a simple heuristic known as Buffon's needle to evaluate nest size. They do this in two stages: first laying a pheromone trail in the nest site, then, after a return to the old nest, coming back and wandering within the site assessing frequency of intersection with the pheromone trail ("two-pass" strategy). If a colony is forced to relocate from its current nest due to destruction of that nest, the time required to find a suitable new nest may be crucial.

Marshall et al. [92] discussed

preliminary results from a computer simulation model of evaluation of nest size. The model aims to study why a "two-pass" strategy is used by ants when a "one-pass" strategy, in which the ant simultaneously lays pheromone and assesses the frequency at which it encounters its own trail, may be more time efficient. Analysis of the results indicates no clear advantage for the "two-pass" strategy, given the assumptions of the model.

"that path will become reinforced even if it not the shortest. To overcome this problem, ACO assumes that virtual pheromones evaporate, thus reducing the probability that long paths are selected" [38, p. 528].[42]

---

[42] In the original *ant system* proposed in 1996 by Dorigo et al. [29], the workings are as follows [38, p.528]:

Initially, ants are randomly distributed on the nodes of the graph. Each artificial ant chooses an edge from its location with a probabilistic rule that takes into account the length of the edge and the amount of pheromones on that edge. Edges leading to nodes that have already been visited by that ant are not considered in the probabilistic choice. Once all ants have completed a full tour of the graph, each of them retraces its own route while depositing on the traveled edges an amount of pheromones inversely proportional to the length of the route. Before restarting the ants from random locations for another search, the pheromones on all edges evaporate by a small quantity. The pheromone evaporation, combined with the probabilistic choice of the edge, ensures that ants eventually converge on one of the shortest paths, but some ants continue to travel also on slightly longer paths.

In 1997, Dorigo and Gambardella [28] developed the *ant colony system* (as opposed to the *ant system* of [29]), in which improvement was achieved by introducing local search heuristics in addition to the virtual ants. Because of the probabilistic edge choice, ACO algorithms have a major advantage over other algorithms for path finding, in that "virtual ants discover and maintain several short paths in addition to the best one" [38, p. 528]. ACO is quite useful for dynamic networks: "If an edge is no longer traversable or a node is unavailable, ants will quickly use and reinforce the second shortest path", with no need to recompute the shortest path on the new graph, which other algorithms must instead do [38, p. 528].

Social odours are also known from mammals [13]. It is important to realize that the ant colony paradigm in operations research and computational intelligence does not exhaust what can be learned from animal pheromone communication. Elsewhere [111], while reviewing [96, 173], I pointed out the following example of robotics displaying *biomimetism:*

A pheromone trail is a concept underlying neurobiologist Frank Grasso's *RoboLobster.* The aim of that project is to produce such a robot that would mimic a lobster's ability to navigate pounding surf, and the intended use is in discovering the scent of chemicals and identifying their sources underwater, such as because of a leakage (e.g., a plume of chemicals was discovered in the Red Sea, in experiments conducted in 2002 on second-generation lobster-like robots in collaboration with the Interuniversity Institute of Eilat, Israel), as well as in clearing mines from shallow water. The underwater trials were conducted at a depth of 5 metres. The substance to be sensed by the robot was marked with dye, so the students who were scoring the robot's behaviour could do so by tracking its movements relative to the dye (Hood 2004). "A small underwater wheeled robot with conductivity sensors was used to test chemical orientation strategies employed by lobsters to locate odor sources" (Beer et al. 1998, p. 779, referring to Grasso et al. 1996; also see Blazis, Grasso 1999, 2001). *RoboLobster* does not look like a lobster, except in that on its front side, it has two antennae, which are parallel with the flanks of the rather flat box which constitutes its body. There is one wheel on each of the flanks of its lower part (a box with a trapeze section), which is surmounted by a parallelepiped of clear plastic.

Natural lobsters sense chemicals which may or may not be produced by their own kind. For example, in his book on pheromones under review here, Wyatt (p. 62, caption of Fig. 3.10) shows: "A female lobster [...], attracted by a male's chemical 'song', jets her own urine towards a male in his shelter. He responds by retreating to the opposite entrance and fanning his pleopods. [...]". The corresponding text (Wyatt, *ibid.,* p. 61) explains: "Males of the lobster *Homarus americanus* create odour currents from their dens, thus 'singing a chemical song' [...] (Bushmann & Atema 1997). Females choose the locally dominant male by his urine signals".

Wyatt (pp. 219–220) explains: "Turbulent odour plumes form as air or water currents disperse odour molecules from their source. Odour plumes are of course normally invisible but swirling smoke clouds from a chimney provide a good visual analogy of the important features", and: "The smoke forms a meandering cloud that snakes down. If you get closer, you can see the fine-scale structure within the clouds, with filaments of high concentration interspersed with cleaner air. As a cloud of odour molecules moves from the source, turbulence tears apart the cloud into elongated odour-containing filaments, each only a few millimetres wide, separated by 'clean' water or air". Importantly for communication: "This fine filament structure is central to the responses evolved by orienting animals. The turbulent effects are greater than diffusion (which is comparatively slow) and an important consequence is that a plume is far from a uniform cloud of pheromone drifting downwind, rather it is composed of filaments that remain relatively concentrated. Thus the pheromone concentrations within the filaments will be above the response threshold much further downstream than a diffusion model would predict — but in a spreading plume, fardownstream [sic], the odour filaments may be widely spaced" (*ibid.*).

Fig. 10.11 on p. 222 in Wyatt's book shows, side by side, two tall, shaded triangles (an idealisation of odour plumes) with two equal edges, topping in a point which corresponds to a chemical source. The flow direction is downwards, i.e., from the top of the triangles, to their basis. On the left-hand triangle, a lobster is shown, zigzagging from outside the triangle on one side, through the triangle to outside the triangle on the opposite side, and then back into the triangle until the lobster reaches (inside the triangle) the top, i.e., the source. By contrast, on the right-hand triangle, an estuarine crab is shown (its body contour being broad, as opposite to the slender lobster). The crab zigzags a little bit, but it does so along the same edge of the triangle, by alternating an α angle, then a $-\alpha$ angle, and so on, until it reaches the top of the triangle. In the caption of that same figure, Wyatt explains:

> Lobsters in turbulent environments, and estuarine crabs in smooth-flowing creeks, use different mechanisms to orient up odour plumes [...] to find the source. Lobsters [...] use tropotaxis, simultaneous bilateral comparisons of odour intensity to turn into the plume, and sequential comparison of odour intensity, klinotaxis, to progress towards the source within the plume. [...] An estuarine crab [...] shows positive rheotaxis to the flow and uses a binary comparison of odour presence – absence to determine that it has left the plume. The crab judges its exit angle (α) relative to the flow direction and uses this information to re-enter the plume at the same angle at which it exited the plume.

Ortiz and his colleagues explained [125]:

> Each heuristic technique is used to design a part of the optimization process. So, the neural network finds an initial fuel loading with a Haling burnup calculation. The ant colony system optimizes full-power control rod pattern of the initial fuel loading. Finally, the genetic algorithm optimizes fuel loading with the optimized control rod patterns. The ant colony system and the genetic algorithm perform an iterative loop until a stop criterion is fulfilled; for example, control rod pattern and fuel-loading convergence. The OCOTH system was tested in an equilibrium cycle of Mexico's Laguna Verde Nuclear Power Plant. We found very good results in control rod pattern and fuel-loading coupled optimization.

In 2009, Juan José Ortiz, Alejandro Castillo, José Luis Montes, Raúl Perusquía, and José Luis Hernández [126] reported about RENO-CC, which they described as "a system to optimize nuclear fuel lattices for boiling water reactors using a multistate recurrent neural network", this being a kind of neural network formed by only one layer of neurons. In their application — Ortiz et al. [126] explained — "Each neuron is associated with a pin of the fuel lattice array." The size was as follows: "RENO-CC was tested through the fuel lattice design of 10×10 arrays with two water channels. Thus, the neural network has a total of 51 neurons; four neurons are associated with the channels (they correspond to a half fuel lattice)." The neural states (i.e., the neuron's outputs) were chosen from an inventory of pins which have different ^{235}U enrichment and concentrations of the burnable poison gadolinium. The neural states are changed, by the neural network of RENO-CC, so that the value of an objective function be decreased or increased. "The objective function includes both the local power peaking factor and the infinite multiplication factor", and these parameters are calculated by using the HELIOS code. The paper explained [126]:

> A fuzzy logic system is applied in order to decide if the designed fuel lattice is suitable to be evaluated by a three-dimensional reactor core simulator. To carry out the assessment, the fuel lattices with the best fuzzy qualification are placed at the bottom zone of a predesigned fuel assembly and predesigned fuel loading and control rod patterns. Fuel lattice performance is verified with the Core Master PRESTO core simulator. According to the obtained results, RENO-CC could be considered as a powerful tool to design fuel lattices.

In 2001, Suetsugu Jagawa, Takashi Yoshii, Akihiro Fukao reported [71] about an automated system for designing a loading pattern (LP) for boiling water reactors (BWR). Their system does not work *ex nihilo*. It requires that a reference loading pattern be given, along with a control rod (CR) sequence. Just as NOXER uses a nodal algorithm, the system described in [71] resorts to a nodal code, SIMULATE-3. The loading pattern optimizer for BWR is a piece of software called FINELOAD-3, which resorts to a simple linear perturbation method and to a modified Tabu search method, in order to select potential optimized loading pattern candidates.

FINELOAD-3 also adjusts deep CR positions to compensate for the core reactivity deviation caused by fuel shuffling. The objective function is to maximize the end-of-cycle core reactivity while satisfying the specified thermal margins and cold shutdown margin constraints. This optimization system realized the practical application for real BWR LP design.

The team from Japan reported that tests they carried out showed that the solutions obtained by using their system "are equivalent or better than the manually optimized LPs" [71].

The development of computer systems for shuffling fuel assemblies in order to obtain a new reload configuration did not die out with the appearance of generators of whole configurations, like FUELCON and FUELGEN. In 1998, K.-J. Lin and Chaung Lin, in Taiwan [87], described pressurized water reactor reload design by an expert system. Their program generated several reload cycles for the Maanshan nuclear power plant in Taiwan. In their system, "an initial loading pattern was generated according to the fuel assembly's infinite multiplication factor, by using heuristic rules. Then, the fuel assembly was swapped or rotated, using heuristic rules, to satisfy an assumed search target" [87].

Let us turn to the development of parameter prediction tools (cf. NOXER). In 2003, Kibog Lee and Chang Hyo Kim [85] presented a least-squares method for three-dimensional core power distribution monitoring calculation in pressurized water reactors (PWR). The application was to a Korean reactor, the Yonggwang Unit 3 (YGN-3) PWR. "The method here makes use of the solution to the normal equation that is derived from solving the overdetermined system of equations comprising the fixed in-core detector response equations and the nodal neutronics design equations in the least-squares principle" [85]. The criteria of evaluation were in terms of computational speed and accuracy. A nodal algorithm was used (like in NOXER) in order to satisfy accuracy requirements: "the nonlinear analytical nodal method (ANM) is employed for accurate core neutronics calculations, and a preconditioned conjugate gradient normal residual iteration algorithm is adopted for speedy solution to the normal equation" [85]. Application to monitoring the Korean reactor of the least-squares method

is examined by pure numerical experiments in which the reference three-dimensional (3-D) power distribution is calculated by the 36 node-per-fuel-assembly (N/A) nonlinear ANM. Simulated detector signals are derived from the reference power distribution to establish detector response equations. The 3-D monitored core power distribution is obtained from the 1 or 4 N/A solution to the normal equation and compared with the reference power distribution to determine the prediction accuracy.

In 2007, David Weber and ten co-authors [172] reported about the Numerical Nuclear Reactor (NNR), a model intended to improve upon three-dimensional reactor analysis for light-water reactors. "High fidelity is accomplished by integrating full physics, highly refined solution modules for the coupled neutronic and thermal-hydraulic phenomena. Each solution module employs methods and models that are formulated faithfully to the first principles governing the physics, real geometry, and constituents" [172]. The requirements were quite demanding. "Specifically, the critical analysis elements that are incorporated in the coupled code capability are a direct whole-core neutron transport solution and an ultra-fine-mesh computational fluid dynamics / heat transfer solution, each obtained with explicit (sub-fuel-pin-cell level) heterogeneous representations of the components of the core" [172]. Of course, this is very costly in terms of computation. "The considerable computational resources required for such highly refined modeling are addressed by using massively parallel computers, which together with the coupled codes constitute the NNR." [172]. The team acknowledged the need "to establish confidence in the NNR methodology", so "verification and validation of the solution modules have been performed and are continuing for both the neutronic module and the thermal-hydraulic module for single-phase and two-phase boiling conditions under prototypical pressurized water reactor and boiling water reactor conditions" [172].

In a paper of 2008, [155], Reuben Sorensen and John Lee described an equilibrium cycle search methodology, for assembly-level fuel cycle analysis in light water reactors (LWR). They developed a "search algorithm that is similar to the REBUS-3 fast reactor methodology but with depletion capabilities typically employed for LWR analysis" [155]. That is, in a sense, they ported a method from fast reactors, to light water reactors.

> Our LWR methodology projects the original coupled nonlinear isotopic balance equations to a series of equations that are piecewise linear in time. Iterations are performed on microscopic reaction rates until the linearized isotopic balance equations yield an ultimate equilibrium state. We further reduce the computational burden associated with LWR analysis by approximating global depletion calculations with assembly-level, collision probability calculations performed by the CASMO-3 code. We demonstrate the benefits of our equilibrium cycle methodology by calculating the true equilibrium [plutonium] inventory of two configurations [...]

In 2007, Marseguerra, Zio and Cadini [91] were concerned with the steam generator of pressurized water reactors. They proposed an optimized adaptive, stable, fuzzy controller of the water level of such a steam generator. The controller's design parameters were optimized by means of a genetic algorithm. "Computer simulations confirm that the devised controller bears good performances in terms of small oscillations and fast settling time even in the presence of steam flow disturbances" [91]. The need for such an improved controller was stated as follows [91]:

> Inefficient control of the water level in a steam generator of a nuclear power plant is responsible for frequent unscheduled reactor trips. This problem is particularly critical at low power, when the steam generator exhibits the "swell and shrink" phenomenon and flow rate measurements are highly unreliable. The design of a proper controller capable of avoiding expensive shutdowns is eagerly sought for increasing the availability of the plant.

In a paper from 2008, [165], Hoai Nam Tran, Yasuyoshi Kato, and Yasushi Muto discussed the optimization of burnable poison loading for HTGR cores with so-called OTTO refuelling.

A burnable poison (BP) loading principle has been proposed for once-through-then-out refueling of a high-temperature gas-cooled reactor (HTGR) core with pebble fuel. The principle holds that an axial core power peaking factor can be minimized when k_∞ [i.e., the infinite multiplication factor] of the fuel pebbles is kept constant during their axial movement from the top to the bottom of the core by adding BP.

In 2006, Alberto Talamo and Waclaw Gudowski [159] were concerned with the incineration of military plutonium. This incineration is to be carried out in the gas turbine-modular helium reactor. "In the future development of nuclear energy, the graphite-moderated helium-cooled reactors may play an important role because of their valuable technical advantages: passive safety, low cost, flexibility in the choice of fuel, high conversion energy efficiency, high burnup, more resistant fuel cladding, and low power density" [159]. This is a type of reactor in which the paper claimed a long experience for General Atomics, "and it has recently developed the gas turbine-modular helium reactor (GT-MHR), a design where the nuclear power plant is structured into four reactor modules of 600 MW(thermal)" [159]. Talamo and Gudowski enumerated, amid the benefits of the GT-MHR, "a rather large flexibility in the choice of fuel type", and thorium, uranium, and plutonium "may be used in the manufacture of fuel with some degrees of freedom". Because of these degrees of freedom, "the fuel management may be designed for different objectives aside from energy production, e.g., the reduction of actinide waste production through a fuel based on thorium"[43] [159].

Talamo and Gudowski had analyzed in previous studies "the behavior of the GT-MHR with a plutonium fuel based on light water reactor (LWR) waste; in the present study we focused on the incineration of military" plutonium [159]. Using such fuel however "requires a detailed numerical modeling of the reactor since a high value of k_{eff} at the beginning of the reactor operation requires the modeling both of control rods and of burnable poison" [159].

The GT-MHR offers advantages, as "by contrast, when the GT-MHR is fueled with LWR waste, at the equilibrium of the fuel composition, the reactivity swing is small" [159]. Talamo and Gudowski [159] proposed a deep burn fuel management strategy for incinerating military plutonium in the GT-MHR, and the modelling is in a detailed three-dimensional geometry, by resorting to

---

[43] It was Alvin Radkowsky, Alex Galperin's former doctoral supervisor, who developed the concept and the design of thorium-based fuel and thorium reactors, in order to prevent the proliferation of plutonium from the waste of civilian nuclear power which could be used for military or even terror purposes. "The proliferation potential of the light water reactor fuel cycle may be significantly reduced by utilization of thorium as a fertile component of the nuclear fuel" [56, p. 265]. The concept of the Radkowsky Thorium Reactor (RTR) was presented in the paper [56]. Other than by Radkowsky or Galperin, thorium reactors are also the subject of, e.g., [21].

the Monte Carlo continuous energy burnup code. Antonino Romano and his colleagues [144] discussed in 2006 the implications of alternative strategies for transition to sustainable fuel cycles. "Fuel cycles employing recycling of actinides in the thermal COmbined NonFertile and UO_2 (CONFU) fuel light water reactor (LWR) or fast Actinide Burner Reactor (ABR) plus standard LWRs are compared to the once-through LWR fuel cycle under the assumption of moderately growing worldwide demand for nuclear energy until 2050" [144]. "Economic analyses show that both closed fuel cycles are more expensive than the reference once-through scheme" [144]. Storage prior to use and final disposal in repositories were important facets in their analysis: "The transuranic elements (TRUs) in temporary storage, the TRUs sent to permanent repositories, and the system cost are taken as key figures of merit" [144]. "Both strategies greatly reduce the total TRU mass destined to the permanent repositories, thus alleviating the burden of licensing a large number of such repositories, and the risk from deliberate or accidental excavation of TRUs from the repositories" [144].

In a paper from 2008, Yonghee Kim and Francesco Venneri [75] were concerned with the optimization of one-pass transuranic (TRU) deep burn (DB) in a block-type modular helium reactor, of a model proposed by General Atomics.

> For three-dimensional equilibrium cores, the performance analysis is done by using McCARD, a continuous-energy Monte Carlo depletion code. The core optimization is performed from the viewpoints of the core configuration, fuel management, tristructural-isotropic (TRISO) fuel specification, and neutron spectrum. With regard to core configuration, two annular cores are investigated in terms of the neutron economy. A conventional radial shuffling scheme of fuel blocks is compared with an axial-only block-shuffling strategy in terms of the fuel burnup and core power distributions. The impact of the kernel size of the TRISO fuel is evaluated, and a diluted kernel, instead of a conventional concentrated kernel, is introduced to maximize the TRU burnup by reducing the self-shielding effects of the TRISO particles. A higher graphite density is also evaluated in terms of the fuel burnup. In addition, it is shown that the core power distribution can be effectively controlled by a zoning of the packing fraction of the TRISO fuels. We also have shown that a long-cycle DB-MHR core can be designed by using a two- or three-batch fuel-reloading scheme, at the expense of only a marginal decrease of the TRU discharge burnup.

In 2009, Sheu, Chen, Liu, and Jiang [148] drew a comparison of discrete ordinates, Monte Carlo, and hybrid methods, for the purposes of shielding calculations for a spent fuel storage cask. The "discrete ordinates and Monte Carlo methods were applied to solve the radiation transport problem for a simplified spent fuel storage cask considering fixed neutron and gamma-ray sources. The results were compared, and the causes for their differences were investigated" [148]. In order to accelerate the Monte Carlo simulations, She et al. [148] adopted "a hybrid method based on the Consistent Adjoint Driven Importance Sampling

(CADIS) methodology": "CADIS utilizes a deterministic adjoint function for variance reduction through source biasing and consistent transport biasing" [148].

Also in 2009, Gasper Zerovnik, Luka Snoj, and Matjaz Ravnik [175] reported about the optimization of spent nuclear fuel filling in canisters for deep repository. One can see then that the panoply of contexts in which optimization methods find application in nuclear engineering is wide indeed.

There is another aspect of nuclear reactors that deserves attention: *vulnerability analysis*. "Since the events of September 11, 2001, the vulnerability of nuclear power plants to terrorist attacks has become a national concern" [134]. In 2004, Peplow et al. [134] pointed out that "[t]he results of vulnerability analysis are greatly influenced by the computational approaches used". The possibility of attacks involves a special challenge: "Standard approximations used in fault-tree analysis are not applicable for attacks, where high component failure probabilities are expected"; therefore, [134] presented "two methods that do work with high failure probabilities". Moreover, vulnerability analysis is sensitive to how one models explosions involved in an attack: "Different blast modeling approaches can also affect the end results" [134]. The calculations in [134] used integrated geometry and event/fault-tree models. "Modeling the structural details of facility buildings and the geometric layout of components within the buildings is required to yield meaningful results" [134].

23   Submarine Refuellings and Victor Raskin's Computational Linguistics Tool for Sensitive Document Declassification

A team in computational linguistics at Purdue University, led by Victor Raskin [142], described in 2001 a hybrid data and text system for downgrading sensitive documents; it is an application of ontologies to eliminating sensitive information while declassifying documents (cf. a discussion of that system when applied to accounts of crime investigation, in [112, Sec. 6.1.7.5]). The tool manipulates documents being declassified, so that information that still must not be released be eliminated, and the wording reformulated so that it would not be included. The project from Purdue University was intended to respond to a real need for handling masses of documents, because of a policy instituted in the mid-1995:

> Since Executive Order 12958, Classified National Security Information, signed by President Clinton on April 17, 1995, most U.S. Government agencies have faced a monumental problem of declassifying millions of pages of its documentation. Many agencies as well as other organizations and corporations are increasingly facing the need of downgrading or sanitizing information that they need or have to share with their various coalition partners, e.g., within the NATO alliance.

Raskin et al. [142] listed different degrees of security requirements while declassifying documents. When the requirement is *weak declassification,* the problem is one of "dividing a set of documents into definitely open ones and others, with a reasonable degree of accuracy". When the requirement is *strong declassification*, the problem is one of "determining the status of each document as unclassified or classified without any margin of error". When the requirement is *downgrading/sanitizing*, the problem is more complex, as it involves "strong declassification coupled with a seamless modification of each classified document to an unclassified version". And finally, the most complex problem in this spectrum is when one has to carry out *"on-the-fly downgrading/sanitizing/surveillance:* filtering out electronic communication in real time." Some information is *top secret,* some other information is merely *secret,* and some other information is merely *confidential* [142]

The report from Purdue University explained [142]:

> In partially automatized textual declassification, there have been two primary approaches to the problem. The keyword- based approach is exemplified by the TapUltra-UltraStructure approach developed for the Department of Energy (see NRC 1995, DPRC 2000 in lieu of unavailable regular publications). The approach is based on an assumption that the classified element will appear as an anticipated word or string of words in the text. This assumption is not always correct, and the result is insufficient accuracy which is unlikely to be improvable in principle. The statistical tagging approach cleverly divides the entire corpus of documents into the training and testing subcorpora. Humans tag the training corpus in a variety of ways and divide it into classified and unclassified subsets. A sophisticated statistical procedure attempts then to relate certain tag clusters to the classified nature of a document and to tag the testing corpus automatically as well as to divide it into the classified and unclassified subsets. If this task is achieved with a high degree of accuracy, the approach succeeds (Hochberg 1999, 2000).

"The existing approaches share an important principle: They do not try to follow the declassification rules for human workers because, of course, humans understand the rules and these approaches do not" [142]. By contrast, the ontological semantic approach in [142] "both for text and for data, is based on the computer understanding of the information, which does make it possible to follow the prescribed declassification rules in every sensitive detail as well as to dynamically modify these rules" [142].

> The ontological semantic approach (see Nirenburg and Raskin [2004]) uses three major static resources, the lexicon (see Nirenburg and Raskin 1987, 1996 and Viegas and Raskin 1998), the ontology (see Mahesh 1996), and the text-meaning representation (TMR) language (see Onyshkevych and Nirenburg 1995). The lexicon contains words of a natural language, whose meanings are explained in terms of an ontological concept and/or its property. The ontology contains a tangled hierarchy of concepts, each containing a set of properties with filler specifications [...]. The TMR language composes the sentential meaning out of ontological concepts and their properties evoked by the words of the sentence with the help of a special formal syntax.

In the approach of Raskin et al. [142], which was to only involve minimal analysis, the use of ontology is confined to crucial terms and concepts, with the "possible addition of a few domain-specific nodes and/or properties of nodes" [142]. The lexicon, too, is a resource only used for crucial terms, with the "possible but rare addition of a terminological lexical entry or sense" [142]. TMR was used primarily for crucial terms. Nevertheless, TMR was to be ready for any paraphrase. The analyzer was fully ready for any paraphrase. As for the text generator, it was to be used only for downgrading and surveillance.

Raskin et al. [142] exemplified their method on several texts. In Sec. 2, entitled "Defining the illegal information", inside the report [142], the discussion was concerning nuclear submarines, including the refulling of such submarines:

> Let us consider a hypothetical example, in which the system is instructed to allow mentions of nuclear submarines but not their specific deployment, reactor capacity, or mode of refueling.[44]
>
> Focusing just on the first of these for the moment, instructing the computer to look for *nuclear submarine* and *deploy* in the text will fail the instruction in many different situations, e.g., when both occur in the text but not in the same sentence or adjacent sentences, and *deploy* does not pertain to the vessel. At the same time, the classified information may be given without using any form of *deploy* but rather with such words as *location*, *is*, or even simply *at*. It is very hard to anticipate all the synonymic substitutions and paraphrases as well as permitted uses with just key-word combinations.

Raskin et al. [142, Sec. 3.1] provided an analysis of that example.

> One would think that simple syntactic parsing will solve at least the question of whether *deploy* pertains to nuclear submarine in a sentence, but, besides the fact that syntactic parsing needs then to be used globally and rather expensively, it will misinterpret such a simple sentence as *Nuclear submarines will be deployed nearby to support ground forces in case of military emergencies.*

---

[44] "In the United States Navy, Refueling and Overhaul (ROH) refers to a lengthy process or procedure performed on nuclear-powered Naval [i.e., U.S. Navy's] ships, which involves replacement of expended nuclear fuel with new fuel and a general maintenance fix-up, renovation, and often modernization of the entire ship. In theory, such a process could simply involve only refueling or only an overhaul, but nuclear refueling is usually combined with an overhaul. An ROH usually takes a year to two years or longer to perform at a Naval shipyard. Time periods between ROH's on a ship have varied historically from about 5–20 years (for submarines) to up to 25 years (for Nimitz-class aircraft carriers). For modern submarines and aircraft carriers, ROH's are typically carried out about midway through their operating lifespan. There are also shorter maintenance fix-ups called availabilities for ships periodically at shipyards. A particularly lengthy refueling, maintenance, and modernization process for a nuclear aircraft carrier can last up to almost three years and be referred to as a Refueling and Complex Overhaul (RCOH)."
http://en.wikipedia.org/wiki/Refueling_and_Overhaul

In case of the occurrence of *nuclear submarine* in the three narrowly defined contexts, this is how the system utilizes the resources. When the analyzer spots *nuclear submarine* or even just *submarine* in a sentence, it immediately evokes the appropriate lexical entry, which, in turn, produces the corresponding ontological concept, [...]

As one can see, application of artificial intelligence to nuclear engineering sometimes even involves computational linguistics.

24   Concluding Remarks

The subject of this paper is the application of artificial intelligence techniques to the problem of designing good loading patterns of nuclear fuel in order to refuel pressurized water reactors. This is a complex combinatorial, multimodal optimization problem. This article discusses a sequence of projects, carried out in Israel and then in London, which resulted in the rule-based expert system FUELCON in the late 1980s, and in the genetic-algorithm based FUELGEN in 1996. This paper also discusses how successive waves within artificial intelligence were reflected in this sequence of projects, and how applications of techniques from artificial intelligence to optimization problems in nuclear engineering have been reported during the 2000s. See Fig. 31.

In over twenty sections, we first provided an introduction to nuclear power plants, to the geometry of a reactor core planar section, to nuclear fuel reload design, and to the batches of fuel assemblies at end-of-cycle. We discussed why it is not possible to forecast the situation at end-of-cycle reliably. We considered the nature of the constraints, before considering the fuel-shuffling tools available before FUELCON, which instead generates families of candidate whole configurations of fuel assemblies inside the core, without shuffling fuel units in the grid based on a previous configuration.

We considered the workings of FUELCON and its significance, also examining a sample ruleset. We turned to the project in which symbolic-to-neural conversion of rules was designed, but not implemented. We then considered the workings of FUELGEN, and the role of macroevolution in that system. We then interpreted FUELCON and FUELGEN in terms of hyperrecursion and hyperincursion from anticipatory computing systems. We discussed the typology of the architectures within the sequence of projects in fuel reload pattern design in which I participated. After dealing with nodal-algorithm based simulators (such as NOXER, which was used in conjunction with both FUELCON and then FUELGEN) for parameter prediction based on the output configurations produced by FUELCON or FUELGEN, we pointed out the emergence of neural tools for calculating the core physics. We mentioned particle swarm optimization as a possible option for refuelling, as well as approaches to the optimization of fuel, and an approach to the combined optimization of fuel rods inside bundles (fuel assemblies), and of fuel assemblies inside the reactor core. We surveyed published applications, from the 2000s, of optimization methods, often

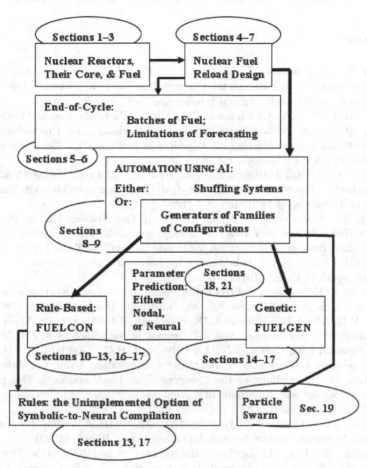

Fig. 31. Topics in this article

from artificial intelligence, to problems in nuclear engineering. Finally we considered Victor Raskin's computational linguistics tool for the automated modification of text enabling the declassification of sensitive documents, and the example Raskin gave of nuclear submarines and their refuelling.

Dedication. This paper is dedicated to the memory of Alvin Radkowsky, the centennial of whose birth will be on 30 June 2015. See notes 25 and 26.

References

1. Ahila, R., Sadavasivam, V., Manimala, K.: Particle Swarm Optimization-Based Feature Selection and Parameter Optimization for Power System Disturbances Classification. Applied Artificial Intelligence 26(9), 832–861 (2012)
2. Alsop, B.H., Chao, Y.A., Johansen, B.J., Morita, T.: Evaluation and Performance of Westinghouse Loading Pattern Search Methodology. In: Proceedings of the International Topical Meeting on Advances in Mathematics, Computations, and Reactor Physics, Pittsburgh, PA, Part 5, 22.2, 2–1 (1991)
3. Alvarenga, M.A.B., Martinez, A.S., Schirru, R.: Adaptive Vector Quantization Optimized by Genetic Algorithms for Real-Time Diagnosis Through Fuzzy Sets. Nuclear Technology 120(3), 188–197 (1997)
4. Bailly, H., Ménessier, D., Prunier, C. (eds.): The Nuclear Fuel of Pressurized Water Reactors and Fast Reactors: Design and Behaviour. Intercept, Andover, Hampshire, England; distrib. USA & Canada by Lavoisier Publ. Inc., c/o Springer Verlag, Secaucus, NJ; distrib. France by Lavoisier Publ., Cachan, dép. Val-de-Marne (south of Paris) (1999)
5. Baranov, S.: Examples of Control Units Design. In his: Logic Synthesis for Control Automata, ch. 8, pp. 340–386. Kluwer, Dordrecht, The Netherlands (1994)
6. Beer, R.D., Chiel, H.J., Quinn, R.D., Ritzmann, R.E.: Biorobotic Approaches to the Study of Motor Systems. Current Opinion in Neurobiology 8, 777–782 (1998)
7. Ben Hmaida, I.A., Carter, J.N., De Oliveira, C.R.E., Goddard, A.J.H., Parks, G.T.: Nuclear In-Core Fuel Management Optimization Using the Tabu Search Method. In: Proceedings of the Conference on Mathematics & Computation, Reactor Physics and Environmental Analysis in Nuclear Applications, Madrid, vol. 2, pp. 1658–1666 (1999)
8. Bernard, J.A., Washio, T.: Expert Systems Applications Within the Nuclear Industry. American Nuclear Society, La Grange Park, Illinois (1989)
9. Billinton, R., Pan, J.: Optimal Maintenance Scheduling in a Two Identical Component Parallel Redundant System. Reliability Engineering & System Safety 59(3), 309–316 (1997)
10. Blazis, D., Grasso, F.W.: Introduction to Invertebrate Sensory Information Processing, Biological Inspiration of Autonomous Robots. Biological Bulletin 200(2), 147–149 (1999)
11. Blazis, D.E.J., Grasso, F.W. (eds.): Proceedings of Invertebrate Sensory Information Processing: Implications for Biologically Inspired Autonomous Systems, Woodshole, MA, April 15-17 (2000), Biological Bulletin 200(2), 147–242 (2001)
12. Blonder, B., Dornhaus, A.: Time-Ordered Networks Reveal Limitations to Information Flow in Ant Colonies. PLoS One 6, e20298 (2011)
http://www.plosone.org/article/info:doi/10.1371/journal.pone.0020298

13. Brown, R.E., Macdonald, D.W. (eds.): Social Odours in Mammals (2 vols.). Oxford University Press, Oxford (1985)
14. Bushmann, P.J., Atema, J.: Shelter Sharing and Chemical Courtship Signals in the Lobster *Homarus Americanus*. Canadian Journal of Fisheries and Aquatic Sciences 54, 647–654 (1997)
15. Cao, T.T., Dornhaus, A.: Ants Use Pheromone Markings in Emigrations to Move Closer to Food-Rich Areas. Insectes sociaux 59, 87–92 (2012)
16. Carter, J.N.: Genetic Algorithms for Incore Fuel Management and Other Recent Developments in Optimisation. Advances in Nuclear Science & Technology 25, 113–154 (2002)
17. Castillo, A., Alonso, G., Morales, L.B., Martín del Campo, C., François, J.L., del Valle, E.: BWR Fuel Reloads Design Using a Tabu Search Technique. Annals of Nuclear Energy 31(2), 151–161 (2003)
18. Chao, Y.A., Alsop, B.H., Johansen, B.J., Morita, T.: Westinghouse Loading Pattern Search Methodology for Complex Core Designs. In: Proceedings of the Annual meeting of the American Nuclear Society (ANS), Orlando, FL, June 2-6 (1991), Transactions of the American Nuclear Society 63, 409–410 (1991)
19. Chapot, J.L.C., Silva, F.C., Schirru, R.: A New Approach to the Use of Genetic Algorithms to Solve Pressurized Water Reactor's Fuel Management Optimization Problem. Annals of Nuclear Energy 26(7), 641–655 (1999)
20. Cho, N.Z., Kim, Y.H., Park, K.W.: Extension of Analytic Function Expansion Nodal Method to Multigroup Problems in Hexagonal-Z Geometry. Nuclear Science and Engineering 126(1), 35–47 (1997)
21. Coates, D.J., Parks, G.T.: Actinide Evolution and Equilibrium in Fast Thorium Reactors. Annals of Nuclear Energy 37, 1076–1088 (2010), http://www-edc.eng.cam.ac.uk/cgi-bin/publications.cgi?542
22. Cochran, R.G., Tsoulfanidis, N.: The Nuclear Fuel Cycle: Analysis and Management. American Nuclear Society, La Grange Park, Illinois (1990)
23. DeChaine, M.D., Feltus, M.A.: Comparison of Genetic Algorithm Methods for Fuel Management Optimization. In: Proceedings of the International Conference on Mathematics and Computations, Reactor Physics, and Environmental Analysis, Portland, Oregon, vol. 1 (1995)
24. DeChaine, M.D., Feltus, M.A.: Nuclear Fuel Management Optimization Using Genetic Algorithms. Nuclear Technology 111, 109–114 (1995)
25. DeChaine, M.D., Feltus, M.A.: Fuel Management Optimization Using Genetic Algorithms and Expert Knowledge. Nuclear Science and Engineering 124(1), 188–196 (1996)
26. Di Caro, G., Dorigo, M.: AntNet: Distributed Stigmergetic Control for Communication Networks. Journal of Artificial Intelligence Research 9, 317–365 (1998)
27. Domingos, R.P., Schirru, R., Pereira, C.M.N.A.: Particle Swarm Optimization in Reactor Core Design. Nuclear Science and Engineering 152(2), 197–203 (2006)
28. Dorigo, M., Gambardella, L.M.: Ant Colony System: A Cooperative Learning Approach to the Traveling Salesman Problem. IEEE Transactions in Evolutionary Computation 1(1), 53–66 (1997)
29. Dorigo, M., Maniezzo, V., Colorni, A.: The Ant System: Optimization by a Colony of Cooperating Ants. IEEE Transactions on Systems, Man and Cybernetics, Part B 26, 1–13 (1996)
30. Dornhaus, A., Franks, N.R.: Individual and Collective Cognition in Ants and Other Insects (Hymenoptera: Formicidae). Myrmecological News 11, 215–226 (2008), http://www.myrmecologicalnews.org/cms/images/pdf/volume11/ mn11_215-226_non-printable.pdf

31. DPRC, Website of the Declassification Productivity Research Center, George Washington University, Washington, DC (2000), http://dprc.seas.gwu.edu/dprc5/research_projects/dwpa_n.htm
32. Duthie, J.C., Robertson, M.I., Clayton, A.M., Lidbury, D.P.G.: Risk-Based Approaches to Ageing and Maintenance Management. Nuclear Engineering and Design 184, 27–38 (1998)
33. Engelbrecht, A.P.: Ant Colony Optimization. In: Computational Intelligence: An Introduction, ch. 17, pp. 199–208. Wiley, Chichester, England (2002)
34. Faught, W.S.: Prototype Fuel Shuffling System Using a Knowledge-Based Toolkit. Technical Report, IntelliCorp, Mountain View, California (1987)
35. Fadaei, A.H., Setayeshi, S., Kia, S.: An Optimization Method Based on Combination of Cellular Automata and Simulated Annealing for VVER-1000 NPP Loading Pattern. Nuclear Engineering and Design 239(12), 2800–2808 (2009)
36. Fischetti, M.A.: Inherently Safe Reactors: They'd Work if we'd Let Them. IEEE Spectrum 24(4), 28–33 (1987)
37. Fitzpatrick, W.E.: Developments in Nodal Reactor Analysis Tools for Hexagonal Geometry. Ph.D. Disseration in Nuclear Engineering (supervisor: A.M. Ougouag), University of Illinois at Urbana-Champaign (1995)
38. Floreano, D., Mattiussi, C.: Bio-Inspired Artificial Intelligence: Theories, Methods, and Technologies. The MIT Press, Cambridge, MA (2008)
39. Franks, N.R., Hooper, J.W., Gumn, M., Bridger, T.H., Marshall, J.A.R., Groß, R., Dornhaus, A.: Moving Targets: Collective Decisions and Flexible Choices in House-Hunting Ants. Swarm Intelligence 1, 81–94 (2007)
40. Franks, N.R., Hooper, J.W., Dornhaus, A., Aukett, P.J., Hayward, A.L., Berghoff, S.: Reconnaissance and Latent Learning in Ants. Proceedings of the Royal Society: Biological Sciences 274, 1505–1509 (2007)
41. Galperin, A.: Utilization of Thorium in Light Water Reactors. Nuclear Science and Engineering 86, 112–115 (1984)
42. Galperin, A.: Exploration of the Search Space of the In-Core Fuel Management Problem by Knowledge-Based Techniques. Nuclear Science and Engineering 119(2), 144–152 (1985)
43. Galperin, A.: Feasibility of the Once-Through Thorium Fuel Cycle for CANDU Reactors. Nuclear Technology (USA) 73, 343–349 (1986)
44. Galperin, A.: Gd Burnable Poison System for Reactivity Control of the First Cycle of a PWR. Annals of Nuclear Energy (UK) 14, 53–57 (1987)
45. Galperin, A., Kimhy[sic], S.: Application of Knowledge-Based Methods to In-Core Fuel Management. Nuclear Science and Engineering 109, 103–110 (1991)
46. Galperin, A., Nissan, E.: Application of a Heuristic Search Method for Generation of Fuel Reload Configurations. Nuclear Science and Engineering 99(4), 343–352 (1988)
47. Galperin, A., Nissan, E.: Discovery as Assisted by an Expert Tool: A Refinement Loop for Heuristic Rules in an Engineering Domain. In: Proceedings of the 16th Convention of Electrical and Electronics Engineers, Paper 1.4.3, Tel-Aviv, March 7-9. IEEE, New York (1989)
48. Galperin, A., Nissan, E.: The FUELCON Meta-Architecture, II: Alternatives for Parameter Prediction. In: Nissan, E. (ed.) Forum on Refuelling Techniques for Nuclear Power Plants: One Decade with FUELCON. Thematic section, New Review of Applied Expert Systems, vol. 4, pp. 151–161 (1998)
49. Galperin, A., Segev, M., Radkowsky, A.: Substitution of the Soluble Boron Reactivity Control System of a Pressurized Water Reactor by Gadolinium Burnable Poisons. Nuclear Technology (USA) 75, 127–133 (1986)

50. Galperin, A., Segev, M., Radkowsky, A.: The Effect of Boron and Gadolinium Burnable Poisons on the Hot-to-Cold Reactivity Swing of a Pressurized Water Reactor Assembly. Nuclear Technology (USA) 75, 123–126 (1986)
51. Galperin, A., Foskolos, K., Grimm, P., Knoglinger, E., Maeder, C.: The Poison Zoning Technique for Power Peaking Control in District Heating Boiling Water Reactors. Kerntechnik (West Germany) 50, 170–172 (1987)
52. Galperin, A., Kimhi, S., Segev, M.: A Knowledge-Based System for Optimization of Fuel Reload Configurations. Nuclear Science and Engineering 102, 43–53 (1989)
53. Galperin, A., Kimhi, S., Nissan, E.: FUELCON: An Expert System for Assisting the Practice and Research of In-Core Fuel Management and Optimal Design in Nuclear Engineering. Computers and Artificial Intelligence 12(4), 369–415 (1993)
54. Galperin, A., Grimm, P., Raizes, V.: Modeling and Verification of the PWR Burnable Poison Designs by Elcos Code System. Annals of Nuclear Energy 22, 317–325 (1995)
55. Galperin, A., Kimhi, S., Nissan, E., Siegelmann, H., Zhao, J.: Symbolic and Subsymbolic Integration in Prediction and Rule-Revision Tasks for Fuel Allocation in Nuclear Reactors. In: Proceedings of the 3rd European Congress on Intelligent Techniques and Soft Computing (EUFIT 1995), Aachen, Germany, vol. 3, pp. 1546–1550 (1995)
56. Galperin, A., Reichert, P., Radkowsky, A.: Thorium Fuel for Light Water Reactors — Reducing Proliferation Potential of Nuclear Power Fuel Cycle. Science & Global Security 6, 265–290 (1997)
57. Galperin, A., Kimhi, S., Nissan, E., Siegelmann, H.: FUELCON's Heuristics, Their Rationale, and Their Representations. In: Nissan, E. (ed.) Forum on Refuelling Techniques for Nuclear Power Plants: One Decade with FUELCON. Thematic section, New Review of Applied Expert Systems, vol. 4, pp. 163–176 (1998)
58. Galperin, A., Segev, M., Todosow, M.: Pressurized Water Reactor Plutonium Incinerator Based on Thorium Fuel and Seed-Blanket Assembly Geometry. Nuclear Technology 132, 214–226 (2000)
59. Galperin, A., Shwageraus, E., Todosow, M.: Assessment of Homogeneous Thorium/Uranium Fuel for Pressurized Water Reactors. Nuclear Technology 138, 111–122 (2002)
60. Ghisu, T., Parks, G.T., Jaeggi, D.M., Jarrett, J.P., Clarkson, P.J.: The Benefits of Adaptive Parametrization in Multi-Objective Tabu Search Optimization. Engineering Optimization 42(10), 959–981 (2010), http://www-edc.eng.cam.ac.uk/cgi-bin/publications.cgi?824
61. Goddard, W.: Mistilings with Dominoes. Discrete Mathematics 137(1-3), 361–365 (1995)
62. Grasso, F., Consi, T., Mountain, D., Atema, J.: Locating Odor Sources in Turbulence with a Lobster Inspired Robot. In: Maes, P., Mataric, M., Meyer, J.-A., Pollack, J., Wilson, S.W. (eds.) Animals to Animats 4: Proceedings of the Fourth International Conference on the Simulation of Adaptive Behavior, pp. 104–113. The MIT Press, Cambridge, MA (1996)
63. Harunuzzaman, M., Aldemir, T.: Optimization of Standby Safety System Maintenance Scheduling in Nuclear Power Plants. Nuclear Technology 113, 354–367 (1996)
64. Havlíček, L.: Nuclear Fuel Cycle Evaluation and Real Options. Acta Polytechnica 48(3), 30–34 (2008), http://ctn.cvut.cz/ap/download.php?id=301

65. Herrera-Martnez, A., Kadi, Y., Parks, G.T.: Transmutation of Nuclear Waste in Accelerator-Driven Systems: Thermal Spectrum. Annals of Nuclear Energy 34, 550–563 (2007)
66. Herrera-Martínez, A., Kadi, Y., Parks, G.T., Dahlfors, M.: Transmutation of Nuclear Waste in Accelerator-Driven Systems: Fast Spectrum. Annals of Nuclear Energy 34, 564–578 (2007)
67. Hochberg, J.: Statistical Approaches to Automatic Identification of Classified Documents. Paper delivered at the CRL/NMSU International Symposium on New Paradigms in Knowledge and Information Processing, Las Cruces, NM (December 13, 1999) Cited in a quotation from Raskin et al. [142]
68. Hochberg, J.: Automatic Identification of Classified Documents. Paper delivered at the CERIAS Security Seminar, Purdue University, West Lafayette, IN (February 25, 2000) Cited in a quotation from Raskin et al. [142]
69. Hood, E.: RoboLobsters: The Beauty of Biomimetics. Environmental Health Perspectives 112(8), A486–A489 (June 2004). Also in EHP Student Edition, pp. A486–A489 (January 2005),
    http://ehp.niehs.nih.gov/members/2004/112-8/innovations.html
70. Jaeggi, D.M., Parks, G.T., Kipouros, T., Clarkson, P.J.: The Development of a Multi-Objective Tabu Search Algorithm for Continuous Optimisation Problems. European Journal of Operational Research 185(3), 1192–1212 (2008),
    http://www-edc.eng.cam.ac.uk/cgi-bin/publications.cgi?981
71. Jagawa, S., Yoshii, T., Fukao, A.: Boiling Water Reactor Loading Pattern Optimization Using Simple Linear Perturbation and Modified Tabu Search Methods. Nuclear Science and Engineering 138(1), 67–77 (2001)
72. Jardon, P., Dubois, D.: NUCLEXPERT: un progiciel d'Intelligence Artificielle pour l'optimisation des séquences de rechargement de centrales nucléaires. Nouvelles de la Science et des Technologies 4(2/3), 99–102 (1986)
73. Jessee, M.A., Kropaczek, D.J.: Coupled Bundle-Core Design Using Fuel Rod Optimization for Boiling Water Reactors. Nuclear Science and Engineering 155(3), 378–385 (2007)
74. Kennedy, J., Eberhart, R.C., with Shi, Y.: Swarm Intelligence. Morgan Kaufmann Publishers, San Francisco, California (2001)
75. Kim, Y., Venneri, F.: Optimization of One-Pass Transuranic Deep Burn in a Modular Helium Reactor. Nuclear Science and Engineering 160(1), 59–74 (2008)
76. Kim, H.G., Chang, S.H., Lee, B.H.: Optimal Fuel Loading Pattern Design Using an Artificial Neural Network and a Fuzzy Rule-Based System. Nuclear Science and Engineering 113, 152–163 (1993)
77. Kim, H.G., Chang, S.H., Lee, B.H.: Pressurized Water Reactor Core Parameter Prediction Using an Artificial Neural Network. Nuclear Science and Engineering 113(1), 70–76 (1993)
78. Kimhi, Y.: A Non-Algorithmic Approach to the In-Core Fuel Management Problem of a PWR Core. Ph.D. Dissertation, Nuclear Engineering, Ben-Gurion University of the Negev, Beer-Sheva, Israel (Kimhi's forename is "Yehoshua"; the form "Shuky" is also used) (1992) (in Hebrew)
79. Kipouros, T., Jaegii, D.M., Dawes, W.N., Parks, G.T., Savill, A.M., Clarkson, P.J.: Biobjective Design Optimization for Axial Compressors Using Tabu Search. AIAA Journal 46(3), 701–711 (2008),
    http://www-edc.eng.cam.ac.uk/cgi-bin/publications.cgi?1205

80. Kropaczek, D.J., Parks, G.T., Maldonado, G.I., Turinsky, P.J.: Application of Simulated Annealing to In-Core Nuclear Fuel Management Optimization. In: Proceedings of the 1991 International Topical Meeting on Advances in Mathematics, Computations and Reactor Physics (1991)

81. Kropaczek, D.J., Parks, G.T., Maldonado, G.I., Turinsky, P.J.: The Efficiency and Fidelity of the In-Core Nuclear Fuel Management Code FORMOSA-P. In: Ronen, Y., Elias, E. (eds.) Reactor Physics and Reactor Computations. Ben Gurion University of the Negev Press, Beer-Sheva, Israel (1994)

82. Lapa, C.M.F.: Análise de confiabilidade do sistema de água de alimentação auxiliar de Angra-I considerando falhas de causa comum pelo modelo das letras gregas múltiplas. Master Thesis, Nuclear Engineering Department, COPPE/UFRJ. Rio de Janeiro, Brazil (1996)

83. Lapa, C.M.F., Pereira, C.M.N.A., de Mol, A.C.A.: Maximization of a Nuclear System Availability Through Maintenance Scheduling Optimization Using a Genetic Algorithm. Nuclear Engineering and Design 196, 219–231 (2000)

84. Lapa, C.M.F., Frutuoso e Melo, P.F.: Indisponibilidade do sistema de água de alimentação auxiliar de Angra-I considerando falhas de causa comum pelo modelo das letras gregas múltiplas. In: Annals of Equipment Technology Meeting (COTEQ 1996), Rio de Janeiro, Brazil (1996)

85. Lee, K., Kim, C.H.: The Least-Squares Method for Three-Dimensional Core Power Distribution Monitoring in Pressurized Water Reactors. Nuclear Science and Engineering 143(3), 268–280 (2003)

86. Li, Z., Levine, H.: AUTOLOAD, an Automatic Optimal Pressurized Water Reactor Reload Design System with an Expert Module. Nuclear Science and Engineering 118, 67–78 (1994)

87. Lin, K.-J., Lin, C.: Pressurized Water Reactor Reload Design by an Expert System. Nuclear Science and Engineering 130(1), 128–140 (1998)

88. Mahesh, K.: Ontology Development for Machine Translation: Ideology and Methodology. Memoranda in Computer and Cognitive Science, MCCS-96-292. Computing Research Laboratory, New Mexico State University, Las Cruces, New Mexico (1996)

89. Maniezzo, V., Carbonaro, A.: Ant Colony Optimization: An Overview. In: Ribeiro, C. (ed.) Essays and Surveys in Metaheuristics, pp. 21–44. Kluwer, Dordrecht (2001)

90. Maniezzo, V., Roffilli, M.: Very Strongly Constrained Problems: An Ant Colony Optimization Approach. In: Nissan, E., Gini, G., Colombetti, M. (eds.) Papers in Sensing and in Reasoning: Marco Somalvico Memorial Issue. Special issue, Cybernetics and Systems 39(4), pp. 395–424 (2008)

91. Marseguerra, M., Zio, E., Cadini, F.: Optimized Adaptive Fuzzy Controller of the Water Level of a Pressurized Water Reactor Steam Generator. Nuclear Science and Engineering 155(3), 386–394 (2007)

92. Marshall, J.A.R., Kovacs, T., Dornhaus, A.R., Franks, N.R.: Simulating the Evolution of Ant Behaviour in Evaluating Nest Sites. In: Banzhaf, W., Ziegler, J., Christaller, T., Dittrich, P., Kim, J.T. (eds.) Advances in Artificial Life: Proceedings of the 7th European Conference on Artificial Life (ECAL 2003). LNCS (LNAI), vol. 2801, pp. 643–650. Springer, Heidelberg (2003)

93. Martín del Campo, C., François, J.L., López, H.A.: AXIAL: A System for Boiling Water Reactor Fuel Assembly Axial Optimization Using Genetic Algorithms. Annals of Nuclear Energy 28(16), 1667–1682 (2001)

94. Martín-del-Campo, C., François, J.L., Avendaño, L., González, M.: Development of a BWR Loading Pattern Design System Based on Modified Genetic Algorithms and Knowledge. Annals of Nuclear Energy 31(16), 1901–1911 (2004)

95. Martín-del-Campo, C., Palomera-Pérez, M.-Â., François, J.-L.: Advanced and Flexible Genetic Algorithms for BWR Fuel Loading Pattern Optimization. Annals of Nuclear Energy 36(10), 1553–1559 (2009)

96. McGregor, P. (ed.): Animal Communication Networks. Cambridge University Press, Cambridge, England (2005)

97. Morozov, A.G., Galperin, A., Todosow, M.: Thorium-Based Fuel Cycle for VVERs & PWRs: A Nonproliferative Solution to Renew Nuclear Power. Nuclear Engineering International 44, 13–14 (1999)

98. Muñoz, A., Martorell, S., Serradell, V.: Genetic Algorithms in Optimizing Surveillance and Maintenance of Components. Reliability Engineering & System Safety 57, 107–120 (1997)

99. Naser, J., Colley, R., Gaiser, J., Brookmire, T., Engle, S.: A Fuel Insert Shuffle Planner Expert System. In: Divakaruni, S.M., Cain, D., Baytch, E., Saylor, C. (eds.) Proceedings of the 1987 Conference on Expert-System Applications in Power Plants, Boston, MA, May 27–29, 1987, pp. 5-19–5-30. Electric Power Research Institute (EPRI), Palo Alto, California (December 1988)

100. Naser, J., Colley, R., Gaiser, J., Brookmire, T., Engle, S.: Fuel Insert Shuffler: A Case Study of Expert System Development. In: Majumdar, D., Sackett, J. (eds.) Proceedings of the ANS International Topical Meeting on Artificial Intelligence and Other Innovative Computer Applications in the Nuclear Industry, Snowbird, Utah, August 31–September 2, pp. 625–633. Plenum Press, New York (1988)

101. Nirenburg, S., Raskin, V.: The Subworld Concept Lexicon and the Lexicon Management System. Computational Linguistics 13(3/4), 276–289 (1987)

102. Nirenburg, S., Raskin, V.: Ten Choices for Lexical Semantics. Memoranda in Computer and Cognitive Science, MCCS-96-304. Computing Research Laboratory, New Mexico State University, Las Cruces, New Mexico (1996)

103. Nirenburg, S., Raskin, V.: Principles of Ontological Semantics. The MIT Press, Cambridge, Massachusetts (2004)

104. Nissan, E.: Intelligent Technologies for Nuclear Power Systems: Heuristic and Neural Tools. Expert Systems with Applications 14(4), 443–460 (1998)

105. Nissan, E. (ed.): Intelligent Technologies for Electric and Nuclear Power Systems. Special issue, Computers and Artificial Intelligence 17(2/3) (1998)

106. Nissan, E.: Forum on Refuelling Techniques for Nuclear Power Plants: One Decade with FUELCON. Thematic section, New Review of Applied Expert Systems 4, 139–194 (1998)

107. Nissan, E.: The FUELCON Meta-Architecture, in the Landscape of Intelligent Technologies for Refuelling. In: E. Nissan (ed.), Forum on Refuelling Techniques for Nuclear Power Plants: One Decade with FUELCON. Thematic section, New Review of Applied Expert Systems, 4, pp. 141–149 (1998)

108. Nissan, E.: Hybrid Techniques. (Five books reviewed.) Computers and Artificial Intelligence 17(2/3), 251–256 (1998)

109. Nissan, E.: Review of: D. Ruan (ed.), Fuzzy Logic Foundations and Industrial Applications (Kluwer, Dordrecht, The Netherlands, 1996). Computers and Artificial Intelligence 17(2/3), 248–249 (1998)

110. Nissan, E.: Review of: D. Ruan et al. (eds.) Intelligent Systems and Soft Computing for Nuclear Science and Industry: Proceedings of the 2nd International FLINS Workshop (World Scientific, Singapore, 1996). Computers and Artificial Intelligence 17(2/3), 250 (1998)

111. Nissan, E.: Review of: P. McGregor (ed.), Animal Communication Networks. (Cambridge University Press, Cambridge, U.K., 2005) and T.D. Wyatt, Pheromones and Animal Behaviour: Communication by Smell and Taste (Cambridge University Press, 2003, reprinted with corrections 2004). Pragmatics & Cognition, 17(2), pp. 482–490 (2005)

112. Nissan, E.: Legal Evidence, Police Investigation, Case Argumentation, and Computer Tools (2 vols.). Law, Governance and Technology Series, vol. 5. Springer, Dordrecht, The Netherlands (2012)

113. Nissan, E., Galperin, A.: Refueling in Nuclear Engineering: The FUELCON Project. Computers in Industry 37(1), 43–54 (1998), http://dx.doi.org/10.1016/S0166-3615(98)00080-3

114. Nissan, E., Siegelmann, H., Galperin, A.: An Integrated Symbolic and Neural Network Architecture for Machine Learning in the Domain of Nuclear Engineering. In: Proceedings of the 12th IAPR International Conference on Pattern Recognition, vol. 2, pp. 494–496 (1994), http://www.cs.umass.edu/~binds/papers/1994_Nissan_ProcPatRec.pdf

115. Nissan, E., Siegelmann, H., Galperin, A., Kimhi, S.: Towards Full Automation of the Discovery of Heuristics in a Nuclear Engineering Project, by Combining Symbolic and Subsymbolic Computation. In: Raś, Z.W., Zemankova, M. (eds.) Proceedings of the 8th International Symposium on Methodologies for Intelligent Systems (ISMIS 1994). LNCS, vol. 869, pp. 427–436. Springer, Heidelberg (1994)

116. Nissan, E., Siegelmann, H., Galperin, A., Kimhi, S.: Upgrading Automation for Nuclear Fuel In-Core Management: From the Symbolic Generation of Configurations, to the Neural Adaptation of Heuristics. Engineering with Computers 13(1), 1–19 (1997)

117. Nissan, E., Soper, A., Zhao, J., Knight, B., Petridis, M.: Fuel Reload Pattern Design Within a Family of Hybrid Architectures. In: Proceedings of FLINS 1998: Third International FLINS Workshop on Fuzzy Logic and Intelligent Technologies for Nuclear Science and Industry (FLINS 1998), Antwerp, Belgium, pp. 408–415 (1998)

118. Nissan, E., Galperin, A., Zhao, J., Knight, B., Soper, A.: From FUELCON to FUELGEN: Tools for Fuel Reload Pattern Design. In: Ruan, D. (ed.) Fuzzy Systems and Soft Computing in Nuclear Engineering. STUDFUZZ, vol. 38, pp. 432–448. Springer, Heidelberg (2000)

119. Nissan, E., Galperin, A., Soper, A., Knight, B., Zhao, J.: Future States for a Present-State Estimate, in the Contextual Perspective of In-Core Nuclear Fuel Management. International Journal of Computing Anticipatory Systems 9, 256–271 (2001)

120. NRC, National Review Council (U.S.) Committee on Declassification of Information for the Department of Energy Environmental Remediation and Related Programs 1995. A Review of the Department of Energy Classification Policy and Practice. National Academic Press, Washington, DC (1995)

121. Onyshkevych, B., Nirenburg, S.: A Lexicon for Knowledge-Based MT. Machine Translation 10(1/2), 5–57 (1995)

122. Ortiz, J.J., Requena, I.: Optimization of Fuel Reload in a BWR Nuclear Reactor Using a Recurrent Neural Network. In: Ruan, D., D'hondt, P., Kerre, E.E. (eds.) Proceedings of the 5th International FLINS Conference on Computational Intelligent Systems for Applied Research, Gent, Belgium, September 16-18, pp. 544–551. World Scientific, Singapore (2002)

123. Ortiz, J.J., Requena, I.: Using Neural Networks to Predict Core Parameters in a Boiling Water Reactor. Nuclear Science and Engineering 143(3), 254–267 (2003)

124. Ortiz, J.J., Requena, I.: An Order Coding Genetic Algorithm to Optimize Fuel Reloads in a Nuclear Boiling Water Reactor. Nuclear Science and Engineering 146(1), 88–98 (2004)

125. Ortiz, J.J., Castillo, A., Montes, J.L., Perusquía, R.: A New System to Fuel Loading and Control Rod Pattern Optimization in Boiling Water Reactors. Nuclear Science and Engineering 157(2), 236–244 (2007)

126. Ortiz, J.J., Castillo, A., Montes, J.L., Perusquía, R., Hernández, J.L.: Nuclear Fuel Lattice Optimization Using Neural Networks and a Fuzzy Logic System. Nuclear Science and Engineering 162(2), 148–157 (2009)

127. Park, T.K., Joo, H.G., Kim, C.H., Lee, H.C.: Multiobjective Loading Pattern Optimization by Simulated Annealing Employing Discontinuous Penalty Function and Screening Technique. Nuclear Science and Engineering 162(2), 134–147 (2009)

128. Parks, G.T.: Multiobjective PWR Reload Core Optimization Using a Genetic Algorithm. In: Proceedings of the International Conference on Mathematics and Computations, Reactor Physics, and Environmental Analyses, Portland, Oregon, vol. 1, pp. 615–624 (1995)

129. Parks, G.T.: Multiobjective Pressurized Water Reactor Reload Core Design by Nondominated Genetic Algorithm Search. Nuclear Science and Engineering 124(1), 178–187 (1996)

130. Parks, G.T.: Multiobjective Pressurised Water Reactor Reload Core Design using a Genetic Algorithm. In: Artificial Neural Nets and Genetic Algorithms, pp. 53–57. Springer, Vienna (1998), http://dx.doi.org/10.1007/978-3-7091-6492-1_12

131. Parks, G.T., Lewins, J.D.: In-Core Fuel Management and Optimization: The State of the Art. Nuclear Europe Worldscan 12(3/4), 41 (1992)

132. Parks, G.T., Turinsky, P.J., Maldonado, G.I.: Solving the PWR Reload Core Optimization Problem. In: Scientific Excellence in Supercomputing, The IBM 1990 Contest Prize Papers, vol. 1, pp. 281–310. Baldwin Press, Athens, Georgia (1992)

133. Parks, G.T., Suppapitnarm, A.: Multiobjective Optimization of PWR Reload Core Designs Using Simulated Annealing. In: Proceedings of the Conference on Mathematics & Computation, Reactor Physics and Environmental Analysis in Nuclear Applications, Madrid, vol. 2, pp. 1435–1444 (1999)

134. Peplow, D.E., Sulfredge, C.D., Sanders, R.L., Morris, R.H., Hann, T.A.: Calculating Nuclear Power Plant Vulnerability Using Integrated Geometry and Event/Fault-Tree Models. Nuclear Science and Engineering 146(1), 71–87 (2004)

135. Pereira, C.M.N.A., Schirru, R., Martinez, A.S.: Learning an Optimized Classification System from a Data Base of Time Series Patterns Using Genetic Algorithm. In: Ebecken, N.F.F. (ed.) Data Mining, 1st edn. Computational Mechanics Publications, WIT Press, Southampton, England (1998), http://dx.doi.org/10.2495/DATA980031

136. Pereira, C.M.N.A., Schirru, R., Martinez, A.S.: Basic Investigations Related to Genetic Algorithms in Core Designs. Annals of Nuclear Energy 26(3), 173–193 (1999)

137. Radkowski, A., Galperin, A.: The Nonproliferative Light Water Thorium Reactor: A New Approach to Light Water Reactor Core Technology. Nuclear Technology 124, 215–222 (1998)

138. Poetschat, G.R., Rothleder, B.M., Faught, W.S., Eich, W.J.: Interactive Fuel Shuffle Assistant Graphics Interface and Automation for Nuclear Fuel Shuffle With PDQ7. In: Proceedings of Topical Meeting on Advances in Fuel Management, Pinehurst, NC, March 2–5, American Nuclear Society, La Grange, Illinois (1986)

139. Poon, P.W.: Genetic Algorithms and Fuel Cycle Optimization. The Nuclear Engineer 31(6), 173–177 (1990)

140. Poon, P.W., Parks, G.T.: Application of Genetic Algorithms to In-Core Nuclear Fuel Management Optimization. In: Proceedings of the Joint International Conference on Mathematical Methods and Supercomputing in Nuclear Applications, p. 777 (1993)

141. Rothleder, B.M., Poetschat, G.R., Faught, W.S., Eich, W.J.: The Potential for Expert System Support in Solving the Pressurized Water Reactor Fuel Shuffling Problem. Nuclear Science and Engineering 100(4), 440–450 (1988)

142. Raskin, V., Mikhail, J., Atallah, M.J., Hempelmann, C.F., Mohamed, D.H.: Hybrid Data and Text System for Downgrading Sensitive Documents. Technical Report, Center for Education and Research in Information Assurance and Security. Purdue University, West Lafayette, Indiana (2001), https://www.cerias.purdue.edu/assets/pdf/bibtex_archive/2001-154.pdf

143. Raza, W., Kim, K.-Y.: Shape Optimization of 19-Pin Wire-Wrapped Fuel Assembly of LMR Using Multiobjective Evolutionary Algorithm. Nuclear Science and Engineering 161(2), 245–254 (2009)

144. Romano, A., Boscher, T., Hejzlar, P., Kazimi, M.S., Todreas, N.E.: Implications of Alternative Strategies for Transition to Sustainable Fuel Cycles. Nuclear Science and Engineering 154(1), 1–27 (2006)

145. Rozon, D., Shen, W.: A Parametric Study of the DUPIC Fuel Cycle to Reflect Pressurized Water Reactor Fuel Management Strategy. Nuclear Science and Engineering 138(1), 1–25 (2001)

146. Schirru, R., Pereira, C.M.N.A., Chapot, L., Carvalho, F.: A Genetic Algorithm Solution for Combinatorial Problems: The Nuclear Core Reload Example. In: XI Encontro Nacional de Fisica de Reatores, Brazil, pp. 357–360 (1997)

147. See, H.J., Parks, G.T., Vassiliadis, V.S., Wilson, D.I.: Simulated Annealing Based Scheduling Algorithm for Selecting Reverse Osmosis Membrane Cleaning Schedules. Water Software Systems: Theory and Applications 1, 149–164 (2001)

148. Sheu, R.J., Chen, A.Y., Liu, Y.-W.H., Jiang, S.H.: Shielding Calculations for a Spent Fuel Storage Cask: A Comparison of Discrete Ordinates, Monte Carlo, and Hybrid Methods. Nuclear Science and Engineering 159(1), 23–36 (2009)

149. Siegelmann, H., Nissan, E., Galperin, A.: A Novel Neural/Symbolic Hybrid Approach to Heuristically Optimized Fuel-Allocation and Automated Fuel-Allocation in Nuclear Engineering. Advances in Engineering Software 28(9), 581–592 (1997), http://dx.doi.org/10.1016/S0166-3615(98)00080-3

150. Silverman, B.G.: Survey of Expert Critiquing Systems: Practical and Theoretical Frontiers. Communications of the ACM 35(4), 106–127 (1992)

151. Silverman, B.G.: Critiquing Human Errors: A Knowledge Based Human-Computer Collaboration Approach. Academic Press, Orlando, Florida (1992)

152. Smith, D.E.: Documentation of Knowledge in the Development of CLEO, a Refueling Assistant for FFTF. In: Majumdar, D., Sackett, J. (eds.) Proceedings of the ANS International Topical Meeting on Artificial Intelligence and Other Innovative Computer Applications in the Nuclear Industry, p. 607 ff. Plenum Press, New York (1988)

153. Smith, D.E., Kocher, L.F., Seeman, S.E.: CLEO: A Knowledge-Based Refueling Assistant at FFTF. (FFTF = Fast Flux Test Facility.) In: Proceedings of the American Nuclear Society Winter Meeting, San Francisco, CA, 10 November 1985, Transactions of the American Nuclear Society 50, 292–293 (1985)

154. Soper, A.: Exploring Genetic Alternative Concepts for FUELGEN. In: Nissan, E. (ed.) Forum on Refuelling Techniques for Nuclear Power Plants: One Decade with FUELCON. Thematic section, New Review of Applied Expert Systems 4, 185–194 (1998)

155. Sorensen, R.T., Lee, J.C.: Light Water Reactor Equilibrium Cycle Search Methodology for Assembly-Level Fuel Cycle Analysis. Nuclear Science and Engineering 158(3), 213–230 (2008)

156. Stephens, G., Smith, K.S., Rempe, K.R., Downar, T.J.: Optimization of Pressurized Water Reactor Shuffling by Simulated Annealing with Heuristics. Nuclear Science and Engineering 121(1995), 67 (1995)

157. Suppapitnarm, A., Parks, G.T., Shea, K., Clarkson, P.J.: Conceptual Design of Bicycle Frames by Multiobjective Shape Annealing. Engineering Optimization 36(2), 165–188 (2004)

158. Tahara, Y., Hamamoto, K., Takase, M.: Computer Aided System for Generating Fuel Shuffling Configuration Based on Knowledge Engineering. Journal of Nuclear Science and Technology 28(5), 399–408 (1991)

159. Talamo, A., Gudowski, W.: A Deep Burn Fuel Management Strategy for the Incineration of Military Plutonium in the Gas Turbine-Modular Helium Reactor Modeled in a Detailed Three-Dimensional Geometry by the Monte Carlo Continuous Energy Burnup Code. Nuclear Science and Engineering 153(2), 172–183 (2006)

160. Tanker, E., Tanker, A.Z.: Application of a Genetic Algorithm to Core Reload Pattern Optimization. In: Proceedings of the International Conference on Mathematics and Computations, Reactor Physics, and Environmental Analysis, Portland, Oregon, vol. 1 (1995)

161. Tanker, E., Tanker, A.Z.: Application of a Genetic Algorithm to Core Reload Pattern Optimization. In: Ronen, Y., Elias, E. (eds.) Reactor Physics and Reactor Computations. Ben Gurion University of the Negev Press, Beer-Sheva, Israel (1994)

162. Todosow, M., Galperin, A., Morozov, A.G.: A Novel Nonproliferative Thorium-Based Seed-Blanket Fuel Concept for PWRs. Transactions of the American Nuclear Society (USA) 80, 46–47 (1999)

163. Todosow, M., Galperin, A., Herring, S., Kazimi, M., Downar, T., Morozov, A.: Use of Thorium in Light Water Reactors. Nuclear Technology 151, 168–176 (2005)

164. Toshinsky, V.G., Sekimoto, H., Toshinsky, G.I.: Multiobjective Fuel Management Optimization for Self-Fuel-Providing LMFBR Using Genetic Algorithms. Annals of Nuclear Energy 26(9), 783–802 (1999)

165. Tran, H.N., Kato, Y., Muto, Y.: Optimization of Burnable Poison Loading for HTGR Cores with OTTO Refueling. Nuclear Science and Engineering 158(3), 264–271 (2008)

166. Turinsky, P.J., Parks, G.T.: Advances in Nuclear Fuel Management for Light Water Reactors. In: Lewins, J., Becker, M. (eds.) Advances in Nuclear Science and Technology, vol. 26, pp. 137–165. Springer, Berlin (2002)

167. Vaurio, J.K.: On Time-Dependent Availability and Maintenance Optimization of Standby Units Under Various Maintenance Policies. Reliability Engineering & System Safety 56, 79–89 (1997)

168. Viegas, E., Raskin, V.: Computational Semantic Lexicon Acquisition: Methodology and Guidelines. Memoranda in Computer and Cognitive Science, MCCS-98-315. Computing Research Laboratory, New Mexico State University, Las Cruces, New Mexico (1998)

169. Wahed, M.E.-S., Ibrahim, W.Z., Effat, A.M.: Multiobjective Optimization of the Plate Element of Egyptian Research Reactor Using Genetic Algorithm. Nuclear Science and Engineering 162(3), 275–281 (2009)

170. Walker, P.M.B.: Chambers Dictionary of Science and Technology. Chambers, Edinburgh, Scotland (1999)

171. Wang, S.: Neural Networks in Generalizing Expert Knowledge. Computers and Industrial Engineering 32(1), 67–76 (1997)

172. Weber, D.P., Sofu, T., Yang, W.S., Downar, T.J., Thomas, J.W., Zhong, Z., Cho, J.Y., Kim, K.S., Chun, T.H., Joo, H.G., Kim, C.H.: High-Fidelity Light Water Reactor Analysis with the Numerical Nuclear Reactor. Nuclear Science and Engineering 155(3), 395–408 (2007)

173. Wyatt, T.D.: Pheromones and Animal Behaviour: Communication by Smell and Taste. Cambridge University Press, Cambridge, England (2003) (reprinted with corrections 2004)

174. Zacharia, J.: Friendly Fuel: A Tel Aviv Scientist Promises an Energy Revolution, Through Nuclear Power That Can't Be Misused for Bomb-Building. The Jerusalem Report, pp. 24–25 (August 7, 1997)

175. Zerovnik, G., Snoj, L., Ravnik, M.: Optimization of Spent Nuclear Fuel Filling in Canisters for Deep Repository. Nuclear Science and Engineering 163(2), 183–190 (2009)

176. Zhao, J.: An Examination of the Macro Genetic Algorithm and its Application to Loading Pattern Design in Nuclear Fuel Management. Ph.D. Dissertation, Computer Science, The University of Greenwich, London (viva in November 1996) (1996)

177. Zhao, J., Knight, B., Nissan, E., Soper, A.: FUELGEN: A Genetic-Algorithm Based System for Fuel Loading Pattern Design in Nuclear Power Reactors. Expert Systems with Applications 14(4), 461–470 (1997)

178. Zhao, J., Knight, B., Nissan, E., Soper, A.: FUELGEN: Effective Evolutionary Design of Refuellings for Pressurized Water Reactors. Computers and Artificial Intelligence 17(2/3), 105–125 (1998)

179. Zhao, J., Knight, B., Nissan, E., Petridis, M., Soper, A.: The FUELGEN Alternative: An Evolutionary Approach. The Architecture. In: E. Nissan (ed.), Forum on Refuelling Techniques for Nuclear Power Plants: One Decade with FUELCON. Thematic section, New Review of Applied Expert Systems 4, pp. 177–183 (1998)

Hypertext Searching - A Survey[*]

Amihood Amir[1,2,5], Moshe Lewenstein[3], and Noa Lewenstein[4]

[1] Department of Computer Science, Bar-Ilan University Ramat-Gan 52900, Israel
amir@cs.biu.ac.il
[2] Department of Computer Science, Johns Hopkins University, Baltimore, MD 21218
[3] Department of Computer Science, Bar-Ilan University, Ramat-Gan 52900, Israel
moshe@cs.biu.ac.il
[4] Department of Computer Science, Netanya Academic College, 42365 Netanya,
Israel
noa@netanya.ac.il

Abstract. The idea of hypertext has been successfully used in Jewish
literature. Its importance has been steadily growing over the last two
decades. Internet and other information systems use hypertext format,
with data organized associatively rather than sequentially or relationally.

A myriad of textual problems have been considered in the pattern
matching field with many non-trivial results. Nevertheless, not much
work has been done on the natural combination of pattern matching
and hypertext. In contrast to regular text, hypertext has a non-linear
structure and the techniques of pattern matching for text cannot be
directly applied to hypertext.

In this paper we survey some of the work that has been done on
exact and approximate pattern matching in hypertext. We show that
in contrast to regular text, it *does make a difference* whether the errors
occur in the hypertext or the pattern. The approximate pattern matching
problem in hypertext with errors in the hypertext turns out to be $\mathcal{NP}$-
Complete and the approximate pattern matching problem in hypertext
with errors in the pattern has a polynomial time solution.

Keywords: Design and analysis of algorithms, combinatorial algorithms
on words, pattern matching, hypertext, pattern matching on hypertext.

1 Introduction

Most digital libraries today appear in *hypertext* form [34], with links between
text and annotations, and, in multimedia libraries, between the text and pictures, video and voice. However, this method has been very successfully used in
Jewish literature. The traditional page format in the Vilna *Shas*, for example,
is a pure use of hypertext. The main text is centered in large letters, the main
commentators are arranged around it in smaller letters, and links to appropriate passages in the Bible and in the main *Poskim* are suitably incorporated.
The printings of many other Jewish texts are in a similar format (e.g. *Rambam,*

---

[*] Partly supported by NSF grant CCR-09-04581 and ISF grant 347/09.

N. Dershowitz and E. Nissan (Eds.): Choueka Festschrift, Part I, LNCS 8001, pp. 364–381, 2014.
© Springer-Verlag Berlin Heidelberg 2014

Shulchan Aruch). These Jewish texts are the most extensive use of windows and hypertext technology prior to the end of the 20th century [3].

Thus, Jewish writings provide a natural motivation for searching hypertexts. The application that directly motivated our research is the *Responsa Judaica library*. Hebrew Law has evolved over two thousand years and is recorded in the Bible, Mishna, Tosephta, Babylonian and Jerusalem Talmud, Maimonides, Shulchan Aruch, Tur, and thousands of published Responsa. This tremendous body of work has been incorporated into the Bar-Ilan Responsa Project. The Responsa Project was conceived in 1963 at the Weizmann Institute by Aviezri Fraenkel. Over the years it migrated to Bar Ilan University. An early version of the system was already running in 1967. In 2007, the Responsa Project was awarded the prestigious Israel Prize for Torah Literature.

The project's "golden age" occurred when Yaakov Choueka was its head. Issues such as full-text-search, searching under Hebrew morphological rules, compression, and man-machine interface, were pioneered and tackled by Choueka and his team. Naturally, The links between the various works in the project create a general hypertext digraph. In this context, one may want to search only a main text, but it is possible that a search is desired through the hyperlinks.

Some of the issues involved are discussed in a manuscript of Fraenkel and Klein [22]. An M.Sc. thesis in the Math and CS department at Bar-Ilan [15] deals with a hypertext system for the Babylonian Talmud. It is clear that algorithms for efficient search of hypertext are crucial.

Classical pattern matching (e.g. [26,21,17,28]) has dealt primarily with unlinked textual files. The 80's have seen research in approximate matching (e.g. [30,33,31]. In the 90's has been interest in nonstandard matching, such as dictionary matching ([11,10]), dynamic indexing ([20,35]) and multidimensional matching ([7,9]). The new millennium saw much effort in geometric modeling ([8,23]), embedding and streaming ([24,14,19,16]), and pattern matching with rearrangements ([5,6,12,4,25]).

This paper summarizes the efforts made in the area of string matching in hypertext.

In a pioneering paper by Manber and Wu [32] a first attempt is made to define pattern matching in hypertext. They suggest the concept of viewing a hypertext library as a general graph of unlinked files. For a formal definition, see section 2.

Akutsu [2], presented an algorithm that would be capable of pattern matching in a hypertext with an underlying tree structure. Park and Kim [27] also use the Manber and Wu model and present a general pattern matching algorithm. Their algorithm assumes that the hypertext links form an acyclic digraph.

All above pattern matching algorithms in the hypertext model ([32,27] assume that the hypertext links form an acyclic digraph. In the Responsa environment, the text files present a general digraph.

In [13] we presented an algorithm for pattern matching in hypertext where the hypertext links form a general graph. The complexity of our algorithm is the same as that of the Park and Kim algorithm, $O(N + |E|m)$, where N is the overall size of the text, m is the pattern length and E is the edge set of the hypertext.

We extended this result to *approximate* matching in hypertext. We began with the hamming distance as our metric. Some very surprising insights are achieved. In classical approximate pattern matching the error locations are *symmetric*. It does not matter if the errors occur in the text or in the pattern. In approximate matching in hypertext there are distinctly different cases.

Pattern matching in hypertext turned out to be the *first case in the literature* where the error location is not symmetric. We showed that it is important to understand whether the mismatches occur in pattern or in the text.

We considered three flavors of the problem: with mismatches in the hypertext only, mismatches in the pattern only and mismatches in both. The first and third turn out to be $\mathcal{NP}$-Complete. For the second type, we present an algorithm that runs in time $O((N\sqrt{m}+m\sqrt{N})\sqrt{\log m}+|E|m)$, where N is the overall size of the text, m the pattern length and E the edge set of the hypertext, over unbounded alphabets. For fixed bounded alphabets the running time is $O(N \log m + |E|m)$.

Finally, we consider edit distance. Once again, this comes in three variations and the variations allowing errors in the hypertext are $\mathcal{NP}$-Complete. If we allow errors in the pattern only, then it is polynomial. We present an algorithm of time complexity $O(Nm \log N+|E|m)$. This problem was already considered by Manber and Wu [32]. As previously mentioned, they assume that the underlying digraph is acyclic. Our algorithm works for an arbitrary graph.

There are some other differences between the Manber-Wu algorithm and ours. Their algorithm does not handle mismatches while ours does. Their algorithm works for non-uniform error cost. Although we considered uniform error cost, our algorithm is constructed in a manner that can be adapted to non-uniform error cost. The time complexity of the Manber-Wu algorithm uses different measures but worst case analysis gives the same results as our algorithm. On the other hand, their algorithm is more space efficient.

2   Pattern Matching in Hypertext

Formally a *hypertext* above alphabet Σ is a triplet $H = (V, E, T)$ where (V, E) is a digraph and $T = \{T_v \in \Sigma^+ \mid v \in V\}$. If for every $v \in V$, $T_v \in \Sigma$ then we call the hypertext a *one-character hypertext*. Let $v_1, ..., v_k$ be a path, possibly with loops, in (V, E) and let $W = T'_{v_1}T_{v_2}T_{v_3}...T_{v_{k-2}}T_{v_{k-1}}T''_{v_k}$ be the concatenation of texts upon this path, where T''_{v_k} is a prefix of T_{v_k} and T'_{v_1} is a suffix of T_{v_1} beginning at location l of T_{v_1}. We say that W *matches* on the path $v_1, ..., v_k$ beginning at location l of v_1 or that $v_1 : l$ is a *W-match location*. In general we say that W *matches* in H. Note that for a one-character hypertext we may disregard the location since there is only one location per vertex.

The *Pattern Matching in Hypertext* problem is defined as follows:
INPUT: A pattern P and a hypertext H.
OUTPUT: All P-match locations.

Initially we solve the problem by transforming a given hypertext into a one-character hypertext. The transformation is done by taking every text T_v and splitting v into $|T_v|$ vertices (saving for each new vertex its origin). For the remainder of this section, we consider the hypertext $H = (V, E, T)$ to be a one-character hypertext. In the next section we discuss general hypertext graphs.

We would like to find all the P-match locations within the hypertext. Since our hypertext is a one-character hypertext, every path that $P = p_1 p_2 ... p_m$ matches upon is exactly of length m, the length of pattern P. To be precise, the path is of the form $v_1, v_2, v_3, ..., v_m$ such that $T_{v_1} = p_1$, $T_{v_2} = p_2$, ..., $T_{v_m} = p_m$. The idea is to create a digraph $G^{(P,H)} = (V^{(P,H)}, E^{(P,H)})$ that depends on the hypertext and the pattern, such that every path of length m in the digraph will represent a match in the hypertext. Corresponding to each vertex in the hypertext there will be m vertices in the digraph that will represent the m pattern locations. Similar to an edge in the hypertext, an edge in the digraph will represent two consecutive characters, but the edge will also represent their location in the pattern, i and $i + 1$. In addition, the edge represents a match between the hypertext character in the source of the edge and the ith pattern character.

Formally, we define the digraph in the following way:

$$V^{(P,H)} = \{v^i \mid v \in V, \ 1 \le i \le m\} \cup \{s, f\}$$

$$E^{(P,H)} = \{(s, v^1) \mid v \in V\} \cup \{(v^i, u^{i+1}) \mid (v, u) \in E, \ T_v = p_i\} \cup \{(v^m, f) \mid T_v = p_m\}.$$

It is easy to see from the definition that $G^{(P,H)}$ is a DAG and the longest path in $G^{(P,H)}$ is of length $m + 1$ (the additional 1 is for the initial vertex s). For our algorithm we need the following lemma.

Lemma 1. *P matches on path $v_1, v_2, ..., v_m$ in H iff $s, v_1^1, v_2^2, ..., v_m^m, f$ is a path in $G^{(P,H)}$.*

Proof: Follows from the definition of $G^{(P,H)}$.   □

Algorithm for Pattern Matching in Hypertext

1. Construct a one-character hypertext $H' = (V', E', T')$ from the original hypertext $H = (V, E, T)$.
2. Construct $G^{(P,H')}$ from the pattern P and the hypertext H'.
3. Do a depth first search in $G^{(P,H')}$ starting from s. Denote by *true* every vertex v^i where there is a path from v^i to f.
4. For every vertex v in the hypertext, check v^1 in the digraph and if marked true announce the vertex and location in H corresponding to vertex v in H' as a P-match location.

Time: Building H' and $G^{(P,H')}$ takes time linear to the size of H', P and $G^{(P,H')}$. The size of $G^{(P,H')}$, where $H' = (V', E', T')$ is $O(m|E'|)$ and this is clearly the largest of the three. Step 3, can likewise be implemented in linear time. Step 4 takes $O(|V'|)$ time. The size of V' is at most $|V| + N$ and the size of E' is at most $|E| + N$ since for every new vertex in the one-character hypertext there is exactly one edge introduced. Therefore the overall time for the algorithm takes $O(m|E'|)=O(mN + m|E|)$. $\square$

Correctness: Follows from the construction of $G^{(P,H)}$ and Lemma 1. $\square$

3   Improved Algorithm for Pattern Matching in Hypertext

We take an approach similar to the previous algorithm without transforming the hypertext into a one-character hypertext. Hypertext vertices may now contain text longer than one-character and possibly even longer than the pattern length. We use conventional pattern matching techniques to find instances of the pattern within vertices that have text longer than the pattern length . To find the other instances of the pattern, i.e. those that cross at least one hyperlink, we will extend the idea from the previous section.

As in the previous section, we create a digraph to model the hypertext and the pattern, but in this case there will be two sets of m vertices for every vertex in the hypertext instead of one set. These two sets will model comparisons of sub-patterns rather than comparisons of characters only. In the case of the one-character hypertext, there is only one possible entrance and one possible exit from every node and only the relative location in the pattern varies. That forced making m copies of every node. Now, however, there may be more than one entrance and more than one exit from each node, *in addition* to the location. For example, a node may end in a number of pattern prefixes, start with a number of pattern suffixes, and be a number of internal sub-patterns. To allow for all these possibilities, we make $2m$ copies of every node, encompassing all "entrance" locations and all "exit" locations.

For a match of T_v from location i to location j in the pattern we set an edge from the ith vertex in the first set to jth vertex in the second set. (These edges are described in the first part of $E^{(P,H)}$ defined below.) We also need to consider a match beginning in the middle of the vertex's text or ending in the middle of the vertex's text. (These edges are described in the second and third part of $E^{(P,H)}$ defined below.)

We will use the following notation. Let x be a string and k an integer. Denote the k length suffix of x by $Suf(x,k)$ and the k length prefix of x by $Pref(x,k)$.

We now give a formal definition of the digraph. Let $H = (V, E, T)$ be a hypertext and $P = p_1p_2...p_m$ be a pattern then $G^{(P,H)} = (V^{(P,H)}, E^{(P,H)})$ is defined in the following way.

$$V^{(P,H)} = \{\overline{v}^i \mid v \in V, \ 1 \le i \le m\} \cup \{\underline{v}^i \mid v \in V, \ 1 \le i \le m\} \cup \{s\}$$

$$E^{(P,H)} = \{(\overline{v}^i, \underline{v}^{i+|T_v|-1}) \mid \ |T_v| < m, \ 1 < i < m - |T_v| + 1, \ T_v = p_i...p_{i+|T_v|-1}\}$$
$$\cup$$
$$\{(\overline{v}^1, \underline{v}^k) \qquad \mid \ Suf(T_v, k) = p_1...p_k, \ 1 \le k < \min\{m, |T_v|\}\}$$
$$\cup$$
$$\{(\overline{v}^k, \underline{v}^m) \qquad \mid \ Pref(T_v, m - k + 1) = p_k...p_m,$$
$$\max\{1, m - |T_v| + 1\} < k \le m\}$$
$$\cup$$
$$\{(\underline{v}^i, \overline{u}^{i+1}) \qquad \mid \ (v, u) \in E, \ 1 \le i < m\}$$
$$\cup$$
$$\{(s, \overline{v}^1) \qquad\qquad \mid \ v \in V\}.$$

Lemma 2. *Let $v \in V$ and l be a location in T_v. If $|T_v| - l + 1 < m$ then there is a P-match location at $v : l$ in H iff there exists a path in $G^{(P,H)}$ beginning with $s, \overline{v}^1, \underline{v}^{|T_v|-l+1}$ and ending with $\underline{u}^m$ for some $u \in V$.*

Proof: Assume that there is a P-match location at $v : l$ in H with $|T_v| - l + 1 < m$. Let $v, v_2, ..., v_k$ be a path such that P matches upon it beginning at location l of v, i.e. $P = T_v' T_{v_2} T_{v_3} ... T_{v_{k-2}} T_{v_{k-1}} T_{v_k}''$. Since $|T_v'| = |T_v| - l + 1$, $(\overline{v}^1, \underline{v}^{|T_v|-l+1}) \in E^{(P,H)}$. It is also immediate that $(s, \overline{v}^1) \in E^{(P,H)}$. Moreover, since the prefix of length $|T_{v_k}''|$ of T_{v_k} matches at pattern location $m - |T_{v_k}''| + 1$, $(\overline{v}_k^{m-|T_{v_k}''|+1}, \underline{v}_k^m) \in E^{(P,H)}$. Also, for every $1 < i < k$, $(\overline{v}_i^{\Sigma_{j=1}^{i-1}|T_{v_j}|+1}, \underline{v}_i^{\Sigma_{j=1}^{i}|T_{v_j}|}) \in E^{(P,H)}$ because $T_{v_i} < m$ and T_{v_i} appears at pattern location $\Sigma_{j=1}^{i} |T_{v_j}| + 1$. Since $(v_i, v_{i+1}) \in E$, for $1 \le i < k$, it follows that $(\underline{v}_i^{|T_{v_i}|}, \overline{v}_{i+1}^{|T_{v_i}|+1}) \in E$. Therefore, we have a path that ends with $\underline{v}_k^m$ as required.

Conversely, a careful analysis of the construction of $G^{(P,H)}$ shows that any path from s to $\underline{u}^m$ for some $u \in V$ must be of the form

$$s, \overline{v}_1^1, \underline{v}_1^{i_1}, \overline{v}_2^{i_1+1}, \underline{v}_2^{i_2}, ..., \underline{v}_{k-1}^{i_{k-1}}, \overline{u}^{i_{k-1}+1}, \underline{u}^m.$$

Similar to the other direction, if $i_1 = |T_v| - l + 1$ it is relatively straightforward to see that this represents a path beginning in v_1 upon which P matches at location l of v_1. $\qquad \square$

Algorithm for Pattern Matching in Hypertext

1. For every vertex v in H do standard pattern matching with pattern P and text T_v.

2. Based on the results of step 1, announce the internal matches as P-match locations.

3. Build $G^{(P,H)}$ from the pattern P and the hypertext H, using step 1 for the first three types of edges.

4. Do a depth first search in $G^{(P,H)}$ starting from vertex s saving at every vertex $w \in V^{(P,H)}$ true, if there is a path from w to $\underline{u}^m$ for some $u \in V$.

5. For every vertex v in the hypertext, check $\overline{v}^1$ in the digraph $G^{(P,H)}$ and if marked true do the following: For each $\underline{v}_j$ s.t. $(\overline{v}^1, \underline{v}^j) \in E^{(P,H)}$, if $\underline{v}^j$ is marked true, announce $v : |T_v| - j + 1$ a P-match location.

Correctness: Matches internal to a vertex will be detected in step 1 and announced in step 2. Now, let $v : l$ be a P-match location that crosses at least one hyperlink. Since it crosses a hyperlink it must be the case that $|T_v| - l + 1 < m$. The conditions of step 4 and step 5, where we set $j = |T_v| - l + 1$, together with Lemma 2 shows that we indeed find this P-match location and announce it in step 5.

Time: Step 1 takes $O(N)$ time since pattern matching is linear for text and N is the overall text size. Step 2 is included in the complexity of the previous step. For step 3, note the size of $G^{(P,H)}$. There are $O(|V|m)$ vertices and there are $O(|E|m)$ edges. Constructing the edges is immediate for those with source s and those of the form $(\underline{v}^i, \overline{u}^{i+1})$. For the others we use the results of the pattern matching from step 1. A possible implementation can be done by slightly modifying the KMP algorithm. Therefore, the construction of $G^{(P,H)}$ is linear in its size. So, step 3 is $O(|E|m)$. Step 4 is, once again, linear in the size of $G^{(P,H)}$ and the time for step 5 is bounded by the size of $G^{(P,H)}$. Therefore, the algorithm runs in $O(N + |E|m)$ time.

4   Approximate Pattern Matching in Hypertext - Hamming Distance

Approximate pattern matching is one of the well-researched problems in pattern matching. Often the text contains errors and searching for an exact match is not sufficient. We present algorithms that search for three types of approximations: a "closest" solution, all "closest" solutions, and for solutions not exceeding k errors. The "closest" solution depends on what type of errors are considered. A mismatch is one of the most common errors. The number of mismatches between two equal length strings is called the *hamming distance*. *Approximate pattern matching with hamming distance* refers to the problem of finding the substring with minimum hamming distance from the pattern or finding all substrings with hamming distance less than a specified distance from the pattern.

Naturally, it would be interesting to investigate approximate pattern matching in hypertext using hamming distance as our metric. This needs some clarification. Historically, whenever hamming distance between two strings is used, it is not specified in which string the error occurred. In our context, the error may occur in the text or in the pattern. This detail is never discussed because, in strings, it really does not make a difference where the error occurred.

In hypertext this is no longer true. Consider a certain path in the hypertext passing through v, k times, where $k > 1$. If we change a character in that hypertext vertex we are changing all k instances on that path. On the other hand, if we are changing the characters in the pattern we can change each instance to a different character. From this reasoning it follows that the fewest number of changes in the pattern required so that the pattern matches may be different than the fewest number of changes required in the hypertext. Moreover, we can always change the pattern so that the pattern will match in the hypertext but it may be the case that we cannot change the hypertext so that the pattern will match. In the example below, assuming that there are two errors in the pattern, we have a match in the hypertext. Assuming a mistake in the text can not give us a match at all!

hypertext: pattern: ABC

In real life, applications vary. In some applications it is reasonable to expect the mismatches to occur in the text while in others the mismatches occur in the pattern. Sometimes we may even expect errors to appear in both. Consider a hypertext similar to the inter net in which information is often inserted quickly and erroneously. Here we would expect the mismatches to be in the text. On the other hand, a relatively constant and well checked hypertext, such as the Responsa project which serves as a query system, is less prone to errors. Nevertheless, for large queries we may expect mismatches in the pattern. The hypertext application actually allows for three versions of approximate pattern matching with hamming distance. In each of these versions the input is a pattern P, a hypertext $H = (V, E, T)$, and an error bound d.

Version 1: Can we change at most d characters in the hypertext H so that P will match in H?
Version 2: Can we change d characters in P so that P will match in H?
Version 3: Can we change d characters in P and H so that P will match in H?

These questions are stated as decision questions but we may also ask, what is the fewest number of changes, min_d, necessary for P to match in H? Or, find all locations where P matches in the hypertext with min_d changes. Note that when the hypertext is a DAG all three versions boil down to the same version. In general for an arbitrary graph we shall see that versions 1 and 3 are $\mathcal{NP}$-Complete and version 2 is polynomial.

Proposition 1. *The Approximate hypertext-hamming distance problem - version 1 is $\mathcal{NP}$-Complete.*

Proof: Clearly the problem is in $\mathcal{NP}$. We will reduce from directed Hamiltonian path.
   Let $G = (V, E)$ be a directed graph in which we seek a Hamiltonian path and let $n = |V|$. Construct a hypertext H over $\Sigma = \{\sigma_1, ..., \sigma_n$ setting $H = (V, E, T)$ where $T_v = \sigma_1$ for every $v \in V$. Take pattern $\sigma_1...\sigma_n$, (note that $\forall i \neq j$, $\sigma_i \neq \sigma_j$) and distance $d = n - 1$. If we have a Hamiltonian path then replacing the i-th vertex's text with σ_i will give us a match of P in the hypertext.

Conversely, if we can make text-changes in the hypertext (which, in our case, clearly, does not exceed n) so that P matches on some path then since $|T| = |V| = n$ and $\forall i \neq j$, $\sigma_i \neq \sigma_j$ it must be the case that the pattern matches on a Hamiltonian path. $\square$

We can not use the same reduction for version 3, since any graph containing a cycle would have returned a match simply by changing all pattern characters to σ_1. However, we use a similar reduction.

Proposition 2. *The Approximate hypertext-hamming distance problem - version 3 is $\mathcal{NP}$-Complete.*

Proof: Clearly the problem is in $\mathcal{NP}$. We will reduce from directed Hamiltonian cycle.

Let $G = (V, E)$ be a directed graph in which we seek a Hamiltonian cycle and let $n = |V|$. Construct a hypertext H setting $H = (V, E, T)$ where $T_v = \sigma_1$ for every $v \in V$. Take pattern $\sigma_1...\sigma_n\sigma_1...\sigma_n$, where $\forall i \neq j$, $\sigma_i \neq \sigma_j$ and distance $d = n - 1$. If we have a Hamiltonian cycle then replacing the i-th vertex's text with σ_i, for $i \geq 2$, making $n - 1$ changes altogether, will give us a match of P in the hypertext.

Conversely, assume we have a match of P in H with at most $n - 1$ changes on P and H together. Consider the path on which P matches in H after the changes were made, call it C, and let k be the number of different characters on C. Note, that it is always true that $k \leq n$ since there are only n characters in the whole hypertext. There are n different characters in the pattern. But since there are only k of these on C, at least $n - k$ of the pattern symbols must be changed. Since each symbol in the pattern appears twice we must make at least $2(n - k)$ changes in the pattern. Now, since we started with the same character in all vertices in the hypertext we must have made at least $k - 1$ changes in the text. So overall there are at least $2(n - k) + k - 1$ changes. Our distance is $d = n - 1$ and therefore it must be that $2(n-k)+k-1 \leq n-1$. This is equivalent to $n \leq k$ and since $n \geq k$ we have $k = n$. This means that after changes every vertex in the hypertext must contain a different character. This already accounts for the $n - 1$ allowed changes. So, the pattern must be in its original form.

C now serves for a Hamiltonian cycle since we first visit the vertex labeled σ_1 and then the vertex labeled σ_2 and so on till we come back to the vertex labeled σ_1 (and then go for another round). $\square$

We now show a polynomial algorithm for version 2. The idea is similar to the algorithm of the previous section.

We build a digraph in a similar fashion to the digraph of section 3 but this time the digraph will be weighted. As in the previous construction, for each vertex in the hypertext we construct two sets of m vertices. All edges that were in the previous construction will also be in this digraph, all having weight zero. The weight zero expresses that there are no mismatches. We add edges that will capture the matches containing mismatches. The weight we assign to such an edge is the number of mismatches occurring between the corresponding sub-pattern and the vertex's text.

We denote the number of mismatches between two equal length strings x and y as $Ham(x,y)$.

Formally we define the directed weighted graph $G^{(P,H)} = (V^{(P,H)}, E^{(P,H)})$, where H is a hypertext (V, E, T) and P is a pattern $p_1 p_2 ... p_m$, as follows:

$$V^{(P,H)} = \{\overline{v}^i \mid v \in V, 1 \le i \le m\} \cup \{\underline{v}^i \mid v \in V, 1 \le i \le m\} \cup \{s\}$$

$$E^{(P,H)} = \{(\overline{v}^i, \underline{v}^{i+|T_v|-1}, w) \mid |T_v| < m, 1 < i \le m - |T_v| + 1,$$
$$w = Ham(T_v, p_i...p_{i+|T_v|-1})\} \cup$$
$$\{(\overline{v}^1, \underline{v}^k, w) \mid 1 \le k < m, w = Ham(Suf(T_v, k), p_1...p_k)\} \cup$$
$$\{(\overline{v}^k, \underline{v}^m, w) \mid 1 < k \le m, w = Ham(Pref(T_v, m - k + 1), p_k...p_m)\} \cup$$
$$\{(\underline{v}^i, \overline{u}^{i+1}, 0) \mid (v, u) \in E, 1 \le i \le m\} \cup$$
$$\{(s, \overline{v}^1, 0) \mid v \in V\}.$$

Here we denoted edges as a triplet (u, v, w) where w is the weight of the edge from u to v. We will alternate between this notation and notation of an edge as (u, v) with a weight function over all edges $w(u, v)$.

Lemma 3. *Every path in $G^{(P,H)}$ from s to $\underline{v}^m$ for some $v \in V$ is of the form $s, \overline{v}_1^1, \underline{v}_1^{i_1}, \overline{v}_2^{i_1+1}, \underline{v}_2^{i_2}, ..., \underline{v}_{k-1}^{i_{k-1}}, \overline{v}^{i_{k-1}+1}, \underline{v}^m$, with $1 \le i_1 < i_2 < ... < i_{k-1} < m$.*

Proof: Let C be a path from s to some $\underline{v}^m$. The only edges leaving s enter vertices of the form $\overline{u}^1$ and all edges leaving vertices of the form $\underline{u}^i$ go to vertices of the form $\overline{w}^{i+1}$. All edges leaving vertices of the form $\overline{u}^i$ go to vertices of the form $\underline{u}^j$ for $j > i$. So the lemma follows.   □

Lemma 4. *Let P be a pattern of length m and $1 \le d \le m$. There exists a pattern P' of length m with $Ham(P, P') = d$ such that P' matches in H iff there exists a path in $G^{(P,H)}$ from s to v^m, for some vertex $v \in V$, with path weight d.*

Proof: Assume that there exists a P' for which the lemma's conditions hold. Let $v_1, ..., v_k$ be the path in H on which P' matches beginning from location l, i.e. $P' = T'_{v_1} T_{v_2} T_{v_3} ... T_{v_{k-2}} T_{v_{k-1}} T''_{v_k}$, where $|T'_{v_1}| = |T_{v_1}| - l + 1$. It is straightforward to check that the following path exists and has weight d:

$$s, \overline{v}_1^1, \underline{v}_1^{|T'_{v_1}|}, \overline{v}_2^{|T'_{v_1}|+1}, \underline{v}_2^{|T'_{v_1}|+|T_{v_2}|}, ...,$$
$$\overline{v}_i^{|T'_{v_1}|+\sum_{j=1}^{i-1}|T_{v_j}|+1}, \underline{v}_i^{|T'_{v_1}|+\sum_{j=1}^{i}|T_{v_j}|}, ..., \overline{v}_k^{m-|T''_{v_k}|+1}, \underline{v}_k^m.$$

Conversely, according to Lemma 3 every path from s to $\underline{v}^m$ is of the form $s, \overline{v}_1^1, \underline{v}_1^{i_1}, \overline{v}_2^{i_1+1}, \underline{v}_2^{i_2}, ..., \underline{v}_{k-1}^{i_{k-1}}, \overline{v}_k^{i_{k-1}+1}, \underline{v}_k^m$ such that $1 \le i_1 < i_2 < ... < i_{k-1} < m$. An analysis of the construction of $G^{(P,H)}$ shows that $(s, \overline{v}_1^1)$ and $(\underline{v}_j^{i_j}, \overline{v}_{j+1}^{i_j+1})$ are edges with weight 0 and that $(\overline{v}_j^{i_{j-1}+1}, \underline{v}_j^{i_j})$ are edges with weight $Ham(T_{v_j}, p_{i_{j-1}+1}...p_{i_j})$ except for $(\overline{v}_1^1, \underline{v}_1^{i_1})$ and $(\overline{v}_k^{i_{k-1}+1}, \underline{v}_k^m)$ which have weight $Ham(Suf(T_{v_1}, i_1), p_1...p_{i_1})$ and $Ham(Pref(T_{v_k}, m - i_{k-1}), p_{i_{k-1}+1}...p_m)$, respectively.

Therefore, the overall weight $d = w(s, \overline{v}_1^1) + w(\overline{v}_1^1, \underline{v}_1^{i_1}) + w(\underline{v}_1^{i_1}, \overline{v}_2^{i_1+1}) + ... + w(\overline{v}_k^{i_{k-1}+1}, \underline{v}_k^m) = Ham(P, T'_{v_1} T_{v_2} T_{v_3} ... T_{v_{k-2}} T_{v_{k-1}} T''_{v_k})$, where $T'_{v_1} = Suf(T_{v_1}, i_1)$ and $T''_{v_k} = Pref(T_{v_k}, m - i_{k-1})$. So, choosing $P' = T'_{v_1} T_{v_2} T_{v_3} ... T_{v_{k-2}} T_{v_{k-1}} T''_{v_k}$ gives a pattern of length m that matches in H with $Ham(P, P') = d$.   □

The following algorithm is designed to output the minimum number of changes necessary to assure a P match. If desired, this can be adapted in a simple way to return P' that does match and is obtained by a minimum number of changes from P. Another modification of our algorithm can allow outputting, for every hypertext location, the number of changes to the pattern that are necessary in order for the pattern to match at that hypertext location.

Algorithm for Approximate Pattern Matching with Hamming Distance in Hypertext

1. For each vertex v in H for which $|T_v| \geq m$, build an array of the hamming distance between pattern P and each substring of the text $\$^{m-1}T_v\$^{m-1}$, where $\$ \notin \Sigma$.
   For each vertex v in H for which $|T_v| \leq m$, build an array of the hamming distance between T_v, viewed as the pattern, and each substring of $\$^{|T_v|-1}P\$^{|T_v|-1}$, viewed as text, where $\$ \notin \Sigma$.
2. For each vertex with $|T_v| \geq m$ use the results of step 1 to find a substring of T_v of length m with least hamming distance from pattern P. Denote the distance $w(v)$.
3. Build $G^{(P,H)}$ from the pattern P and the hypertext H, using the results of step 1.
4. Do a depth first search in $G^{(P,H)}$ starting from vertex s finding the shortest path from s to $\underline{u}^m$ for some $u \in V$ and denote the length of the shortest (weighted) path w.
5. **Output:** $\min(\{w\} \cup \{w(v) \mid v \in V, |T_v| \geq m\})$.

Correctness: If the substring with shortest hamming distance from the pattern appears within a vertex then we will find it in step 2 and announce it in step 5. If the pattern crosses at least one hyperlink then by Lemma 4 there is a path of the form described in Lemma 4 with this weight. Since by Lemma 3 all paths from s to $\underline{v}^m$ for some $v \in V$ have this form which by Lemma 4 correspond to paths which model comparisons of P in the hypertext, it is sufficient to find the shortest path from s to some $\underline{v}^m$. This is exactly what we do in step 4. We implement it with a depth first search since $G^{(P,H)}$ is a DAG. In step 5 we announce the shortest.

Time: Assume the alphabet is unbounded. For each vertex, if $|T_v| > m$ then step 1 takes time $O(|T_v|\sqrt{m \log m})$ [1,29] and if $m > |T_v|$ then step 1 takes time $O(m\sqrt{|T_v| \log m})$, for an overall time of $O((N\sqrt{m} + m\sqrt{N})\sqrt{\log m})$. If the alphabet is fixed, then by the Fischer-Patterson method [21] step 1 can be solved in time $O(N \log m)$. Step 2 is linear in the size of the text within the vertices, i.e. $O(N)$. Step 3 is linear in the size of $G^{(P,H)}$, which has a vertex set of size $O(|V|m)$ and edge set of size $O(|E|m)$. Step 4 is linear in the size of $G^{(P,H)}$ and step 5 costs $O(|V|)$. So, we have an overall complexity of $O((N\sqrt{m} + m\sqrt{N})\sqrt{\log m} + |E|m)$. ($O(N \log m + |E|m)$ over fixed bounded alphabets.)

5 Approximate Pattern Matching in Hypertext - Edit Distance

While it is true that mismatches are a common error in texts, often other errors occur such as accidentally deleting a character or inserting a superfluous character. The minimal number of insertions, deletions and changes necessary to transfer one string into another is called the *edit distance* of these two strings. In this section we consider approximate pattern matching in hypertext with edit distance as our metric.

Similar to the previous section we have three versions to the problem and, not surprisingly similar results. We will first show that if the insertions, deletions and changes can be done only in the hypertext, then the problem is $\mathcal{NP}$-Complete. We then give an outline how to extend this result to the case when the errors occur both in the pattern and in the hypertext. Afterwards we present a polynomial algorithm for the case when errors occur in the pattern only. Note that the insertions or deletions are always on the characters whether in the pattern or in the hypertext, never on the structure of the hypertext. The underlying digraph always remains in its original form. Different from what we have seen up till now, it may be that after a deletion of a character of text in a vertex, the text is the empty word ϵ.

The *Approximate Hypertext Matching-Edit Distance in Hypertext* problem is defined as follows:

Input: A pattern P, a hypertext $H = (V, E, T)$ and a distance d.

Output: *True*, if with d error-corrections (insertions, deletions and changes) we can change the hypertext so that P matches in H. *False*, otherwise.

Proposition 3. *The Approximate Matching-Edit Distance in Hypertext problem is $\mathcal{NP}$-Complete.*

Proof: Clearly the problem is in $\mathcal{NP}$. We will reduce from directed Hamiltonian path.

Let $G = (V, E)$ be a directed graph in which we seek a Hamiltonian path and let $n = |V|$. Set $P = \$\sigma_1 \# ... \$\sigma_n \#$, where $\forall i \neq j$, $\sigma_i \neq \sigma_j$ and $\$, \# \notin \{\sigma_1, ..., \sigma_n\}$ and set the hypertext $H = (V, E, T)$ where $T_v = \$\#$ for every $v \in V$. Set the distance $d = n$. If we have a Hamiltonian path then by inserting σ_i in between the $\$$ and the $\#$ of the i-th vertex will give us a match of P in the hypertext with n error-corrections.

Conversely, assume we have a match of P in H with at most n error-corrections on H. Since $\sigma_1, ..., \sigma_n$ do not appear in the hypertext before the error-corrections and must appear after the error-corrections and since $\forall i \neq j$, $\sigma_i \neq \sigma_j$ it must be the case that the n error-corrections are either changes or insertions intended for inserting $\sigma_1, ..., \sigma_n$ into the hypertext.

Consider the path C in the hypertext that P matches upon after the error-corrections. If this path is not Hamiltonian then one of the following must be true: (a) there is a vertex that does not appear on C, (b) there is a vertex that appears twice, not including the first or last vertex on the path or (c) the first or last vertex appear a second time along the path.

If (case (a)) there is a vertex that does not appear on C then there must be a different vertex in which both σ_i and σ_{i+1} appear. But this other vertex must contain text $\sigma_i\#\$\sigma_{i+1}$. This cannot be, because at least $n-2$ error corrections are necessary for the other vertices and four corrections are necessary for the vertex containing $\sigma_i\#\$\sigma_{i+1}$.

If (case (b)) there is a vertex in C that appears twice, this vertex may not contain σ_j for any j. But then there must be a vertex with σ_i and σ_{i+1} which, as in case (a), is impossible. Case (c) is also impossible following similar reasoning. Therefore, C is a Hamiltonian path.   □

If we modify the definition of the problem to allow errors in the hypertext and the pattern then it is once again $\mathcal{NP}$-Complete. This can be proved reducing from the directed Hamiltonian cycle problem with pattern $P = \$\sigma_1\#...\$\sigma_n\#\$\sigma_1\#...\$\sigma_n\#$, using a similar claim to Proposition 2 to show that there cannot be changes in the pattern and then the rest is similar to the proof of Proposition 3.

We now consider the version with errors in the pattern only. For this problem we present a polynomial algorithm that, once again, extends the previous ideas. We start with a formal definition.

The *Approximate Hypertext Matching-Edit Distance in Pattern* problem is defined as follows:

Input: A pattern P and a hypertext $H = (V, E, T)$.

Output: The minimum d such that with d error-corrections (insertions, deletions and changes) in the pattern, P, it will match in H.

The best known algorithms [31] for approximate pattern matching with edit distance in regular text have complexity of $O(nm)$, where n is the text length and m is the pattern length. In a hypertext a vertex may contain $O(N)$, where N is, as before, the overall size of the text in the vertices. So applying regular approximate pattern matching techniques would cost $O(Nm)$ for this vertex alone. Therefore, for simplicity, without sacrificing efficiency, we will turn the hypertext into a one-character hypertext.

As in section 2, for each vertex v in the hypertext the digraph contains the vertex set $\{v^i \mid 1 \le i \le m\}$, where v^i represents the comparison of T_v and p_i. The edges will be weighted in a fashion similar to the previous section. There will be edges with weight 0 to account for an exact match and edges with weight 1 to account for mismatch. We also add edges with weight 1 to account for insertion and deletion of a character.

We now describe the edges in the digraph. We have (a) edges describing an exact match of ith pattern character, (b) edges describing a mismatch at location i, (c) edges describing insertion of a character to the pattern before pattern location i, (d) edges describing deletion of the ith character of the pattern and (e) edges from the start vertex s to all the first location vertices.

Formally,
$$V^{(P,H)} = \{v^i \mid v \in V, 1 \le i \le m\} \cup \{s\} \cup \{f\}$$

$$E^{(P,H)} = (a) \; \{(u^i, v^{i+1}, 0) \mid (u,v) \in E, T_u = p_i\} \cup$$
$$\{(u^m, f, 0) \quad \mid T_u = p_m\} \cup$$
$$(b) \; \{(u^i, v^{i+1}, 1) \mid (u,v) \in E, T_u \neq p_i\} \cup$$
$$(c) \; \{(u^i, v^i, 1) \quad \mid (u,v) \in E, \; 2 \leq i \leq m\} \cup$$
$$(d) \; \{(v^i, v^{i+1}, 1) \mid v \in V, \; 1 \leq i \leq m-1, \; T_v \neq p_i \, or \, (v,v) \notin E\} \cup$$
$$\{(v^m, f, 1) \quad \mid T_v \neq p_m\} \cup$$
$$(e) \; \{(s, v^1, 0) \quad \mid v \in V\}.$$

Lemma 5. *Let P be a pattern of length m and $1 \leq d \leq m$. There exists a pattern P' formed by d error-corrections of P such that P' matches in H iff there exists a path in $G^{(P,H)}$ from s to f with path weight d.*

Proof: Let $P = p_1 \cdots p_m$, $P' = p'_1 \cdots p'_k$. The proof of the lemma follows immediately from the following observation.

Let $e_1, ..., e_d$ be the edit operations performed on P to achieve P'. Denote each e_i by a triple $\langle j_i, E_i, \sigma_i \rangle$, where $j_i \in \{1, ..., m\}$, $\sigma_i \in \Sigma$, and $E_i \in \{M, I, D\}$. The meaning of E_i is:

$$E_i = \begin{cases} M, & \text{means ``change } p_{j_i} \text{ to } \sigma_i\text{''} \text{ (mismatch)}; \\ I, & \text{means ``insert } \sigma_i \text{ before } p_{j_i}\text{''}; \\ D, & \text{means ``delete } p_{j_i}\text{''}. \end{cases}$$

Let $\#_i^I$ be the number of E_ℓ's that are I, for $\ell = 1, ..., i$. Let $\#_i^D$ be the number of E_ℓ's that are D, for $\ell = 1, ..., i$, and let $\#_i = \#_i^I - \#_i^D$.

Without loss of generality, assume that $e_1, ..., e_d$ are sorted by increasing values of j.

By definition of edit distance, the following is true:

$p_1 \cdots p_{j_1-1} = p'_1 \cdots p'_{j_1-1}$
If $E_1 = I$ then $p'_{j_1} = \sigma_1$ and $p'_{j_1+1} = p_{j_1}$.
If $E_1 = M$ then $p'_{j_1} = \sigma_1$.
$p_{j_1+1} \cdots p_{j_2-1} = p'_{j_1+\#_1+1} \cdots p'_{j_2+\#_1-1}$

$\vdots$

If $E_i = I$ then $p'_{j_i+\#_{i-1}} = \sigma_i$ and $p'_{j_i+\#_{i-1}+1} = p_{j_i}$.
If $E_i = M$ then $p'_{j_i+\#_{i-1}} = \sigma_i$.
$p_{j_i+1} \cdots p_{j_{i+1}-1} = p'_{j_i+\#_i+1} \cdots p'_{j_{i+1}+\#_i-1}$

$\vdots$

If $E_d = I$ then $p'_{j_d+\#_{d-1}} = \sigma_d$ and $p'_{j_d+\#_{d-1}+1} = p_{j_d}$.
If $E_d = M$ then $p'_{j_d+\#_{d-1}} = \sigma_d$.
$p_{j_d+1} \cdots p_m = p'_{k+j_d+1-m} \cdots p'_k$.

Assume now that P' matches in H. Then there exists a path $v_1, ..., v_k$ in H where P' matches, i.e. $P' = T_{v_1} T_{v_2} \cdots T_{v_k}$.

The following path in $G^{(P,H)}$ starts at s, ends at f and has weight d. Start with type (e) edge $(s, v_1^1, 0)$ followed by j_1 type (a) edges $(v_i^i, v_i^{i+1}, 0)$, for $i = 1, ..., j_1 - 1$.

Inductively assume that we have constructed a path of weight $i - 1$ until $p'_{j_i + \#_{i-1} - 1}$. The following three cases are possible:

1. $E_i = M$. Follow one type (b) edge $(v^{j_i}_{j_i + \#_{i-1}}, v^{j_i+1}_{j_i + \#_i + 1}, 1)$.
2. $E_i = I$. Follow one type (c) edge $(v^{j_i}_{j_i + \#_{i-1}}, v^{j_i}_{j_i + \#_i}, 1)$, and one type (a) edge $(v^{j_i}_{j_i + \#_i}, v^{j_i+1}_{j_i + \#_i + 1}, 0)$.
3. $E_i = D$. Follow one type (d) edge $(v^{j_i}_{j_i + \#_{i-1}}, v^{j_i+1}_{j_i + \#_i}, 1)$.

Continue with $j_{i+1} - j_i - 1$ type (a) edges, $(v^{\ell}_{\ell + \#_\ell}, v^{\ell+1}_{\ell + \#_\ell + 1}, 0)$, $\ell = j_i + 1, ..., j_{i+1} - 1$ until the next edit operation.

For the final operation, end it with a type (a) edge to f if $j_d \neq m$, and with a single type (d) edge to f if $j_d = m$.

The converse is similar. Simply construct the edit operations from the path in $G^{(P,H)}$. □

Algorithm for Approximate Hypertext Matching - Edit Distance in Pattern

1. Create a one-character hypertext $H' = (V', E', T')$ from H.
2. Build $G^{(P,H')}$ from the pattern P and the one-character hypertext H'.
3. Find the shortest path from s to f and announce its weighted length.

Correctness: Follows directly from Lemma 5.

Time: Step 1 takes time linear to H' and step 2 time linear to $G^{(P,H')}$. $|V'| = O(|V| + N) = O(N)$ and $|E'| = O(|E| + N)$. $G^{(P,H')}$ has vertex size $O(|V'|m) = O(mN)$ and edge size $O(m|E'|) = O(mN + m|E|)$. Using Dijkstra's algorithm implemented with Fibonacci heaps the third step can be done in $O(Nm \log N + |E|m)$ time [18].

Acknowledgement. In my elementary school year book, under the "what would you like to be when you grow up?" heading, I unhesitatingly put down: *mathematician*. Indeed, when I started college at Bar Ilan University in 1972, I was one of four people who were chosen for a special program in advanced mathematics. These four always remind me of the four who entered the *Pardess* (Orchard – symbolising the Jewish Mysticism, Kabala). In the Talmud, tractate *Hagiga*, page 14. an interesting *braita* is brought, describing four sages who entered the Pardess. "Ben Azai glimpsed and died, and about him he Scriptures say: "It is precious in the Eyes of God the death of his *Hassidim*". Ben Zoma glimpsed and was injured, and about him the Scriptures say: "If you find honey eat (only) to your capacity, else you will overfill and vomit it". The Other uprooted the saplings. Rabbi Akiva departed in peace."

I jocularly fancy the *Orchard* as the hallowed field of pure mathematics. One of the four of us, glimpsed, but "died" to Math. He became one of the leading Rabbis of the Breslav Hassidut. The second, saw "honey" and "sold out" to high tech. The math he uses is "impure" and "injured". The third departed in peace and he is today a professor of mathematics at Hebrew University. I uprooted the saplings – I made the transition to the nascent field of computer science. This change can be likened to "uprooting the saplings" for more reasons than the obvious one – where the back is turned on pure math. Note also that, unlike in mathematics, trees in computer science are drawn with the root up and the leaves down - thus "uprooted".

The person most responsible for my traitorous treatment of mathematics is Professor Yaakov Choueka. He taught me the Computability class. His clear style, impeccable exposition, perfect imparting of the intuitions, and straightforward reasoning, caused an upheaval in my life. After over a decade of conviction that pure mathematics is my future, I underwent emotional turmoil when I realized that I am enjoying theoretical computer science much more. My father, *alaiv hashalom* helped me make the final decision by quoting Rabbi Yehuda Hanasi who taught that a person should study what he enjoys most. I transfered to a computer science minor and my life was changed forever.

It was natural that I turned to Professor Choueka as my M.Sc. adviser, and consequently published my first papers with him. In Judaism, the person who is most influential on one's Judaic studies is called *Rabo Muvhak*. Professor Choueka is my Rav Muvhak in computer science. A role model and inspiration to me, and by transitivity, to the over 20 Ph.D. students I have supervised, and even their students and their students' students.

Professor Choueka – thank you!

References

1. Abrahamson, K.: Generalized string matching. SIAM J. Comp. 16(6), 1039–1051 (1987)
2. Akutsu, T.: A linear time pattern matching algorithm between a string and a tree. In: Apostolico, A., Crochemore, M., Galil, Z., Manber, U. (eds.) CPM 1993. LNCS, vol. 684, pp. 1–10. Springer, Heidelberg (1993)
3. Amir, A.: Entry: Computer Science. In: Berenbaum, M. (ed.) Encyclopaedia Judaica, McMillan's Reference and Keter Publishing (2006)
4. Amir, A., Aumann, Y., Indyk, P., Levy, A., Porat, E.: Efficient computations of ℓ_1 and ℓ_∞ rearrangement distances. In: Ziviani, N., Baeza-Yates, R. (eds.) SPIRE 2007. LNCS, vol. 4726, pp. 39–49. Springer, Heidelberg (2007)
5. Amir, A., Aumann, Y., Benson, G., Levy, A., Lipsky, O., Porat, E., Skiena, S., Vishne, U.: Pattern matching with address errors: rearrangement distances. In: Proc. 17th ACM-SIAM Symposium on Discrete Algorithms (SODA), pp. 1221–1229 (2006)
6. Amir, A., Aumann, Y., Kapah, O., Levy, A., Porat, E.: Approximate string matching with address bit errors. In: Ferragina, P., Landau, G.M. (eds.) CPM 2008. LNCS, vol. 5029, pp. 118–129. Springer, Heidelberg (2008)
7. Amir, A., Benson, G., Farach, M.: An alphabet independent approach to two dimensional pattern matching. SIAM J. Comp. 23(2), 313–323 (1994)
8. Amir, A., Butman, A., Crochemore, M., Landau, G.M., Schaps, M.: Two-dimensional pattern matching with rotations. Theoretical Computer Science 314(1-2), 173–187 (2004)
9. Amir, A., Calinescu, G.: Alphabet independent and dictionary scaled matching. In: Hirschberg, D.S., Meyers, G. (eds.) CPM 1996. LNCS, vol. 1075, pp. 320–334. Springer, Heidelberg (1996)

10. Amir, A., Farach, M., Giancarlo, R., Galil, Z., Park, K.: Dynamic dictionary matching. Journal of Computer and System Sciences 49(2), 208–222 (1994)
11. Amir, A., Farach, M., Idury, R.M., La Poutré, J.A., Schäffer, A.A.: Improved dynamic dictionary matching. Information and Computation 119(2), 258–282 (1995)
12. Amir, A., Hartman, T., Kapah, O., Levy, A., Porat, E.: On the cost of interchange rearrangement in strings. In: Arge, L., Hoffmann, M., Welzl, E. (eds.) ESA 2007. LNCS, vol. 4698, pp. 99–110. Springer, Heidelberg (2007)
13. Amir, A., Lewenstein, N., Lewenstein, M.: Pattern matching in hypertext. J. of Algorithms 35, 82–99 (2000)
14. Andoni, A., Deza, M., Gupta, A., Indyk, P., Raskhodnikova, S.: Lower bounds for embedding of edit distance into normed spaces. In: Proc. 14th Annual ACM-SIAM Symposium on Discrete Algorithms (SODA), pp. 523–526 (2003)
15. Aviad, A.: Hypertalmud: a hypertext system for the babylonian talmud and its commentaries. Master's thesis, Bar-Ilan University, Department of Mathematics and Computer Science (1993)
16. Batu, T., Ergun, F., Sahinalp, C.: Oblivious string embeddings and edit distance approximations. In: Proc. 17th Annual ACM-SIAM Symposium on Discrete Algorithms (SODA), pp. 792–801 (2006)
17. Boyer, R.S., Moore, J.S.: A fast string searching algorithm. Comm. ACM 20, 762–772 (1977)
18. Cormen, T.H., Leiserson, C.E., Rivest, R.L.: Introduction to Algorithms. MIT Press and McGraw-Hill (1992)
19. Cormode, G., Datar, M., Indyk, P., Muthukrishnan, S.: Comparing data streams using hamming norms (how to zero in). IEEE Transactions on Knowledge and Data Engineering 15(3), 529–540 (2003)
20. Ferragina, P., Grossi, R.: Fast incremental text editing. In: Proc. 7th ACM-SIAM Symposium on Discrete Algorithms, pp. 531–540 (1995)
21. Fischer, M.J., Paterson, M.S.: String matching and other products. In: Karp, R.M. (ed.) Complexity of Computation. SIAM-AMS Proceedings, vol. 7, pp. 113–125 (1974)
22. Fraenkel, A.S., Klein, S.T.: Information retrieval from annotated texts with applications to hypertext (submitted for publication, 1996)
23. Fredriksson, K., Navarro, G., Ukkonen, E.: Optimal exact and fast approximate two dimensional pattern matching allowing rotations. In: Apostolico, A., Takeda, M. (eds.) CPM 2002. LNCS, vol. 2373, pp. 235–248. Springer, Heidelberg (2002)
24. Indyk, P.: Stable distributions, pseudorandom generators, embeddings and data stream computation. In: Proc. 41st IEEE FOCS, pp. 189–197 (2000)
25. Kapah, O., Landau, G.M., Levy, A., Oz, N.: Interchange rearrangement: The element-cost model. In: Amir, A., Turpin, A., Moffat, A. (eds.) SPIRE 2008. LNCS, vol. 5280, pp. 224–235. Springer, Heidelberg (2008)
26. Karp, R., Miller, R., Rosenberg, A.: Rapid identification of repeated patterns in strings, arrays and trees. In: Symposium on the Theory of Computing, vol. 4, pp. 125–136 (1972)
27. Kim, D.K., Park, K.: String matching in hypertext. In: Galil, Z., Ukkonen, E. (eds.) CPM 1995. LNCS, vol. 937, Springer, Heidelberg (1995)
28. Knuth, D.E., Morris, J.H., Pratt, V.R.: Fast pattern matching in strings. SIAM J. Comp. 6, 323–350 (1977)
29. Rao Kosaraju, S.: Efficient string matching (1987) (manuscript)
30. Landau, G.M., Vishkin, U.: Efficient string matching with k mismatches. Theoretical Computer Science 43, 239–249 (1986)

31. Landau, G.M., Vishkin, U.: Fast parallel and serial approximate string matching. Journal of Algorithms 10(2), 157–169 (1989)
32. Manber, U., Wu, S.: Approximate string matching with arbitrary cost for text and hypertext. In: Proc. Int'l Workshop on Structural and Syntactic Pattern Recognition, pp. 22–33 (1992)
33. Miller, W., Myers, E.: Sequence comparison with concave weighting functions. Bulletin of Mathematical Biology 50, 97–120 (1988)
34. Nielsen, J.: Hypertext and Hypermedia. Academic Press Professional, Boston (1993)
35. Sahinalp, S.C., Vishkin, U.: Efficient approximate and dynamic matching of patterns using a labeling paradigm. In: Proc. 37th FOCS, pp. 320–328 (1996)

Search Engines and Hebrew - Revisited

Judit Bar-Ilan

Department of Information Science, Bar-Ilan University, Ramat Gan, 52900, Israel
`barilaj@mail.biu.ac.il`

Abstract. In previous studies, carried out in 2002 [3] and in 2005 [2] we showed, that Google, the most popular search engine in Israel, does not take into account any of the morphological complexities of Hebrew, while Morfix, a Hebrew search engine, handles Hebrew very well, but has limited coverage and freshness. In the current study we revisit these search engines and explore the situation as of 2007. Our findings show some improvement in Google's Hebrew retrieval capabilities.

Keywords: Hebrew queries, search engines.

1   Introduction

During its short existence, the Web has already become a major information source. Although English is the lingua franca of the Web, and Hebrew is spoken only by a small fraction of the Web users, users whose mother tongue is Hebrew prefer to search in Hebrew even though much less information is available in Hebrew than in English.

It is not easy to estimate the number of Hebrew speaking Internet users in the world, since not all Israelis are Hebrew speakers and there are Hebrew speakers living in other parts of the world (see [9]). If we take the number of Israeli Internet users as a rough estimate for Hebrew speaking Internet users then according to the latest data from Internet World Stats [12], the estimated 3.7 million Israeli Internet users make up about 0.3% of the total Internet population. We were unable to find updated information on the percentage of Hebrew language pages on the Web; information from 2000 states that 0.06% of the pages on the Web were written in Hebrew [15] and Gey's [8] estimate as of 2003 is that 0.153% of the Web pages were in Hebrew.

Over the years we witness considerable growth in the amount of information in Hebrew available on the Web. According to "Dapey reshet" [7], in January 1997 there were 300 sites that supported Hebrew (about 30% of the total Israeli sites). By the end of 1997, Dapey reshet estimated that the number of Hebrew language sites is around 2,500. In January 2005, based on data from Google [2], there were 4,140,000 pages in the domain .il (Israel). As of September 2007, Google reported to have indexed about 13,400,000 pages from the domain .il, out of which it reported that its database contains 2,520,000 pages in Hebrew. It also indexed Hebrew language pages outside the domain .il (although it is impossible to get an estimate for the number of Hebrew

N. Dershowitz and E. Nissan (Eds.): Choueka Festschrift, Part I, LNCS 8001, pp. 382–394, 2014.

language pages through a direct query), since for the query ישראל (Israel in Hebrew) and limiting the search to pages written in Hebrew, it reported to have found 3,970,000 pages.

The Web is an important information source to Hebrew speaking Web users. Based on data from the latest TIM survey [17] the most frequently visited site by Israelis is Google with more than 3 million visitors per week, followed by the Walla portal and ynet the Internet portal of the newspaper Yedioth Aharonot. Besides Google, in the list of the twenty most visited sites by Israelis there are six other search sites and portals that enable searching. In addition, two of the major newspaper sites (HaAretz and Maariv) also feature search boxes that allow searching the Internet. For Israelis, searching is one of the major activities on the Web [4].

What is special about searching in Hebrew? Hebrew, unlike English is a morphologically complex language. Most of the research in information retrieval is geared towards English. Simple application of information retrieval techniques that were developed for English is not sufficient for Hebrew. Hebrew is a Semitic language, thus many of the challenges of Hebrew language information retrieval in are similar to the issues related to Arab language retrieval [14]

Perhaps the most important aspect of Hebrew when searching the Web is its extensive use of prefixes added to nouns. The definite article (ה – the) and most of the prepositions (e.g., ב – in, ל – to) are prefixed to the nouns. Several layers of prefixes can be added to a word (e.g., מה – from the). Prefixes are so prevalent in the Hebrew language, that any search engine that does not strip these prefixes looses a lot of information.

An additional challenge is that modern Hebrew is written most of the time without vowels, and as a result of this a given string of letters often has several quite different meanings. As an example consider the string מספר. If one consults the dictionary, for example the Morfix Hebrew-English dictionary at http://milon.morfix.co.il/MorDictFirstPage.htm), it provides fourteen different meanings including: number, to cut hair, storyteller, from a book and related. Some of the missing vowels are replaced by consonants resulting in different spelling styles, KTIV MALE and KTIV HASSER (plene spelling and vocalized spelling).

Thus it is much easier tools for English than for Hebrew, and it is also much more worthwhile financially because of the differences in the number of English speaking and Hebrew speaking users. In spite of this, there are a number of studies on Hebrew language information retrieval – some of the theoretical studies and systems are reviewed in [16]. Especially outstanding are works of the Responsa project, headed by Prof. Choeuka and Prof. Fraenkel in this area [1, 5, 6]. The Web search engine Morfix (http://www.morfix.com) integrates technologies developed in collaboration with Prof. Choeuka [13].

In two previous studies we have already explored some search engines' information capabilities in Hebrew. In [3] the searches were carried out in November of 2002. The general search engines tested by us were: Google (the Hebrew interface as http://www.google.co.il), AlltheWeb (FAST) (http://www.alltheweb.com) and AltaVista (http://www.altavista.com) – at that time AltaVista and AlltheWeb were independent search engines. In addition to the general search engines, the local search tools Morfix (http://www.morfix.co.il –morphological search and exact search options) and Walla (http://www.walla.co.il – both partial word and full word options of the directory listings) were tested. The queries were chosen to test whether the search engines take into account different word forms – prefixes and suffixes. We tested different forms of the word *university* (אוניברסיטה – *university*, האוניברסיטה – *the university*, with the definite article prefixed to the word, באוניברסיטה – *in the/a university*, with the preposition in prefixed to the word, אוניברסיטת - *university of*, possessive postfixed, results in the change of the final character, ושהאוניברסיטה – *and that the university*, three levels of prefixes), for two forms of the word house/home (בית – *house* and מהבית – *from the house*, two prefixes the definite article and then from) and the word מדבר that can mean *speaks*, *desert* and *from a thing*, in the last case the word is prefixed by the preposition from). The findings showed that the major search engines searched for the exact form only, i.e., when searching for university, they missed all the appearances of *the university*, *in the university*, *university of*, from *the university*, etc. Morphological search on Morfix was successful for the different forms of the word *university*, however for מדבר seemingly not all forms were retrieved. In the paper, we also noted the low coverage of Morfix. Walla had very low coverage and mixed results, but this could be expected since the searches were carried out in the directory listings.

At the beginning of 2005 the Hebrew search capabilities of Google, Morfix, Walla and another Hebrew search tool Nana (http://www.nana.co.il) [2] were tested. This study in addition to testing whether the search tool is capable of handling different word forms; we also examined up-to-dateness, KTIV MALE vs. KTIV HASSER (plene spelling vs. vocalized spelling), precision@5 of the retrieved results and the effects of using the " sign in Hebrew abbreviations (a pair of quotation marks in most search engines is used for phrase searching, whereas in Hebrew a single " is used a sign of abbreviation). Again, we found that Morfix handles best the morphological issues, but its coverage is low and at the time it was rather out-dated. Nana and Walla displayed even less results than Morfix, but the result were fresher than Morfix's results. These two tools, like Google searched for the exact word form only.

2   Methods

In the current study we examine the Hebrew search capabilities of all the sites in the list of the twenty most popular sites for Israelis as of July 2007 [17] that offer Web search (this excludes sites that offer directory or archive search only). The sites are:

♦ Google - in this paper we test google.co.il (the Hebrew interface to Google)
♦ Walla, www.walla.co.il - search engine based on Yahoo search (search.yahoo.com) [16]; results not identical to those provided by Yahoo
♦ MSN, msn.co.il – provides a Hebrew interface to Microsoft's Live Search, results similar, but not identical to those provided by Live Search (www.live.com)
♦ Nana, www.nana10.co.il – search "enhanced by Google" (www.nana10.co.il); results more similar to google.com than to google.co.il, but not identical; no phrase search; number of reported results smaller than on Google. Since the search is based on Google, this site was not tested.

- Nrg, www.nrg.co.il – the Internet site of the daily newspaper Maariv. Allows searching the Web through a customized Google (http://www.google.com/coop/cse/?hl=iw). Not tested.
- Tapuz, www.tapuz.co.il – serach engine devloped by Arnevet Search. Searches both the Web and content of the Tapuz site. Only Web search was tested. Searching Google from Tapuz is also possible, but this option was not tested.
- Yahoo!, search.yahoo.com. Since it is unknown how Walla is based on yahoo, it was decided to test both search sites.
- Haaretz, www.haaretz.co.il – the Internet site of the daily newspaper Haaretz. Has interface to google.com, google.co.il and walla. Not tested.
- Start, start.co.il – a portal that allows searching the Web through several search engines, including msn, google and walla. Not tested.

Thus in the current study we test Google.co.il, Walla, MSN, Tapuz and Yahoo!. We also test Morfix (www.morfix.co.il), even though it is not included in the twenty most frequently visited sites by Israelis, but previous studies [2,3] showed that it has far superior morphological capabilities compared to the other search engines.

All the searches were carried out at the end of September 2007. Each query was submitted to all the search engines within a ten-minute time period. We tested:

1. Up-to-datedness of the search engine by searching for
    a. Boaz Mauda (בועז מעודה) the recent winner of the Israeli version of the American Idol competition. The competition ended on August 29, 2007.
    b. The National Library Law ("חוק הספריה הלאומית") – this law was approved for second and third reading by the Knesset (the parliament) on September 11, 2007.
2. Word forms by searching for different forms of the word university (אוניברסיטה)
3. Plene spelling vs. vocalized spelling (KTIV MALE vs KTIV HASSER) by searching for two spellings of the word library (ספריה vs. ספרייה)
4. Submitting some of the more popular queries issued by Israelis, as reported by the Google Zeitgeist [10]. Here again we chose linguistically problematic queries.
    a. Different word forms of recipes (מתכונים) - recipe (מתכון), the recipe (המתכון), the recipes (המתכונים)
    b. Mobile phone/mobile phones (both forms are listed) – (טלפון סלולרי, טלפונים סלולריים). We will also test the alternative spelling טלפון סלולארי.
    c. Western Galilee College, listed in the March 2007 Zeitgeist as מכללת גליל מערבי (Michlelet Galil Maaravi) although the official name of the college is המכללה האקדמית גליל מערבי (HaMichlala HaAcademit Galil Maarvi).

3   Results and Discussion

3.1   Freshness of Search Results

The first query was Boaz Mauda, the winner of the 5th "A star is born" competition (the Israeli version of the "American Idol"). The finals took place on August 29, 2007, but the competition started during the spring of 2007. Google.co.il reported 69,100 results; walla 2,621 results; msn 2,596 results; tapuz 1,110 results; Yahoo! reported 52,900 results and Morfix reported 56 results for the query. When looking at the first page of results for all the search engines, except for Morfix, all the results related to Boaz Mauda, the winner of the contest. When looking at the results of Morfix, none of them were related to Boaz Mauda. The name Boaz appeared in all the results, but Mauda could not be found, instead in most cases the search engine highlighted the word OD (עוד – more) – it assumed that Mauda was a morphological variant of OD. When searching for the exact phrase "Boaz Mauda" on Morfix, not a single result was retrieved. It seems that Morfix is either totally outdated or it does not cover popular topics.

The second query testing freshness was the "National Library Law" ("חוק הספריה הלאומית"). The National Library which used to be the Jewish National & University Library (University Library of the Hebrew University of Jerusalem) is in the process of separation from the Hebrew University, and this is the reason for the recent legislation. The law was approved for second and third reading in the Parliament by the Parliament Committee on Education, Culture and Sport on September 11, 2007. The law was first proposed in 2004. Google.co.il reported 154 results, including reports from the recent committee meeting. Walla retrieved seven results, three results relate to the September 11 meeting of the Committee. Msn retrieved four results, one of them a news item that was published on September 12, 2007 with a report from the Committee meeting. Tapuz retrieved a single result, the protocol of a meeting that was held in November 2005. Yahoo! reported 35 results, out of the top-ten results; six results mention the Committee meeting of September 11, 2007. Morfix retrieved 19 pages, but none of them included the phrase "National Library Law", even though the query terms were enclosed in quotation marks, and Morfix's about page (http://www.morfix.co.il/al-morfix.htm) states (in Hebrew) that query terms enclosed within quotation marks are treated as phrases and are searched "as-is".

These two examples illustrate that all of the examined search tools, except for Morfix are updated. We see considerable differences in the number of results reported. We also saw that Morfix's phrase search is not working properly.

3.2   Word Forms

In this section we examined different forms of the word university. In our previous test, Morfix was the only search tool capable of handling different word forms. In this case too, for most queries Morfix returned the same number of results, from which we conclude that all the queries are considered different forms of the same word. An exception was the query "*to the university*", which for some reason retrieved a much smaller number of results. We have no explanation for this. The search engine is supposed to handle disjunctions, but probably the last query had too many terms in it and this is the reason for the reported 0 results.

Walla, Yahoo and MSN do not seem to apply any morphological transformations, they search for the occurrence of the query term "as-is". The version of Live Search running at msn.co.il does not support conjunctions (this is a beta version of Live Search), and neither does Walla's search tool. On Yahoo! we were able to run the searches: *university, universities, university* AND *universities, university* OR *universities*. The number of reported results seem to support the assumption that currently no morphological transformations are applied by Yahoo!.

Table 1. Word forms

Query term	Google. co.il	Walla	MSN	Tapuz	Yahoo!	Morfix
University אוניברסיטה	654,000	15,960	30,435	85,579	332,000	8,594
Universities אוניברסיטאות	355,000	12,531	21,024	33,687	251,000	8,594
The university האוניברסיטה	1,100,000	34,230	68,242	88,132	734,000	8,594
To the university לאוניברסיטה	258,000	9,277	15,094	26,810	183,000	137
In the university באוניברסיטה	788,000	24,719	43,806	67,842	474,000	8,594
From the university (two prefixes) מהאוניברסיטה	111,000	4,010	7,582	12,006	73,400	8,594
University of אוניברסיטת	1,490,000	46,527	95,437	116,333	1,170,000	8,594
The university OR of the university OR in the university OR האוניברסיטה OR אוניברסיטת באוניברסיטה	1,610,000	2,882	4,937	3,209 OR is probably not supported	1,950,000	8,594
University OR universities OR the university OR to the university OR in the university OR from the university OR university of OR אוניברסיטה OR אוניברסיטאות OR האוניברסיטה OR לאוניברסיטה OR באוניברסיטה OR מהאוניברסיטה אוניברסיטת	1,590,000	20	24	System error	2,370,000	0

Tapuz does not support conjunctions either, but it seems to apply some stemming of prefixes, as can be seen in Figure 1 for the query *university*. The term *university* is highlighted even when it is prefixed by "in" or "the". On the other hand, for all the other queries the highlighted words were exactly in the form the word was entered into to the search box, without any pre or postfixes. Thus one may be tempted to deduce, that a search for university will retrieve all the occurrences of university, even when prefixes are added to the word (but without the plural or the possessive forms). However, if we also assume that the numbers reported by the search engine are also correct, we run into a problem: a search for *university* is assumed to include all the occurrences of *the university* and more, however the search engine reports more results for the query *the university* than for the query *university*, thus it is not clear how and to what extent the morphological transformations are applied.

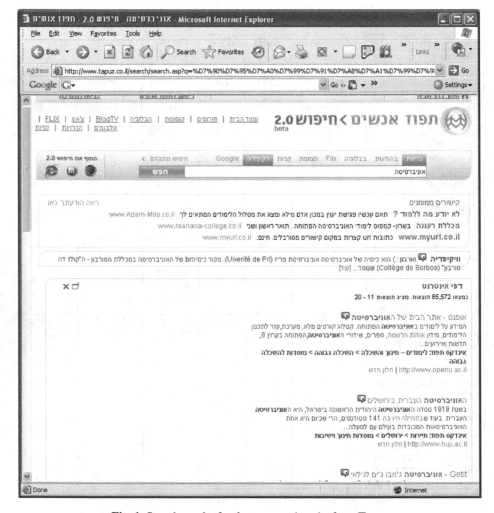

Fig. 1. Search results for the query *university* from Tapuz

In our previous tests Google retrieved the query term in its exact form only. This time we observed that for the query university, Google highlighted also occurrences of *universities* and *university of* and the occurrence of the word *university* in the prefixed terms *to the university* and *the university*. Does this mean that Google when searching for *university* Google retrieves all morphological forms? The reported number of results suggest otherwise: the query *the university* had many more results than the query *university*. To further test this point, we constructed the obscure query *university humus rhinoceros* (35 results) with *the university humus rhinoceros* (15 results). We chose a query that only has a small number of results, which allowed us to compare the two result sets. For both queries we clicked on the option *"If you like, you can repeat the search with the omitted results included"*, in order to see the whole set of results. Even though the number of results for the version with *the university* was smaller than without *the*, it turned out that the result set for *the university* included URLs that did not appear in the query without *the*. Thus it is not clear how and when Google applies morphological transformations. Unlike Tapuz, Google seems to apply morphological transformations not only to the base form of the word, but to other forms as well, as can be seen in Figure 3.

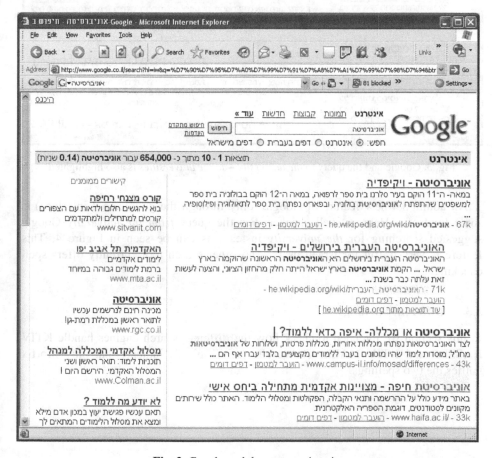

Fig. 2. Google and the query *university*

Fig. 3. Google and the query *to the university – to the universities* is also highlighted

An additional new feature of Google (only through the google.co.il interface) is some kind of a Hebrew spell checker. For the query *from the university* Google suggested searching for *the university* instead, as can be seen in Figure 4. This feature is very useful for Israeli users – no other search tool currently offers spell checking.

3.3 Different Spellings

In this section we intended to check how the different search engines handle KTIV HASSER and KTIV MALE. The results (see Table 2) indicate that only Morfix unifies the two spellings.

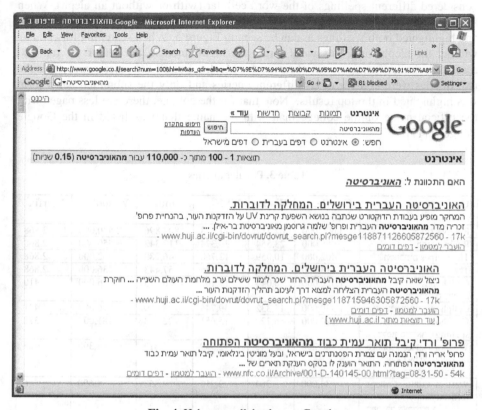

Fig. 4. Hebrew spellchecker on Google

Table 2. Spelling variants

Query term	Google.co.il	Walla	MSN	Tapuz	Yahoo!	Morfix
Library ספריה	652,000	20,769	60,211	75,127	381,000	21,299
Library ספרייה	339,000	10,398	27,840	39,172	182,000	21,299

3.4 Popular Queries from Google's Zeitgeist

In this section we experimented with a few queries (see Table 3) that appeared in the Google Zeitgeist – these queries are either very popular, or gained popularity during the specific month, i.e., the query was submitted with much higher frequency than in the previous month. The results for the different forms of the word *recipe* are in line with the searches we carried out for *university*. For the query *cellular phone*, we considered different spellings of the word cellular (with or without an aleph). When searching for cellular with an aleph, Google suggested the spelling without the aleph and highlighted both spellings as can be seen in Figure 5. When searching for *cellular* without the aleph, only this word form was highlighted in the set of the top 100 results. A similar behavior was observed for Morfix. For all the other search tools the two queries were considered as different queries and only the submitted word form was highlighted in the top results. Note that for the college, there are less pages with the official name of the college than with the name that was listed in the Google Zeitgeist [17].

Table 3. Popular queries

Query term	Google.co.il	Walla	MSN	Tapuz	Yahoo!	Morfix
Recipes מתכונים	3,600,000	62,417	117,393	804,896	2,530,000	2,868
Recipe מתכון	955,000	23,554	30,374	117,342	550,000	2,868
The recipes המתכונים	402,000	10,059	12,768	46,289	262,000	2,868
The recipe המתכון	413,000	9,980	13,346	57,443	236,000	2,868
Cellphones טלפונים סלולריים	1,320,000	8,044	17,165	56,313	166,000	410
Cellphone טלפון סלולרי	1,330,000	15,332	39,745	95,479	316,000	431
Cellphone (alternative spelling) טלפון סלולארי	1,170,000	6,720	15,651	22,633	181,000	377
Western Galilee College (as recorded by Google) מכללת גליל מערבי	80,200	746	2,949	3,613	14,300	25
Western Galilee College (official name) המכללה האקדמית גליל מערבי	34,000	384	2,317	4,857	4,600	6

Fig. 5. Alternative spellings of *cellular* on Google

4   Conclusions

This is the third time that we examined the Hebrew language search capabilities of some popular search tools. Google was the most popular search engine in Israel when it had no Hebrew spellchecker and searched for the exact form of the word only. Now that it has improved Hebrew language capabilities it seems that it will be even more difficult to compete with it. It is still not clear when and to what extent it applies morphological transformations. We can only hope that these features will be documented in Google's help section in the near future. The Walla search engine was launched as a competitor with Google and it was announced that it will be able to handle different word forms, but so far it does not. We will have to wait and see when this occurs and to carry out further tests in the meanwhile. Morfix handles the morphological forms correctly most of the time, but its coverage and timeliness have to be improved if it wants to compete with Google in Israel.

References

1. Attar, A., Choueka, Y., Dershowitz, N., Fraenkel, A.S.: KEDMA - Linguistic tools for retrieval systems. Journal of the Association for Computing Machinery 25(1), 52–66 (1978)
2. Bar-Ilan, J.: Demonstrating the Hebrew language information retrieval capabilities of Web search engines at the beginning of 2005. MEIDAAT 2, 68–79 (2006) (in Hebrew)
3. Bar-Ilan, J., Gutman, T.: How do search engines respond to some non-English queries? Journal of Information Science 31(1), 13–28 (2005)
4. Berkovits, U. In: July 2006 too – more surfers surf more (2006) (in Hebrew), http://net.nana10.co.il/Article/?ArticleID=386560&sid=127
5. Choueka, Y.: Computerized full-text retrieval systems and research in the humanities: The responsa project. Language Resources and Evaluation 14(3), 153–169 (1980)
6. Choueka, Y., Cohen, M., Dueck, J., Fraenkel, A.S., Slae, M.: Full text document retrieval: Hebrew legal texts. In: Proceedings of the 1971 International ACM SIGIR Conference on Information Storage and Retrieval, pp. 61–79. ACM Press, New York (1971)
7. Dapey Reshet: Israeli site index (1998), http://dapey.reshet.co.il/help/2067.htm (Hebrew)
8. Gey, F.: ECDL2004 Tutorial – Multilingual information access (2004), http://ucdata.berkeley.edu:7101/projects/ecdl2004/ecdl-2004-MLIA-tutorial-web-page.htm
9. Global Internet Statistics: Sources & References (2004), http://www.glreach.com/globstats/refs.php3
10. Google Zeitgeist, http://www.google.com/press/intl-zeitgeist.html
11. HaNer, U.: There are no search engines that speak Hebrew (2007), http://themarker.captain.co.il/captain/pages/ShArtCaptain.jhtml?contrassID=11&subContrassID=0&itemNo=815537 (in Hebrew)
12. Internet World Stats: Middle East Internet Usage and Population Statistics (2007), http://www.internetworldstats.com/stats5.htm
13. Melingo: Natural language processing – About Morfix (in Hebrew), http://www.melingo.com/hb_morfix_ab.htm
14. Moukdad, H., Large, A.: Information retrieval from full-text Arabic databases: Can search engines designed for English do the job? Libri 51(2), 63–74 (2001)
15. Pastore, M.: Web pages by language (2000), http://www.clickz.com/showPage.html?page=408521
16. Wintner, S.: Hebrew computational linguistics: Past and future. Artificial Intelligence Review 21(20), 113–138 (2004)
17. Zoref, A: Internet sites in July (in Hebrew), http://advertising.themarker.com/tmc/article.jhtml?ElementId=ats20070814_109109190

Matching with a Hierarchical Ontology

Yaacov Choueka[1,2], Nachum Dershowitz[3], and Liad Tal[4]

[1] Department of Computer Science, Bar-Ilan University, Ramat Gan 52900, Israel
[2] The Friedberg Genizah Project, Jerusalem 95483, Israel
[3] School of Computer Science, Tel Aviv University, Tel Aviv 69978, Israel
[4] Equivio, Rosh Haayin 48091, Israel

Abstract. We describe how hierarchical ontologies are used for classifying products, as well as for answering queries. For classifying and scoring product descriptions and queries in an electronic-commerce search engine, we make use of declarative subset/superset and part/whole hierarchies, such as the sense hierarchies provided by WordNet. Retrieval is also aided by use of the ontology. Results of experiments were encouraging.

Keywords: ontologies, search, ecommerce.

> *I now see the hierarchical as both beautiful and necessary.*
> —Camille Paglia (1992)

1 Introduction

Consider a search engine, geared to electronic commerce. Each user query retrieves a ranked list of matching products and a dialogue is initiated to refine the search results down to a short list of quality matches.[1] For example, a search for "black bags" might return hundreds of products. Since there are many different types of bags, in addition to displaying a ranked list of black bags, the system allows an online customer to choose from various categories, such as handbags, briefcases, doctor bags, or backpacks. Products in the store's catalogue are classified (either on-the-fly or in a pre-processing stage) to each of the possible categories and subcategories. The ideal refining question, taking the attributes in the query and of the items in stock into account, can be chosen according to entropy considerations; see [2]. See Fig. 1.

We describe in the following sections how hierarchical ontologies are used for classifying products, as well as for answering queries.

2 Hierarchical Ontologies

For classifying and scoring product descriptions, as well as queries, we make use of declarative hyponym/hyperonym[2] (*is-a*) and meronym/holonym (*part-of*) hierarchies, such as the sense hierarchies provided by WordNet [4]. We assume these ontologies are organized as directed acyclic graphs. Each node—representing a class

---

[1] Celebros Ltd. markets such a site-search engine, formerly called Qwiser™ [5].
[2] More often written "hypernym".

N. Dershowitz and E. Nissan (Eds.): Choueka Festschrift, Part I, LNCS 8001, pp. 395–398, 2014.

Fig. 1. Sample search dialogue

of objects (commodities and commodity categories, in our case)—may be related by *is-a* and *part-of* edges to other nodes. For example: a rucksack *is-a* kind of a backpack, which *is-a* kind of bag (in the sense of container), jet black *is-a* shade of black, and a clasp is a *part-of* a handbag, as is a handle.

3   Classification

Making use of a hyponym taxonomy has long been a tool in hierarchical classification. See, for example, [6,3,7].

There are several novel ways in which an ontology can help:

1. Consider rival classifications, B (e.g. bag) and C (container), of some item, be they derived by linguistic or statistical means.
   (a) If C is a hyperonym of B, then the more specific classification B is preferred.
   (b) If neither is a hyperonym of the other (shirt and cardigan, say), then their closest common ancestor (*least upper bound*) A (garment) is a better classification than either.
   (c) If several sibling meronyms are competing, this suggests their shared holonym, especially when the latter is also a contender.
2. To decide between rival meronym and holonym (lens and camera), additional criteria are called for (e.g. the likelihood that a camera lens is sold alone).
3. Even weak indications of relevance to a hyperonym/hyponym/meronym/holonym can help in word sense disambiguation.

For example, consider a product labelled "Zombie Costume," and described as a "Mask from the Buffy the Vampire Slayer collection of masks. From 'Movie Originals' at The Fright Catalog – Halloween 2001." Linguisitic analysis suggests it may be a *costume* or a *mask*. Since *mask* is a hyponym of *costume*, the former, more specific, category is preferred. On the other hand, *mask* may also be a meronym of *costume*, but since only one part of a *costume* is mentioned in the description, the category *mask* wins out.

4 Retrieval

It is standard to organize retrieved items according to a predetermined hierarchy, as illustrated in the example in Fig. 1. See [1].

There are several additional ways in which some search engines take advantage of hierarchical ontologies. These include:

1. Retrieve all hyponyms (e.g. rucksacks and etuis) of query terms (bag), but not their hyperonyms.
2. If the query ("orange leather briefcase") is for a subcategory in which there are too few elements, one may wish to suggest siblings (orange leather backpacks; red leather briefcases) or cousins from the hyperonym hierarchy.
3. In some contexts, a query for a category might also propose its meronym classes (lenses for "cameras") as also of relevance.

If hyponym/hyperonym and meronym/holonym links have meaningful weights attached, they can be used to assign probabilities to matches and improve the quality of the ranking of retrieved items. For example, links from W (e.g. watch) to its hyperonyms I (instrument) and J (jewelry) may be weighted by the likelihood that an item classified as W is an I or a J, respectively; the reverse, hyponym link, from J to W, may be qualified by the chance that someone who asked for J will choose an item from W. Similarly, one may label the link from meronym C (clasps) to holonym H (handbags) by the likelihood that a C is part of an H and, in the reverse direction, that an H has part C.

5 Results

We tested the method described above on eight different e-commerce stores. The stores' domains vary between mainstream domains (such as apparel, sports, and books), and specialty stores (such as survival gear and wine products). Seven of the catalogs were in English, and one in German. The number of products in each catalog vary between 500 and 70,000.

The test was conducted as follows. We used a classification algorithm that included the method described here to classify every product in every store into some appropriate ontology. Two things were checked: first, whether the method was used in the classification process of the product, and second, whether it was right – did it point to the correct classification, thereby helping the algorithm reach the correct decision. The results are given in Table 1.

Table 1. Test Results

Language	Domain	#Products	%Unaffected	%Right	%Wrong
English	Kitchen Supplies	68430	70.3	29.5	0.1
English	Survival Gear	3146	78.5	20.1	1.4
English	Apparel	6521	89.4	8.8	1.8
English	Everything	38123	68.3	31.2	0.5
English	Specialty – Wine	35758	82.4	17.5	0.1
English	Specialty – Sea	1008	98.0	1.9	0.1
German	Sports	2686	86.5	13.5	0.0
English	Books	663	78.0	19.6	2.4
Average:			**81.4**	**17.8**	**0.8**

On average, the method described applies to 18.6% of the products – 18.6% of the products had hyponym-hyperonym relations that could be extracted from their descriptions. For these 18.6%, in 95.6% of the cases (17.8% of the total number of products), the method was correct, and it helped the classification algorithm classify the product in the correct place. These are encouraging results – the algorithm affects a large percentage of the products, and using it almost never causes erroneous results.

Acknowledgements. We thank Michael Flor for his large share in this effort and Yael Villa for her comments and encouragement.

References

1. Chen, H., Dumais, S.: Bringing order to the Web: Automatically categorizing search results. In: Proceedings of the SIGCHI Conference on Human Factors in Computing Systems, The Hague, The Netherlands, pp. 145–152. ACM Press (2000)
2. Dershowitz, N.: Entropic questioning (2005), Unpublished note at http://nachum.org/papers/entropy.pdf
3. Dumais, S.T., Chen, H.: Hierarchical classification of Web content. In: Belkin, N.J., Ingwersen, P., Leong, M.K. (eds.) Proceedings of SIGIR-00, 23rd ACM International Conference on Research and Development in Information Retrieval, Athens, GR, pp. 256–263. ACM Press (2000)
4. Fellbaum, C.: WordNet: An Electronic Lexical Database. MIT Press, Cambridge (1998)
5. Rubenczyk, T., Dershowitz, N., Choueka, Y., Flor, M., Hod, O., Roth, A.: Search engine method and apparatus (2004), Patent pending
6. Scott, S., Matwin, S.: Text classification using WordNet hypernyms. In: Proceedings of the COLING/ACL Workshop on Usage of WordNet in Natural Language Processing Systems, Montréal, Canada, pp. 45–52 (1998)
7. Sun, A., Lim, E.-P., Ng, W.-K.: Hierarchical text classification methods and their specification. In: Chan, A.T.S., Chan, S.C.F., Leong, H.V., Vincent, Ng, T.Y. (eds.) Cooperative Internet Computing, pp. 236–256. Kluwer Academic, Boston (2003)

Analyzing Product Comparisons on Discussion Boards

Ronen Feldman[1], Moshe Fresko[1], Jacob Goldenberg[1], Oded Netzer[2], and Lyle Ungar[3]

[1] School of Business Administration,
The Hebrew University of Jerusalem, Jerusalem, Israel
{ronen.feldman,freskom,msgolden}@huji.ac.il
[2] Columbia Business School, Columbia University
on2110@columbia.edu
[3] Computer and Information Science, University of Pennsylvania
ungar@cis.upenn.edu

Abstract. Product discussion boards are a rich source of information about consumer sentiment about products, which is being increasingly exploited. Most sentiment analysis has looked at single products in isolation, but users often compare different products, stating which they like better and why. We present a set of techniques for analyzing how consumers view product markets. Specifically, we extracted relative sentiment analysis and comparisons between products, to understand what attributes users compare products on, and which products they prefer on each dimension. We illustrate these methods in an extended case study analyzing the sedan car markets.

Keywords: sentiment analysis, information extraction, text mining.

1 Introduction

There is increasing recognition that product reviews by consumers can provide important insight into how they view products, and that automated text analysis methods can be fruitfully used to extract such information [1, 2]. For example, the rapidly growing field of sentiment analysis looks to extract how authors feel about different products [3-6]. Such work has tended to look at single products, in spite of the fact that many of the purchase decisions, and hence much of the marketing effort, is based on product comparisons. This paper describes a methodology for automatically analyzing products and comparisons between them. Given a (possibly ungrammatical) sentence such as "Sonata has soft ride similar to Camry and Accord" we automatically extract the products (Sonata, Camry and Accord) and what attributes they are compared on ("soft ride"). Our goal is to automatically determine which products are compared with each other, what attributes they are compared on, and which products are preferred on different attributes. We term this process "comparative sentiment analysis."

The first step in comparative sentiment analysis is extracting from discussion boards the co-occurring product names and other frequently occurring terms and the phrases they occur in. The extracted phrases provide snippets of text, similar to those

N. Dershowitz and E. Nissan (Eds.): Choueka Festschrift, Part I, LNCS 8001, pp. 399–408, 2014.

in product reviews such as those provided by Zagat ®. The extracted products and attributes can be used to construct product comparison tables and graphs, which can be used either by consumers or by firms.

Even noting what pairs of products are mentioned together gives valuable insight into the structure of the market and how consumers view products. We build on previous work on entity recognition dealing with entity extraction from text and visualization of the co-occurrence of these entities in the same sentence or paragraph [7-9]. Entity recognition have been often used to find pairs of companies or genes that are mentioned together, sometimes in the context of a word such a "merger." These relationships are then displayed as graphs [10]. Such work has been directed at corpora such as newswire articles or scientific abstracts. We extend these methods to the more informal styles common in consumer product reviews and blogs, and extract the type and sentiment of the relationship as well as simply co-occurrence. We locate snippets such as "...*Sonata* pricing is pretty similar to the *Fusion*", identify the brands (shown here in italics), and extract the relations between them. We show how multi-dimensional scaling (MDS) can be fruitfully used to provide a "perceptual map" of an industry, with products being related to each other either by co-occurrence (which products are being compared) or by the similarity of the terms used to described these products.

This paper describes an implemented system that extracts product mentions and comparisons from user discussion forums. The following sections describe the underlying methodology, and then show results obtained from a set of 868,174 reviews of cars, extracted from the sedans section of the forum at Edmund's Car Space (http://townhall-talk.edmunds.com/WebX/.ee9e22f/) .

2   Methodology for Analyzing Messages

Extracting structured product comparison data from product forum messages requires several processing steps. Html-pages are downloaded from a given forum site and html-like tags and non-textual information such as images, commercials, etc. are cleaned from the downloaded files. Products and product attributes are then extracted from the messages. The extracted products and attributes then allow us to visualize which products are compared against each other, showing the overall market structure, which terms are used in the comparisons, and the direction of the comparison, giving detailed insight into consumer preferences.

The key steps involve tagging the product mentions ("information extraction"), extracting snippets containing pairs of product mentions, and extracting the terms used in product descriptions of comparisons.

2.1   Information Extraction

We first extract the brand names (28 car companies) and model names (180 car models) from the discussion board messages. Brand names were relatively easy to extract – one can just string-match on the names – while model names showed significant variation and ambiguity. Extraction by string matching on names was not suitable for extracting models because of the variations in the writing styles. Instead, a set of regular expressions was developed for recognizing models from the model-names appearing in these informal texts [11].

The last decade has seen a profusion of papers on information extraction [7,9], mostly using machine learning methods such as HMMs, CRFs, and other maximum entropy models, and primarily looking at formally written texts such as newswire articles or scientific abstracts [12] or partially structured web pages (e.g., seminar announcements). Entity extraction and resolution from user reviews is much trickier than from the corpora used in classic IE research. Product names vary more than personal names, and clues such as capitalization that exist in formal text are not reliable in user reviews.

Although hand-crafting extraction rules is out of fashion, we believe that there are cases, such as these informal product reviews, when it is substantially faster to build rules by hand than to label data, write feature extractors, and train models. This is particularly true since we want not only to tag terms as products, but also to resolve which product is being referred to.

The key to constructing such entity extraction tools is to note that lists of product brands and models are easy to come by on the web; the trick is to generalize the formal product names to the many variants used. Terms referring to products generally consist of a subset of the brand name, model name, and model number. Any combination of the three components can be kept or dropped. Different delimiters (e.g. space, hyphen, or nothing) can also be used between them. Brand names are mostly clean string matches to a list, while model names are often abbreviated (or misspelled). Numbers can be Roman or Arabic.

Matching is handled in two stages. First there is a tagging stage that is based on regular expressions and a list of search strings. This stage is greedy and tries to match as many terms as possible, giving high recall. After that, a second stage removes or modifies the falsely extracted entities in order to improve the precision. Based on a random sample of 500 messages and manual evaluation of the results we achieved recall of 89.4% and precision of 96.7% leading to F1 of 92.9%.

2.2   Snippet Extraction

We are interested in seeing which products are compared to one another, which terms show up most often in connection with a product or pair of products and what attributes consumers are using when they compare products. A term recognizer was built by using a CRF [9] model trained on the CoNLL-2000 shared task corpus [13]. It uses two consecutive CRF models - one for part of speech tagging and another for chunking. After chunking, there is filtering step, which retains only noun phrases that contain actual nouns (and not, pronouns, for instance).

The terms extracted for cars fall into several categories such as: Driving Experience (safety, aerodynamic, suspension, control, maneuverable, noise, performance, power, reliability, speed), Short and Long-Term Costs (aging, trade_in, holds_value, insurance_cost, fuel_economy, maintenance_expense, price), Internal

Construction (brakes, construction, engine, platform, materials), Internal Comfort (seats, leg_room, interior_space, higher, size), and External Design (interior, design, sportive, weight, look, paint, features).

The snippet extraction component takes as input a large set of sentences in which the relevant product models are labeled. The output is a set of *snippets* – small sentence fragments, each containing a description of opinion, either *factual* (e.g., "Model A's X is Y", or "Model A has X), *sentiment-relating* (e.g. "Model A is good", or "I like model A's X) or *comparative* (e.g., "Model A is better than model B", or more generally, "Model A's X is better than model B"). We focus here on the comparative snippets.

Snippet extraction is done using the following steps:

Preprocessing: The texts are tagged with parts of speech (PoS) and chunked into noun phrases using a CRF-based tagger and chunker, both trained on CoNLL-2000 shared task training set. During preprocessing, we also find lists of models ("Models X, Y, and Z") and convert them into a single term, so that the system can more easily extract opinions expressed about multiple models simultaneously.

Pattern Extraction: We generate the set of surface patterns by a suitable modification of the Apriori association mining algorithm. Each such pattern is a sequence of tokens including the special slot-mark tokens for product names and (optionally) *skips*, which indicate gaps in the pattern. First, we extract all sequences (without gaps) of tokens, PoS tags, and noun phrase (NP) chunks that appear in the set of all sentences with frequency greater than a given minimal support value. Then we mine the sentences (as ordered sets of such sequences) for frequent item-sets. The result is the set of all sufficiently surface patterns.

Pattern Filtering: In order to reduce the number of irrelevant patterns, we keep only patterns that contain specified words. In the first set of results, for the two-model case, we require at least one of the words "more", "less", or "than", or at least one adjective. Also, all of the patterns must start with a model. If a pattern contains two models, then the pattern must also end with a model. We also tried simple parsing, but we found that fairly simple pattern matching works better than an off-the-shelf parser. Empirically, sentences are often ungrammatical, and comparisons in these corpora often span sentence boundaries, but generally fit the pattern *model ... comparative than ... model*.

Snippet Extraction: Snippets from the user reviews are extracted by matching the patterns against the corpus. Matching is conceptually straightforward. We use a fast algorithm that finds all matches of all patterns with complexity logarithmic in the number of patterns and linear in the corpus size. We used two very general patterns to extract snippets:

```
<Model> * /JJ than * <Model>
<Model> * /JJ * to * <Model>
```

where /JJ means "adjective" and "*" means a gap is allowed. This produced 3,025 snippets. When the snippets are extracted, we obtain the pairs of products and the comparative term used between them. This information can be extracted and put into a table or a graph. We describe such analysis below.

3   Example Results

Starting with 868,174 messages containing 5,972,695 sentences, we extracted 28 car brands, 180 car models and 1,037 different terms. There were 20,768 mentions of brand, 575,110 of car models, and 6,194,507 of terms.

3.1   Co-occurrence Results

One can examine the comparisons consumers make at the brand or model level to draw a "perceptual map" of the similarities between car companies. We looked at several different ways of displaying co-occurrence data, and found that the most informative is plotting brands using multi-dimensional scaling (MDS) [20] on co-occurrence lift -- the ratio of the actual appearance of two nodes together to the frequency we would expect to see them together. Using MDS on the lift of the comparisons between each pair of the 28 car brands mentioned in the sedan cars forum we create a perceptual map of the car brands, where the axes represent perceptual dimensions inferred solely from co-occurrence of mentions in user comments. As can be seen in Fig.1, as we go from left to right the brands seem to be decreasing in prestige, and from bottom to top the brands decreasing in the age of the target market they appeal to. Furthermore, similarly perceived cars are clustered together in this space. On the left of the map we find the luxury car brands: the Japanese: Acura, Lexus and Infinity on the top, the German: BMW, Audi and Mercedes in the top middle, the other European: Volvo, Saab and Jaguar in the bottom middle, and the two American brand that seem to be perceived as more luxurious (Lincoln and Cadillac) at the bottom. On the right of the figure, from top to bottom, we find the high share Japanese cars (Honda, Mazda, Nissan and Toyota) followed by some Korean and lower market share Japanese in the middle, to the majority of the American brands at the bottom. Note that Ford, which has a stronger international presence, is positioned closer to the non-US brands. The lower share Japanese Mitsubishi and Suzuki brands are clustered together with the Korean cars.

Such a perceptual map could be very informative in determining the market structure and competitive landscape as well as in understanding the word-of-mouth pattern expressed in the forum. The perceptual map seems to provide strong face validity to the information provided from brand comparisons in forums. While for cars, this analysis provides few surprises, for less well-studied product categories, such an analysis might be far more informative.

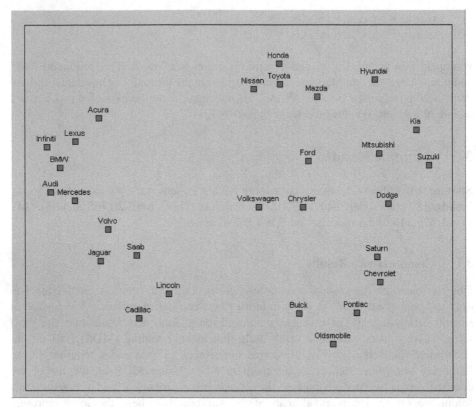

Fig. 1. A Perceptual Map of Car Brands

We also built an MDS map using the raw co-occurrence data, and using the terms mentioned in connection with each car. The maps generated in each case share gross characteristics but are different in their details.

Snippets were classified into three categories, depending on whether the pair of cars was judged to be (a) similar, (b) different or (c) neither. Similarity of products is fairly reliably indicted by the word "similar" (e.g., "*Sonata* has soft ride similar to *Camry and Accord*"), while differences between products rarely mention the word 'different'; they say how it is different (e.g., "*300 C* Touring looks so much better than the Magnum", "I drove the Honda Civic, it does not handle better than the TSX, not even close"). Many snippets neither indicate similarity nor difference, but merely mention a pair of products, for example asking how they compare.

We tried training a support vector machine to predict the category labels of the snippets. We manually labeled 200 snippets each containing pairs of car models and of shoe models.   (We found a similar set of user comments on shoes in *RunnersWorld*[1] *Magazine Discussions*[1] and used these to see how well models developed for one product on one web site generalize to a different product on a different site.; See [11] for a description and more analysis of the shoe discussions.)

---

[1] http://forums.runnersworld.com/eve/forums/a/frm/f/687106477/p

Training on cars and testing on shoes gave a micro-averaged F1 of 0.66; training on shoes and testing on cars gave an F1 of 0.76. (Coincidently, precision was equal to recall in both cases, so these are also the precision and recall accuracies.) We also wrote a very simple rule-based classifier of the following form: label as similar if it contains the words "similar or "comparable" or as different if it contains the words "differ", "more", "less" or any comparative adjective. All other snippets are labeled as "other". These gave significantly better micro-averaged F1's of 0.785, and 0.82 on the same shoe and car test sets.

Focusing in on the snippets classified as "different," we can easily extract from those snippets which car or shoe was labeled as better, and the keyword or phrase (if any) indicating on what attribute they were better. The result is a count of occurrences of 4-tuples of the form: *4 compare(Camry, Accord, noise, better)*. This should be interpreted as "there were 4 snippets in which the Camry was judged to be better than the Accord in terms of noise".

A summary of the results for comparisons between the Accord and Camry gives the flavor of what is learned. The "vote" is 12 to 8 saying the Accord is better than the Camry (these are general comparisons, where no attribute was found) but there is almost an even split on which has a better price. The count is 5 to 0 saying the Accord has worse noise than the Camry and 3 to 0 saying the Accord has a better interior. The Accord is perceived to be more sportive, and better to drive, but the Camry is bigger, has more leg room and looks better.

For objective facts such car theft, size, or sales, one can ask how accurate the sentiment is. For example, we compared user sentiment about cars being stolen with the reported rates at which the cars were stolen. The **National Insurance Crime Bureau** (NICB®) has compiled a list of the 10 vehicles most frequently reported stolen in the U.S. in 2005. Six of these appear in the top 10 cars mentioned with "stealing" phrases in our data ("Stolen," "Steal," "Theft"). The top five from each source are shown below; the left column gives the NICB stolen car list; the right column gives our extracted "stealing" brands, along with the number of times they were mentioned in connection with stealing.

National Insurance Crime Bureau	Consumer Discussion Boards
1) 1991 Honda Accord	1) Honda Accord (165)
2) 1995 Honda Civic	2) Honda Civic (101)
3) 1989 Toyota Camry	3) Toyota Camry (71)
4) 1994 Dodge Caravan	4) Nissan Maxima (69)
5) 1994 Nissan Sentra	5) Acura TL (58)

4   Conclusions

As is clear from the growing scholarly [1,3,4,5,16,17,18] and commercial interest in sentiment analysis (commercial companies include BuzzMetrics, Reputica, Umbria, Cymfony, BuzzLogic, and SentiMetrix), discussion boards provide a potentially attractive source of information about how consumers view products. None of these researchers except for [19, 21] focused on the relationships among or comparisons between different products. We believe that in addition to the more widely studied work on sentiment analysis for individual products, useful insight can be gained by extracting pairs of products. At the highest level, graphs of co-mentions of pairs of products give an overview of one type of market structure: what is compared against what. MDS on co-occurrence lift provides good visualization of the market. At a more detailed level, comparative sentiment analysis provides insight into what attributes products are compared on, and which products are preferred to others.

At several points in the extraction process we compared state-of-the-art machine learning methods against simple hand-coded patterns. Although CRFs were useful for part-of-speech tagging, and the part of speech tags were useful in extracting comparisons, it was often the case (e.g., when resolving forms of mentions of model numbers to the actual model, or in classifying messages into "similar", "different", or "other") that surprisingly simple rules worked well, and worked well for the disparate domains of shoes and cars. No doubt, if we used the right feature set and more training data, better results could have been obtained with CRFs or SVMs, but the point is that the right features (e.g., the presence of a comparative adjective or of an Arabic or Roman numeral) make the deciding difference in the quality of the results. Note that this contrasts the dominant direction of current research in information extraction [22]. User discussion boards differ significantly from the text used in competitions such as MUC, TREC and CoNLL [13] , which focused on extracting entities (typically people, places and organizations) from relatively carefully written formal text such as that of newswire articles. Although more careful study is required, preliminary experiments suggest that parsing is far less helpful on informal texts. As a further difficulty, there does not appear to be any good collection of resolved informal product model names that can serve as a basis for supervised learning methods. We thus rely more on hand-built regular expressions.

Marketing campaigns are often designed in part based on product comparison tables: what is my product compared against, and on what dimensions? Extracting co-mentioned pairs of products and the terms that show up frequently with them provides precisely this kind of table. Cars are a widely studied and a relative stable market, providing nice face validity to our extraction system. However, for markets such as computer games, electronics, movies and music, which change rapidly, one can utilize our method to better analyze and understand the market. We suspect that for such dynamic markets the attributes used as the basis of comparison such as disk size, latency, interface and color may become more or less important as differentiators. In such cases, even knowing what dimensions products should be compared on is nontrivial. Even in relatively low tech markets such as running shoes, it is common to see sites such as SportsAuthority offering comparisons of 65 shoe models, with no mechanism for selecting a subset other than picking a brand. With evidence accumulating that offering more choices can lead to lower consumer satisfaction and lower purchase rates [23], it is becoming ever clearer that picking the right set of products for comparison is of great value for both consumers and retailers. Mining consumer product reviews provides a relatively inexpensive mechanism not only for selecting potential products to compare against a given product, but also the dimensions on which to compare the products on.

References

1. Popescu, A.-M., Etzioni, O.: Extracting Product Features and Opinions from Reviews. In: Proceedings of HLT-EMNLP, pp. 339–346 (2005)
2. Dave, K., Lawrence, S., Pennock, D.M.: Mining the Peanut Gallery: Opinion Extraction and Semantic Classification of Product Reviews. In: Proceedings of the 12th International World Wide Web Conference WWW 2003 (2003)
3. Kim, S.-M., Hovy, E.: Identifying and Analyzing Judgment Opinions. In: Proceedings of HLT/NAACL-2006, New York City, NY, pp. 200–2007 (2006)
4. Turney, P.D.: Thumbs Up or Thumbs Down? Semantic Orientation Applied to Unsupervised Classification of Reviews. In: Proceedings of ACL 2002 (2002)
5. Hu, M., Liu, B.: Mining and Summarizing Customer Reviews. In: Proceedings of the 10th ACM SIGKDD International Conference on Knowledge Discovery and Data Mining, pp. 168–177 (2004)
6. Pang, B., Lee, L., Vaithyanathan, S.: Thumbs up? Sentiment Classification Using Machine Learning Techniques. In: Proceedings of EMNLP-02, 7th Conference on Empirical Methods in Natural Language Processing, Association for Computational Linguistics, Morristown, US, pp. 79–86 (2002)
7. Miller, D., Schwartz, R., Weischedel, R., Stone, R.: Named Entity Extraction from Broadcast News. In: Proceedings of DARPA Broadcast News Workshop, Herndon, VA (1999)
8. Feldman, R., Rosenfeld, B., Fresko, M.: TEG – A Hybrid Approach to Information Extraction. Knowledge and Information Systems 9(1), 1–18 (2006)
9. McCallum, A., Li, W.: Early Results for Named Entity Recognition with Conditional Random Fields, Feature Induction and Web-Enhanced Lexicons. In: Proceedings of CoNLL-2003, Edmonton, Canada, pp. 188–191 (2003)
10. Feldman, R., Kloesgen, W., Zilberstein, A.: Visualization Techniques to Explore Data Mining Results for Document Collections. In: Proceedings of KDD 1997 (1997)
11. Feldman, R., Fresko, M., Goldenberg, J., Netzer, O., Ungar, L.: Extracting Product Comparisons from Discussion Boards. In: Proceedings of ICDM 2007, Omaha, NE (2007)
12. Yeh, A., Hirschman, L., Morgan, A., Colosimo, M.: BioCreative task 1a: Gene Mention Finding evaluation. In: BMC Bioinformatics, p. 6 (2005)
13. Sang, E.F.T.K., Buchholz, S.: Introduction to the CoNLL-2000 Shared Task: Chunking. In: Proceedings of 4th Conference on Computational Natural Language Learning, pp. 127–132 (2000)
14. Etzioni, O., Cafarella, M., Downey, D., Popescu, A.-M., Shaked, T., Soderland, S., Weld, D.S., Yates, A.: Unsupervised Named-Entity Extraction from the Web: An Experimental Study. Artificial Intelligence 165(1), 91–134 (2005)
15. Rosenfeld, B., Feldman, R.: Using Corpus Statistics on Entities to Improve Semi-supervised Relation Extraction from the Web. In: Proceeding of ACL 2007 (2007)
16. Esuli, A., Sebastiani, F.: Determining the Semantic Orientation of Terms through Gloss Classification. In: Proceedings of CIKM 2005, Bremen, DE (2005)
17. Chklovski, T.: Deriving Quantitative Overviews of Free Text Assessments on the Web. In: Proceedings of 2006 International Conference on Intelligent User Interfaces (IUI 2006), Sydney, Australia (2006)
18. Gregory, M., Chinchor, N., Whitney, P., Carter, R., Turner, A., Hetzler, E.: User-Directed Sentiment Analysis: Visualizing the Affective Content of Documents. In: Sentiment and Subjectivity in Text Workshop at the Annual Meeting of the Association of Computational Linguistics ACL 2006 (2006)

19. Jindal, N., Liu, B.: Mining comparative sentences and relations. In: Proceedings of AAAI 2006 (2006)
20. Lattin, J.M., Green, P.E., Carroll, J.D.: Analyzing Multivariate Data. Thomson Brooks/Cole, Pacific Grove (2003)
21. Jindal, N., Liu, B.: Identifying Comparative Sentences in Text Documents. In: Proceedings of the 29th Annual International ACM SIGIR Conference on Research and Development in Information Retrieval, pp. 244–251 (2006)
22. Information Extraction: Distilling Structured Data from Unstructured Text. Andrew McCallum. ACM Queue 3(9) (November 2005)
23. Schwartz, B.: The Paradox of Choice: Why More Is Less (2004)

Benchmarking Applied Semantic Inference: The PASCAL Recognising Textual Entailment Challenges

Roy Bar-Haim, Ido Dagan, and Idan Szpektor

Computer Science Department, Bar-Ilan University, Ramat-Gan 52900, Israel
{barhair,dagan,szpekti}@cs.biu.ac.il
http://www.cs.biu.ac.il/~{barhair,dagan,szpekti}

Abstract. Identifying that the same meaning is expressed by, or can be inferred from, various language expressions is a major challenge for natural language understanding applications such as information extraction, question answering and automatic summarization. Dagan and Glickman [5] proposed *Textual Entailment*, the task of deciding whether a target text follows from a source text, as a unifying framework for modeling language variability, which has often been addressed in an application-specific manner. In this paper we describe the series of benchmarks developed for the textual entailment recognition task, known as the PASCAL RTE Challenges. As a concrete example, we describe in detail the second RTE challenge, in which our methodology was consolidated, and served as a basis for the subsequent RTE challenges. The impressive success of these challenges established textual entailment as an active research area in natural language processing, attracting a growing community of researchers.

1 Introduction

1.1 Textual Entailment as a Unifying Framework for Semantic Inference

Identifying that the same meaning is expressed by, or can be inferred from, various language expressions is one of the main challenges in natural language understanding. The need to recognize such semantic variability is common to various applications such as information extraction, question answering, automatic summarization, and information retrieval. However, despite the common need, resolving semantic variability has been studied largely in an application-specific context, by disjoint research communities. This situation led to redundant research efforts, and hampered the sharing of new advancements across these communities.

This observation led Dagan and Glickman to propose in 2004 a unifying framework for modeling language variability, which they termed *Textual Entailment* [5]. Textual entailment recognition is the task of deciding, given two text fragments, whether the meaning of one text is entailed (can be inferred) from another text. They showed that this task captures generically a broad range of

N. Dershowitz and E. Nissan (Eds.): Choueka Festschrift, Part I, LNCS 8001, pp. 409–424, 2014.

inferences that are relevant for multiple applications. For example, a Question Answering (QA) system has to identify texts that entail the expected answer. Given the question *"Who is John Lennon's widow?"*, the text *"Yoko Ono unveiled a bronze statue of her late husband, John Lennon, to complete the official renaming of England's Liverpool Airport as Liverpool John Lennon Airport."* entails the expected answer *"Yoko Ono is John Lennon's widow"*. Similarly, semantic inference needs of other text understanding applications such as Information Retrieval (IR), Information Extraction (IE), and Machine Translation (MT) evaluation can be cast as entailment recognition [6].

An important feature of the textual entailment framework is that its formulation as a mapping between texts makes it theory-neutral, independent of concrete semantic interpretations. In other words, semantic interpretation becomes a possible means for performing inference, rather than a goal of its own. For example, in word sense disambiguation, it is not always easy to define explicitly the right *set of senses* to choose from. In practice, however, it is sufficient for most applications to determine whether a word meaning in a given context *entails* another word. For instance, the occurrence of the word *"chair"* in the sentence *"IKEA announced a new comfort chair"* entails *"furniture"*, while its occurrence in the sentence *"MIT announced a new CS chair position"* does not. Thus, proper modeling of lexical entailment in context may alleviate the need to *interpret* word occurrences into explicitly stipulated senses.

The long-term goal of textual entailment research is the development of robust entailment "engines". Such engines would be used as a generic component in many text understanding applications, which encapsulates all the required semantic inferences, analogously to the use of part-of-speech taggers and syntactic parsers in today's natural language processing (NLP) applications.

1.2   The Recognising Textual Entailment Challenges

A necessary step in transforming textual entailment from a theoretical idea into an active empirical research field was the introduction of benchmarks and an evaluation forum for entailment systems. Dagan, Glickman and Magnini [6] initiated in 2004 a series of contests under the PASCAL Network of Excellence, known as *The PASCAL Recognising Textual Entailment Challenges* (*RTE* in short). These contests provided researchers concrete datasets on which they could evaluate their approaches, as well as a forum for presenting, discussing and comparing their results. The RTE datasets were freely available also for non-RTE participants, so as to further facilitate research on textual entailment.

The RTE challenges attracted an increasing number of researchers from leading groups worldwide, from both academia and industry. The impressive success of these challenges established textual entailment as a rapidly-growing research field. It became the subject of various papers in recent NLP conferences, and is consequently being listed regularly as one of the solicited topics in calls for papers.

In this paper we survey the first four textual entailment challenges, held between 2005 and 2008. As a concrete example, we focus on our experience with organizing the second RTE challenge (RTE-2). In RTE-2, the methodology for data collection and annotation, as well as the evaluation metrics have matured, and served as the basis for the two subsequent RTE challenges.

The rest of the paper is organized as follows: Section 2 briefly overviews the RTE-1 challenge, in which the basic task definition was introduced. Section 3 describes in detail the RTE-2 dataset. Section 4 summarizes the participation in the RTE-2 Challenge. It covers the various approaches, presents the obtained results, and provides some analysis. Section 5 surveys subsequent developments of the RTE task in the third and fourth challenges. Finally, Sect. 6 concludes the survey of the RTE challenges and their impact, and suggests future enhancements for the task.

2   The First RTE Challenge

The first RTE challenge[1] (RTE-1) introduced the first benchmark for textual entailment recognition [6]. The RTE-1 dataset consisted of manually collected text fragment pairs, termed *text (t)* (1-2 sentences) and *hypothesis (h)* (a single sentence). The participating systems were required to judge for each pair whether the meaning of t entails the truth of h. The pairs represented success and failure settings of inferences in various application types (termed *"tasks"*), including, among others, the QA, IE, IR, and MT evaluation mentioned above. The dataset was split into a development set, containing 567 pairs, and a test set, containing 800 pairs. The pairs were balanced between positive (entailing) and negative (non-entailing) pairs.

The challenge raised noticeable attention in the research community, attracting 17 submissions from diverse groups. The relatively low accuracy achieved by the participating systems (best results below 60%) suggested that the entailment task is indeed a challenging one, with a wide room for improvement.

3   The RTE-2 Dataset

Following the success and impact of RTE-1, the main goal of the second challenge[2] [2] was to support the continuation of research on textual entailment. Four sites participated in the data collection and annotation: Bar-Ilan University (Israel, coordinator), CELCT (Italy), Microsoft Research (USA) and MITRE (USA). Our main focus in creating the RTE-2 dataset was to provide more "realistic" text-hypothesis examples, based mostly on outputs of actual systems. As in the previous challenge, the main task is judging whether a hypothesis h is entailed by a text t. The examples represent different levels of entailment reasoning, such as lexical, syntactic, morphological and logical. Data collection and annotation processes were improved, including cross-annotation of the examples across the organizing sites (most of the pairs were triply annotated). The data collection and

---

[1] http://www.pascal-network.org/Challenges/RTE
[2] http://www.pascal-network.org/Challenges/RTE2

annotation guidelines were revised and expanded. In order to make the challenge data more accessible, we also provided some pre-processing for the examples, including sentence splitting and dependency parsing.

3.1   Dataset Overview

The RTE-2 dataset consists of 1600 text-hypothesis pairs, divided into a development set and a test set, each containing 800 pairs. We followed the basic setting of RTE-1: the texts consist of 1-2 sentences, while the hypotheses are a single (usually short) sentence.

We chose to focus on four out of the seven applications that were present in RTE-1: Information Retrieval (IR), Information Extraction (IE), Question Answering (QA), and multi-document summarization (SUM[3]). Within each application setting the annotators selected positive entailment examples (annotated *YES*), where t does entail h, as well as negative examples (annotated *NO*), where entailment does not hold (50%-50% split, as in RTE-1). In total, 200 pairs were collected for each application in each dataset. Each pair was annotated with its related task (IE/IR/QA/SUM) and entailment judgment (YES/NO, released only for the development set). Some of the pairs in the development set are listed in Table 1.

The examples in the dataset are based mostly on outputs (both correct and incorrect) of Web-based systems, while most of the input examples which were fed to these systems were sampled from existing application-specific benchmarks[4]. Thus, the examples give some sense of how existing systems could benefit from an entailment engine validating their output. The data collection procedure for each task is described in sections 3.3 through 3.6.

3.2   Defining and Judging Entailment

We consider an applied notion of textual entailment, defined as a directional relation between two text fragments, termed t - the entailing text, and h - the hypothesized entailed text.

> *Definition: t entails h* if, typically, a human reading t would infer that h is most likely true.

This somewhat informal definition is based on (and assumes) common human understanding of language as well as common background knowledge. Textual entailment recognition is the task of deciding, given t and h, whether t entails h.

Some additional judgment criteria and guidelines are listed below (examples are taken from Table 1):

– Entailment is a directional relation. The hypothesis must be entailed from the given text, but the text need not be entailed from the hypothesis.

---

[3] Equivalent to the CD task in RTE-1.

[4] See the Acknowledgments section for a complete list of systems and benchmarks used.

Table 1. Examples of text-hypothesis pairs, taken from the RTE-2 development set

ID	Text	Hypothesis	Task	Judgment
77	Google and NASA announced a working agreement, Wednesday, that could result in the Internet giant building a complex of up to 1 million square feet on NASA-owned property, adjacent to Moffett Field, near Mountain View.	Google may build a campus on NASA property.	SUM	YES
110	Drew Walker, NHS Tayside's public health director, said: "It is important to stress that this is not a confirmed case of rabies."	A case of rabies was confirmed.	IR	NO
294	Meanwhile, in an exclusive interview with a TIME journalist, the first one-on-one session given to a Western print publication since his election as president of Iran earlier this year, Ahmadinejad attacked the "threat" to bring the issue of Iran's nuclear activity to the UN Security Council by the US, France, Britain and Germany.	Ahmadinejad is a citizen of Iran.	IE	YES
387	About two weeks before the trial started, I was in Shapiro's office in Century City.	Shapiro works in Century City.	QA	YES
415	The drugs that slow down or halt Alzheimer's disease work best the earlier you administer them.	Alzheimer's disease is treated using drugs.	IR	YES
691	Arabic, for example, is used densely across North Africa and from the Eastern Mediterranean to the Philippines, as the key language of the Arab world and the primary vehicle of Islam.	Arabic is the primary language of the Philippines.	QA	NO

– The hypothesis must be fully entailed by the text. Judgment would be NO
  if the hypothesis includes parts that cannot be inferred from the text.
– Cases in which inference is very probable (but not completely certain) are
  judged as YES. For instance, in pair #387 one could claim that although
  Shapiro's office is in Century City, he actually never arrives to his office, and
  works elsewhere. However, this interpretation of t is very unlikely, and so
  the entailment holds with high probability. On the other hand, annotators
  were guided to avoid including vague examples for which inference has some
  positive probability which is not clearly very high.
– Our definition of entailment allows presupposition of common knowledge,
  such as: a company has a CEO, a CEO is an employee of the company, an
  employee is a person, etc. For instance, in pair #294, the entailment depends
  on knowing that the president of a country is also a citizen of that country.

3.3   Collecting IE Pairs

The collection of these pairs is inspired by the Information Extraction (and Relation Extraction) application. In IE, the task is to correctly extract from texts arguments of a predicate template, such as 'X acquire Y'. We adapt the setting to pairs of texts rather than a text and a structured template by phrasing the template as a sentence in which the extracted arguments replace the slot variables. For example, given the relation 'X acquire Y' and the text *"Microsoft announced the acquisition of Zoomix."* (t), a hypothesis *"Microsoft acquired Zoomix."* is created from the extracted arguments $X = Microsoft$ and $Y = Zoomix$, producing an entailing pair.

The pairs were generated using four different approaches. In the first approach, ACE-2004 relations (the relations tested in the ACE-2004 RDR task) were taken as templates for hypotheses. Relevant news articles were collected as texts (t). These collected articles were then given to actual IE systems for extraction of ACE relation instances. The system outputs were used to fill the argument slots in the hypothesis template, generating both positive examples (from correct outputs) and negative examples (from incorrect outputs). In the second approach, the output of IE systems on the dataset of the MUC-4 TST3 task (in which the events are acts of terrorism) was similarly used to create entailment pairs.

In the third approach, additional entailment pairs were manually generated from both the annotated MUC-4 dataset and news articles collected for the ACE relations. For example, given the ACE relation 'X work for Y' and the text *"An Afghan interpreter, employed by the United States, was also wounded."* (t), a hypothesis *"An interpreter worked for Afghanistan."* is created, producing a non-entailing (negative) pair.

In the fourth approach, hypotheses which correspond to new types of semantic relations (not found in the ACE and MUC datasets) were manually generated for sentences in collected news articles. These relations were taken from various domains, such as sports, entertainment and science. These processes simulate the need of IE systems to validate that the given text indeed entails the semantic relation that is expected to hold between the extracted slot fillers.

3.4   Collecting IR Pairs

In this application setting, the hypotheses are propositional IR queries, which specify some statement, e.g. "Alzheimer's disease is treated using drugs". The hypotheses were adapted and simplified from standard IR evaluation datasets (TREC and CLEF). Texts (t) that do or do not entail the hypothesis were selected from documents retrieved by different search engines (e.g. Google, Yahoo and MSN) for each hypothesis. In this application setting it is assumed that relevant documents (from an IR perspective) should entail the given propositional hypothesis used as a query.

3.5   Collecting QA Pairs

Annotators were given questions, taken from TREC-QA and QA@CLEF datasets and the corresponding answers extracted from the Web by QA systems. Transforming a question-answer pair to a text-hypothesis pair consisted of the following stages: First, the annotators picked from the answer passage an answer term of the expected answer type, either a correct or an incorrect one. Then, the annotators turned the question into an affirmative sentence with the answer term "plugged in". These affirmative sentences serve as the hypotheses (h), and the original answer passage serves as the text (t). For example (pair #575 in the development set), given the question *"How many inhabitants does Slovenia have?"* and an answer text *"In other words, with its 2 million inhabitants, Slovenia has only 5.5 thousand professional soldiers"* (t), the annotators picked *"2 million"* as the (correct) answer term, which was used to turn the question into the statement *"Slovenia has 2 million inhabitants"* (h), producing a positive entailment pair. Similarly, a negative pair could have been generated by picking "5.5 thousand" as an (incorrect) answer term, resulting in the hypothesis *"Slovenia has 5.5 thousand inhabitants"*. This process simulates the need of a QA system to verify that the retrieved passage text in which the answer was found indeed entails the selected answer.

3.6   Collecting SUM Pairs

In this setting t and h are sentences taken from a news document cluster, a collection of news articles that describe the same news item. Annotators were given output of multi-document summarization systems, including the document clusters and the summary generated automatically for each cluster. The annotators picked sentence pairs with high lexical overlap, preferably where at least one of the sentences was taken from the summary (this sentence played the role of t). For positive examples, the hypothesis sentence was simplified by removing sentence parts, until it was fully entailed by t. Negative examples were simplified similarly. This process simulates the need of a summarization system to identify information redundancy, which should be avoided in the summary, and may also be considered to increase the assessed importance of such repeated information.

3.7   Creating the Final Dataset

Cross-annotation of the collected pairs was done between the organizing sites. Each pair was judged by at least two annotators and most of the pairs (75% of the pairs in the development set, and all of the test set) were triply judged. As in RTE-1, we filtered out pairs on which the annotators disagreed. The average agreement on the test set (between each pair of annotators who shared at least 100 examples), was 89.2%, with average Kappa level of 0.78, which corresponds to "substantial agreement" [17]. 18.2% of the pairs were removed from the test set due to disagreement. The following situations often caused disagreement:

- t gives approximate numbers and h gives exact numbers.
- t states an asserted claim made by some entity, and the h drops the assertion and just states the claim. For example:
  t: *"Scientists say that global warming is made worse by human beings."*
  h: *"Global warming is made worse by human beings."*
- t makes a weak statement, and h makes a slightly stronger statement about the same fact.

Additional filtering was done by two of the organizers, who discarded pairs that seemed controversial, too difficult, or redundant (too similar to other pairs). In this phase, 25.5% of the (original) pairs were removed from the test set.

We allowed only minimal correction of texts extracted from the web, e.g. fixing spelling and punctuation but not style, therefore the English of some of the pairs is less than perfect. In addition to the corrections made by the annotators along the process, a final proof-reading pass over the dataset was performed by one of the annotators.

4   The RTE-2 Challenge

4.1   Submission Instructions and Evaluation Measures

The main task in the RTE-2 challenge was *classification* – entailment judgement for each pair in the test set. The evaluation criterion for this task was *accuracy* – the percentage of pairs correctly judged.

A secondary optional task was *ranking* the pairs according to their entailment confidence. In this ranking, the first pair is the one for which the entailment is most certain, and the last pair is the one for which the entailment is least likely (i.e. the one for which the judgment as "NO" is the most certain). A perfect ranking would place all the positive pairs (for which entailment holds) before all the negative pairs. This task was evaluated using the *Average precision* measure, which is a common evaluation measure for ranking (e.g. in information retrieval), and is computed as the average of the system's precision values at all points in the ranked list in which recall increases, that is at all points in the ranked list for which the gold standard annotation is YES [22]. More formally, it can be written as follows:

$$\frac{1}{R} \sum_{i=1}^{n} \frac{E(i) \times \#PositiveUpToPair(i)}{i} \tag{1}$$

where n is the number of the pairs in the test set, R is the total number of positive pairs in the test set, $E(i)$ is 1 if the i-th pair is positive (in the gold standard) and 0 otherwise, and i ranges over the pairs, ordered by their ranking (note that this measure is different from the *Confidence Weighted Score* used in RTE-1).

Participating teams were allowed to submit results of up to two systems, and many of the participants made use of this option, and provided the results of two runs.

4.2   Submitted Systems

Twenty-three teams participated in the challenge, a 35% growth compared to RTE-1. Table 2 lists for each submitted run the methods used and the obtained results. These methods include lexical overlap, based on lexicons such as WordNet [8] and automatically acquired resources which are based on statistical measures; n-gram matching and subsequence overlapping between t and h; syntactic matching, e.g. relation matching and tree edit distance algorithms; semantic annotation induced using resources such as FrameNet [1]; logical inference using logic provers; statistics computed from local corpora or the Web (including statistical measures available for lexical resources such as WordNet); usage of background knowledge, including inference rules and paraphrase templates, and acquisition (automatic and manual) of additional entailment corpora. Many of the systems derive multiple similarity measures, based on different levels of analysis (lexical, syntactic, logical), and subsequently use them as features for a classifier that makes the final decision, trained on the development set.

Overall, the common criteria for entailment recognition were *similarity* between t and h, or the *coverage* of h by t (in lexical and lexical syntactic methods), and the ability to *infer* h from t (in the logical approach). Zanzotto et al. [23] also measured the similarity between different *(t,h) pairs* (cross-pair similarity). Some groups tried to detect non-entailment, by looking for various kinds of mismatch between the text and the hypothesis. This approach is related to an earlier observation in [21], which suggested that it is often easier to detect false entailment.

4.3   Results

The accuracy achieved by the participating systems ranges from 53% to 75% (considering the best run of each group), while most of the systems obtained 55%-61%. Two submissions, Hickl at el. (accuracy 75.4%, average precision 80.8%) and Tatu at el. (accuracy 73.8%, average precision 71.3%), stand out as about 10% higher than the other systems. The top accuracies are considerably higher than the best results achieved in RTE-1 (around 60%).

The results show, for the first time, that systems that rely on deep analysis such as syntactic matching and logical inference can considerably outperform lexical systems, which were shown to achieve around 60% on the RTE datasets. In the RTE-1 challenge, one of the two best performing systems was based on lexical statistics from the web [11]. Zanzotto at el. experimented with baseline lexical systems, applied to both RTE-1 and RTE-2 datasets. For RTE-1 they found that even a simple statistical lexical system, based on IDF measure, gets close to 60% in accuracy. Bar-Haim et al. [3] also showed by manually analyzing the RTE-1 dataset, that lexical systems are expected to achieve up to around 60%, if we require that h is fully lexically entailed from (covered by) t. For the RTE-2 test set, Zanzotto et al. found that simple lexical overlapping achieves accuracy of 60%, better than any other sophisticated lexical methods they tested (Katrenko and Adriaans [16] report 57% for a slightly different baseline).

Table 2. Submission results and system description. Systems for which no component is indicated used lexical overlap only

First Author (Group)	Accuracy	Average Precision	Lexical Relation DB	n-gram/ Subsequence overlap	Syntactic Matching/ Alignment	Semantic Role Labelling/ Framenet/ Propbank	Logical Inference	Corpus/ Web-Based Statistics	ML Classification	Paraphrase Templates/ Background Knowledge	Acquisition of Entailment Corpora
Adams (Dallas)	0.6262	0.6282	X						X		
Bos (Rome & Leeds)	0.6162	0.6689	X					X	X		
	0.6062	0.6042	X				X	X	X	X	
Burchardt (Saarland)	0.5900		X			X					
	0.5775		X		X	X			X		
Clarke (Sussex)	0.5275	0.5254		X				X			
	0.5475	0.5260		X							
de Marneffe (Stanford)	0.5763	0.6131	X		X			X	X	X	
	0.6050	0.5800	X		X			X	X	X	
Delmonte (Venice)	0.5475	0.5495	X		X	X				X	
Ferrández (Alicante)	0.5563	0.6089	X		X			X			
	0.5475	0.5743	X		X						
Herrera (UNED)	0.5975	0.5663	X						X		
	0.5887		X		X				X		
Hickl (LCC)	0.7538	0.8082	X	X	X	X		X	X		X
Inkpen (Ottawa)	0.5800	0.5751	X	X	X				X		
	0.5825	0.5816	X	X	X				X		
Katrenko (Amsterdam)	0.5900				X						
	0.5713										
Kouylekov (ITC-irst & Trento)	0.5725	0.5249	X		X			X			
	0.6050	0.5046	X		X			X	X		
Kozareva (Alicante)	0.5487	0.5589	X	X				X	X		
	0.5500	0.5485	X	X				X	X		
Litkowski (CL Research)	0.5813										
	0.5663				X						
Marsi (Tilburg & Twente)	0.6050		X		X			X			
Newman (Dublin)	0.5250	0.5052	X	X				X	X		
	0.5437	0.5103	X	X	X			X	X		
Nicholson (Melbourne)	0.5288	0.5464	X		X				X		
	0.5088	0.5053	X		X				X		
Nielsen (Colorado)	0.5962	0.6464		X	X			X	X		
	0.5875	0.6487		X	X			X	X		
Rus (Memphis)	0.5900	0.6047	X		X						
	0.5837	0.5785			X						
Schilder (Thomson & Minnesota)	0.5437			X	X			X	X		
	0.5550			X	X			X	X		
Tatu (LCC)	0.7375	0.7133	X				X			X	
Vanderwende (Microsoft Research & Stanford)	0.6025	0.6181	X		X			X	X		
	0.5850	0.6170	X		X			X			
Zanzotto (Milan & Rome)	0.6388	0.6441	X		X			X	X		
	0.6250	0.6317	X		X			X	X		

4.4   The Contribution of Knowledge and Training Data

Although it is clear that deeper analysis is a must for achieving high accuracy, most of the systems which participated in RTE-2 that employed deep analysis did not improve significantly over the 60% baseline of lexical matching. The participants' reports point out two main reasons for the shortcoming of current systems: the size of the training corpus (RTE-2 development set and the RTE-1 datasets together contain less than 2,200 pairs), and the lack of semantic and background knowledge.

It seems that the best performing systems were those which better coped with these issues. Hickl et al. utilized a very large entailment corpus, automatically collected from the web, following [4]. In addition, they manually annotated a corpus of lexical entailment, which was used to bootstrap automatic annotation of a larger lexical entailment corpus. These corpora contributed 10% to the overall accuracy they achieved. Tatu et al. developed an entailment system based on logical inference, which relies on extensive linguistic and background knowledge from various sources.

The success of these systems suggests that perhaps the most important factors for deep entailment systems are the amount of linguistic and background knowledge, and the size of training corpora, rather than the exact method for modeling t and h and the exact inference mechanism.

4.5   Per-task Analysis

Per-task analysis shows that systems scored considerably higher on the multi-document summarization task (SUM). The same trend was observed in RTE-1 for the comparable documents (CD) task, which was similar to the RTE-2 summarization task. For most systems, the lowest accuracy was obtained for the IE task. Katrenko and Adriaans report that simple lexical overlapping was able to predict correctly entailment for 67% of the SUM pairs, but only for 47% of the IE pairs.

Some of the participants took into account such inter-task differences, and tuned the parameters of their models separately for each task. Given the observed differences among the tasks, it seems that better understanding of how entailment in each task differs might improve the performance of future systems.

4.6   Additional Observations

Some participants tested their systems on both RTE-1 and RTE-2 datasets. Some systems performed better on RTE-1 while others performed better on RTE-2, and the results were usually quite close, with up to 5% difference for either side. This indicates similar level of difficulty for both datasets. However, simple lexical overlap systems were found to perform better on the RTE-2 test set than on RTE-1 test set - 60% on RTE-2 vs. 53.9% on RTE-1, as reported by Zanzotto et al., (although for the RTE-1 development set they obtained 57.1%). Interestingly, de Marneffe et al. [7] and Zanzotto et al. [23] report that adding the RTE-1 data to the RTE-2 training set decreased the accuracy, which indicates the variance between the two datasets (notice that the RTE-1 datasets include three tasks not present in RTE-2. Inkpen at el. [15] showed that the results somewhat improve if only the compatible tasks in RTE-1 are considered). Schilder and McInnes [20] found that classification using only the lengths of t and h as features could give accuracy of 57.4%.

In the RTE-2 dataset (both the development set and the test set), multiple IR pairs were created for a single IR query (where t was extracted from different documents retrieved), and similarly, multiple QA pairs were created for a single question (where t was extracted from different answer passages). Some of the groups (de Marneffe et al., Nicholson et al. [7, 18]) noted that these dependencies between the pairs could potentially have a negative effect on the learning, and somewhat bias the evaluation on the test set. In practice, however, there was no evidence that systems perform significantly worse on the RTE-2 test set than on the RTE-1 test set (using RTE-2/RTE-1 development sets, respectively, for training), and, as described above, similar scores were obtained for both datasets.

5   The Third and Fourth RTE Challenges

RTE-3[5] [9] followed the same basic structure of RTE-1 and RTE-2, in order to facilitate the participation of newcomers and to allow "veterans" to assess the improvements of their systems in a comparable setting. The main novelty of RTE-3 was that part of the pairs contained longer texts (up to one paragraph), encouraging participants to move towards discourse-level inference. 26 Teams participated, and the results were presented at the ACL 2007 Workshop on Textual Entailment and Paraphrasing.

The fourth challenge[6] [10] was co-organized, for the first time, under the umbrella of the U.S. National Institute of Standards and Technology (NIST), together with CELCT (Italy), which co-organized previous RTE campaigns. RTE-4 was included as a track in the newly-established NIST Text Analysis Conference (TAC), together with question-answering and summarization tracks, and was supported by the PASCAL-2 European Network of Excellence. Hopefully, bringing these tracks together would promote the use of generic entailment technology within these applications. The major innovation of the fourth challenge was three-way classification of entailment pairs, which was piloted in RTE-3. In three-way judgment, non-entailment cases are split between *contradiction*, where the negation of the hypothesis is entailed from the text, and *unknown*, where the truth of the hypothesis cannot be determined based on the text. Participants could submit to either the three-way task, the traditional two-way task, or to both. As in RTE-3, 26 teams have participated, some of which also participated in other TAC tracks.

---

[5] http://www.pascal-network.org/Challenges/RTE3
[6] http://www.nist.gov/tac/tracks/2008/rte/

6   Conclusion

The textual entailment task, proposed only five years ago, is now an established research field studied by dozens of research groups worldwide. The RTE challenges described in this paper have played a crucial role in this success story. The challenges stimulated researchers to attempt diverse approaches, and papers about many of the RTE submissions were published later in prominent venues. Although the RTE task is very hard, the performance improvement obtained in the last four years is impressive (with best system achieving accuracy of 80% in RTE-3). Recently, some researchers have reported on successful integration of their entailment technology in various applications, such as question-answering [13, 14], multi-document summarization [12] and intelligent tutoring [19].

While the RTE task gradually evolved over the years (mainly three-way classification and longer texts mentioned above), the basic setting was maintained. We believe that next challenges will further develop the task, making it more realistic and closer to actual application settings. One possible enhancement is to compliment the *validation* setting, where the text and the hypothesis are given, with a *search* setting, where only the hypothesis is given, and the task is to find all the entailing texts in a given corpus. This would provide a more natural distribution of pairs, compared to the relatively small set of manually-collected pairs in the previous RTE datasets.

Acknowledgment The following sources were used in the preparation of the RTE-2 data:

- AnswerBus question answering system, provided by Zhiping Zheng, Computational Linguistics Department, Saarland University.
  http://answerbus.coli.uni-sb.de/
- PowerAnswer question answering system, from Language Computer Corporation, provided by Dan Moldovan, Abraham Fowler, Christine Clark, Arthur Dexter and Justin Larrabee.
  http://www.languagecomputer.com/solutions/question_answering/power_answer/
- Columbia NewsBlaster multi-document summarization system, from the Natural Language Processing group at Columbia University's Department of Computer Science.
  http://newsblaster.cs.columbia.edu/
- NewsInEssence multi-document summarization system, provided by Dragomir R. Radev and Jahna Otterbacher from the Computational Linguistics and Information Retrieval research group, University of Michigan.
  http://www.newsinessence.com/
- IBM's information extraction system, provided by Salim Roukos and Nanda Kambhatla, I.B.M. T.J. Watson Research Center.
- New York University's information extraction system, provided by Ralph Grishman, Department of Computer Science, Courant Institute of Mathematical Sciences, New York University.

- ITC-irst's information extraction system, provided by Lorenza Romano, Cognitive and Communication Technologies (TCC) division, ITC-irst, Trento, Italy.
- MUC-4 information extraction dataset, from the National Institute of Standards and Technology (NIST).
  http://www.itl.nist.gov/iaui/894.02/related_projects/muc/
- ACE 2004 information extraction templates, from the National Institute of Standards and Technology (NIST).
  http://www.nist.gov/speech/tests/ace/
- TREC IR queries and TREC-QA question collections, from the National Institute of Standards and Technology (NIST).
  http://trec.nist.gov/
- CLEF IR queries and CLEF-QA question collections, from DELOS Network of Excellence for Digital Libraries.
  http://www.clef-campaign.org/, http://clef-qa.itc.it/

We would like to thank the people and organizations that made these sources available for the RTE-2 challenge. In addition, we thank Oren Glickman and Dan Roth for their assistance and advice.

We would also like to acknowledge the people and organizations involved in creating and annotating the data: Malky Rabinowitz, Dana Mills, Ruthie Mandel, Errol Hayman, Vanessa Sandrini, Allesandro Valin, Elizabeth Lima, Jeff Stevenson, Amy Muia and the Butler Hill Group.

This work was supported in part by the IST Programme of the European Community, under the *PASCAL Network of Excellence*, IST-2002-506778. This publication only reflects the authors' views. We wish to thank the managers of the PASCAL challenges program, Michele Sebag, Florence d'Alche-Buc, and Steve Gunn, and the PASCAL Challenges Workshop Chair, Rodolfo Delmonte, for their efforts and support, which made the RTE-2 challenge possible.

References

[1] Baker, C., Fillmore, C., Lowe, J.: The Berkeley Framenet project. In: Proceedings of the COLING-ACL, Montreal, Canada (1998)
[2] Bar-Haim, R., Dagan, I., Dolan, B., Ferro, L., Giampiccolo, D., Magnini, B., Szpektor, I.: The Second PASCAL Recognising Textual Entailment Challenge. In: The Second PASCAL Challenges Workshop on Recognizing Textual Entailment (2006)
[3] Bar-Haim, R., Szpecktor, I., Glickman, O.: Definition and analysis of intermediate entailment levels. In: Proceedings of the ACL Workshop on Empirical Modeling of Semantic Equivalence and Entailment, Ann Arbor, Michigan, pp. 55–60. Association for Computational Linguistics (June 2005)
[4] Burger, J., Ferro, L.: Generating an entailment corpus from news headlines. In: Proceedings of the ACL Workshop on Empirical Modeling of Semantic Equivalence and Entailment, Ann Arbor, Michigan, pp. 49–54. Association for Computational Linguistics (June 2005)

[5] Dagan, I., Glickman, O.: Probabilistic textual entailment: Generic applied modeling of language variability. In: PASCAL Workshop on Text Understanding and Mining (2004)

[6] Dagan, I., Glickman, O., Magnini, B.: The PASCAL Recognising Textual Entailment Challenge. In: Quiñonero-Candela, J., Dagan, I., Magnini, B., d'Alché-Buc, F. (eds.) MLCW 2005. LNCS (LNAI), vol. 3944, pp. 177–190. Springer, Heidelberg (2006)

[7] de Marneffe, M.C., MacCartney, B., Grenager, T., Cer, D., Rafferty, A., Manning, C.D.: Learning to distinguish valid textual entailments. In: The Second PASCAL Challenges Workshop on Recognizing Textual Entailment (2006)

[8] Fellbaum, C. (ed.): WordNet: An Electronic Lexical Database. Language, Speech and Communication. MIT Press (1998)

[9] Giampiccolo, D., Magnini, B., Dagan, I., Dolan, B.: The Third PASCAL Recognizing Textual Entailment Challenge. In: Proceedings of the ACL-PASCAL Workshop on Textual Entailment and Paraphrasing (2007)

[10] Giampiccolo, D., Trang Dang, H., Magnini, B., Dagan, I., Dolan, B.: The Fourth PASCAL Recognizing Textual Entailment Challenge. In: Proceedings of the TAC 2008 Workshop (2008)

[11] Glickman, O., Dagan, I., Koppel, M.: A lexical alignment model for probabilistic textual entailment. In: Quiñonero-Candela, J., Dagan, I., Magnini, B., d'Alché-Buc, F. (eds.) MLCW 2005. LNCS (LNAI), vol. 3944, pp. 287–298. Springer, Heidelberg (2006)

[12] Harabagiu, S., Hickl, A., Lacatusu, F.: Satisfying information needs with multi-document summaries. Inf. Process. Manage. 43(6), 1619–1642 (2007)

[13] Hickl, A., Harabagiu, S.: Methods for using textual entailment in open-domain question answering. In: Proceedings of the 21st International Conference on Computational Linguistics and 44th Annual Meeting of the ACL. Association for Computational Linguistics (2006)

[14] Iftene, A., Balahur, A.: Answer validation on English and Romanian languages. In: Peters, C., Deselaers, T., Ferro, N., Gonzalo, J., Jones, G.J.F., Kurimo, M., Mandl, T., Peñas, A., Petras, V. (eds.) CLEF 2008. LNCS, vol. 5706, pp. 448–451. Springer, Heidelberg (2009)

[15] Inkpen, D., Kipp, D., Nastase, V.: Machine learning experiments for textual entailment. In: The Second PASCAL Challenges Workshop on Recognizing Textual Entailment (2006)

[16] Katrenko, S., Adriaans, P.: Using maximal embedded syntactic subtrees for textual entailment recognition. In: The Second PASCAL Challenges Workshop on Recognizing Textual Entailment (2006)

[17] Landis, J.R., Koch, G.G.: The measurements of observer agreement for categorical data. Biometrics 33, 159–174 (1997)

[18] Nicholson, J., Stokes, N., Baldwin, T.: Detecting entailment using an extended implementation of the basic elements overlap metric. In: The Second PASCAL Challenges Workshop on Recognizing Textual Entailment (2006)

[19] Nielsen, R.D., Ward, W., Martin, J.H.: Classification errors in a domain-independent assessment system. In: Proceedings of the Third Workshop on Innovative Use of Natural Language Processing for Building Educational Applications, at the Forty-Sixth annual meeting of the Association for Computational Linguistics. ACL (2008)

[20] Schilder, F., McInnes, B.T.: Word and tree-based similarities for textual entailment. In: The Second PASCAL Challenges Workshop on Recognizing Textual Entailment (2006)

[21] Vanderwende, L., Dolan, W.B.: What syntax can contribute in the entailment task. In: Quiñonero-Candela, J., Dagan, I., Magnini, B., d'Alché-Buc, F. (eds.) MLCW 2005. LNCS (LNAI), vol. 3944, pp. 205–216. Springer, Heidelberg (2006)
[22] Voorhees, E.M., Harman, D.: Overview of the seventh text retrieval conference. In: Proceedings of the Seventh Text REtrieval Conference (TREC-7). NIST Special Publication (1999)
[23] Zanzotto, F.M., Moschitti, A., Pennacchiotti, M., Pazienza, M.T.: Learning textual entailment from examples. In: The Second PASCAL Challenges Workshop on Recognizing Textual Entailment (2006)

A Retrospective of a Pioneering Project. Earlier Than XML, Other Than SGML, Still Going: CuProS Metadata for Deeply Nested Relations and Navigating for Retrieval in RAFFAELLO

Ephraim Nissan[1] and Jihad El-Sana[2]

[1] Department of Computing, Goldsmiths College, University of London,
25–27 St. James Street, New Cross, London SE14 6NW, England, U.K.
ephraim.nissan@hotmail.co.uk
[2] Department of Computer Science,
Ben-Gurion University of the Negev, Beer-Sheva, Israel
el-sana@cs.bgu.ac.il

Abstract. The spread of XML vindicated a project that the present authors developed earlier, independently of SGML, the parent-language of XML (SGML was originally devised for communicating structured documents). Our own project was the NAVIGATION component of the RAFFAELLO retrieval system. The latter was originally devised for managing the deeply nested, flexible relations that constituted the lexical database of the ONOMATURGE expert system for Hebrew word-formation. Whereas RAFFAELLO within ONOMATURGE was a simpler version, such that retrieval was done by means of retrieval functions implemented in LISP and reflecting the actual structure of the nested relations as known beforehand, the version of NAVIGATION that was implemented by El-Sana under Nissan's supervision used a metadata schema. The syntax for describing metadata in RAFFAELLO was in a language defined by Nissan, CuProS (short for *Customization Production System*). Whereas a few articles about RAFFAELLO were published, none explained CuProS and the NAVIGATION tool as implemented by El-Sana. The unabated interest in XML, Web technology, and ontologies (an area relevant for the database of ONOMATURGE) have vindicated Nissan's contention that *nested relations* (a research area in database design) should be allowed not only unlimited depth of nesting, but also extreme flexibility of structure. This is now taken for granted because of how metadata are defined for XML, but the feasibility of the idea was shown by El-Sana's managing to implement retrieval as based on metadata description, along the lines of CuProS syntax. In this article, apart from explaining the syntax of CuProS and also describing El-Sana's implementation of retrieval, we also illustrate the approach to metarepresentation through an exemplification from the structure of lexical frames in ONOMATURGE. In particular, we discuss variants of a given derivational pattern of word-formation, and we also discuss the evolution of terminology for given lexical concepts, throughout historical strata of Hebrew. We show how

N. Dershowitz and E. Nissan (Eds.): Choueka Festschrift, Part I, LNCS 8001, pp. 425–583, 2014.
© Springer-Verlag Berlin Heidelberg 2014

this is handled in nested relations, but a fuller discussion is provided in appendices. The approach is also exemplified based on a project applied to Italy's regional constitutions.

Keywords: Metadata, knowledge-representation, retrieval, RAFFAELLO, CUPROS, ONOMATURGE, ontologies, nested relations, XML, lexicography, hospitality management, legal computing, history of computing.

Table of Contents of the Article

1.   Background of the Project
  1.1.   A Lexicographical Database of Deeply Nested Relations
  1.2.   A Project for a Corpus in Constitutional Law
  1.3.   Another Application, in Retrospect a Precursor
  1.4.   The Nested Relations Approach in Database Research
  1.5.   "Denormalized Relations" in Cornell University's
          Uto-Aztecan Project
2.   Nested Relations, and Passive Frames vs. Active Frames
3.   RAFFAELLO: A Toolkit for Retrieval from Nested Relations
  3.1.   A History of the RAFFAELLO Project
  3.2.   Operational Aspects of RAFFAELLO
4.   The Metarepresentation
  4.1.   Preliminary Remarks
  4.2.   From the Object-Level, to the Meta-Level
  4.3.   A Concrete Example of Object-Level vs. Meta-Level Structure
5.   XML Comes into the Picture
  5.1.   General Considerations
  5.2.   The Significance of the Rise of XML for the
          the Precursor Status of RAFFAELLO and
          the Deeply Nested relations from Which it Retrieves
  5.3.   Well-Formedness in XML and the SIMPLE NAVIGATION
          Version of RAFFAELLO, vs. the Validity of
          an XML Document and the CUPROS-Directed
          NAVIGATION Version of RAFFAELLO
  5.4.   A Project for Traslating Our Representation into XML
6.   For Comparison: Data and Metadata in XML
7.   Early Versions of RAFFAELLO
  7.1.   The Basics: RAFFAELLO's Original Tasks
  7.2.   Why a Production-System as Metarepresentation,
          While the Object-Level is in Nested-Relation Frames?
  7.3.   SIMPLE NAVIGATION vs. NAVIGATION
  7.4.   A Protocol Integrating NAVIGATION and SIMPLE NAVIGATION
8.   Queries
  8.1.   The Specification of NAVIGATION's Queries
  8.2.   Queries with Variables
  8.3.   Motivation of the Metarepresentation
          from the Viewpoint of Queries:
          Consulting Keys, and Allowing Incomplete Paths

9.   The Early Version of RAFFAELLO That Maps
          Nested Relations to INGRES Flat Relations
   9.1.   An Overall View
   9.2.   Query Handling in the INGRES-Oriented
          Version of RAFFAELLO
   9.3.   Details of the Representation Under INGRES
10.   The CuPROS Metarepresentation, vs. Data-Dictionaries
   10.1. A Separate Nesting-Schema, vs.
          an All-Encompassing Data-Dictionary
   10.2. Indexing for Large Frames
11.   Syntactic Elements of CuPROS,
          the Metarepresentation Language of RAFFAELLO
   11.1. Basic Terminology
   11.2. Parsing the Labels in the Metarepresentation
   11.3. A Sample Metarepresentation. Part I
   11.4. A Sample Metarepresentation. Part II
   11.5. A Sample Metarepresentation. Part III
   11.6. Slot-Synonymy, and Contextual Disambiguation of Slot-Polysemy
   11.7. More Conventions
   11.8. Slotless-Facet Identifiers, and Repeatable Facet-Schemata
   11.9. Ancestor-Identifying Descendants
          of Repeatable Facets: Attributes Storing
          Identifiers of Subframe-Instances
   11.10. Multi-Attribute or Multi-Facet Identification-Keys
   11.11. Facets Containing Local Navigation-Guides
12.   Sample Rules from the Metarepresentation
          of the Lexical Frames of ONOMATURGE
   12.1. The Top Few Levels in Lexical Frames
   12.2. The Metarepresentation Rules for Facets of
          Individual Lexemes or Acceptations
   12.3. Facets for Semantic, Morphological,
          and Historical Information
   12.4. Considerations About Facets in the Lexical Frames
   12.5. The Effects of Omission from a Noun Phrase
   12.6. Socio-Cultural Change, and Morphological Gender
   12.7. More Concerning Morphological Gender
13.   More Syntax for CuPROS Metarepresentations
   13.1. Mutual Exclusion of Sub-RHSs
   13.2. Pointers to an Exceptional Position in the Hierarchy
   13.3. Ancestry-Statements That Constrain the Schema of
          an Attribute to the Context of a Given Sub-RHS
   13.4. Cartesian Spaces of Attributes
14.   Conclusions
References
Appendix A: Kinds of /Pa^oL/ Among $C_1aC_2oC_3$ Hebrew Derivational Patterns
Appendix B: Historical Strata, and Verbs That Took Over
Appendix C: The Code of NAVIGATION
Appendix D: The Metarepresentation of the Lexical
             Frames in ONOMATURGE

1   Background of the Project

1.1   A Lexicographical Database of Deeply Nested Relations

ONOMATURGE is an expert system developed by Nissan in 1983–1987. Its area of expertise is word-formation, within computational linguistics. Its task was to generate and propose a gamut of new Hebrew terms (candidate neologisms that express a concept whose definition was entered as input), and to evaluate how 'good' those terms would seem to native or fluent speakers of Hebrew. That is to say, the program also had to produce an estimate of the psychosemantic transparency of the coinages it generated, and according to that estimate, it would rank them. The control of ONOMATURGE was described by Nissan in [71], whereas the structure of the database was dealt with in [72]. In the present volume set, see [82].

The lexical database of ONOMATURGE consists of a collection of large chunks of lexicographic knowledge; each entry is structured as a deeply nested database relation.[1] A refined structure was envisaged in a sequel multilingual project, which is described in another article in the present volume set [79]. In the multilingual project, lexical frames are separate from semantic frames, and moreover there are onomasiological frames (i.e., about how given lexical concepts are named across languages; in particular, semantic shifts are described in such frames).

In the database of ONOMATURGE, retrieval is performed by a tool, RAFFAELLO, whose early versions were described in part of Nissan's PhD thesis [75, Sec. 7 and Appendices E and F], and then, in a more limited fashion, in the articles [68, 73, 74]. In ONOMATURGE, a procedural control component accesses nested

---

[1] Nissan's earlier research in database design had adopted the *universal relation* approach instead [64, 65, 69]. In the universal relation approach to the design of relational databases, there is a conceptual phase such that there virtually is only one relation. The latter is global, is defined by all attributes that are relevant for the database, and its set of attributes forms a space in which the values are coordinates on the respective attribute's axis, thus identifying all those individuals (points in the space) that match a query. In the words of Ullman [106], in the universal relation approach, "the objects are [...] the smallest sets of attributes for which a significant connection is represented in the database", but even though object-based semantics of universal relations has been defined in those terms, it is the opposite approach with respect to nested relations. The universal relation's goal is relieving users from having to use schemata; for certain applications, this approach remains very interesting. However, mapping complex objects onto the universal relation model is a very elaborate task, as early as the database design stage. As Ullman [106], in polemising with Kent [37], recognised, the universal relation model does not improve, with respect to previous relational models, in requiring that attribute-names be made unambiguous by unnatural-sounding strings; this may be inconvenient for objects with a deep part-explosion hierarchy. The universe of attributes should be flattened since the design phase, whereas the nested-relation model keeps the object's structure explicit. Because of all the mapping involved, universal relations don't seem adequate for situations where nested relations could give the best.

relations and then, based on values found there, further nested relations are sometimes accessed, and rules fire (which in turn execute programs in derivational morphology); that is, substantially, control first accesses frames, and then it accesses
rules.

Importantly, within ONOMATURGE, not only retrieval but also a few other
functions were associated with RAFFAELLO, the main of these being having the
word-formation patterns triggered across several programming languages.[2] This
was described in [75, Subsec. 7.3.1, 7.3.2, 7.3.3], and will not be dealt with in
the present article, because it is outside the scope of showing how we combined
a rule-driven metarepresentation language with an object-level representation in

---

[2] RAFFAELLO allows to access and exploit parts of the knowledge-base that are coded
in languages different from LISP. This applies to frames simulated under INGRES,
but — and this was especially important for the version of ONOMATURGE that was
in actual use — this applies also to program-bases heterogeneously implemented: for
ONOMATURGE, the collection of derivational programs. Some of them were implemented in LISP (according to different programming approaches), but most of them
were implemented in the Shell or CShell languages of the UNIX operating system.
"Some Unix systems support more than one Shell. For example, on the Berkeley
UNIX system both the Bourne Shell and the C-Shell are available, as the programs
sh and **csh** respectively." [57, p. 417]

What were the respective advantages of LISP and of Shell or CShell, in the implementation of derivation programs? On the one hand, LISP was found to be best suited
for those kinds of inflection where *string explosion* is needed. On the other hand,
when *concatenation* (but not explosion) was needed, Shell or CShell implementations proved to be *compact* and relatively *readable*. Moreover, a relevant ruleset
was already implemented by Nissan in Shell or CShell, before he finally decided to
focus on LISP, while implementing ONOMATURGE.

Rules in ONOMATURGE are specialised in Hebrew word-formation, because the task
of the expert system was to generate, evaluate, rank, and propose candidate neologisms in Hebrew. Some such word-formation patterns (patterns of derivation rather
than compounding) are suffixes, but usually, they are *free-place formulae* — which
is typical of the morphology of Semitic languages. Some rules of ONOMATURGE were
coded in LISP (following one out of several possible conceptions and implementations
in the same language), or in the Shell or CShell command languages of UNIX. The
control programs of ONOMATURGE ask RAFFAELLO to trigger a certain rule, whose
name was retrieved from some frame instance, but without knowing where it belongs to, from the implementational viewpoint. The format of arguments in different
implementations (e.g., in different programming languages) may happen to differ.
The input arguments are transformed suitably, and then executed. RAFFAELLO returns the result to the program that invoked it. Unlike **exec** — a FRANZ LISP
function that accesses Shell and executes Shell commands from inside LISP, Nissan's
interface suitably converts the format of argument-lists, special characters, and so
forth. This was performed according to information introduced by the user in the
clone (i.e., modified copy: a copy of the file, with some modifications introduced)
of the interface that was customised for the given application. This provides more
flexibility in the integration, as it wouldn't be realistic to assume that heterogeneous
implementations (which possibly were developed differently, without the future need
of their integration in mind), would share *a priori* conventions on lists of arguments.

nested relations with no conceptual limit on depth and flexibility, well before this has become commonplace with XML.

1.2   A Project for a Corpus in Constitutional Law

A similar encoding in nested relations was applied by Nissan to Italy's regional constitutions (*Statuti Regionali*) [102], trying to exploit their similarities. The description of that project as can be found in Nissan's paper [76] pays much attention to the metarepresentation whose object-level representation is constituted by the nested relations inside which, the regional constitutional provisions are encoded.

In that project, it was envisaged that nested relations be used at an intermediate level of the knowledge representation, a level unsuitable for interfacing the user, but suitable for knowledge-engineering and -acquisition. It was also envisaged that another part of the knowledge representation (actually, its lower level), as well as possibly queries, would be logic-based, and coded in PROLOG; for example, a rule about the Regional Executive Council (*Giunta Regionale*) of Lombardy in 1972–1976 was formulated as follows:

```
in_office( giunta_regionale,
          [ [ president, tizio ] ,
            [ aldermen,   [ caio, sempronio, etc ] ]
          ]
       ) :- region_is( lombardia ), period_is( 1972, to, 1976 ).
```

In this article, part of the exemplification (in Subsec. 4.4) is going to be drawn from work originally done for this application to Italy's regional constitutions. This is worthwhile, as the metarepresentation that defines and regulates the nested relations of this project had interesting aspects that made good use of the syntax of the CuProS metarepresentation language, which itself had been originally defined by Nissan for it to subserve the development of the ONOMATURGE expert system for word-formation.

1.3   Another Application, in Retrospect a Precursor

This subsection describes the second application of the approach to database structure that had been inaugurated with ONOMATURGE. This second application was a program whose role was as an adviser for terminal food-processing: meal configuration under constraints on ingredient quantities, and so forth. Implementors of various phases (in 1986 and 1987) included Edith Marmelstein and Gabi Shahar; Tzafrir Kagan and Benny Trushinsky; Gilla Shluha, Tzvi Getzel, and Adi Gavish; Dorit Nogah and Nava Sha'ya. They were supervised by Nissan.

A database of deeply nested relations, again similar to the database of ONOMATURGE, was applied to the database of this expert system prototype for planning in large kitchens, thus the application domain was within hospitality management [70]: FIDEL GASTRO (so named after *gastronomy*) plans cooking or terminal food-processing (its intended use being at institutional or hotel kitchens) by configuring meals, as constrained by available quantities of (mandatory or optional) ingredients, and by various kinds of other constraints. Kinds of food, and ingredients, are represented in an inheritance network whose vertices are deeply nested relations. the procedural control component of FIDEL GASTRO first accesses heuristics (that can be conceived of as rules operating on sets), and then accesses frames (and then again it accesses more frames).

Even though FIDEL GASTRO was a relatively minor project that Nissan had his undergraduate students implement in 1987, it was considered valuable enough for a journal in hospitality management to publish a paper on this application to large kitchens. Moreover, it finds now a parallel in a function of the so-called Microsoft Home, introduced in 2004, and first inhabited by Bill Gates and his family. Even though the Microsoft Home uses radio-frequency identification tags for inventory tracking, the basic function is like that of the 1987 project, FIDEL GASTRO. James Barron [7], describing the Microsoft Home, wrote: "The network knows, for example, what ingredients are available in the kitchen. If the makings for chocolate chip cookies are not at hand, it will suggest a recipe for oatmeal cookies, assuming these ingredients are on the shelf" — and this is precisely what FIDEL GASTRO was doing.

While representation in the frame-bases of ONOMATURGE and FIDEL GASTRO is similar, the architecture of the *dynamics* (the control flow) of the two expert systems is different (and somewhat "upside down" with respect to each other). In fact, in ONOMATURGE, a large procedural control component intensively accesses frames, the process identifies suitable rules in a ruleset, and triggers modules that perform the action part of the rule. In FIDEL GASTRO instead, frames are accessed by a procedural control, whose structural regularities suggest macro-based reimplementation in terms of a deterministic production-system storing meta-level knowledge on the dynamics.

In ONOMATURGE, a procedural and retrieval-intensive control accesses a database of frames. Among other things, upon retrieving from the frame-base certain properties that indicate rules of word-formation that are suitable in the current context, the control heuristics of Onomaturge access a program-base of modules, implementing procedural rules, and which is heterogeneous. Relevant rules fire, while a scoring procedure evaluates the application of rules to data instances by retrieving declarative knowledge on rules from another frame-base, whose frames describe single rules.

By contrast, in FIDEL GASTRO, kinds of food, ingredients, and so forth are described in an *inheritance network* of frame-instances. The frame-base is accessed by a procedural control. Control heuristics generate and constrain the search-space where a solution is sought for the problem proposed by the task. A procedural program coded in LISP fulfilled the role of control. However, this code could be easily rewritten as decomposed into a production-system of control heuristics: the ruleset would access frames, whereas in ONOMATURGE, frames cause the ruleset elements to fire. Besides, FIDEL GASTRO's control component could be repeated for different tasks, and task-oriented versions would anyway access the general frame-base on food. The first task implemented proposed possible meals, once it had learnt about ingredients or dishes that are available in a kitchen. Incrementally, it could conceivably be expanded with new constraints, which in turn would possibly need further accesses in frames, or would instead perform only computations that are not specific of *semantic* knowledge about certain kinds of food, but involve *contingent* data (i.e., *episodic* knowledge). For example, such contingent (session-dependent) constraints may involve quantities: an operations research problem should be solved, in trials to optimise heuristically (or, anyway, to enhance) the exploitment of ingredients.

In FIDEL GASTRO, one can identify two macro-components: the *database* — where detailed general information is stored about kinds of food and ingredients — and *task-oriented programs*. These programs embody a set of rather modular *heuristics* for performing a given task, and a general *control* that orders and organises the application of the heuristics to the data. Heuristics access the database intensively. Besides, they are applied to input data. The task implemented consists of checking qualities and quantities of stocks available in a kitchen, and then in proposing the kinds of food that could be prepared with the basic or intermediate ingredients available, in order to constitute a meal, under constraints.

Constraints may be *quantitative:* you cannot use twice the same flour. They may be temporal, and involve sequences of actions or absolute amounts of time, in presence of a limited amount of cooking facilities. On the other hand, constraints may be *qualitative,* and refer to any out of several domains: social etiquette, dietetic, medical, religious, and so forth.

The control programs of FIDEL GASTRO tackle the hierarchy of ingredients to prepare a given candidate kind of food that is being considered by the program; limited availability of ingredients is accounted for. The organisation of knowledge chunks in the database as implemented includes many attributes that can be exploited to impose constraints: actually, more than the control as implemented was actually exploiting (the same is also true of ONOMATURGE). Chunks of knowledge about single kinds of food (or of ingredients that cannot be served as food on their own) are organised in data-structures of the same kind of frames in ONOMATURGE.

Let us consider, now, the *statics* of FIDEL GASTRO as reflected in the structure of single entries in its database. Afterwards, we are going to look at the *dynamics* of the system, as embodied in the control programs and in the heuristics they apply. The control programs of FIDEL GASTRO exploit only a small part of the information that can be stored in frames, according to the following organisation. Inside each frame that describes a kind of food, an attribute IS_A lists such concepts of which the current concept is a subclass. It is useless to state, inside the frame of a concept, C_1, i.e., such properties that are coincident with properties as found in frames of concepts

$$\{C_2, C_3, \ldots\}$$

of which C_1 is a subclass. In fact, those properties are enforced for C_1 as well, unless the frame of C_1 explicitly states different values that supersede the inherited property. On the other hand, the attribute PARTICULAR_CASES lists subclasses belonging to the current concept.

An attribute IS_INGREDIENT_FOR states for what kinds of food the present entry could be used as ingredient. Often, food that can be served on its own has no such value of IS_INGREDIENT_FOR. Knowledge stored under the attribute INGREDIENTS lists various properties, subdivided according to the kind of MANDATORY_INGREDIENTS or OPTIONAL_INGREDIENTS.

In terminal kinds of food (as opposed to general classes), the QUANTITY of ingredients is stated. Besides, the SPECIFICITY is tentatively quantified: this is resorted to by the control programs, in order to avoid looking for candidate dishes first according to those ingredients (such as salt or water) that do not typify only a reasonably small set of kinds of food of which they are an ingredient. For optional ingredients, a tentative quantification of the extent to which they may be renounced is also stated. Besides, standard units of measure are defined for different kinds of food.

Social information is gathered in properties nested inside the property SOCIAL_INFO. Namely, information on suitable occasions (events, or calendar recurrences) for serving a given kind of food fits in the property OCCASION_STATUS. Information on the social status of food fits in the property SOCIAL_STATUS. Price information fits in properties nested inside the property PRICE. Medical constraints and fitness constraints respectively fit in properties nested inside MEDICAL_CONSTRAINTS (subdivided by pathological condition, drug-dependent prohibitions, therapy-dependent prohibitions, and so forth), and FITNESS_CONSTRAINTS (subdivided by kind of diet). RELIGIOUS_CONSTRAINTS are subdivided by religious denomination, and include constraints that depend upon a particular status of a person, upon place, on calendar time, upon time past since the consumption of other given kinds of food, upon contemporaneousness of consumption, and so forth.

MORAL_CONSTRAINTS is an attribute actually more closely related to lifestyle than to ethos, and includes information on VEGETARIAN habits (of various kinds: e.g., admitting fish, admitting eggs, excluding meat but not animal fats, etc., with default assumptions), on ANTI_HUNT, or ANTI_SMELL (thus excluding garlic), or FLORA_CONSERVATION considerations and sentiments (e.g., either persons, or legal systems, object to palm cabbage, as one palm is killed for each cabbage). LEGAL_CONSTRAINTS can be of various kinds: e.g., the prescribed addition of sesam-oil to ersatz to make it easily identifiable, or other laws against adulteration, or protectionist or prohibitionist norms, as dictated by economic considerations or by health hazards. Etiquette is described also under the attribute HOW_TO_SERVE. Other attributes refer to CALORIES, CONSERVATION, TASTE, ODOR, CONSISTENCE, and so forth. PREPARATION_PROTOCOL lists the attributes TOTAL_TIME, MACHINES, and PROCEDURE.

Let us turn to the control flow of FIDEL GASTRO. At the beginning of each session, the program interacts with the user, ideally a cook or the manager of an institutional kitchen. The control of FIDEL GASTRO takes a list of stocks (with the respective quantities) that are available in a kitchen, and then it proposes possible lists of dishes to be prepared.

First of all, for each kind of stock, the system determines whether it can be served as food on its own, or it is just a possible ingredient. (This is done according to the properties IS_INGREDIENT_FOR and HOW_TO_SERVE, as found in the frame of each item in the list.) Then, FIDEL GASTRO tries to figure out what dishes could be prepared by means of the list of ingredients it has in the kitchen. It should not begin by considering ingredients that are very often used, such as salt. Instead, FIDEL GASTRO tries to direct its search into small classes of candidate dishes. Thus, for each item in the list of available ingredients, the control program checks its IS_INGREDIENT_FOR property, and begins by considering those ingredients that could fit only in few dishes. Besides, this check is done recursively; that is, if you have flour, yeast, and water in the kitchen, then you would find out that you can prepare dough (an intermediate ingredient), but then, those kinds of food that can be prepared by means of dough should also be looked for.

Mandatory ingredients in the list of candidate dishes are retrieved from the frame of each item, and this is done (recursively) also for intermediate ingredients. FIDEL GASTRO checks whether it has, in the kitchen, all of the ingredients necessary to prepare the candidate currently considered. After having checked the actual presence of all of the ingredients required, FIDEL GASTRO checks also whether the available quantities of ingredients: not only the initial quantities should be available for a single considered candidate dish, but interactions are also considered between the requirements of different candidate dishes as considered for inclusion in the same menu. It may happen indeed that if you employ a certain quantity of a certain ingredient for the first candidate dish in the current candidate menu, then an insufficient quantity would be left for preparing a given dish that was also a candidate for inclusion in the menu. Feasible candidate menus are then displayed.

1.4   The Nested Relations Approach in Database Research

When the *nested relation* approach appeared in database design research, nested relations were also called *non-1NF relations* (where 1NF refers to Codd's First Normal Form of database relations), or *relation-valued relations*. The latter name highlights the recursive structure of nested relations. Namely, values may themselves be relations. At the time, in the 1980s, it looked like the ascent of knowledge-based systems (expert systems, or, more in general, computer systems that exploit knowledge-representation), as well as the need to model complex objects (a need subserved also, in another manner, by object-oriented programming) was vindicating a school, in relational-database research, that during the 1970s already existed but was by far in the minority: this was the school advocating processing relations as being nested (this was felt by proponents to be a natural description of objects in the world as modelled), without transforming them into shallow tables through Codd normalisations. In fact, expert database systems, CAD/CAM knowledge-bases, and so on — it was already felt in the

1980s — need to represent complex objects, whose part-explosion representation naturally leads to nested relations. In relational databases with shallow relations, the universe of attributes is "flattened" as early as the design phase, whereas the nested-relation model instead keeps the object's structure explicit.

Deeply nested relations allow to define attributes by decomposing and refining the universe of notions of a given application-domain. Nissan's approach in the database of ONOMATURGE concentrated on static properties of complex objects (as opposed to active networks of objects), and thus on the very identification of attributes that fit into the database schema as nested inside each other: according to the intuitive semantics of instances of nested attributes, whenever the need was felt to articulate information associated with a given attribute, Nissan nested inside that attribute further attributes, which classify the concerned information according to a hierarchical structure. More detail involves deeper nesting just as it may involve "broadening" the set of attributes found on the same hierarchical level.

Nested relations emerged, in relational database design research, out of the desire to generalise flat relations, so that hierarchically structured objects could be modelled directly. Paper collections appeared [1, 88]. Normal forms were introduced for nested relations [89]. Mark Levene introduced important variants of nested relations [44–47].

In particular, Levene combined the universal relation model (which allows the user to view the database as though it was just one flat relation, in the space of all attributes of the database), with nested relations, into an approach called the *nested universal relation model* [44]. That model offered the following advantages [44, Abstract]:

> Functional data dependencies and the classical notion of lossless decomposition are extended to nested relations and an extended chase procedure is defined to test the satisfaction of the data dependencies. The nested UR model is defined, and the classical UR model is shown to be a special case of the nested model. This implies that an UR interface can be implemented by using the nested UR model, thus gaining the full advantages of nested relations over flat relations

Levene's formalisation incorporated null values into the model. More recent work on nested relations includes [8, 25, 26]. Georgia Garani [26] distinguishes nested attributes as decomposable and non-decomposable. She has proven that — overcoming a once popular maxim in nested relations research ("Unnesting and then nesting on the same attribute of a nested relation does not always yield the original relation") — "for all nested relations, unnesting and then renesting on the same attribute yields the original relation subject only to the elimination of duplicate data" (in the wording of the abstract of [26]).

1.5 "Denormalized Relations" in Cornell University's Uto-Aztecan Project

In the 1980s, it looked like in computational lexicography there were developments being published (already in the early years of that decade), that were well suited by the nested-relation approach. Grimes, who was researching the lexicon of Huichol, a Native American language in Mexico (one result was a dictionary, [33]), had developed an approach to lexicographical databases that was based on what Grimes called *denormalized relations* [32], that is to say, on nested relations. The ones proposed by Grimes were not deeply nested however, unlike the nested relations in ONOMATURGE. In 1984, Grimes [32] expressed his opinion that relations in Codd normalisation are not suited for the representation of natural-language dictionaries: "It appears as if the better the dictionary in terms of lexicographic theory, the more awkward it is to fit relational constraints".

An application developed by Grimes and others was [33], the already mentioned dictionary of Huichol. Definitions were in Spanish, and the lexicon was that of a Uto-Aztecan language of Mexico. However, since the work as reported in 1984 [32], which had adopted denormalised relations, Grimes had been reconsidering the feasibility of "traditional", normalised relations for lexicography (personal communication from Grimes to Nissan, 1985). By contrast to Grimes, who was a linguist affiliated with a linguistics department at Cornell University, Nissan's main concern was with the computer science aspect of his own project in word-formation (after all, his doctoral project was in computer science), even as he strove for a linguistically rigorous treatment. Therefore, Nissan did not shy away from sticking with his deeply nested relations, as being applied to representing the lexicon, for the needs of ONOMATURGE and beyond.

2 Nested Relations, and Passive Frames vs. Active Frames

A nested relation is a *tree of properties*. In the lexical database exploited by ONOMATURGE, each entry is organised as a nested relation, and is owned by a word, a collocational compound,[3] or a lexical root (i.e., a consonantal stem as typical of Semitic languages, as ONOMATURGE is applied to Hebrew word-formation). Besides, derivational morphemes as well are allowed to have a nested relation associated, whose attributes often are the same as those of lexical entries. In ONOMATURGE, chunks of knowledge are large: tens or hundreds of (indented and possibly commented) lines can correspond to a single entry, if much information is stated.

For the purposes of the expert system using the database, each entry in the database is a *passive* frame. A frame is a representation of an object in terms of its properties; it is passive if no *procedural attachment* is found that is automatically triggered on access: in programs such as ONOMATURGE and FIDEL

---

[3] An interesting thing about collocations, is that sometimes usage flexibilises them; see e.g. [27].

GASTRO (the latter was described in Subsec. 1.3 above), it is the responsibility of control programs, exploiting the database, to perform suitable actions after consultation; in particular, the action taken could be the execution of some retrieved value. But even though from the viewpoint of knowledge engineering, these nested relations are basically passive frames (accessed by an external control), conceivably a control component in a program exploiting such a database of nested relations could exploit them as embodying active data, too: actions firing as soon as they are read.

3   RAFFAELLO: A Toolkit for Retrieval from Nested Relations

3.1   A History of the RAFFAELLO Project

As mentioned, from late 1983 to 1987, Nissan developed by himself ONOMATURGE, an expert system for Hebrew word-formation, in which a lexical database of deeply nested relations was a component. This was the original background for all subsequent work done on RAFFAELLO, whose potential for application was of course believed to be wider. Retrieval functions of RAFFAELLO's various versions, always applied to deeply nested relations such as those of ONOMATURGE, were first implemented by Nissan in the FRANZ LISP programming language, as part of the ONOMATURGE project. Moreover, also in 1984–1986, he had different groups of students also do some work on RAFFAELLO by using FRANZ LISP. Afterwards, Nissan had his students develop further versions of RAFFAELLO, and these versions were implemented in either PROLOG (this was the version developed by Jihad El-Sana in 1989), or the C programming language (which was the case of a version developed in 1989 especially by Ziad Ashkar).

As said, the earliest version of RAFFAELLO was developed by Nissan, who implemented retrieval functions in FRANZ LISP: these functions carried out retrieval from the nested relations of a lexical database, and were invoked by the control component of Nissan's ONOMATURGE expert system. Between 1984 and 1990, his students who were involved in the development of the RAFFAELLO toolkit for retrieval from deeply nested relations were, at first, Gai Gecht and Avishay Silbeschatz, and next, for different versions,

- on the one hand Jihad El-Sana, who developed in PROLOG a version of RAFFAELLO that carries out retrieval from nested relations by consulting a metarepresentation coded in the CuPROS language as defined by Nissan,
- and on the other hand Ziad Ashkar, Ilia 'Ablini, Muataz Abusalah, and Fadel Fakher-Eldeen. These other students developed, in the C programming language, a version of RAFFAELLO that does not consult the metarepresentation.

In 1985, Yehudit Shakhi and 'Irit Dahan implemented under Nissan's direction a nested-relations based representation of semantic componential analysis (in lexical semantics). This project was inspired by Nissan's concomitant work in computational linguistics, but did not contribute to ONOMATURGE itself. By

1988, Nissan was developing a multilingual schema for the lexis and semantics. In 1989, his student Barak Shemesh developed a program transforming a nested subrelation into a visual representation, by applying this to diachronic onomasiological relations, that is to say, to how a given lexical concept came to be expressed by a different set of terminology over time, in different historical strata of the same language. This application is discussed in Appendix B, at whose end Barak Shemesh's project is briefly described.

In 1989, Nissan designed an adaptation of deeply nested relations to the representation of legal or constitutional concepts, namely, a representation that exploited similarities among Italy's regional constitutions: some of our exemplification in the present article is taken from that project in legal computing, as there were niceties to the metarepresentation of the nested relations that it is worthwhile to reproduce here.

3.2   Operational Aspects of RAFFAELLO

The PROLOG version of RAFFAELLO converts the syntax of the nested relations (originally developed so it would be handled in a LISP environment) into nested lists as in a syntax that PROLOG can handle; then, retrieval from the nested relation is performed, according to a database schema (i.e., a metarepresentation) that specifies legal nesting of properties. The PROLOG version of RAFFAELLO stands out among the other versions, in that it navigates inside the nested relations by using the metarepresentation to guide it.

A query addressing the nested-relation representation is a predicate that takes a list as argument; the list is the *retrieval path* through the nested levels of the frame: the path consists of the name of a frame, followed by a sequence of names of nested attributes, from the outermost, to the innermost interested. Incomplete but unambiguous paths are also allowed. As for traversing an unnamed chunk, instead of naming the attribute (that in this case is implicit), one has to state the key value (that is identified as such because unlike names of attributes, it includes at least one lower-case letter). As for the case when repeated chunks of different attributes occur — that is, in the generalised multiset case — the path has to include the name of the attribute, followed by the key value that identifies the particular chunk.

The PROLOG-coded retrieval tool consults the metarepresentation, and is able to analyse its syntax: Nissan defined a language, named CuPROS, short for *Customization Production System,* as it is rule-based. Writing down a metarepresentation coded in CuPROS customises the kind of knowledge representation for the given application. Likewise, using that metarepresentation coded in CuPROS customises the retrieval tool for the particular application. Each rule describes legal nesting in a given attribute, which is named in the left side; implicit attributes (those with unnamed chunks) have a conventional name, in use only inside the metarepresentation, and written (at least partly) in lower case.

4   The Metarepresentation

4.1   Preliminary Remarks

As early as the ONOMATURGE project, and regardless of the fact that the kind of retrieval used inside that expert system did not consult the metarepresentation while accessing the nested relations of the lexical database, the relation between the nested relations and the formalism by which their structure is regulated was clearly defined. The nested relation itself is at the *object-level* of representation, as opposed to the *meta-level representation* (or *metarepresentation*). Each kind of nested relation may have several instances at the object level, and one metarepresentation.

What was special (before the widespread adoption of XML) about our kind of frames (beside their being passive rather than active, i.e., beside the absence of *procedural attachments* being triggered on access), is these frames being structured as deeply nested relations. The nesting schema of attributes is flexible: its instances in different frames are likely to vary even considerably. This makes it relatively easy to add new kinds and new formats of information.

Control, as subserving the specific task of ONOMATURGE, exploits information found under several attributes inside frames. However, attributes as actually found — with values filled in — in implemented instances of database entries, are only a subset of attributes that are allowed to appear, according to a *meta-level representation* (or *metarepresentation*) stating legal nesting of attributes, and expressed in terms of a *production system* augmented with the syntax of a special language, CUPROS. This metarepresentation reflects a decomposition of the knowledge-domain into a large set of attributes, and flexibility as allowed is far-reaching.

Meta-level representation, as opposed — in frame-systems and knowledge-bases — to the *object-level representation* that it defines and regulates, is the equivalent of what a *data-dictionary* is for a traditional *database.* Metarepresentation, in knowledge-based systems, is not necessarily limited to describing the structure of the database component: in fact, a meta-level description can be given as well of sets of heuristic rules, or even of the control component. Our retrieval tool, RAFFAELLO, resorts however to metarepresentation (in the one RAFFAELLO version that does access the metarepresentation indeed) only as defining the database of nested relations.

4.2   General Aspects of the Object-Level Representation

Bear in mind that from the viewpoint of LISP, a nested relation (no matter how deeply nested it is) is a recursive list of lists. It is only the semantics, to the human beholder, that interprets such nested relations as being trees of properties. By convention, each property is identified by an attribute, which usually is explicitly named in upper-case, but that can be implicit, in certain contexts that are specified in the metarepresentation. Each property is delimited by the parenthesis enclosing it This parenthesis includes the name of the attribute first, followed by either one or more terminal values, or one or more inner properties. Comments may be inserted, in the part of a line that follows a semicolon. Consider the following example (the first of eleven, taken from [76]):

Example 1.

```
(ATTRIBUTE_1
     (ATTRIBUTE_2   ( value_a   value_b )  )
     (ATTRIBUTE_3   ( value_c )
     (ATTRIBUTE_4
             (ATTRIBUTE_5   ( value_d  value_e )  )
             (ATTRIBUTE_6
                     (ATTRIBUTE_7 ..........    ; further
                                  ..........    ; nesting.
                     )
                     ........................
             )
     (ATTRIBUTE_8   ( textual_value )  )
)
```

These nested properties can be all different (every kind occurs once), so they are explicitly identified by the upper-case name of their respective attribute. But sometimes chunks with the same subschema of attributes can be repeated after each other, appearing with more or less the same attributes, but with different values. That is to say, the nested properties can constitute a sequence of one or more instances of one or more attributes. If several instances of just one attribute occur in the same sequence, then it is superfluous to state the name of the attribute explicitly: each property will be an *unnamed chunk,* which can contain either terminal values, or further nested properties. For example, in the following piece of code, two unnamed chunks are nested inside the property named after **ATTRIBUTE_1**, and they each have the same structure, in the sense that all or some of the attributes nested inside one chunk, occur (with possibly different values) in the following chunk.

Example 2.

```
(ATTRIBUTE_1
     (   (ATTRIBUTE_2    ( value_a    value_b )  )
         (ATTRIBUTE_3    ( value_c )  )
         (ATTRIBUTE_4    ........      )
         (ATTRIBUTE_5    ........      )
     )
     (   (ATTRIBUTE_2    ( value_d )  )
         (ATTRIBUTE_3    ( value_e )  )
         (ATTRIBUTE_5    ........      )
     )  )
```

One or more of the attributes have their value providing the identification *key* of the repeated chunk. For example, let `ATTRIBUTE_3` in the example be the key, but a key could even be multiple, and involve several (or even all) of the attributes occurring in a given chunk.

Unnamed chunks introduce, in our syntax, *multisets* (as opposed to *simple sets,* that is sets of such elements that can occur just once). In fact, unnamed chunks allow several instances of the same (implicit) attribute to be nested side by side. However, the limitation is that several occurrences are allowed for just one attribute. The most general case of multiset is allowed by the following syntactic feature; in fact, we are interested in admitting repeatable chunk-patterns even as instances of one out of a set of attributes; in such cases, it is obvious that the name of the relevant attribute — notwithstanding the repetition — must be stated explicitly (except at most one of the attributes), as in the following sample code:

Example 3.

```
(ATTRIBUTE_1
        (ATTRIBUTE_2   (ATTRIBUTE_3    (  value_a  )  )
                       (ATTRIBUTE_4    (  value_c  )  )
                       (ATTRIBUTE_5    ........      )
                       (ATTRIBUTE_6    ........      )
        )
        (ATTRIBUTE_2   (ATTRIBUTE_3    (  value_d  )  )
                       (ATTRIBUTE_4    (  value_e  )  )
                       (ATTRIBUTE_6    ........      )
        )
        (ATTRIBUTE_7   (ATTRIBUTE_8    (  value_f  )  )
                       (ATTRIBUTE_9    (  value_g  )  )
        )
        (ATTRIBUTE_2   (ATTRIBUTE_3    (  value_h  )  )
                       (ATTRIBUTE_5    ........      )
        )
        (ATTRIBUTE_7   (ATTRIBUTE_8    (  value_i  )  )
                       (ATTRIBUTE_9    (  value_j  )  )
        )   )
```

We could have omitted the name of either `ATTRIBUTE_2` or `ATTRIBUTE_7`, because the occurrence of two open parenthesis characters, successively with no other characters between (excepts blanks, newlines, or comments following a semicolon), at the level nested immediately inside `ATTRIBUTE_1`, ensures that the first parenthesis opens an unnamed chunk, to be associated with the one implicit attribute allowed.

4.3   From the Object-Level, to the Meta-Level

Example 4 is a piece of metarepresentation, concerning the object-level code of Example 1.

Example 4.

```
(ATTRIBUTE_1        (   ATTRIBUTE_2
                        ATTRIBUTE_3
                        ATTRIBUTE_4
                        ATTRIBUTE_8
)                   )
(ATTRIBUTE_4        (   ATTRIBUTE_5
                        ATTRIBUTE_6
)                   )
(ATTRIBUTE_6        (   ATTRIBUTE_7
                        . . . . . . . . . . .
)                   )
```

As for Example 2, its metarepresentation is in the following Example 5:

Example 5.

```
(ATTRIBUTE_1     (   n:   chunk_under_Attribute_1 )   )

(chunk_under_Attribute_1    (   ATTRIBUTE_2
                                i:   ATTRIBUTE_3
                                ATTRIBUTE_4
                                ATTRIBUTE_5
)                               )
```

In the latter example, one can see that the right-side part of rules can be interspersed with labels (ending by a colon, and typically being a letter); these labels are meant to convey information concerning the following attribute, or — as the case is of other labels, such as x: (which corresponds to an *exclusive or* of substructures of frame) — of a sub-unit of the right-side part of the rule, listing one or more attributes.

The label n: indicates that the following attribute can have repeated chunks; in the example, that attribute has its name containing lower-case letters (only one letter happens to be capitalised), thus the repeatable chunk is an unnamed chunk, at the object level.

The label i: indicates that the attribute that follows it, is the key attribute of the chunk-pattern. By contrast, according to the code in the following Example 6, the key includes two attributes, preceded by the label i2: (and being unmistakably a label, because of its ending in a colon).

Example 6.

```
(ATTRIBUTE_1     (  n:  chunk_under_Attribute_1 ) )

(chunk_under_Attribute_1   (  i2:  ATTRIBUTE_2
                              i2:  ATTRIBUTE_3
                                   ATTRIBUTE_4
                                   ATTRIBUTE_5
)                                )
```

The code in the following Example 7 is the metarepresentation of the object-level code of Example 3:

Example 7.

```
(ATTRIBUTE_1         (  n:  ATTRIBUTE_2
                        n:  ATTRIBUTE_7
)                     )
(ATTRIBUTE_2         (  ATTRIBUTE_3
                        ATTRIBUTE_4
                        ATTRIBUTE_5
                        ATTRIBUTE_6
)                     )
(ATTRIBUTE_7         (  ATTRIBUTE_8
                        ATTRIBUTE_9
)                     )
```

4.4   A Concrete Example of Object-Level vs. Meta-Level Structure

Recall the project, mentioned earlier (in Subsec. 1.2), which encoded in nested relations Italy's regional constitutions (*Statuti Regionali*), trying to exploit their similarities [76]. The following Example 8 is the nested relation of the concept `Giunta_regionale`, that is, 'Regional Executive Council'. In the code shown, we are going to provide in detail only the representation of knowledge on how many members (i.e., regional aldermen, in Italian *assessori alla Regione*) belong to the Executive Councils of the various Regions:

Example 8.

```
(assign_frame      Giunta_regionale
   (  (DEFINITION  ( ( Every region has a Giunta_regionale )
                    ( The Giunta_regionale is the
                      Executive_organ of the Region      )
                    ( The Giunta_regionale has
                      one Presidente_della_Giunta and
                      many an Assessore_alla_Regione
```

```
                              (SEE  ATTRIBUTE  ALDERMEN  )            )
                         ( The Giunta_regionale usually has
                              one Vice_Presidente_della_Giunta    )
                    )
    (APPOINTMENT_MODALITIES        ...................... )
    (COMPETENCES                   ...................... )
    (ALDERMEN
       (HOW_MANY
         (  (IF              ( Region is Abruzzo )  )
            (VALUE_IS        (         10           )  )
         )
         (  (IF              ( Region is Basilicata )  )
            (VALUE_IS        (          6             )  )
         )
         (  (IF              ( Region is Calabria
                                or  Emilia-Romagna
                 )             )
            (VALUE_IS
              (AND
                  ( >=  8 )  ;  the same as:  ( at least 8 )
                  ( <= 12 )  ;  the same as:  ( at most 12 )
         )  )  )
         (  (IF        ( Region is Campania or Toscana )  )
            (VALUE_IS
              (AND
                  ( >=   #X / 10  )
                  ( <=   #X / 5  )
                  (DEFINE
                      ( #X  is  how many a
                            Consigliere_regionale
                            the Region has
         )  )  )  )  )
         (  (IF              ( Region is Lazio or Piemonte )  )
            (VALUE_IS        (         at most  12          )  )
         )
         (  (IF              ( Region is Liguria )  )
            (VALUE_IS        (   at most 9      )  )
         )
         (  (IF              ( Region is Lombardia )  )
            (VALUE_IS        (    at most  16      )  )
         )
         (  (IF              ( Region is Marche or Molise )  )
            (VALUE_IS        (         at most  8           )  )
         )
         (  (IF              ( Region is Puglia )  )
```

```
                    (VALUE_IS      (         12         ) )
             )
             (  (IF          ( Region is Umbria )  )
                (VALUE_IS      (          8         ) )
             )
             (  (IF          ( Region is Veneto )  )
                (VALUE_IS      ( at most one fifth of
                                how many a Consigliere_regionale
                                the Region has
             ) )                  )
             ...................................
       )  ;   end of  HOW_MANY
             ...................................
       )  ;   end of  ALDERMEN
             ...................................
)  )         ;   end of frame.
```

A relatively more concise representation, which however, would require a separate formulation of the criterion of interpretation, is the following, in Example 9:

Example 9.

```
(ALDERMEN
  (HOW_MANY
    ( (CRITERION              ( fixed number )  )
      (SCHEMA_OF_ATTRIBUTES    ( ( Region )  ( Value )  ) )
      (TYPE_OF_ATTRIBUTES      ( ( strings )  ( number )  ) )
      (RELATION
                      (  (  Abruzzo   )      ( 10 )   )
                      (  ( Basilicata )      (  6 )   )
                      (  (  Puglia    )      ( 12 )   )
                      (  (  Umbria    )      (  8 )   )
    ) )
    ( (CRITERION              ( at most )  )
      (SCHEMA_OF_ATTRIBUTES    ( ( Region )  ( at most )  ) )
      (TYPE_OF_ATTRIBUTES      ( ( strings )  ( number )  ) )
      (RELATION
                      (  ( Lazio  Piemonte )     ( 12 )   )
                      (  (     Liguria     )     (  9 )   )
                      (  (     Lombardia   )     ( 16 )   )
                      (  (  Marche   Molise )     (  8 )   )
    ) )
    ( (CRITERION              ( constantly delimited range )  )
      (SCHEMA_OF_ATTRIBUTES ( (Region )  (at least)  (at most)  ) )
      (TYPE_OF_ATTRIBUTES    ( (strings)  ( number )  (number )  ) )
      (RELATION    ( ( Calabria
```

```
                              Emilia-Romagna )   ( 8 )     ( 12 )    )
    ) )
    ( (CRITERION    ( depends on variable )   )
      (DEFINE       ( #X  is how many a Consigliere_regionale
                           the Region has
      )           )
      (SCHEMA_OF_ATTRIBUTES ( (Region ) (at least) (at most) ) )
      (TYPE_OF_ATTRIBUTES    ( (strings) ( text ) ( text ) ) )
      (RELATION     (   ( Campania  Toscana )
                        ( one tenth  of  #X )
                        ( one fifth  of  #X )
                    )
                    (   ( Veneto )
                        ( unspecified )
                        ( one fifth  of  #X )
) ) ) )                 )
```

In the case of the criterion constantly delimited range, only one instance — the chunk comprising the Calabria and Emilia-Romagna regions — occurs under RELATION; thus, having to define three more properties (CRITERION, SCHEMA_OF_ATTRIBUTES, and TYPE_OF_ATTRIBUTES) according to the new format of Example 9, yields, for the instance considered, a representation that is even more prolix than in Example 8.

Then, for the situation when the number of regional aldermen is constantly and explicitly delimited by a lower and an upper bound, the chunk identified by the key property

```
        ( (CRITERION ( constantly delimited range ) )
```

and repeated hereby for the reader's convenience (**Example 9′**):

```
( (CRITERION              ( constantly delimited range )  )
  (SCHEMA_OF_ATTRIBUTES ( ( Region  ) ( at least ) ( at most ) ) )
  (TYPE_OF_ATTRIBUTES   ( ( strings ) (  number  ) ( number ) ) )
  (RELATION    ( ( Calabria  Emilia-Romagna ) ( 8 )    ( 12 )    )
) )
```

could usefully be replaced by this other code (**Example 10**):

```
      (  (IF       ( Region is Calabria or Emilia-Romagna )  )
         (VALUE_IS  (AND ( at least 8 )   ( at most 12 ) )  )
      )
```

in the framework of the code of Example 9, but according to the format of Example 8. According to the syntax of the CuPROS metarepresentation language

we defined, such flexibility in the format of the frame portion under HOW_MANY
is expressed, in a global metarepresentation file, as follows (**Example 11**):

Example 11.

```
(executive_organism          ;   It is the kind of frame that
 ( DEFINITION                 ;   Giunta_regionale belongs to:
   APPOINTMENT_MODALITIES     ;   the attributes may appear at
   COMPETENCES                ;   the upper level of nesting.
   x: ALDERMEN       ;   x: stands for  "either... or..."
   x: MINISTERS      ;   and delimits one or more attributes.
 ) )


(ALDERMEN           ( HOW_MANY  ..........  )   )

(HOW_MANY           ( n:  if-value_chunk
                      n:  criterion-dependent_chunk  )  )

(if-value_chunk     ( i: IF              ; key.
                      VALUE_IS  )  )

(criterion-dependent_chunk
 ( i: CRITERION   ; key.
   DEFINE
   par: SCHEMA_OF_ATTRIBUTES (applies_to: RELATION)
   par: TYPE_OF_ATTRIBUTES  (applies_to: SCHEMA_OF_ATTRIBUTES)
   multi-par: RELATION
 ) )
```

The par: labels, in the last rule of Example 11, state that the ordered set
of elements given, in the object-level representation, as value of the attributes
SCHEMA_OF_ATTRIBUTES and TYPE_OF_ATTRIBUTES, have to be considered as
parallel. We have seen indeed, for instance, in Example 9′, that we have the
correspondence:

```
(SCHEMA_OF_ATTRIBUTES  ( ( Region  ) ( at least ) ( at most ) ) )
(TYPE_OF_ATTRIBUTES    ( ( strings ) (  number  ) ( number ) ) )
```

where the second property defines the type of the elements listed under the
first property, which, in turn, is the schema of a tabular relation, stated under the RELATION attribute. By contrast, the label multi-par: (which, in the
metarepresentation formulated in the last rule of Example 11, precedes the attribute RELATION) states that, in the object-level representation, the property
RELATION consists of the name of the attribute RELATION followed by a sequence
of rows in a table, that is, followed by a list of elements, each being parallel to
those properties, whose attribute name in the same metarepresentation rule is
preceded by the label par:

To specify some semantics for the attributes of the right-side part of the rule, the optional, parenthesised statement `applies_to`: that accompanies the attributes labelled with `par`: stipulates, in the last rule of Example 11, that the values of `TYPE_OF_ATTRIBUTES` are applied to the respective elements of `SCHEMA_OF_ATTRIBUTES` that, in turn, are applied to the respective elements of the rows of elements (rows) of `RELATION`. The inner level (elements of elements, instead of elements) is conventionally due to the label `multi-par`: that appears before RELATION, instead of the `par`: label.

The intricacy of the `par`: and `multi-par`: syntax is due to the fact that they define the metarepresentation of properties that, in turn, are a local metarepresentation inserted in object-level representation code (indeed, the attribute `SCHEMA_OF_ATTRIBUTES` defines a syntactic schema for attributes included in the same chunk of object-level representation, while `TYPE_OF_ATTRIBUTES` defines some *data semantics*, corresponding to the local syntactic metarepresentation provided by `SCHEMA_OF_ATTRIBUTES`). These features of our metarepresentation language are meant to enhance its expressive flexibility, but are not indispensable, if one adopts our representation formalism: indeed, one can adopt the schema of Example 8, which is simpler than the schema of Example 9. Further details of the metarepresentation in Nissan's *Statuti Regionali* project can be found in [76] and — in the present Choueka Jubilee set of volumes — in [85, Sec. 3].

5   XML Comes into the Picture

5.1   General Considerations

XML, the Extensible Markup Language, is currently a very popular representation language. It is at the foundation of the field known now as the *semantic Web*. Now XML is even appearing as a data type in some other languages. The popularity of XML stems from its role as a standard within Web technology (it was endorsed institutionally), and is reflected in a multitude of languages and applications making use of it, as well as in a literature comprising textbooks or reference books [53, 35, 62], conference proceedings [24, 9, 120], and dissertations [58], as well as in reports in the information media.

The project described in this article, RAFFAELLO, originated in the 1980s, independently of SGML (the Standard Generalized Markup Language), that itself was later simplified into XML, with which our approach is compatible, and of which it is a precursor. Most of XML comes from SGML unchanged. Our own project in knowledge-representation in deeply nested relations, flexibly structured, with no limit on the depth of the nesting, and with retrieval guided by metadata, originated separately from XML's parent language, namely, SGML [29, 10, 101, 100], which was also designed in the 1980s, and is defined in ISO Standard 8879. SGML enabled a formal definition of the component parts of a publishable data set, and when designed, it was primarily intended as a tool enabling publishable data (such as technical documentation) to be interchanged between, e.g., authors or originators, and publishers. By the late 1980s, early digital media publishers had understood the versatility of SGML for dynamic information display. The main historical interest now of SGML is that it was simplified into XML. This ought to be enough for preserving interest in SGML.

5.2   The Significance of the Rise of XML for the Precursor Status of RAFFAELLO and the Deeply Nested Relations from Which It Retrieves

The spread of XML vindicated the project that is the subject of the present paper and that the present authors developed earlier, independently of SGML, the parent-language of XML (SGML was originally devised for communicating structured documents). At the apex of our own project, there was the NAVIGATION component of the RAFFAELLO retrieval system. The latter was originally devised for managing the deeply nested, flexible relations that constituted the lexical database of the ONOMATURGE expert system for Hebrew word-formation. Whereas RAFFAELLO within ONOMATURGE was a simpler version, such that retrieval was done by means of retrieval functions implemented in LISP and reflecting the actual structure of the nested relations as known beforehand, the version of NAVIGATION that was implemented by El-Sana under Nissan's supervision used a metadata schema.[4]

The unabated interest in XML, Web technology, and ontologies (an area relevant for the database of ONOMATURGE) have vindicated Nissan's contention that *nested relations* (a research area in database design) should be allowed not only unlimited depth of nesting, but also extreme flexibility of structure. This is now taken for granted because of how metadata are defined for XML, but the feasibility of the idea was shown by El-Sana's managing to implement retrieval as based on metadata description, along the lines of CuProS syntax: as seen, the syntax for describing metadata in RAFFAELLO was in a language defined by Nissan, CuProS (short for *Customization Production System*).

5.3   Well-Formedness in XML and the SIMPLE NAVIGATION Version of RAFFAELLO, vs. the Validity of an XML Document and the CuProS-Directed NAVIGATION Version of RAFFAELLO

There is one aspect of XML that was first formalised in XML, but had been first successfully implemented in a number of projects, one of these being in lexicography: the software from the University of Waterloo New Oxford English Dictionary Project. That aspect is the notion of well-formedness, as opposed to validity. Well-formedness enables parsing without a schema. By contrast, an XML document being valid means that it contains a reference to a schema (a Document Type Definition, or DTD), and abides by that schema. The schema itself is a grammar. There are various schema languages for XML. The oldest of these is DTD, which XML inherited from SGML. But XML DTDs are simpler than SGML DTDs.

---

[4] Whereas a few articles about RAFFAELLO were published, none explained CuProS and the NAVIGATION tool as implemented by El-Sana.

The distinction between well-formedness and validity in XML is at the heart of the difference between the various versions of RAFFAELLO. A well-formed XML document can be parsed without a schema. The versions of RAFFAELLO that carry out retrieval from deeply nested relations according to an input retrieval path, and do not consult the metarepresentation, are able to do so because the nested relation they access is well-formed. These were the SIMPLE NAVIGATION versions of RAFFAELLO.

By contrast, the NAVIGATION version of RAFFAELLO that was implemented by El-Sana carries out the retrieval by being directed by the metarepresentation (a grammar) coded in CuProS and which the retrieval program consults, in order to be able to navigate correctly. Thus, it is essential that the nested relation abides by the metarepresentation, and this foregrounds the notion of validity, as being now familiar from XML.

It must be said however that (as can be seen from the PROLOG code in Appendix C) even the NAVIGATION version of RAFFAELLO was exclusively guided by the metarepresentation: some of the PROLOG predicates were customised for features in the structure of a particular terminological database. Nevertheless, NAVIGATION was the most important step forward, in generalising RAFFAELLO. The next step would have been to produce a more sophisticated version, which would replace that subset of the NAVIGATION predicates with ones which would not be tailored for an attribute taken to be a constant, but could treat it instead as a variable, within a context entirely dictated by the metarepresentation.

5.4   A Project for Traslating Our Representation into XML

In 2001, Monica Larussa did as a BSc project in London — under the supervision of Ala Al-Zobaidie and Ephraim Nissan — some preparatory work [52] (including some preliminary code in JAVA) for the project building a translator into XML from nested relations as described by a metarepresentation coded in CuProS. Because of reasons other than any technical problem inherent in the project (it rather was the departure of one of the co-investigators), this did not develop further.

And yet, if the kind of representation that is associated with the lexical frames of ONOMATURGE and with a sequel multilingual project [79] hopefully comes to be known better, it stands to reason that developing such a translator would be a worthwhile undertaking. What is more, it would be a relatively simple software project.

A possibility that was envisaged was to resort to YACC, as being a widespread tool for the construction of compilers for programming languages, in order to handle at least part of the translation from CuProS-regulated nested-relation representations into XML, and from the CuProS-coded metarepresentation itself into the *Document Type Definition* (*DTD*) that describes admissible structures of the semantic attributes with respect to each other, the way they can appear inside the XML document.

6   For Comparison: Data and Metadata in XML

It is typical for webpages to be coded in HTML: labels of HTML are interspersed within the textual content, and the identifiers of graphic material. HTML handles presentation, not content, which is what XML is supposed to do. If one was to search an HTML Web page for content, one could only look for the occurrences of given strings. This is because the only function of the syntax of HTML is to structure the presentation, regardless of the meaning of the content. In XML, instead, the syntax is meant to describe the semantics of the content, whereas a separate module, called a stylesheet, states how the syntactic units extracted from an XML document are to be displayed. It is not the case that the entire content of the stored data has to be displayed, only their layout will be different. In fact, it may be possible to only extract some of the information, as enclosed by given tags which constitute semantic attributes; it's the data retrieved in response to a query that will be displayed as instructed by the stylesheet, and the query itself is actually specified inside the stylesheet along with the specification of how to display the results. Furthermore, a separate module, called DTD (for *Document Type Definition*) will describe admissible structures of the semantic attributes with respect to each other, the way they can appear inside the XML document. That is to say, the DTD is the schema of a database, whose instances are the respective XML documents.

There are some minor problems with terminology, when dealing with both XML and databases, because the term 'attribute' and the term 'entity' are used differently in the XML literature and in the database literature. Here is a standard XML definition for 'attribute': "A name-value pair, separated by an equals sign, included inside a tagged element that modifies certain features of the element. All attribute values, including things like size and width, are in fact text strings and not numbers. For XML, all values must be enclosed in quotation marks". This is very much like some HTML declarations of tables, or of the inclusion of images, and the like. What is meant by 'attribute' in database terminology, is called an 'element' in the jargon of XML, and what in database terminology is 'the value of the attribute', in XML is the content of the element. If a string, this is referred to as data of the PCDATA type. If, instead, something is nested inside the current element, then this aggregate is made of sub-elements of that element.

Consider a database relation schema, whose attributes ("attributes" as meant in database terminology, that is, "elements" in XML) are: FORENAMES, SURNAME, EMPLOYMENT, PLACE_OF_RESIDENCE, MARITAL_STATUS, DEPENDENTS, and REFERENCES.

One straightforward way to represent in XML such a relation for the given individual, Donald Duck, would be to simply enclose the value of each relation attribute between two tags, <FORENAME> and </FORENAME>, and so forth:

```
<PERSON>
        <FORENAMES>      Donald          </FORENAMES>
        <SURNAME>        Duck            </SURNAME>
        <EMPLOYMENT>     unemployed      </EMPLOYMENT>
```

```
            <PLACE_OF_RESIDENCE>  Duckburg  </PLACE_OF_RESIDENCE>
            <PLACE_OF_BIRTH>  Granny McDuck's Farm  </PLACE_OF_BIRTH>
            <MARITAL_STATUS>  unmarried  </MARITAL_STATUS>
            <DEPENDENTS>        Hewey              </DEPENDENTS>
            <DEPENDENTS>        Louie              </DEPENDENTS>
            <DEPENDENTS>        Dewey              </DEPENDENTS>
            <REFERENCES>        Scrooge McDuck     </REFERENCES>
            <REFERENCES>        Daisy Duck         </REFERENCES>
            <REFERENCES>        Mickey Mouse       </REFERENCES>
</PERSON>
```

Such a slavish rendering into XML of the database relation lifted from a relational database grossly underexploits the capabilities of XML. To start with, mainstream relational database technology stores the data in flat relations, that is, tables. In the 1980s and early 1990s, several database researchers tried to promote an alternative kind of relational databases, in which tables could be nested inside each other, or, to say it otherwise, attributes may be nested as being the value of another attribute. In artificial intelligence representations, too, frames usually are hierarchies of properties: the values are the terminal nodes in a tree with, say, three generations. Conceptually, such were some of the ideas that can be detected behind the rise of XML, as being a coding in which you can actually nest any levels of attributes inside each other. For example, the same XML file could store a much richer relation than the above, still for the individual whose name is Donald Duck:

```
<PERSON>
        <NAME>
            <FORENAME>  Donald   </FORENAME>
            <SURNAME>
                        <CURRENT>    Duck     </CURRENT>
                        <AS_RECORDED_AT_BIRTH>
            </SURNAME>
        </NAME>
        <EMPLOYMENT_RECORD>
            <CURRENT_EMPLOYMENT>
                    unemployed
            </CURRENT_EMPLOYMENT>
            <PREVIOUS_EMPLOYMENT>
                        <CATEGORY>    sailor      </CATEGORY>
                        <CATEGORY>    farm hand   </CATEGORY>
                        <FROM>        1936        </FROM>
                        <UNTIL>       1937        </UNTIL>
            </PREVIOUS_EMPLOYMENT>
            <PREVIOUS_EMPLOYMENT>
                        <CATEGORY> factotum     </CATEGORY>
                        <EMPLOYER> Scrooge McDuck </EMPLOYER>
```

```
                    <WHEN>        often          </WHEN>
                    <MODE> short-term informal contract </MODE>
            </PREVIOUS_EMPLOYMENT>
        </EMPLOYMENT_RECORD>
        <PLACE_OF_RESIDENCE>
                <TOWN>          Duckburg       </TOWN>
                <STATE>         California     </STATE>
        </PLACE_OF_RESIDENCE>
        <PLACE_OF_BIRTH>
                <PLACE> Granny McDuck's Farm   </PLACE>
                <COUNTY>        Duckburg       </COUNTY>
                <STATE>         California     </STATE>
        </PLACE_OF_BIRTH>
        <MARITAL_STATUS>  unmarried   </MARITAL_STATUS>
        <DEPENDENTS>
            <MINOR>
                    <NEPHEW>      Hewey    </NEPHEW>
                    <NEPHEW>      Louie    </NEPHEW>
                    <NEPHEW>      Dewey    </NEPHEW>
            </MINOR>
            <SENIOR>
                    <UNCLE>     Scrooge McDuck    </UNCLE>
            </SENIOR>
        </DEPENDENTS>
        <REFERENCES>        Daisy Duck      </REFERENCES>
        <REFERENCES>        Mickey Mouse    </REFERENCES>
</PERSON>
```

The syntax of XML requires that the hierarchical structure have one and just one root, which here is PERSON. This happens to be the case with nested relations from which retrieval is handled by RAFFAELLO. This was the case of lexical frames in the database of the ONOMATURGE expert system for word-formation, as well as of a few other applications of the database concept.

Let the XML code of the example given above be stored in a file called duck1.xml It will have to be preceded by two initial XML statements, respectively specifying under which version of XML and with which alphanumeric encoding that file has to be processed; and to which stylesheet type and given stylesheet file the given XML file should be linked:

```
<?xml version="1.0" encoding="UTF-8"?>
<?xml-stylesheet type="text/xsl"  href="nicestyle3.xsl"?>
```

Now, let us define the DTD for the XML nested relation in which we stored information about Donald Duck. We want to state that:

- The root element is PERSON
- The root element contains one NAME element

- The root element contains zero or one elements of each of the following: EMPLOYMENT_RECORD, PLACE_OF_RESIDENCE, PLACE_OF_BIRTH (it may be absent for some reason), MARITAL_STATUS (it also may be absent, for example if unknown, or not relevant, or even deliberately withheld), and MARITAL_STATUS may or may not include an element SPOUSE.
- The root element contains zero or more elements of each of the following: DEPENDENTS (not everybody has other people legally depending on him or her), REFERENCES.
- Each NAME element is expected to contain either one or more strings (the symbol standing for a string in a DTD is #PCDATA), or one or more FORENAME and one or more SURNAME, and moreover, these may contain just a value, or, then, zero or more CURRENT, PREVIOUS, and AS_RECORDED_AT_BIRTH. The symbol | stands for 'or'.
- Element EMPLOYMENT_RECORD may include one or more strings, or then, zero or more elements for CURRENT_EMPLOYMENT and for PREVIOUS_EMPLOYMENT, and these possibly contain a further level of nesting, including zero or more CATEGORY elements and zero or one FROM, UNTIL, or WHEN elements.
- Elements PLACE_OF_RESIDENCE and PLACE_OF_BIRTH include some string, or zero or one PLACE, COUNTY, STATE, and COUNTRY.
- DEPENDENTS may include some string, or zero or more of: MINOR, SENIOR.
- SPOUSE, REFERENCES, or elements inside MINOR or SENIOR may each include just a string, or a NAME element, or a LINK_TO_PERSON element.
- MINOR may include one or more of: CHILD,GRANDCHILD, NEPHEW, GREATNEPHEW, and COUSIN.
- SENIOR may include zero or more of: PARENT, GRANDPARENT, UNCLE, GREATUNCLE, and COUSIN (a child may be grown-up and thus no longer of minor age, yet be otherwise legally a minor)

The DTD is coded as follows.

```
<?xml version="1.0"?>
<!ELEMENT    PERSON   (NAME, EMPLOYMENT_RECORD+,
                       PLACE_OF_RESIDENCE+,  PLACE_OF_BIRTH+,
                       MARITAL_STATUS+, DEPENDENTS*, REFERENCES*)>
<!ELEMENT    NAME        (#PCDATA+ | (FORENAME*, SURNAME*))>
<!ELEMENT    FORENAME
                (#PCDATA+ | (CURRENT*, PREVIOUS*,
                             AS_RECORDED_AT_BIRTH*))>
<!ELEMENT    SURNAME    (#PCDATA+ | (CURRENT*,
                         PREVIOUS*, AS_RECORDED_AT_BIRTH*))>
<!ELEMENT    CURRENT    (#PCDATA*)>
<!ELEMENT    PREVIOUS   (#PCDATA*)>
<!ELEMENT    AS_RECORDED_AT_BIRTH    (#PCDATA*)>
<!ELEMENT    EMPLOYMENT_RECORD
                (#PCDATA+ | (CURRENT_EMPLOYMENT*,
                             PREVIOUS_EMPLOYMENT*))>
<!ELEMENT    CURRENT_EMPLOYMENT
             (#PCDATA+ | (CATEGORY*, FROM+, UNTIL+, WHEN+))>
```

```
<!ELEMENT   PREVIOUS_EMPLOYMENT
                (#PCDATA+ | (CATEGORY*, FROM+, UNTIL+, WHEN+))>
<!ELEMENT   PLACE_OF_RESIDENCE
                (#PCDATA+ | (PLACE+, COUNTY+, STATE+, COUNTRY+))>
<!ELEMENT   PLACE_OF_BIRTH
                (#PCDATA+ | (PLACE+, COUNTY+, STATE+, COUNTRY+))>
<!ELEMENT   MARITAL_STATUS  (#PCDATA*, SPOUSE*)>
<!ELEMENT   DEPENDENTS  (#PCDATA*, MINOR*, SENIOR*)>
<!ELEMENT   MINOR  (#PCDATA*, CHILD*, GRANDCHILD*,
                    NEPHEW*, GREATNEPHEW*, COUSIN*)>
<!ELEMENT   SENIOR (#PCDATA*, PARENT*, GRANDPARENT*,
                    UNCLE*, GREATUNCLE*, COUSIN*)>
<!ELEMENT   SPOUSE     (#PCDATA*, NAME+, LINK_TO_PERSON)>
<!ELEMENT   LINK_TO_PERSON    (#PCDATA*)>
<!ELEMENT   CHILDN     (#PCDATA*, NAME+, LINK_TO_PERSON)>
<!ELEMENT   PARENT     (#PCDATA*, NAME+, LINK_TO_PERSON)>
<!ELEMENT   GRANDPARENT  (#PCDATA*, NAME+, LINK_TO_PERSON)>
<!ELEMENT   UNCLE   (#PCDATA*, NAME+, LINK_TO_PERSON)>
<!ELEMENT   GREATUNCLE    (#PCDATA*, NAME+, LINK_TO_PERSON)>
<!ELEMENT   NEPHEW    (#PCDATA*, NAME+, LINK_TO_PERSON)>
<!ELEMENT   GEATNEPHEW    (#PCDATA*, NAME+, LINK_TO_PERSON)>
<!ELEMENT   COUSIN    (#PCDATA*, NAME+, LINK_TO_PERSON)>
<!ELEMENT   PLACE     (#PCDATA*)>
<!ELEMENT   COUNTY    (#PCDATA*)>
<!ELEMENT   STATE     (#PCDATA*)>
<!ELEMENT   COUNTRY   (#PCDATA*)>
<!ELEMENT   CATEGORY  (#PCDATA*)>
<!ELEMENT   FROM      (#PCDATA*)>
<!ELEMENT   UNTIL     (#PCDATA*)>
<!ELEMENT   WHEN      (#PCDATA*)>
```

The meaning of the notation can be understood by comparing this code with the explanation with which it was foreworded. The following is an example of nested relation coded in XML, and representing an aspect of the content of this quotation from the very beginning of a paper in literary studies, "Falstaff's Monster", by Clayton Mackenzie [54], concerning the plot of a famous Shakespeare play:

> In *1 Henry IV*, II.iv, Falstaff presents his account of the Gadshill fiasco. What begins as 'two rogues in buckram suits' (line 184) grows to four (lines 188–9), then to seven (line 194), then to nine (line 204) and ends as a veritable army of eleven men in buckram (line 210) all assailing the beleaguered hero.

As an exercise, we represent the content of this quotation in XML, by analysing its sense into hierarchy of XML elements rooted in account. We are only interested in Falstaff's account, and nothing else, focusing on its consecutive

variants by which the number of rogues is increased from time to time.[5] Note the
use we are making of linking values such as `Tag1` and the like, to which we are
giving a meaning as though they were variables, which, however, is something
XML does not know about. It's only the user, and the user's queries, that will
have to take this meaning into account.

```xml
<?xml version="1.0" encoding="UTF-8"?>
<?xml-stylesheet type="text/xsl"  href="nicestyle3.xsl"?>


<account>
  <about>
      <event>              Gadshill fiasco      </event>
      <protagonist>        Falstaff             </protagonist>
  </about>
  <reported_by>            Falstaff      </reported_by>
  <textual_reference>
      <identifying_tag> Tag1             </identifying_tag>
      <play>
              <title>    Henry the Fourth    </title>
              <part>     1                   </part>
              <act>      2                   </act>
              <scene>    4                   </scene>
      </play>
  </textual_reference>
  <content>
      <sub-event>
          <identifying_tag>    Tag2      </identifying_tag>
          <action>
                  <is>         assault      </is>
                  <is>         fight        </is>
                  <agent>      Tag3         </agent>
                  <object>     Tag4         </object>
          </action>
          <action>
                  <is>         fight back   </is>
                  <agent>      Tag4         </agent>
                  <object>     Tag3         </object>
          </action>
      </sub-event>
```

---

[5] Actually, the dialogue in the play is even more complex. All of the following is taken
from Falstaff's own words: "a hundred upon poor four of us", "at half-sword with a
dozen of them two hours together", "Sixteen, at least, my lord", and so forth. The
rogues clad in clothing of buckram are the supposed assailants whom Falstaff claims
to have killed in a fight. He actually was trying to rob innocent travellers, but this
is irrelevant for the encoding to be generated, as this exercise is only interested in
an aspect of his own account.

```
    <sequence>  Tag2    <contains/>    Tag5    </sequence>
    <sub-event>
        <identifying_tag>    Tag5      </identifying_tag>
        <action>
                <is>        kill        </is>
                <agent>     Falstaff    </agent>
                <object>    Tag6        </object>
        </action>
    </sub-event>
</content>
<explain_the_tags>
    <explain_this_tag>
            <tag_is>      Tag3        </tag_is>
            <tag_means>
                        <some/> rogues
            </tag_means>
    </explain_this_tag>
    <explain_this_tag>
            <tag_is>      Tag4        </tag_is>
            <tag_means>
                    Tag4  <contains/> Falstaff
            </tag_means>
    </explain_this_tag>
    <explain_this_tag>
            <tag_is>      Tag6        </tag_is>
            <tag_means>
                    Tag3  <contains/> Tag6
            </tag_means>
            <tag_means>
                        <some/> men
            </tag_means>
            <tag_means>
                    <description>
                        clad in buckram suits
                    </description>
                    <how_many>
                        <claim>
                            <number> 2  </number>
                            <according_to>
                                <version_of_account> 1
                                </version_of_account>
                                <textual_reference>
                                    <in>  Tag1 </in>
                                    <line> 184 </line>
                                </textual_reference>
```

```
                    </according_to>
          </claim>
          <claim>
               <number>  4  </number>
               <according_to>
                  <version_of_account> 2
                  </version_of_account>
                  <textual_reference>
                    <in> Tag1 </in>
                    <line> 188-189 </line>
                  </textual_reference>
               </according_to>
          </claim>
          <claim>
               <number>  7  </number>
               <according_to>
                    <version_of_account> 3
                    </version_of_account>
                    <textual_reference>
                       <in> Tag1 </in>
                       <line> 194 </line>
                    </textual_reference>
               </according_to>
          </claim>
          <claim>
               <number>  9  </number>
               <according_to>
                    <version_of_account> 4
                    </version_of_account>
                    <textual_reference>
                       <in> Tag1 </in>
                       <line> 204 </line>
                    </textual_reference>
               </according_to>
          </claim>
          <claim>
               <number>  11  </number>
               <according_to>
                    <version_of_account> 5
                    </version_of_account>
                    <textual_reference>
                       <in> Tag1 </in>
                       <line> 210 </line>
                    </textual_reference>
               </according_to>
```

```
            </claim>
          </how_many>
        </tag_means>
      </explain_this_tag>
<account>
```

7 Early Versions of RAFFAELLO

7.1 The Basics: RAFFAELLO's Original Tasks

The retrieval component is the main component of RAFFAELLO, so much so that we have been describing the latter as being a toolkit for retrieval. Within ONOMATURGE, all aspects of handling the nested relations were conceptually associated with RAFFAELLO. Originally, RAFFAELLO was developed in FRANZ LISP, for it to perform some given tasks supporting the ONOMATURGE expert system. The main component of RAFFAELLO is the one that, invoked by the LISP control of an expert system, retrieves the requested data from the proper location inside deeply nested frames. In ONOMATURGE, this component is intensively resorted to, in order to access the frame-base. Another component of RAFFAELLO had the task of interfacing the LISP control of an expert system with a possibly outer program-base, through the C and Shell or CShell languages of UNIX. In ONOMATURGE, this serves the purposes of one of its architectural components, the MORPHOLOGICAL COINER when it needs to have lexical derivation or compounding programs triggered (disregarding the fact they are functions defined in LISP, or Shell or CShell programs).

There also was a third task, ascribed to a particular component of RAFFAELLO, and conceived with ONOMATURGE in mind, but not integrated in that expert system. That component was concerned with output-acquisition, as being a form of machine-learning. Thus, as seen, the pool of tasks of RAFFAELLO within the ONOMATURGE project was broader that merely carrying out retrieval. In a sense, those functions of ONOMATURGE that were of general interest for knowledge-based systems, and were not specific for computational linguistics, were ideally moved within the delimitation of RAFFAELLO.

7.2 Why a Production-System as Metarepresentation, While the Object-Level Is in Nested-Relation Frames?

The very choice of how to structure the relations in the database, the decision to have a meta-level representation, and the decision to have it in the form of a ruleset (in practice, a grammar), was taken by Nissan early in his doctoral project.[6] By that time, the very idea of *knowledge-representation metadescriptive languages* was already found in the scholarly literature (in [31, Sec. 6], and in [28]). Greiner [31, Sec. 6] termed such a language, a *representation language language* (or *rll* for short); the language RLL-1 he introduced and described was

---

[6] This subsection is based on [75, Subsec. 7.2.2.8].

intended to be a *proto-rll,* that is the first of a class of knowledge-representation metalanguages. According to Greiner, "every part of an rll system must be visible", that is: the rll should be self-describing; every component of an rll (slots, data types, modes of inheritance, data-accessing function) must be explicitly represented in the system [31, Subsec. 6.1].

Even earlier, in the 1970s, in databases, attributes were already being described by means of a *data dictionary.* Integrated *metadata* management provides a sort of self-description in the database [55]. In the database design literature, this is the equivalent of metarepresentation as found in the knowledge representation sector. The difference mainly stems from the difference in the object-level representation models.

More in general, *metamodelling* investigates reasoning and knowledge acquisition processes as used in *modelling,* that is to say, in the representation of reality to obtain knowledge for problem solving. Not limited to computing, *metamodelling* fits in the systemic approach to organization and management, and concerns the design of systems to control banking or financial systems, health care systems, the environment, and so forth.[7]

According to Greiner's 1980 approach to metarepresentation, frames are described by frames. Each attribute is also the owner of a frame (at a metalevel), where information is found that describes the conventions about the attribute. Nevertheless, Greiner mentioned pedagogic difficulties with the use of levels of frame-representations. In Nissan's CuPROS approach, a production system states the legal class of hierarchical structures inside frames. Each rule expresses the legal childset of a given attribute.[8]

---

[7] For example, van Gigch had been publishing epistemic papers in metamodelling [109, 110]. But this was within general systems theory [107], a rather unprestigious area of scholarship, arguably for good reason. Conferences in the domain certainly used to be omnia gatherum, if not anything goes. At any rate, [111] is a book on metamodelling in decision making. Van Gigch [108] discussed the relation between *metadesign* and system failure, and also elaborated about the difference between modelling and metamodelling. At the time, van Gigch was affiliated with the School of Business and Public Administration at California State University in Sacramento.

[8] It can be shown that CuPROS production systems are related to *tree-grammars.* As soon as 1973, Barry K. Rosen defined *subtree replacement systems* [92]. In formal language theory (this is well known), *grammars* are *generating devices,* whereas *automata* are *accepting devices.* Metarepresentation with RAFFAELLO as being automatically processed in its version called NAVIGATION (which, anyway, consults it, does not compile it), concerns the *accepting* side of the medal. As being dual with *graph-grammars,* Witt [118] formally defined *finite graph-automata* as *graph-acceptors.* By contrast, our implementations (Nissan's in LISP, and El-Sana's in PROLOG) of NAVIGATION was *ad hoc,* with no sound formal support. John Barnden, at a conference talk, subdivided (not the first one to do so) scholars and practitioners of artificial intelligence into two branches: the *messies,* and the *neaties.* The neaties are the theorists. The others are the messies, and the term is not used with any derogatory intention. CuPROS (like most of Nissan's work in artificial intelligence) fits in the messies' camp. Not that the two camps have been doing war on each other. Rather, they have been complementary, in the history of the discipline.

A rule expressed in CuPros may be considered to be an attribute/value tree with only one level: the left-hand side and the right-hand side may be considered to be, each, a property. In order to describe the semantics of attributes, one should augment the internal structure of each rule in the metarepresentation, with *meta-attributes* other than FATHER (that is, the left-hand side) and CHILDSET (that is, the right-hand side). Thus, the metarepresentation would be brought back to metalevel frames.

Nissan had found out however that — from the software engineering viewpoint — keeping all of the "genealogical" information on attributes in one structure (a production system) is an easy style of metaknowledge acquisition. Further, semantic details may follow (possibly in another structure). Strings that synonymously refer to the same attribute are listed in a different structure (a list of synonym-lists, in RAFFAELLO). We preferred to *separate* such structures that are meant to store those secondary details: stating such full-fledged metaknowledge details would cause the advancing front of the knowledge analysis (it was feared) to slow down. In Nissan's experience with frame-bases, *attribute genealogy* is the proper carrier of the thrust forward, in this analysis. Now, a *production system* as metarepresentation allows to *focus* on attribute genealogy. By contrast, metarepresentational *frames* would lead you to *schedule* entering secondary details early, together with the genealogical information for each attribute: Nissan believed that this is undesirable. Good metarepresentation structures ought to elicit a proper style of metarepresentation.

7.3   SIMPLE NAVIGATION vs. NAVIGATION

The earlier three versions of RAFFAELLO were implemented in 1984–1986. None of those versions actually required the metarepresentation, which was defined nevertheless within ONOMATURGE, in order to regulate the structure of its nested relations, and enable it to be flexible. During that stage, the metarepresentation was still only a tool for humans, rather than a tool for an automated component to make use of it.

We have already seen that at the metalevel of representation, a schema — a metarepresentation — stating what is valid nesting among attributes, is drawn in terms of a *production system* (a ruleset, in practice a formal grammar) augmented with the syntax of the CuPros language of metarepresentation; that language was specifically defined by Nissan in the framework of the RAFFAELLO project. That syntax was defined especially in 1984–1985, in connection with the first application to ONOMATURGE.

As opposed to the *metalevel,* the *object level* of representation is constituted by instances of nested relations, whose internal organisation of attributes fits in a space of possibilities as allowed by the metarepresentation. Instances describing the same kind of object are allowed to look even very differently, when it comes to the hierarchy of nested attributes: nevertheless, such freedom is constrained by the specifications in the metarepresentation.

The retrieval component comes in two branches of versions: SIMPLE NAVIGATION, vs. NAVIGATION. Of the latter, a partial implementation was first done in LISP by Nissan, but the fuller specification of NAVIGATION only came to fuller fruition when El-Sana implemented it. SIMPLE NAVIGATION is the version that Nissan integrated into ONOMATURGE as being his own doctoral project. In 1984–1985, Nissan implemented low-level parts of SIMPLE NAVIGATION: basic retrieval functions, attribute-synonymy management, and so forth. In 1984–1986, SIMPLE NAVIGATION was developed and applied to ONOMATURGE, as being (*per se*) a clonable program-base specialised in the internal topology of frames structured as deeply nested relations. In 1986–1987, SIMPLE NAVIGATION was applied to FIDEL GASTRO, an expert system for short-term planning in large kitchens.

A more sophisticated version is NAVIGATION. Retrieval, as performed by NAVIGATION, proceeds by consulting the query, the metarepresentation, and the concerned instances of nested relations. This way, NAVIGATION is independent from the application-domain, from which it is uncoupled by means of the application-dependent metarepresentation.

On the other hand, SIMPLE NAVIGATION is an alternative version, consisting of a modular program-base that can be cloned for specific applications. A customisation of SIMPLE NAVIGATION is easily constructed by the human developer consulting the metarepresentation that was previously drawn as a specification, design and reference tool, but the programs themselves do not consult the metarepresentation. The human developer consults it, in order to adapt or compose retrieval functions needed by the control. In fact, SIMPLE NAVIGATION is a module-base of retrieval functions, specialised for a taxonomy of topological situations of property-nesting inside frames. Only the low-level functions of SIMPLE NAVIGATION exhibit some intricacy, and once Nissan had coded them, there was no need to touch them again; rather, those functions that are defined to retrieve the value (or the subframe) found in a specific attribute described in the metarepresentation were very simple, composable, and easily reused in new applications.[9]

The ideal respective role of NAVIGATION and SIMPLE NAVIGATION suits different phases of the development of an expert system. NAVIGATION is suited for early phases when the creative impetus should not be fettered by rote tasks of providing an (efficient) access from the control programs of the expert system being developed, to knowledge chunks that are being developed.

In such perspective, SIMPLE NAVIGATION can be customised for the application in later, calmer moments in the development process. Once the control programs of the expert system have been shaped, and it is clear what information

---

[9] In the application to ONOMATURGE, the retrieval functions of SIMPLE NAVIGATION were stored in several directories (i.e., folders). Each directory includes one or several retrieval functions, being either simple compositions of other functions, or simple functions that are "drains" (terminal "leaves") in the direct acyclic graph of invoking among the functions of the customisation of SIMPLE NAVIGATION for ONOMATURGE. Terminal functions of the customisation invoke lower-level functions of SIMPLE NAVIGATION, that is, such functions that their code does not need to be touched when customising SIMPLE NAVIGATION for a knowledge-based system.

is needed at what points, NAVIGATION queries can be replaced by invocations to modules of the customised SIMPLE NAVIGATION, which no longer involve the steps taken in the general case by NAVIGATION, but instead are specialised for given paths of retrieval as preferred by the control programs of the particular application.

One of the motivations of our approach to metarepresentation finds application not only in the framework of NAVIGATION (which has to consult it), but more in general in RAFFAELLO. Metarepresentation is a handy tool during the the specification, knowledge analysis, design, and knowledge-acquisition phases (including instance coding). The metarepresentation specifies the statics of the knowledge-base. The control of the application is woven by referring to the set of attributes that are already present in the metarepresentation, and by motivating the insertion of new attributes.

In the SIMPLE NAVIGATION version, alternative to NAVIGATION, the metarepresentation is not consulted by that program while it is running, but the customisation of SIMPLE NAVIGATION for a given application is developed according to the specific needs of the control programs of the application, and the programmer constantly refers to the metarepresentation while he or she composes modules to retrieve specifically along preferred paths.

See in Fig. 1 how the control of NAVIGATION proceeds, on processing a query, once the frame involved has been loaded. The top level of frames is processed in a slightly different manner with respect to nested levels, because on processing the top level, low-level functions invoked resort to property-retrieval functions in FRANZ LISP, but eventually El-Sana implemented the system in PROLOG). On processing inner levels of nesting, instead, NAVIGATION has to make headway on its own, recursively for each level. As shown in Fig. 1, three data-structures are considered concomitantly: the path provided in the query, the metarepresentation, and the frame-instance as reduced to a currently relevant subtree.

Different kinds of actions have to be taken, whenever the currently considered token in the path provided by the query is an attribute-name, as opposed to a value (interpreted as identifying a slotless facet). The test is: "Consult the next token, $Y := TOKEN(j)$, in the path provided by the query". If the token is an attribute, then consult production, $P(j)$, with $TOKEN(j)$ as left-hand side. But if the token is a value instead (interpreted as identifying a slotless facet), then Y is needed to identify the proper facet instance in a sequence of nested facets with a similar nesting-schema (i.e., the same production).

Besides, one should consider also that data-structures in RAFFAELLO include a list of lists of synonymy among attribute-names. For example, MORPHO_CAT is the same as MORPHOLOGICAL_CATEGORY in the lexical frames of ONOMATURGE. Such equivalent attribute-names are handled by SIMPLE NAVIGATION. The same feature could be added to NAVIGATION.

In 1986, a core of NAVIGATION was implemented that tackles the major syntactic features of the CUPROS metarepresentation language; implementers are students of the *Expert Systems* course taught at the time by Nissan; those students were Ofer Hasson, Orly Priva, Ilan Shaked and Ronen Varsano. A fuller

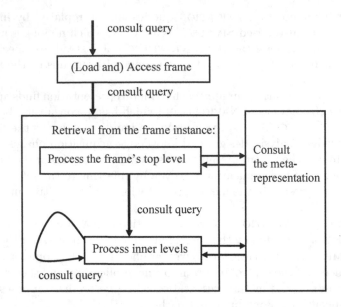

Fig. 1. An outline of the control flow in NAVIGATION

version was implemented from scratch by El-Sana, that also resorted to a different programming language in order to do so.

There also was a third version, a rather early one, of the retrieval component of RAFFAELLO: it retrieves from nested relations that are reconstructed after having been mapped onto INGRES flat relations.[10] However, this version was very slow, as one virtual step of retrieval corresponds to several actual steps. By comparison, the INGRES-oriented version indicated the advantages of direct manipulation of nested relations. The INGRES-oriented version was implemented in 1985 by two students of the *Expert Systems* course taught by Nissan, namely, Gai Gecht and Avishay Silberschatz. This INGRES-oriented version is described in Sec. 9.

7.4   A Protocol Integrating NAVIGATION and SIMPLE NAVIGATION

This subsection is based on [75, Subsec. 7.2.3.2]. NAVIGATION is an "expert" version, and a tool independent from the application-domain: NAVIGATION is expert in looking into a frame in a "new" application-domain for which it wasn't specifically coded (which is the case of SIMPLE NAVIGATION instead). On penetrating frames, NAVIGATION consults their legal schema, like a tourist who normally lives in a city, and therefore knows how to go around in an urban environment, but does not know the particular city he or she is visiting, and

---

[10] INGRES is a relational database management system (DBMS) available under the UNIX operating system: see [18, 119].

nevertheless manages to visit it, by consulting a map. NAVIGATION is itself an "expert", at least in the sense that its *data, rules,* and *control* are separate, and that control determines the application of rules to data according to the context (as was expected of expert systems).

- In fact, as we already know, the *ruleset* accessed by NAVIGATION is the CuProS metarepresentation of the application.
- By contrast, the attribute-names of the application are the *data* of NAVIGATION, and are described in the metarepresentation. Frame-instances accessed are also data.
- *Control* performs *conflict resolution,* in order to disambiguate attribute-names that refer to the roots of different hierarchies (nesting-schemata). Control has to disambiguate attribute-names according to the context ("ancestry"), which is the same as having to select rules among a collection of rules with the same lefthand side. The need for this stems from the fact that the syntax of CuProS is as liberal as to allow the same attribute-name to be the father of different subschemata, according to its own ancestry in the metarepresentation, that is in different contexts.

In terms of computational steps, NAVIGATION "thinks a lot", and therefore is slower than SIMPLE NAVIGATION. This clearly was the case of the LISP version, the earlier one implemented. By contrast, SIMPLE NAVIGATION is not an "expert" program itself, as it just executes an algorithm with no distinction between a general control and rules and data. (Let us consider again the tourist metaphor: SIMPLE NAVIGATION could not visit a foreign city, as it has no general knowledge of "walking". It can only follow a very specific path.)

With NAVIGATION, you place an invocation to *one* standard primitive function, independent from the application-domain, whenever, in the control programs of the application, you need knowledge to be retrieved from frames. On invoking that NAVIGATION function, you give it, as argument, the name of the frame (or a variable representing that value), followed by a list of attributes: a path along which NAVIGATION is going to visit the tree of properties, and retrieve what it finds at the end of the path. In order to do that, NAVIGATION consults a ruleset describing legal structures of frames for the given application (terminology, in the case of ONOMATURGE), and it retrieves the required values (possibly, not just a value, but a subtree of properties: a subframe).

By contrast, with SIMPLE NAVIGATION, you use not one general function, but several different functions for each path of retrieval, in the specific schema of attributes of your application; therefore, you need to invest time to develop this gamut of functions. True, it is easily done, but if you do that in the initial phases of implementing a prototype of the control programs of your application, devoting time to the customisation of a SIMPLE NAVIGATION version — that is to do trivial work — would slow you down, right when you should concentrate on creative work, that is on modelling expertise. This is why it is preferable to begin developing a prototype of the control programs of an expert system, by using NAVIGATION instead of SIMPLE NAVIGATION. Afterwards, once you find some spare time, you can install SIMPLE NAVIGATION instead. Typically, this moment will come once the schema of legal frames — that is to say, the metarepresentation — of the given application is settled reasonably, as one can tell because the growth of the schema, and especially the modification rate, has slowed down, and because the preferred invocations of retrieval in your control programs have been individuated (by then, the control programs exploiting the frame-base are already in a rather advanced phase of development.)

Retrieval efficiency enhancement can be obtained by programmers, by replacing the "expert" NAVIGATION with the faster but "dumb" SIMPLE NAVIGATION. By using a metaphor from the domain of programming language compilers, turning to the SIMPLE NAVIGATION option is a kind of *manual* knowledge compilation, if you would pass us this expression.[11] Think of a human being who, on becoming skilled in a given task, acquires habits and shortcuts (or in a learning machine compiling its heuristics for more particular, but frequently occurring classes of situations). Similarly, the difference between how NAVIGATION and then SIMPLE NAVIGATION work, is that certain heuristics are no longer thought about, steps are skipped, and performance is faster.

Now, let us consider in further detail the *protocol* of project management integrating the use of NAVIGATION and SIMPLE NAVIGATION. Using both these alternative versions of the retrieval component of RAFFAELLO, according to the protocol, is meant to enhance *prototyping*. SIMPLE NAVIGATION is (we have seen) a modular collection of retrieval functions, specialised for the metarepresentation instance — describing attribute-nesting inside frames — of the knowledge-based system for some particular application. It is quite easy, even though not a creative phase in projects, to apply that software again: modules may be *reused* as they are, to construct composites, but in order to maintain identifiers in the source code semantically adherent to the application, Nissan around 1987–1988 used to *clone* modules, and in copies he just modified attribute-names. NAVIGATION is domain-independent, and metarepresentation-driven.

NAVIGATION is able to visit new topologies (we used earlier the metaphor of a tourist who is visiting a foreign city and consults a guide), and this is useful to avoid a long preparation of access to frames on the part of control: this way, you are allowed to prototype control expeditiously. Functions in SIMPLE NAVIGATION are specialised for *paths of intensive retrieval.*

The programmer consults the metarepresentation, while building the SIMPLE NAVIGATION instance: this is a shortcut with respect to the way NAVIGATION (that is to say, the metarepresentation-driven version) performs

---

[11] In artificial intelligence, if an artificial agent is able to optimise its heuristics by itself (thus, unlike RAFFAELLO), for a class of situations that recur often, then we speak about self-improving automatic learning, and, in particular, about *knowledge compilation* into ready patterns. (*Compilation* is the term, as opposed to a thoughtful, step-by-step, *interpretive,* and therefore slow execution of rational heuristics). We should stress that this does *not* mean that RAFFAELLO is a *learning* machine: the optimisation of retrieval is not performed automatically; it is human intervention on the programs that replaces NAVIGATION with SIMPLE NAVIGATION.

retrieval, and thus spares execution time, but such "optimisation" is obtained at the expense of coding-time. This way, a way was found for transferring the investment in terms of coding time: using NAVIGATION first, allows *rapid prototyping*. See below a list of the steps of the protocol, which schedules first the most creative work.

Step 1. First, one draws the metarepresentation, by trying to identify relevant parameters or objects in the considered area of knowledge, writing a production, and then refining the analysis recursively. The bulk of attribute-genealogy elicitation comes first; secondary details follow (e.g., attribute-name synonyms, or any non-genealogical metaknowledge). The production system stemming out of top-down refinement may be integrated with productions generated by considering specific examples, that is by a bottom-up analysis. According to needs, the metarepresentation may be augmented or corrected even during the remaining steps.

Step 2. Implement the control programs of the application, where NAVIGATION is invoked by means of the call

```
(navigate_and_retrieve <frame-name> <attribute> ... <attribute>)
```

which states a path for visiting the frame's internal hierarchy. You see the prototype running on few sample object-level frames.

Step 3. Fill object-level knowledge in more frames, and possibly rulesets.

Step 4. When you have time, you may "optimise" (actually, just enhance the efficiency of) the retrieval, by adapting a SIMPLE NAVIGATION module-base for your application, and by replacing the application-control's calls to NAVIGATION, with calls to SIMPLE NAVIGATION functions. Step 4 is easy, but not creative.

The protocol we described allows to concentrate one's efforts on creative work first. The knowledge structures are defined in the metarepresentation, and then work proceeds with control. Seeing the *prototype* running is not delayed beyond what is strictly necessary.[12] Enhancing access efficiency is allowed to be delayed until it has become clear what are the accesses that control needs, or needs more intensively. If and when a group of personnel takes over, and is not acquainted with the metarepresentation (e.g., because the latter was developed by somebody else), then one or more *system rebirth sessions* with a trainer may be useful: he or she would simulate regenerating the metarepresentation, along the already threaded path of knowledge analysis. The group would penetrate the structure organically, and thus profitably. This protocol wasn't applied to ONOMATURGE: when Nissan began to build the frame-base of ONOMATURGE, he built the SIMPLE NAVIGATION component of RAFFAELLO, whereas the NAVIGATION component became available only later. The principle that Nissan was nevertheless advocating, of using NAVIGATION first, was a lesson he drew *a posteriori*. It was hoped that it would become useful for future new applications of RAFFAELLO.

---

[12] Approaches to *rapid prototyping* for expert systems were described, e.g., in 1988 by Shaw et al. [98].

8   Queries

8.1   The Specification of NAVIGATION's Queries

This subsection is based on [75, Subsec. 7.2.2.2]. It defines the format of queries, as addressed to the knowledge-base by the control programs of an expert system, by invoking the main function of NAVIGATION, namely, the function `Navigate_and_retrieve`. A simple query, consulting just one frame, and selecting there information that is located by means of a given path, can be described by the following grammar:

```
<simple_query> ::=  (navigate_and_retrieve
                          '( <frame-instance_name>
                             <path>
                   )        )


<path>  ::=  <facet-identifier>  |  <facet-identifier> <path>

<facet-identifier> ::= <attribute-name>
                     | <slotless-facet_identification_value>
```

Conventionally, attribute-names in our frames include at least one capital letter, and never include a character in lower case. Digits and special characters can be included, except characters that are special for LISP (e.g., a dot).

In the framework of the lexicographical database of ONOMATURGE, specifications for NAVIGATION prescribed that one should be able to formulate a query like the following:

```
(navigate_and_retrieve
      '(gid~ul ACCEPTATIONS ARE tumor RELATED_TO RULES
        SUFFIXES   omt   RELEVANCE_ORDINAL)
)
```

This query consults just one frame-instance: the one for `gid~ul` (the noun *giddúl* in Hebrew has the acceptations 'tumour' and 'growth'). That acceptation had this subframe in ONOMATURGE's database:

```
( RELATED_TO
    ( RULES
       ( SUFFIXES
          ( ( IS  ( omt ) )
             ( RELEVANCE_ORDINAL  ( 1.5 ) )
       ) )
       ( COMPOUND-FORMATION_PATTERNS
          ( ( IS   (giddul_ba-X) )  ;  X is a metasymbol.
             (RELEVANCE_ORDINAL   ( 1 ) )
       ) )
     ( LIKELY_CONTEXT     ( medicine )  )
```

```
( NEAR-SYNONYMS
    ( ARE  ( ( TERM_IS        ( sarTan ) )
            ( KEYWORD_IS      ( cancer ) )
            ( RELATIONSHIP  ( particular_case ) )
          )
          ( ( TERM_IS        ( neo-plasTi ) )
            ( KEYWORD_IS      ( neoplastic ) )
            ( RELATIONSHIP  ( expresses_quality ) )
          )  )
    ( FREQUENCY_SCORE_AMONG_ACCEPTATIONS    ( 1 ) ) )
```

For the other acceptation, 'growth', the value 2 was given for frequency score among acceptations; this is a subjective estimate, and the context is Israeli Hebrew. For the acceptation 'tumour', associated word-formation patterns were listed under RULES. Names for particular kinds of tumour are formed in Israeli Hebrew as compounds (literally, 'tumour in the X'). Moreover, apart from present-day standard medical terminology (let alone medical terminology in medieval Hebrew), there was an attempt made by Even-Odem and Rotem in 1975 to introduce much medical terminology [19], which however did not get institutional approval, and therefore did not gain acceptance and did not enter use. Even-Odem and Rotem's medical dictionary (and in particular, Rotem's introduction) proposed to translate the international derivational suffix *-oma* for names for tumours,[13] with a Hebrew suffix *ómet* (phonemically: /-omt/). This was applied throughout their dictionary, using Hebrew stems.

In the example from ONOMATURGE, the acceptation-identifier is the value of an attribute, KEYWORD, found as nested under MEANING, which is nested inside the acceptation-chunk. As we want to access the acceptation identified by tumor under KEYWORD, we include tumor after ARE, in the query: by consulting the metarepresentation, NAVIGATION will learn it should access KEYWORD (in the proper location), to check the identity of acceptation-chunks, and thus select the acceptation-chunk in which we are interested. Inside that chunk, we want to have the facet of the attribute RELATED_TO selected, and thereinto, we specify the selection of the attribute RULES. The subframe whose top attribute is RELATED_TO clusters such linguistic information that would not fit under the attribute MEANING, in the acceptation-chunk. RULES lists word-formation morphemes possibly employed to convey the meaning of the acceptation.

The suffix-chunk identifier is the value of the attribute IS, nested inside the suffix-chunk. We specify, in the path, that we are interested in the chunk describing the suffix identified by omt (i.e., the phonemic transcription of the suffix proposed by Even-Odem and Rotem; in ONOMATURGE, phonemic transcription was used throughout). Inside the suffix-chunk, we are interested in the value of the attribute RELEVANCE_ORDINAL — this being a numerical estimate of the frequency of use of the suffix omt in forming modern Hebrew terms indicating specific tumours, with respect to other suffixes or different kinds of formative morphemes

---

[13] For example, in English, *epithelioma* denotes an epithelial tumor, *endothelioma* denotes an endothelial tumor, and so forth.

that in Hebrew are able to convey the same meaning, as being identified by the keyword `tumor` (but it must be said that the frame under consideration was developed for the sake of the example: actually, that particular suffix did not manage to get acceptance in Israeli Hebrew medical terminology).

8.2   Queries with Variables

In this subsection, we continue with the specification for the format of queries, the way it was defined for NAVIGATION in [75, Subsec. 7.2.2.3]. According to the syntax of FRANZ LISP, whenever a list is preceded by a quote sign, then it is interpreted as consisting of constants only. Without the quote before the parenthesis, the first token found inside the parenthesis would be assumed to be the name of a function. On the other hand, the syntax of FRANZ LISP allows to insert variables inside a list of constants. Then, the parenthesis should be preceded by a backquote sign, instead of the quote, and the variables inside the parenthesis should be preceded by a comma. (Whenever a quote can be used before a parenthesis, a backquote, too, can be used. If no comma is included, then the effect is the same.) This syntax was incorporated in the specification of the syntax of queries as allowed by NAVIGATION, according to the definition in [75, Subsec. 7.2.2.3]. Cf. [115, pp. 202–206]. For example,

```
(navigate_and_retrieve '( ,object  MORPHOLOGICAL_CATEGORY ) )
```

would retrieve the value of the attribute MORPHOLOGICAL_PROPERTY, as found at the top level of the frame-instance whose name is the value of the variable `object` which is assumed to have been assigned a value before.

By contrast, if we want a variable inside a path as stated in a query, to qualify all of the instantiated range at the current range of nesting, then the syntax of NAVIGATION queries, as originally defined, envisages another feature: *variable-names* that are not preceded by a comma, but, instead, by an underscore. Each string beginning by an underscore — if used where a *chunk-identifying value* would fit (like `omt` in the example given in the previous subsection) qualifies a fan of values, whose type is determined by the position in the path. In his doctoral project, Nissan had not implemented yet the specific handling of variable-names beginning by an underscore, but this could be easily done in LISP, because in LISP any data can be evaluated, and interpreted as a variable or as a function. In the event, once El-Sana implemented an operational version of NAVIGATION, queries conformed to the syntax of PROLOG instead. See the code of NAVIGATION in Appendix C, and the metarepresentation of how attributes in ONOMATURGE are nested, in Appendix D.

For example, in the query

```
(navigate_and_retrieve
  '(gid~ul ASSOCIATIONS_OF_IDEAS ARE _Any_value FOR_WHOM) )
```

the variable `_Any_value` qualifies the values `Goedel` and `giddily` — supposing that you bothered to include such values in the frame of `gid~ul` in a subframe whose top attribute is `ASSOCIATIONS_OF_IDEAS`. By lexicographers' practice, there is no reason in the world to list something like this subframe in a lexical entry, but we are making up an example for the sake of illustrating the syntax:

```
( ASSOCIATION_OF_IDEAS
    ( ARE ( ( IS    ( Goedel )
            ( FOR_WHOM ( ( FOR ( computation-theorists ) )
                        ( LIKELIHOOD    ( 0.05 - 0.3 )  )
                        )
                      ( ( FOR    ( mathematicians
                                    computer-scientists
                        )    )
                        ( LIKELIHOOD    ( 0 - 0.1 )  )
                        )
                      ( ( FOR    ( laypersons ) )
                        ( LIKELIHOOD    ( 0 ) )
            )  )          )
            ( ( IS    ( giddily ) )   ..... )
) )    )
```

The query

```
(navigate_and_retrieve
      '(gid~ul  ACCEPTATIONS  ARE  _Any_acceptation
                RELATED_TO    LIKELY_CONTEXT          ) )
```

qualifies the value of `LIKELY_CONTEXT` inside both acceptations (e.g., the value is `medicine` when `LIKELY_CONTEXT` is under `RELATED_TO` inside the acceptation-chunk of `tumor`), and should return the list of lists

```
    ( ( medicine )    ( quantifiable_thing  life ) )
```

where the order among the inner lists carries no meaning. Another kind of variable to be introduced, is a variable representing any attribute that is found as nested directly inside the current level of nesting. Such variables are identified by a plus symbol prefixated. For example,

```
(navigate_and_retrieve
      '(gid~ul  ACCEPTATIONS  ARE  tumor
                RELATED_TO  RULES  +Any_rule ) )
```

should retrieve all of the single-rule chunks, found either under `SUFFIXES`, or under `COMPOUND-FORMATION_PATTERNS`, which are the two attributes matching `+Any_rule` in the example we have been considering in this subsection. Thanks to the built-in syntax of FRANZ LISP, according to the original definition of NAVIGATION users would be able to include a sub-path as being the value of a variable included inside a path stated in a query. For example, if the variable `subpath1` was previously assigned, as value, the list

```
      '(ARE  _Any_acceptation  RELATED_TO)
```

then the query

```
(navigate_and_retrieve
  '(gid~ul  ACCEPTATIONS  ,@subpath1  LIKELY_CONTEXT ) )
```

would be interpreted just as:

```
(navigate_and_retrieve
     '(gid~ul  ACCEPTATIONS  ARE  _Any_acceptation
              RELATED_TO   LIKELY_CONTEXT          ) )
```

According to that specification of the syntax, ,@ (not just a comma) would have had to be prefixated before the variable-name (i.e., subpath1). If only a comma was prefixated, then the value of subpath1 would have been inserted inside the path as being an internal list:

```
     '(gid~ul  ACCEPTATIONS
              ( ARE  _Any_acceptation RELATED_TO )
              LIKELY_CONTEXT
     )
```

8.3   Motivation of the Metarepresentation from the Viewpoint of Queries: Consulting Keys, and Allowing Incomplete Paths

One could ask, why should a metarepresentation be used at all, as retrieval could just select the specified nested attribute, in the current facet.[14] One reason is ascertaining the identity of slotless facets, by accessing their identification key in the proper location, as indicated by the metarepresentation. This could not be done just by sticking to the actual nesting instantiation as found in frame-instances, if application-dependent information on the position of keys of given kinds of slotless facets is not provided to the retrieval programs. Such information is incorporated in modules of SIMPLE NAVIGATION as composed according to the application. NAVIGATION, instead, is an application-independent program, and draws information about the application from an interface, constituted by the metarepresentation.

Another reason for using a metarepresentation, when Nissan defined it for the lexical frames of ONOMATURGE, concerns extensions he envisaged for NAVIGATION. This motivation consists of the aim of freeing users from having to know exactly the path of nesting reaching the attribute whose value they need, or reaching the nonterminal where the subtree they need is rooted. We wanted to allow paths, as stated in queries, to include just some necessary elements ("landmarks"), along the nesting path as found in the schema, or in the frame-instances. This is an extension of NAVIGATION that eventually was implemented by El-Sana.

By using a metarepresentation, freedom degrees are provided for stating a simple query without specifying the whole path: it would be sufficient to state

---

[14] The present subsection is based on [75, Subsec. 7.2.2.4].

just the final facet-identifier in the path, and some intermediate facet-identifiers included as being "landmarks". Such landmarks are necessary only when ambiguity is involved because of attributes with the same name but with different "ancestry" (i.e., with a different sequence of nesting).

Just a few facets — those whose schema is repeated in a sequence nested at the same level — have facet-identifiers, in our approach. Such facet-identifiers can be found either at the top level of the repeatable subframe, or even at a deeper level, according to definitions in the metarepresentation. Another approach, that was described by Setrag Khoshafian, Patrick Valduriez, and George Copeland [39], introduces system-generated identifiers termed *surrogates*, independent of any physical address, and being the value of a special attribute, SURROGATE, for each and every tuple object in a nested structure. (See Subsec. 10.2.)

9   The Early Version of RAFFAELLO That Maps Nested Relations to INGRES Flat Relations

9.1   An Overall View

In 1985, a program was developed by two of Nissan's students under his supervision, that on the one hand, maps Nissan's LISP nested relations onto flat relations under INGRES and, on the other hand, reconstructs the LISP frame instance according to relations stored in INGRES, and then answers queries.[15]

The INGRES-oriented version of retrieval with RAFFAELLO was developed and tried as being an alternative to frames as built in files and processed by the

---

[15] This section is based on [75, Subsec. 7.2.5]. The implementors of the INGRES-oriented version of RAFFAELLO were Gai Gecht and Avishay Silberschatz, who had taken the *Expert Systems* course taught by Nissan. INGRES is a relational database management system (DBMS) available under the UNIX operating system: see [18, 119]. The overall project we are describing was given by Nissan the name RAFFAELLO, because of the same semantic motivation by which the name POSTGRES was given to a successor of INGRES. But RAFFAELLO was obtained by pseudo-algebraic reasoning. When Nissan began the ONOMATURGE project, initially (in 1984) it was considered whether to implement the database of that expert system in INGRES, for all of there going to be nested relations. What happened instead was that Nissan carried out the all-in-LISP implementation of the SIMPLE NAVIGATION version of RAFFAELLO. The database management system (DBMS) of UNIX was called INGRES after the painter Ingres, who influenced the Lyon School, itself related to the Pre-Raffaellites. For the sake of simplicity, Ingres was assimilated to a Pre-Raffaellite. Then, from

$$\text{AFTER} + \text{INGRES} = \text{AFTER} + \text{PRE} + \text{RAFFAELLO}$$

we obtain: AFTER + INGRES = RAFFAELLO. This is how the name RAFFAELLO was devised. Afterwards, Nissan learned that Stonebraker and Rowe, the developers of INGRES, presented [103] in 1986 the POSTGRES database management system, intended to be the successor of INGRES. The name POSTGRES was derived from *post + INGRES*.

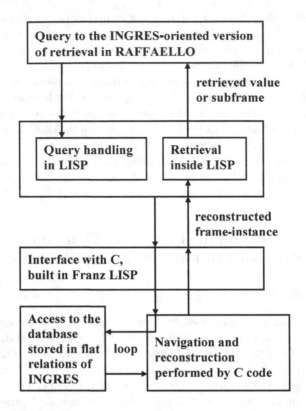

Fig. 2. Retrieval with the INGRES-oriented version of RAFFAELLO

all-in-LISP versions of the retrieval component of RAFFAELLO. The INGRES-oriented component was meant to probe certain opinions on the implementation of nested relations. In nested relations, each *compound tuple* may be considered to an instance of a frame-instance *à la* RAFFAELLO (in the latter, however, the nesting hierarchy of attributes is more flexible).

The RAFFAELLO/INGRES interface proved to be slow, due to cumulation. This was ascribed especially to the elaborate mapping as supported specifically by INGRES, and, besides, to the path of retrieval, as shown in Fig. 2.

One virtual step of retrieval may require, say, forty actual retrieval steps in INGRES, if the query requires access into a deep level of nesting inside the simulated frame-instance. Also storage actions are slow; see Fig. 3.

From this viewpoint, our experience corroborated the claims motivating the efforts to build DBMSs based on a nested-relation algebra, without any stage of mapping into flat relations. The relative slowness of the INGRES-oriented version of retrieval with RAFFAELLO was taken to be indicative of the advantages

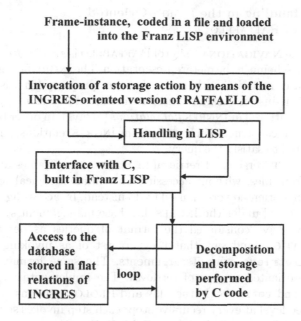

Fig. 3. Storage with the INGRES-oriented version of RAFFAELLO

one could expect to accrue from direct manipulation of nested relations with RAFFAELLO. Some approaches to nested relations in the early 1980s used to accept nested relations at the user front-end, and internally transform nested relations into flat relations. Office forms, input as nested relations, are transformed into flat relations inside APAD, as described by Kitagawa & al. in 1981 [41].

Because of the cost of the transformation, an alternative idea was more appealing: a more efficient solution would resort to such database management systems that are specifically devised for processing nested relations. Projects in this direction were under way during the 1980s in various places. As a matter of fact, prototypes were being built by researchers (in industry, IBM had been developing a tool), but at the time Nissan started to develop the ONOMATURGE project, such nested-relation based database management systems were not commercially available as yet.

Nested relations research was published, e.g., in [1, 88]. Such research was carried out in Darmstadt (West Germany) and at the IBM Research Center in Heidelberg, as well as by groups of researchers in Paris, in Austin (Texas), in Tokyo, and elsewhere. In personal communication to Nissan (1985), Prof. Hans-Jörg Schek remarked: "It would be important to support AI data structures by DB data structures. The more similar these structures are, the more effective is the support which expert systems layers can get from a DB kernel".

9.2   Query Handling in the INGRES-Oriented
Version of RAFFAELLO

Retrieval with the NAVIGATION version of RAFFAELLO is *syntax-directed,* as it consults the nesting-schema in the metarepresentation. The INGRES-oriented *instance-directed:* attributes nested directly inside the same property (that is, *childsets*) as found in the frame-instance under consideration are stored as mapped onto a set of *tuples* (rows) scattered in INGRES *flat relations* (arrays). In order to retrieve, the frame-instance is reconstructed in LISP from the INGRES relations, and the relevant data are extracted to satisfy the query.

In the all-in-LISP versions of retrieval in RAFFAELLO, frames are loaded into LISP directly from files, without accessing any different logical representation, which the INGRES-oriented version used to do instead, by accessing a transformed representation stored under the INGRES database management system.

In Sec. 8, we have considered the format of queries as per the specification of NAVIGATION, and saw that they consist of as invoking the function `navigate_and_retrieve` with its arguments. The same format was adopted by the INGRES-oriented version of retrieval. The implementation of the function `navigate_and_retrieve` in the LISP and PROLOG versions of NAVIGATION accesses one tree-level at every recursive step; each step invokes several function-levels, each processing one of the labels of the CUPROS metarepresentation language, with which the productions of the nesting-schema are interspersed. Some frame facets are not headed by any attribute-name: such properties are *slotless facets,* also called *slotless chunks.* They are identified by the value of a suitable "child" or "grandchild", being the identifying key of the slotless chunk among its similarly structured siblings. Access to the proper instance of repeated slotless facet requires consulting (by backtracking) instances of a certain attribute meant for identification: either a directly nested property (a "child"), or an attribute nested even more deeply (a "grandchild"), devised for identifying the slotless chunk. The *filler* of a property (i.e., of a *facet*) is whatever follows the attribute-name inside the parenthesis, if the property is slotted, or the parenthesis itself, if the property is slotless.

Refer to Fig. 4. The query (`navigate_and_retrieve` '(<path>)) where let <path> be

        (<A>_slot <AB>_slot <ABAAA>_value <ABAB>_slot)

retrieves the filler of <ABAB>_facet after consulting <ABAAA> in order to identify <ABA> as opposed to <ABB> or <ABC>. The INGRES-oriented version of retrieval, in RAFFAELLO, transforms <path> into a path such that <ABAAA>_value is explicitly preceded by a flag signalling that grandfather-identification is needed. Then, accessing INGRES, search is performed by backtracking.

The RAFFAELLO/INGRES interface exploits the option, which FRANZ LISP offers [43], to access functions external to LISP that are themselves in the C language. C itself [38] allows a UNIX Shell command to be executed, by assigning it as argument to the function `system`. Then, if the Shell command invokes

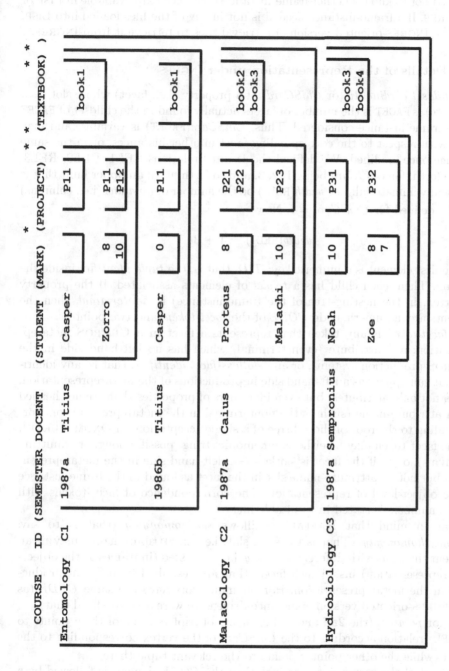

Fig. 4. Hierarchical schema of a frame-instance (ignoring actual attribute-names)

INGRES, we access INGRES from inside FRANZ LISP; see Fig. 2 and Fig. 3. Heuristics need not to know whether frame-instances referenced are available in LISP or in INGRES. If a frame-instance needed is not in any of the files loaded into LISP, then the INGRES-oriented version of retrieval tries to retrieve it from INGRES.

9.3   Details of the Representation under INGRES

The *childset cardinality* (or *ChiSCard*) of a property (i.e., facet) whose slot (i.e., attribute) is FACET is the number of facets actually found in the childset of FACET in the frame-instance considered. Thus, *ChiSCard*(FACET) is variable, and may differ with respect to the corresponding facet in other instances, or in the same instance once modified. We defined the INGRES relations REL1, REL2, REL3, and so forth, for *ChiSCard* being 1, 2, 3, and so forth, until an upper limit that is practically immaterial. Let *width*(REL$_i$) be the number of *domains* (i.e., columns) of REL$_i$ defined for *ChiSCard* $= i$. Now,

$$width(\text{REL}_i) = 1 + 3i$$

The first element is a numeric key: *TID*, that is, the *tuple identifier* inside the relation. Then, each child has a *triplet* of elements associated. If the property (a vertex, in the nesting-tree of the frame-instance) is *nonterminal*, then the elements are: a numeric code *CODE* of the *facet-token*, and two pointers.

A *facet-token* is any token that represents a facet in a CUPROS metarepresentation: any attribute (even terminal, which has no left-hand side in the CUPROS production system), or any *slotless-facet identifier*, that is, any identifier that can appear as a left-hand side in productions of the metarepresentation, hence, not only attributes, but even identifiers of properties that are not headed by an attribute-name (such as the nonterminal in the metarepresentation, corresponding to the root of the subtree of a single acceptation, in ONOMATURGE).

The facet-token may be either a mnemonic string (possibly long, or admitting synonyms), or — if the facet is slotless — a left-hand side in the metarepresentation but not an attribute-name slot in the facet as found in the frame-instance at the object-level of representation. The correspondence of facet-tokens with *CODE* numbers is stated in a suitable file.

Bear in mind that RAFFAELLO allows *slot-homonymy* (that is to say, *attribute-homonymy*). That is to say, a slot, i.e., an attribute-name, may mean different things as with different *ancestry*, i.e., as nested (in frames at the object-level representation) inside such facets that are described by different productions in the metarepresentation. Homonymous slots have the same *CODE* (as the INGRES-oriented version is instance-driven, we were able to afford that).

As for *pointers* (the 2nd and 3rd elements of triplets), one of them points to the REL$_i$ relation according to the *ChiSCard* of the vertex corresponding to the triplet, while the other pointer points to the relevant tuple there.

Instead, if the vertex is a *terminal*, then the *CODE* element is followed by a pointer to the relation *LEAVES*, and by a pointer to the tuple, there, that stores the value of that terminal property.

Let us consider the frame-instance of Fig. 4. The root (and the name) is
<A>. In our database in INGRES, the relation ROOT has a tuple listing <A> and
pointers to a particular tuple of 10 elements in REL3 (as <A> has 3 children):

```
{  <A>_TID      ,
   <AA>_CODE    ,    "REL2"     ,   <AA>_TID   ,
   <AB>_CODE    ,    "REL3"     ,   <AB>_TID   ,
   <AC>_CODE    ,    "LEAVES"   ,   <AC>_TID       }
```

In the case of slotless facets, as the subtree-root is not an identifying slot, the
search process checks, say, a certain grandchild to be distinguished. (Actually,
repeated instances of the same facet in the same childset may either be slotless,
or have all the same slot that by itself does not provide identification.)

Tuples consist of the tuple key (TID) and of triplets, whose 1st elements are
$CODEs$ of facet-tokens. An alternative solution could eliminate that element,
and reduce triplets to just pairs, at the cost of having another element in the
tuple: a pointer to a tuple in a CHILDREN$_i$ relation with i columns. Tuples there
would be ordered sets of $CODEs$ of facet-tokens, for every childset met with
$ChiSCard = i$. The identity of pairs in REL$_i$ tuples would depend on the order
found in the tuple of CHILDREN$_i$ that is being pointed to.

10 The CuProS Metarepresentation, vs.
Data-Dictionaries

10.1 A Separate Nesting-Schema, vs. an All-Encompassing
Data-Dictionary

The CuProS metarepresentation is useful as a knowledge-analysis tool, a specification, and a reference during the design, implementation and maintenance
phases. Why should a metarepresentation of legal nesting among attributes, be
better than an all-encompassing schema, including type definitions of the value-
sets of each attribute?[16] In RAFFAELLO, we separate the data-dictionary from
the nesting-schema, by reckoning that developing first just a skeleton, in terms of
nesting, subserves the knowledge-analysis better, without fettering it with type
definitions that could follow in calmer moments, or even directly after a session
of skeleton-development.

We have investigated also a metarepresentation involving data-types, separately
from the nesting-schema. In 1985, *Expert Systems* students, Yehudit Shakhi and
'Irit Dahan, coded under Nissan's supervision a data-type schema for a certain
application, in the framework of *local* metarepresentation subtrees, which can be
occasionally found inside (or pointed to from inside) a frame-instance, and which
are meant to be applied to a portion of that instance, and possibly to a class of
inheriting instances. This feature however was not integrated into the control of
NAVIGATION. For the time being, it was felt, it was quite adequate to have just

---

[16] This section is based on [75, Subsec. 7.4].

one data-structure storing a metarepresentation, and this would be processed by NAVIGATION by default; optionally, the name of the metarepresentation structure can be provided explicitly. Switching from a global metarepresentation to a local metarepresentation is envisaged by the **g**: label in the syntax of the CuProS metarepresentation language, but this was not handled yet by the implementations of NAVIGATION. We are going to see that on an example in Subsec. 11.5 below.

10.2   Indexing for Large Frames

Let us consider possible ways of access to frame instances, of the kind dealt with by RAFFAELLO. The simplest way (the one that was implemented) is finding the name of the frame-instance, and then accessing it: knowledge coded procedurally in the control component embodies the indication of the particular attribute whose value it needs. Another way that is allowed by NAVIGATION is accessing a particular attribute, once the name of the frame-instance is provided in a list together with the path from the root of the frame to the attribute considered.

The name of frame-instances can be found in other frames, or is drawn from the input of the expert system using RAFFAELLO. While we didn't implement any inheritance manager in RAFFAELLO or RAFFAELLO (but did so in FIDEL GASTRO),[17] such a component has to draw upon chains of pointers from given properties in given frame-instances, to other frame-instances. The way RAFFAELLO was actually developed, if no list of frame-instances to be accessed is known *a priori*, then we have to perform brute-force search. In ONOMATURGE, such situations do not occur, but for the sake of generality, this problem should be taken into consideration. If we have no way of knowing in what subset of frame-instances, certain values are likely to be found inside the instances (even though we know what attribute to look for), then we can gain insight into the contents of the frame-instance only by entering it from the root of the property-tree, and by performing a blind search.

To make search "smarter", we could develop an approach for accessing frame-instances according to their contents. One idea is to have an *index* or a *concordance* of frame-instances automatically generated and updated. *Indices* are well-known not only from textual document processing, but from from database organisation as well.[18]

By the time Nissan and his students were developing RAFFAELLO, the issue of indexing for nested relational structures has already been investigated, in the literature. Khoshafian et al. [39] discussed in 1986 an approach to complex objects (nested structures) that identifies *every* tuple object by means of a unique

---

[17] FIDEL GASTRO is the expert system for gastronomy and planning at institutional kitchens we described in Subsec. 1.3 above.

[18] Principles of *secondary indexing* — as well as *indexing* in general — in traditional database approaches current in the 1980s were discussed, e.g., by Cardenas [11, Sec. 2], Ullman [105, Secs. 2.7 to 2.9], Hatzopoulos and Kollias [34], and Schkolnik [95]. Cf. Ghosh [30, Secs. 3.4, 5.1] and, in Wiederhold [114], Subsecs. 4-2, 4-3, but in particular his Subsec. 4-4, which deals with indexing for *tree-structured files*.

identifier, termed a *surrogate* (or a *level-id surrogate*). With RAFFAELLO, identifiers of nested facets (i.e., *subframes*) are necessary only for sequences of repeated subframe-instances with the same schema; our approach is more flexible because of other reasons, as well: it enables flexibility concerning the location, inside the subframe, of the key, i.e., subframe-identifying attribute. Khoshafian et al. [39] described an approach to indexing: the *Fully Inverted Hierarchical Storage Model* (*FIHSM*).

Consider the following code:

```
C1: {[ SURROGATE:      sur_1      ,
       COURSE:         Entomology ,
       BY_SEMESTER: { {[ SURROGATE:      sur_2 ,
                         SEMESTER_IS     1987a ,
                         DOCENT:         Titius ,
                         STUDENTS:  { {[ SURROGATE: sur_3 ,
                                         IS:        Casper ,
                                         MARK:          nil ,
                                         PROJECT:       P11
                                     ]} ,
                                     {[ SURROGATE: sur_4 ,
                                        IS:           Zorro ,
                                        MARK: { 8 , 10 } ,
                                        PROJECT:
                                            { P11 , P12 }
                                     ]} ,
                                   } ,
                         TEXTBOOK:       book1
                      ]} ,
                      {[ SURROGATE:      sur_5 ,
                         SEMESTER_IS     1986b ,
                         DOCENT:         Titius ,
                         STUDENTS:  { {[ SURROGATE: sur_6 ,
                                         IS:        Casper ,
                                         MARK:      0       ,
                                         PROJECT: P11
                                     ]} ,
                                   } ,
                         TEXTBOOK:       book1
                      ]}
                  }
   ]}
```

This is an example of an adaptation of that approach to express our frames equivalently. It is the equivalent, with surrogates as described by Khoshafian and colleagues, of the frame instance of an academic course shown in the following code:

```
(assign_frame    C1
    (  (COURSE           Entomology)
      (BY_SEMESTER
          (  (SEMESTER_IS    1987a)
            (DOCENT          Titius)
            (STUDENTS
                (  (IS       Casper)
                  (PROJECT   P11) )
                (  (IS       Zorro)
                  (MARK         8 10)
                  (PROJECT P11 P12)))
            (TEXTBOOK        book1) )
          (  (SEMESTER_IS    1986b)
            (DOCENT          Titius)
            (STUDENTS
                (  (IS       Casper)
                  (MARK         0  )
                  (PROJECT    P11)))
            (TEXTBOOK        book1     ]
```

that is itself a coding in frame-form of the nested database relation shown in Fig. 4, and whose metarepresentation in CuPRoS is shown in the following code:

```
(setq  CuProS_of_course-database
   '( (root   ( COURSE BY_SEMESTER ) )
     (BY_SEMESTER
         ( n: semestral_chunk) )
         ; after "n:", a repeatable subtree-schema.

     (semestral_chunk   ; the attribute
         ( i: SEMESTER_IS   ; after "i:"
          DOCENT            ; identifies
          STUDENTS          ; the nameless
          TEXTBOOK ) )      ;        father.

     (STUDENTS (n: student_individual))

     (student_individual
         ( i:  IS
          MARK
          PROJECT )  )
```

Judging from the nested relation in Fig. 4, it would appear to be the case that Khoshafian et al. [39] in 1986 were considering such complex objects, that just one complex object or atomic value can appear as being the value of an attribute, but other approaches (including RAFFAELLO) allow sequences of values (possibly, even sequences of complex objects with the same schema) to appear as the instance of the same attribute. { } denotes set objects, whereas [ ] denotes tuple objects (i.e., sets of attribute/value elements). The example is stated not according to the same representation method as the one proposed by Khoshafian et al. [39], but instead by means of an adaptation: sequence-valued attributes are included.

In the following code, we show a collection of binary relations, meant to be kept for indexing purposes, and which biunivocally correspond to the complex object shown in the previous codes in this subsection, as well as in Fig. 4:

```
C1_1:    {[ SURROGATE:      sur_1                    ,
            COURSE:         Entomology               ]}
C1_2:    {[ SURROGATE:      sur_1                    ,
            BY_SEMESTER:    { sur_2 , sur_5 }        ]}
C1_3:    {[ SURROGATE:      sur_2                    ,
            SEMESTER_IS:    1987a                    ]}
C1_4:    {[ SURROGATE:      sur_2                    ,
            DOCENT:         Titius                   ]}
C1_5:    {[ SURROGATE:      sur_2                    ,
            STUDENTS:       { sur_3 , sur_4 }        ]}
C1_6:    {[ SURROGATE:      sur_3                    ,
            IS:             Casper                   ]}
C1_7:    {[ SURROGATE:      sur_3                    ,
            MARK:           nil                      ]}
C1_8:    {[ SURROGATE:      sur_3                    ,
            PROJECT:        P11                      ]}
C1_9:    {[ SURROGATE:      sur_4                    ,
            IS:             Zorro                    ]}
C1_10:   {[ SURROGATE:      sur_4                    ,
            MARK:           { 8 , 10 }               ]}
C1_11:   {[ SURROGATE:      sur_4                    ,
            PROJECT:        { P11 , P12 }            ]}
C1_12:   {[ SURROGATE:      sur_2                    ,
            TEXTBOOK:       book1                    ]}
C1_13:   {[ SURROGATE:      sur_5                    ,
            SEMESTER_IS:    1986b                    ]}
C1_14:   {[ SURROGATE:      sur_5                    ,
            DOCENT:         Titius                   ]}
C1_15:   {[ SURROGATE:      sur_5                    ,
            STUDENTS:       sur_6                    ]}
C1_16:   {[ SURROGATE:      sur_6                    ,
            IS:             Casper                   ]}
C1_17:   {[ SURROGATE:      sur_6                    ,
            MARK:           0                        ]}
C1_18:   {[ SURROGATE:      sur_6                    ,
            PROJECT:        P11                      ]}
C1_19:   {[ SURROGATE:      sur_5                    ,
            TEXTBOOK:       book1                    ]}
```

This is a collection of binary relations equivalent to the complex object of Fig. 4. Whereas the latter is meant to be kept as being the primary copy, these binary relations, instead, are meant to be kept for indexing purposes. This approach is adapted from Khoshafian et al. [39], but we allow the attribute (other than the surrogate) in these binary relations to be set-valued, in order to cope with the primary copy, a complex object that admits as values even sequences of complex objects with the same schema. This extension requires that surrogates be easily identified as being such, at least whenever they appear as values of the second attribute (the one after SURROGATE) in the binary relation. Besides, relational operators should suitably account for the extension.

Let us go back to the subject of indexing frames of the kind from which RAFFAELLO carries out retrieval. One consideration about full indexing of the hierarchical structure of frame-instances is that it could prove too costly to keep whole paths from the root of the tree (frame-instance) until the leaf, to locate each occurrence: then, just a certain subtree could be pointed to, leaving it to the retrieval component, to search the subtree for the value requested. That is, such a choice for the index would ignore the internal structure of the subtree. This constitutes a trade off between memory efficiency and time efficiency requirements. Besides, once a frame-instance is loaded, pointers are valid if referring to nodes of its hierarchical structure, while the contents *files* in the database, even though the latter store frame-instances, could possibly be referred to by means of other kinds of coordinates (e.g., with a *concordance*, as if frames were text; this would allow to refer to *user comments* in the files of frames, without having to introduce COMMENT attributes in the frames, that would use up memory when loaded, or reconstruction-time to delete them on loading).

The metarepresentation in RAFFAELLO, the way it was developed, is a metarepresentation of attributes, and, therefore, a *metastructure of the type*, not of the *values*. In order to access the proper instances of frames, or at the very least, to access promising frame-instances, we would need indications on values, too.

Nevertheless, *frame-indices* have their own limitations: they would point just to *disaggregated* values, i.e., to an index of values as found in terminal properties in the tree of attributes. This is not enough to enable a synthetic grasp of what is represented in subframes containing a given set of values. Owing to the hierarchical structure of frames, secondary indices as known from databases, or concordances as known from full-text information retrieval, may obviate to problems with search in trees, but, if bare values do not refer to clear contexts, entries in the index or the concordance would point to too many occurrences with respect to what queries intend, and thus concordances would just reduce — not eliminate — search in trees: sets of coordinates for a given entry in the concordance (a value in the frame) could be seen as a forest of hierarchical "skeletons" drawn out of the frame-base, and search should check there whether the value occurrence is relevant or not.

Perhaps, semantically coherent portions of frame-instances — likened to chapters in a book — could be *labelled* with indicators of the topic, for insertion in the index. This is something familiar, by now, from Web technology. Webpages have lists of keywords, in order to attract search engines, and this is (apart from the misuse of keywords at webpages) like keyword-lists in scientific papers.

11   Syntactic Elements of CuProS, the Metarepresentation Language of Raffaello

11.1   Basic Terminology

Raffaello provides the possibility of representing nested relations inside the property-lists of Lisp atoms: the top-level attributes in the frame are properties in the property-list. Nested properties however obey a syntax defined in the metarepresentation language of Raffaello, and not belonging to Lisp. In fact, basically the syntax is independent of Lisp.

By *slot*, we are going to refer to any attribute in a tree of properties. By *facet*, we refer to any attribute together with its value. The value, which we term a *filler*, is either a terminal value or value-list (if the facet is a leaf in the tree of properties), or — if the facet is a nonterminal vertex in the tree of properties — a subtree (or even a list of subtrees). In practice it has never happened, in our frames, for the filler to include a terminal value and also further levels of nested facets, as being brothers. We term a subtree of properties, a *subframe*.

Attribute-schemata are described — at a *meta-level* of representation (*metarepresentation*) — by means of a production system, where *productions* state legal genealogies of slots, and are augmented with *labels* that express particular conventions for conveying particular features (e.g., slotless repeatable subframes,

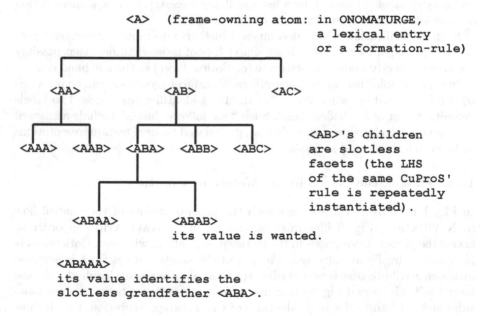

Fig. 5. Processing input facet-identifiers

as identified by the value of some child or grandchild facet defined in the schema itself). See Fig. 5.

The metarepresentation, according to our approach, consists of a data-structure storing a *production system*. Each *production* is a parenthesis including a *left-hand side* and a *right-hand side*. This set of rules constitutes a grammar, specifying valid structures of nested relations for the given application.

Let us refer to the *left-hand side* of productions by the acronym *LHS*, and to the *right-hand side* of productions by the acronym *RHS*. The RHS lists attributes constituting the legal childset of the attribute that is the LHS. We sometimes refer to a *nesting level* by the name *generation* (i.e., a generation in a tree).

Each LHS is either a *facet-identifier*, or a parenthesis including several facet-identifiers. Facet identifiers are either *attribute-names* (and then, they do not include lower-case letters), or *implicit nonterminals*. Implicit nonterminals are lower-case names that, in the metarepresentation, represent what in frame-instances are *slotless facets*. In ONOMATURGE, acceptation-chunks and rule-chunks (where rules are lexical derivation patterns) are examples of slotless facets, that is, they each are a nonterminal nested parenthesis that does not begin by an explicit attribute-name.

Right-hand sides are either *structured*, or *simple* lists of facet-identifiers. Structured right-hand sides are subdivided by means of *labels* belonging to the reserved lexicon of the CuPROS language.

The higher level of subdivision can be according to "ancestry", that is, to the nesting-context: the legal schemata of nesting inside the facet represented by the left-hand side are different according to the different ancestry possible for that left-hand side. Thus, the right-hand side is subdivided into parts constituted by an ancestry label (f: or a:), by a list specifying ancestry, and by a specification of legal sets of facet-identifiers that can be nested.

Such a specification can be decomposed further, into mutually exclusive portions — preceded by x: — which are simple lists of facet-identifiers that possibly are nested directly under the attribute (or slotless facet) in the left-hand side.

In such "simple" lists of facet-identifiers, some facet-identifiers can be preceded by a label describing some feature of the facet-identifier (as opposed to labels delimiting a set of facet-identifiers). Such "one-follower labels" include n: as well as c: and i: (related to slotless facets), g: (related to local metarepresentations to be switched to), and so forth.

11.2   Parsing the Labels in the Metarepresentation

In Fig. 1 in Subsec. 7.3, we have seen the general outline of the control flow in NAVIGATION. Fig. 6 illustrates actions taken by NAVIGATION in order to access the proper productions in the metarepresentation, whenever slotless facets (symbolised by F) are involved. The *key* of the single slotless facet is accessed inside an attribute that is nested (directly, or at a deeper level) inside the slotless facet itself. Fig. 6 and Fig. 7 show how processing switches between right-hand sides and left-hand sides in productions of the metarepresentation, that is, how productions are *chained*.

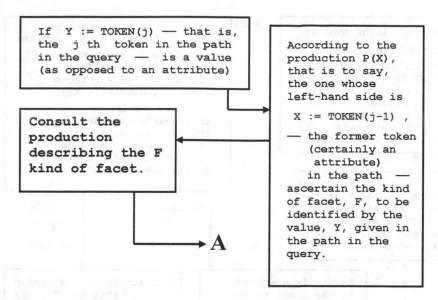

Fig. 6. The way left-hand sides of productions inside the metarepresentation are handled when the latter is consulted, in order to chain productions

Fig. 8 and Fig. 9 show how labels found inside (possibly structured) right-hand sides guide the processing. That way, whenever the same attribute-name (e.g., ARE) is found in different nesting contexts (*ancestry contexts*) inside frames, then according to its production in the metarepresentation, the proper childset of nested facets (attributes, or slotless facets) is selected.

At an inner level inside right-hand sides, possibly x: labels (for "exclusive or") delimit mutually exclusive sets of facet-identifiers. Labels with different priorities are processed at different points in the schema, as indicated in Fig. 8 and Fig. 9. See further, at the end of Subsec. 11.4, the two parts in Fig. 10 and Fig. 11. Boxes with a grey bottom right ("southeast") corner were not implemented in the 1988 version in LISP of NAVIGATION.

11.3   A Sample Metarepresentation. Part I

In Subsec. 8.2, we have considered how to formulate queries containing variables, in the path leading to what is sought. Such queries were exemplified on a rather simple lexical frame, a simplification of the kind found in the database of the ONOMATURGE expert system for word-formation. The following code shows a metarepresentation of the nesting structure for such frames. This will enable us to get a taste of what the labels in a CuProS metarepresentation mean, before we turn to explaining the syntax more systematically.

Consider, first of all, that setq is the assignment operator in LISP. Considering the attribute name MORPHOLOGICAL_CATEGORY bear in mind that MORPHO_CAT is a synonym for that name. Such synonyms of attribute names are declared in a separate data structure, not the CuProS ruleset we are considering.

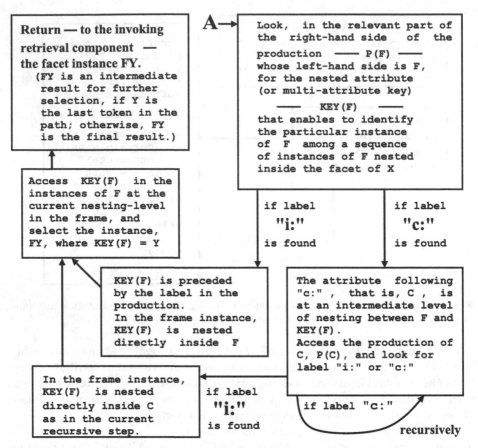

Fig. 7. The way left-hand sides of productions inside the metarepresentation are handled when the latter is consulted, in order to chain productions

```
(setq  metarepresentation_1
    '(
        (pointer_atom        ( POINTER ) )

        (atom                ( INFLECTION
                              MORPHOLOGICAL_CATEGORY
                              ACCEPTATIONS
                              ASSOCIATION_OF_IDEAS
                              FRAME_GENERATED_ON
                              CODED_BY              ) )

    (MORPHOLOGICAL_CATEGORY   ( x: terminal_list
                                x: See_ACCEPTATION ) )
```

Bear in mind that the label x: stands for "exclusive or". Also, bear in mind that it is possible to add comments to a CuProS metarepresentation: this is

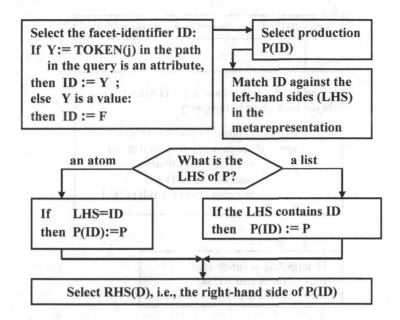

Fig. 8. Manipulation by RAFFAELLO as triggered by syntactic features detected inside the metarepresentation, starting with labels whose priority is highest. These boxes were already implemented in the LISP version of NAVIGATION as developed by Nissan by 1988, except — in Fig 10 and 11 — boxes with a grey bottom right corner.

done in what remains of a line after a semicolon, because this is how in LISP one adds comments.

Pay attention to the syntax of the attribute ARE if found nested inside ACCEPTATIONS. ARE is a *polysemous* attribute-name, that in different contexts refers to different slots. That is to say, it may happen we find ARE nested in some slot, i.e., under some attribute, different from ACCEPTATIONS. Parsing disambiguates polysemous slots according to their ancestry in the property-tree. The label f: is followed by a parenthesis stating ancestry (in our present example, the ancestor ACCEPTATIONS), and then by a separate childset of attributes. When found nested under ACCEPATIONS, the attrubute name ARE is followed by a sequence of facets with no attribute-name at the their beginning, and whose schema is the one stated in the production whose left-hand side is the string `single_acceptation` — but then also consider that it may happen we find ARE nested under the attribute ASSOCIATION_OF_IDEAS (in which case, ARE introduces a list of at least one "association chunk"), or then ARE may be found nested under either SYNONYMS or NEAR-SYNONYMS and this in turn involves two alternative syntactic features. The first option is captured by n: `syno_chunk` and this means that one finds under ARE a sequence of at least one "synonym chunk". That is to say, a sequence only of chunks each describing a single (near-)synonym, and sharing the nesting-schema, so an attribute-name would be superfluous, and this is why the "synonym chunk" is slot-less, i.e., it is not preceded by an attribute name. The alternative option is captured

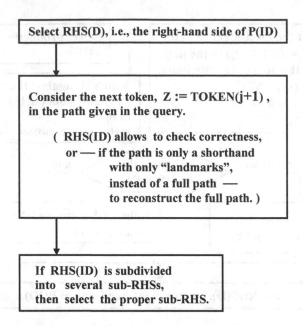

Fig. 9. Manipulation by RAFFAELLO as triggered by syntactic features detected inside the metarepresentation

by the label x: being followed by both n: SINGLE_SYNO and n: SYNO_CLUSTER. The code of the metarepresentation rules for ACCEPTATIONS and for ARE is as follows:

```
(ACCEPTATIONS          ( ARE ) )

(ARE    ( f: ( ACCEPTATIONS )
              n: single_acceptation

        f: ( SYNONYMS  NEAR-SYNONYMS )
              x:   n: syno_chunk
              x:   n: SINGLE_SYNO
                   n: SYNO_CLUSTER

        f: ( ASSOCIATION_OF_IDEAS )
              n: association_chunk
   )        )
```

The reason why under the label x: one finds two attributes, each preceded by the label n: is that a sequence where two kinds of facets may occur, so we must name the proper attribute.

11.4   A Sample Metarepresentation. Part II

Let us turn to the metarepresentation production that describes the valid structure of an "association chunk". There are alternatives, so we use the high-priority label x: followed by one of the options. Therefore, we find indeed an option whose syntax is captured by x: i: IS and this means that one finds in the slotless association chunk just the key for a siungle attribute, and this key value is preceded by the attribute IS. Otherwise, we have the option captured by the syntax x: is: TERM and this means that at most two more attributes may appear in the key, and that this is signalled by finding (instead of IS) the attribute name TERM, along with one or two more attributes. Which ones? This is captured by the syntax j: KEYWORD and this means: a keyword disambiguating the meaning of the term. But the syntax j: SCRIPT tells us that we may also find an identification of the script of the keyword. We may have chosed instead to identify the language, or the spelling of a language, instead of the script. Envisaging having several scripts was premature in 1988, but is now quite a possibility, with the spread of Unicode and of XML, which may accommodate various scripts thanks to Unicode.[19]

---

[19] At a later time, for a while, Nissan was member by invitation of a Unicode definition committee in England, with the role of making proposals concerning the Hebrew script, and for that purpose, he prepared specifications that included typographical needs from various contexts of use of the script, from scholarly transcriptions, to lexicographic practice as being instantiated in various Israeli dictionaries, to the practice of typesetters of devotional literature. For example, an early Israeli dictionary of Amharic had used a reversed *qamats* Hebrew diacritical mark in order to render what Romanisation expresses by means of a reversed e and Nissan included that. Philological works from Israel that need to account for Syriac data, transliterate them into the Hebrew script letter by letter, but as Syriac scriptorial practice is to express a plural word by writing the word in the singular and adding two dots side by side over the end of the word, also Israeli transliterations from Syriac do likewise, and Nissan included that diacritical mark. Medieval Judaeo-Arabic, and the usual scripts of the various modern Jewish vernaculars (e.g., modern Judaeo-Arabic, Judaeo-Spanish, and Judaeo- whatever, apart from Yiddish that was dealt with in Unicode separately) have their own needs in terms of diacritical marks.

Besides, the history of diacritical marks for the Hebrew scripts includes not only the Tiberian system currently in use, but also the Babylonian system, still in use by some philologists, and that survived in the Yemeni Jewish community. There also existed the simpler Palestinian system. The Babylonian and Palestinian systems added marks above letters, in between, whereas the Tiberian system mostly adds marks under each letter. Moreover, the history of the Tiberian system itself gives rise to Unicode needs: the late linguist Shlomo Morag pointed out, as can be seen in his collected papers, that historically some grammarians also envisaged the semivowel *ḥataf-ḥiriq*, just as there is a diacritical mark for the semivowels *ḥataf-qamats*, *ḥataf-pataḥ*, and *ḥataf-segol*. Nissan pointed out that much to the committee. The popular Megiddo English-Hebrew dictionary [49] introduced special diacritical marks for transliterating English into the Hebrew script. Devotional literature has specific needs, e.g., with the last letter of the Tetragrammaton containing in smaller type the word indicating how that divine name needs to be pronounced. Whereas this is traditional

Moreover, whereas by now we are acquainted with the x: label for "exclusive or", we are going to see an example of the y: label as well. The y:-preceded segment lists optional content that may appear in any of the x:-preceded segments (which, instead, are mutually exclusive).

in typesetting, there is a modern practice (promoted by one publisher of prayer books, Moreshet) of distinguishing between the mark for a *qamats* when it stands for /a/ and the same mark when is stands for /o/ (in the latter case, it is called a "small *qamats*", but is usually printed the same; the innovation was in making the "small *qamats*" look different, by making a vertical line longer). Other *desiderata* include the bent-neck and the beheaded versions of the letter *lamed* (traditional in Hebrew typesetting, historically out of the need to reduce spacing between lines, but the practice still exists in prayer books), the ligature of the letters *aleph* and *lamed* (a requirement for the devout), and the variant of the letter *vav* cut in the middle (a famous *hapax* from the Pentateuchal weekly reading of *Phineas*).

All of this was pointed out to the committee. Moreover, there are the Masoretic marks, indicating prosody in the Hebrew Bible. Whereas the committee was initially eager to listen, eventually nothing was taken on board, with no explanations given, and no further contact from the committee. An Israeli professor, Uzzi Ornan, was in the committee. He is known for his publicly expressed dislike for the Hebrew script. His minimalistic preferences prevailed. This is apparently why the Hebrew script is not well subserved by Unicode, with some glaring and dismal inadequacies. This did not need to be the case. By contrast, the Arabic and Arabic/Persian script is subserved beautifully (evidently because the respective committee did an excellent job), with diacritical signs subserving niche communities of users, and some typographical signs traditional from devotional literature (a cultural need that is as legitimate as any other). Extensions of the Arabic script from Asia are included, but one would also like to see such extensions from Africa (where modified Arabic letters appear in at least one textual genre: magic), as shown in Dalby's papers from 1967 and 1968 that also described autonomously developed West African scripts [13, 14].

Dalby enumerated so-called *sub-Arabic* scripts with the function of magico-cryptic alphabets. There are several of them: in the Hodh region of the south-western Sahara, eleven secret alphabets were recorded ([60, 59] and [14, p. 172, fn. 45]). Apart from the *al-Yāsīnī* alphabet, other sub-Arabic scripts include the *al-Qalfatīrī, al-Falaluīsī, al-Ṭabī'ī* and *al-'Ajamī* alphabets, these being alphabets recorded by Monteil [60], the *'Ibrāniyya* ("Hebrew") alphabet recorded by Monod [59], the "amulette" alphabet of Mauchamp [56, p. 208], and Ibn Waḥshiya's collection of 84 alphabets (the latter is controversial). Ancient Epigraphical South Arabian characters occur in an early 19th-century navigational guide from Kuwait, and were apparently used for magical nautical calculations. Also note special characters used in some Arabic books of magic ([pp. 150–167] [117] and [16, pp. 158–159], cited in [14, pp. 173–174]), as well as Arabic cryptography, e.g., the secret writing ascribed to the secretary of the Sultan Aḥmad al-Manṣūr of Morocco (1578–1603) ([12], cited in [14, p. 172, fn. 45]). "One of the scripts from the Hodh which is particularly rich in non-Arabic characters is the *al-Yāsīnī* alphabet, named either after its inventor (the mage Yāsīn?) or after the two 'mystic' letters which open the *Yāsīn* sura of the Koran (sura 36)" [14, p. 172]. (Nissan is thankful to Dr. Dorit Ofri of Geneva for making him aware in 1995 of David Dalby's papers [13, 14] and supplying him with photocopies, while she was preparing her Bern thesis about the Vai culture of Liberia, which has a peculiar alphabet of modern origination.)

```
(association_chunk     ( x:   i:  IS
                         x:   i2: TERM
                              j:  KEYWORD
                              j:  SCRIPT
                         y:   FOR_WHOM
)                        )
```

Under the attribute FOR_WHOM one may find one or more slotless chunks. Inside each such chunk, it is expected one would find the attributes FOR and LIKELIHOOD (the latter expresses a numerical range, which may be, e.g., hyperfuzzy). Pay attention to the syntax i_inc: FOR that conveys the prescription that FOR contains a variant of a key, allowing inclusion: for example, the values may be mathematicians or computer-scientists or both. It is valid to list either or both of them, if under FOR we find both of them listed.

```
(FOR_WHOM          ( n: for-whom_chunk ) )

(for-whom chunk   ( i_inc:  FOR
                    LIKELIHOOD
)                   )
```

In the following, we make use of the c: label. In the example, it precedes the attribute name MEANING and this means that inside the slotless chunk of a single lexical acceptation, one may find MEANING nested as intermediate: it is inside the facet to be identified by the key, but the key itself is nested deeper.

```
(single_acceptation  ( c: MEANING
                       CONNOTATION
                       RELATED_TO
                       FREQUENCY_SCORE_AMONG_ACCEPTATIONS
)                      )

(MEANING             ( i: KEYWORD
                       TEXTUAL_DEFINITION
                       DENOTATIONAL_FEATURES   )  )

(CONNOTATION         ( POS/NEG
                       CONNOTATIONAL_FEATURES   )  )

(POS/NEG             ( x:  terminal_singleton
                       x:  AT_FIRST
                       IN_CONTEXT              )  )
```

We are going to encounter the a: label. It is a high-priority label (like f:), and its syntax only differs from that of f: in that what follows a: needs to be enclosed by a parenthesis. Both those labels are about ancestry. The following means that the attribute IN_CONTEXT may be found nested inside the POS/NEG facet inside the `CONNOTATION` facet, or then alternatively one may find `IN_CONTEXT` nested directly under the attribute `BLA_BLA_BLA`.

```
(IN_CONTEXT        ( a:   ( POS/NEG CONNOTATION )
                          IMPRESSION_IS
                          IF_CONTEXT_IS
                   f:   ( BLA_BLA_BLA )
                        n: bla_bla_bla_chunk
  )                     )
```

What follows is the production for the `RELATED_TO` facet inside the lexical frames of ONOMATURGE. In a separate structure, the attribute name `RULES` is declared to be synonymous with `FORMATION_RULES` (as those rules are linguistic rules for word-formation. In Semitic languages, *free-place formulae* are a typical kind of derivational pattern).

```
(RELATED_TO        ( RULES
                     PECULIAR_FACETS
                     LIKELY_CONTEXT
                     SYNONYMS
                     NEAR-SYNONYMS     )   )


(RULES             ( SUFFIXES
                     PREFIXES
                     FREE-PLACE_FORMULAE
                     REDUPLICATIVE_PATTERNS
                     COMPOUND-FORMATION_PATTERNS ))
```

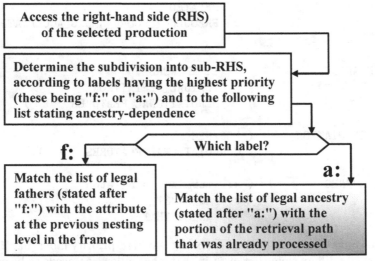

Fig. 10. Manipulation by RAFFAELLO as triggered by syntactic features being the f: label or the a: label. The grey box was not implemented.

Fig. 10 shows the control flow of interpretation which enables to handle appropriately the f: label and the a: label. Fig. 11 shows the control flow of interpretation which enables to handle appropriately the x: label, the n: label, and the g: label. Boxes with a grey bottom left corner were not implemented in the 1988 version in LISP of NAVIGATION.

11.5   A Sample Metarepresentation. Part III

The following production stands out, because its left-hand side is multiple: it is a list of five attribute names. This is equivalent to having five separate productions with the same right-hand part, and *atomic* left-hand sides.

```
(  ( SUFFIXES
     PREFIXES
     FREE-PLACE_FORMULAE
     REDUPLICATIVE_PATTERNS
     COMPOUND-FORMATION_PATTERNS  )
   ( n: formation-rule_chunk )  )
```

We may have listed these five rules instead:

```
(SUFFIXES
         ( n: formation-rule_chunk )  )

(PREFIXES
         ( n: formation-rule_chunk )  )

(FREE-PLACE_FORMULAE
         ( n: formation-rule_chunk )  )

(REDUPLICATIVE_PATTERNS
         ( n: formation-rule_chunk )  )

(COMPOUND-FORMATION_PATTERNS
         ( n: formation-rule_chunk )  )
```

The following rule prescribes the valid structure for a slotless "formation-rule chunk". The i2: label along with the j: label prescribe that the key has at least one attribute (it is IS), and at most further two attributes, which is useful in case rule-names are ambiguous.

```
(formation-rule_chunk       ( i2: IS
                              RELEVANCE_ORDINAL
                              j: INFLECTION_PARADIGM
                              j: MORPHO_CAT_IS        ) )

(INFLECTION_PARADIGM  ( FORM_IDENTIFICATION
                        INFLECTED_FORM_IS      ) )
```

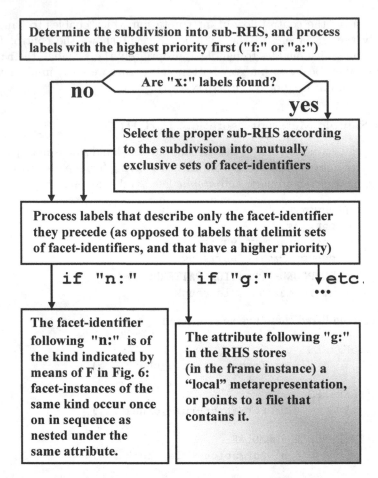

Fig. 11. Manipulation as triggered by syntactic features being the x: label, or the n: label, or the g: label

We allow the global metarepresentation to be supplemented with some local metarepresentation, either stored directly in a part of the lexical frame, or pointed to from that same facet. This is enabled by using the g: label, as already mentioned at the end of Subsec. 10.1 above. The following rule states that under the attribute PECULIAR_FACETS one should expect to find a local metarepresentation stored or pointed to from inside the facet whose slot is LOCAL_METAREPRESENTATION. By the reserved word etc in the context of this kind of rule, we mean: further attributes, as described in the local metarepresentation.

```
(PECULIAR_FACETS      ( g: LOCAL_METAREPRESENTATION
                        etc
)                     )
```

We have seen earlier the rule for ARE. But here in the following we have rules that state that the structure of SYNONYMS and of NEAR-SYNONYMS is just that we should expect to find the ARE facet nested inside them, and to find nothing else (i.e., no sibling facet of ARE) nested inside them. Moreover, we give the rule prescribing the valid structure of the slotless "synonym chunk". In each such chunk, we may find the key, and moreover the non-key facet whose attribute name is RELATIONSHIP. The value of the key is found in the facet whose attribute is TERM_IS but as this may not be sufficient for unambiguous identification, the i1: label stipulates that the key may be augmented by at most one other key facet, this being (as the j: label informs us) the facet whose attribute is KEYWORD_IS.

```
        (SYNONYMS                ( ARE ) )

        (NEAR-SYNONYMS           ( ARE ) )

        (syno_chunk        ( i1: TERM_IS
                             j:  KEYWORD_IS
                             RELATIONSHIP   ) )
]
```

The symbol] is standard syntax in FRANZ LISP for closing all open parentheses.[20] This is why this symbol is found at the end of CuPROS metarepresentation, as well as at the end of the lexical frames of ONOMATURGE, unless one wants to close down all levels of parenthesis one by one.

11.6   Slot-Synonymy, and Contextual Disambiguation of Slot-Polysemy

Our metarepresentation syntax allows *slot-synonymy*. That is to say, you may refer to the same attribute by different names; for example, MORPHO_CAT is (by convention in the ONOMATURGE expert system) a legal synonym of MORPHOLOGICAL_CATEGORY. Besides, the metarepresentation syntax allows *slot-polysemy*. That is to say, the same attribute-name may refer to slots that in different contexts, may father different subframe-schemata (not just variants of RHS meant to describe the same kind of knowledge).

For example, ARE is a dummy slot, which in the frames of ONOMATURGE may be the child of ACCEPTATIONS, or of SYNONYMS. Therefore, ARE is a *polysemous* attribute-name, which in different contexts refers to different slots. NAVIGATION (i.e., the component of RAFFAELLO that is guided by the metarepresentation), according to its fuller specification, disambiguates polysemous slots according to their ancestry in the property-tree. In such cases, the metarepresentation syntax subdivides the RHS of the production whose LHS is S, into parts headed by the

---

[20] Wilensky's [115] *LISPcraft* is a book about FRANZ LISP, whereas his [116] *Common LISPcraft* is a book about the COMMON LISP dialect of the LISP programming language. FRANZ LISP was also described by Larus [43].

label f: or a: followed by a parenthesis stating ancestry, and then by a separate childset of attributes (an f:-*sub-RHS* body, or an a:-*sub-RHS* body).

The labels f: and a: differ according to the conventions of the ancestry-list following the label, and preceding the body. In the case of the f: label, the parenthesis is a list of slots possibly fathering the LHS in the case where the legal childset of the LHS is as stated in the body. By contrast, in the case of the a: label, the parenthesis is a list of lists of slots: each innermost list states a possible father, its own father as well, and so forth. That is to say: a: is useful whenever ambiguity involves more than a single generation.

Another case (far more frequent) is possible: instances — S1, S2, ... — of the same slot S may happen to be children of different slots (say, P, Q, and R), and yet S1, S2, and so forth refer to the same meaning of S, and their legal childset is as stated, in the production of S, for the same meaning of S. The metarepresentation syntax expresses this by having S listed in different productions with different LHSs, while in the production whose LHS is S, no f: or a: label is included (that is: S is *monosemous,* unambiguous), or otherwise, P, Q, and R belong to the same ancestry-list, so the same f:-sub-RHS or a:-sub-RHS is referred to by S1, S2, and so forth.

Metarepresentation labels are in lower case, and usually end by a colon. The syntax of the label a: is just like the syntax of f: except that a: requires one more level of parenthesis, in the *ancestry-statement.*

$$\text{f:} \quad (\; <slot> \;) \quad \text{is equivalent to:} \quad \text{a:} \quad (\; (\; <slot> \;) \;)$$

$$\text{f:} \quad (\; A \; B \;) \quad \text{is equivalent to:} \quad \text{a:} \quad (\; (\; A \;) \; (\; B \;) \;)$$

By contrast, neither

$$\text{a:} \quad (\; (\; X \; Y \;) \;)$$

nor

$$\text{a:} \quad (\; (\; X \; Y \;) \; (\; Z \;) \;)$$

can be expressed in terms of the f: option.

a: is suited when stating just the father would be ambiguous. Then, the ancestry is stated in a list, beginning by the father, followed by the grandfather, and so forth, until no more ambiguity remains.

11.7   More Conventions

The kind of *sub-RHS* as distinguished according to ancestry is not the only kind of RHS subdivision allowed, even though it ranks as having the highest precedence among *RHS-subdividing labels.* A slot may father different attribute-schemata in the same context, that is, as having the same ancestry itself: our metarepresentation syntax envisages RHSs that are possibly subdivided into several alternative sub-RHSs, even nested.

At the same level of subdivision of an RHS, both f:-sub-RHSs and a:-sub-RHSs are allowed to appear. At inner level, the sub-RHS body may include further subdivisions as stated by means of a lower-priority RHS-dividing label, such as x: (See in Subsec. 13.1).

RHSs list possible children of the LHS: not all of the slots listed *must* appear in actual instances. This is, after all, intuitive for one used to formal grammars. It stands to reason that flexibility in nesting is subserved by a spectrum of alternatives being envisaged.

According to our conventions about the syntax of frames (our nested relations), slots (attributes) are in upper case, and possibly include underscores or digits as well. Values in frame instances — not in the metarepresentation — are either numbers, or special-symbol strings, or strings which contain lower-case letters and possibly also digits, special symbols, or upper-case letters. Values are not listed in the kind of metarepresentation we are describing.

In the metarepresentation, *slots* are only a particular case of *facet-identifier*. A facet-identifier is *nonterminal,* if and only if beside appearing inside some RHS or RHSs, it is also the LHS of some production (a *different* production, as we do not admit cyclical productions).

11.8   Slotless-Facet Identifiers, and Repeatable Facet-Schemata

There may be, in a metarepresentation, such nonterminal facet-identifiers that are in lower-case. This convention is needed, in order to represent, in the metarepresentation, such *slotless facets* as occasionally appear inside frames. Why do frames include facets with no expressly named slot?

Slotless facets are *repeatable* under the same father (that is: the sub-RHS body that is nested deepest, in the RHS subdivision into alternative sub-RHSs), and if that father does not have any other kind of child facet-identifiers, then putting a slot would not bear identifying information. However, not every repeatable facet is slotless: slots may be put there even if unnecessary, and moreover, if a repeatable child is not a singleton child-set in the considered RHS, then it should have a slot. That slot would not distinguish facet instances with the same slot, but it would distinguish them from children with any other slot.

n: precedes a facet-identifier that, as instantiated in the same facet whose slot is the LHS, can be repeated there several times. This is a frequent case in the metarepresentation. Most often, *repeatable-facet identifiers* (that is, facet-identifiers preceded by n:) in the metarepresentation are in lower-case, that is, they identify a *slotless* facet. Bear in mind that n: is not an RHS-subdividing label.

In fact, an *RHS-subdividing label* does not head a body. A *sub-RHS body* includes one or several facet-identifiers, and ends as soon as another RHS-subdividing label with the same precedence is met. (For example, an f:-sub-RHS body or an a:-sub-RHS body ends as soon as the successive *ancestry-disambiguating label* (that is, f: or a:) is met.

By contrast, n: (like several other labels) does not head a sub-RHS body, but it qualifies only the facet-identifier being its immediate successor. We say, then, that n: is a *one-successor label.*

11.9   Ancestor-Identifying Descendants of Repeatable Facets: Attributes Storing Identifiers of Subframe-Instances

i: is one more one-successor label. In order to enable the identification of the proper instance of a certain repeatable facet — when a path is given as input to the **navigate_and_retrieve** function of NAVIGATION, or when a path is the value in a **PATH** or **POINTER** facet — each repeatable-facet identifier has a *father-identifying child* (or an *ancestor-identifying descendant* in general, if the c: label is also used: see below).

A *father-identifying nonterminal* always corresponds to a *slotted* facet (as opposed to a *slotless* facet). In the path given as argument to the function **navigate_and_retrieve** the filler of the *father-identifying facet* (or *ancestor-identifying facet*) fits in the place of the identified father (or ancestor) — if the latter is a slotless facet — or follows its slot, in the path (if the father is an instance of a slotted repeatable facet).

Every *ancestor-identifying descendant* is preceded by i: in the RHS where it appears. Let us consider the case where A1 is a *repeatable-facet identifier,* and A2 is its *ancestor-identifying descendant.* Then, A1 is preceded by n: in the RHS(s) where it appears. Besides, if A2 is a direct child of A1 (that is to say: in frames, A2 is nested immediately under A1), then, in the production whose LHS is A1, the RHS lists A2 as preceded by the label i:

However, it may also happen that the *ancestor-identifier* A2 is not an immediate child of the ancestor A1 it identifies. In the lexical frames of Nissan's ONOMATURGE expert system, this happens with the single acceptations, which are identified by the value of the facet **KEYWORD**. The latter is a child of the facet **MEANING,** that in turn, is a child of the facet storing the single acceptation. Then, A2 is the facet **KEYWORD,** whereas A1 is the slotless-facet identifier **single_acceptation** under **ARE** — which itself is under **ACCEPTATIONS**.

The metarepresentation syntax provides the one-successor label c: that in the production whose LHS is **single_acceptation** precedes the attribute **MEANING** as listed in the RHS. Then — in the production whose LHS is **MEANING** — the RHS lists the attribute **KEYWORD** as being preceded by the label i:

Visiting the metarepresentation, the *inter-production path* between *single_acceptation* (as being preceded by n:) and the RHS where **KEYWORD** is listed (as being preceded by i:), it deserves notice that the *signal* represented by the label c: occurs only once: **KEYWORD** is a *grandfather-identifying grandchild.* Ancestry more remote than that could correspond to a longer inter-production path, along which c: would appear several times.

11.10   Multi-attribute or Multi-facet Identification-Keys

A rather infrequently occurring label is i<*digit*> : of which an example is i2: The label i<*digit*> : — also a one-successor label for ancestor-identification — states that the slot stated as following it in an RHS, is a component in an *identification-key,* but that it is not necessarily a *singleton key:* at most <*digit*> further attributes could appear in the key.

Let us explain that by means of an example, drawn from the ONOMATURGE expert system for word-formation. In ONOMATURGE, most word-formation rules are templates, where an exploded stem fits. This is typical of the morphology of Semitic languages. The lexical root is a sequence of radical consonants, which generally speaking need not be consecutive, and they fit inside empty "plugs" interspersed inside the template, which apart from the plugs also includes substrings of vowels and possibly formative consonants that are not part of the lexical root.

This corresponds, e.g., to suffixes in English: the suffix -*able* means 'that can be done' whereas the equivalent derivational template in Hebrew is /PaˆiL/, where P, ˆ, L are metasymbols representing the consonants of a "triliteral" root consisting of three radical consonants. This way, by inserting the letters of the root $\sqrt{\text{lmd}}$, (that denotes 'learn') in the derivational template /PaˆiL/, one obtains the adjective /lamid/, i.e., 'learnable'. Once you obtain a word from the word-formation template, that word is in its lemmatised or lexematised, i.e., uninflected form, that is to say, this is the form the way you could insert it as a headword of some entry in the dictionary. Now, let us consider inflected forms, out of the inflected paradigm of the considered word-formation pattern from which the word derived. For example, /PaˆiL/ is the uninflected pattern, whereas its plural form is /PˆiLim/, as instantiated in the word /lmidim/ for the sense 'which are learnable'.

Sometimes, the uninflected identifier of a word-formation pattern happens to "homonymously" refer to different patterns (possibly with the same meaning) that are inflected according to (at least partially) different inflection paradigms.[21] One such derivational pattern is /PaˆoL/. One variant of it has the plural /PaˆoLim/, and another variant has the plural /PaˆoLot/.

Then, let us think about any facet (for example, in the RULES subtree, in the subframe of an acceptation inside a lexical frame) that has to list /PaˆoL/, as being associated with only one of the two inflection paradigms. The *single_rule* slotless facet would then contain an identification-key, as well as non-key attributes. For unambiguous pattern-names, it would be enough to state:

```
( (IS  <pattern-name> )
  (RELATED_INFO  <dependent information> )  )
```

---

[21] We explain this in some detail in the Appendix A to the present article. In this footnote, suffice it to concisely explain that this is the case of the uninflected pattern-identifier /PaˆoL/, of which one variant shortens the first syllable's *a* in the inflected forms, and another variant retains it instead. The latter is not as productive in the Hebrew lexicon, i.e., its derivatives are rarer, and moreover, in Israeli Hebrew no new derivatives are formed by using it any more.

It was typically productive in the Roman era, because of the influence of Aramaic, and by applying it, masculine nominalised participles are generated. Moreover, both the *a*-shortening /PaˆoL/ and the *a*-retaining /PaˆoL/ have two subvariants, according to whether the ending of the plural is -*im* or -*in*, or is -*ot* instead.

Of the *a*-retaining /PaˆoL/, there exists in Hebrew a pattern whose plural form is /PaˆoLot/, but there also exists in Hebrew the *a*-retaining pattern /PaˆoL/ whose plural form is /PaˆoLim/, and which is seldom instantiated, and most examples of which belong to Tannaic Hebrew (also known as Tannaitic Hebrew or Middle Hebrew, from the Roman age), and are often obsolete in contemporary Hebrew.

where the nested facet (IS <pattern-name>) is the *father-identifying facet*. In the metarepresentation, the corresponding productions are:

```
(PATTERNS    ( n:    pattern_with_information ) )
(pattern_with_information    ( i:    IS
                                     RELATED_INFO ) )
```

That way, IS is a *singleton key*, that is, a key including a single attribute. By contrast, in the case of the /Pa^oL/ derivational pattern of Hebrew, the inner facet (IS Pa^iL) is not enough for identification, inside the *single_rule* slotless facet. Correspondingly, in the metarepresentation, IS alone is not enough, in the key. Therefore, the productions resort to the label indicating the possibility of an extended key being used:

```
(PATTERNS    ( n:    pattern_with_information ) )
(pattern_with_information    ( i2:    IS
                                      RELATED_INFO
                                      j:  INFLECTION_PARADIGM
                                      j:  MORPHO_CAT_IS
 )                                    )
```

By this syntax, we mean that the key may include *at most* <*digit*> +1 (here: 3) facets, that in our example are: IS, INFLECTION_PARADIGM, and MORPHO_CAT_IS.

Instances could be those included in the following code, being an example of different single-rule subtrees. They are legal inside the subtree rooted in RULES, inside an acceptation of different lexical entries. The pattern-name /Pa^oL/ is ambiguous (because it is associated with two different inflection paradigms, whose salient feature is the form of the the plural). Therefore, a multi-attribute key is stated.

```
( (IS  Pa^iL)  (RELATED_INFO  <dependent information> ) )

( (IS  Pa^oL)
  (INFLECTION_PARADIGM  ( (FORM_IS Pa^oLot)
                          (FORM_CLASSIFICATION plural)
  )                     )
  (RELATED_INFO  <dependent information> )
)

( (IS  Pa^oL)
  (INFLECTION_PARADIGM  ( (FORM_IS Pa^oLim)
                          (FORM_CLASSIFICATION plural)
  )                     )
  (RELATED_INFO  <dependent information> )
```

We have used, in the previous code, the j: label, a one-successor label that precedes each legal *key-completion* attribute. In the code given earlier, we used the slot INFLECTION_PARADIGM (which is the slot of a nonterminal facet), in order to obtain a 2-facet key (including the attributes inside the `INFLECTION_PARADIGM` nested facet belonging to the key).

Conceptually, the same pair { IS, `INFLECTION_PARADIGM` } could even not be enough, as words of some different morphological category may be generated out of the same pattern, even once its paradigm has been stated. For example, we could have masculine as opposed to feminine nouns, or we could have adjectives vs. adverbs, and so forth. Then, a 3-facet key should be used.

As a matter of fact,

- { `IS` }   keys are frequent inside `RULES` subtrees;
- { `IS, INFLECTION_PARADIGM` }   keys are the most likely exception;
- { `IS, MORPHO_CAT_IS` }   keys are expected to be rarer;
- { `IS, INFLECTION_PARADIGM, MORPHO_CAT_IS` }   keys are unlikely, but not ruled out by the metarepresentation syntax of ONOMATURGE.

Besides, bear in mind that there is no need to distinguish between AND and OR, in this representation of the frame-schema AND/OR tree; however, optionally, one could state *mutually exclusive* parts of the same RHS (or sub-RHS), by means of the `x:` label. (See in Subsec. 13.1).

`i`<*digit*> `p`<*digit*> : is another kind of label. Just as `c:` has been introduced in order to allow having the `i:` facet in a level of facets nested more deeply than just the children of the facet of the `n:`-preceded slot considered, the option `i`<*digit*> `p`<*digit*> : enables having a facet — whose slot is preceded in the RHS by `j:` (key-completing) — in a level nested more deeply than just that of the `i`<*digit*> : facet.

When the slot preceded by the `j:` label is a "nephew" in the tree, rather than a brother, of the slot preceded by `i`<*digit*> :, then let `i`<*digit*> `p`<*digit*> : precede what should have been the `i`<*digit*> :-preceded slot in the proper RHS.

The digit between `i` and `p` may be zero, or a greater natural number, and has just the semantics of the digit of the `i`<*digit*> : label. That is to say, that digit indicates that that particular number of `j:`-preceded slots are present in the same RHS (if undivided), or in the same innermost sub-RHS.

As for the digit between `p` and the colon, it indicates that that particular number of `p:`-preceded slots are present in the same RHS or innermost sub-RHS.

Now, let us consider the `p:` label. When a key-completing facet is at the same tree-level of the key necessary component — this being the facet whose slot is preceded by `i`<*digit*> : or `i`<*digit*> `p`<*digit*> : — then its slot is preceded by `j:` in the proper RHS or sub-RHS.

By contrast, when a key completing facet is at the level nested immediately more deeply (i.e., is a "nephew" of the key necessary component), then the father of that key-completing nephew is a brother of the key necessary component, and is listed in the same RHS or sub-RHS, and is preceded by the `p:` label.

As for the "nephew" itself, the label `q:` should precede that slot, in the RHS or sub-RHS where it is listed.

11.11   Facets Containing Local Navigation-Guides

The syntax of CUPROS is as flexible as to allow a subtree of a frame instance to contain a metarepresentation specifying how to navigate locally. That is to say, there is the option of the metarepresentation and the object-level representation (the latter being the frame instance) commingling together. This is not a situation we would normally envisage or recommend (while recognising that in some future application, a local metarepresentation may be convenient). In fact, in the implementation of NAVIGATION we did not include also the parsing of such a local metarepresentation by switching to it as found inside the frame instance being visited; it would be straightforward however to allow the parser such switching.

g: should precede slots of *navigation-guide facets* mentioned in the frame instance itself, and describing the access to instance-specific schemata of subframes.

While frame-representation in frames is the *object-level* of representation, the production-system stating legal schemata of frames is the *meta-level* representation, or *metarepresentation.*

The **g:** option enables the object-level representation to include subframes described by *local metarepresentations:* such a description is stored in — or pointed to from — facets whose slot is preceded by the label **g:** in the *global metarepresentation* (or, more generally, in the metarepresentation that is immediately more general, if several levels of locality of metarepresentations are present).

12   Sample Rules from the Metarepresentation of the Lexical Frames of ONOMATURGE

12.1   The Top Few Levels in Lexical Frames

Thus far, we have explained various labels that may occur inside a CUPROS metarepresentation. Further options as expressed by means of labels in a CUPROS metarepresentation will be explained by referring to the sample metarepresentation code shown in the following. These are productions from the metarepresentation of the lexical entries of the ONOMATURGE expert system.

```
(atom                   ( INFLECTION
                        MORPHO_CAT
                        x: ACCEPTATIONS
                        x: LEXEMES
                . . . . . . . )  )
```

The root of the lexical frame is represented by *atom.* A lexical entry or a rule may have more than one meaning (i.e., acceptation). That is why there is a subtree rooted in ACCEPTATIONS. Sometimes acceptations are clustered in lexemes of the same entry. If LEXEMES is under the root, then ACCEPTATIONS is not there at the same nesting level. Such being the case, ACCEPTATIONS may be found instead as being a child of the slotless nonterminal *single_lexeme* — which is itself a child of LEXEMES.

```
(MORPHO_CAT          ( x: terminal_list
                       x: ARE
                       y: s: single_lexeme
                          s: single_acception ) )
```

Under MORPHO_CAT, a possible example of *terminal_list* is

(noun masculine plural)

A very important part of a lexical frame is the part where different meanings are distinguished and described:

```
(ACCEPTATIONS        ( ARE ) )
```

Acceptations are distinct meanings (especially such word senses that — unlike lexemes — are related to each other) of a lexical entry, or even of a word-formation rule (this is so, because some given derivational pattern may be productive of agent nouns, for example).

```
(LEXEMES             ( ARE ) )
```

When the etymology is different, or when meanings are unrelated, then dictionaries would rather list the lexical entry under distinct paragraphs, and these are called *lexemes*. Each lexeme may include even several acceptations.

12.2 The Metarepresentation Rules for Facets of Individual Lexemes or Acceptations

Consider the structure of the subtree of an individual lexeme:

```
(single_lexeme   ( i: LEXEME_KEYWORD
                     INFLECTION
                     MORPHO_CAT
                     ACCEPTATIONS ) )
```

Inside the facet of LEXEME_KEYWORD, in the lexical frames of the ONOMATURGE expert system, one expects to find an English-like, unambiguous identification string. By "English-like", we mean that the string looks like an English word or compound, but this string is conventional, so one should not mistake this for an actual description in English of what the given lexeme means.

Concerning the facets INFLEXION and MORPHO_CAT, facets with those slots may also be found directly under the root of the lexical entry, that is to say, directly in the metarepresentation production rule whose left-hand side is the string atom (the labels s: and z: are relevant for this).

```
(single_acception  ( c: MEANING
                       CONNOTATIONS
                       RELATED_TO
                       AURO
                       . . . . . . ) )
```

In the latter CuPros production, the slot MEANING is the root of a subtree that may include any out of different kinds of artificial intelligence representations for expressing the meaning of the same semantic concept. Actually the ONOMATURGE expert system did not require accessing the MEANING facet, because the manipulation of the English-like descriptors of acceptations or lexemes was enough for getting reasonable results.

The AURO facet was used by the control component of the ONOMATURGE expert system in order to rank the candidate neologisms that it generates in output. AURO is a fuzzy mark of a subjective estimate of frequency vs. rarity. For both the stem employed in a coinage trial, and the rule if owning a frame, the main scores retrieved and employed are AURO and AURC as well as NORMATIVITY (if found). AURO stands for *Actual Use Relevance Ordinal*, whereas AURC stands for *Actual Use Relevance Cardinal*.

AURO describes context-independent subjectively rated frequency of the acceptation with respect to the other acceptations of the same lexical entry. AURO = 1 means that the acceptation considered has the subjectively rated highest frequency among those associated with the acceptations of the given frame. Note however that scores are neither necessarily consecutive numbers, nor unique. Two acceptations may happen to both have the same AURO score; if no smaller AURO value is found in any AURO facet of any other acceptation in the same frame, then we are facing the worst case of ambiguity (provided that context is ignored, and of course this is quite a big methodological assumption, and possibly a flaw of the design; the proof however is in the pudding, and the results of ONOMATURGE looked reasonable).

AURC describes context-independent subjectively rated frequency of the acceptation with respect to the whole lexicon. That is, AURC states how rare the term is, as used in a certain acceptation, in the contemporary use of the given natural language. AURC values around 250 are associated with frequent acceptations of frequent terms. AURC values around 800 indicate that the term (as in the acceptation considered) is considerably rare. We must stress that numerical information that we provide on diffusion, is *not* statistically based on the frequency of occurrences in document corpora. Our frequency degrees are subjectively estimated diffusion degrees, where scaling is also conventional and "naive", with no claim of precision in terms of frequency, or even of emulating actual values of frequency: Nissan, while developing ONOMATURGE, took the liberty to exaggerate the diffusion or the rarity of terms, acceptations, and rules. By contrast, rigorous investigation into *term frequency* has been carried out in several places, concerning various languages or corpora.

12.3   Facets for Semantic, Morphological, and Historical Information

Now, let us turn to the metarepresentation of the RELATED_TO facet. Inside it, the RULES facet lists such word-formation rules that have a meaning coincident with the given meaning of the lexical-entry atom. In the ONOMATURGE expert system, derivational patterns were implemented either in LISP, on in the UNIX Shell language. For example, the Hebrew derivational pattern Pa^~aL was implemented as template-rule called Pa^~aL and meaning 'any professional'. Therefore it could be expected to be listed in the RULES facet inside the lexical frame of a word meaning 'a professional'.

Under the facet PECULIAR_FACETS it was envisaged that one could include a possible local guide, that is to say, a "private" metarepresentation to be stored inside the lexical frame itself, instead of separately.

```
(RELATED_TO        ( RULES
                   g: PECULIAR_FACETS
                   CONTAINED_IN_THE_IDIOMS
                   SYNONYMS
                   NEAR_SYNONYMS
                   CONTRARIES
                   MOP
          . . . . . . ) )
```

Actually MOP facets were not included inside the lexical frames in the ONOMATURGE expert system, but the very possibility of inclusion was envisaged. Roger Schank's and Michael Dyer's *Memory Organization Packets,* or *MOPs* [17], enable to represent an abstraction of goal-driven scripts, corresponding to an abstract contractual relation (such as a shop, without the need to stick to a particular kind of shop), and with several characters being associated with various roles, each with its own chain of goals and plans. This enables interpretation by default, when something is not stated explicitly in the story analysed by Dyer's BORIS automated story-understanding program. About story understanding, see, e.g., [77, 78] in Vol. 2 of the present volume set.

```
(ARE            ( f: ( SYNONYMS  NEAR_SYNONYMS )
                    n: componential_difference_doubleton
                f: ( ACCEPTATIONS )
                    n: single_acceptation
                f: ( LEXEMES )
                    n: single_lexeme
                f: ( MORPHO_CAT )
                    n: HISTORY
                    n: MORPHO_WITH_WEIGHT
)          )

(componential_difference_doubleton
                        ( i: IS
                          DIFFERENCES ) )
```

The latter production rule is suitable for a semantic componential analysis. For example, under the IS facet, one may find (IS sofa) in the frame of the term that denotes the general lexical concept 'chair' (for sitting). Eventually, componential analysis was not used by the control component of the ONOMATURGE expert system, but some of the preparatory work [66, 67] considered the use of componential analysis indeed.

```
(MORPHO_WITH_WEIGHT    ( i: MORPHO_CAT_IS
                         RELEVANCE_IS ) )
```

Sometimes, the morphological gender of a noun, or — in general — the morphological category of a word or of a template, differs in different historical strata of the given language.[22] Besides, when a noun has been, e.g., masculine and feminine in the same stratum, one ought to state what was the relative frequency in use, e.g., that feminine was far more frequent than masculine. This is shown in the following metarepresentation code.

Take notice of how we position the CONTEXT facet: this way, the same MORPHO_CAT_IS may refer to several contexts, with different relevance.

```
(HISTORY (  x:    i1: MORPHO_CAT_IS
                      RELEVANCE_IS
                  j:  STRATUM
            2x:   i:  MORPHO_CAT_IS
                  n:  CONTEXT
            3x:   i:  MORPHO_CAT_IS
                  d:  DEFINE_RELATION
                  rel: MORPHO_CAT_IS
                  rel: CONTEXT
            x:    i:  MORPHO_CAT_IS
                      RELEVANCE_IS
                      ORDINAL
            x:    i:  MORPHO_CAT_IS
                      RELEVANCE_IS
                      CAME_AFTER
            y:    s:  single_lexeme
                  s:  single_acceptation
         )          )
```

The CAME_AFTER facet states some historical sequence. The argument of CAME_AFTER is the value of another MORPHO_CAT_IS, or some pointer to any atom or frame-vertex. As for *single_lexeme* and *single_acceptation* — consider that sometimes, the morphological category (e.g. masculine noun or feminine noun) depends upon the particular meaning of the word or of the template-rule. Then,

---

[22] This was historically the case of the Hebrew noun *śadé,* i.e., 'field'. It is masculine in Biblical and Modern Hebrew, but feminine in Tannaic Hebrew. It was also the case of *lašón,* the name for 'tongue' in Hebrew. In Biblical Hebrew it is feminine, but in Tannaic (or Tannaitic) Hebrew it is sometimes masculine, and sometimes feminine. By contrast, *šémeš* — the name for 'sun' in Biblical Hebrew — is feminine but on occasion masculine (but it is always feminine in Israeli Hebrew), whereas in Tannaic Hebrew the term itself was replaced with the feminine noun *ḥammá* (literally, 'hot one'), just as *yaréaḥ,* the masculine noun by which Biblical Hebrew refers to the moon (and that is also the term in use in Israeli Hebrew), was replaced in Tannaic Hebrew with the feminine noun *levaná* (literally, 'white one').

a `MORPHO_CAT` facet (the root of a subtree) should be looked at, under the particular acceptation or lexeme.

```
(CAME_AFTER        ( n: MORPHO_CAT_IS
                     n: POINTER        ) )
```

As we are not sure that `HISTORY` will remain unique, in the metadata schema, we give its proper ancestry. `ARE` is ambiguous. Therefore, its father is given, too:

```
(CONTEXT           ( a: ( (HISTORY 2x ARE MORPHO_CAT) )
                     n:  stratum_information
)                  )


(stratum_information ( i: STRATUM
                       RELEVANCE_IS ) )

(DEFINE_RELATION   ( a: ( (HISTORY 3x ARE MORPHO_CAT) )
                     n: relation
)                  )
```

12.4   Considerations about Facets in the Lexical Frames

In the introduction to Menaḥem Moreshet's *A Lexicon of the New Verbs in Tannaic Hebrew* [61, Sec. III.4, p. 75 ff], one finds this example of disappearance or shrinking use of Biblical Hebrew verbs from given lexical roots in the Tannaic stratum of Hebrew, and the emergence of a new verb that took over for denoting the same sense 'to be in charge (of)':

$$\sqrt{\text{šrt}}\ ,\ \ \sqrt{\text{khn}}\ \ \ —\ \ \ \sqrt{\text{šmš}}$$
$$\downarrow \qquad \downarrow \qquad\qquad \uparrow$$

(shrank) disappeared   appeared,
                        took over

In the frame of the root $\sqrt{\text{šmš}}$, or of the verb /šimmeš/, derived from it, and which means 'to be in charge (of)', it makes sense to include this information about the history of those verbs:

```
(EVOLUTION
   ( (FROM_STRATUM   ( Biblical_Hebrew ) )
     (TO_STRATUM     ( Tannaic_Hebrew ) )
     (PHENOMENA
             ( (ROOT  ( $rt ) )
               (DID   ( shrink ) )   )
             ( (ROOT  ( khn ) )
               (DID   ( disappear ) ) )
             ( (ROOT  ( $m$ ) )
               (DID   ( appear  take_over ) ) )
   ) ) )
```

This is a kind of phenomenon to which we are going to devote some attention in Appendix B. In the present subsection, instead, we are going to make a few more general considerations. Let us consider a particular kind of facet from the lexical frames of ONOMATURGE: HISTORY under MORPHO_CAT. Its purpose is to store knowledge about the evolution of how a certain lexical entry used to belong to *morphological categories*, throughout history as documented in different *historical strata* of the language.[23]

Such knowledge is not resorted to by the control of ONOMATURGE, but in general, knowledge-bases in lexicography may involve also such information; for example:

- for such lexical entries that used to be both *masculine* and *feminine* in the same stratum or in different strata;
- or for lexical entries that used to be *singularia tantum* (i.e., only in the singular) — or, instead, *pluralia tantum*, i.e., only in the plural — during a certain historical period, while admitting both singular and plural forms in some other historical periods;
- Sets of semantically related lexical entries happen to share particular morphological features, in given languages: even only the gender.[24]
- More in general, morphological evolution for large classes of terms sometimes concerns change of morphological gender, especially the terms evolve from a language (or stratum) admitting the neuter, to a language with only masculine and feminine.

---

[23] In the present volume, the articles [80, 81] are concerned with historical linguistics, and in part the approach to representation is akin to lexical nested relations as discussed here.

[24] Of course, gender alone is far less significant, semantically, than a formation-pattern with a small set of acceptations. Nevertheless, in given contexts, gender still gives useful indications. For example, Italian *pera*, in the feminine, denotes 'pear' (the fruit), whereas *pero*, masculine, denotes 'pear-tree' (and etymologically corresponds a neuter Latin noun). In most cases of fruits that belong, as concepts, to traditional culture (thus, excluding some exotic fruits), gender distinguishes fruits from trees, in Italian. In Florence in 1974, at a conference on Camito-Semitic, W. Vycichl remarked that in Coptic, to refer to a statue of a male god a masculine form, *twōt*, of the noun for 'statue' was used, but the feminine form, *twoote*, if the statue was of a goddess. Just one exception is recorded, of the feminine form of the noun for 'statue' being used when referring to the statue of a male god, and Vycichl suggested that this exception is from a late period — the Christian era of Egypt, and he tentatively proposed that this was by influence of the gender of a noun, *eikōn*, for 'statue' being feminine in Greek (a language that was quite influential on Coptic after Christianisation) [112, p. 71].

Gender is somewhat relevant also for *zoonyms*, that is, names of animals. According to the historical period and to the dialect (as it happened in Italian) certain zoonyms had their masculine form used as being the *unmarked* form (that is: the general term, denoting both males and females), while, instead, the feminine form (derived morphologically from the entry in the masculine form) was capable of indicating both females and indistinctly males and females. The distinction between *marked* vs. *unmarked* terms in semantics and in morphology is standard knowledge in linguistics; see, e.g., [50, Vol. 1, Ch. 9.7]. The evolution of the gender of Italian *zoonyms* was discussed by Rohlfs [90, §381, cf. §353].

Let us elaborate about the latter. A quantitatively relevant, heterogeneous class of Latin neuter nouns are masculine or feminine in Romance languages that have no neuter gender. This phenomenon is related to the partition of nouns belonging to the five Latin nominal declensions, among new paradigms in Romance languages or dialects; cf., e.g., §§350–355 and 383–385 in [90]. A similar phenomenon, perhaps simpler as it involves only the morphological gender, occurred with Yiddish terms in the neuter, that became either masculine or feminine in the Lithuanian dialect of Yiddish, that, because of the influence of the Lithuanian language, had no neuter gender.

Morphological phenomena sometimes involve the gender of *phytonyms* (that is, names of plants), in a given language. This is the case of Italian terms indicating fruit-bearing trees: they often share the treatment of the gender, in opposition to the gender of names of fruits. In Romance languages, names of trees (and fruits) correspond to nouns belonging to declensions (and genders) as in Latin. The morphology of phytonyms in Italian was discussed by Rohlfs [90, §382]. Let us consider one more example involving phytonyms and gender. In Latin, the suffix *-ago* was resorted to in order to form phytonyms, and was preserved in Italian in this role, having become *-àggine* in some feminine Italian phytonyms [91, §1058]. In some Italian dialects, the suffix developed a masculine variant (see [91, §1058]), perhaps because of the final *-o* of the third Latin nominal declension, which was attracted into the set of masculine nouns of the second declension (ending in *-us* in the nominative, but in *-o* in the ablative and dative); cf. [90, §§352, 353]. Nevertheless, in Sicilian one finds *piràinu* (see [91, §1058]), i.e., 'pear-tree' (applying the suffix, as opposed to Italian *pero* and to Latin), the masculine suffix and gender were adopted, probably by attraction into the class of tree-names, which are used to be in the masculine, in Italian and in its dialects.

The morphology of Hebrew (and Aramaic), too, is concerned, as phytonyms are involved. A *phytonym-formation pattern* in Talmudic Aramaic is the rare /Pa^PLina/, instantiated in /parphina/ (from the root $\sqrt{prh}$, associated with the meanings 'flower' and 'to flower'), and in /harhbina/ (which has become *harhăviná* in Israeli Hebrew), from the root $\sqrt{hrb}$, associated with the meaning 'sword' (of the Hebrew noun /herb/ *hérev*), and also with the meanings 'dry' and 'destroyed' of the Hebrew adjective /hareb/ *harév*. In Hebrew, the few instances of the derivational pattern /Pa^PLina/ are in the feminine, by interpreting the final *-a* as indicating the gender, whereas in Aramaic instead the final *-a* originally was equivalent to the article 'the'. In Aramaic, the final *-a* originally was the suffixed definite article, but this role, which was still found in Biblical Aramaic, was lost in later strata, that kept the ending in nouns as found in any syntactic position. A likely conjecture is that the article suffix derived from /ha/, for the demonstrative 'this', which on the other hand also became the Hebrew prefix /ha-/, with the role of definite article and interrogative particle. Cf. the evolution of the Latin demonstrative *ille,* i.e., 'that', which evolved into the Italian prefixed definite articles, as opposed to an areal feature from the Balkans, including, e.g., the Rumanian suffix *-ul* for the determinative article: Italian *il lupo,* Rumanian *lupul,* English *the wolf.*

In a footnote in Alinei and Nissan [3], it was suggested that the immigration of agriculturalists speaking a version of Northwest Semitic in which the demonstrative became the article suffix (like in Aramaic) may be what gave raise to the Balkan areal feature (found in Bulgarian, Macedonian, Rumanian, and Albanian) by which the determinative article is a suffix. This conjecture pinpointed the suggestion made by Alinei in [2, pp. 215–216] that it was an "unknown language" from the Fertile Crescent, at the time of the introduction of agriculture into the Balkans, that introduced into the Balkanic *Sprachbund* the suffixation of the demonstrative article.

12.5   The Effects of Omission from a Noun Phrase

If one term, or a class of terms, evolved from a noun phrase that included the term considered and an accompanying term, by omitting of the latter, then gender (or number) agreement in the original noun phrase often determines the gender (and number) of the resulting term.

Omissions may imply assumptions, and assumptions often evolve with technology. Even tramway lines, as opposed to bus or trackless-trolley lines, happen to involve conventions on gender: in Milan, in order to reach the university where he was studying, Nissan used to take *la 60* (a bus route), and then *il 23* (a tram route), instead of taking *la 90* (the route of a *filobus*, i.e., a trolleybus, a trackless trolley). Whereas numbers (or letters) are the name of lines of the urban public transports, the name of tramway lines is in the masculine, by implying *tram,* which is masculine and indicates the vehicle (i.e., the tramcar) or the route, as opposed to the rather affected *tranvia,* that is feminine and indicates the route, and as opposed to *linea autofilotranviaria* that is in the feminine, and indicate any bus (*autobus*), trolleybus (from *filobus*), or tramway route. By contrast, bus routes are in the feminine, by implying *linea (automobilistica),* as opposed to *autobus,* which is in the masculine, and indicates the vehicle. A trackless trolley (a trolleybus) is termed a *filobus,* which is morphologically masculine, but its routes are referred to in the feminine, by implying *linea.*

12.6   Socio-cultural Change, and Morphological Gender

Socio-cultural change is sometimes at the root of morphological gender change, in the way professionals are usually termed. As an example of culture-bound morphological change of gender, consider the names for such professions that, because of varying socio-cultural conditions, used to be typically carried out by men, while at present they are typically carried out by women, so the unmarked form used to follow the prevailing situation. For example: Italian *segretario* and Hebrew /mazkir/ denote 'secretary' and, as they are in the masculine form, at present they are typically used in order to indicate especially a leader in the parties or trade-unions, as well as political advisers, while today, the unmarked term for a secretary at commercial firms, or in low ranks of the administration, is in the feminine: Italian *segretaria,* and Hebrew /mazkira/, which properly, indicate a 'lady secretary'. In Israeli Hebrew, you record a phone message on the "automated /mazkira/", thus implying that had there been a human being to answer your call, a lady secretary would have taken it. In English, the referent of *typist* is usually assumed by default to be a woman, but in the early 20th century, lady typists wcrc still a novelty. The lexical concept 'lady typist' therefore underwent a transition from being the marked subordinate concept of 'typist' (because a typist was assumed to be a man), to being the unmarked subordinate concept (when one would rather expect a woman to fill the job). In some historical cultures, therefore, 'secretary' was assumed to be male, and this was reflected in the default morphological gender. On the other hand, the *secretary* of a political organisation is still masculine by default (also morphologically if the given language has a morphological gender, or at any rate in the conceptual map), even in such cultures where *secretary* — a subaltern office worker — is feminine by default.

12.7   More Concerning Morphological Gender

As one can see, there are good reasons — at least, for certain purposes — for dealing with morphological features, e.g., with morphological gender, from the historical viewpoint, when one is representing lexicographical information. In the next section, we are going to discuss the syntax of the metarepresentation portion of the example. Incidentally, not all of the semantic phenomena we listed are suited by the metarepresentation productions in the metarepresentation excerpt whose syntax we are going to discuss, but our previous discussion provides a motivation for defining facet-subschemata on the history of morphological gender for given lexical entries.

Concerning morphological gender in various languages including Hebrew, Alan D. Corré (in a posting dated 4 May 1990, which appeared in the e-list *Humanist Discussion Group,* Vol. 4, No. 5, circulated on 7 May 1990) made the following remarks, which we reproduce by kind permission given by Corré to Nissan on 8 May 1990:

> Clearly there is some connection between sex and gender, but in most languages it is not clear cut. English pays little attention to sex/gender. It differentiates chiefly in the third person singular pronouns. Occasionally inanimate things are called "she" but this is often rather deliberate. (Consider the news item that went something like this: "Her Grace christened the ship by breaking a bottle of champagne over her bows, after which she gently slid into the water.") Tamil, a Dravidian language quite unrelated to English behaves in much the same way. It has three third person pronouns like English, but there is no adjectival concord by gender. The third person verb does have separate endings though. On the other hand, German, a language closely related to English, has complex gender distinctions that often relate to the shape of the word rather than the sex of the object referred to. Thus the word for "girl" is neuter, and referred to as "it" because the word has a diminutive ending which selects the neuter gender. The Romance languages lack a neuter gender, or largely so, and squeeze all objects into the masculine/feminine dichotomy. This is often

determined by the shape of the word. Thus the word for "sentry" in French is feminine, and referred to as "she" although women rarely fulfill this role. In Latin some words of typically feminine shape can however be masculine, *poeta,* for example. One looks in vain for logic in natural languages which constantly change, ironing out some irregularities while creating others. We may ask why the distinction exists at all. Professor Rabin of the Hebrew University told me of an individual of his acquaintance who had unilaterally decided that gender distinctions in Hebrew were unnecessary in the modern world, and refused to use any feminines, referring even to his wife as "he". (I mean the English "he"; the word "he" in Hebrew happens to mean "she"). I imagine that most people would find this quite difficult. It is worth pointing out that Semitic languages are particular to distinguish gender in the "you" forms, even where some other distinctions are obliterated in modern dialects. Accordingly one finds that the recipes on the side of food packages in Hebrew ("take one tablespoon... add water... stir") are invariably in the feminine, while the instructions for operating a hacksaw will be in the masculine. It's easy to see how this fosters sex roles, and probably this is part of the key to the whole issue. Natural languages have many subtle markers which put varying degrees of space between interlocutors. In a recent showing of *People's Court* Judge Wapner chastised a defendant who addressed him as "man". The individual replied: "Sorry, judge." I also once had occasion to calm a colleague who was incensed at a student who had used the expression "... and all that shit..." in an exam paper. I pointed out that the student was probably unaware that such a locution may be OK in the local bar, but is not to be used in written English, and he simply should be advised accordingly. These expressions give cues as to the relationship between speakers, and sometimes misfire. French has a familiar *tu* and a formal *vous* and even verbs to indicate the usage (*tutoyer* — 'to call someone *tu*'). Whether one uses one or the other can sometimes be a matter of difficulty. It's interesting to note that in local Tunisian French, *tu* is routinely used, presumably because the colonists didn't see fit to address the locals ever by the polite form, which is itself a comment on social attitudes. Gender differences are probably tied up with these subtle ways that we differentiate you/me boy/girl lower/higher and so on. Such things can be exasperating or fascinating, and that will probably determine whether you enjoy studying foreign languages, or avoid them like the plague.

13   More Syntax for CuProS Metarepresentations

13.1   Mutual Exclusion of Sub-RHSs

Let us explain the supplementary syntax we introduced in the sample of metaprepresentation given in the previous section. We are going to do so by referring to that example itself. In the production of HISTORY in the metarepresentation, we find the x: label, which subdivides the RHS into *mutually exclusive*

sub-RHS bodies. One more sub-RHS may be present at the same level, as preceded by the label y: This is in order to indicate a portion that can be present
with facet-structure instantiations according to any of the sub-RHSs that in
the metarepresentation, are preceded by x: inside the same RHS of the same
production.

In the simplest case, the x: label can be exploited to impose an *exclusive
or* between attributes as found in instances. More generally, x: is an RHS-
subdividing label, and is used to state *mutually exclusive* sets of attributes. x:
has a lower priority with respect to f: and a: Therefore, x: can be nested inside
a sub-RHS subdivided according to ancestry, while the opposite cannot occur.
For example, the following production lists x:-sub-RHSs inside an f:-sub-RHS:

```
(ARE     (f:  ( <father> )
              x:  ....
                  ....
              x:  ....
                  ....
         a:  ( <ancestry_list> )
              x:  ....
                  ....
              x:  ....
                  ....
 )       )
```

The use of the y: label is meant to spare code. A y:-sub-RHS may appear
after x:-sub-RHSs, and list facet-identifiers that *can* be (and are meant to be)
different from those of the x:-sub-RHSs of the same level, even though the
content of the y:-sub-RHS body is not necessarily disjoint with respect to the
set of facet-identifiers as appearing in the preceding x:-sub-RHS.

Bear in mind that not all of the slots (or, generally, facet-identifiers) listed in
a RHS or sub-RHS, should necessarily appear in given frame instances.

The rarely used label yx: precedes mutually exclusive y:-sub-RHSs.

13.2   Pointers to an Exceptional Position in the Hierarchy

In the production whose LHS is HISTORY and that was introduced in Subsec. 13.2,
the y:-sub-RHS includes two slotless-facet identifiers. These are single_lexeme
and single_acceptation They are each preceded by the label s: That means
that in certain instances, HISTORY should not be put under the global MORPHO_CAT
facet of the lexical entry as a whole, but instead in the facet of a single lexeme
or of a single acceptation. This occurs when the morphological category depends
on the specific meaning in which the lexical entry is being used.

More generally, s: is occasionally useful because sometimes, the localisation of
a nonterminal slot (together with the subtree stemming out of it) is unsuitable,
in some particular instance. It may happen that elsewhere in the hierarchy, a
certain position be suitable instead for that nonterminal. Then, s: means that

the following slot (an s:-preceded) slot is a "suitable father", that is to say, the slot that should be the father of the slot being the LHS of the considered production. The *pointer* is *implicit* in s: (unlike z:).

z: also indicates an alternative location in the hierarchy. However, the pointer — with the z: option — should be an explicit facet. That liberalises the way of pointing, and moreover allows to point to a slot being polysemous (cf. f: and a:), and thus ambiguous.

Suitable formats for z:-preceded slots are as follow:

```
(LOOK_UNDER    <suitable_father> )
```

is suitable when the slot `<suitable_father>` can be identified unambiguously. Else, a PATH or POINTER facet would be a suitable *filler* of the LOOK_UNDER facet:

```
(LOOK_UNDER    (PATH    <path> )  )
```

as following z: in the production, inside the metarepresentation. This way, z: is a one-successor label, but it is followed by a facet, instead of a slot or a slotless-facet identifier.

`<path>` is a full path from the frame-root until `<suitable_father>`. By `<path>` a list is meant, whose first element is the name of the entry owning the frame, and whose last element is *<suitable_father>* One could develop alternative formats to point to *<suitable_father>* For example, by devising a one-successor label — a variant of s: — to be followed (like z:) by a facet, but with that facet containing an *ancestry-statement* (cf. a:), instead of a *full path* as required by z:

13.3   Ancestry-Statements That Constrain the Schema of an Attribute to the Context of a Given Sub-RHS

Labels may have the form *<digit> <label>* : For example, the label *<digit>* x: is derived from x: Digits are added before literal labels of the RHS-subdividing kind, in order to provide identification for given sub-RHS, in complicated cases when ancestry-statements should specify a particular context as prescribed by a given sub-RHS of a production whose LHS is the preceding slot (or facet-identifier in general).

An example of this is an ancestry-statement inside the RHS of the production of the slot CONTEXT as shown in the following:

```
(CAME_AFTER    ( n: MORPHO_CAT_IS
                 n: POINTER       ) )


(CONTEXT       ( a: ( (HISTORY 2x ARE MORPHO_CAT) )
                 n:   stratum_information
 )             )
```

Concerning ((HISTORY 2x ARE MORPHO_CAT)) the reason for stating that path in the tree is that as we are unsure whether HISTORY will remain unique, we give its proper ancestry. We could have just given the immediate ancestor, which is ARE. Nevertheless, ARE is ambiguous, as it may occur at different places in the tree. Therefore, its father is given, too.

```
(stratum_information ( i: STRATUM
                         RELEVANCE_IS ) )


(DEFINE_RELATION  ( a: ( (HISTORY 3x ARE MORPHO_CAT) )
                    n: relation
)                 )
```

Let us consider, in particular, $<digit>$ x: labels. If the ancestry-statement is

```
( ....... <slot>   <digit>x ....... )
```

then the x:-sub-RHS (inside the RHS of that production whose LHS is <slot>) whose initial x: is replaced by $<digit>$ x: (with the digit as suitable), should be selected. That is to say: if the ancestry statement is, for example,

```
( SLOT1   3x   SLOT2 )
```

then the proper x:-sub-RHS in the production of SLOT1 is the one beginning by 3x: Actually $<digit>$ is not necessarily the ordinal number of the sub-RHS (in the subdivision at the same level). In fact, $<digit>$ is used as being an indicator — like line labels in FORTRAN — with no numeric meaning (if not a mnemonic role) attached to it. On the other hand, the very fact that a x:-sub-RHS has been labelled by $<digit>$ x: should not be taken to imply that all of the x:-sub-RHSs of the same production should be labelled by digits.

Moreover, more than a single x:-sub-RHS of the same production can be pointed to at once, by formulating the ancestry-statement as follows:

```
( ..... SLOT_i+1 <digit>x <digit>x SLOT_i ..... )
```

where:

- the two digits are different,
- the order between the $<digit>$ x: labels is indifferent,
- and $i + 1$ is the index of a "younger generation" of slots (that is: of facets nested deeper).

That definition is extended to such sub-RHSs that are not x:-sub-RHSs. Then, since it is possible to nest sub-RHSs of different kinds, a hierarchy of nested levels could be stated in the ancestry-statement, inside parentheses:

```
( ...
  SLOT_i+1
             ( <digit><outer_label>
               <inner_label>
             )
  SLOT_i
  ...
)
```

is an example of a legal way of stating an ancestry-statement.

<digit> <label> <digit>   is a generalisation of `label><digit>`: For example,
<digit> x*<digit>* is to x*<digit>* (see below), as *<digit>* x is to x:

x*<digit>*   is a generalisation of x: It enables us to state an *inclusive or* of different *exclusive-or fans* inside the same RHS (or inside the same sub-RHS, at the same level). For example:

```
x1:    SLOT1
       SLOT2
x1:    SLOT2
       SLOT3
       SLOT4
       SLOT5
x2:    SLOT6
       SLOT7
x2:    SLOT8
x2:    SLOT9
```

means that all of the sets

```
{ SLOT1 , SLOT2 , SLOT6 , SLOT7 }  ,
{ SLOT1 , SLOT6 }  ,
{ SLOT2 , SLOT3 , SLOT5 , SLOT6 , SLOT7 }  ,
{ SLOT2 , SLOT4 , SLOT7 }  ,
{ SLOT3 , SLOT5 , SLOT8 }  ,
{ SLOT4 , SLOT5 , SLOT9 }  ,
```

and so forth, are slots of facets that can be legally co-present as nested immediately inside that facet whose facet-identifier is the LHS of the considered production in the metarepresentation.

13.4   Cartesian Spaces of Attributes

Whenever a hierarchical organisation of facets would be cumbersome, you can resort to the label `rel`: in order to define an *n*-to-*n* shallow relation in the space of several attributes. Let us refer again to the metarepresentation:

```
(atom                ( INFLECTION
                     MORPHO_CAT
                     x: ACCEPTATIONS
                     x: LEXEMES
                         . . . . . . . ) )

(MORPHO_CAT          ( x: terminal_list
                     x: ARE
                     y: s: single_lexeme
                        s: single_acceptation ) )

(ACCEPTATIONS        ( ARE ) )
(LEXEMES             ( ARE ) )
(single_lexeme       ( i: LEXEME_KEYWORD
                     INFLECTION
                     MORPHO_CAT
```

```
                         ACCEPTATIONS ) )
(single_acceptation    ( c: MEANING
                         CONNOTATIONS
                         RELATED_TO
                         AURO
                         . . . . . ) )
(RELATED_TO            ( RULES
                         g: PECULIAR_FACETS
                         ;    A possible local guide:
                         ;    a metarepresentation.
                         CONTAINED_IN_THE_IDIOMS
                         SYNONYMS
                         NEAR_SYNONYMS
                         CONTRARIES
                         MOP  ;   a graph of goals and plans.
                         . . . . . . ) )
(ARE          ( f: ( SYNONYMS  NEAR_SYNONYMS )
                n: componential_difference_doubleton
              f: ( ACCEPTATIONS )
                n: single_acceptation
              f: ( LEXEMES )
                n: single_lexeme
              f: ( MORPHO_CAT )
                n: HISTORY
              n: MORPHO_WITH_WEIGHT
)        )
(componential_difference_doubleton
          ( i: IS
            DIFFERENCES ) )
(MORPHO_WITH_WEIGHT   ( i: MORPHO_CAT_IS
                       RELEVANCE_IS ) )
(HISTORY              (  x:  i1: MORPHO_CAT_IS
                             RELEVANCE_IS
                         j:  STRATUM
                        2x:  i:  MORPHO_CAT_IS
                             n:  CONTEXT
                        3x:  i:  MORPHO_CAT_IS
                             d:  DEFINE_RELATION
                             rel: MORPHO_CAT_IS
                             rel: CONTEXT
                         x:  i:  MORPHO_CAT_IS
                             RELEVANCE_IS
                             ORDINAL
```

```
                    x:    i:  MORPHO_CAT_IS
                          RELEVANCE_IS
                          CAME_AFTER
                    y:    s:  single_lexeme
                          s:  single_acceptation
)           )

(CAME_AFTER         ( n:  MORPHO_CAT_IS
                      n:  POINTER        ) )
(CONTEXT            ( a:  ( (HISTORY 2x ARE MORPHO_CAT) )
                        n:   stratum_information
)                   )
(stratum_information ( i:  STRATUM
                          RELEVANCE_IS ) )
(DEFINE_RELATION   ( a:  ( (HISTORY 3x ARE MORPHO_CAT) )
                      n:  relation
)                   )
```

An extension of the first x:-sub-RHS in the RHS of the production of HISTORY is the x:-sub-RHS that begins by 2x: That label allows the same MORPHO_CAT_IS facet to refer to several contexts, with different relevance degrees (which are quantified, say, numerically, possibly by means of fuzzy values).

A 1-to-n correspondence is allowed. Let us see that in an example from the history of derivation in Hebrew. In Hebrew, the word-formation pattern /PoˆeL/ generates *verb participles* of the Hebrew basic active conjugation in all historical strata. The relevance in use of /PoˆeL/, in all those strata, is very high. Besides, such participles may happen to be nominalised. The same pattern, /PoˆeL/, has also generated *departicipial nouns* in every historical stratum, but the relevance degrees in each single stratum differ. On the other hand,[25] in Tannaic Hebrew — that is, the historical stratum of Hebrew in which the *Mishnah* (the nucleus of the Talmud) was compiled ca. 200 C.E. — the purpose of generating *departicipial nouns* was satisfied by adopting the pattern /PaˆoL/. In Aramaic, the etymologically equivalent pattern, /PaˆoLa/, generated participles of the same verbal conjugation. From /PaˆoL/, Hebrew departicipial nouns were generated, albeit rarely so; some of them are still in use. See Appendix A. There are two /PaˆoL/ homonymous polytemplates (i.e., procedural code items) in Onomaturge: one whose plural form is /PaˆoLot/, and another one, instantiated in some obsolete terms of post-Biblical formation, whose plural is /PaˆoLim/. In relation to this example, the following exemplifies, from inside a frame, different single-rule subtrees. They are legal inside the subtree rooted in RULES, inside an acceptation of different lexical lexical entries. A multi-attribute key is stated, because of the existence of the same pattern as with two different forms of the plural.

---

[25] See Bar-Asher [6]. The paragraphs referred to are 16–20 (pp. [13]–[20] in the paper itself; pp. 94–102 as first published in *Leshonenu;* pp. 135–142 as reprinted in 1979/80).

```
( (IS  Pa^oL)
  (INFLECTION_PARADIGM  ( (FORM_IS Pa^oLot)
                          (FORM_CLASSIFICATION plural)
  )                     )
  (RELATED_INFO  <dependent information> )
)
( (IS  Pa^oL)
  (INFLECTION_PARADIGM  ( (FORM_IS Pa^oLim)
                          (FORM_CLASSIFICATION plural)
  )                     )
  (RELATED_INFO  <dependent information> )
)
```

The triplet

```
atom = /Pa^oL/
MORPHOLOGICAL_CATEGORY = (departicipial noun)
STRATUM = later_Prophets
```

may have a numerical score associated, which expresses the salience in documented use. In fact, even as their text provides evidence for the introduction of /Pa^oL/ into Hebrew just for generating departicipial nouns, some of the later Prophets kept using /Po^eL/ not just for the participle, but also for departicipial nouns. In a later stratum of Hebrew, Tannaic Hebrew, /Pa^oL/ remained in use (along with /Po^eL/) for generating departicipial nouns, so a particular value of salience ("relevance") in the use of that particular historical stratum should be stated.

In such a situation, it is suitable to represent a 1-to-n correspondence, by resorting to the CONTEXT facet, as indicated in the sub-RHS of HISTORY that begins by 2x: In the metarepresentation, this corresponds to this rule:

```
(CONTEXT    ( a: ( (HISTORY 2x ARE MORPHO_CAT) )
              n:  stratum_information
)           )
```

A further generalisation allows n-to-n correspondence. It is suitable when a hierachical organisation is not the most natural one.[26] For example, let us consider the relation shown in Fig. 12. Then, its adjacency matrix will be an array of zeros and ones, as in Table 1.

MORPHO_CAT_IS facets state the morphological category. According to the schema allowed by the production of CONTEXT in the metarepresentation,

---

[26] Six [99] formalised a framework for data structures, in terms of a general class of objects: "arbitrary directed rooted graphs in which the information associated with each node is either empty, elementary or an object in the general class. Since many data structures cannot be modelled by tree structures in a natural way, such a generalisation to graphs is desirable. Furthermore, the concept of hierarchy in which a node may serve for an arbitrary complex substructure supports a structured view of complex data objects."

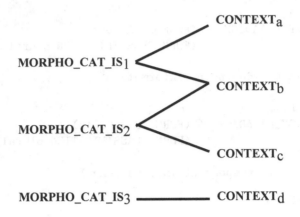

Fig. 12. An *n*-to-*n* relation defined in the space of two attributes

Table 1. The adjacency matrix of the *n*-to-*n* relation of Fig. 12

	a	b	c	d
1	1	1	0	0
2	0	1	1	0
3	0	0	0	1

MORPHO_CAT_IS facets are *repeatable*, as nested under CAME_AFTER — as per the following metarepresentation rule expressed as a CuProS production:

```
(CAME_AFTER    ( n: MORPHO_CAT_IS
                 n: POINTER          ) )
```

Then, at the same hierarchical level of the repeated MORPHO_CAT_IS facets, one could include a DEFINE_RELATION facet, and also repeated CONTEXT facets. DEFINE_RELATION itself is not a keyword of the CuProS language: this is the reason for having this slot preceded by the d: label, in the RHS or sub-RHS where it is stated.

See in the sub-RHS body preceded by 3x: in the production having HISTORY as LHS, namely:

```
(HISTORY ( x:    i1:  MORPHO_CAT_IS
                      RELEVANCE_IS
                 j:   STRATUM
           2x:   i:   MORPHO_CAT_IS
                 n:   CONTEXT
           3x:   i:   MORPHO_CAT_IS
                 d:   DEFINE_RELATION
                 rel: MORPHO_CAT_IS
                 rel: CONTEXT
```

```
          x:    i:    MORPHO_CAT_IS
                      RELEVANCE_IS
                      ORDINAL
          x:    i:    MORPHO_CAT_IS
                      RELEVANCE_IS
                      CAME_AFTER
          y:    s:    single_lexeme
                s:    single_acceptation
)         )
```

Let the label **d:** define relations represented by a binary matrix. The attributes MORPHO_CAT_IS and CONTEXT, involved in the relation, are stated to be brothers of DEFINE_RELATION in the same sub-RHS. Now, consider the production having DEFINE_RELATION as LHS:

```
(DEFINE_RELATION  ( a: ( (HISTORY 3x ARE MORPHO_CAT) )
                       n: relation
)                      )
```

In the **a:**-sub-RHS considered of the production whose LHS is the attribute DEFINE_RELATION, after the ancestry statement, only **relation** is stated to be repeatable (because of the **n:** label). This should help to avoid redundancy, as the attributes involved in the relation are stated as "uncles" in the facet-hierarchy, each preceded by the **rel:** label.

Let us see a portion of a *frame-instance* (not of the metarepresentation, this time). The following is a possible portion of a frame-instance; an n-to-n relation is represented:

```
(DEFINE_RELATION  ( ( MORPHO_CAT_IS CONTEXT )
                        ( 1 a )  ( 1 b )
                                 ( 2 b )  ( 2 c )
                                          ( 3 d )
                    )
                        ( < another_relation> ..... )
                          . . . . . . . .
)
(MORPHO_CAT_IS  (ID 1)   <value or value_list
                          or frame_subtree> )
(MORPHO_CAT_IS  (ID 2)   <value or value_list
                          or frame_subtree> )
                          . . . . . . . .
(CONTEXT        (ID a)   <value or value_list
                          or frame_subtree> )
(CONTEXT        (ID b)   <value or value_list
                          or frame_subtree> )
                          . . . . . . . .
```

The sets {1,2,3} and {a,b,c,d} are just sets of labels of facets nested deeper. Then the label/value, or label/value_list, or even label/subtree association is made in those facets that in the metarepresentation are preceded by the label `rel:` It would be possible to generalise that n-to-n correspondence in several ways. First of all, we have imposed a constraint, in the frame-schema, on the identity of the attributes involved in the relation. An extension could be introduced, allowing to define their identity instance-wise, and not rigidly in the schema. Moreover, by no means should a relation only involve two attributes: once the arity is liberalised, more coordinates could be stated for each case. This is allowed with the `d:` option itself. Moreover, such tables can be envisaged, that are not arrays of zeroes and ones. Some convention can be devised, for expressing the case value in the table-representation inside the frame hierarchy.

The `l:` label (i.e., lower-case L followed by a colon) allows relations to be defined as being represented by labelled graphs, and then by matrices with whatever values. The syntax for the coordinate-list representing table-cases could be extended as follows:

```
( <coordinate>    ...    <coordinate>
  VAL       <value or value_list> )
```

Whenever a value-list is stated after VAL, a relation corresponding to a multi-labeled graph is represented.

14   Conclusions

In this article, we have presented the RAFFAELLO project in data storage and retrieval, and the related CuProS syntax for metarepresentation of the schemata of deeply nested relations. The main application, in the 1980s and early 1990s, was in the domain of lexicography and word-formation. There were other applications, which we mentioned and briefly described. The importance of the project has been meanwhile vindicated by the popularity that similar notions have gained with the widespread acceptance of XML.

Whereas the full syntax of CuProS was originally presented in an appendix to Ephraim Nissan's doctoral thesis (in computational linguistics, its main supervisor was Yaacov Choueka, the Jubilarian of the present volume set), this is the very first time that the syntax of CuProS is published in full. It arguably still has features to recommend it, even in an era that has grown accustomed to XML. Even at the risk of this article partly resembling a manual, we feel it is important that we have gone here into the details, and that moreover, in the sections and appendices we have dealt to some extent with the application to lexicography and derivational morphology. This makes that kind of application more readily available for, hopefully, further future adoption of CuProS.

For retrieval from deeply nested, flexibly structured frame-instances as described by means of a metarepresentation coded in CuProS, the most developed tool, the one that fully met the specifications, was NAVIGATION, the version of RAFFAELLO that was implemented by Jihad El-Sana, whose own scholarly career next unfolded in the disciplinary context of image processing. By contrast to NAVIGATION, Nissan's, ONOMATURGE expert system (for Hebrew word-formation and the evaluation of psychosemantic transparency of lexical coinages generated by ONOMATURGE itself) retrieved data from the frame-instances of lexical entries or derivational morphemes by resorting to SIMPLE NAVIGATION, a tool implemented by Nissan and tailored to the specific frame-structure adopted in ONOMATURGE.

Even though Nissan has also defined CuPROS, and had coded in CuPROS the structure of the frames of ONOMATURGE, it wasn't until El-Sana's implementation of NAVIGATION that CuPROS became a language actually being parsed by computer tools. This is rather like what happened with XML: that language existed, and was studied, well before implementations became available. That CuPROS and XML were developed in mutual independence of each other bears witness to the times having been mature for the appearance of their underlying idea. It was a more radical idea than the one advocated by the nested relations school within database research.

References

1. Abiteboul, S., Fischer, P.C., Schek, H.-J. (eds.): Nested Relations and Complex Objects in Databases, NF2 1987. LNCS, vol. 361. Springer, Heidelberg (1989)
2. Alinei, M.: Continuità dal Mesolitico all'età del Ferro nelle principali aree etno-linguistiche. Vol. 2 of his: Origini delle lingue d'Europa. Il Mulino, Bologna, Italy (2000)
3. Alinei, M., Nissan, E.: L'etimologia semitica dell'it. *pizza* e dei suoi corradicali est-europei, turchi, e semitici levantini. Quaderni di Semantica: An International Journal of Semantics and Iconomastics 28(1), 117–135 (2007)
4. Alterman, R.: A Dictionary Based on Concept Coherence. Artificial Intelligence 25(2), 153–186 (1985)
5. Ayali, M.: A Nomenclature of Workers and Artisans in the Talmudic and Midrashic Literature. (in Hebrew.) Hakibbutz Hameuchad, Tel-Aviv (1984)
6. Bar-Asher, M.: Rare Forms in the Tannaitic Language. (In Hebrew.) Lěšonénu 41, 83–102 (1976/1977=5737 of the Hebrew calendar). Also in Bar-Asher, M.: Collected Papers in Tannaitic Hebrew, vol. 2, pp. 123–142. The Hebrew University, Jerusalem (1979/1980=5740)
7. Barron, J.: In a Futuristic House, Speak Clearly and Carry a Manual. In The New York Times selection supplement, p. 7, of The Daily Telegraph, London (28 October 2004)
8. Bertino, E., Catania, B., Wong, L.: Finitely Representable Nested Relations. Information Processing Letters 70(4), 165–173 (1999)
9. Bressan, S., Chaudhri, A.B., Li Lee, M., Yu, J.X., Lacroix, Z. (eds.): Efficiency and Effectiveness of XML Tools and Techniques (EEXTT), and Data Integration over the Web (DIWeb 2002): Revised Papers from the VLDB Workoshop, at the 28th Very Large Data Bases International Conference, Hong Kong, China, 2002. LNCS, vol. 2590. Springer, Heidelberg (2003)
10. Bryan, M.: SGML and HTML Explained, 2nd edn. Addison Wesley Longman, Harlow, Essex, England (1997)
11. Cardenas, A.F.: Data Base Management Systems, 2nd edn. Allyn and Bacon, Boston (1985)
12. Colin, G.S.: Note sur le système cryptographique du sultan Aḥmad al-Manṣūr. Hespéris 7(2), 221–228 (1927)

13. Dalby, D.: A Survey of the Indigenous Scripts of Liberia and Sierra Leone: Vai, Mende, Loma, Kpelle and Bassa. African Language School of Oriental and African Studies, London, distrib. Luzac, London, 8, 1–51 + initial map (1967)

14. Dalby, D.: The indigenous scripts of West Africa and Surinam: Their Inspiration and Design. African Language Studies 9, 156–197 (1968)

15. Dor, M.: Ha-ḥay bi-ymei ha-Miqra ha-Mishnah ve-ha-Talmud (Hebrew: The Fauna at the Times of the Bible, the Mishnah and the Talmud). Grafor-Daftal Books, Tel-Aviv (1987)

16. Doutté, E.: Magie et réligion dans l'Afrique du Nord. Adolfe Jourdan, Algiers (1909); J. Maisonneuve & P. Geuthner, Paris (1984)

17. Dyer, M.G.: In-Depth Understanding: A Computer Model of Integrated Processing of Narrative Comprehension. The MIT Press, Cambridge, MA (1983)

18. Epstein, R.: A Tutorial on INGRES. Memo ERL-M77-25, Electronics Research Laboratory, University of California, Berkeley (1977)

19. Even-Odem, J., Rotem, Y.: New Medical Dictionary. Rubin Mass Publ., Jerusalem (1975) (in Hebrew)

20. Even-Shoshan, A.: Millón Ḥadáš Menuqqád uMeṣuyyár (4 vols., Hebrew: New Vowelled, Illustrated Dictionary), 3rd edn., Kiryath Sepher, Jerusalem (1953)

21. Even-Shoshan, A.: HaMillón heḤadáš — haMahadurá haMešullévet (5 vols., Hebrew: The New Dictionary — The Combined Version), Kiryath-Sepher, Jerusalem (1997)

22. Fischler, B.: Mass'ei ha-shemot. (Hebrew: The Trajectories of Names: On the Development of the Terminology of Birdnames (1866–1972)). Lashon ve-Ivrit: Language & Hebrew 4, 6–35 (1990)

23. Freedman, D.N., Rittersprach, A.: The Use of Alef as a Vowel Letter in the Genesis Apocryphon. Revue de Qumran 6, 293–300 (1967)

24. Fuhr, N., Lalmas, M., Malik, S., Kazai, G. (eds.): Advances in XML Information Retrieval and Evaluation: 4th International Workshop of the Initiative for the Evaluation of XML Retrieval (INEX 2005), Dagstuhl Castle, Germany, November 28–30, 2005. Revised and Selected Papers. LNCS, vol. 3977. Springer, Heidelberg (2006)

25. Garani, G.: A Temporal Database Model Using Nested Relations. Ph.D. Dissertation, Computer Science and Information Systems Engineering, Birkbeck College, University of London, London (2004)

26. Garani, G.: Nest and Unnest Operators in Nested Relations. Data Science Journal 7, 57–64 (2008)

27. García-Page Sanchez, M.: Sobre los procesos de deslexicalización en las expresiones fijas. Español actual 52, 59–79 (1989)

28. Genesereth, M.R., Lenat, D.B.: Meta-Description and Modifiability. Technical Report HPP-80-18, Heuristic Programming Project, Computer Science Dept., Stanford University, Stanford, California (1980)

29. Goldfarb, C.F.: The SGML Handbook. Clarendon Press, Oxford (1990); Y. Rubinsky (ed., introd.); repr. (2000)

30. Ghosh, S.P.: Data Base Organization for Data Management. Academic Press, New York (1977)

31. Greiner, R.: RLL-1: A Representation Language Language [sic]. Technical Report 80-0, Heuristic Programming Project, Computer Science Dept., Stanford University, Stanford, California. An expanded version of the paper was published in the Proceedings of the First National AAAI Conference, Stanford (1980)

32. Grimes, J.E.: Denormalization and Cross-Referencing in Theoretical Lexicography. In: Proceedings of the COLING 84 Conference, pp. 38–41 (1984)

33. Grimes, J.E., de la Cruz Ávila, P., Carrillo Vicente, J., Díaz, F., Díaz, R., de la Rosa, A., Rentería, T.: El Huichol: Apuntes sobre el léxico. Department of Modern Languages and Linguistics, Cornell University, Ithaca, NY (1981) (in Spanish, abstracted in English on pp. 283–291)
34. Hatzopoulos, M., Kollias, J.G.: A Dynamic Model for the Optimal Selection of Secondary Indexes. Information Systems 8(3), 159–164 (1983)
35. Holzner, S.: XML Complete. McGraw-Hill, New York (1998)
36. Jastrow, M.: Dictionary of the Targumim, the Talmud Babli and Yerushalmi, and the Midrashic Literature. (Definitions are in English). 2 vols. G.P. Putnam's Sons, New York; Trübner, Leipzig, and Luzac, London (1886–1903). Reprints: Choreb, New York (2 vols. in 1, 1926, later reprinted by Chorev, Jerusalem); Shapiro [i.e., Shapiro & Vallentine], London (1926); Title Publ., New York (1943); New York: Pardes Publ., New York (2 vols., 1950), and with a new title: Hebrew-Aramaic-English Dictionary... (2 vols., 1969). Also (with the standard title), Judaica Press, New York, 1971 (2 vols. in 1); Jastrow Publishers, New York, 1903, repr. 1967 (2 vols. in 1); Shalom, Brooklyn, 1967 (2 vols.); Hendrickson Publ., Peabody, Massachusetts, 2005 (in 1 vol. of 1736 pp.). Also accessible on the Web, vol. 1: http://www.etana.org/sites/default/files/coretexts/14906.pdf, vol. 2: http://www.etana.org/sites/default/files/coretexts/14499.pdf, Arranged for alphabetical access online at Tyndale House: http://www.tyndalearchive.com/tabs/jastrow/
37. Kent, W.: The Universal Relation Revisited. ACM Transactions on Database Systems 8(4), 644–648 (1983)
38. Kernighan, B.W., Ritchie, D.M.: The C Programming Language. Prentice-Hall, Englewood Cliffs, New Jersey (1978)
39. Khoshafian, S., Valduriez, P., Copeland, G.: Parallel Query Processing for Complex Objects. MCC Technical Report DB-397-86, Microelectronics and Computer Technology Corporation, Austin, Texas (November 1986)
40. Kimron, E.: Middle Aleph as a Mater Lectionis in Hebrew and Aramaic Documents from Qumran, as Compared to Other Hebrew and Aramaic Sources. (In Hebrew.) Lĕšonénu 39. The Academy of the Hebrew Language, Jerusalem 5735 (1974/1975), pp. 133–164, Also in: Bar-Asher, M. (ed.), Collected Papers in Tannaic Hebrew, Vol. 2. The Hebrew University, Jerusalem 5740, pp. 335–348 (1979/1980)
41. Kitagawa, H., Kunii, T.L., Ishii, Y.: Design and Implementation of a Form Management System, APAD, Using ADABAS/INQ DBMS. Report 81-18, Information Science Dept., University of Tokyo, Tokyo (1981)
42. Kutscher, E.Y.: Trivia (in Hebrew: Zutot). In: Kutscher, E.Y. (ed.) Archive of the New Dictionary of Rabbinical Literature, vol. 1, Bar-Ilan University, Ramat-Gan, Israel, pp. 95–105; English summary on pp. XXX–XXXII (1972)
43. Larus, J.R.: Parlez-Vous Franz? An Informal Introduction to Interfacing Foreign Functions to Franz LISP. Technical Report PAM-124, Center for Pure and Applied Mathematics, University of California, Berkeley (early 1980s)
44. Levene, M.: The Nested Universal Relation Database Model. LNCS, vol. 595. Springer, Heidelberg (1992)
45. Levene, M., Loizou, G.: The Nested Relation Type Model: An Application of Domain Theory to Databases. The Computer Journal 33(1), 19–30 (1990)
46. Levene, M., Loizou, G.: Semantics of Null Extended Nested Relations. ACM Transactions on Database Systems 18, 414–459 (1993)
47. Levene, M., Loizou, G.: The Nested Universal Relation Data Model. Journal of Computer and System Sciences 49, 683–717 (1994)

48. Levene, D., Rothenberg, B.: A Metallurgical Gemara: Metals in the Jewish Sources. Metal in History series, vol. 4. Institute for Archaeo-Metallurgical Studies, Institute of Archaeology, University College London, London (2007); distributed by Thames & Hudson, London (except in the USA and Canada)

49. Levenston, E.A., Sivan, R.: The Megiddo Modern Dictionary. (English-Hebrew dictionary), Megiddo, Tel-Aviv (1966) (in one volume), repr. 1982 (in two vols., in other respects identical)

50. Lyons, J.: Semantics, 2 vols.. Cambridge University Press, Cambridge, U.K. (1977)

51. Lamping, J., Rao, R.: The Hyperbolic Browser: A Focus + Context Technique for Visualizing Large Hierarchies. Journal of Visual Languages & Computing 7(1), 33–55 (1996)

52. Larussa, M.: Building a Translator for Nested-Relation into XML Document. Dissertation for a BsC degree in Computing Science (supervised by A. Al-Zobaidie, E. Nissan). University of Greenwich, London (2001)

53. Light, R.: Presenting XML. Sams.net, Indianapolis, Indiana (1997)

54. Mackenzie, C.: Falstaff's Monster. AUMLA: Journal of the Australasian Universities Language and Literature Association (New Zealand), 83, pp. 83–86 (May 1995)

55. Mark, L., Roussopoulos, N.: Metadata Management. IEEE Computer 19(12), 26–36 (1986)

56. Mauchamp, E.: La sorcellerie au Maroc. Oeuvre posthume. Dorbon-ainé, Paris, n.d. (1911)

57. McGilton, H., Morgan, R.: Introducing the UNIX System. McGraw-Hill, New York (1983)

58. Minh, T.T.H.: Approaches to XML Schema Matching. Ph.D. Thesis. University of East Anglia, Norwich, England (2007)

59. Monod, T.: Systèmes cryptographiques. In: Monod, T. (ed.), Contributions à l'étude du Sahara occidental, Fasc. 1: Gravures, peintures et inscriptions rupestres. Comité d'Études Historiques et Scientifiques de l'Afrique Occidentale Française, Publications, Série A, no. 7. Librairie Larose, Paris, pp. 114–126 (1938)

60. Monteil, V.: La cryptographie chez les maures. Bulletin de l'I.F.A.N., 13(4), pp. 1257–1264 (1951)

61. Moreshet, M., A Lexicon of the New Verbs in Tannaic Hebrew. Bar-Ilan University Press, Ramat-Gan, Israel (1980) (In Hebrew)

62. Nakhimovsky, A., Myers, T.: XML Programming: Web Applications and Web Services with JSP and ASP. The Expert's Voice Series. APress, Berkeley, CA (2002)

63. Nini, Y. (ed., introd.), Gamlieli, N.B. (trans.): Al-Misawwadeh: Bēth-Dīn (Court) Records of the Ṣanʻānī Jewish Community in the Eighteenth Century. Vol. 1: Ms. Heb. 38° 3281/2, The Jewish and University Library, Jerusalem. Publications of the Diapora Research Institute, Book 145. The Diaspora Research Institute, Tel Aviv University, Tel Aviv (2001) (in Hebrew, with Judaeo-Arabic. English abstract.)

64. Nissan, E.: Proprietà formali nel progetto logico-concettuale di basi di dati. (Italian: Formal Properties in the Logical and Conceptual Design of Databases.) Tesi di Laurea in Ingegneria Elettronica, Dipartimento di Elettronica, Politecnico di Milano, 2 vols., pp. 400+200. Awarded the Burroughs Italiana Prize (1982)

65. Nissan, E.: The Info-Spatial Derivative: A New Formal Tool for Database Design. In: Proceedings of the AICA 1983 Conference, Naples, vol. 2, pp. 177–182 (1983)

66. Nissan, E.: The Twelve Chairs and ONOMATURGE. Part I of: The Representation of Synonyms and of Related Terms, in the Frames of an Expert System for Word-Coinage. In: Proceedings of the 5th International Workshop on Expert Systems & Their Applications, Avignon, France, vol. 2, pp. 685–703 (June 1985)

67. Nissan, E.: On Lions, Leopards and ONOMATURGE. Part II of: The Representation of Synonyms and of Related Terms, in the Frames of an Expert System for Word-Coinage. In: Nissan, E. (ed.) Proceedings of the 5th International Workshop on Expert Systems & Their Applications, Avignon, France, vol. 2, pp. 705–741 (June 1985)

68. Nissan, E.: The Frame-Definition Language for Customizing the RAFFAELLO Structure-Editor in Host Expert Systems. In: Ras, Z., Zemankova, M. (eds.) Proceedings of the First International Symposium in Methodologies for Intelligent Systems (ISMIS 1986), Knoxville, Tennessee, pp. 8–18. ACM SIGART Press, New York (1986)

69. Nissan, E.: Data Analysis Using a Geometrical Representation of Predicate Calculus. Information Sciences 41(3), 187–258 (1987)

70. Nissan, E.: The Wining and Dining Project. Part II: An Expert System for Gastronomy and Terminal Food-Processing. International Journal of Hospitality Management 6(4), 207–215 (1987)

71. Nissan, E.: ONOMATURGE: An Expert System for Word-Formation and Morpho-Semantic Clarity Evaluation. Part I: The Task in Perspective, and a Model of the Dynamics of the System. In: Czap, H., Galinski, C. (eds.) Terminology and Knowledge Engineering: Proceedings of the First International Conference, Trier, Germany, pp. 167–176. Indeks Verlag, Frankfurt/M (1987)

72. Nissan, E.: ONOMATURGE: An Expert System for Word-Formation and Morpho-Semantic Clarity Evaluation. Part II: The Statics of the System. The Representation from the General Viewpoint of Knowledge-Bases for Terminology. In: Czap, H., Galinski, C. (eds.) Terminology and Knowledge Engineering: Proceedings of the First International Conference, Trier, Germany, pp. 177–189. Indeks Verlag, Frankfurt/M (1987)

73. Nissan, E.: Nested-Relation Based Frames in RAFFAELLO. Meta-representation Structure & Semantics for Knowledge Engineering. In: Schek, H.-J., Scholl, M. (eds.) International Workshop on Theory and Applications of Nested Relations and Complex Objects, Darmstadt, Germany, April 6-8, pp. 95–99 (1987) Handouts printed as a report of INRIA, Rocquencourt, France.

74. Nissan, E.: Knowledge Acquisition and Metarepresentation: Attribute Autopoiesis. In: Ras, Z.W., Zemankowa, M. (eds.) Proc. 2nd International Symposium Methodologies for Intelligent Systems (ISMIS 1987), pp. 240–247. North-Holland, Amsterdam (1987)

75. Nissan, E.: ONOMATURGE: An Expert System in Word-Formation (3 vols., in English). Ph.D. Dissertation in Computer Science, Ben-Gurion University of the Negev, Beer-Sheva, Israel (1988)

76. Nissan, E.: Deviation Models of Regulation: A Knowledge-Based Approach. Informatica e Diritto, year 18, 2nd Series 1(1/2), 181–212 (1992)

77. Nissan, E.: Narratives, Formalism, Computational Tools, and Nonlinearity. In: Dershowitz, N., Nissan, E. (eds.) Choueka Festschrift, Part II. LNCS, vol. 8002, pp. 270–393. Springer, Heidelberg (2014)

78. Nissan, E.: Tale Variants and Analysis in Episodic Formulae: Early Ottoman, Elizabethan, and "Solomonic" Versions. In: Dershowitz, N., Nissan, E. (eds.) Choueka Festschrift, Part II. LNCS, vol. 8002, pp. 138–192. Springer, Heidelberg (2014)

79. Nissan, E.: Multilingual Lexis, Semantics, and Onomasiology by Using the CuProS Metarepresentation Language: An XML-Compatible XML-Precursor Enabling Flexible Nested-Relation Structures. In: Dershowitz, N., Nissan, E. (eds.) Choueka Festschrift, Part III. LNCS, vol. 8003, pp. 122–173. Springer, Heidelberg (2014)

80. Nissan, E.: Which Acceptation? Ontologies for Historical Linguistics. In: Dershowitz, N., Nissan, E. (eds.) Choueka Festschrift, Part III. LNCS, vol. 8003, pp. 174–206. Springer, Heidelberg (2014)

81. Nissan, E.: Etymothesis, Fallacy, and Ontologies: An Illustration from Phytonymy. In: Dershowitz, N., Nissan, E. (eds.) Choueka Festschrift, Part III. LNCS, vol. 8003, pp. 207–364. Springer, Heidelberg (2014)

82. Nissan, E.: Knowledge Engineering for Word-Formation: Generating and Evaluating Candidate Neologisms. In: Dershowitz, N., Nissan, E. (eds.) Choueka Festschrift, Part III. LNCS, vol. 8003, pp. 365–434. Springer, Heidelberg (2014)

83. Nissan, E.: A Study of Humorous Explanatory Tales, 2 parts (In a book in preparation)

84. Nissan, E., HaCohen-Kerner, Y.: Information Retrieval in the Service of Generating Narrative Explanation: What We Want from GALLURA. In: Proceedings of KDIR 2011: International Conference on Knowledge Discovery and Information Retrieval, Paris, October 26–29, pp. 487–492 (2011)

85. Nissan, E., Asaro, C., Dragoni, A.F., Farook, D.Y., Shimony, S.E.: A Quarter of Century in Artificial Intelligence and Law: Projects, Personal Trajectories, a Subjective Perspective. In: Dershowitz, N., Nissan, E. (eds.) Choueka Festschrift, Part II. LNCS, vol. 8002, pp. 452–695. Springer, Heidelberg (2014)

86. Ornan, U.: Hebrew Word Formation. In: Bar-Asher, M., et al. (eds.) Volume in Honor of Z. Ben-Hayyim, year 5743, pp. 13–42. Magnes Press, The Hebrew University, Jerusalem (1982/3) (in Hebrew)

87. Osborne, W.R.: A Linguistic Introduction to the Origins and Characteristics of Early Mishnaic Hebrew as it Relates to Biblical Hebrew. Old Testament Essays, New Series 24(1), 159–172 (2011)

88. Özsoyoğlu, M.Z. (ed.): Nested Relations. Special issue, The IEEE Data Engineering Bulletin, 11(3) (1988)

89. Özsoyoğlu, Z.M., Yuan, L.Y.: A New Normal Form for Nested Relations. ACM Transactions on Database Systems 12, 111–136 (1987)

90. Rohlfs, G.: Grammatica storica della lingua italiana e dei suoi dialetti. Vol. 2: Morfologia. Piccola Biblioteca Einaudi (PBE), vol. 149, Einaudi, Torino, Italy (1968). Revised edition, translated from: Historische Grammatik der Italienischen Sprache und ihrer Mundarten. vol. 2: Formenlehre und Syntax. A. Francke AG, Bern, Switzerland (1949). The sections cited are in the 1968 edn.

91. Rohlfs, G.: Grammatica storica della lingua italiana e dei suoi dialetti. Vol. 3: Sintassi e formazione delle parole. Piccola biblioteca Einaudi (PBE), vol. 150. Einaudi, Torino, Italy (1969). Revised edition, translated from: Historische Grammatik der Italienischen Sprache und ihrer Mundarten, vol. 3: Syntax und Wortbildung. A. Francke AG, Bern, Switzerland (1954). The sections cited are in the 1969 edn.

92. Rosen, B.K.: Tree-Manipulating Systems and Church-Rosser Theorems. Journal of the ACM 20(1), 160–187 (1973)

93. Sáenz-Badillos, A.: A History of the Hebrew Language, Elwode, J. (trans.) Cambridge University Press, New York & Cambridge, U.K. (1993)

94. Sarkar, M., Brown, M.H.: Graphical Fisheye Views. Communications of the ACM 37, 73–84 (1994)

95. Schkolnick, M.: The Optimal Selection of Secondary Indices for Files. Information Systems 1, 141–146 (1975)

96. Segal, M.H.: A Grammar of Mishnaic Hebrew. Clarendon, Oxford, 1978 (Reprint of 1st edn., with corrections). Previously published in 1927, 1958 (repr. lithographically from corr. sheets of the 1st edn.) (1970, 1978, 1980)

97. Schwartz, S.: Were the Jews a Mediterranean Society? Reciprocity and Solidarity in Ancient Judaism. Princeton University Press, Princeton, NJ (2010)

98. Shaw, M.L.G., Bradshaw, J.M., Gaines, B.R., Boose, J.H.: Rapid Prototyping Techniques for Expert Systems. In: Proceedings of the Fourth IEEE Conference on Artificial Intelligence Applications, San Diego, California, March 14–18 (1988)

99. Six, H.-W.: A Framework for Data Structures. In: Noltemeier, H. (ed.) Graphtheoretic Concepts in Computer Science: Proceedings of the International Workshop WG80, Bad Honnef, West Germany, June 1980. LNCS, vol 100, pp. 250–267. Springer, Heidelberg (1981)

100. Smith, J.M.: SGML and Related Standards: Document Description and Processing Languages. Ellis Horwood Series in Computers and Their Applications. Ellis Horwood, New York and London (1992)

101. Spivak, J.: The SGML Primer. CTI, Cambridge, Mass., and London (1996)

102. Gli Statuti Regionali. Supplement to no. 1 (January 1972) of Vita Italiana: Documenti e Informazioni. Servizi delle Informazioni e della Proprietà Lette-raria, Presidenza del Consiglio dei Ministri della Repubblica Italiana. Istituto Poligrafico dello Stato, Roma (1972)

103. Stonebraker, M., Rowe, L.A.: The Design of POSTGRES. In: Proceedings of the 1986 ACM SIGMOD International Conference on Management of Data, Washington, D.C., May 1986. SIGMOD Record, 15(2), June, 340–355 (1986)

104. Ta-Shma, I.: Dates and Localities in the Life of Rabbi Zeraḥyah Ha-Levy of Lunel. In: Kaddari, M.Z., Katzburg, N., Sperber, D. (eds.)Bar-Ilan: Annual of Bar-Ilan University Studies in Judaica and the Humanities, vol. 12, pp. 118–136 (Hebrew); English summary: pp. XIII-XIV. Bar-Ilan University, Ramat-Gan, Israel (1974)

105. Ullman, J.D.: Principles of Database Systems, 2nd edn. Computer Science Press, Rockville, MA (1982)

106. Ullman, J.D.: On Kent's "Consequences of Assuming a Universal Relation". ACM Transactions on Database Systems 8(4), 637–643 (1983)

107. van Gigch, J.P.: Applied General Systems Theory, 2nd edn. Harper & Row, London and New York (1978)

108. van Gigch, J.P.: Modeling, Metamodeling, and Taxonomy of System Failures. IEEE Transactions on Reliability R-35(2) (1986)

109. van Gigch, J.P.: Beyond Modeling: Using Metamodeling for Design and Creativity. In: Proceedings of the 1987 Annual Meeting of the International Society for General Systems Research, Budapest, Hungary (June 1987)

110. van Gigch, J.P.: The Metasystem Paradigm as an Inductive Methodology for Critical Thinking. In: Proceedings of the 1987 Annual Meeting of the International Society for General Systems Research, Budapest, Hungary (June 1987)

111. van Gigch, J.P.: Decision Making About Decision Making: Metamodels and Metasystems. Abacus Press, Tunbridge Wells, Kent, England (1987)

112. Vycichl, W.: L'état actuel des études chamito-sémitiques. In: Fronzaroli, P. (ed.) Atti del Secondo Congresso Internazionale di Linguistica Camito-Semitica, Florence, Italy, 16–19 April 1974. Quaderni di Semitistica, vol. 5, pp. 63–76. Istituto di Linguistica e di Lingue Orientali, Università di Firenze, Florence (1978)

113. Weinberg, W.: The History of Hebrew Plene Spelling. Hebrew Union College Annual 46, 457–487 (1975), 47, 237–280 (1976), 48, 291–333 (1977), 49, 311–338 (1978), 50, 289–317 (1979)

114. Wiederhold, G.: Database Design. McGraw-Hill, New York (1977)
115. Wilensky, R.: LISPcraft. Norton, New York (1984)
116. Wilensky, R.: Common LISPcraft. Norton, New York (1986)
117. Winkler, H.A.: Siegel und Charaktere in der Muhammedanischen Zauberei. W. de Gruyter, Berlin & Leipzig (1930)
118. Witt, K.-U.: Finite Graph-Automata. In: Mühlbacher, J. (ed.) Proceedings of the 7th Conference on Graphtheoretic Concepts in Computer Science (WG81), Linz (Austria), June 15-17, pp. 45–53. Carl Hanser Verlag, Munich and Vienna (1981)
119. Woodfill, J., Siegel, P., Ranstrom, J., Meyer, M., Allman, E.: INGRES Version 7 Reference Manual. Bell Laboratories (1983)
120. XML and Information Retrieval: Proceedings of the 2nd Workshop, Tampere, Finland. ACM Special Interest Group on Information Retrieval. ACM, New York (August 2002)

Appendix A: Kinds of /Pa^oL/ among $C_1 a C_2 o C_3$ Hebrew Derivational Patterns

In footnote 21 to Subsec. 11.10, we referred to this Appendix. We are going to exemplify extensively from the lexicology of such terms that instantiate a given class of derivational patterns, and in order to make reference easier, we are going to number the paragraphs.

1. Sometimes, the uninflected identifier of a word-formation pattern in Hebrew (but this may be generally true also of derivational patterns in other Semitic languages as well) happens to "homonymously" refer to different patterns (possibly with the same meaning) that are inflected according to (at least partially) different inflection paradigms. This is the case of the Hebrew uninflected pattern-identifier /Pa^oL/, of which one variant shortens the first syllable's a in the inflected forms, and another variant retains it instead. The latter is not as productive in the Hebrew lexicon, i.e., its derivatives are rarer, and moreover, in Israeli Hebrew no new derivatives are formed by using it any more. It was typically productive in the Roman era, because of the influence of Aramaic, and by applying it, masculine nominalised participles are generated. Moreover, both the a-shortening /Pa^oL/ and the a-retaining /Pa^oL/ have two subvariants, according to whether the ending of the plural is -im or -in, or is -ot instead.

2. Examples of a-shortening /Pa^oL/ include /gadol/ (adj.) for 'big' (plural: $gdolim$); /šalom/ (noun m.) for 'peace' (plural, especially in the sense 'greetings': both $šlomim$ and $šlomot$); /qarob/ (pronounced [ka'rov], plural [kro'vim]) that as an adjective denotes 'close by', and as a noun denotes 'next of kin'.

3. In the *Babylonian Talmud,* at tractate *Siṭah,* 47b, one finds the plural compound *zeḥoḥei-hallév,* i.e., literally, 'those wanton of heart', thus 'boastful ones', 'ones prepossessing'. As the so called constructed state (denoting 'X of') of the masculine plural of the /Pa^oL/ term inside the compound is *zeḥoḥei-,* the masculine plural (in its absolute state) is not *zaḥoḥót,* but rather the morphologically normal *zeḥoḥím* /zḥoḥim/, with the less likely possibility that the form should be *zaḥoḥim,* as per a rare Tannaic Hebrew pattern found in the word *bazozím* for 'robbers'. (There also exists *haróg* for 'murderer', 'murderous robber', in the *Palestinian Talmud,* tractate *Qiddushín,* 66:2; the plural is *harogót* [20, Vol. 1, p. 506, s.v.])

In the *Sifra* at *Aḥăré* 12:9, one finds the noun *nagód* for 'guide' (cf. Aramaic *nagóda*), and the plural is *nagodím*. The word *nagod* 'leader', 'guide', is found in the saying "Not the teaching is the guide, but the practice", in *Sifra*, pericope *Aḥărei*, 12:9 (referring to *Leviticus* 18:4), but as pointed out by Jastrow [36, p. 873, s.v.], in the writings of Rabad (Ravad, Ra'avad) the word *nagod* was replaced with the more usual *nagid* (which is what philologists call *lectio facilior*). Rabad is Abraham ben David, a Provençal rabbi born ca. 1120 in Narbonne, and who died in Posquières in 1198. He was a commentator of Maimonides.

One finds the noun *ṣaróf* 'smelter', 'goldsmith' in the *Palestinian Talmud*, at *Megillah* III, 74a, bottom (the standard Israeli Hebrew term is *ṣoréf*), and in the same sense, one finds *ṣaróv* (with a final /b/ [v] instead of /p/ [f]) in the *Babylonian Talmud*, tractate *Kiddushin*, 82a, according to the version in the *'Arúkh* (a medieval glossary), the plural of *ṣaróv* being *ṣarovín*. But in the printed editions of tractate *Kiddushin*, 82a, one finds the spelling *ṣwrpym* — this being the regular Hebrew plural, *ṣorfím,* of the singular *ṣoréf* (itself a departicipial noun) for 'smelter', 'goldsmith'.

In the *Mishnah*, tractate *Kelim*, 14:3, one finds the name of an instrument, *daqór* (literally, 'piercer'), which Jastrow's dictionary [36, p. 318] defines as "*chisel* or *borer*". In the Mishnaic passage, it is an instrument of a carpenter (*ḥaráš*). The plural form is unknown. The Even-Shoshan dictionary [20] does not have that entry.

4. Distinguish between those four kinds of /PaˆoL/ patterns, and the fifth pattern (typical of adjectives and names for colour), which in its inflected forms, is both *a*-shortening and last-radical redoubling (i.e., /LL/, but the convention in ONOMATURGE is to indicate redoubling by the tilde sign ˜ following the consonant it redoubles, i.e., here, /L˜/. As any transcription between slashes is phonemic, also the uninflected form reflects the consonant redoubling: /PaˆoL˜/. Its plural form is /PˆuL˜im/. An example is *yaróq* for 'green', whose plural form is *yeruqqím*. This is also the pattern of the adjective *'arókh* for 'long', its plural being *'arukkím*.

5. There even is a sixth variant of /PaˆoL/, such that the place of the stress does not move in the plural (because this is the word-form of a European modern loanword into Hebrew): this fifth pattern is instantiated in the noun *fagóṭ* for 'bassoon' (a musical instrument, in Italian *fagotto*), the plural form being *fagóṭim*. As in Israeli Hebrew, the most prestigious kind of pronunciation degeminates (i.e., double consonants are not audibly double), if follows that the word-form of *fagóṭ* is in practice the same as that of *gazóz* for 'fizzy drink', and the plural form is *gazózim* — but lexicographers prefer to consider the derivation pattern of *gazóz* to be /gazzoz/, by deriving it directly in Hebrew from the loanword [gaz] /gazz/ for 'gas' (the plural 'gasses' being denoted by /gazzim/).

6. In the Roman period, Hebrew used to have the noun /qaron/ for 'cart', (animal-driven) 'wagon' (it was a loanword from Latin through Greek), and the plural form was /qaronot/. But Israeli Hebrew has the noun /qaron/ especially for 'wagon' (of a train), and the plural is /qronot/. That is to say, the noun was switched from the *a*-retaining /PaˆoL/ pattern, to the *a*-shortening /PaˆoL/ pattern.

The word /maḥoq/ (which instantiates the /PaˆoL/ pattern, because the initial /m/ is a radical) occurs e.g. in the *Mishnah* in tractate *Kelim* 17:16, denoting an instrument, shaped as a cylindrical cane, for levelling a measure of a dry staple, by removing its excess. Was the plural *maḥoqim*? Jastrow's dictionary [36, p. 758] listed the entry under two headwords, *mĕḥoq* and *maḥaq* (the latter, with both vowels long), which he defined as "strike, an instrument for levelling a measure of grain &c." He gave the plural as *mĕḥoqim* (it occurs in the inflected form spelled *mhwqyhn* (for *mĕḥoqeihen*) 'their canes for taking off the excess' in *Leviticus Rabbah* 21. Whether historically the plural form was *mĕḥoqim* or *maḥoqim*, at any rate the documented occurrence of the inflected form *mĕḥoqeihén* proves that the plural form was not *maḥoqót*. Also Even-Shoshan's dictionary [20] gives the plural as /mḥoqim/. The singular form *máḥaq* (thus, derivationally a "segolate" term, unlike the form of which Jastrow's dictionary [36, p. 758] reconstructed the vowels as *maḥaq* with both vowels long), is now in use in Hebrew in the sense 'eraser' (of rubber, used in order to erase what was written with a pencil).

7. Of the *a*-retaining /PaˆoL/, there exists in Hebrew a pattern whose plural form is /PaˆoLot/, but there also exists in Hebrew the *a*-retaining pattern /PaˆoL/ whose plural form is /Paˆolim/ or /Paˆolin/, and which is seldom instantiated, and most examples of which belong to Tannaic Hebrew (also known as Tannaitic Hebrew or Middle Hebrew, from the Roman age), and often are obsolete in contemporary Hebrew.[27]

8. For example, in Tannaic Hebrew *laqóaḥ* means 'buyer', 'customer', the plural being *laqoḥót*. In Biblical and Modern Hebrew, the transitive verb *laqáḥ* means 'to take', but in Tannaic Hebrew its denotation was restricted to 'to buy', whereas the sense 'to take' was taken over by the transitive verb *natál*. The noun *laqóaḥ* is still in use in Israeli Hebrew, and has retained the sense it had in Tannaic Hebrew. So is the term for 'candlestick': *pamót* (the plural is *pamotót*). In the *Tosefta* at tractate *Bava Metsi'a* 9:14, one finds *hafór* 'digger', and the plural is *haforót*. In the *Mishnah* at tractate *Kelim* 26:5, one finds *saróq* for 'dealer in hatchelled wool of flax', 'hatcheller', the plural being *saroqót* (see *Mishnah* at *Kelim* 12:2) or *saroqín* (in the *Babylonian Talmud* at *Qiddushin* 82a according to the version in the medieval glossary *'Arukh*). Uncertainty about forms is more extensive for *šavóy* 'captor', 'enslaver', 'slaverer', plural *šavoyín* (see in the *Palestinian Talmud* at tractate *Giṭṭín* 45:4), whereas one would expect in Tannaic Hebrew *šabbay* (the plural being *šabba'im* or *šabba'in*) and in Aramaic *šabba'ah* or *šabboya* or *šavoya*, the Aramaic plural being *šabba'ei* or *šabboyei* 'captors', cf. *šabboyinhi* 'their captors' in Aramaic in the *Babylonian Talmud* at tractate *Ketubbot* 23a.

---

[27] Typically, the masculine plural ending in Tannaic Hebrew is -*in* where Biblical Hebrew has -*im*. That some occurrences of terms peculiar of Tannaic Hebrew have been traded down with the -*im* ending rather than -*in* can typically be ascribed to scribal modification while copying the manuscripts (they often applied forms with which they were familiar from Biblical Hebrew), or when the texts were prepared for printing.

9. A term that is no longer in use, even though the concept it denotes is still current, is /qaroy/ (plural: /qaroyot/) — found in the *Palestinian Talmud,* at tractate *Megillah,* 75a — for 'congregant called to read in public a liturgical reading', such as a passage from the weekly portion of the Pentateuch (for this sense, the standard term at present is the compound *ha'olé lasséfer,* literally: 'he who goes up to [reading] the Book'), or one of the five *megillót* ("rolls" from the Hagiographa), but the present-day term is either a generic *haqqoré* (literally, 'the reader'), or *ha'olé laddukhán* (literally, 'he who goes up to the platform', but it may also refer to the lay officiant of prayer).

10. We have in Tannaic Hebrew *naṭoším* for 'fugitives whose estate is abandoned', *raṭoším* for 'absentees whose estate is abandoned and whose whereabouts are unknown, but who left of their own accord (and not fleeing under duress)', both these terms belonging to legal terminology. (In the late Roman Empire, the case was frequent of landowners who left their estate, either because they had estates elsewhere, or because they wanted to escape the fiscal liabilities of being appointed a city councillor: they rather fled away, the tax burden being unbearable.)[28]

11. There also exists, in Tannaic Hebrew, *la'ozót* for 'ones who speak a foreign language and do not know Hebrew' (even though they are Jewish), and the latter term has remained in rabbinic discourse. The Tannaic Hebrew *pa'oṭót* for 'toddlers' (found in the *Mishnah* at tractate *Giṭṭin,* 5:7) means 'toddler', and is still in use in Israeli Hebrew. But the variant *payoṭót* for 'toddlers' is obsolete; it is found in the *Palestinian Talmud* at tractate *Érubin,* 7, 24c, bottom. Tannaic Hebrew also had *masorót* for 'informers' ('traitors'), the singular being *masór,* but in Israeli Hebrew by *masorót* one understands 'traditions', being the plural of *masóret* ('tradition'). Both terms are associated with the Hebrew verb *masár* for 'to consign', just as in English both *traitor* and *tradition* (as well as *tradent,* for 'one handing down a tradition') are ultimately derived from the Latin verb for 'to consign'. In Hebrew from the 19th century, instead of *masór* for 'informer' (more precisely: 'one who consigns people unjustly to ones who would harm them') the regular Hebrew participle *mosér* would often rather be used (the plural being *mosrim*).

An inflected form of the Hebrew verb *masár* — as in the sense 'to denounce unjustly' — made its way into the 18th-century rabbinic court records (written in Judaeo-Arabic in Hebrew characters) of the city of Ṣan'a in Yemen, which have been published by Nini [63]. In entry 897 on p. 312 in Nini's edition, recorded in the summer of the year 2076 of the Seleucid calendar, i.e., in 1765, one finds a tax collector, Yiḥya (this name is the Yemeni form of *Yaḥya*), who had been accused of embezzlement, and therefore ended up in prison for a while. Because of this, he had incurred costs that he recovered from the taxes he collected from the Jews of 'Amrān, but part of them sued him in the rabbinic court, and the court ruled that he was in the wrong and must return the money he had recovered in that manner, and if anything, should Yiḥya have a complaint against any particular person for having denounced him unjustly (spelt in Hebrew characters as < 'nh msrw>), then Yiḥya should sue that person, and the court case would be between those two. It is

---

[28] On the *bouleutai* (city councillors), seized lands, and squatters, see e.g. in Seth Schwartz's recent book [97], on p. 107 and 115–116 (especially the long fn. 15).

quite likely that < *'nh msrw*> is to be read *ánna msáru* (thus, with the verbal form being inflected as in the vernacular Arabic, the verb being a technical loanword from Hebrew fully integrated into the lexicon and grammar of Judaeo-Arabic). But it may also be that < *'nh msrw*> is to be read *ánna mesaró* (thus, with the Hebrew verbal form appearing the way it is inflected according to the Hebrew grammar: the technical term would then have been inserted in its Hebrew form, as a *Fremdwort,* into the Judaeo-Arabic context).

12. In Israeli Hebrew, *pagóš* (whose plural form is *pagoším*) means 'bumper' (of a car), but in Tannaic Hebrew, that term means 'battering projectile', 'catapult stone' (in *Mishnah,* at *Kelim,* 16:8). In that sense, there also used to exist the variant *pagóz* (in Aramaic *pagóza*), whose plural form is *pagozín*. In Israeli Hebrew, that variant no longer exists, but in a modified form (*pagáz*) it means 'shell', i.e., 'projectile' (of artillery). By contrast, in Israeli Hebrew an ancient catapult stone is called *éven-balístra.*

13. The departicipial noun *ḥokhér* denotes 'land tenant'. In the *Mishnah,* tractate *Bikkurím* 1:2 and 1:11, the plural *ḥakhorót* is found, from a singular form *ḥakhór.* In the context, the *ḥakhorót* are juxtaposed to the *arisín.* The *arisín* owe the landowner a given share of the harvest, and cultivate the land for their own share; whereas the *ḥakhorót* owe the landowner a fixed amount of produce, no matter how large or small the yield of the harvest has been. Therefore, *ḥakhorót* denotes 'tenants on a fixed rent payable in kind (irrespective of the yield of the crops)'.

We also have *laqoṭót* for 'poor persons who come into a field in order to collect the ears of grain that fell while being cut, and were left behind on purpose for the poor', 'grain-gleaner', and there is as well *namošót* for 'ones from amongst the weakest of mendicants', 'ones from amongst the slowest among the poor who are allowed to collect the remainder of the crop in a field': the earliest interpretations were given in the *Talmud* itself, and vary between 'those who gather after the gatherers', and 'old people who walk with the help of a walking stick'. There also was a variant of *namošót* being *mašošót* and meaning the same (*Palestinian Talmud,* at tractate *Pe'ah,* VIII, beginning of 20d). Actually, Jastrow [36, p. 850, s.v. *mašoš*] defined it "groper, slow walker", and in the same talmudic passage, one also finds the idiom *memašméš uvá* — a couple of participles that literally means 'touching and coming' (i.e., 'feeling one's way and coming'), but idiomatically means 'coming gropingly', 'coming slowly', or 'coming nearer and nearer'. Moreover, consider the term for 'surveyor', still in use in Israeli Hebrew for one who measures a field: *mašóaḥ,* whose plural is *mašoḥót.* It occurs as early as the *Mishnah* in tractates *Erubin* 4:11, and *Kelim* 13:3.

14. In Modern Hebrew, the word *namošót* was sometimes used as a very negatively connotated word for 'epigons'. In Israeli Hebrew, there has been some metaphorical use of *namošót* (but in a substandard pronunciation: *n(e)mušót*) for 'wimps', most infamously when a politician who will remain unnamed stated that Israelis who live abroad are *nfólet šel namošót,* i.e., "scraps (*nfólet*) of *namošót*". The connotation was reversed, with respect to the historical context: he came out as being utterly inconsiderate (a constant with him), whereas the original cultural context was one of caring and sharing, even though with a streak of condescending pity. Also see point 25 below. (The Israeli Hebrew noun *nfólet* for 'scrap', 'produce waste', is derived from the root for 'to fall', and therefore the semantic motivation is like that of the Italian name for the same concept, *cascàme,* and in the plural: *cascàmi* — literally, 'things fallen down'.)

15. Of *karóz* — for 'herald' (e.g., 'Temple herald' in Graeco-Roman age Jerusalem) or 'city crier' — the plural is *karozót.* That term is standard in Israeli Hebrew for 'city crier', even though in the last two centuries you would have been quite hard pressed to find any city crier around. Tannaic Hebrew *karóz* has an antecedent in Biblical Aramaic, /karoza/, in *Daniel,* 3:4. But there is possibly a relation to the Greek κήρυξ. Incidentally, Korazin (Chorazin) was a Roman-age town north of Capernaum, which itself was on the northern shore of the Sea of Galilee. The spelling *Chorazin* reflects ancient phonetics: the Hebrew phoneme has currently the allophones [k] and [x] (i.e., *kh*), but in the Roman period, apparently even after a consonant or at the beginning of a word, one would hear *kh* (judging from the evidence of transcriptions into the Greek and the Roman alphabets).

16.   Here is another example of the pattern /PaˆoL/: in the homiletical collection *Genesis Rabbah,* 86, one finds the descriptor *géver qafóz* (literally, "a man [who is a] runner/jumper"), spelled *gbr qpwz,* in the sense 'a runner', 'a quick man'. There is no instance of the plural of *qafóz* documented. The descriptor is metaphorically applied to Joseph, who in Egypt was a diligent, quick, and successful worker.

The Hebrew noun /naqor/ is mentioned in the plural /naqorot/ among such professionals whose dealings are with women (in the *Tosefta* in tractate *Kiddushin* 5:14, and in the *Babylonian Talmud* in tractate *Kiddushin* 82a). These were artisans (known in Arabic by the name *naqqār*) who used to restore a rough surface on millstones once these had become too smooth for grinding [5, p. 67].

The Hebrew noun *ṣayyár* means 'painter'. Apparently there also used to exist the synonym *ṣayor,* because its plural *ṣayorot* is documented. In fact, the frame of a painter or embroiderer is called an *'arisa* ('cradle') of painters, *ṣayyarin* in *Tosefta Kelim* at *Bava Batra* 2:9, but *ṣayorot* according to Zuckermandel's edition of the *Tosefta.* Therefore, the frame of a painter or embroiderer was called either *'arisa šel ṣayyarin,* or *'arisa šel ṣayorot.*

17.   In the Hebrew Bible, the noun *taqoa'* (in the singular) for 'trumpet' or 'horn' — a musical wind instrument — is found in *Ezekiel,* 7:14: "they blew the trumpet/horn", *taqe'ú battaqóa'.* Clearly, the noun which is the direct object and the verb are co-derivatives of the same lexical root, which is semantically associated with conative action, such as thrust, sticking in, driving in, plugging in, or blowing into a horn. The entry for the noun *taqóa'* in the standard Even-Shoshan dictionary [20, 21] gives the plural as *taqo'ót,* thus making a choice about which variant of the /PaˆoL/ variant to choose. The choice was in line with the typical choice that Tannaic Hebrew would make.

18.   Consider the Modern Hebrew agent noun /garos/ 'grist maker' or 'grist dealer' (from the plural noun /grisim/ 'grist', for the product). The Even-Shoshan dictionary [20] gives as correct forms of the plural both *garosím* and *garosót.*

Note however that this Hebrew term may or may not be merely an adaptation of the Aramaic *garosa* (spelt *grwsh*) for 'grit-maker' or 'grist-dealer', as found more than once in the *Palestinian Talmud,* and of which such early rabbinic texts also give two forms of the plural in Hebrew: *garosím* and *garosót.* In the *Mishnah,* at tractate *Mo'ed Katan,* 2:5, one finds yet another agent noun, in Hebrew, *dašóš* for 'wheat-stamper' or 'groats-maker' (as grist was made by stamping upon the wheat). The term is found there in the plural form *dašošót.* In particular, the *Mishnah,* at tractate *Mo'ed Katan,* 2:5, mentions "the hunters and the *dašošót* [variant: *rašošót*] and the *garosót*". The alternation of the forms *dašošót* and *rašošót* is easily explained by the shape of the Hebrew letters for /d/ and /r/ being similar. The *dašošót* are those whose occupation was to pound or tread wheat into a pap, i.e., into grit (cf. the Aramaic noun *daysa* written with a final letter *aleph,* and the Israeli Hebrew noun *daysa* written with a final letter *he,* for 'pap', and cf. the Hebrew verb *daš* for 'to tread upon', 'to stamp upon', and the Arabic verb *dās* for 'to press', 'to squeeze'). The *garosót* instead used to pound wheat or beans into ground stuff (*grisím*) more coarse than a pap. Moreover, in the *Mishnah,* at tractate *Terumot,* 3:4, one finds (in the plural) the Hebrew agent noun *darokhót* for 'grape treaders' or 'olive treaders'. For both *dašóš* and *darókh* the etymology is quite transparently from verbs for 'to stamp upon'.

19. The standard Hebrew term for 'miller' is *tohén,* and its plural is *tohăním* [20, Vol. 1, p. 474, s.v.]. This term is in use in Modern and Israeli Hebrew, and has been in use for centuries. But in medieval Provence, Meiri[29] (writing about tractate *Pesahim,* p. 142 in the Jerusalem edn. of 1963/4) related that "I found that in Narbonne it happened that the *tahonót* (millers) were fixing (or: arranging) a sack full of wheat on the edge of a pit/well", and out of concern lest the wheat had become humid, the question rose whether that wheat could be permissibly used in order to prepare unleavened bread for Passover (quoted in [104, p. 125]). Clearly the plural *tahonót* for 'millers' instantiates a word-form available from Tannaic Hebrew. And yet, that word is not found in the extant corpus of texts in Tannaic Hebrew from the Roman period. In the early (i.e., Roman-age) rabbinic literature, one does find, in the singular, the Aramaic form *tahona,* and the plural is *tahonayya* or *tahonin* (spelt *thwnyn*), and one even finds — in *Pesikta Rabbati,* 23–24 — *tahonim* (spelt *thwnym*), thus a Hebrew plural form. This suggests that the form *tahonót* was reconstituted in the Middle Ages, as both writers and readers mastered the word-formation of Tannaic Hebrew, and based on the Aramaic cognate were inspired to make up an adaptation to Hebrew, as the textual context required a Hebrew word. The Even-Shoshan dictionary [20] has, for 'miller', apart from the usual *tohén,* which is a departicipial noun [20, Vol. 1, p. 474, s.v.], also the term *tehán* (formed as an agent noun) [20, Vol. 1, p. 478, s.v.], and yet another entry, *tahón* [20, Vol. 1, p. 478, s.v.], and for the latter term the plural is given as *tahonót,* with no mention of the sources (which that dictionary usually indicates). At any rate, the etymon of the Hebrew noun *tahón* 'miller' is its Talmudic Aramaic derivational and semantic equivalent *tahóna* [36, p. 528, s.v.], whose plural is *thonin* or *thonayya.*

---

[29] Rabbi Menachem ben Solomon Meiri was born in 1249 and died in 1315.

20. The following example is from zoonymy (i.e., names for animal kinds). The noun *'aród* has two lexemes, and both of them denote a given animal kind. In the *Mishnah,* at tractate *Kil'áyim,* 1:6, the noun *'aród* means 'onager' (a species of wild donkey). This noun is still in use in Israeli Hebrew, for the sense 'onager', and its modern plural (e.g., in the Even-Shoshan Hebrew dictionary [20]) is *'ărodím.* The *a* of the singular is shortened into what in traditional Hebrew grammar is considered to be a semivowel, even though the current pronunciation retains the *a.* Still, morphologically it is the *a*-shortening /Pa︠oL/ pattern that is applied to that noun. In Roman-age rabbinic texts, one finds two forms of the plural of *'aród* as meaning 'onager':

- one form of the plural that is spelt *'rwdwt* (found in the *Palestinian Talmud,* at tractate *Shekalim,* VIII, beginning of 51a), and may be either
  - *'ărodót* (thus, an instance of the *a*-shortening /Pa︠oL/ pattern),
  - or, more likely, *'arodót* (thus, an instance of the *a*-retaining /Pa︠oL/ pattern),
- and the plural form *'ărodi'ót* (in the *Babylonian Talmud,* at tractate *Menahot,* 103b).

21. In the early rabbinic literature, one also finds (only in the singular) the noun *'aród* (according to the usual reading of the spelling *'rwd*) denoting a kind of rather large reptile, thought to be poisonous,[30] and whose birth was fabled to be as a hybrid.[31] Note however that modern philological research has shown that apparently the original form of the noun when referring to a reptile was *'arvád.*[32] Therefore, in that sense the noun was not an instance of the pattern /Pa︠oL/.

---

[30] According to a tale, a sage was bitten by it. He didn't die, but the reptile died. So the sage carried the carcass of the reptile to the house of learning and told those present that as they could see, it is not the *'aród* that kills, but it is sin that kills. This tale appears in the *Babylonian Talmud,* at *Berakhot* 33a.

[31] So Rashi's commentary to the *Babylonian Talmud* at *Berakhot,* 33a: "*'Aród:* From the *nahás* (snake) and the *tsav* it comes [i.e., it is born], as they mate with each other and from both of them, what comes out is an *'aród*". This notion is turn is based on a passage in the *Babylonian Talmud,* at *Hullin,* 127a. Whereas in Israeli Hebrew, *tsav* means 'turtle' or 'tortoise', in Biblical and Tannaic Hebrew it apparently meant the same as *dabb* in Arabic, i.e., a large lizard: the spiny-tailed agama (*Uromastix*), but apparently also the other local large meat-yielding lizard, the desert monitor (*Varanus griseus*). Dor discussed this [15, pp. 163–165], as well as how the tortoise was referred to in those textual corpora [15, pp. 167–168].

[32] A synonym used to be *hăvarbar.* Dor [15, p. 163] claimed that the *'arvád* or *hăvarbar* could be identified with a large limbless lizard, the glass snake (*Ophiosaurus apodus,* which in Israeli Hebrew is called *qamtán ha-hóreš*). When threatened, the glass snake squirts a green, smelly liquid. According to Dor, this may have been reason enough for this species to become the subject of folktales. Maybe the glass snake squirting green liquid was considered similar to poisonous snakes that release a poisonous liquid? At any rate, it makes sense that if this identification of the *'arvád* is correct, its bite was not lethal, albeit it was expected to be.

22. It is important to realise that not all nouns or adjectives of the word-form $C_1aC_2oC_3$ (where C_i is a consonant) are necessarily an instance of one of the /PaˆoL/ patterns. One needs to be especially careful when the first consonant is /m/ or /n/. Is that a radical (thus, /P/, the first radical), or rather a preformative that belongs in the pattern itself? In fact, the pattern of the passive participle, /niPˆaL/, becomes /naPoL/, when the middle radical (i.e., /ˆ/) is a mute w. Examples include the noun *mazón* 'food', whose plural /mzonot/ *mezonót* means 'foods' but also 'alimony'; and the adjectives *namókh* (phonemically /namok/) for 'low'; the medieval and modern *namóg* for 'melting away'; as well as /naloz/, whose plural /nlozim/ appears in the Bible (*Proverbs,* 2:15) in the sense 'wayward', but which in Israeli Hebrew is a rather formal term for 'contemptible'.

23. It is likely that the noun /mazor/, that in the Hebrew Bible means either 'bandage' (or 'compress') — which is the sense in *Jeremiah,* 30:13 (but also in the *Palestinian Talmud,* at tractate *Shabbat,* 5:1) — or 'ailment' (which is the sense in *Hoshea,* 5:13) was derived by applying the /maPoL/ pattern. In those sources, that noun is only found in the singular. The term is not in use in Israeli Hebrew, but the Even-Shoshan dictionary [20] gives a plural form *mĕzorím.* Thus, this is an *a*-shortening form of $C_1aC_2oC_3$, as could be expected indeed of a pattern that is not /PaˆoL/, even though both the /maPoL/ pattern and the various kinds of /PaˆoL/ match the word-form $C_1aC_2oC_3$.

24. A clear example of the /maPoL/ pattern is the Biblical *Magog* (cf. Arabic *Majūj,* English *Magog,* Italian *Magoga*), all the more so as the context in Ch. 38 of *Ezekiel* states "Gog, from the land of Magog", and the m preformative often appears in the role of forming nouns for place. From the proper name *Gog* (which is apparently related to the Anatolian name preserved in the Classical sources as *Gyges* and in Akkadian as *Gugu*), Biblical Hebrew derived the root $\sqrt{\mathrm{g(w)g}}$, whence the proper name for Gog's country, *Magog.* This is an instance of the /maPoL/ pattern, such that it happens to be the case that /P/ = /L/ = /g/.

The /maPoL/ pattern is frequent in Hebrew, and has been productive in both Biblical Hebrew and Modern Hebrew. An example of a modern term is /maḥoš/ 'antenna' (of invertebrates), and its plural is *mĕhoším.* The etymological sense is 'instrument for sensing'. Biblical Hebrew examples of instances of the pattern /maPoL/ includes for example /maṣoq/ 'distress' (*Deuteronomy* 28:53), and /maṣor/. The Even-Shoshan dictionary [20] gives the plural form of neither term. The term /maṣor/ is now used in the sense 'siege' (which occurs in *2 Kings* 24:10), but in the Hebrew Bible it also had the acceptations 'fortress' (*2 Chronicles* 11:5), and 'distress' (*Jeremiah* 19:9 juxtaposes both terms in that sense: "in /maṣor/ and /maṣoq/"). Another instance of the /maPoL/ pattern is /maṣod/ 'hunt' (it is now used for 'hunt' in the sense of the police hunting for a criminal), but in *Ecclesiastes* 9:14 the acceptation is 'fortress', and the term occurs there in the plural form *mĕṣodím.* Therefore, in the entry for /maṣod/, the Even-Shoshan dictionary [20] gives it as the plural form.

25. We have already discussed (see point 14 above) *namošót* for 'ones from amongst the weakest of mendicants', 'ones from amongst the slowest among the poor who are allowed to collect the remainder of the crop in a field'. Even that one may be (it was proposed by some) an instance of the /naPoL/ pattern (as being a particular case of the /niP^aL/ passive participle pattern), but it is legitimate to analyse it as an instance of /Pa^oL/ anyway (actually, such ambiguity of analysis is what historically caused the emergence of new lexical roots). As a matter of fact, Kutscher [42, Sec. 5 on pp. 98–99 (Hebrew) and p. XXXI (English)] claimed that the root of the word spelt *nmwšwt* is $\sqrt{\text{nmš}}$, and rejected Epstein's claim that the root is $\sqrt{\text{m(w)š}}$ instead, in which case, Kutscher argued, the *a* would be shortened, and the word would be *nemošot* instead of *namošot*. Kutscher was able to marshal as evidence an authoritative manuscript in which a diacritical sign for *a* appears indeed, as well as another manuscript in which the presence of an *a* is incontrovertibly indicated by a mute *aleph* letter. Thus, this being a *scriptio plena* instead of defective spelling, as the place of some vowels is indicated by the presence of letters (*matres lectionis*) with the role of being mute instead of consonantal: see [113] for the history of Hebrew plene spelling, and see [40, 23] for the emergence of *aleph* as a *mater lectionis* in the Qumran texts.

26. Also the derivational pattern /PaLon/ has the word-form $C_1aC_2oC_3$, where not all three consonants are radicals (only the first two are, the third one being in this case "inorganic", i.e., a non-radical). An example is the noun *ratsón* (phonemically: /rason/) for 'will' (i.e., the action of wanting). It shortens the *a* in its inflected forms, e.g., (/rasoni/>)/rsoni/ *rtsoní* for 'my wish', and in derived terms such as the adjective /rsoni/ 'voluntary' such as in *tnu'á rtsonít,* 'voluntary movement'. Also note the word (only singular) *latsón* (phonemically: /lason/) for 'clowning' or 'pranking', for which the Even-Shoshan dictionary [20] gives an inflected form with a shotrtened *a,* namely, *letsonó* ('his clowning', 'his pranking'). But take /garon/ 'throat'. It was apparently formed according to the derivational pattern /PaLon/, but then it was reanalysed as being an instance of the derivation pattern /Pa^oL/, when /garon/ became itself the stem of a modern verb from which the form in use is the participle /mgurran/ *megorán* 'gutturalised'. That is to say, all three consonants of /garon/ were treated as though they were the radicals of the neologism.

27. In the *Mishnah,* at tractate *Kelim,* 11:3, names for products of metal working are enumerated, and these include the words spelt as *grwdwt* and *qswswt* which — unless they are to be pronounced *grudót* and *ketsutsót* — could rather be *garodót* and *katsotsót*. Nevertheless, instead of the spelling *grwdwt* (which is per force associated with the plural), in some manuscripts one finds the form spelt *grwdt,* thus a singular feminine term (*gródet*). In a book about metals and metal working in Jewish (especially talmudic) sources [48, Sec. 5.5, pp. 158–160], Dan Levene[33] and Beno Rothenberg explain *grwdwt* and *qswswt* as being names

---

[33] Because of their respective disciplines being far apart, it is for sure a rare thing to be able to cite (which we do), in the selfsame paper, both Mark Levene, the computer scientist from Birkbeck College of the University of London, and his younger brother Dan Levene of the University of Southampton, best known for his research about the magic spells found in incantation bowls from Mesopotamia in late antiquity. Here we are citing his book in archaeo-metallurgy.

for different waste products of metal working, respectively 'filings and shavings', and 'cut bits of metal'.

28.   The derivational pattern /PaˆoL/, plural /PaˆoLot/, appears to no longer be available for neologisation in present-day Hebrew. This does not mean it couldn't turn up in some given literary idiolect (i.e., in the peculiar language of some given author). In Nissan's own literary writings, there is an occurrence of *békher hannavonót* for 'young giraffe'. Literally, this compound means "*békher* ('young camel') of the *navonót*" — plural of *navón*. The masculine noun *navón* is a neologism for 'giraffe' after the term *nabun*. The latter is an Africanism in Pliny the Elder's Latin treatise *Historia Naturalis*. Pliny's *nabun*, transcribed into the Hebrew script as <nbwn> , is then read as the extant Hebrew word spelled that way, i.e., /nabon/ *navón*, which means 'intelligent' (m. sing.). The plural of that adjective is *nevoním* 'intelligent' (m. pl.), vs. *nevonót* 'intelligent' (f. pl.) being the plural of *nevoná* 'intelligent' (f. sing.). Therefore, the neologised plural *navonót* 'giraffes' (which is found in a text written in the Hebrew script and including also the diacritical marks for vowels) enables differentiation, and because the vowel /a/ is maintained in the first syllable even though the stress is only on the syllable following the next, this word must be the plural of the pattern /PaˆoL/, plural /PaˆoLot/. A playfully etymologising backup story for the neologism claims that being called *navón* is apt for the giraffe, because (this is true) it is the most intelligent ruminant. (Ruminants, however, are among the least intelligent among the Mammals.) In the same literary corpus, Nissan also neologised in Hebrew the name *aholót* for the axolotl (a Mexican amphybian), by emulating the phonetics of the Mexican Spanish and general standard Spanish name for the same animal, *ajolote,* and by adapting it into the Hebrew derivational pattern with which we are concerned. The plural ending in -*ot* as used for a word in the singular is found in Hebrew *běhemót* 'hippopotamus' (cf. *Job* 40:15),[34] and rarely in a man's name:

---

[34] The Hebrew word *běhemót* as being used not in the masculine singular, but in the feminine plural, means 'beasts' or 'domestic beasts'. Note morever the animal name spelled *'yšwt* or *'šwt* in the early rabbinic literature. It occurs in the *Mishnah* at *Mo'ed Katan* 1:4 and at *Kelim* 21:3. That spelling is read by some as *išut,* or then as *ešut* or *ašut* (or the Ashkenazi pronunciations *óšis, áyšis,* or *íšis*), but we cannot take it for granted that historically or in some historical receptions, there was here the ending -*ot* instead.

The *Babylonian Talmud* at *Mo'ed Katan* 6b states: "What is *'yšwt*? Rav Judah said: 'a creature that has no eyes'". This is now understood to have been the mole-rat, not to be confused for the mole. There exist no moles in nature in Israel. What does exist is the mole-rat, a blind fossorial rodent of the genus *Spalax,* now called *ḥóled* in Israeli Hebrew (by reapplication or by tentative identification of a biblical zoonym). The mole is outwardly similar, but is an insectivore, and does not belong to the rodents. The mole-rat has no eyes at all, whereas in the mole, tiny residual eyes can still be found, even though they cannot see.

In another early rabbinic text, in *Genesis Rabbah,* 51, the word *'yšwt* or *'šwt* denotes an animal "which sees not the light". The word as occurring there is used in order to explain *Psalms* 58:9 homiletically. In that verse from *Psalms,* in whose

- *Maḥăzi'ót*, in *1 Chronicles* 25:4 and 25:30;
- *Mĕrayót*, in *Ezra* 7:3, *Nehemiah* 11:11, and *1 Chronicles* 5:32, 5:33, 6:37, and 12:15;
- *Mĕremót*, in *Ezra* 8:33 and 10:36, and in *Nehemiah* 3:4, 3:21, 10:6, and 12:3;
- *Mĕšillemót*, in *Nehemiah* 11:13 and *2 Chronicles* 28:12;
- *Šĕlomót*, in *1 Chronicles* 24:22, 26:26;
- *Šammót*, in *1 Chronicles* 11:27;
- *Šĕmiramót*, in *1 Chronicles* 15:18, 15:20, 16:5, and *2 Chronicles* 17:8;
- *Lappidót*, in *Judges* 4:4 (if this is the name of Deborah's husband indeed, when she is described as "woman of Lappidot");
- *Aḇót*, in *1 Chronicles* 24:31;
- *Naḇót*, in *1 Kings*, Ch. 21;
- *Yĕrimót*, in *1 Chronicles* 7:7, 12:5, 24:30, 25:4, and 27:19, and in *2 Chronicles* 11:18 and 31:13;
- whereas *Yĕri'ót* instead (found in *1 Chronicles* 2:18) is understood to have been the name of a woman.

29. The derivational pattern /PaˆoL/, plural /PaˆoLot/, also occurs in neologisation in Nissan's literary writings in the plural *la'osót* for 'chewers', 'ones who chew'. It is patterned after the Tannaic Hebrew word *la'ozót* for 'ones who speak a foreign language and do not know Hebrew' (even though they are Jewish), a term from rabbinic discourse for which see in §11 above. The neologism *la'osót* occurs in a playfully etymologising backup story, set in the aftermath of the Tower of Babel, and combines an explanation of why it is that a country is called *Laos* and that in Greek, λαός means 'people', 'population'. That Hebrew-language story is discussed by Nissan and HaCohen-Kerner [84], as an example in the context of illustrating the control sequence in the designed multiagent architecture of the GALLURA project in automated generation of playful explanation. For the conceptual background of that project, see [83] in this set of volumes.

---

second hemistich (i.e., second part out of two) the words *néfel éšet* occur, the sense of these is probably "a woman's miscarried fetus", and it is stated that it does not see light (because dead before being born). As the first hemistich of the same verse refers to a snail proceeding in its mucus, and as in *Psalms* semantic parallelism of the two hemistichs of a verse is frequent, apparently for those two reasons, in *Genesis Rabbah* 51 it was assumed that also in the second hemistich an animal was being named.

The Hebrew zoonym *išút* is a homonym, or should we rather say, *išút* is polysemous in Hebrew. As Hebrew *iš* denotes 'man' and *iššá* denotes 'woman', the noun *išút*, formed with the abstraction suffix *-út*, means 'sexual life', such as in the compound *dinei išút* for 'norms of marital life' (from Jewish law).

Moreover, in the *Babylonian Talmud*, tractate *Ḥullin*, 62b, there is an occurrence of the Aramaic bird name *giruta*, written *gyrwt'*. In the early 20th century, the zoologist Israel Aharoni adapted it into the Hebrew neologism *girút*, written *gyrwt*, which he applied to a species of waterfowl, the coot (*Fulica atra*). It is now called *agamiyyá* in Israeli Hebrew. How those names for this particular bird species evolved in Hebrew is the subject of a table entry in a paper by Fischler [22, pp. 10-11, no. 1, and p. 10, note 1].

30. Let us conclude this appendix by quoting from an article by Osborne [87], whose subject is Early Mishnaic Hebrew, in relation to Biblical Hebrew. We replace the words which appear in Osborne's original in the Hebrew script, with a transcription enclosed (according to the convention we applied elsewhere in this paper) in single guillements. Moreover, we replace the exponents of Osborne's footnotes 53 and 54 with the respective citations of [96] and [93]. Bear in mind that MH stands for Mishnaic Hebrew, and BH stands for Biblical Hebrew:

> MH developed the qāṭôl patterns as a *nomina agentis*. In BH nouns of agency are often patterned after the participle form <qwṭl>. The following examples demonstrate the change observed in MH: <ṭḥwn> "miller", <srwq> "wool-comber", and <lqwḥ> "buyer" [96, 106]. Agency in MH is also expressed by the suffix <-n>, as in <gzln> "robber" [93, 187].

Appendix B: Historical Strata, and Verbs That Took Over

In Subsec. 12.4, we gave an example based on the introduction to Menaḥem Moreshet's *A Lexicon of the New Verbs in Tannaic Hebrew* [61, Sec. III.4, p. 75 ff]. We are going to repeat it here in this Appendix B, and to give further examples of how verbs belonging to given lexical roots evolved from Biblical Hebrew to Tannaic Hebrew.

But first of all, note this explanation about transliteration in the following example, reflecting how the coding was done in the ONOMATURGE expert system. *Phonemic transcription* is between slashes, whereas *lexical roots* (Semitic consonantal stems) are between backslashes (but in the diagrams as shown here, appear under the mathematical root symbol). Such roots of which there was more than one lexeme are distinguished by a numeric subscript. By % we transliterate the letter *aleph;* the phoneme /%/ is a glottal stop (or zero). Inside roots, the letters %, h, w, y may be mute. By $ we transcribe the phoneme /š/, which is like *sh* in the English adjective *sheer.* /$/ is one of the two phonemes indicated by the Hebrew letter *shin,* which corresponds also to the phoneme that we write as /S/, and which phonetically is [s], the same as the phoneme /s/ that corresponds to the letter *samekh.* By H we transliterated, in ONOMATURGE, the phoneme /ḥ/ (a voiceless pharyngeal fricative, but many Israelis pronounce it as [x], a voiceless uvular fricative). It is represented by the Hebrew letter *ḥet.* By & we indicate the letter and phoneme *'ayin,* which some people pronounce as a voiced pharyngeal fricative, but others pronounce as a glottal plosive, or as zero. The phoneme expressed by the Hebrew letter *tsadi* is indicated by /c/ and its modern phonetic value is [ts], even though historically (and in the liturgical Hebrew of Oriental Jews) it is [ṣ], a velarised sibilant. By /t/ the Hebrew letter *tav* is transcribed. By contrast, /T/ transcribes (in ONOMATURGE) the velarised phoneme /ṭ/, expressed by the Hebrew letter *ṭet.* We transliterate as /q/ the phoneme expressed by the letter *qof,* whose phonetic value is [k] in Israeli Hebrew, but which historically (and in the traditional liturgical pronunciation of many Oriental Jews) is pronounced as [q], a voiceless uvular plosive, a consonant preserved in Modern Standard Arabic (while often not by Arabic vernaculars).

Now, let us turn to the exemplification of how verbs developed from Biblical Hebrew to Tannaic (or Tannaitic) Hebrew. According to the notation in Moreshet [61], provenience from the older, Biblical stratum (independently from its being characterised by disappearance, or decrease in use, or even increase in use), is indicated by a downward arrow, while the adoption of a stem, in Tannaitic Hebrew, to denote a certain meaning, is indicated by an upward arrow. Evolution modifies the roles of lexical entries (terms and roots) in the concerned semantic field: for example, Moreshet [61, p. 77] discussed the shrinking, from Biblical Hebrew to Tannaitic Hebrew, of the pool of verbs expressing the concept 'seeing'. Several examples follow; all of them are drawn from Moreshet, and are so processed as to yield a representation in a portion of a nested relation:

A) Disappearance or shrinking use, in the Tannaic stratum of Hebrew, Biblical Hebrew verbs derived from given lexical roots, and the emergence of a new verb that took over for denoting the same sense 'to be in charge (of)':

$$\sqrt{\text{šrt}} \;,\quad \sqrt{\text{khn}} \quad - \quad \sqrt{\text{šmš}}$$
$$\downarrow \qquad\qquad \downarrow \qquad\qquad \uparrow$$

(shrank) disappeared   appeared,
took over

In the frame of the root $\sqrt{\text{šmš}}$, or of the verb /šimmeš/, derived from it, and which means 'to be in charge (of)', it makes sense to include this information about the history of those verbs:

```
(EVOLUTION
   ( (FROM_STRATUM    ( Biblical_Hebrew ) )
     (TO_STRATUM      ( Tannaitic_Hebrew ) )
     (PHENOMENA
                 (  (ROOT  ( $rt ) )
                    (DID   ( shrink ) )   )
                 (  (ROOT  ( khn ) )
                    (DID   ( disappear ) )   )
                 (  (ROOT  ( $m$ ) )
                    (DID   ( appear  take_over ) ) ) )
  ) ) )
```

B) Evolution from Biblical Hebrew to Tannaic Hebrew of verbs belonging to given lexical roots, and which denote 'to ask for'; one root shrank, another one disappeared, yet another one remained in use roughly to the same extent, and a new verb from a new root made its appearance, all of these conveying 'to ask for':

$$\sqrt{\text{drš}} \;,\quad \sqrt{\text{nšh}_1} \;,\quad \sqrt{\text{bqš}} - \sqrt{\text{tb\&}}$$
$$\downarrow \qquad\quad \downarrow \qquad = \qquad \uparrow$$

(shrank) disappeared   appeared

The symbol $=$ indicates that the lexical root was shared by both strata, namely, Biblical Hebrew and Tannaic (or Tannaitic) Hebrew. The following nesting of attributes conveys a somewhat richer representation than the diagram:

```
(EVOLUTION ((FROM_STRATUM ( Biblical_Hebrew )  )
            (TO_STRATUM  ( Tannaitic_Hebrew )  )
            (PHENOMENA   ( (ROOT     ( dr$ ) )
                           (KEYWORD ( to_look_for  to_ask_for ))
                           (DID     ( shrink ) )
                           (INTO    ( to_propose_as_exegesis )))
                         ( (ROOT    ( n$h ) )
                           (KEYWORD ( to_exact_debts ) )
                           (DID     ( disappear ) )        )
                         ( (ROOT    ( bq$ ) )
                           (KEYWORD ( to_ask_for ) )
                           (DID     ( remain ) )    )
                         ( (ROOT    ( tb& ) )
                           (DID     ( appear  share_spoils ) )
                           (INTO    ( to_demand_peremptorily ))))
)           )
```

C) Evolution from Biblical Hebrew to Tannaic Hebrew of the presence of such lexical roots, that verbs derived from them denoted the sense 'to hide':

$$\sqrt{\text{Tmn}} \ , \ \sqrt{\text{Hb\%}} \ , \ \sqrt{\text{cpn}} \ , \ \sqrt{\text{str}} - \sqrt{\text{Tmr}} \ , \ \sqrt{\text{kmn}}$$
$$= \quad \downarrow \quad\quad \downarrow \quad\quad \downarrow \quad\quad \uparrow \quad\quad \uparrow$$
disappeared disappeared (shrank)   appeared appeared

The following nested subrelation (a subtree of attributes) conveys a somewhat richer representation than the diagram, because also some data appear that identify semantic shifts (such as specialisation into a narrower word-sense):

```
(EVOLUTION ( (FROM_STRATUM ( Biblical_Hebrew )  )
             (TO_STRATUM   ( Tannaitic_Hebrew )  )
             (PHENOMENA
               ( (ROOT     ( Tmn ) )
                 (DID      ( remain ) ) )
               ( (ROOT     ( Hb% ) )
                 (DID      ( disappear ) ) )
               ( (ROOT     ( cpn ) )
                 (DID      ( disappear ) ) )
               ( (ROOT     ( str ) )
                 (KEYWORD  ( to_hide ) )
                 (DID      ( shrink ) )
                 (INTO
                   (to_meet_alone_person_of_opposite_sex)))
               ( (ROOTS    ( Tmr  kmn ) )
                 (DID      ( appear  share_spoils ) ) )
)          ) )
```

D) Evolution from Biblical Hebrew to Tannaic Hebrew of verbs belonging to given lexical roots, and which denote 'to see'. The verb *ra'á* retained its use.

The verb *hibbiṭ* disappeared in the Tannaic A stratum (i.e., the stratum mainly represented by the *Mishnah,* when Hebrew was still a living language spoken as a vernacular), but was revived in the Tannaic B stratum (i.e., in Hebrew the way it appears in the *Talmud,* by which time it was a literary language). In the diagram, we use "dis." as an abbreviation for "disappeared". The verbs *hitbonén* and *ṣafá* shrank very much. The verbs *šur, ḥazá,* and *hišqif* disappeared. The verb *heṣíṣ* expanded a little bit. The verbs *histakkél* and *sakhá,* also for 'to see', made their appearance in Tannaic Hebrew, being absent from Biblical Hebrew.

$$\sqrt{\text{r%h}} \;,\quad /\text{hibbiT}/ \;,\quad /\text{hitbonen}/ \;,\quad \sqrt{\text{cph}} \;,\quad \sqrt{\text{\$wr}} \;,\quad \sqrt{\text{Hzh}} \;,$$

$$= \qquad\quad \downarrow \qquad\qquad \downarrow \qquad\qquad \downarrow \qquad \downarrow \qquad \downarrow$$

dis. in T-A,   (shrank   (shrank   dis.   dis.

revived in T-B.   very much)   very much)

$$/\text{hi\$qip}/ \;,\quad \sqrt{\text{cyc}} \;\; — \;/\text{histakkel}/ \;,\quad \sqrt{\text{skh}}$$

$$\downarrow \qquad\qquad \downarrow \qquad\qquad\quad \uparrow \qquad\qquad \uparrow$$

dis.   (expanded   appeared   appeared

a little)

We show an excerpt from the `EVOLUTION` chunk corresponding to the latter diagram:

```
(EVOLUTION
   ( (FROM_STRATUM   ( Biblical_Hebrew ) )
     (TO_STRATUM     ( Tannaitic_Hebrew ) )
     (PHENOMENA      ( (VERB    ( hitbonen ) )
                       (DID     ( shrink++ ) ) )
 ) )
   ( (FROM_STRATUM   ( Biblical_Hebrew ) )
     (TO_STRATUM     ( Tannaitic_Hebrew_A ) )
     (PHENOMENA      ( (VERB    ( hibbiT ) )
                       (DID     ( disappear ) ) )
 ) )
   ( (FROM_STRATUM   ( Tannaitic_Hebrew_A ) )
     (TO_STRATUM     ( Tannaitic_Hebrew_B ) )
     (PHENOMENA      ( (VERB    ( hibbiT ) )
                       (DID     ( revive ) ) )
 ) ) )
```

But the following:

```
( (THROUGH_STRATA ( Biblical_Hebrew
                    Tannaitic_Hebrew_A
                    Tannaitic_Hebrew_B ) )

  (TRANSITIONS    ( (VERB ( hibbiT ) )
                    (DID  ( disappear --> revive ) ) ) )
) )
```

is a shorter alternative to this portion of code:

```
( (FROM_STRATUM    ( Biblical_Hebrew )  )
  (TO_STRATUM      ( Tannaitic_Hebrew_A )  )
  (PHENOMENA       (  (VERB    ( hibbiT ) )
                      (DID      ( disappear ) )  )  )
) )
( (FROM_STRATUM    ( Tannaitic_Hebrew_A  )  )
  (TO_STRATUM      ( Tannaitic_Hebrew_B )  )
  (PHENOMENA       (  (VERB    ( hibbiT ) )
                      (DID      ( revive ) )  )  )
) )
```

Moreshet remarked that it is difficult to delimit the role of each entry (verb or root) in this example. A list of contexts is appropriate in order to try and convey their historical meaning. A suitable representational choice, at the implementational level, for this example, is indicating just the *trend* (as for diffusion and semantics) inside the EVOLUTION chunk in the nested relations (thus indicating the occurrence of shrinking, appearance, and so forth), possibly by distinguishing, for the verb /hibbiT/, between substrata of Tannaic Hebrew.

One could extend the schema described in order to account also for the influence of similar terms or roots as belonging to *adstrata* (i.e., adjacent strata), especially of languages in contact. That way, some suitable attributes in the lexical frames could provide reference to (some given stratum of) Aramaic, believed to have influenced the appearance of some term in Tannaic Hebrew.

E) This other example is about the evolution, from Biblical Hebrew to Tannaic Hebrew, of verbs expressing the lexical concept 'to fail'. The use of one root shrank, and another root disappeared, whereas a new root made its appearance.

$$\sqrt{k\check{s}l} \quad , \quad \sqrt{nq\check{s}} \quad - \quad \sqrt{tql}$$
$$\downarrow \qquad\qquad \downarrow \qquad\qquad \uparrow$$

(shrank) disappeared   appeared,
took over

Correspondingly, in the frame of $\sqrt{k\check{s}l}$ (coded as \k$l\); or of the verb /nik$al/ (pronounce: *nikhšál*), itself derived from $\sqrt{k\check{s}l}$, and which denotes 'to fail'; or then in the frame of the root $\sqrt{tql}$, one may incorporate this chunk:

```
(EVOLUTION
  ( (FROM_STRATUM    ( Biblical_Hebrew )  )
    (TO_STRATUM      ( Tannaitic_Hebrew )  )
    (PHENOMENA       (  (ROOT  ( k$l ) )
                        (DID   ( shrink ) )  )
                     (  (ROOT  ( nq$ ) )
                        (DID   ( disappear ) )  )
                     (  (ROOT  ( tql ) )
                        (DID   ( appear  take_over ) )  )  )
) ) )
```

F) When it comes to verbs denoting 'to look for', one Biblical Hebrew lexical root disappeared, but two new roots made their appearance in Tannaic Hebrew:

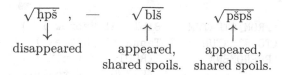

$$\sqrt{\text{ḥpš}} \ , \quad - \qquad \sqrt{\text{blš}} \qquad \sqrt{\text{pšpš}}$$

$$\downarrow \qquad\qquad \uparrow \qquad\qquad \uparrow$$

disappeared   appeared,   appeared,

shared spoils.   shared spoils.

Correspondingly, in the frame of any of the roots $\sqrt{\text{ḥpš}}$, $\sqrt{\text{blš}}$, or $\sqrt{\text{pšpš}}$ (which are respectively coded as `\HpS\`, `\bl$\`, and `\p$p$\`), denoting 'to look for', in the subtree of the acceptation whose `KEYWORD` value is `to_look_for`, one may incorporate this chunk:

```
(EVOLUTION
  ( (FROM_STRATUM   ( Biblical_Hebrew )  )
    (TO_STRATUM     ( Tannaitic_Hebrew )  )
    (PHENOMENA      ( (ROOT    ( HpS ) )
                      (DID     ( disappear ) )  )
                    ( (ROOTS   ( bl$  p$p$ ) )
                      (DID     ( appear  share_spoils ) ) )
) ) )
```

G) Evolution, from Biblical Hebrew to Tannaic Hebrew, of verbs denoting 'to convince' or 'to entice' saw one root disappear, two roots shrink, and one new lexeme of a root make its appearance. For example, the semantics of the root $\sqrt{\text{skh}}$ shrank from 'to entice', to the legal technical term for 'to seduce' (the direct object being a maiden of minor age).

$$\sqrt{\text{nš'}} \ , \quad \sqrt{\text{šwt}} \ , \quad \sqrt{\text{pth}} \quad - \quad \sqrt{\text{šdl}}_1$$

$$\downarrow \qquad\quad \downarrow \qquad\quad \downarrow \qquad\qquad \uparrow$$

disappeared (shrank) (shrank)   appeared,

took over.

Correspondingly, the representation in nested relations is as follows:

```
(EVOLUTION
  ( (FROM_STRATUM   ( Biblical_Hebrew )  )
    (TO_STRATUM     ( Tannaitic_Hebrew )  )
    (PHENOMENA      ( (ROOT    ( n$% ) )
                      (DID     ( disappear ) )  )
                    ( (ROOTS   ( $wt  pth ) )
                      (DID     ( shrink ) )  )
                    ( (ROOT    ( Sdl ) )
                      (KEYWORD ( to_convince ) ) )
                      (DID     ( appear  take_over ) ) )
) ) )
```

More accurately, the following coding could be used, by incorporating it in the frame of any of the roots of the semantic field of 'convincing' or 'instigating':

```
(EVOLUTION  ( (FROM_STRATUM  ( Biblical_Hebrew )  )
              (TO_STRATUM    ( Tannaitic_Hebrew )  )
              (PHENOMENA     (  (ROOT     ( n$% ) )
                                (KEYWORD ( to_lure ) )
                                (DID      ( disappear ) ) )
                             (  (ROOT     ( swt ) )
                                (KEYWORD ( to_instigate ) )
                                (DID      ( shrink ) )
                                (INTO
                                  ( to_instigate_to_heresy ) ) )
                             (  (ROOT     ( pth ) )
                                (KEYWORD ( to_lure ) )
                                (DID      ( shrink ) )
                                (INTO ( to_seduce_a_maiden ) ) )
                             (  (ROOT     ( $dl ) )
                                (DID       ( appear  take_over ) )
                                (KEYWORD ( to_convince ) ) )
)             ) )
```

The indication — for the attribute KEYWORD — of the value to_convince (the broadest meaning in the semantic field) for the root √šdl (coded as Sdl) is necessary, in order to distinguish this lexeme of the root from the lexeme instantiated in the verb /hi$taddel/ (pronounced *hištaddél*), i.e., 'to try', 'to do efforts' (in this lexeme, the Hebrew root √šdl is a semantic equivalent of the Arabic lexical root √jhd).

H) Barak Shemesh, at the time a student of Nissan, in late 1989 wrote a LISP program that accepts as input a PHENOMENA subtree of an EVOLUTION chunk of nested code, and transforms it into a diagram in Ascii. The input is in a file called **sample_input** and is loaded into LISP before the program is loaded. The program can only handle triliteral roots (and not, For example, quadriliteral roots, or some specific verb such as /hitbonen/ rather than its root). Also, synonyms of attribute names were not handled (e.g., the program would take ROOT but not its synonym ROOTS).

Function **get_roots_and_events** takes the input, invokes the function **get_and_print** to find the roots to be shown, and afterwards invokes it to find the events that are connected to each root:

```
(defun  get_roots_and_events  (list)
        (terpri) (terpri)
        ( setq roots ( cdr list ) )
        ( setq counter 1 )
        ( get_and_print roots counter )
```

```
( setq counter 4 )
( setq events roots )
( get_and_print roots counter )  )
```

Function `get_and_print` finds all roots to be shown, and also finds the event which connects to each root. After finding all roots, it invokes the functions `print_roots` and `print_middle_lines` After finding all events, it invokes the function `print_events`

```
(defun get_and_print (object counter)
  (if
    (equal counter 1)
  then ( setq root1 ( cdaar object) )
       ( setq counter 2 )
       (setq object1 (cdr object ) )
       (get_and_print object1 counter )
  elseif
       (equal counter 2 )
  then ( setq root2 ( cdaar object ))
       ( setq counter 3 )
       (setq object2 (cdr object ) )
       (get_and_print object2 counter )
  elseif
       (equal counter 3 )
  then ( setq root3 ( cdaar object ))
          ( print_roots root1 root2 root3)
          ( print_middle_lines)
)
  (if
    (equal counter 4 )
  then ( setq event1 (cdadar object))
       ( setq counter 5 )
       (setq object1 (cdr object ) )
       (get_and_print object1 counter )
  elseif
       (equal counter 5)
  then ( setq event2 (cdadar object))
          ( setq counter 6 )
          (setq object2 (cdr object ) )
          (get_and_print object2 counter )
  elseif
       (equal counter 6)
  then ( setq event3 (cdadar object))
          ( print_events event1 event2 event3)
) )
```

Function `print_roots` prints the given roots in the wanted format:

```
(defun print_roots (root1 root2 root3)
 (patom '|    |)         (patom root1)
 (patom '|   ,   |)      (patom root2)
 (patom '|   ---   |)  (patom  root3)
 (terpri)  )
```

Function `print_middle_lines` handles the arrows in the output diagram:

```
(defun print_middle_lines ()
 (patom '|       !        !            ^        |)
 (terpri)
 (patom '|       !        !            !        |)
 (terpri)
 (patom '|    V        V            !        |)
 (terpri) )
```

The latter function could have been made with more sophistication, in order to handle any number of roots being involved. Besides, function `print_events` prints the given events in the output diagram:

```
(defun print_events (event1 event2 event3)
 (patom '|   |) (patom event1)
 (patom '|   |) (patom event2)
 (patom '|   |) (patom event3)
 (terpri) (terpri) (terpri)      )
```

Clearly, such a visualisation was rudimentary, even for one entirely relying on Ascii graphics. Example D, involving a large number of roots or verbs, could not have been handled. Note however that if this set is conceptualised as the first generation in a tree under one root, then one may resort to techniques for visualising even large hierarchies. One such technique was described by Lamping and Rao [51], but that one is suitable for a large hierarchy with much branching: it visualises a tree inside a circle, based on hyperbolic geometry. This is somewhat similar to graphical fisheye views of graphs [94].

Appendix C: The Code of NAVIGATION

This appendix is based on material completed in March 1990 by Jihad El-Sana, within a project supervised by Nissan. It introduces and explains the PROLOG code units of the NAVIGATE AND RETRIEVE software. For each code unit, we explain the predicate, its parameters, and the task or workings of the code unit. As can be seen, the code does handle the labels of the syntax of CuPROS, but neverthelss the code is customised for the metarepresentation of the frames of the ONOMATURGE expert system for Hebrew word-formation, or then of the multilingual Semitic dictionary project that was a sequel of the ONOMATURGE project. More sophisticated software would have been really general, the way such software that processes XML is when using a metarepresentation of the structure of deeply nested relations.

In `navigate_and_retrieve` the parameters are `Word` (the name of the frame instance that is being searched); `Path` (a path inside the frame); and `Result` (the output information). The main program invokes the predicate `navigate` for it to look for the information using the path.

```
navigate_and_retrieve(Word,Path, Result ) :-
        consult(Word),
        assign_frame(Word,Frame_list ),
        meta('BEGIN',Meta_list),
        navigate(Path,Meta_list,Frame_list,
                 []/Fathers,[]/Keys,Result).
```

In the `meta` predicate, metarepresentation rules are stated. The first parameter is the left-hand part of the rule, the returned output being the value of the second parameter. The latter is called `Meta_list`.

```
meta( 'BEGIN'  ,     [  'IDENTITY'
                     ,'AVAILABLE_FRAMES'
                     ,'ROOTS_WITH_ALTERNANCE'
                     ,'CURSORY_LEVEL'
                     ,'DETAIL_LEVEL'
                     ]
    ).

meta('IDENTITY' , terminal ).
meta('CURSORY_LEVEL' ,  [  'ACCEPTATIONS'  ]  ).
meta('AVAILABLE_FRAMES',[  'n:','kind-of-frame_chunk']).
meta('kind-of-frame_chunk',[ 'i:','OF_KIND','ARE' ] ).
meta('ACCEPTATIONS',[ 'n:','acceptation_chunk'  ] ).


meta('acceptation_chunk',[  'i:' ,'IS'
                                 ,'ETYMOLOGICAL_ANTERIORITY'
                                 ,'ROUGH_DIFFUSION'
                            ]
    ).

meta('DETAIL_LEVEL' ,  [  'ACCEPTATION_CLUSTERS' ] ).


meta('ACCEPTATION_CLUSTERS'
                    ,[  'n:' , 'acceptation-cluster_chunk'
                      ,'n:'     ,'SEMANTIC_CHANGE'
                     ]
    ).
```

```
meta('acceptation-cluster_chunk'
                      ,[  'i:'   ,'IS'    /* identifier*/
                          ,'DERIVATIVES_SPECIALIZATION'
                          ]
).


meta('DERIVATIVES_SPECIALIZATION'
                      ,[  'n:', 'particular-acceptation_chunk'
                          ,'SEMANTIC_CHANGE'
                          ]
).


meta('SEMANTIC_CHANGE'    ,[ 'x:', 'terminal_value',
                             'x:', 'n:','arc_chunk'
                          ]
    ).


meta('particular-acceptation_chunk'
                      ,[  'i:'   ,'PARTICULAR_ACCEPTATION'
                          ,'DERIVATIVES'
                          ]
).

meta('DERIVATIVES'        ,[  'n:'   ,'derivative_chunk' ] ).


meta('derivative_chunk' ,[  'i:'    ,'x:'   ,'IS'
                                     ,'x:'   ,'ARE'
                                     ,'LANGUAGE'
                          ]
).


meta('IS'        ,[  'f:'   ,['acceptation-cluster_chunk'],
                             'terminal_value'
                     ,'f:'   ,['derivative_chunk']
                        ,'x:'   ,'terminal_value'
                        ,'x:'   ,'PHONEMIC'
                           ,'VOCALIZED'
                      ]
).
```

```
meta('terminal_value'
                ,[ 'string'
                 ,'list_of_strings'
                 ,'SAME'
                 ,'logic_expression'
                 ]
).


meta('arc_chunk',[ 'i2:'  ,  'DIRECTION',
                   'i2:'  ,'x:', 'PARTICULAR_ACCEPTATION',
                   'x:', 'ACCEPTATION_CLUSTER',
                   'x:', 'SEMANTIC_CONCEPT',
               'WHY'
               ]
   ).
```

Let us turn to the **navigate** predicate. Its first parameter is **Path**. After the parameters **Meta_list** and **Frame_list**, the next parameter is **Fathers/Next_fathers**, where **Father** is the immediate ancestry in the way down, whereas **Next_fathers** takes into account one more level of ancestry. Similarly, with the parameter **Keys/Next_keys**, by **Keys** we convey the value of the keys we meet on the way down, whereas by **Next_keys** we convey the value of the keys we meet on the way down and up. As for the **Ans** parameter, this is the information list which we are looking for.

If the **meta** head is terminal we finish searching and stop, and put the terminal value in the **Ans** list. If the path head is an attribute value, it's a value of a key so we invoke **key_chunk**. In order to make the path to the key name, **get_key_chunk** is invoked. To get the chunk which contains the key value which exist in the path, invoke **navigate** recursively.

If **SAME** appears in the **meta** head, the info we are looking for is the head of the **Value_key** list. If **SEE** appears in the head of the meta list, then **do_see** is invoked. It returns the answer resulting from the SEE step. If the **meta** list head is the **i:** or **j:** label, then we get the value of its key by invoking the **get_one_after** predicate, then we save the value thus obtained in a list. If the **meta** list head is **i1:** we search for two keys values and save them. We invoke **get_j_key** in order to get the first key. If the **meta** list head is **i2:** we take two keys from the set of of the keys by invoking **good_i2** twice. After such label processing, **navigate** is invoked. If the **meta** head is a label other than **i:** and the like, the predicate **process_label** is invoked in order to get the new **meta** list. Next, **navigate** is invoked recursively. In case the **meta** list is a list rather than an individual variable, we search for the frame in this list. If it exists, we assign its **meta** as being the new **meta**, by invoking **get_tail_of** in order to get the tail of the head in the frame list as the new frame list, and next, **navigate** is invoked. If the path head did not exist in the **meta** list, then it is inferred that there is something missing in the path (which is legitimate, as it is permissible to only list milestones in the path). Therefore, we get the `meta` of the first variable in the frame list, and `navigate` is invoked.

```
navigate([],Meta_list,Frame_list,
        Fathers/Next_fathers,Keys/Next_keys,Frame_list):-
                            move(Fathers,Next_fathers),
                            move(Keys,Next_keys),!.


navigate(Path,Meta_list,Frame_list,
        Fathers/Next_fathers,Keys/Next_keys,Ans):-
      list(Path,Path_head,Path_tail),
      list(Meta_list,Meta_head,Meta_tail),
      list(Frame_list,Frame_head,Frame_tail),
      ( ( ( Meta_head = terminal),
              /* if the item is terminal,
                 the value searched is reached */
            navigate([],Meta_tail,Frame_list,
                  Fathers/Next_fathers,Keys/Next_keys,Ans)
        );
      /* if the path head is an attribute value, then it is
         a key value, so we search for the key name and get
         the path to go there, then we get the chunk that
         has the same key value and continue with the rest
         of the path.
      */

         ( is_attr_value(Path_head),
           key_chunk(Meta_list,Fathers/Next_Fathers,Key_path),
           get_key_chunk(Path,Key_path,Frame_list,
                   Fathers/Next_Fathers,
                   Keys/Next_Keys,New_frame),
           navigate(Path_tail,Meta_list,New_frame,
                   Fathers/Next_fathers,New_keys/Next_keys,Ans)
        );
         ( ( Frame_head = 'SAME' ),
           head(Keys,Value_key),
           move(Value_key,Ans),
           move(Fathers,Next_fathers),
           move(Keys,Next_keys)
        );
         ( ( Frame_head = 'SEE' ),
           do_see(Frame_tail,Ans)
        );
```

```
/* deal with the i labels or j labels */
(   ( if_exist(Meta_head,['i:','j:']),
      head(Meta_tail,Head1),
      get_one_after([Head1],Frame_list,Key_value),
      append(Key_value,New_Keys,N_keys),
      navigate(Path,Meta_tail,Frame_list,
               Fathers/Next_fathers,N_keys/Next_keys,Ans)
    );


    (   ( Meta_head = 'i1:'),
      list(Meta_tail,Head2,Tail2),
      get_j_key(Tail2,KK),

      append([Head2],KK,Keys_name),
      get_one_after(Keys_name,Frame_list,Key_value),
      append(Key_value,Keys,N_keys),
         navigate(Path,Meta_tail,Frame_list,
                  Fathers/Next_fathers,N_keys/Next_keys,Ans)
    );

    (   ( Meta_head = 'i2:' ),
      good_i2(Meta_list,Keys1,Rest1),
      good_i2(Rest1,Keys,keys2,Rest2),
      get_one(Keys1,K1),
      get_one(Keys2,K2),
      append([K1],[K2],KEYS),
      get_one_aftre(KEYS,Frame_list,Key_value),
      navigate(Path,Meta_tail,Frame_list,
               Fathers/Next_fathers,N_keys/Next_keys,Ans)
) );

/* if it is not an i label but some other label,
   then process_label will deal with this. */
(label(Meta_head),
 process_label(Meta_head,Meta_list,Fathers/New_fathers,
                          Keys/New_key,New_meta),
 navigate(Path,New_meta,Frame_list,
         New_fathers/Next_fathers,New_keys/Next_keys,Ans)
);


/* if the meta list is a list rather than just one item,
   we check if the head of the path exists, and use this
   to continue navigating. Otherwise, something appears
   to have been skipped in the path. */
```

```
( is_list(Meta_list),
  ( ( if_exist(Path_head,Meta_list),
      append(Fathers,[Path_head],New_fathers),
      get_tail_of(Path_head,Frame_list,New_frame),
      ((( Path_tail \== [] ),
         meta(Path_head,New_meta)
       );
         true
      ),
      navigate(Path_tail,New_meta,New_frame,
               New_fathers/Next_fathers,
               Keys/Next_keys,Ans)
    );
    ( meta(Meta_head,New_meta),
      append(Fathers,[Meta_head],New_fathers),
      navigate(Path,New_meta,Frame_list,
               New_fathers/Next_fathers,
               Keys/Next_keys,Ans)
    );
      navigate(Path,Meta_tail,Frame_list,
               Fathers/Next_fathers,Keys/Next_keys,Ans)
) ) ).
```

The predicate key_chunk gets the path to the key in a chunk. The returned value is the value of the Path parameter. If the meta list head is an atom, then labels of the i: kind are dealt with as explained above in this appendix. By contrast, if the meta list head is a: or f: then the processaf predicate is invoked, and next, key_chunk is invoked recursively. If the meta head is a list, we invoke key_chunk with just the head of that list. Failing that, we invoke key_chunk with the tail of the Meta_head list. If the meta list head is an atom being an attribute name, we get the meta of this head, and invoke key_chunk with the new meta, and append this head to the path. If none of the above succeeds, we invoke navigate with the tail of the main meta list that appears as parameter.

```
key_chunk([],Fathers/Next_Fathers,Path):-fail,!.
key_chunk(Meta_list,Fathers/Next_Fathers,Path):-
    list(Meta_list,Meta_head,Meta_tail),
    ((
      /* If the head is an atom rather than a list */
      atom(Meta_head),
      (( (
          /* if we found an i label we do as in navigate */
          if_exist(Meta_head,['i:','j:']),
          head(Meta_tail,Head1),
          move([Head1],P),
```

```
                move([P],Path)
            );

        ( ( Meta_head = 'i1:'),
            list(Meta_tail,Head2,Tail2),
            key_chunk(Tail2,Fathers/Next_Fathers,P),
            append([[Head2]],P,Path)
        );

        ( ( Meta_head = 'i2:' ),
            good_i2(Meta_list,Keys1,Rest1),
            good_i2(Rest1,Keys,keys2,Rest2),
            get_one(Keys1,K1),
            get_one(Keys2,K2),
            append([K1],[K2],Keys),
            move([Keys],Path)
    ) );

    /* If we found a: or f: then processaf is invoked */
    (   ( ( Meta_head = 'a:' );
        ( Meta_head = 'f:' )
        ),
        processaf(Meta_list,Fathers/Next_fathers,Res),

        key_chunk(Res,Fathers/Next_Fathers,Path)
)));

    /* If the meta head is a list we should try to get   */
    /* the path to the label via the head; failing that, */
    /* we try via the rest of the list                   */

( is_list(Meta_head),
    ( key_chunk(Meta_head,Fathers/Next_Fathers,Path);
      key_chunk(Meta_tail,Fathers/Next_Fathers,Path)
) );

( atom(Meta_head),
    is_attr_name(Meta_head),
    meta(Meta_head,New_Meta),
    append([Meta_head],Fathers,N_fathers),
    key_chunk(New_Meta,N_fathers/Next_Fathers,P),
    append([Meta_head],P,Path)
);
    key_chunk(Meta_tail,Fathers/Next_Fathers,Path)
).
```

The is_list predicate checks whether the argument is or is not a list. If it is not a list, then failure is returned. A list has a head and a tail (i.e., whatever remains after the head of the list), so we continue until the tail is null.

```
is_list([]):- !.
is_list([H|T]):- is_list(T).
```

The is_attr_name predicate checks whether the variable is an attribute name, by checking that there is no lower-case letter inside it. This is because there is such a convention in the terminological and other databases that historically, RAFFAELLO had to process.

```
is_attr_name(T) :- name(T,L),!, value(L,F).
value([],F):- ( F = 1),!.
value([H|T],F):-
          ( ( H >= 65 ),( H =< 90 ),(F is 1),!,value(T,F)) ;
          ( not( low_case(H)),value(T,F)).
low_case(Char) :- ( Char >= 97 ), ( Char =< 122 ).
```

The is_attr_value predicate checks whether its input is an attribute value. If it is not, then the predicate returns failure. The test carried out checks whether there is any lower-case letter inside the input string.

```
is_attr_value(Var) :- name(Var,L),!, contain_low(L).
contain_low([]):- fail ,!.
contain_low([H|T]):- ( ( H >= 97), ( H =< 122),!);
                     contain_low(T).
```

The good_i2 predicate deals with the case that the i2: key label is found. If there is more than one key, then that many keys have to be handled. The program stops looking for keys once either i_label or the word WHY is found. The input parameter I_list is a list containing the i-labels to be processed. If such a label is immediately followed by an x: label, then the predicate get_x_key is invoked, in order to select the key name from the x: label. If there is no x: right after the i-label, it means that what does follow it is a key name. If instead of i2: what is found instead is j: then the predicate get_j_key is invoked, in order to get the key. If the head is an attribute name, then good_i2 is invoked recursively.

```
good_i2(I_list,K_list,R_list):-
      list(I_list,I_head,I_tail),
      ( ( ( 'i2:' = I_head ),
          list(I_tail,Key,New_tail),
          ( ( ( Key = 'x:' ),
             get_x_key(I_tail,K_list,R_list)
           );
           (   move([Key],K_list),
               move(New_tail,R_list)
           ) ));
```

```
    ( ( I_head = 'j:' ),
      get_j_key(I_list,K_list),
      move([],R_list)
    );
    ( is_attr_name(I_head),
      good_i2(I_tail,K_list,R_list)
  ) ).
```

The `do_see` predicate takes as input the parameter `See_list` being the list containing the word `SEE` in its head. The output parameter is `Result` which is the processed list. The `do_see` predicate makes the path to the `SEE` information then invokes the predicate `do_under` to get this information according to the property and the list following the key word in the variable `Under`.

```
do_see(See_list,Result) :-
        find_by_index(2,See_list,Property),
        find_by_rang(3,See_list,Under_list),
        do_under(Property,Under_list,Result).
```

The `do_under` predicate takes as input the parameters `Property` (that is, the property that appears in the `SEE` list), and `Under_list` (that is, the list following the key word in the variable `Under`). The output parameter is `Result` which contains the information we are looking for. The variable `Under` may contain more than one under-list, so we invoke the predicate `do_one_under` in order to process just one under-list. Next, the `do_under` predicate is invoked recursively, in order to process the tail (i.e., the remnant) of the list of under-lists, once its head (i.e., the first under-list) has been taken away from the list of under-lists. The result from all the under-lists is saved in the final result list.

```
do_under(Property,[],[]) .
do_under(Property,[Under_head|Under_tail],Result) :-
            do_one_under(Property,Under_head,ResHead),
            do_under(Property,Under_tail,ResTail),
            append(ResHead,ResTail,Result).
```

The `do_one_under` predicate takes as input the parameters `Property` (being the variable following the key word property), and `Under_list`, and returns the output parameter `Result`. The `do_one_under` predicate makes the path to the `SEE` information using the `Property` and the `Under_list` it made. The path is generated by invoking the predicate `make_path` after using subservient predicates in order to collect information for path-making. (The predicate `key_chunk` constructs a path to a key.) Then, the `Property` is appended to the path, and the predicate `navigate_and_retrieve` is invoked with the root and the path.

```
do_one_under(Property,Under_List,Result):-
                    find_by_index(1,Under_List,Root_list),

                    find_by_index(3,Root_list,Root),
                    find_by_rang(1,Under_List, Under),
                    make_path(Under,Path),
                    append([Property],Path,NPath),
                    navigate_and_retrieve(Root,NPath,Result).
```

The parameters of the get_j_key predicate are J_list (the list containing all the keys to be selected) and Keys (the keys selected from the list). If we found the label j: we know that the item following it is the key name we have been looking for. If we didn't find the label j: as yet, then we invoke the get_j_key predicate recursively.

```
get_j_key([],[]):- !.
get_j_key(J_list,Keys):-
      list(J_list,J_head,J_tail),
      ( ( (J_head = 'j:' ),
        list(J_tail,Key,New_tail),
        get_j_key(New_tail,K),
        append([Key],K,Keys)
      );
        get_j_key(J_tail,Keys)
      ).
```

The parameters of the get_key_chunk predicate are Path (the path leading to the key name in the chunk intended), key_path (the value of the key we are looking for), Chunks (the list containing all those chunks which contain the key name), and Good_chunk (the chunk containing the key value which is equal to the value key_path). Once the attributes in the path are obtained (from the first three parameters in the parameter list of get_key_chunk), the get_value predicate is invoked, in order to get the value of the key in that chunk. If this value is a sublist of the attribute list, then this is the chunk we are looking for. Otherwise, we invoke get_key_chunk recursively.

```
get_key_chunk(Path,Key_path,Chunks,Good_chunk):-
        get_the_2attr(Path,Attrs),
        list(Chunks,One_Chunk,Res_chunks),
        ( get_value(Path,One_Chunk,Value),
          sub(Attrs,Value),
          move(One_chunk,Good_chunk)
        );
        get_key_chunk(Path,Key_path,Res_Chunks,Good_chunk).
```

The sub predicate verifies whether the first list (the first parameter) is a sublist of the other list (the second parameter).

```
sub([],List):- !.
sub(List1,List2):-
      list(List1,Head,Tail),
      if_exist(Head,List2),
      sub(Tail,List2).
```

The key_chunk predicate constructs the path to the key in the chunk in order to return that path.

```
key_chunk([],Fathers/Next_Fathers,Path):-fail,!.
key_chunk(Meta_list,Fathers/Next_Fathers,Path):-
   list(Meta_list,Meta_head,Meta_tail),
   ( ( atom(Meta_head),
       (( ( if_exist(Meta_head,['i:','j:']),
            head(Meta_tail,Head1), /* we have one key name  */
            move([Head1],P),       /* in order to get the   */
            move([P],Path)         /* key in []             */
         );

         ( ( Meta_head = 'i1:'),
            list(Meta_tail,Head2,Tail2),
            key_chunk(Tail2,Fathers/Next_Fathers,P),
            append([[Head2]],P,Path)
         );

         ( ( Meta_head = 'i2:' ),
            good_i2(Meta_list,Keys1,Rest1),
            good_i2(Rest1,Keys,keys2,Rest2),
            get_one(Keys1,K1),
            get_one(Keys2,K2),
            append([K1],[K2],Keys),
            move([Keys],Path)
       ) );

       (   ( ( Meta_head = 'a:' );
           ( Meta_head = 'f:' )
         ),
         processaf(Meta_list,Fathers/Next_fathers,Res),
         key_chunk(Res,Fathers/Next_Fathers,Path)
     )));

     ( is_list(Meta_head),
       ( key_chunk(Meta_head,Fathers/Next_Fathers,Path);
         key_chunk(Meta_tail,Fathers/Next_Fathers,Path)
     ) );
```

```
( atom(Meta_head),
  is_attr_name(Meta_head),
  meta(Meta_head,New_Meta),
  append([Meta_head],Fathers,N_fathers),
  key_chunk(New_Meta,N_fathers/Next_Fathers,P),
  append([Meta_head],P,Path)
);
  key_chunk(Meta_tail,Fathers/Next_Fathers,Path)
).
```

The get_2attr predicate gets the first two attribute values. The input parameter is List and contains the set of attributes to be chosen from. The output parameter is Attrs which contains the chosen attributes.

```
get_2attr(List,Attrs):-
     list(LIst,Head,Tail),
     list(Tail,Head1,Tail1),
     list(Tail1,Head2,Tail2),
     append([Head],[Head1],L1),
     append(L1,[Head2],LIST1),
     ch_attr(LIST1,Attrs).
ch_attr([],[]).
ch_attr([H|Tail],R):-
     ( is_attr_value(H),
       ch_attr(Tail,R1),
       append([H],R1,R)
     );
       ch_attr(Tail,R).
```

The get_one predicate gets one item R from a list [R|Tail].

```
get_one([R|Tail],R).
get_one([R|Tail],Result):-
            get_one(Tail,Result).
```

The get_one_after predicate is used in order to get a key value after its name. The get_one_after predicate takes as input the parameters Key_names (the names of the chunk-identifying keys), and Frame (the list from which we select the item), and returns the selected item, this being the value of the output parameter Values.

```
get_one_after([],Frame,[]):- !.
get_one_after(Key_names,Frame,Values):-
   list(Key_names,Key_name,Keys_names),
   get_tail_of(Key_name,Frame,Tail),
   list(Tail,Value,New_tail),
   get_one_after(Keys_names,Frame,N_values),
   append(Value,N_values,Values).
```

The `get_tail_of` predicate take a list (this is the parameter called `Variable`) and a frame list which contains the list which is the value of `Variable`, and returns (in the output parameter `Result`) the tail of `Variable`. If the list head is an atom, then if it is equal to `Variable`, then the result is the tail of the list. If the head is a list instead, then we invoke the procedure `get_tail_of` recursively, passing to it as input the head of that list. If this fails, we look for `Variable` in the tail of the main list by invoking the procedure `get_tail_of` recursively.

```
get_tail_of(Variable,[],Result):- fail,!.

get_tail_of(Variable,
        [[ Attr_head | Attr_head_tail] | Attr_Tail],Result):-
    (  atom(Attr_head),
        (    (Variable = Attr_head ),
            put_off(Attr_head_tail,Attrheadtail),
            move(Attrheadtail ,Result)
        );
        get_tail_of(Variable,Attr_head_tail,Result);
        get_tail_of(Variable,Attr_Tail,Result)
    );
    get_tail_of(Variable,Attr_head,Result)  ;
    get_tail_of(Variable,Attr_head_tail,Result);
    get_tail_of(Variable,Attr_Tail,Result).

get_tail_of(Variable,[ Attr_head | Attr_Tail],Result) :-
    (atom(Attr_head),
        (   (Variable = Attr_head ),
            debracket(Attr_Tail,Attrtail),
            move(Attrtail ,Result)
        );
        get_tail_of(Variable,Attr_Tail,Result)
    );
    get_tail_of(Variable,Attr_head,Result);
    get_tail_of(Variable,Attr_Tail,Result).
```

The `get_x_key` predicate handles the appearance of the `x:` label. The input parameter is `X_list` (a list containing the `x:` label). The output parameters are `K_list` (a list containing the keys found in the above), and `R_list`, this being the final tail after allocating all the keys. If `x:` is found in the `X_list`, we expect the item following the label to be a key name, so we get the rest of the keys by invoking the procedure `get_x_key` recursively. All the key names are collected in `K_list` by appending them inside it. If the head of the `X_list` is not `x:` we move the list to the `R_list`, and the `K_list` is nil.

```
get_x_key([],[],[]).
get_x_key(X_list,K_list,R_list):-
    list(X_list,Head,Tail),
    ( ( Head = 'x:' ),
      list(Tail,Key_name,New_tail),
      get_x_key(New_tail,K_list,R_list),
      append([Key_name],K_list,K_list)
    );
    ( move(X_list,R_list),
      move([],K_list)
    ).
```

The `do_xy` predicate handles the co-occurrence of the x: and y: labels. The `do_xy` predicate takes as input the parameters `Xlist` (a list containing the x: label), and `Ylist` (a list containing the y: label). `Res` is the resulting list, and is the output parameter. The `do_xy` predicate divides the `Xlist` into lists containing the items which follow every x: and then a permutation of x: and y: is sought.

```
do_xy(Xlist,Ylist,Res):-
                divid('x:',Xlist,Dx),
                divid('y:',Ylist,Dy),
                permut(Dx,Dy,Res).
```

The `process_label` predicate deals with the occurrence of labels such as a: or f: or i: or x: or y: and so forth, by invoking a special predicate devised for every such case. The parameters of the `process_label` predicate include L (a variable whose value is the label), `Meta_list` (this being the metarepresentation list), `Fathers/New_fathers`, `Keys/New_keys`, and the processed list given as the result, `Res`. If the label is a: or f:, then the `processaf` predicate is invoked. If the label is n: or c:, then we get the `meta` of the item which follows the label, and next move the new `meta` into the `Res` parameter, and the keys into `New_keys`. If the label is x: or y:, then the `processxy` predicate is invoked, a sublist is in the result, and moreover fathers are moved into the new fathers, and the keys are moved into the new keys.

```
process_label(L,Meta_list,Fathers/New_fathers,Keys/New_keys,Res):-
        (    ( ( L = 'a:' );( L = 'f:' )),
             processaf(Meta_list,Fathers,Res),
             move(Fathers,New_fathers)
        );

        (    ( ( L = 'n:' );
               ( L = 'c:' );
               ( L = 'g:')
             ),
             find_by_index(2,Meta_list,Item),
             append([Item],Fathers,New_fathers),
```

```
            meta(Item,New_Meta),
            move(New_Meta,Res),
            move(Keys,New_keys)
    );

    (   ( ( L = 'x:');
          ( L = 'y:')
        ),
        head(Path,Path_head),
        processxy(Meta_list,R),
        get_one(R,Res),
        move(Fathers,New_fathers),
        move(Keys,New_keys)
    ).
```

The processxy predicate processes the labels x: and y: by subdividing the input list List into two lists, one for x: and the other one for y:, and then every such list is subdivided into lists that only contain one label. The result R is the output parameter. The predicate do_xy is invoked so that x: and y: would each be dealt with.

```
processxy(List,R):-
        separate('x:','y:',List,Xlist,Ylist),
        do_xy(Xlist,Ylist,R).
```

The processaf predicate processes the labels a: and f: by dividing the input list List (being the metarepresentation list) into two lists, one for the a: label, and the other one for the f: label. The first such list is placed in Fathers, whereas the other list is placed in Grands. Then every such list is subdivided into lists that only contain one label. The parameter Fathers contains the fathers we meet on our way down. By invoking the predicates do_a and do_f the two labels are handled separately. The list found is returned as a result in the variable Res (the output parameter).

```
processaf(List,Fathers,Res):-
        super_separate('a:','f:',List,Alist,Flist),
        list(Fathers,Father,Grands),
        head(Grands,Grand),
        ( do_a(Alist,Father,Grand,Res);
          do_f(Flist,Father,Res)
        ).
```

The get_value predicate gets the tail of the last attribute in the path, that is to say, the predicate gets whatever, in the path, follows the attribute. This predicate is suitable for obtaining a value. The parameters are Path (the path of the attribute for whose value we are looking), Frame_list (the actual frame instance which contains the attribute), and Value (the list of the values we get).

If the head of the list `Path` is itself a list, then we get the value of the key in the list if it exists, by invoking the procedure `get_one_after` and then invoking `get_value` recursively, in order to get the value of the tail, and then we append inside `Value` the values found.

```
get_value([],Frame_list,[]):- !.
get_value(Path,Frame_list,Value):-
          list(Path,Path_head,Path_tail),
          ( ( is_list(Path_head),
              get_one_after(Path_head,Frame_list,V),
              get_value(Path_tail,Frame_list,V2),
              append(V,V2,Value)
            );
            (  get_tail_of(Path_head,Frame_list,New_frame),
               get_value(Path_tail,New_frame,Value)
          ) ).
```

The `do_f` predicate divides the input list `Flist` into a list of `f:` lists, every one containing a `f:` label; that is, `Flist` is divided into a list of lists stating the fathers nested in the list containing the attributes. Then the predicate looks for the attribute of the list which contains the father. The father for whose list we are looking is in the variable `Father`. The list of the father is returned in the output parameter `Res`.

```
do_f(File,Flist,Father,Res):-
          divid('f:',Flist,Dlist),
          find(Dlist,[Father],Res).
```

The `do_a` predicate divides the input list `Alist` into lists containing the items following every occurrence of the `a:` label. Then the predicate finds out whether the father `Father` and the grandfather `Grand` exist in the divided list. The output is in the parameter `Res` and is the list of the father which has been obtained.

```
do_a(File,Alist,Father,Grand,Res):-
          divid('a:',Alist,Dlist),
          find(Dlist,[Father,Grand],Res).
```

The following predicate checks whether a string is a label. It concludes that it is a label, if the last character in the string is a colon.

```
label(Label):-
          atom(Label),
          name(Label,Lablist),
          last(Lablist,Last),
          (Last = 58 ).
```

The following predicate finds the last item of a list.

```
last([A],A):- !.
last([H|T],L) :- last(T,L).
```

The following predicate returns success if its argument, LABEL, contains any of the labels i: or j: or i1: or i2: or j2:

```
i_label(LABEL):-
     ( ( LABEL = 'i:' );
       ( LABEL = 'i1:' );
       ( LABEL = 'i2:' );
       ( LABEL = 'j:' );
       ( LABEL = 'j1:' );
       ( LABEL = 'j2:' )
     ),!.
```

The following predicate gets the head (i.e., the first element) of the argument list, and discards the rest of the list (i.e., the tail of the list).

```
head([Head|Tail],Head):- !.
```

The following predicate instead returns the first atomic element in its input. That is to say, if the head of the list being the input is itself a list, the predicate gets its head, and if it, too, is a list, then it gets its head, and so on, recursively.

```
main_head([HEAD|TAIL],HEAD,TAIL) :- atom(HEAD),!.
main_head([Head_List | Tail_List],HEAD,TAIL) :-
                         main_head(head_List,HEAD,TAIL).
```

The following predicate takes a list as input, and returns its head and its tail.

```
list([Head|Tail],Head,Tail):- !.
```

The following predicate checks whether the value of the input parameter, Item, exists inside a list or its nested sublists, recursively. If it does exist, then the predicate succeeds, otherwise the predicate fails.

```
if_exist(Item,[]):- fail,!.
if_exist(Item,[Head|Tail]) :-
          ( atom(Head), Item = Head,! );
          ( is_list(Head), if_exist(Item,Head));
          if_exist(Item,Tail).
```

The following predicate takes a list as input, and only returns its tail, by discarding the head of the input.

```
tail([Head|Tail],Tail):- !.
```

The following predicate appends a list L2 at the end of a list L1. Recursively, when L1 becomes nil, the tail L3 is assigned to L1 and is treated as L1 in the next step of the recursion.

```
append([],L,L):- !.
append([H|L1],L2,[H|L3]) :-
        append(L1,L2,L3).
```

In the copy predicate, the first parameter is a list. The second parameter is Until, which is where the predicate must stop when copying the input list and placing the sublist Until in the third parameter, which is returned as the result when the recursion stops.

```
copy([],Until,[],[]):- !.
copy([Head|Tail],Til,[],[Head|Tail]):- if_exist(Head,Until).
copy([Head|Tail],Until,Res,T):-
    copy(Tail,Until,L,T),
    append([Head],L,Res).
```

The divide predicate transforms the list of labels found at the same level, into a list of such sublists that they each begin by a label. For example, if the input is

[a:,hghh,hghghdghg,a:,ghghghghd,a:,dhghgdhdg]

then the output will be:

[[a:,hghh,hghghdghg],[a:,ghghghghd],[a:,dhghgdhdg]]

The code is as follows:

```
divide(Index,[],[]):- !.
divide(Index,List,Dlist):-
  copy(List,Index,One,R),
  length(One,L),
  ( L \== 0 ),
  divide(Index,R,DL),
  append([One],DL,Dlist).
```

The separate predicate subdivides an input list into two lists. The first resulting list contains all the label L1, whereas the second resulting list contains all the label L2 and whatever follows.

```
separate(L1,L2,[],[],[]):- ! .
separate(L1,L2,[L2|Tail],[],[L2|Tail]):- ! .
separate(L1,L2,[Head|Tail],Xlist,Ylist) :-
        separate(L1,L2,Tail,X,Ylist),
        append([Head],X,Xlist).
```

Also the super_separate predicate subdivides an input list into two lists. The first resulting list contains all the labels L1, whereas the second resulting list contains all the labels L2 and whatever follows.

```
super_separate(L1,L2,[],[],[]):- !.
super_separate(L1,L2,[L1|Tail],Alist,Blist):-
            copy(Tail,[L2,L1],Befor,After),
            super_seprate(L1,L2,After,Alist1,Blist),
            append([L1],Befor,A),
            append(A,Alist1,Alist).
super_separate(L1,L2,[L2|Tail],Alist,Blist):-
            copy(Tail,[L2,L1],Befor,After),
            super_seprate(L1,L2,After,Alist,Blist1),
            append([L2],Befor,B),
            append(B,Blist1,Blist).
```

The move predicate scans two lists of the same length. Its code is as follows:

```
move([],[] ) :- !.
move( [H | A] , [H | B] ) :- move(A,B) .
```

The equal predicate succeeds if the two input lists are equal; else it fail.
If the heads are atoms, they must be equal for the predicate to succeed. If the
heads are lists, then the predicate is invoked recursively. The tails of the list are
checked by invoking the equal predicate recursively.

```
equal([],[]):- !.
equal([H | T] , [H2 | T2] ) :-
      (atom(H), H = H2 ,equal(T , T2 ));
      (not(atom(H)), equal(H,H2), equal(T,T2)).
```

The find and exist predicates subserve the need to handle lists beginning by
the label a: or by the label f:, by checking whether inside those lists, a nested
list exists, and then the attributes found there are returned.

```
find([],Looked,Res):- fail,!.
find([Head|Tail],Looked,Res) :-
                exist(Looked,Head,Res);
                find(Tail,Looked,Res).


exist(L,[H|T],T):-
                ( atom(L),
                  if_exist(L,H)
                );
                sublist(L,H).
```

The find_index predicate finds the place of an item in the input list

```
find_index(Item,[Item | Tail ],I):- ( I is 1 ).
find_index(Item,[Head | Tail ],I):-
                find_index(Item,Tail,J),
                ( I is J + 1).
```

The `find_by_index` predicate gets the I-th item in the input list, and returns that item in the output parameter `Res`. Every time we check the head, we subtract 1 from I until I is 1 (cf. `find_by_rank`).

```
find_by_index(I,[Head | List],Head):- ( I =  1 ).
find_by_index(I,[Head | List],Res):-
                ( J is I-1 ),
                find_by_index(J,List,Res).
```

The `find_by_rank` predicate returns the entire sublist beginning immediately after the item I (the idea being the same as in `find_by_index`).

```
find_by_rank(I,[Head | Res],Res) :- ( I = 1 ).
find_by_rank(I,[Head | Tail ],Res) :-
        ( J is I-1 ),
        find_by_rank(J,Tail,Res).
```

The `debracket` predicate removes the outer brackets [ ] from the input list. This predicate is only successful if what remains is also a list.

```
debracket([T],T):- is_list(T).
debracket(T,T):- !.
```

The `simple_list` predicate returns success if the input list is not nested. If anything in the list is not an atom, the predicate fails.

```
simple_list([]):- !.
simple_list([ Head | Tail]) :-
        ( ( not(atom(Head)),fail);
          atom(Head)
        ),
        simple_list(Tail).
```

To load all files containing the code, the go predicate used to be run:

```
go :- g([head,do_lab,do_one_under,do_see,
        do_under,find,get_2att,get_j_key,
        get_one,get_one_after,get_one,good_i2,
        get_x_key,navigate_and_retrieve,navigate,
        debracket,sub,list,i_label,is_attr_name,
        is_attr_value,is_list,key_chunk,label,
        main_head,simple_list,tail,append,move,
        get_value,get_tail_of,copy,divide,
        get_key_chunk,equal,meta,process_label,
        separate,exist,find_by_index,superseparate]).
g([]).
g([H|T]):- reconsult(H),g(T).
```

Appendix D: The Metarepresentation of the Lexical Frames in ONOMATURGE

This appendix shows extensive excerpts from the metarepresentation of lexical frames in the ONOMATURGE expert system. The metarepresentation of frames of formation-rules is very similar. Semicolons precede comments, as per the syntax of LISP.

```
(setq  facet_children_schema

      '(
         (pointer_atom        ( POINTER ) )

         (atom                ( INFLECTION
                                MORPHO_CAT
                                ETYMOLOGY
                                LEXEMES
                                ACCEPTATIONS
                                TOP_RELATED_TO
                                ORTHOGRAPHY
                                ETHICAL_FILTER
                                NORMATIVITY
                                INVENTED_ON    ) )

         (NORMATIVITY         ( x: normativity_info
                                x: ARE  ) )
```

The attribute TOP_RELATED_TO is used for example for stating homographs. As for the attribute ARE, consider that for those top-level facets that may have several inner facets, we have to give the top-filler as being a single list, because of the syntax of Franz LISP. This is the reason why Nissan defined the dummy level whose attribute is ARE, as nested inside ACCEPTATIONS, LEXEMES, TOP_RELATED_TO, NORMATIVITY, ETYMOLOGY (the latter attribute was not actually coded, let alone used in ONOMATURGE), and ORTHOGRAPHY. This is also the reason why Nissan defined FORMS_ARE as nested inside INFLECTION. For the same reason, Nissan introduced (in principle) such dummy nonterminals as normativity_info, orthographic_info, etymological_info, and so forth.

```
         (normativity_info    ( NORMATIVITY_DEGREE
                                SEE_LEXEME
                                SEE_ACCEPTATION ) )

         (ORTHOGRAPHY         ( x: orthographic_info
                                x: ARE  ) )
```

```
(orthographic_info
                        ( VOCALIZED
                          PLENE_NON_VOCALIZED
                          DEFECTIVE_NON_VOCALIZED   ) )


(extended_orthographic_info      ; under INFLECTION.
                        ( VOCALIZED
                          PLENE_NON_VOCALIZED
                          DEFECTIVE_NON_VOCALIZED   ) )


(INFLECTION             ( x: terminal_list
                          x: FORMS_ARE
                          y: SEE_LEXEME
                             SEE_ACCEPTATION ) )


(FORMS_ARE              ( SINGULAR_CONSTRUCTED
                          PLURAL_ABSOLUTE
                          PLURAL_CONSTRUCTED
                          SINGULAR_POSSESSIVE_MINE
                          SINGULAR_FEMININE
                          SINGULAR_CONSTRUCTED_FEMININE
                          PLURAL_CONSTRUCTED_FEMININE
                          SEE_LEXEME
                          SEE_ACCEPTATION ) )
```

The following is a shorthand: a multi-LHS, which states at once the left-hand side of the rule for several attributes, which all have the same right-hand side.

```
(  ( SINGULAR_CONSTRUCTED
     PLURAL_ABSOLUTE
     PLURAL_CONSTRUCTED
     SINGULAR_POSSESSIVE_MINE
     SINGULAR_FEMININE
     SINGULAR_CONSTRUCTED_FEMININE
  )
```

The corresponding right-hand side is as follows:

```
                    ( x: ARE
                      x: PHONEMIC
                         VOCALIZED
                         PLENE_NON_VOCALIZED
                         DEFECTIVE_NON_VOCALIZED
                      y: SEE_LEXEME
                         SEE_ACCEPTATION ) )
```

where the second x: chunk is the unparenthesised childset of the attribute `extended_orthographic_info`, and where the y: chunk states the possibility that pointers to the attribute `INFLECTION` be found inside acceptations or lexemes.

```
(MORPHO_CAT          ( x: terminal_list_of_lists
                       x: ARE
                       y: SEE_LEXEME
                          SEE_ACCEPTATION ) )


(ETYMOLOGY           ( x: etymological_info
                       x: ARE
                       x: SEE_LEXEME ) )


(etymological_info   ( ROOT
                       PATTERN_APPLIED
                       WORD_OF_ORIGIN
                       SUFFIX_APPLIED
                       SEM_PRE_ROOTS
                       DERIVED_ROOTS
                       DERIVED_WORDS
                       DERIVED_PATTERNS
                       COMPOSED_OF
                       CONJECTURES
                       SEE_LEXEME
                       SEE_ACCEPTATION ) )
```

The attribute `COMPOSED_OF` is for compounds. In contrast, the attribute `DERIVED_PATTERNS` concerns emulative coinage (metanalysis), something that Nissan discussed in Sec. 3.6 in his Ph.D. thesis [75]. The attribute `SEM_PRE_ROOTS` ("semantics-preserving roots": a concept explained in Sec. 3.3.3.21 of Nissan's Ph.D. thesis [75]) is for either the root being the etymon, or secondary roots derived from the entry itself and keeping its semantics, or "basic elements" squeezed out of the entry itself. Such roots that have many lexemes, or at any rate are very polysemous, as such derivatives that are semantically disparate were formed out of them, should have a very low semantics-preservation numeric degree associated, and this holds true even though the root considered is neither an actual etymon, nor a derived root.

The attribute `DERIVED_ROOTS` is for derived roots. A derived root (called *néṭaʿ* by the linguist Uzzi Ornan [86], or "basic element") is a kind of lexical root, which is derived from a term which is itself the derivative of some historical root. For example, the Hebrew term for 'donation' or 'contribution' is /truma/, historically from the root $\sqrt{r(w)m}$ of the verb /herim/ 'to raise', the adjective /ram/ 'high', and the like. In Tannaic Hebrew, from /truma/ the secondary root $\sqrt{trm}$ was introduced. Therefore, in the frame instance of /truma/, under the attribute ETYMOLOGY one would have to list r(w)m under ROOT, and trm under both DERIVED_ROOTS and SEM_PRE_ROOTS.

In slangish Israeli Hebrew, the verb *hizdangef* was derived from the name of the central Dizengoff Square in Tel-Aviv, and means 'to idle in Dizengoff Square'. The derived root is $\sqrt{zngf}$ (actually the last radical is a foreign phoneme, even though it could be treated here as though it was the native Hebrew phoneme /p/). This is because the /d/ is interpreted as an infix of the verbal conjugation which forms reflexive verbs. Therefore, /d/ is excluded from the derived root.

```
(ROOT                    ( terminal
                           n: root_doubleton ) )


(root_doubleton          ( i: IS
                           PLAUSIBILITY ) )

(COMPOSED_OF             ( n: lexical_doubleton ) )

(WORD_OF_ORIGIN          ( n: lexical_doubleton ) )


(lexical_doubleton       ( TERM_IS
                           KEYWORD_IS ) )

(ACCEPTATIONS            ( ARE ) )

(LEXEMES                 ( ARE ) )


(ARE                     ( f: ( SYNONYMS  PARASYNONYMS )
                             n: syno_chunk
                           f: ( ACCEPTATIONS )
                             n: single_acceptation
                           f: ( LEXEMES )
                             n: single_lexeme
                           f: ( MORPHO_CAT )
                             n: HISTORY
                             n: WEIGHTED


                           f: ( TOP_RELATED_TO )
                             ASSOCIATION_OF_IDEAS
                             HOMOGRAPHS
                             PARA_HOMOGRAPHS


                           f: ( NORMATIVITY )
                             NORMATIVITY_DEGREE
                             SEE_LEXEME
                             SEE_ACCEPTATION
```

```
f: ( ORTHOGRAPHY )
     VOCALIZED
     PLENE_NON_VOCALIZED
     DEFECTIVE_NON_VOCALIZED
     SEE_LEXEME
     SEE_ACCEPTATION


f: ( SINGULAR_CONSTRUCTED
     PLURAL_ABSOLUTE
     PLURAL_CONSTRUCTED
     SINGULAR_POSSESSIVE_MINE
     SINGULAR_POSSESSIVE_MINE
     SINGULAR_FEMININE
     SINGULAR_CONSTRUCTED_FEMININE
   )
; for each inflection variant:
     n: extended_orthographic_info


f: ( ETYMOLOGY )
     ROOT
     PATTERN_APPLIED
     WORD_OF_ORIGIN
     SUFFIX_APPLIED
     SEM_PRE_ROOTS
     DERIVED_ROOTS
     DERIVED_WORDS
     DERIVED_PATTERNS
     COMPOSED_OF
     CONJECTURES
     SEE_LEXEME
     SEE_ACCEPTATION
)                     )
```

The latest f: chunk is the childset of etymological_info.

```
(WEIGHTED              ( i: MORPHO_CAT_IS
                         RELEVANCE_IS ) )
```

Whereas the attribute HISTORY may be found under the attribute for the morphological category, MORPHO_CAT, by contrast the attribute ACPT_STRATUM (for the historical stratum of a semantic acceptation) may be found inside an acceptation. Owing to CONTEXT, the same MORPHO_CAT_IS may refer to several contexts, with different relevance degrees.

```
(HISTORY
                        ( x:   i1:  MORPHO_CAT_IS
                                    RELEVANCE_IS
                               j:   STRATUM

                  2x:   i:   MORPHO_CAT_IS
                        n:   CONTEXT

                  3x:   i:   MORPHO_CAT_IS
                             DEFINE_RELATION
                       rel:  MORPHO_CAT_IS
                       rel:  CONTEXT

                   x:   i:   MORPHO_CAT_IS
                             RELEVANCE_IS
                             ORDINAL

                   x:   i:   MORPHO_CAT_IS
                             RELEVANCE_IS
                             CAME_AFTER
                        y:   SEE_ACCEPTATION
                             SEE_LEXEME
      )                     )
```

The value of the attribute CAME_AFTER is the value of another MORPHO_CAT_IS, or some pointer to an atom or to a vertex in the tree of properties in the frame.

```
(CAME_AFTER           ( n: MORPHO_CAT_IS
                        n: POINTER        ) )


(CONTEXT      ( a: ( (HISTORY 2x ARE MORPHO_CAT) )
                    n:  stratum_information
       )            )
```

Concerning CONTEXT, note that as Nissan was unsure whether the attribute named HISTORY would remain the only one so named, in the metarepresentation schema he gave the proper ancestry of the attribute CONTEXT. Moreover, ARE is ambiguous; therefore, its father is stated, too.

```
(stratum_information      ( i: STRATUM
                            RELEVANCE_IS ) )
```

The STRATUM chunk provides "stratum_information" that is found under CONTEXT as nested inside HISTORY, in the subtree of the MORPHO_CAT attribute. Another STRATUM facet (with a terminal, or a terminal-list), may be found directly under HISTORY. Besides, ACPT_STRATUM may be found inside an acceptation.

```
(STRATUM            ( terminal_list ) )

(ACPT_STRATUM       ( terminal_list ) )

(DEFINE_RELATION    ( a: ( (HISTORY 3x ARE MORPHO_CAT) )
)                        n: relation
                    )

(single_lexeme      ( i: LEXEME_KEYWORD
                         INFLECTION
                         MORPHO_CAT
                         ETYMOLOGY
                         RELATED_TO
                         ACCEPTATIONS ) )

(single_acceptation ( c: MEANING
                         CONNOTATIONS
                         RELATED_TO
                         AURO
                         AURC ) )

(CONNOTATIONS       ( POS/NEG
                         QUALITIES_OF_CONCEPT
                         QUALITIES_OF_TERM/ACPT ) )
```

An example at the object-level representation could be as follows:

```
(QUALITIES_OF_CONCEPT  ( huge
                          strong
                          slow
                          unaesthetic
                          (HAS memory)
                          (PRODUCES ivory)
    )                   )
```

as a simplified way to state qualities of elephant. Frame-instances found may include a more complex format of this attribute, including information on typicality and necessity. Now, let us revert back to the metarepresentation.

```
(LIKELY_CONTEXT     ( n: CONCEPT_IS ) )

(CONCEPT_IS         ( ATOM_IS
                         KEYWORD_IS ) )
```

```
(CONTRARY              ( ABSOLUTE
                         RELATIVE ) )

(RELATIVE    ( n: contextual_contrary_doubleton ) )

(contextual_contrary_doubleton       ( i: IS
                                         CONTEXT ) )


(RULES                 ( POLYTEMPLATES
                         SUFFIXES
                         PREFIXES
                         IDIOMS
                         COMPOUNDS
                         ROOT_PATTERNS
                         REDUPLICATIVE_PATTERNS ) )
```

Root patterns are clusters of related roots, either alloroots, or a primary root with some related reduplicative root. This is rather frequent in Semitic languages.

```
(POLYTEMPLATES        ( n: rule_doubleton ) )

(SUFFIXES             ( n: rule_doubleton ) )

(PREFIXES             ( n: rule_doubleton ) )

(IDIOMS               ( n: rule_doubleton ) )

(COMPOUNDS            ( n: rule_doubleton ) )

(rule_doubleton       ( i2: IS
                        RO
                        j: INFLECTION_PARADIGM
                        j: MORPHO_CAT_IS         ) )


(INFLECTION_PARADIGM  ( FORM_IDENTIFICATION
                        INFLECTED_FORM_IS        ) )


(PECULIAR_FACETS      ( g: PECULIAR_SLOTS
                        etc    ;   the slots listed
                               ;   in  PECULIAR_SLOTS .
                        TOOLS
                        NEXUS  ;   Event/state description
 )                      )      ;   a' la NEXUS .
```

```
(NEXUS              ( SC       ;  subclass.
                     SUBSEQ    ;  subsequence.
                     COORD     ;  coordinated action.
                     ANTE      ;  antecedent.
                     PREC      ;  precedent.
                     CONSEQ    ;  consequent.
                     SEQ       ;  sequence.
)                  )
```

NEXUS, described by Alterman in 1985 [4] (Alterman had just earned a Ph.D. at the University of Texas in Austin, then moved to Berkeley), is a text-understanding system that uses a dictionary of event/state concepts whose relation is described in a network with various links.

```
(SYNONYMS           ( ARE ) )

(PARASYNONYMS       ( ARE ) )


(syno_chunk         ( i: IS
                    ORTHOGRAPHY
                    KEYWORD_IS
                    DIFFERENCES
                    RELATIONSHIP
                    REL_FREQ_VS_FRAME_OWNER ) )
```

ORTHOGRAPHY as nested in syno_chunk is optional: it is useful in case you state a rare synonym, or a mere variant, which does not deserve a frame-instance on its own, but has such an idiosyncratic spelling that it could not be reconstructed by a "phonemic antitransform".

KEYWORD_IS as nested in syno_chunk is also optional; it is necessary however when near-synonyms are listed, if keywords are not the same.

The attribute RELATIONSHIP may occur as a grand-grandchild of the attribute PARASYNONYMS, and then it indicates such a relationship that it involves concepts (as opposed to terms): for example, values could be

$$((metonymy: kind\_contains))$$

or

$$((metonymy: kind\_contained))$$

On the other hand, RELATIONSHIP may appear as a grand-grandchild of SYNONYMS, too, even in order to provide some unsophisticated indications about the term itself in a cross-linguistic framework:

$$((standard))$$

or

```
                    ( ( cross-language: Phoenician ) )
or

        ( ( cross-language_reconstruction: Phoenician ) )
```

The metarepresentation rule for RELATION is as follows:

```
    (RELATIONSHIP           ( terminal_list ) )
```

According to the following metarepresentation rule, under the attribute COMPONENTIAL_ATTRIBUTES a local metarepresentation is given inside the frame-instance, with instance-specific facets.

```
    (DIFFERENCES           ( g: COMPONENTIAL_ATTRIBUTES
                           ; a local metarepresentation.
                           etc
    )                      )


    (COMPONENTIAL_ATTRIBUTES
              ( terminal
                n: componential_attribute_doubleton ))


    (componential_attribute_doubleton  ( i: IS
                                         VALUESET
                                         VALUE_TYPE
                                         VALUE_ACTION ) )

    (VALUE_ACTION          ( n: value_action_doubleton ) )


    (value_action_doubleton    ( i: IF
                                 THEN  ) )


    (THEN                  ( terminal
                             CONSULT_ATTRIBUTE ) )

    (HOMOGRAPHS            ( n: homograph ) )


    (homograph            ( IN_WHAT_WRITING
                            i: STRING_IS
                            INFLECTED_FORM_IS
                            HOMOGRAPHY_IS_WITH ) )
```

```
(para_homograph        ( IN_WHAT_WRITING
                         i: STRING_IS
                         INFLECTED_FORM_IS
                         HOMOGRAPHY_IS_WITH ) )
```

The use of HOMOGRAPHY_IS_WITH is in order to deal with situations where there are roots similar to some other roots, because of either etymology, or coincidence (and then, there is potential for puns).

```
(INFLECTED_FORM_IS    ( f: ( homograph )
                        IS
                        MORPHOLOGICAL_ANALYSIS
                      f: ( INFLECTION_PARADIGM )
                        terminal
 )                    )

  (HOMOGRAPHY_IS_WITH ( IS
                        MORPHOLOGICAL_ANALYSIS
                        ATOM_OF_NON_INFLECTED_IS ) )

 )
]
```

According to the syntax of LISP, the] character closes all parentheses still open.

Arabic Character Recognition

Nachum Dershowitz and Andrey Rosenberg*

School of Computer Science, Tel Aviv University, Ramat Aviv, Israel

Abstract. Although optical character recognition of printed texts has been a focus of research for the last few decades, Arabic printed text, being cursive, still poses a challenge. The challenge is twofold: segmenting words into letters and identifying individual letters. We describe a method that combines the two tasks, using multiple grids of SIFT descriptors as features. To construct a classifier, we do not use a large training set of images with corresponding ground truth, a process usually done to construct a classifier, but, rather, an image containing all possible symbols is created and a classifier is constructed by extracting the features of each symbol. To recognize the text inside an image, the image is split into "pieces of Arabic words", and each piece is scanned with increasing window sizes. Segmentation points are set where the classifier achieves maximal confidence. Using the fact that Arabic has four forms of letters (isolated, initial, medial and final), we narrow the search space based on the location inside the piece.

The performance of the proposed method, when applied to printed texts and computer fonts of different sizes, was evaluated on two independent benchmarks, PATS and APTI. Our algorithm outperformed that of the creator of PATS on five out of eight fonts, achieving character correctness of 98.87%–100%. On the APTI dataset, ours was competitive or better that the competition.

1 Introduction

After more than forty years of research, *optical character recognition* (OCR) systems for machine-printed text show impressive performance [5]. However, printed Arabic texts still present difficult challenge. The reasons are manifold:

(a) Even printed text is semi-cursive. Each word consist of one or more *pieces (of an Arabic word)* (paws). The letters inside a paw are connected (as in cursive script) and cannot be easily separated, since finding the correct segmentation point is itself a challenge.

(b) Many Arabic letters are distinguished one from another only by diacritical dots or strokes. Misclassifying them can lead to a completely different word. Diacritical marks representing vowels are often left out and the meaning of a word is identified from the context.

---

* This paper is based on A.R.'s M.Sc. thesis, *Using SIFT Descriptors for OCR of Printed Arabic*, Tel Aviv University, Feb. 2012 (available at http://nachum.org/papers/AndreyThesis.pdf).

N. Dershowitz and E. Nissan (Eds.): Choueka Festschrift, Part I, LNCS 8001, pp. 584–602, 2014.
© Springer-Verlag Berlin Heidelberg 2014

ﺍ ﻒ ﺍ ﻩ

Fig. 1. Initial, medial, final and isolated forms of the letter hā' in the Arial font

(c) The same letter may be written differently, depending on its location in the word, as there are up to four different variations in form for each letter, isolated, initial, medial and final (see Fig. 1).

(d) For some fonts, some combinations of letters may result in a new symbol (ligature). These multiple forms and combinations of letters significantly increase the number of different graphically-represented symbols a classifier needs to recognize to well over a hundred, besides punctuation marks and numerals.

By using features extracted with a grid of scale invariant feature transform (SIFT) descriptors and a sliding-window technique, we aim to *jointly* solve the segmentation and recognition problems for printed Arabic. We scan each paw and consider different segmentations of it into letters. Each form (initial, medial, final and isolated) has its own classifier. For each possible segmentation and based on the location of the window inside the paw, an appropriate classifier is chosen and a set of letters is suggested. The algorithm chooses those segmentation points for which the classifier achieves its highest confidence in the recognized letters.

Given a font, we construct a classifier based purely on the images of letters in all possible forms or combinations of letters that are graphically-represented by a single symbol. Our classifier does not undergo the classical training phase, where a part of a tested dataset is used for training, while the other part is used for performance evaluation. We did not use language models, morphological information, word lists or any other language resources that are commonly used to improve performance.

Recently, SIFT descriptors [8] have been suggested for use in OCR. They were used for Chinese character recognition in [15] and [6], and were applied to degraded handwritten Latin manuscripts in [4]. The authors of [1] showed that a SIFT descriptor outperform the classical feature representation methods, such as PCA, when performing word based classification of cursive Pashto printed text (very similar to the Arabic printed text). They used the keypoints suggested in [9] as centres of the SIFT descriptors. SIFT descriptors were also used to recognize the font of an Arabic printed text [16].

As described in [14], Hidden Markov Model (HMM) serve as a base for most of the methods that perform recognition of cursive scripts. The author of PATS dataset [3], the first dataset we used to test our algorithm, uses HMM and a sliding window to segment and recognize Arabic scripts. See also the recent [2]. In a competition [13] recently conducted by the authors of APTI dataset [12], the second data set we used to test our algorithm, participated two HMM based systems. The system that was suggested by the authors themselves did not participate in the competition, but was also HMM based. The first system that participated in the competition is based on the Hidden Markov Model Toolkit (a toolkit that was originality designed to be used for speech recognition), which was customized to a purpose of character recognition. The second system that participated in the competition is based on Bernoulli HMMs (BMMs), that is, HMMs in which conventional Gaussian mixture density functions are replaced with Bernoulli mixture probability functions.

The remainder of this paper is organized as follows: In the next section, we present our proposed algorithm. In Sect. 3, we describe the datasets that were used to measure performance, compare the results of other OCR algorithms that were evaluated on those datasets, and analyze the results. Finally, we conclude with a few observations.

2   SOCR Algorithm

Our algorithm, which we call *SOCR* for "SIFT-based OCR", segments and recognizes the letters of an image containing a single paw, and is described in Sect. 2.7. Using a sliding-window technique a candidate letter is isolated inside each window (see Sect. 2.6) and classified using the appropriate classifiers (see Sect. 2.4). The appropriate classifiers are chosen base on the location of the window inside the paw and can be either of the four form classifiers (see Sect. 2.3). The best segmentation points and letters are chosen based on the confidence of the classifier for the letter to end at this segmentation point.

We assume that the image passed a preprocessing phase and contains only Arabic text consisting of letters of a predefined alphabet located on a white background and the baselines are horizontally aligned. We also assume that the image contains only one line of text. An accurate segmentation of an image containing more than one line of text to a set of images where each image contains only one line is out of the scope of this work. While the segmentation of a line or a word to paws is a significant part of the algorithm and described in Sect. 2.5, a segmentation of a line into words is required only when the performance in terms of word recognition rate is a significant performance metric (see Sect. 3.1). A segmentation into words can be achieved by distinguish between white spaces and spaces between paws inside a word. We suggest a method for this in Sect. 3.2. For each input image, we estimate the baseline to be the row having the most black ink among all rows. The baseline is needed to correctly split the image to paws (see Sect. 2.5) and to isolate correctly a letter inside a window see Sect. 2.6). A more accurate baseline estimation that was designed for handwritten texts and considers the diacritical dots and marks of Arabic [17] was considered, but not used in this work.

The extraction of features lies at the core of any classification process. The features of all the unique symbols of a given font (limited to an alphabet) are extracted during the construction of the classifier as described in Sect. 2.3. Those features are later compared to the features extracted from the image of a letter that we are trying to classify as described in Sect. 2.4.

We use a multiple grids of SIFT descriptors as the main feature set. The structure and extraction process of the grids of descriptors are described in Sect. 2.1. To fine-tune the classification results produced by the use of SIFT descriptors, we use additional features. The structure and extraction process of those additional features are described in Sect. 2.2.

2.1 Extracting a Grid of SIFT Descriptors

Given an image that contains a whole paw or a part of a paw, the following steps are executed to extract the grid of SIFT descriptors:

1. The image is padded with white to the size of the smallest bounding *square* of the paw.
2. The image is split into $G \times G$ identical squares, where G is a small constant.
3. Let W be the width of each square and the scale be $W/4$.
4. In the middle of each square, extract N descriptors, where $M = \{m_1, \ldots, m_N\}$ are the magnification factors.
5. Each extracted descriptor is identified by $D_{x,y,m}$, where x, y are the coordinates of the square in the grid and m is the magnification factor.

When no magnification is used, by design, the grid of descriptors should cover the whole image without overlapping each other; hence the scale of the descriptor is always set to $W/4$ due to the fact that each descriptor has 4 spatial bins in each spatial direction. Throughout this work, $G = 3$ and $M = \{0.5, 1.0, 1.5\}$. Figure 2 shows an example of a grid of SIFT descriptors that were extracted without using magnification.

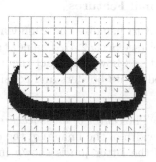

Fig. 2. A grid of 3×3 SIFT descriptors of the letter tā' of isolated/final form. Each descriptor is separated by a dashed (red) line.

Alternative Points for SIFT Descriptors Extraction. It was suggested by the author of SIFT to extract descriptors at keypoints where maxima and minima of the result of difference-of-Gaussians function applied in scale-space to a series of smoothed and re-sampled images is achieved [9]. While this method might perform well for complex images, it achieved very low performance on Arabic letters and had major disadvantages:

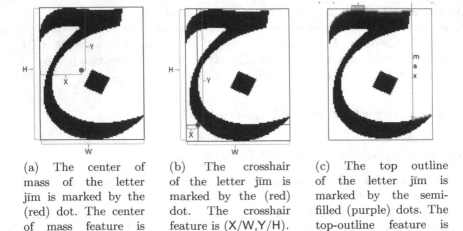

(a) The center of mass of the letter jīm is marked by the (red) dot. The center of mass feature is (X/W,Y/H).

(b) The crosshair of the letter jīm is marked by the (red) dot. The crosshair feature is (X/W,Y/H).

(c) The top outline of the letter jīm is marked by the semi-filled (purple) dots. The top-outline feature is $(t_1, \ldots, 1, \ldots, 0, \ldots, t_W)$.

Fig. 3. Additional features of the letter jīm

a) The number of keypoints depends on the resolution.
b) For some simple letters, the method did noy produce any keypoints at all.
c) Similar shapes can have almost identical sets of descriptors.

Those findings were later, independently, reported in [1]. We overcame these disadvantages by combining padding to the bounding square, a constant-size grid of descriptors and the quantization process described in Sect. 2.3.

2.2 Extracting Additional Features

Additional features are used to penalize the confidence of letters that are suggested by the SIFT classifier (see Sect. 2.4). The next sections describe the additional features that we used and how to extract them. We assume that the text inside the image is bounded by its borders and consists of black pixels located on a white background.

Center of Mass Feature. The *center of mass feature* f_m is the relative location (relative to the height and width of the image) of the center of mass of the black ink. The center of mass of the letter jīm is shown in Fig. 3a. Given an image and a letter, where c and c' are their centers of mass, respectively, the *center of mass penalty* used is $p_m = 1/(1 + d^{\frac{1}{2}}(c, c'))$, where $d^{\frac{1}{2}}$ gives the square-root of the Euclidean distance (a commonly used measure).

Crosshair Feature. The *crosshair feature*, f_c, is the relative location (relative to the height and the width of the image) of the vertical and horizontal slices with the largest portion of black ink compared to the white background. The crosshair of the letter jīm is shown in Fig. 3b. Given an image and a letter, where c and c' are their crosshair features, respectively, the *crosshair penalty* used is $p_c = 1/(1 + d^{\frac{1}{2}}(c, c'))$.

Ratio Feature. The *ratio feature*, f_o, is the height divided by the width of the bounding box of the black ink. Given an image and a letter, where o' and o are their ratio features, respectively, the *ratio penalty* used is $p_o = 1/(1 + (o' - o)^2)$. The exponent was arbitrary set to be 2 without being optimized for any of the datasets tested in Sect. 3.

Outline Features. Each image has four *outline features*, top, left, bottom and right. The top-outline feature, $f_t = (t_1, \ldots, t_W)$, where W is the width of the bounding box of the black ink, is calculated as follows:

1. For $i = 1, \ldots, W$, let d_i be the distance from the top of the bounding box to the first occurrence of a black pixel in the ith column of the image.
2. For $i = 1, \ldots, W$, let t_i be $(\max\{d_j\} - d_i)/(\max\{d_j\} - \min\{d_j\})$, where maximum and minimum are taken over all columns.

The left (f_l), bottom (f_b) and right (f_r) outline features are calculated in a similar manner. The top-outline of the letter jīm is shown in Fig. 3c.

Given an image and a letter, where t and t' are its top-outline features, respectively, the *top-outline penalty*, p_t, is calculated as follows:

1. If the two feature vectors are of unequal length, downscale the longer one, so they are both of some length n.
2. Define $p_t = 1/(1 + \text{avg}_{i=1}^n |t_i - t'_i|)$, where avg takes the average.

The left (p_l), bottom (p_b) and right (p_r) outline penalties are calculated in a similar manner.

Black Ink Histogram Features. Each image has a horizontal *black ink histogram feature* and a vertical one. The horizontal black ink histogram feature, $f_h = (h_1, \ldots, h_H)$, where H is the height of the bounding box of the black ink, is calculated as follows:

1. For $i = 1, \ldots, H$, let b_i be the number of black ink pixels in row i.
2. For $i = 1, \ldots, H$, let h_i be $b_i/\max\{b_i\}$.

The vertical black ink histogram feature (f_v) is calculated in a similar manner.

Given an image and a letter, where h and h' are its horizontal black ink histogram features, respectively, the horizontal *black ink histogram penalty*, p_h, is calculated as follows:

1. If the two feature vectors are of unequal length, downscale the longer one, so they are both of some length n.
2. Define $p_h = 1/(1 + \text{avg}_{i=1}^n |h_i - h'_i|)$.

The vertical black ink histogram penalty (p_v) is calculated in a similar manner.

2.3 Constructing a Classifier

For each classifier C for font F and an alphabet Σ, we execute a series of operations as described below. In Sect. 2.3, we explain how we generated high-resolution images, each one containing a unique symbol of the alphabet Σ written in font F. In Sect. 2.3, we explain how to extract the SIFT descriptors and additional features from each image and group the SIFT descriptors into four groups based on the location where the unique symbol can appear in a word (isolated, initial, medial and final). In Sect. 2.3, we describe the *quantization* process on the SIFT descriptors and group them into four groups creating a separate classifier for each of the four forms of letters. Finally, in Sect. 2.3, we compute a *base confidence* for each unique symbol.

Creating Images for All Possible Symbols. To create an image for each unique symbol for the alphabet Σ written in font F, a Word® document that contains $|\Sigma|$ rows, representing all possible letters of the alphabet, and four columns, representing the different possible letter forms (isolated, final, medial and initial) is created. Since some letter combinations are graphically-represented by a single symbol (ligature), these combinations are referred to as letters and belong to Σ. Each row can have one to four symbols, since some letters do not have all four letter forms, but only isolated or initial forms, or even only an isolated form. The resulting document is exported as a high resolution image. See Sect. 3 for details about the alphabet and the resolution of the image that was exported for each tested font. The exported image is split into lines and each line is split into the number of unique symbols it contains resulting in an image for each possible symbol. We denote each image by $L_{i,r}$, where $r \in \{$isolated, initial, medial, final$\}$ is the form of the ith letter of the alphabet Σ.

Feature Extraction. Before we extract features, we assign to each image $L_{i,r}$ a unique identification number σ. We extract SIFT descriptors and additional features as described in Sects. 2.1 and 2.2, respectively. The number of extracted SIFT descriptors per symbol is NG^2, where, as we said, N is the number of different descriptor magnifications used and G is the size of the grid of descriptors that were extracted. Each SIFT descriptor of symbol σ is denoted $D^\sigma_{x,y,m}$, where x,y and m are as described in Sect. 2.1. We group the descriptors into $4NG^2$ groups, each SD_g, for a combination of $g = (x, y, m, r)$, containing all the relevant descriptors $D^\sigma_{x,y,m}$.

Quantization. For each SD_g, a quantization is performed using k-means clustering. For each g, k_g is chosen to be the largest number such that the smallest energy among 1000 runs of k_g-means is smaller than E. For more information about how E was chosen, see Sect. 3. The k-means process is executed 1000 times to insure, with a high probability, that the clustering solution is near optimal (has the smallest energy) and consistent over many runs. The centers of each of the k_g clusters are the quantized descriptors of SD_g and denoted QD_g. Each quantized descriptor $QD \in QD_g$ is assigned a unique identification number, τ. For each τ, we save a mapping, MAP^τ_g, to the σs of the descriptors that QD is their quantized descriptor; $id \in MAP_g^\tau$ iff $QD_\tau \in QD_g$ is the center of the cluster to which $D_{id} \in SD_g$ belongs. We divide all QD_g into four groups, based on r, the form of the letter. Each group serves as the SIFT classifier for that form.

The quantization process is designed to improve the recognition rate. Since there are letters that look similar, their descriptors might also be very close to each other. By quantizing, we allow a letter descriptor $D_{x,y,m}$ to be matched to one $QD_\tau \in QD_g$, but since $|MAP_g^\tau| \geq 1$, the descriptor can be matched to more than one symbol.

Base Confidence. For each symbol, we compute its base confidence. The base confidence is the confidence value returned by executing the classification process described in Sect. 2.4 on the image $L_{i,r}$ that the σ of the symbol was assigned to. Since the base confidence is used to divide the confidence as the last step in the classification process, its initial value is set to 1. Since all additional feature penalties will be equal to 1, the base confidence is actually the SIFT confidence.

In the classification process, the SIFT confidence of the classifier in the symbol σ is divided by its base confidence to create a more "comparable metric" between different symbols of the same form.

2.4   Single Letter Classification

Given an image I, a classifier C and a letter form r, the classification process returns the pair (σ, c), where c is the confidence of the classifier that I contains just the symbol σ.

First, SIFT descriptors and the additional features are extracted as described in Sect. 2.1 and Sect. 2.2, respectively. The grid size, G, and the magnification factors, M, must be the same once that were used to create C. The extracted features of I are: a) SD, the set of descriptors $D_{x,y,m}$, where $x, y \in \{1, \ldots, G\}$ and $m \in M$; b) the additional features $f_m, f_c, f_o, f_t, f_r, f_b, f_l, f_h, f_v$. Next, we execute the following operations:

1. Let P' be an empty list that will hold the predicted σs. The σs in P' can repeat since two descriptors can be matched to the same σ, as can be seen in the next step.
2. For each $D_{x,y,m} \in SD$, we execute the following:
   (a) Find $QD_\tau \in QD_g$, where $g = (x, y, m, r)$, such that Euclidean distance between $D_{x,y,m}$ and QD_τ is smaller or equal to any other descriptor in QD_g.
   (b) Add all the σs of MAP_g^τ to P'.
3. Let P be the set of unique values of P'.
4. For each $\sigma \in P$ execute the following:
   (a) Calculate the additional feature penalties $p_m, p_c, p_o, p_t, p_l, p_b, p_r, p_h, p_v$ as described in Sect. 2.2.
   (b) Let the SIFT confidence, p_s, be the number of occurrences of σ in P' divided by $|P'|$.

(c) Let the confidence, c_{id}, of the classifier C in I being the symbol σ, be $p_s p_m p_c p_o p_t p_l p_b p_r p_h p_v$/(base confidence of id).

5. The pair (σ,c) is the result of the classification process, where $c = \max_{id \in P} c_\sigma$ and σ is such that $c_\sigma = c$.

2.5 Splitting Words into Paws

The classification process described in Sect. 2.7 requires that the classified image contain a single piece of Arabic word (paw). Given an image containing one line of Arabic text, we split it into paws.

First, we find and label in ascending order, based on the horizontal position of the first pixel, all *8-connectivity* connected components (CCs). Next we group the CCs into "rough" paws by executing the following steps for each CC starting from the one labelled using the smallest label until the one labelled with the largest label:

1. If the CC does not belong yet to any "rough" paw, add the CC to the paw.
2. While there are CCs that vertically intersect with the "rough" paw, add them to the paw. A CC and a paw vertically intersect if there is a column of pixels in the image that contains both pixels that belong to the CC and the paw.

Next, we split each "rough" paw into "regular" paws (referred to as just paws) by first finding and labelling in ascending order, based on the horizontal position of the first pixel, all *4-connectivity* CCs. At this point, each 4-connectivity CC has 2 labels, one 8-connectivity label and one 4-connectivity label. Next, all 4-connectivity CCs that are located on the *baseline* are marked as the anchors of each paw. For each anchor CC, we execute the following steps:

1. Add the anchor CC to the paw.
2. All CCs that have the same 8-connectivity label as the anchor, that either vertically intersect only with the anchor, or do not intersect with any other CC at all, are added to the paw.
3. All CCs that are not an anchor, but intersect by more than $X\%$ with the anchor of the current paw are added to the paw.
4. All other CCs that have the same 8-connectivity are added to the paw only if their width is 10 times smaller or less than the width of the paw. The value 10 was chosen arbitrarily without being optimized for any of the datasets tested in Sect. 3.

Each "rough" paw is eventually split to a number of paws as the number of anchor CCs. The percentage of intersection, X, is a font-specific characteristic that can be a priori calculated for each font. For each font, X will be the minimal amount of vertical intersection that a diacritical dot or a mark has with the other parts of the letter. In this work, we used an intersection percentage of 50% to all fonts but Andalus, which had an intersection percentage of 30%.

2.6 Isolating a Letter Inside a Window

Given a paw and starting and ending positions inside this paw, we would like to isolate the black ink that belongs to the possible letter that starts and ends at those positions. If we will always take all the ink between the starting and ending positions of the window, we might get black ink that belongs to the next or previous letter. Instead of taking all the black ink, we remove black ink that is located on the external side of the borders of the window and on the baseline of the paw. If no black ink is located on the baseline, we remove all the black ink located on the outer side of the border of the window. This process is expected to create three connected components that are located on the baseline. On the image with the cut baseline, we execute the process described in Sect. 2.5, which splits an image into paws. The second paw retuned by this process is the isolated letter. If the starting point of the window is the beginning of the paw, the first paw returned by this process is the isolated letter.

2.7 Paw Classification

The classifications of a paw is one of the main challenges we address in this work. A paw can consist of one or more letters of different forms depending on their location in the paw. Since we do not know where one letter ends and the next letter begins we use a sliding window to scan for letters throughout the paw. A paw can be one of the three types described below:

- **Type 1**: A paw that contains one isolated letter.
- **Type 2**: A paw that starts with initial letter, ends with a final letter and contains zero or more middle letters.
- **Type 3**: A paw that contains two isolated-form letters. This case is very rare and happens when the algorithm that splits words into paws (see Sect. 2.5) fails to split an image containing two isolated letter into two paws of type 1.

A high level overview of the steps of classifying a paw are as follows:

1. Scan for an initial or isolated letter at the beginning of the paw.
2. Scan for a final or isolated letter at the end of the paw.
3. Decide if the paw is of type 1, 2 or 3.
4. If the paw is of type 1 or type 3, then return the best isolated letters and the confidence in them.
5. Otherwise, if the paw is of type 2, scan for a middle or final letter until some final letter is found.
6. Return the list of one initial letter, zero or more middle letters and one final letter. Also return the confidence of the classifier in those letters.

Steps 1, 2 and 3 are explained in detail in Sect. 2.7; step 5 is explained in detail in Sect. 2.7. The scanning procedure in steps 1, 2 and 5 is described in Sect. 2.7.

Scanning. Given a letter form r and a starting point inside the paw, scanning is done by classifying a set of windows of increasing sizes, starting at the given point. Inside each window, a letter is isolated as described in Sect. 2.6 and then classified using the classifier of form r as described in Sect. 2.4. Each window of size s is assigned with the result of the classifier on it, (σ_s, c_s), and the following is executed:

1. Let B be the window size that has the highest classifier confidence c_B.
2. Let σ_B be the σ that was assigned by the classifier to the window of size B.
3. Return σ_B and a list of all pairs (p, c_s), where p is the ending point of a window that the classifier assigned the letter σ_B and c_s is the confidence of the classifier for the isolated letter inside the window to be σ_B.

Scanning is done by increasing the window size from the starting point either towards the end of the paw or towards the beginning of the paw. The latter scanning is used when scanning for the best starting point of a final or isolated letter that end exactly at the end of a paw.

Scanning for Initial and a Final Letter or an Isolated Letter. We execute this kind of scan to identify the type of the paw. First we scan for an initial letter candidate that starts at the beginning of a paw and a final letter candidate that ends at the end of the paw, assuming the paw is of type 2:

1. Scan for σ_0 and $P_0 = \{(p_1, c_1), \ldots, (p_n, c_n)\}$, where σ_0 is the σ of the best initial letter starting at the beginning of the paw and P_0 are the possible ending positions and confidences of the letter to end at those positions.
2. Scan for σ_* and $P_* = \{(p_1, c_1), \ldots, (p_n, c_n)\}$, where σ_* is the σ of the best final letter ending at the end of the paw and P_* are the possible starting positions and confidences of the letter to start at those positions.

Second, we scan for an isolated letter candidate that begins at the beginning of the paw and an isolated letter candidate that ends at the end of the paw, assuming the paw is either of type 1 or type 3:

1. Scan for $\sigma_{@..}$ and $P_{@..} = \{(p_1, c_1), \ldots, (p_n, c_n)\}$, where $\sigma_{@..}$ is the σ of the best isolated letter starting at the beginning of the paw and $P_{@..}$ are the possible ending positions and confidences of the letter to end at those positions.
2. Scan for $\sigma_{..@}$ and $P_{..@} = \{(p_1, c_1), \ldots, (p_n, c_n)\}$, where $\sigma_{..@}$ is the σ of the best isolated letter ending at the end of the paw and $P_{@_c b}$ are the possible starting positions and confidences of the letter to start at those positions.

Third, we calculate some intersection ratios between the windows of the candidates as follows:

1. Let the intersection ratio, $I_@$, between the isolated letters, $\sigma_{@..}$ and $\sigma_{..@}$, be twice the number of pixels shared by the windows with the highest confidence of $\sigma_{@..}$ and $\sigma_{..@}$ divided by the sum of the window sizes.
2. Let the intersection ratio, I_{0*}, between the initial and final letters, be twice the number of pixels shared by the windows with the highest confidence of σ_0 and σ_* divided by the sum of the window sizes.

3. Let the "unclassified ratio", $I_{@@}$, be one minus the ratio of the number of pixels not covered by the windows with the highest confidence of $\sigma_{@..}$ and $\sigma_{..@}$ and the width of the paw.

Fourth, we calculate the confidence of a paw to be one of the three possible types:

- The confidence of a paw to be of type 1 is $C_1 = c_{@..}c_{..@}I_@$
- The confidence of a paw to be of type 2 is $C_2 = c_0 c_*(1 - I_{0*})$
- The confidence of a paw to be of type 3 is $C_3 = c_{@..}c_{..@}I_@(1 - I_@)$
- For C_3 to be taken into account, it has to be significantly bigger than C_2, i.e. if $C_2/C_3 > 0.9$, then $C_3 = 0$. The value 0.9 was arbitrary.

Finally, based on the type confidences, we decide whether to return the isolated letter or letters that we found or to continue and scan for medial letters that are located between the initial and the final letter that we found:

1. If C_3 is the largest confidence, return $\sigma_{@..}, \sigma_{..@}$, the σs of the 2 isolated letters that were found.
2. If C_1 is the largest confidence and $\sigma_{@..} = \sigma_{..@}$, return $\sigma_{@..}$.
3. If C_1 is the largest confidence and $\sigma_{@..} \neq \sigma_{..@}$, choose the better isolated letter. Since the paw is a single isolated letter, taking the confidences of both possible isolated letters is not enough. It should be taken into account how many pixels were left outside the best window for each isolated letter. Based on that, a revised confidence for each isolated letter is calculated:
   (a) $c_{@..} = c_{@..}$ (size of the window that was classified to be $\sigma_{@..}$ and confidence $c_{@..}$)
   (b) $c_{..@} = c_{..@}$ (size of the window that was classified to be $\sigma_{..@}$ and confidence $c_{..@}$)
   If $c_{@..} > c_{..@}$, return $\sigma_{@..}$, otherwise return $\sigma_{..@}$.
4. If C_2 is the largest confidence continue scanning for medial letters as described in Sect. 2.7.

Scanning for Medial Letters. We scan for medial letters if the paw was classified as type 2. At this point, we know the initial letter, σ_0, and it possible ending positions and the confidences for the letter to end at those positions, P_0. We also know the final letter that ends at the end of the paw, σ_*, and its possible starting positions and the confidences for it to start at those positions, P_*. We do the scanning for medial letters until we find a final letter as follows:

1. Let p_f be the first possible starting position of σ_*.
2. Let p_l be the last possible starting position of σ_*.
3. Let p_{pre} be the position where the previous letter has the highest confidence for ending. At the first iteration of this process, the previous letter is σ_0, while on the next iterations, this letter is the previous medial letter.
4. For windows ending before p_l, scan for σ_m and $P_m = \{(p_1, c_1), \ldots, (p_n, c_n)\}$, where σ_m is the σ of the best middle letter starting at p_{pre} and P_m in the set of possible ending positions and confidences of the letter to end at those

positions. Let $(p_m, c_m) \in P_m$ be the ending position and the confidence for σ_m to end at this position, where c_m is the highest confidence among all possible ending positions.

5. For windows ending after p_f, scan for σ_{b*} and $P_{b*} = \{(p_1, c_1), \ldots, (p_n, c_n)\}$, where σ_{b*} is the σ of the best final letter starting at p_{pre} and P_{b*} is the possible ending positions and confidences of the letter to end at those positions. Let $(p_{b*}, c_{b*}) \in P_{b*}$ be the ending position and confidence for σ_{b*} to end at this position, where c_{b*} is the highest confidence among all possible ending positions.

6. Let the intersection ratio, I_{m*}, between the middle letter, σ_m, and the final letter, σ_*, be twice the number of pixels shared by the windows with the highest confidence of σ_m and σ_* divided by the sum of the window sizes. Update c_m to be $c_m \sqrt{1 - I_{m*}}$.

7. Let the intersection ratio, I_{**}, between the final letter, σ_{b*}, and the final letter, σ_*, be twice the number of pixels shared by the windows with the highest confidence of σ_{b*} and σ_* divided by the sum of the window sizes. Update c_{fl_b} to be $c_{fl_b} \sqrt{I_{**}}$.

8. If the SIFT confidence part, p_s, of the higher confidence between c_m and c_{b*} is less than 0.9 (the value 0.9 was chosen arbitrary without being optimized for any of the datasets tested in Sect. 3), retry and scan starting from all possible ending positions of the previous letter as follows:

   (a) Normalize the confidences of all ending points of the previous letter by dividing them by the value of the maximal confidence.

   (b) Repeat steps 3–7 to get σ_m, c_m and σ_{b*}, c_{b*}, the best middle and final letters and their confidences starting at all possible ending points of the previous letter.

   (c) For each possible ending point of the previous letter, multiple c_m and c_{b*} by the normalized confidence of the previous letter ending at this position.

   (d) Choose σ_m, $P_m = \{(p_1, c_1), \ldots, (p_n, c_n)\}$ and σ_{b*}, $P_{b*} = \{(p_1, c_1), \ldots, (p_n, c_n)\}$ to be the ones with the highest c_m and c_{fl_b} among all possible ending positions of the previous letters.

9. If $c_m > c_{fl_b}$, save σ_m as the next letter and scan, stating from step 3, for the next letter starting at the position, where the medial letter found has the highest confidence to end.

10. Otherwise if $c_m \le c_{fl_b}$, return the initial letter σ_0, all medial letters and the final letter that has the higher confidence. If $c_{b*} > c_*$ return σ_{b*}; otherwise return σ_*.

3   Experimental Results

To test the performance of SOCR, two different datasets were used. First, in Sect. 3.2, we describe how the PATS dataset was constructed [3] and compare the results of the algorithm suggested by the author of PATS to the results of SOCR. then, in Sect. 3.3, we describe how the APTI benchmark was constructed [12] and provide some initial tests results we did on parts of the dataset.

Common Parameter Configuration

Although all the parameters used in SOCR can be configured, the parameters that a priori cannot be automatically computed were the same for all datasets and fonts. The following list contains the common configuration of parameters:

- G – the number grid elements, SIFT descriptors, in each spatial direction extracted from each given image was set to 3.
- M – the set of descriptor magnification factors was set to $\{0.5, 1.0, 1.5\}$.
- E – the energy used to compute the optimal k for k-means clustering of the descriptors as described in Sect. 2.3 was set to 10^4.

3.1   Performance Metrics

The performance is reported in terms of character recognition rate (CRR) and word recognition rate (WRR). CRR was measured using the Levenshtein edit distance [7] between the predicted word and ground truth. WRR is the ratio of the number of words having all its letter recognized correctly to the total number of words. WRR is an important performance parameter for algorithms that take a language-specific approach, such as using word lists, for training or for improving the results of the classification process. Since we do not use a language-specific approach, WRR is less important for our algorithm and reported only in cases where we were able to split the input images into words.

3.2   PATS Dataset

The PATS dataset consists of 2766 text-line images that were selected from two standard classic Arabic books. The images were split into images that each contain one line. The dataset includes the fonts Arial, Tahoma, Andalus, Simplified Arabic, Akhbar, Thuluth, Naskh and Traditional Arabic. Lines written using Arial, Tahoma, Andalus and Simplified Arabic use 41 different letters and ligatures (see Table 1a). Akhbar uses three more symbols, while Thuluth, Naskh and Traditional Arabic use several more symbols that were not taken into consideration when creating the classifier (see Table 1b).

Using tables like 1a and 1b, a classifier was constructed for each font, as described in Sect. 2.3. Using the classifier, the SOCR algorithm was executed on all 2766 lines of each font. See Fig. 4 for a sample line of Tahoma, Andalus and Thuluth fonts.In Table 2 the performance, in terms of CRR and WRR, is reported for all 2766 lines and the last 266 lines, along side with the CRR of executing on the last 266 lines the algorithm suggested by the author of PATS. SOCR outperforms the algorithm suggested by the author of PATS on Tahoma, Arial, Andalus, Simplified Ararbic and Akhbar fonts. The classifier constructed for fonts Thuluth, Naskh and Traditional Arabic was constructed using a table of 44 unique letters and combination of letters, but the lines in PATS dataset included some more combinations. This resulted in a constant failure of the classifier on those missing combinations and a poor CRR performance.

Table 1. Tables of unique symbols that are used to construct classifiers

(a) Arial

	و	و	ﺵ	ﺵ	ش	ش		ا	ا
ﻳ	ﻳ	ي	ي	ﺻ	ﺻ	ص	ص		ى	ى
ﻻ	ﻻ	ﺿ	ﺿ	ﺿ	ض	ﺑ	ﺑ	ﺑ	ب
أ	أ	ﻃ	ﻃ	ﻃ	ط	ﻧ	ﻧ	ﺗ	ت
	ﻇ	ﻇ	ﻇ	ظ	ة	ة	ث
	ﻋ	ﻋ	ﻋ	ع	ﺛ	ﺛ	ﺟ	ج
آ	آ	ﻐ	ﻐ	ﻏ	غ	ﺟ	ﺟ	ح	ح
ﺈ	ﺈ	ﻓ	ﻓ	ﻓ	ف	ﺣ	ﺣ	ﺧ	خ
ﺉ	ﺉ	ﻗ	ﻗ	ﻗ	ق	ﺧ	ﺧ	د	د
ﺋ	ﺋ	ﻛ	ﻛ	ﻛ	ك		ذ	ذ
	ﻼ	ﻼ	ﻟ	ﻟ	ﻟ	ل		ر	ر
	ﻸ	ﻸ	ﻢ	ﻢ	م	م		ز	ز
	ﻺ	ﻺ	ﻦ	ﻦ	ن	ن		ﺳ	ﺳ
		ﻪ	ﻬ	ﻬ	ه	ﺳ	ﺳ

(b) Naskh

	ﻻ	ﻻ	ﺻ	ﺻ	ص	ص		ا	ا
	أ	أ	ﺿ	ﺿ	ﺿ	ض		ﺑ ﺗ ة	ﺑ ت ى
	ﻃ	ﻃ	ﻃ	ط	ﺛ ﺟ	ث ج
	ﻇ	ﻇ	ﻇ	ظ	ﺣ	ح
آ	آ	ﻋ	ﻋ	ﻋ	ع	ﺧ	خ
ﺈ	ﺈ	ﻏ	ﻏ	ﻏ	غ		ﺧ د ذ ر	خ د ذ ر
ﺉ	ﺉ	ﻓ	ﻓ	ﻓ	ف	ﺣ	ح
ﺋ	ﺋ	ﻗ	ﻗ	ﻗ	ق	ﺧ	خ
ﻼ	ﻼ	ﻛ	ﻛ	ﻛ	ك		ز ز س	ز س
ﻸ	ﻸ	ﻟ	ﻟ	ﻟ	ل		ﺳ ﺳ	س ش
ﻺ	ﻺ	ﻢ	ﻢ	م	م	ﺳ	ش
	ﻦ	ﻦ	ن	ن	و
	ﻪ	ﻬ	ه	و
	ي	ي

حدثهم أن رجلا نادى النبي صلى الله عليه وسلم وهو في المسجد

(a) Tahoma

حدثهم أن رجلا نادى النبي صلى الله عليه وسلم وهو في المسجد

(b) Andalus

حدثهم أن رجلا نادى النبي صلى الله عليه وسلم وهو في المسجد

(c) Thuluth

Fig. 4. Line 88 of various fonts in the PATS dataset

Table 2. Performance in terms of CRR and WRR of SOCR and the algorithm suggested by the author of PATS executed on PATS dataset

Font	SOCR CRR-266	PATS CRR-266	SOCR CRR-2766	SOCR WRR-2766
Tahoma	**100.0%**	99.68%	100.0%	100.0%
Arial	**99.98%**	99.90%	99.96%	99.90%
Andalus	**98.87%**	97.86%	98.58%	94.90%
Simplified Arabic	**99.72%**	99.70%	99.73%	99.00%
Akhbar	**99.83%**	99.34%	99.89%	99.72%
Thuluth	87.23%	**97.78%**	86.16%	N/A
Naskh	87.38%	**98.09%**	85.69%	N/A
Traditional Arabic	92.56%	**98.83%**	91.53%	N/A

3.3 APTI Dataset

The Arabic printed text image database (APTI) [12], was created to address the challenges of optical character recognition of printed Arabic text of multiple fonts, multiple font sizes and multiple font styles. APTI is designed for the evaluation of screen-based OCR systems. The authors suggested numerous OCR evaluation protocols and conducted a competition [13] to test the performance of state of the art OCR systems. The dataset is split in to six sets, where five of the six sets of the dataset were publicly available for research and training, while set number 6 was used for evaluating the submitted systems and known only to the creators of APTI.

Table 3 shows the performance comparison, in terms of CRR and WRR, of SOCR and the systems submitted to the competition running the first APTI protocol. The first protocol tests the ability of a system to recognize the images

Fig. 5. A word in Arabic Transparent and sizes 6, 8, 10, 12, 18 and 24 (from left to right)

of words written using Arabic Transparent font (very similar to Arial) in six different sizes (6, 8, 10, 12, 18 and 24). See Fig. 5 for a sample image of a word in the dataset in Traditional Arabic and the six fonts sizes used. Each system is tested on all six sizes, while the size is known to the system. Three different systems, IPSAR, UPV-PRHLT and DIVA-REGIM, were evaluated in the competition using the first protocol on the unpublished set number 6, while the latter system was declared out of the competition since it was built by the creators of APTI and optimized for more than a year on the first five sets. The other two systems also used the first fives sets for training. Since set number 6 is not publicly available, SOCR was evaluated (on the randomly chosen) set number 4 [11, No. 221] in two different modes. The first mode considers the variations of the letter alif (no diacritic marks, hamza above, hamza below and tilda above) as different letters, while the second mode considers all the variation of alif as the same letter. The approach of the second mode, measuring the quality of Arabic OCR while considering the different variations of the letter alif as the same letter, was previously suggested in [10]. Since SOCR assumes that the input images are black ink on white background, each image was converted to a black and white image using a dynamic threshold. Assuming that the value 0 represents a black pixel and value 1 represented a white pixel, the dynamic threshold was calculated as follows:

- Let s be the standard deviation of the pixel values in the image.
- Let m be the mean value of all the pixels that are smaller than $1 - s$.
- Let $t = m + s$ be the dynamic threshold.

All pixels smaller than t are transformed into 0, while all pixels larger or equal to t are transformed into 1. The APTI dataset uses an alphabet of 43 uniquely represented letters and combination of letters for Arabic.

From Table 3 it can be seen that SOCR performs competitively with the other systems, mostly on the larger font sizes. It is important to mention that all the other three systems used the first five sets to train their classifiers, while SOCR did not perform any training using those sets. SOCR also used the same classifier for all font sizes. The difference in performance between the first and second mode shows that a training phase can be used to create an SOCR classifier for each font size to significantly improve the performance when running in the first mode. The training phase can fine tune the SIFT descriptors for each font size of the different variations of the letter alif.

Table 3. Performance in terms of CRR and WRR of SOCR and the algorithm suggested by the author of PATS executed on PATS dataset

System/Size		6	8	10	12	18	24
SOCR	WRR	23.5%	61.9%	63.5%	71.2%	84.0%	97.0%
	CRR	64.7%	90.1%	92.7%	93.2%	97.1%	99.2%
SOCR	WRR	27.6%	78.9%	89.8%	94.0%	99.0%	98.5%
Ignore Alif Variation	CRR	68.2%	94.4%	97.5%	97.6%	99.8%	99.6%
IPSAR	WRR	5.7%	73.3%	75.0%	83.1%	77.1%	77.5%
	CRR	59.4%	94.2%	95.1%	96.9%	95.7%	96.8%
UPV-PRHLT	WRR	94.5%	97.4%	96.7%	92.5%	84.6%	84.4%
	CRR	99.0%	99.6%	99.4%	98.7%	96.9%	96.0%
DIVA-REGIM	WRR	86.9%	95.9%	95.7%	93.9%	97.9%	98.9%
	CRR	98.0%	99.2%	99.3%	98.8%	99.7%	99.7%

4   Conclusion

We have seen how SIFT descriptors can be successfully used as features of individual letters to perform OCR of Arabic printed text. We overcame the challenge of printed Arabic being a cursive text by performing, jointly, segmentation into letters and their recognition. While enjoying the benefit of not having a need for a training set, our method performs competitively compared to other, recently purposed methods, which require large training sets. More work can be done to address the scenarios where the method showed a relatively high failure rate. In the situation where the method fails to distinguish between the variations of the letter alif, which differ only in diacritical marks, post-processing can be used to correct the misclassification by matching the recognized word against a pre-defined list of words. In the situation where the method fails due to a failure to split two paws, which happens mostly with low resolution fonts, this post-processing might not suffice, since the probability that most of the letters of the second paw will not be recognized correctly is high.

Since our classifier consists of four classifiers, one for each possible location of a letter inside a paw, creating one classifier for all forms can help overcome the failures that happen when a split fails. On top of that, introducing a learning phase can, potentially, improve performance by finding the best weights for penalties and their combination with the segmentation and recognition scores.

Also, image-based verification can be added. By generating an image of the predicted word or paw, we can measure its visual similarity to the word we are trying to recognize. Future work should focus on a larger variety of fonts and sizes and the algorithm should be extended to work well on texts containing multiple fonts.

References

1. Ahmad, R., Amin, S.H., Khan, M.A.: Scale and rotation invariant recognition of cursive Pashto script using SIFT features. In: 6th International Conference on Emerging Technologies, pp. 299–303 (2010)
2. Ahmed, I., Mahmoud, S.A., Parvez, M.T.: Printed Arabic text recognition. In: Märgner, V., El Abed, H. (eds.) Guide to OCR for Arabic Scripts, pp. 147–168. Springer, London (2012)
3. Al-Muhtaseb, H.A., Mahmoud, S.A., Qahwaji, R.S.R.: Recognition of off-line printed Arabic text using Hidden Markov Models. Signal Processing 88, 2902–2912 (2008)
4. Diem, M., Sablatni, R.: Recognition of degraded handwritten characters using local features. In: International Conference on Document Analysis and Recognition, pp. 221–225 (2009)
5. Fujisawa, H.: Forty years of research in character and document recognition-an industrial perspective. Pattern Recognition 41, 2435–2446 (2008)
6. Gui, J.P., Zhou, Y., Lin, X.D., Chen, K., Guan, H.B.: Research on Chinese character recognition using bag of words. Applied Mechanics and Materials 20-23, 395–400 (2010)
7. Levenshtein, V.I.: Binary codes capable of correcting deletions, insertions, and reversals. Soviet Physics Doklady 10, 707–710 (1966)
8. Lowe, D.G.: Object recognition from local scale-invariant features. In: Proceedings of the International Conference on Computer Vision. ICCV 1999, vol. 2, pp. 1150–1151 (1999)
9. Lowe, D.G.: Distinctive image features from scale-invariant keypoints. International Journal of Computer Vision 42, 91–110 (2004)
10. Magdy, W., Darwis, K.: Arabic OCR error correction using character segment correction, language modeling, and shallow morphology. In: Proceedings of the 2006 Conference on Empirical Methods in Natural Language Processing, pp. 408–411 (2006)
11. Munroe, R.: Random number, xkcd.com/221
12. Slimane, F., Ingold, R., Kanoun, S., Alimi, A., Hennebert, J.: A new Arabic printed text image database and evaluation protocols. In: International Conference on Document Analysis and Recognition, pp. 946–950 (2009)
13. Slimane, F., Kanoun, S., Abed, H.E., Alimi, A.M., Ingold, R., Hennebert, J.: Arabic recognition competition: Multi-font multi-size digitally represented text. In: Eleventh International Conference on Document Analysis and Recognition, pp. 1449–1453. IEEE (2011)
14. Steinherz, T., Rivlin, E., Intrator, N.: Offline cursive script word recognition – a survey. International Journal on Document Analysis and Recognition 2, 90–110 (1999)
15. Wu, T., Qi, K., Zheng, Q., Chen, K., Chen, J., Guan, H.: An improved descriptor for Chinese character recognition. In: Third International Symposium on Intelligent Information Technology Application, pp. 400–403 (2009)
16. Zahedi, M., Eslami, S.: Farsi/Arabic optical font recognition using SIFT features. Procedia Computer Science 3, 1055–1059 (2011)
17. Ziaratban, M., Fae, K.: A novel two-stage algorithm for baseline estimation and correction in Farsi and Arabic handwritten text line. In: 19th International Conference on Pattern Recognition (2008)

Author Index

Amir, Amihood   I-364
Asaro, Carmelo   II-452

Bar, Kfir   III-54, III-64
Bar-Haim, Roy   I-409
Bar-Ilan, Judit   I-382
Bar-Ilan, Meir   II-406
Barringer, Howard   I-103

Calzolari, Nicoletta   III-103
Chandar, Subha   II-424
Choueka, Yaacov   I-1, I-395, III-1,
   III-54
Cohen, Mark R.   II-38

Dagan, Ido   I-409
Dershowitz, Nachum   I-19, I-395,
   I-584, III-54
Diab, Mona   III-64
Dragoni, Aldo Franco   II-452

El-Sana, Jihad   I-425
Erlich, Ofir Tzvi   III-36

Farook, Dany Yamen   II-452
Feldman, Ronen   I-399
Finkel, Olivier   I-50
Fraenkel, Aviezri S.   I-37
Fredj, Erick   I-252
Fresko, Moshe   I-399

Gabbay, Dov   I-103
Goldenberg, Jacob   I-399
Goldstein, Moshe   I-252
Goren-Bar, Dina   II-47
Gorfinkel, Ariel   II-47

HaCohen-Kerner, Yaakov   III-36,
   III-82, III-780
Harel, David   I-156
Hawwari, Abdelati   III-64

Jbara, Sadek   II-47
Jefferson, Rebecca J.W.   II-9

Kannai, Ruth   II-440
Kantor, Amir   I-156
Kashtan, Nadav   II-47
Kats, Shahar   II-47
Klein, Shmuel T.   I-197
Koppel, Moshe   II-1
Kraus, Sarit   I-180
Kuflik, Tsvi   II-47

Lancashire, Ian   II-88
Lewenstein, Moshe   I-364
Lewenstein, Noa   I-364
Lin, Raz   I-180
Lister, Kendall   I-225

Manistersky, Efrat   I-180
Martino, Antonio A.   II-696, II-721
McCarty, Willard   II-103
Monachini, Monica   III-103

Netzer, Oded   I-399
Nissan, Ephraim   I-19, I-263, I-425,
   II-138, II-193, II-270, II-452, III-82,
   III-122, III-174, III-207, III-365,
   III-435, III-483, III-537, III-562,
   III-593, III-612, III-642, III-780

Peleg, David   I-168

Quochi, Valeria   III-103

Reingold, Edward M.   I-213
Rosenberg, Andrey   I-584
Rydeheard, David   I-103

Schild, Uri J.   II-440
Schmidt, Klaus M.   III-14
Sheidin, Julia   II-47
Shimony, Solomon Eyal   II-452
Soria, Claudia   III-103
Sterling, Leon   I-225

Stock, Oliviero　II-47
Szpektor, Idan　I-409

Tal, Liad　I-395
Toral, Antonio　III-103

Ungar, Lyle　I-399

Vardi, Moshe Y.　I-78

Winer, Dov　II-72, II-394

Zancanaro, Massimo　II-47
Zarri, Gian Piero　II-118
Zeleznikow, John　II-424, II-440
Zuckermann, Ghil'ad　III-537